D1277151

György Matolcsy

ECONOMIC BALANCE AND GROWTH
Consolidation and stabilisation in Hungary
2010–2014

© György Matolcsy, 2015

Technical editor: Dániel Palotai, Executive Director for Economic Sciences
and Priority Matters

Published: 2015
Book Series of the Magyar Nemzeti Bank
ISBN: 978-615-5318-03-0
ISSN 2416-3503

Print: Prospektus–SPL consortium
English translation: Kendall Logan, Bence Gáspár and Douglas Arnott

GYÖRGY MATOLCSY

Economic Balance and Growth

Consolidation and stabilisation in Hungary 2010-2014

György Matolcsy

Economic Balance and Growth

Consolidation and stabilisation in Hungary

2010-2014

© György Matolcsy, 2015

Technical editor: Dániel Palotai, Executive Director for
Economic Sciences and Priority Matters

Published: 2015
Book Series of the Magyar Nemzeti Bank

ISBN: 978-615-5318-03-0
ISSN 2416-3503
Published by Kairosz Kiadó, on behalf of the Magyar Nemzeti Bank

Typography: Ilona Németh
Printing: SPL – Prospektus Nyomda consortium
English translation: Kendall Logan, Bence Gáspár and Douglas Arnott

Contents

Preface

This work focuses on the significant success of the Hungarian economy in the period from 2010 to 2014, the return to a balanced budget and the stabilisation of the economy which led to a recovery in Hungarian growth. At the same time, it discusses the first ten years of Hungary's membership of the European Union, examining the mistakes made in economic policy in the period 2004–2014. It analyses why it was not possible to take advantage of the historic opportunities opening up following accession in 2004 and why a fundamental change in economic policy was required even before the crisis in 2008–2009.

Focusing on the two decades of flawed, unsuccessful economic development in the period 1990–2010, it discusses why the economic policy, tools and solutions which proved successful in the period 2010–2014 were not used earlier in Hungary and why these were only used after the political transformation, when the country had no alternatives, because of the evident complex crisis situation.

It is worthwhile to compare Hungary's economy in the period 1990–2010 with the other economies in the Visegrád region. The Czech Republic, Poland and Slovakia started the 1990s with similar historical legacies and economic structures. Over the last two decades, the convergence process in these countries was not accompanied by excessive growth in external or internal debt indicators, and thus their convergence has proven to be sustainable from a financing perspective. By contrast, for the entire period of 1990 to 2010 the Hungarian economy was characterised by a situation in which either balance indicators deteriorated due to the structure of growth, or growth was retarded because it was necessary to remedy imbalances. Throughout the period 1990–2010, the economic policy dilemma in Hungary was always "economic balance or growth". This was resolved by the successful restoration of balance between 2010 and 2014, and the recovery in economic growth as a result of economic stabilisation.

This book also discusses the last 50 years, as the dilemma of "economic balance or growth" was a recurring feature starting from the early 1960s all the way to the start of the 2010s. During this period of economic history, this economic dilemma arose time and time again: economic growth resulted in a deterioration of the trade balance and budget balance. Consequently, various governments made efforts to correct this, but these measures either slowed down or stopped growth. This was repeated on several occasions under the centrally planned economic regime in place before 1990. After 1990, this misguided economic policy approach was repeated under market economy conditions and in the four-year cycles of democratic elections. During the first half of the political cycle, attempts were made to rectify the imbalances which had accumulated, after which growth was promoted for the new elections, or vice-versa.

Hungary's economic history over the last 100 years is also analysed, as the successful consolidation and stabilisation which was achieved in 2010–2014 is unique in Hungary's economic history and in the entire 20th century.

The true value of the successful consolidation of the public budget and stabilisation of the real economy in 2010–2014 is reflected by the fact that Hungary was able to achieve better results than most of its peers. What Hungary was able to do was hardly replicated by anyone else, while at the same time almost all of Hungary's competitors in the European Union were struggling with a similar legacy, namely the burdens of the 2008–2009 crisis. The achievements in Hungary after 2010 were exceptional, viewed from a four-year perspective, from the perspective of several decades and even from the perspective of fifty or a hundred years. This is what my book is about: the means and ways by which Hungary achieved this success.

A breakthrough in economic history

During the last century, Hungary experienced several major economic shocks which had massive impacts on its economic growth and financial balance. During the first half of the 20th century, three external shocks hit the Hungarian economy: the First World War, the Great Depression of 1929–1933 and the Second World War. While the two World Wars caused the greatest damage to the Hungarian economy, the Great Depression also had very strong impact. During the second half of the century, Hungary was hit by another three economic shocks: the 1956 revolution, the oil crisis in the 1970s, and the transition to a market economy in the first half of the 1990s. Although none of these were on the same order of magnitude as the two World Wars, these shocks still hampered the development of the Hungarian economy for many years.

The economic shock from the 1956 revolution was relatively short-lived, as Hungary's national income returned to the earlier level after around two years. By contrast, the external/internal shock from the transition to a market economy in the 1990s was only overcome around 2000. Although the economic setback was smaller than during the two World Wars, it took almost an entire decade for the economy to recover. The economic crisis in 2008–2009 caused a smaller downturn, but in addition to the losses in gross domestic product, the sudden rise in government debt and the impact of the exchange rate exposure inherent in foreign currency loans also resulted in an internal shock in Hungary.

The situation was similar to that seen in the 1970s, when Hungary's debt surged around the middle of the decade, as government borrowing snowballed; these debt problems remained a secret of the country's central leadership, until they erupted into an open crisis in 1990. Confronted with high debt and low FX reserves, Hungarian economic policy opted for a shock therapy transition, resulting in distortions to the structure of the country's market economy from the very beginning.

The process of debt accumulation initiated in the 1970s had a negative impact for decades to come. Similar developments were seen in the period of new debt accumulation from 2002–2010, but while the pre-1990 system was unable to find an adequate response, in the market economy system it should have been possible to find a solution by pursuing the correct economic policy. Unfortunately, exactly the opposite occurred.

The significance of the financial consolidation and economic stabilisation achieved in Hungary after 2010 is underlined by the fact that an open financial crisis and a hidden growth crisis were both overcome in a very short period of time. While the renewed episode of borrowing between 2002 and 2010 will cast a long shadow over Hungary, its historical impact will likely be measured only in years and not in decades, thanks to the successful consolidation and stabilisation in 2010–2014.

Amidst these significant external and internal shocks, Hungary's per capita GDP grew at an average rate of 1.5% in the period 1900–2010, which falls short of the pace of growth registered in developed countries and in the European countries which have managed to converge successfully. Thus, despite Hungary's favourable starting position, its convergence efforts have consistently failed in the last one hundred years and more (Table 1).

During the fifty years between 1960 and 2010, the Hungarian economy was typically only able to achieve rapid growth at the cost of large-scale external borrowing. Of the indicators that best reflect a country's macroeconomic balance, and thus its state of health – the fiscal balance, the trade balance and inflation (mirroring market balance) – the trade balance is the best indicator of a country's vulnerability, and thus the sustainability of its economic growth. Unless a country is numbered amongst the most advanced, it will not be able to balance a trade deficit with a positive income balance. This is typically the situation in Hungary, and thus developments in the trade balance precisely foreshadow the path of the current account balance and the country's external balance in general.

Table 1. Economic growth in Hungary and certain countries, 1900-2010

Per capita GDP (PPP) average annual growth 1900-2010 (in %)	
Hungary	1.5
Poland	1.8
Czech Republic*	1.9
Slovakia*	1.8
Austria	1.9
Germany	1.8
France	1.8
Italy	2.1
Spain	2.1
UK	1.5
USA	1.8
Japan	2.7
China	2.5

Source: Maddison database   ** Czechoslovakia before 1993*

During the 1960s, Hungary's trade balance tended to be positive and – with the exception of the setback that occurred around the middle of the decade – GDP growth moved in a favourable range of 5% until the end of the 1970s. Between 1960 and 1980, however, it was only possible to achieve GDP growth in a range of 2.5% to 5%, in conjunction with increasing deterioration in the trade balance. The first major imbalance appeared in the early 1970s, and subsequently Hungary's trade balance steadily continued to deteriorate as a result of the two oil price shocks. Looking at the two decades between 1960 and 1980, the first decade was marked by good growth data, while the second decade was characterised by mounting problems in the trade balance, in the form of increasing imbalances. Although the growth figures of around 5% for the period 1960–1980 appear favourable, they masked a dualistic economic structure, which looked to be healthy from the top down, but showed a different picture from the bottom up.

With the strong weighting of industry, the sectoral structure was similar to that of advanced economies, but the structure at the micro level, the state of the technologies and products, and the level of productivity were closer to that of less developed economies. This dualistic structure ran into problems as a result of the external shocks, and it turned out that, compared to its competitors, the Hungarian economy was actually not suited for economic convergence. In the decade between 1980 and 1990, growth fell to between 0% and 2.5%, indicating that the Hungarian economy had decelerated from the earlier growth range of around 5% into a range allowing for a surplus on the trade balance. The Hungarian economy sacrificed growth in the interests of balance.

By the 1980s, Hungary was unable to maintain the stable growth from the previous two decades, because the structure of the economy made it impossible to apply a viable formula for high growth and favourable balance. It was possible to achieve one or the other, but not both at the same time. The shock therapy transition to a market economy implemented in the 1990s came with a high growth sacrifice, which kept Hungary's economy in a modest growth range for two decades and generated significant economic imbalances. The trade and budget deficit resulted in rising public debt, and the shock from the transition to a market economy in the 1990s proved to be a long-lasting shock to economic balance: the current account balance, inflation, the state budget and the government debt-to-GDP ratio all pointed towards a deterioration in Hungary's economic balance.

Hungary was impacted by yet another external shock in 2008–2009, as the global financial crisis caused a significant setback in growth, while the trade surplus rose. The reason for this was the balance sheet adjustment of the sectors. In order to reduce their accumulated debts, economic agents had to increase their savings, and they scaled back their demand to a great degree to achieve this. Economic policy also had to adjust to the situation after 2008. The growth rate of less than 2.5% was accompanied by an improvement in balance, as the economic policy measures to restore balance came with a growth sacrifice. As in the past, the traditionally negative Hungarian economic policy formula once again came to the fore during the years around the 2008–2009 crisis: if growth is strong, macroeconomic balance deteriorates, and if macroeconomic balance is good, growth declines.

A deterioration in the balance of the real economy, as reflected in trade deficits, is almost always accompanied by a deterioration in financial balance. This is generally reflected in the path of government debt, but is also mirrored by developments in two other items of external debt: the outstanding debt of households and enterprises. On numerous occasions, Hungarian fiscal policy became expansive during periods when households' propensity to save was also on the decline or had settled at a low level. Consequently, the budget's rising financing needs were almost immediately translated into an increase in the national economy's reliance on foreign borrowing. Figure 1, which shows the development of Hungarian government debt, illustrates this Hungarian pattern surprisingly well. The path of Hungarian government debt depends strongly on the fiscal policy which is pursued, and thus there is close correlation with the political cycles.

In 1998, the first Orbán Government inherited public debt amounting to 61% of GDP, which was reduced to 53% by mid-2012, before rising again to almost 70% of GDP during the 2002–2006 political term. During the political cycle from 2006 to 2010, Hungary's debt continued to rise from nearly 70% to reach a level of 85% of GDP. During the 2010–2014 political term, government debt hovered around 80%, showing how much more difficult it is to bring down public debt from a level of above 80%, as compared to a level around 60%. In addition to the elevated risk premium due to the higher government debt ratio, the budget's interest expenses are also higher, and furthermore – in addition to possible consolidation needs – following a crisis it is particularly difficult to lower the debt-to-GDP ratio if economic growth is lower.

Figure 1. Government debt, GDP and current account balance in Hungary

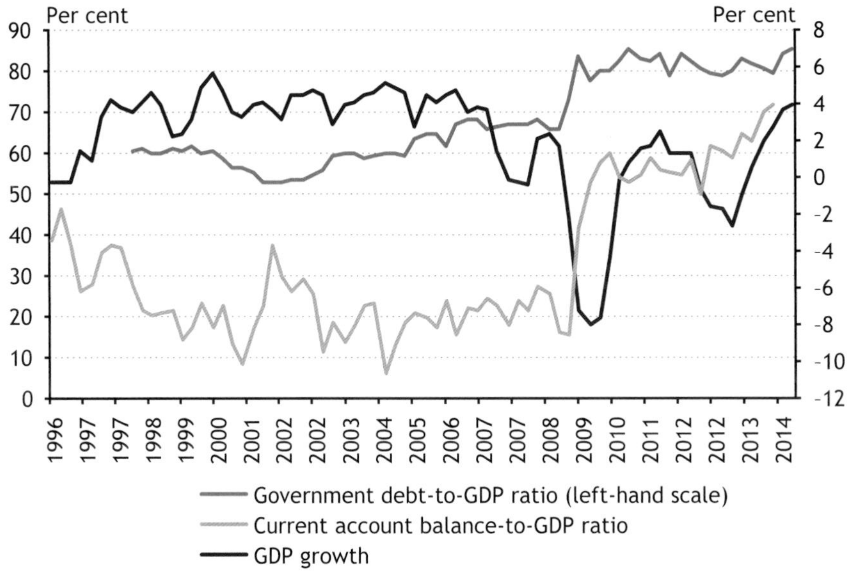

Source: Eurostat

Reviewing the Hungarian economy over the last one hundred years, it is clear that economic balance deteriorates as a result of external and internal shocks, but internal shocks are almost always due to flawed economic policy. The external shocks (the first and second World Wars, the Great Depression of 1929–1933, the two oil price crises and the 2008–2009 global financial crisis), together with poor economic policy led to balance and growth shocks. In each and every case, the internal shocks (the shock during the mid-1960s, the market economy transition in the 1990s, the Bokros package in 1995–1996 and the austerity policies of 2006–2008) stemming from poor economic policy decisions led to a growth sacrifice, while at the same time the measures taken did not or only moderately addressed the structural deficiencies of the economy and were consequently only able to improve economic balance on a temporary basis.

The reason for the internal shocks was economic imbalances, and the need to re-establish balance resulted from the mistaken economic policy. Until 2010, restoring economic balance after an internal shock always went hand in hand with sacrificing growth, thus perpetuating the formula for the "economic balance or growth" trap.

The external or internal shocks during the five decades following 1960 constantly maintained this incorrect economic policy formula. With successful fiscal consolidation and economic stabilisation, the Hungarian economy was able to break out of this vicious circle after 2010 and achieve a favourable pattern of "economic balance and growth".

A breakthrough in economic history: successful crisis management

In the four decades from 1974 to 2014, one of the most characteristic features of the Hungarian economy was the lack of long-term financial balance. At the beginning of the 1970s, due to the shock of the oil price crisis, Hungary's current account balance began to deteriorate sharply, and by the end of the second oil crisis in the 1970s the deficit amounted to 8% of GDP. During that decade, the budget deficit fluctuated in a range of roughly 6–10% of GDP, and this high budget deficit represents the other fundamental feature of the lack of financial balance. The external shock caused by the two oil crises was the reason behind both of these deficits, but the combination of the lack of a market economy structure and the centralised political regime transformed this external shock into an internal shock: the economic and financial system was not able to manage the effects of the external shocks in the 1970s and these consequently led to a deterioration in economic balance and a sharp rise in government debt.

From the late 1970s to the early 1980s, an adjustment to restore economic balance started in the Hungarian economy and positive results were achieved: 10 years after the oil price shock, balance was restored in 1983–1984, as the current account balance and the fiscal balance both returned to levels around zero. The unsustainable imbalance in these two financial indicators disappeared temporarily, but this achievement proved ephemeral. In the decade from 1974 to 1984, the Hungarian economy generally ran a twin deficit: negative balances were typical both for the budget and the current account, and these eventually reached an unsustainable level. The twin deficit disappeared between 1984 and 1990, but the unsustainable current account deficit remained in place. One can see that this period of economic balance was temporary, as the current account deficit between 1984 and 1988 was already around 4–6% of GDP, which is clearly an unsustainable level.

By contrast, the fiscal deficit hovered in a range of 0–4%. This did not represent a twin deficit, and compared to the previous decade and the coming decade it marked exceptionally good fiscal performance.

In the first half of the 1990s, as a result of the shock therapy transition to a market economy, both of these balance indicators simultaneously nosedived, and a large twin deficit was typical during this key phase of the transition period. After a brief period with a surplus, the current account balance moved steeply into a deficit of almost 10% of GDP, and the fiscal deficit also plunged to a level of 8% of GDP. In 1991–1994, at the decisive point of the shock therapy transition to a market economy, the balance indicators of the Hungarian economy deteriorated to a degree last seen as a result of the external shocks from the two oil price crises in the 1970s.

This forced shock therapy transition was an internal shock for the Hungarian economy: there were massive terminations of state-run enterprises and public sector jobs, and government investment and consumption plunged. As a result of this, budget revenues dried up and imports replaced the disappearing domestic production. During the 1970s, the external shock was transformed into an internal shock by the workings of economic policy, and a sharp rise in government debt was registered in conjunction with the twin deficits. In the first half of the 1990s, the internal shock and the external shock stemming from the collapse of the Eastern markets occurred simultaneously. The consolidation measures adopted in 1995–1996 attempted to address this situation, in the form of the so-called Bokros package and the related decisions on privatisation. Again, however, the improvement in balance indicators proved to be temporary: by the election year of 1998, the budget deficit had once again swelled to an unmanageable 8% of GDP. Similarly, the temporary improvement in the current account also turned around in 1996 and by 2000 a deficit of 8% of GDP had developed, which is also unsustainable over the long term.

Between 1998 and 2002, the budget situation improved significantly, but the current account deficit steadily remained at a level of 6–8% of GDP, in an unsustainable range.

Between 2002 and 2006, Hungary's economy is once again marked by a twin deficit, as the fiscal balance consistently showed a deficit between 6–8% of GDP until consolidation measures were launched in the second half of 2006, while the current account deficit was also steadily in a range of 6–8% of GDP. Although the fiscal balance improved between 2006 and 2008, the lack of economic balance continued, because this period occurred after Hungary's accession of the European Union: as part of joining the Union in 2004, Hungary undertook to maintain its budget deficit below 3% of GDP, a target which was clearly missed every single year in the period 2004–2010.

With the onset of the global financial crisis in autumn 2008, improving the current account balance became a necessity required by the response to the crisis. Neither the consolidation programme to restore economic balance in 2005–2008, nor the efforts to improve economic balance from 2008 to mid-2010 met with success in remedying the imbalances in Hungary's budget. Only in 2011 was Hungary was able to meet its EU obligation to achieve a fiscal deficit below 3% of GDP (according to the methodology valid at that time).

Starting from mid-2010, Hungary's new political approach and new economic policy led to a turnaround: between 2011 and 2014, fiscal balance was restored and the budget deficit target of less than 3% of GDP was achieved in a sustainable manner, while at the same time a steady, sustainable surplus was registered on the current account.

The development of balance indicators during the four decades between 1974 and 2014 shows that Hungarian economic policy and the structure of the Hungarian economy were not able to simultaneously achieve sustainable balance in the budget and the current account over the long term, all the way up until 2010. Either one or the other indicator deteriorated, leading to the balance being upset. Indeed, for long periods deterioration was seen in both of these indicators, resulting in a twin deficit. In 1983–1984 and in 1989–1990 there were two-year "grace periods", but otherwise Hungary was incapable of maintaining an environment of financial balance.

Starting from mid-2010 Hungary's macroeconomic balance started to improve, leading to a reversal of the trend in the general government deficit as early as 2011.

In the four years following 2010, Hungary's economic policy was able to achieve a sustainable fiscal balance and a sustainable current account balance at the same time. In respect of the former, this means a budget deficit of less than 3% of GDP. In respect of the latter, this is reflected by the surplus on the current account.

From the perspective of economic history, four decades is a span of time which is suitable for identifying the patterns characterising the operation of an economy. Clearly, over the span of several decades the Hungarian economy exhibits a tendency towards a loss of financial balance. With regard to these financial imbalances, both worsen as a result of external shocks, but the deterioration in the current account is worse than that seen in the fiscal balance. This allows us to draw the conclusion that the trade performance of the Hungarian economy is better than the resilience of its domestic economy to shocks. This suggests a deep-seated duality in the structure of the Hungarian economy: the sectors participating in foreign trade show better performance, even during periods of shock, than the sectors of the economy producing for the domestic market.

Another special feature of the decades between 1974 and 2014 is that the two balance indicators tend to move in tandem: in the event of deterioration in the fiscal balance, the current account balance also worsens; in the event of improvement in the fiscal balance, the current account balance is also more favourable. Again, this underlines the weak ability to weather shocks, and again the dualistic economic structure is behind this. Simultaneous deterioration in the two balance indicators is linked to external shocks and economic policy efforts to restore balance, and thus to internal shocks. In the absence of external and internal shocks, both indicators improve, if the economic policy approach is correct. This occurred for part of the 1980s, but did not occur in the period from 2002 to 2006, when almost the entire global economy was in a simultaneous economic upturn. Hungarian economic policy initially provided an unsuccessful response to the 2008 crisis in the field of fiscal policy, but economic agents responded appropriately in relation to the current account.

During the four decades under review, three external shocks impacted Hungary's economy: the oil price crisis of the 1970s, the collapse of the Eastern markets in 1990 and the 2008 global financial crisis. In each of these three cases, balance indicators in the Hungarian economy deteriorated in response.

The most severe deterioration in balance indicators was seen when the external shock was intensified by an internal shock. This occurred in the second half of the 1990s, when transition to a market economy was triggered both by the collapse of the Eastern markets and withdrawal from the Eastern political system, using an economic policy of shock therapy.

As a result of the deep-seated dualistic structure of the Hungarian economy, its ability to resist shocks is weak, because the sectors playing a role in foreign trade are able to adjust quickly, while agents mainly producing for the domestic market are only able to adjust slowly. On the other hand, there is a strong link between economic policy and imbalances: this was the case between 2002 and 2006 (the years marked by twin deficits), when both the fiscal balance and the current account showed deficits running between 6% and 10% of GDP (Figure 2).

Another feature of the Hungarian economy is that it responds to both external and internal shocks with a strong rise in government debt. This was seen in the 1970s, and in the period between 2002 and 2010, but is also occurred in a hidden form in the second half of the 1990s. At that time, economic policy was not fundamentally characterised by new borrowing, but rather by the sale of state assets: a reduction in the state assets backing the earlier level of public debt actually results in a higher level of indebtedness.[1] To a great extent, the revenues from privatisation in 1994–1998 were used to pay off earlier government debts. This is what happened with the USD 3 billion in revenue from the privatisation of the hydrocarbons industry, but in the case of other privatisation projects, for example power utilities, the reduction in the state's assets did not equal the decline in government debt through the privatisation revenues (Figure 3).

---

[1] In official statistics, it is mainly the figure for gross general government debt which is published, but from an economic point of view, net debt is also of similar significance. This is because in the case of gross debt, one must take into account that states also have financial receivables. Net debt can be interpreted as the difference between gross debt and the state's gross financial assets, although there is no exact definition. In relation to the definition, the unanswered question is precisely what parts of a state's financial assets are to be taken into consideration in the calculation (e.g. in addition to deposits and debt-type receivables, should equity shares and non-liquid items also be considered?). If we also take into account equity shares in the calculation of net debt, then net debt cannot be reduced by privatisation, because in this case the receivables decline to the same degree as the debts.

Figure 2. Current account balance and fiscal balance in Hungary, 1974-2014

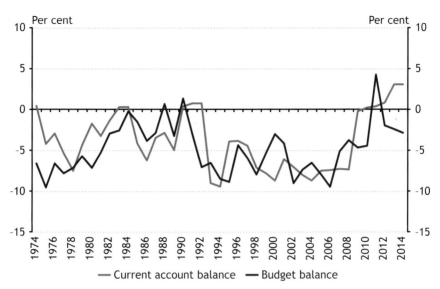

Source: MNB   % of GDP

In addition to the external and internal shocks, the differing economic policies and the dualistic structure of the economy, there is another factor behind the tendencies towards deterioration in macroeconomic balance before and after 1990: the cyclical nature of fixed investments. In the centrally planned economy system prior to 1990, it was essentially the investment projects by large, state-owned enterprises and the state's infrastructure investments which were reflected in developments in balance indicators. The upward leg of the investment cycle was also behind the deterioration in the current account as well as in the fiscal balance: this leg involved imports for investment purposes, along with the need for working capital for the operation of the investment and capacities. In the Hungarian economy before and after 1990, a substantial portion of this came from imports.

Figure 3. Government debt and GDP growth, 1974-2014

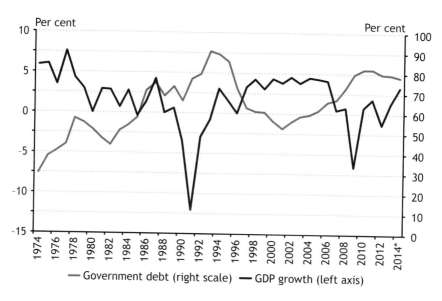

*estimate

Source: MNB, HCSO, Mihályi (2013): A magyar gazdaság útja az adósságválságba 1945–2013

Hungary's propensity for economic imbalance is also reflected in the link between the trade balance and GDP growth. Based on more than five decades of data from 1961 to 2014, it can be seen that – compared to the average GDP growth rate of 2.7% for this half century – higher rates of growth were generally accompanied by deterioration in the trade balance and tended to lead to a deficit on this balance. During the 1960s and the first half of the 1970s, until the oil crisis of 1973–1974, growth was significantly higher than the historical rate of GDP growth for the half century, and aside from a few years this was accompanied by a negative balance on the trade account.

During the lengthy period from the second half of the 1970s to the end of the 1980s, the rate of GDP growth remained lower than this 2.7% historical average, while at the same time a substantial positive balance was recorded on the foreign trade account for most of this period.

The shock therapy transition to a market economy in the first half of the 1990s temporarily upset this connection: the massive contraction in GDP was linked to a sharp deterioration in the trade balance, and thus to a large trade deficit. The original strong connection between the trade balance and GDP growth reappears around 2000, as GDP growth above the historical average is associated with a deficit on trade again.

Figure 4. Economic growth and trade balance in Hungary, 1961-2014

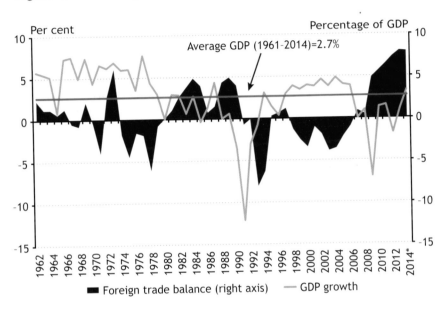

Source: HCSO, MNB Inflation Report (September 2014)   * estimate

A shift had already occurred before the 2008 global crisis: from spring 2005 the investment rate in Hungary begins to fall and from autumn 2006 a new policy of austerity measures is launched. As a result of these developments, the rate of Hungarian GDP growth was lower than the historical average from 2006 to autumn 2008, during a period of economic upturn on Hungary's external markets.

Low GDP growth is once again accompanied by an improvement in the trade balance. In 2009, GDP plunges while the trade balance improves, and then thanks to the successful crisis management measures taken until 2014 growth returns to the Hungarian economy, but does not result in deterioration in the trade balance (Figure 4).

Naturally, from an economic history perspective, the period from 2010 to 2014 is too short to make a definitive statement that a lasting change has taken place in the Hungarian economy in terms of the link between GDP growth and the trade balance, but during the five years of crisis management we clearly see a new correlation for this period. GDP growth was higher than the historical average for the last fifty years, but this did not occur in conjunction with renewed deterioration in the trade balance. Indeed, the trade surplus continued to rise, and at the same time a substantial surplus was also registered on the current account. The large improvement in the terms of trade also made a contribution to this growth in the trade surplus: while changes in export and import prices had a negative impact on the trade balances of countries in the region after the crisis, these changes were very supportive of growth in Hungary (Figure 5).

Figure 5. Terms of trade in the region

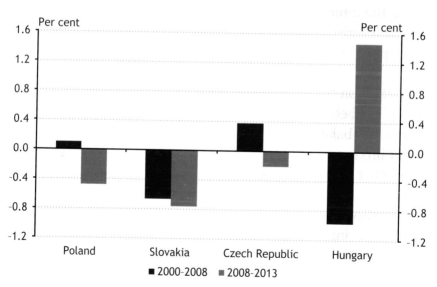

Source: MNB

After showing a tendency to become imbalanced during the four decades between 1974 and 2010, the first real change in Hungary's economy occurred between 2011 and 2014. A sustained surplus was recorded on the current account, and a balanced level was reached for the fiscal deficit within the framework of the European Union. Lasting improvement in economic balance was achieved in the two most important financial balance indicators.

What might be the reason for the change in the previously asymmetric relationship between the trade balance and economic growth? Before 1990, under the planned economy and centralised political regime, it was the state and politics which determined the course of economic policy, and through this also set the tone for developments in economic balance and growth. This economic policy allowed for rising deficits, including the fiscal deficit, the trade deficit and the current account deficit, but this was already unsustainable in the prevailing non-market environment: economic policy measures intended to restore economic balance depressed the rate of economic growth below the historical average. In the economic system before 1990, the state played the main role, and the interests of the political and state leaders, and the heads of large enterprises resulted in the long-standing "economic balance or growth" paradigm.

Even in the non-market economy functioning before 1990, there was a strong link between financial balance, the current account balance and the fiscal balance, and GDP growth. Within the current account, a similar linkage is found between developments in the trade balance and the rate of GDP growth.

What is really interesting, however, is that similar relationships are also found during the period 1990–2010, when the Hungarian economy was already operating under market conditions. The change of political regime and the introduction of a new economic model did not result in any major change in the relationship between economic balance and growth: the formula of "economic balance or growth" also remained intact in this new political and economic system.

Examining market balance, we also find a similar relationship in the development of inflation: in the event of economic growth above the historical average, the balance indicators deteriorate, adjustment programmes are launched, these retard growth, and the pattern is repeated.

Deterioration in market balance appears in different forms in the Hungarian economy in the periods before and after 1990. Both economic logic and the actual developments demonstrate that hidden inflation (a shortage of goods) and open inflation (increases in consumer prices) are closely related to Hungarian GDP growth rates being below or above the historical average.

All of this clearly underlines the underlying tendency towards imbalances in the Hungarian economy, and indeed in Hungarian society. Before 1990, the deterioration in the balance indicators was caused by the state's desire for growth and accumulation. The same outcome was seen in the market economy framework, with all economic agents pursuing these goals. And finally, after 2002, economic balance again deteriorated as both the state and households focused on growth and accumulation. By 2014, the inverse relationship between economic balance and growth had been broken, because the system of values and method of operation of Hungarian society and economic agents underwent significant changes. The state now pays serious attention to one of the key economic balance indicators, fiscal balance, and thus a sea change has occurred in the government's system of values and operation of the largest participant in the economy (the state is responsible for redistribution of approximately 50% of GDP). Households' behaviour has also changed: accumulation of wealth by borrowing has been replaced with savings and the reduction of past debts. One major change is that the goal of accumulation has been replaced with the goal of security. Values and approaches have also changed in the corporate sector: investment financed with companies' rising savings has taken the place of investment and decisions financed by borrowing, typically using foreign currency loans.

While the structure of the economy continues to be characterised by duality, sensible decision-making by SMEs in Hungary has caught up with the rational investment decisions made by developed sectors which are active on the global markets.

The change in the previous paradigm of economic balance or growth and the shift to a new formula of simultaneous economic balance and growth in the Hungarian economy was made possible by this fundamental change in the behaviour of all economic agents.

If only the behaviour of the state had changed, the earlier pattern of borrowing and accumulation followed by the corporate sector and households would have continued to disturb financial balance in Hungary. If only the behaviour of enterprises and households had shifted towards greater rationality, the regular increase in the budget deficit would have led to repeated consolidation programmes, preserving the paradigm of "economic balance or growth". Because the behaviour of all three economic agents changed, and because this change was significant and concerted, it was possible to overcome the inadequate paradigm of the last fifty years and replace "economic balance OR growth" with "economic balance and growth" (Figure 6).

Figure 6. GDP, fiscal and current account balance,
and inflation in Hungary, 1974-2014

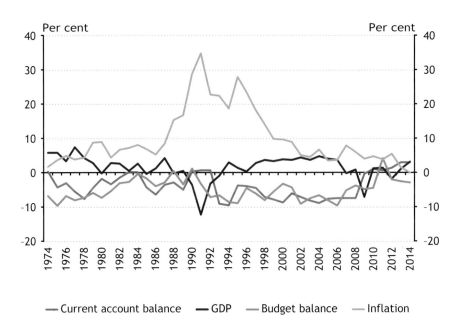

Source: MNB

Looking at the main players in the global economy, one can see that there is a mildly negative correlation between economic growth and the current account balance, and the strength and direction of this connection can change from time to time.

In the wake of the crisis, the issue of financial sustainability has become more important in the assessment of long-term growth prospects. In line with this, the equilibrium growth rate is a rate of economic growth which does not result in an unsustainable financing position or debt path. Clearly, in the period before the successful crisis management in 2010–2014, the Hungarian economy repeatedly moved on an unsustainable path according to this definition. It was possible to achieve a turnaround in this regard, because in addition to economic policy, which mainly determines the balance and growth indicators, the way Hungarian society works also underwent a fundamental change. A society's system of values goes beyond the annual scope of the government budget and the four-to-five year horizon of economic policy cycles and influences the growth path of an economy through deeper relationships (Figure 7).

Figure 7. GDP growth and current account balance

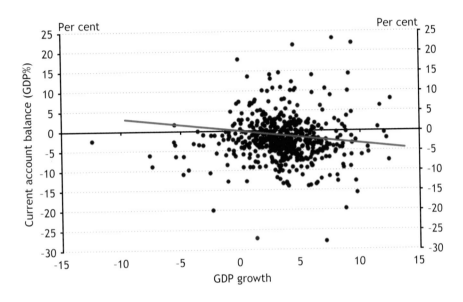

Source: IMF–IFS, WDI

The fundamental system of values of Hungarian society is Anglo-Saxon in nature. In this system, individual and family values are key aspects, with the value of wealth accumulation at the core. During the non-market economy period from 1960 to 1990, almost the only way that individuals and families were able to pursue this value of wealth accumulation was through the acquisition of real property.

For lack of private economic opportunities and under the centralised political system, acquiring moveable and real property was the only way that families could express this fundamental value of wealth accumulation. It was hardly possible to build up one's own company, a family firm or to increase one's financial wealth or collect valuable items: the value of wealth accumulation was reflected in the acquisition of real property and moveable goods primarily through consumption (durable consumer goods).

After 1990, there was a major change: the development of one's own company, the expansion of a family firm, accumulation of savings and other valuables became more common ways of expressing people's desire for wealth accumulation and their related decisions. In the 2000s, however, another significant change occurred: investment in real property reappeared as an option, alongside the accumulation of business wealth.

During the period of misguided economic policy from 2002 to 2010, the unbridled rise in foreign currency lending and the ballooning of the banking sector's balance sheet were actually the consequences of decisions by the state, and in most cases the consequences of the state's failure to make decisions. Thus, the state in fact reinforced Hungarian society's wealth accumulation values, whereas it would have been in the interests of economic policy to channel these desires for wealth accumulation towards success in business. From a social and economic point of view, the development of a family company is a better form of wealth accumulation than an investment on the real estate market financed with a foreign currency loan. Financial savings are also more favourable, as they create the future foundations for investment decisions by companies or families.

The main factor behind the major change that occurred and paved the way for the simultaneous development of sustainable financial balance and long-term economic growth is that the state is no longer influencing the decisions of individuals and families in a negative manner; it is no longer fuelling the desire for wealth accumulation found at the core of the Hungarian system of values. The state no longer promotes the expansion of real property assets; instead, it provides incentives for the development of business wealth and financial savings. In doing so, it cools the Hungarians' desire for the acquisition of physical assets and channels this into a direction which is favourable from an economic policy perspective.

This all occurred in a time frame which is very short from the point of view of economic history, during the period 2010–2014. Two mutually reinforcing factors played a key role in this: the dual crisis which happened after 2006 and the change in the functioning of the state after 2010.

Taking a longer perspective, during the six decades between 1947 and 2007 Hungarian economic growth showed significant fluctuations in terms of the historical trend in GDP growth. The two to three years of reconstruction after 1945 saw Hungarian GDP growth start out below the historical trend, followed by above-trend economic growth for the period from 1957 to 1989. Growth developed below the trend during the shock therapy transition to the market economy and the related losses from the start of the 1990s all the way until 2007.

During the three decades between 1957 and 1989–1990, Hungarian GDP expanded at a rate above the historical trend, but in many respects this growth was unsustainable. On the one hand, almost two hundred years of economic history shows that in a market economy it is not possible to sustain growth above its trend in a closed economy or a closed integration: the centralised political system and command economy achieved this artificial growth in an internally closed integration which was open to the East.

While the method of transition to a market economy which had to be chosen, i.e. shock therapy, entailed greater sacrifices than necessary, in terms of GDP all of the countries which moved from a non-market economy system to a market economy experienced these sacrifices: the losses incurred during the market transition reflect the unsustainability of the earlier non-market economy system. In fact, the transition to a market economy merely brought to the surface the losses which were hidden under the earlier economic system.

Thus, from a historical perspective, we must consider the period between 1957 and 1990 as a phase of unsustainable growth: it was merely a question of time as to when the change of political regime and transition to the market economy would occur.

After 1990, the losses from the earlier non-market system which were exposed and the losses stemming from the shock therapy market transition were combined: this is reflected in the Hungarian GDP growth rate falling below the historical trend for the period from 1990 to 2007.

The global financial crisis then erupted in 2008, and Hungarian GDP plunged again in 2009. Following this, new losses were realised; these were not losses from the market transition and the earlier non-market economic system, but rather the risks and losses stemming from the misguided economic policy pursued after 2002 (Figure 8).

Figure 8. Per capita GDP growth in Hungary, 1947-2010

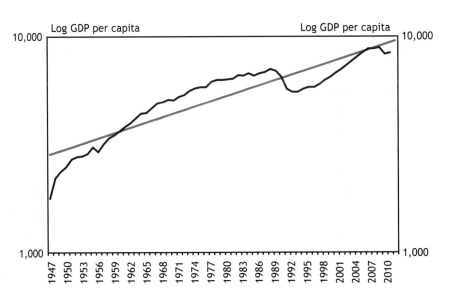

Source: Maddison project

The real question in the coming years and decades will be whether the new economic policy formula, i.e. expanding employment and long-term growth equals sustainable economic balance, is able to produce and sustain a rate of GDP growth which is above the historical trend.

Hungary has a good chance of achieving this, because the previous three decades of above-trend economic growth were unsustainable due to the centralised political system and the non-market economy, but the economic policy and unsuccessful consolidation attempts between 2002 and 2010 occurred in a democratic system in a market economy which is open to the global market. In the period 2002–2010, economic output improved, as evidenced by GDP growth approaching the trend, but this was accompanied by mounting imbalances, which were also responsible for the lower growth during the years following the crisis. Hungary remedied its flawed economic policy in 2010–2014, leading to a recovery in growth in a very short period of time in terms of economic history and sustained Hungarian GDP growth above the historical trend, from the perspective of a decade.

This is also backed by the fact that the Hungarian economy has significant growth reserves: the activity rate continues to be low, several hundred thousand Hungarians are working abroad, the investment rate only increased to around 20% in one single year (2014), and household consumption is still being hindered by the outstanding foreign currency loans, as well as earlier borrowing in forints.

Thanks to these significant growth reserves and the new structure for using the more than EUR 34.5 billion in EU funds available during the EU's seven-year financing period 2014–2020, there is a very real chance that Hungarian GDP growth will be higher than the trend in the coming years and even in the coming decades.

Comparing the trend for the growth rate in the USA with the Hungarian trend, one sees an interesting difference: the trend growth rate for 1883–2003 fits quite closely with the actual path of GDP growth in the US economy. There are two major deviations: one upwards and one downwards. These were the prolonged effects of the 1929–1933 economic crisis, which was only ended by the war-time economic upturn, and then the effect of that upturn in the 1940s, when the US economy produced GDP growth higher than the trend. The difference between the growth trends in Hungary and the USA actually stems from the differences in economic policy. The US economy was always a market economy, and thus its economic policy was continuously formulated and measured in a market economic environment. The switchover to a war-time economy in the 1930s and 1940s was the exception, while the market economy was the rule.

Comparison of the US and Hungarian growth rates reveals several things. First, that while it was possible to boost GDP growth above the trend in Hungary under non-market economy conditions, this growth proved to be unsustainable. Second, that external and internal shocks resulted in below-trend growth in both economies. Third, the state plays a substantial role in the development of growth rates which deviate from the trend: prior to the 1929–1933 crisis, it was the lack of intervention by the US government which significantly diverted US growth from the trend, and later it was the economic policies which led to recovery from the crisis and the economic policies during the war. The case is similar in the Hungarian economy: the quality of economic policy and the use of the correct or the incorrect policy tools indicates that – in terms of producing GDP growth below or above trend – the modern state plays a significant role in the USA, but that it plays a decisive role in the Hungarian economy (Figure 9).

Figure 9. Per capita GDP growth in the USA, 1883-2010

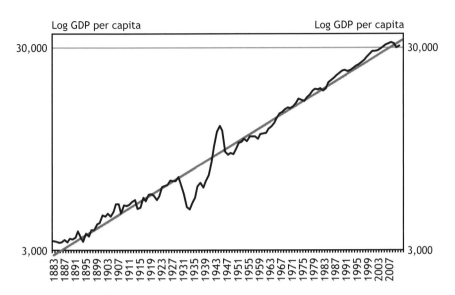

Source: Maddison project

Bearing in mind that the simultaneous fiscal consolidation and stabilisation of the economy was unique in the first decade of EU membership, as well as the two decades of the new market economy after 1990 and indeed for the last fifty years and even more than one hundred years of Hungarian economic history, one must necessarily ask a fundamental question: how was it possible?

The need for successful consolidation and stabilisation after 2010 stemmed from the country's high external debt and government debt. The opportunity to achieve this, however, was opened up by the political transition in 2010, when the victorious political parties secured a two-thirds majority in the Hungarian parliament. The strong support for the governing parties paved the way to launch reforms in areas which were crucial in terms of the structural deficiencies of the Hungarian economy, often involving politically sensitive issues. The change in Hungarian politics allowed for the re-orientation of economic policy, redirecting the economy towards a new, sustainable formula for development. The goal was to achieve sustainable economic balance by expanding employment and restarting economic growth.

The results are all the more impressive because in early 2010 the Greek financial crisis erupted, and consequently the EU did not support a Hungarian policy aimed at gradually restoring economic balance and demanded immediate fiscal consolidation. It almost seemed like 1990 all over again: back then, instead of a gradual transition to a market economy, the new Western allies demanded shock therapy, and their arguments were backed by the very high levels of Hungarian general government debt compared to the peers in the region (and the fact that much of this debt was held by precisely these allies). A gradual move towards economic balance was rejected again in 2010, and again their argument rested on the high level of debt. But this is where the first turnaround occurred: economic policy started by reversing its own formula. First, economic balance was restored and at the same time the structure for a new growth path was created, and then following successful budget consolidation, economic growth was restarted.

In contrast to the other EU countries, however, Hungary not only achieved the deficit target of 3% of GDP indicating a balanced government budget for the first time since accession of the EU in 2004, it carried out this fiscal consolidation in a sustainable manner, by implementing structural reforms.

Consolidation of the Hungarian budget after 2010 was exceptional, because it did not merely achieve the 3% deficit over the short term, but rather over the long term. With the exception of 2011 which also involved one-off expenses,[2] the general government deficit has continuously remained below 3% since 2010. This is already a striking

[2] Due to the methodological revisions of the European system of national accounts (ESA-2010), the revenues for 2011 do not include the revenues stemming from the private pension fund savings of persons returning to the public pension system and as a result according to the latest statistical data a deficit of 5.5% of GDP was registered instead of the previous surplus.

medium-term achievement and has been accompanied by positive trends in consumption, investment and economic growth.

A new employment policy and new tax system were at the heart of these structural reforms. In the following chapters, we will see how many critics of Hungary's economic policy consider the bank levy, the crisis taxes and a number of other measures to be temporary, and thus do not believe that this consolidation is sustainable. They fail to see, however, that this consolidation was followed by economic stabilisation and then by a recovery in growth, which will lead to new fiscal revenues, while at the same time employment is steadily expanding. Over the long run, all of these factors will render this consolidation sustainable.

The structural reforms made the new economic balance sustainable, and also helped to trigger economic growth in a new structure. Over the long term, sustainable economic balance creates favourable conditions for the stable functioning and growth of the real economy. Hungary's successful consolidation and stabilisation after 2010 is built on an economic policy vision according to which if employment expands dynamically and growth starts again, this will automatically preserve economic balance.

Thus, in 2010 Hungarian economic policy simultaneously applied a long-term formula, employment + growth = sustainable economic balance, and a short-term formula, fiscal balance + rising employment = growth, with the latter formula paving the way for the success of the former.

Had it proven impossible to turn around the budget from 2010 to 2011, there would have been no chance to transition to a formula for sustainable, long-term development.

There is, however, a hidden connection between these two formulas: they are actually in harmony with one another. Restoring fiscal balance essentially only used tools which did not hinder economic growth.

Indeed, many of the tools used to achieve the fiscal turnaround, such as the restructuring of the private pension system, budgetary spending freezes, reform of the tax system, the bank levy, crisis taxes and other measures, actually helped to foster growth again after economic balance had been re-established. In fact, the short-term decisions did not undermine the transition to a successful, long-term economic policy, they actually supported it. The hidden, indirect and delayed effect of sector-specific taxes actually leads to structural changes: a healthier ownership structure and stronger competition develops in the banking sector and in the energy sector. The sector-specific taxes are not in fact temporary sources of revenue, but rather the source of structural reforms.

Thanks to the structural reforms, fiscal balance has been restored, employment has been on a continuous upward trend, and consolidation has created the basis for a re-orientation of Hungary's monetary policy as well. In mid-2013, the new leadership of the Magyar Nemzeti Bank changed the direction of Hungary's monetary policy, simultaneously reinforcing price stability, sustainable economic balance, rising employment and economic growth. Thus, the political change in Hungary resulted in a fresh economy policy, which in turn triggered structural reforms, as a result of which fiscal balance was restored, which paved the way for a new approach in monetary policy, facilitating a recovery in Hungarian economic growth. Following the re-establishment of economic balance in 2011–2012, a recovery in economic growth was seen in 2013–2014. With this, Hungary has left behind the trap of "economic balance or growth" and entered a new era of "economic balance and growth".

Part One

From crisis to crisis

Chapter 1

Legacy of the global and European crisis

In mid-2010, Hungary was confronted with the necessity of consolidating its finances, due to the flawed economic policy pursued after 2002 and the consequences of the 2008 global financial crisis. These were the two problems which rendered the Hungarian crisis so serious, and both of them had to be solved at the same time.

Crisis of the Western economic model

The global financial crisis in 2008–2009 which started in the developed Western economies eventually evolved into an extremely complex, prolonged balance sheet crisis at the global level. Initially, the problems in the financial system appeared in the market of the most developed banks (theorically) using the most advanced risk management methods, before spreading to affect the systems of less developed economies.

Actually, however, the events of 2008–2009 plunged the very model of the free market economy based on the free market philosophy and the consumer society into crisis. The central precept of this model is the belief in the self-regulating ability of the markets, and thus the idea that market forces must be allowed to operate freely, because any imbalances in supply and demand will eventually be remedied by an internal, self-correcting mechanism. According to this idea, only one agent would be able to take the place of the market, namely the state, but there is no need for this to occur, since the market can take care of everything itself. Indeed, not only is there no need for the state, its presence on the market is actually harmful because it is not a natural market agent when dealing with companies and individuals and therefore its intervention can only cause distortion: its operation does not improve, but rather worsens the situation. This is the train of thought behind the points of the "Washington consensus", but it is in reality a belief and not a proven fact, and indeed experience tends to refute its validity, rather than confirm it.

Over two hundred years of financial and economic crises, this belief has led to failure over and over again, because the participation of the state was always needed to manage crises, and the prevention of crises by state regulation would have resulted in smaller losses than the crises and the subsequent efforts to deal with them. Its failure was complete, however, during the 1929–1933 world economic crisis, because without exception all of the economies affected were only able to emerge from the crisis with the help of the state. In fact, all the way up until the 1980s market balance and economic growth could only be maintained with the increasing participation of the state.

The crises occurring in market economies are no accident, they are an inevitable outcome. Crises reflect the joint failure of the markets and state regulation. In each and every case, bad decisions by market agents are behind a crisis. If each and every market participant would always make the right decision, internal factors in an economy could not trigger a crisis. If, at the global level, all market participants in every country would always made the right decisions, then a global crisis could also not occur, neither as a result of external nor internal factors.

However, the market is experiencing a series of crises every single moment, because complete and total balance between supply and demand never occurs anywhere. While this balance is possible in theory, it is impossible in the real world. The reason for this is quite simple: all of the necessary information has to be available to make the right decision. Indeed, for everyone to always be able to make the right decision everywhere, it is not enough for some market participants to have all of the necessary information. For this to occur, all market participants would always have to have all of the necessary information. But no market participants anywhere ever have all of the necessary information, and thus they are unable to always make the right decisions.[3]

If many agents make good decisions for a long period of time, then no crisis develops, but if many participants make bad decisions which have an increasingly significant negative impact, then a crisis erupts. Tiny, unnoticed crises, however, are always occurring on every market: deviation between supply and demand is natural, and it is based on lack of information; this is at once the engine which drives development. Otherwise, a crisis always represents a lack of regulation, or the failure of regulation. The state has the responsibility of ensuring the framework conditions for the functioning of the market economy and remedying its errors. Proper state regulation can help achieve a situation in which too many market participants do not make bad decisions for too long.

The 2008–2009 global financial crisis had its origins in the US financial system, and this was no coincidence. Starting from the early 1980s, the US financial system was gradually able to have its own interests accepted as being the interests of the national economy: this ultimately led to a crisis. US financial institutions successfully promoted the pretence that "what is good for the banks is good for the country". In the 1930s, President Roosevelt reformulated the regulation of the financial markets, because the financial system was also responsible for the 1929–1933 financial crisis. By the end of the 1990s, however, the mega-banks in the USA had once again become so strong that they were able to exert control over the political parties and Congress. They

---

[3] The Austrian neo-liberal economist Friedrich Hayek argued that individual participants in the economy did not have to have all the information, they only needed to know the market price. This is because the price formed on the market transmits all of the information on developments in supply and demand which is essential for the participants. In practice, two arguments can be made against this assertion. First, enterprises with significant market power can influence the prices, and thus distort the information which they contain. Second, it is not possible to assign a price to all goods which are valuable for a society. See: Hayek (1945): The Use of Knowledge in Society. American Economic Review, Vol. 35, No. 4, pp. 519–530.

successfully argued that the wider use of financial innovations and the dismantling of the state's regulation of the financial markets would be beneficial for the economy. In their opinion, market self-regulation also functioned on the financial market: in 2007–2008 it finally turned out that this market was not able to regulate itself and that dismantling government regulation was a mistake.

The greed of the US mega-banks led to the financial crisis. This was backed by the loose monetary policy of the US central bank, and the absence of the earlier government regulation which had been dismantled also contributed to the crisis. Financial globalisation opened up a new chapter for the global economy and speeded up development, but it also exacerbated the risks involved in lending. The real risk in lending is a crisis, i.e. that borrowers will not be able to repay their debts, and this risk increased with financial globalisation.

Consequently, crises occurred more and more frequently.[4] Financial crises became larger and larger, and more and more expensive. Lending money, i.e. providing financing, is an unusual activity, in the sense that it is founded on promises. If I take out a loan, I trust the party from whom I have borrowed and, vice-versa, that party trusts me. The global financial world is like a pyramid built on promises, and this pyramid can easily turn into a house of cards over time. Catastrophic

---

[4] Based on the frequency of financial crises, modern economic history can be divided into three periods. The first period lasted up until the crisis of the Great Depression and was marked by loose regulation and strong international financial integration. During this period, financial crises were relatively frequent events. The second period roughly corresponds to the duration of the Bretton Woods system, starting from the end of WWII until the 1970s. This period was characterised by strict regulation and weak global financial integration, but at the same time financial crises also became less frequent. The third period, which is currently occurring, is characterised by the features of the first period: relaxation of regulation and the strengthening of international integration. This may partly be why the frequency of crises has increased again. See: Schularick et al. (2012): Credit Booms Gone Bust: Monetary Policy, Leverage Cycles, and Financial Crises, 1870–2008. American Economic Review, Vol. 102, No. 2, pp. 1029–1061.

situations can develop quickly if one part fails, for example because panic breaks out on the financial markets and everyone realises that financial promises are actually not made of stone, but are really just like cards. This is precisely what happened when the crisis in the USA erupted: part of the US financial system collapsed like a house of cards.

The US financial crisis turned into a global crisis, the financial crisis triggered an economic crisis in the European Union and the developed world, and the economic crises led to political and social crises. The series of global crises in 2008–2009 resulted in a significant change in the earlier trends in the global economy. The exponential growth trend previously seen in world trade was interrupted, and the growth rate of global trade in goods decelerated in particular. The crisis caused a sharp break in world trade in 2009, and this setback had still not been overcome by 2013: the pace of growth in global trade has changed over the long term. In Asia, savings are too high and consumption is too low, while in the USA and in the Western world in general, consumption is too high and savings are too low. The internal imbalance in the global economy of the early 21st century were exposed and it became clear that this imbalance was not sustainable (Figure 10).

The crisis of the West and the bursting of the real estate bubble also represent a breaking point for the Western model of the free market economy.

The cause of the financial crisis was that the US financial system was able to elevate its own interests above the interests of the state and the country. But there was also another reason behind the financial crisis: the doubling of the financial world. The virtual world of the financial markets outgrew the tangible, real economy and these markets became several times larger than the value of a nation's assets and the real economy. This is also reflected by the excessive attention paid to the interests of the financial markets.

Figure 10. Ratio of import-based and GDP-based external demand

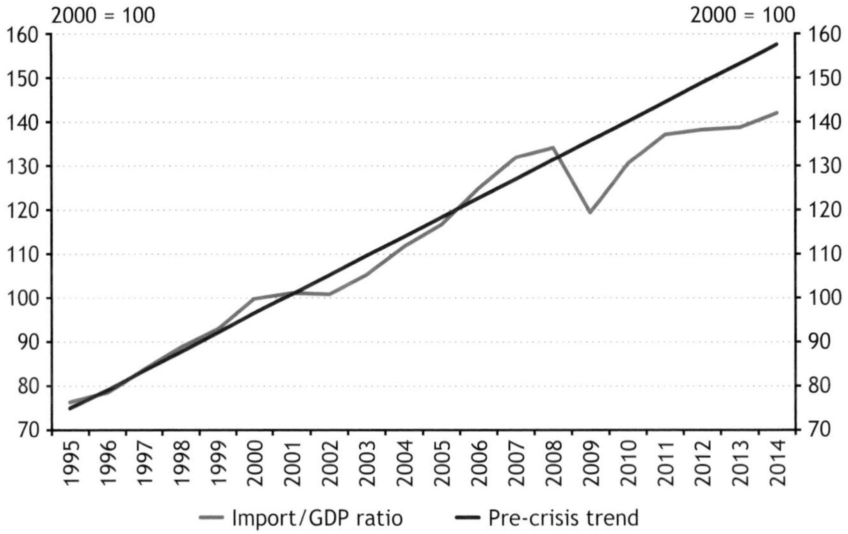

Source: MNB Inflation Report, December 2013

Debt crisis in the developed Western economies

Debt accumulation in the West and the debt crisis in the advanced economies were the factors behind the 2008–2009 global financial crisis. In the Western countries, while all economic agents took on debt, the growth in government debt was the largest problem. After 2007, the level of government debt in the Western countries suddenly surged higher, and the Anglo-Saxon countries were in a worse position than the member states of the European Union. The global financial crisis exposed the internal inequalities of globalisation and resulted in the indebtedness of the developed countries (Figure 11).

Figure 11. General government gross debt as a percentage of GDP in
developed and emerging G20 countries, 2004-2014

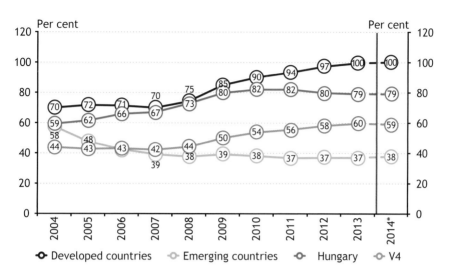

Source: IMF   * estimate

The rapid rise in government debt in the developed economies is
actually a sickness. It reflects an imbalance between the state and the
market, between regulation and freedom. The market has obtained
excessive power vis-à-vis the state. In the USA and the European
Union, it is as if the fate of the British Empire was playing out again:
Great Britain entered the First World War in 1914 as the world's largest
creditor, and ended the war in 1918 as the world's largest debtor. The
West entered into the struggle of globalisation going on behind the
scenes between the developed and emerging markets as the world's
largest creditor and capital investor, but after the crisis in 2008–2009
government debt rose sharply in many of the developed countries,
indicating that the West does not appear to be winning this struggle. The
elevated government debt levels in these countries will be increasingly
difficult to finance in the coming decades, because the central banks
supported the accumulation of debt with historically low base interest
rates and loose monetary policy.

In the years ahead, the monetary policy of central banks may return to the historically higher levels of interest rates: this will make the financing of the elevated levels of government debt in the USA and the European Union more and more expensive. The challenges faced by the European Union are even more serious because while some countries have preserved their economic balance and competitiveness (and even built up surpluses), others have fallen deep into debt.

Crisis in the euro area

The total debt of the 28 member states of the European Union amounts to more than EUR 11,000 billion. The annual cost of servicing this debt (interest and redemption) is EUR 2,000 billion. The economies in the European Union accumulate EUR 1,200 billion of new debt every day. Within this, the debts of the euro area countries are backed by the euro. The decision to introduce the euro was a political one, involving the financial integration of economies which exhibited differences of more than 25 percentage points in terms of their level of development:[5] this caused a hidden crisis for the use of the single currency right from the very moment of its inception. While the Union accounts for 25% of the world's economic output, it also pays 50% of the world's total social expenditure. Accordingly, the internal crisis in the Union can be traced back to two fundamental reasons: first, the financing crisis of the welfare state, which basically affects all of the developed member states, and second, the crisis of the euro as the common currency in the euro area (Figure 12).

Starting from autumn 2008, in response to the global financial crisis the European Central Bank started to reduce its base interest rate, which ensured cheap funds for the countries to manage the crisis. This move, however, did not do anything to address the fundamental problem of the euro area, namely that regions which were very different in terms of their economic structures, institutional systems and regulatory

[5] Expressed in PPP-based GDP per capita.

frameworks had been combined under a common currency. The European Union and within this, the euro area, are in the midst of a continuous financial crisis, as is clearly reflected by the fact that high fiscal deficits are tolerated and the level of public debt is steadily rising.

The southern countries in the euro area are struggling with severe fiscal and debt problems, as a combined result of the unsustainable growth paths which were mainly financed by the accumulation of debt at low interest rates in the years before the crisis and the massive fiscal austerity measures implemented during the period when the recovery was still fragile. Through the close foreign trade relations, the persistent weakness of the economies in the euro area periphery also hampered growth in the core countries and exacerbated the deflationary risks. Over the long run, the slower increase in nominal GDP may also force the social and welfare states which are in a stronger initial position to take corrective measures, due to the slowdown in public revenues.

Figure 12. Gross government debt as a percentage of GDP in the euro area and the European Union

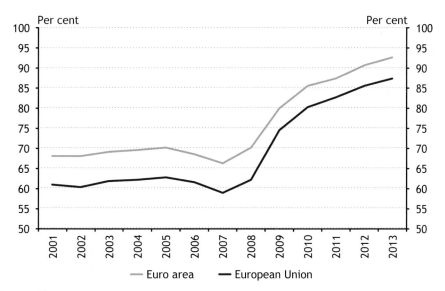

Source: Eurostat

Within the euro area, the euro is weak for the developed countries and strong for the group of southern countries, while the former group, in particular the German economy, is providing financing to the southern countries in the euro area. The crisis emerging in the euro area at various different levels, for example the crisis of the welfare state and the internal crisis of the euro, has combined and become evident in the southern member states of the euro area, whereas it has remained hidden in the northern and western member states, although it is starting to show in the growth and productivity data there.

In the southern group, the crisis has already emerged over the short run, while it will surface over the long term in the group of developed member states (Gossé – Serranito, 2014).

The crisis in the euro area is actually a political crisis. In planning the euro, the European powers – France and Germany – imagined that they could re-establish their status as global superpowers by way of the euro area. They planned on elevating the euro to the same status as the US dollar, or even to supersede the US dollar, envisioning a global currency and intending the euro area to play the role of a global superpower. The logic behind the development of the European Union and its system of institutions, however, did not make it possible to establish firm financial foundations to underpin the single currency. The euro area does not have a common budget or finance ministry and nor was a European monetary fund created. The activities of the European Central Bank were only reinforced in response to external pressures, in this case the financial crisis, because in fact the Union is only able to move forward when it is in crisis. Today's Union and European integration as a whole has always deepened and widened as a result of crises. This is a strange modern European paradox: integration progresses as a result of crises, but the crises reinforce the differences within and between the member states.

The euro area was designed for positive economic performance and was not prepared for crises. Introduction of the euro occurred between 1999 and 2001 during a period of exceptionally strong, simultaneous economic growth, and they were unable to devise an institutional system for the efficient functioning of the currency union and its ability to handle crises. This shortcoming is now evident, and this is a factor behind the continuous, partially open, partially hidden crisis affecting the euro. The internal crisis is exacerbated by the faulty crisis management strategy being pursued by the euro area, because this strategy prioritises the interests of the strong members over those of the weak ones. There is no effort to reform the welfare state among the strong members, whereas this is demanded of the weaker members of the euro area. Fiscal austerity programmes are being forced upon the southern members, instead of promoting an economic policy focused on growth.[6]

In reality, the European Union, and within it the euro area's crisis management strategy, are based on the Anglo-Saxon model of the free market. The goal is to lift the crisis-ridden southern countries of the euro area out of the crisis using fiscal tools, rather than focusing on the political, social and economic problems which are the deep underlying causes of the crisis. Financial crises are always caused by distortions in economic structure, the society's system of values and the political and governmental framework (including the regulatory framework). A financial crisis is always a reflection, the superficial manifestation of deeper crises: if only the consequences are addressed and not the causes, the crisis will only deepen and become permanent.

This is because in the crisis-stricken parts of the euro area, the crisis is a combination of a Western-style structural crisis, a crisis of the European-style welfare state and a unique financial crisis within the euro area itself. Together, these three crises are too much for the economies in the southern part of the euro area, and furthermore it is impossible to overcome the third one without finding a solution to the first two. The crisis of the European welfare state may also surface in

---

[6] See: Lapavitsas et al. (2012): Crisis in the Eurozone, and Lane (2012): The European Sovereign Debt Crisis, The Journal of Economic Perspectives, Vol. 26, pp. 49–67.

the developed, stronger members of the currency union, but in their case the favourable EUR/USD exchange rate conceals the structural weaknesses. There is one ratio which has the strongest impact on the Union and the future of the euro: if the euro appreciates versus the US dollar, then the economies of the southern members weaken. If the euro is stronger than its historical peak, the strongest German economy will also not be able to handle this for a longer period of time. If the EUR/USD exchange rate remains in the middle of the range seen since the crisis, it is good for the strong economies in the euro area and bad for the weak ones: in the years following the crisis, this has mainly been the case. For the German economy, this EUR/USD exchange rate represents a global competitive advantage, but this rate is also good for the US national strategy. Most of the euro area is weakening, and thus the euro cannot usurp the role of the US dollar (Figure 13).

Figure 13. Real effective exchange rates in the euro area

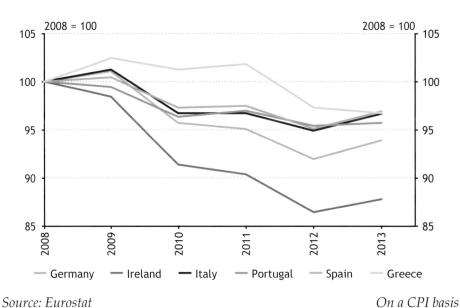

Source: Eurostat   *On a CPI basis*

Since crisis management in the weaker members of the euro area is focused on financial and budgetary issues rather than addressing the structural issues in the economy, these economies are becoming weaker, while the economies benefiting from the strong euro continue to strengthen. The economy of the euro area as a whole is stagnating, which means a setback for the weakest members and slack growth in the case of the stronger members. The euro no longer looks to unseat the US dollar, as it struggles to even survive.

Labour market indicators in the countries in the currency union have deteriorated significantly, and compared to their competitors in the global economy – the Anglo-Saxon countries and East Asia – they are gradually at a competitive disadvantage. The rate of unemployment in the euro area is two to three times higher than in its global competitors: even in its own right this renders the welfare state unsustainable. The large number of unemployed in the weaker euro area members leads to a permanently unstable political and social situation, which hampers the initiation and implementation of structural reforms, with the result that competitiveness is continuing to decline (Figure 14).

Figure 14. Unemployment in the world's major economic regions

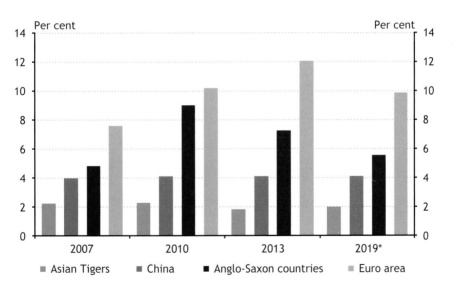

Asian Tigers: Hong Kong, Singapore, Thailand, South Korea; Anglo-Saxon countries: Australia, Canada, New Zealand, UK, USA

Source: IMF WEO, April 2014   ** estimate*

Naturally, the internal crisis of the euro area is only one part of the complex crisis afflicting the Western economy as a whole. Both before and after 2008, the Western world became indebted because of cheap loans, as governments, households and companies amassed the biggest debt in Western economic history. In a period of six years, total global debt increased from USD 85 trillion to almost USD 200 trillion, with the Western economies leading the way in this regard. The Irish borrowed 25 times the amount of annual tax revenues, the French and the Spanish 10 times this amount, and this money went into inflating bubbles in numerous countries such as Iceland, Spain, Ireland and naturally the USA. Cheap money triggered a boom on the real estate market. The Irish bought property from each at higher and higher prices, the Spanish, Portuguese and Greeks built homes for foreigners and the Icelanders bought up practically everything they could get their hands on. First, the bubble burst in Iceland, then the US crisis erupted, followed by crises in Greece, Ireland and Portugal.

The crisis is concealed in a number of euro area members which are currently still thought to be strong, because (with the exception of the German economy) the citizens of the euro area tried to get rich by borrowing, and spent their money on bubbles instead of on education, innovation and industrial development.

Around the turn of the millennium when the euro was introduced, money was being pumped into the US economy, which reinforced the business cycle. Between 2008 and 2011, this previous, artificial stimulus and the massive amount of money used to manage the crisis in the USA caused a small degree of contraction in GDP, but by 2011 the previous trend had returned, and economic growth in the USA began to accelerate more and more in the subsequent years. In conjunction with the accelerating growth, the amount of financing is being reduced, and the additional money supply stemming from the loose monetary policy is being cut back (Figure 15).

Figure 15. Business cycle and financial cycle in the USA

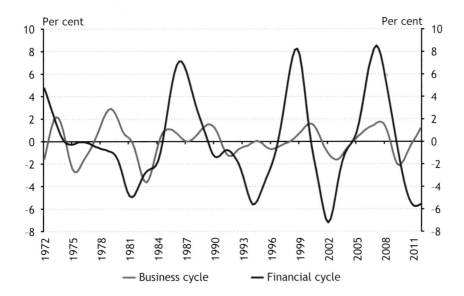

Business cycle is the 1.5-8 year frequency variation of output. Financial cycle is the medium term variation of the credit-to-GDP ratio obtained by frequency filter.

Source: MNB Growth Report, November 2014

The weak points of the euro area are the uncompetitive economic structure at a certain euro exchange rate, the high fiscal deficits and the high level of government debt in the southern members. With the outbreak of the global financial crisis and crisis management based on loose monetary policy, the USA has won back its global role in politics and economics. Even though the unipolar world has not been re-established, the USA has become stronger vis-à-vis the European Union, and the US dollar has underlined its role as the leading global currency versus the euro. In the meantime, the budget deficit in the USA quadrupled during the crisis and government debt surged higher, but nevertheless the US dollar remained the safe-haven currency of choice for the world's investors.

The global financial crisis has turned out to be asymmetrical: it started in the USA, but the shocks suffered by peripheral countries were more severe than those felt in the core countries.[7] On the whole, the USA has been a winner from the crisis, while its competitors have lost ground. The US strategy pursued in the internal financial struggles in the West was successful, because the crisis management strategy pursued in the euro area was a failure.

After hitting the low point of the crisis, when the euro area's members perceived the first fragile signs of recovery they decided that the solution was to embark on a strong programme of budget consolidation. In the particularly fragile economies of the peripheral economies, the decline in public spending, dismantling of the welfare state and enforcement of extremely modest wage agreements with the goal of internal depreciation of the real exchange rate resulted in severe real economic sacrifices. Measures intended to improve fiscal balance can have a particularly strong negative impact on growth when carried out during a period in which over-indebted private agents in the economy are already focused on paying back their debts and lowering their consumption expenditures.

On the one hand, the jump in unemployment and the drastic deterioration in growth conditions blocks the ultimate goal of reducing the debt, and on the other hand, the rise in social and political tensions renders the execution of any later reform programmes impossible.

---

[7] A disproportionately large amount of US (sub-prime) mortgage securities, in particular the more risky ones, were purchased by European banks. Between 2007 and the end-2008, more than one half of the losses on US debt instruments was realised in the euro area. Consequently, the losses suffered on these "toxic" US investments made a significant contribution to the crisis in the euro area's banking sector. See: Gourinchas et al. (2012): The financial crisis and the geography of wealth transfers. Journal of International Economics, Vol. 88, No. 2, pp. 266–283.

Similar to the approach taken in the USA, a correct strategy would have been based on three pillars: 1) softening the impact of budget consolidation measures and distributing the costs of crisis management; 2) pursuing a strongly supportive monetary policy; and 3) moving quickly to clean up the banking sector's balance sheet.

The requirement to remedy the fiscal deficits was imposed too early, in a flawed structure and concentrated manner in the economies which were most severely impacted by the crisis. Instead of focusing on the extent of the fiscal deficit, the emphasis in the beginning should have been on improving the structure of the budget to promote growth, since the economic environment was already suffering from anaemic demand anyway. A suitable tool to achieve this would have been to reduce taxes on labour and promote public investment, which could have been financed by increasing consumption and environmental protection taxes, along with a reduction in interest expenses.

While the European Central Bank did endeavour to play a supportive role through its interest rate policy, in contrast to the Fed's moves to expand its balance sheet, the ECB's balance sheet already started to shrink gradually from 2012, and in relative terms this ultimately amounted to a tightening of monetary conditions. Due to the fragmentation of the European banking sector, the interlinking of sovereign and bank risks, fading risk tolerance and the slow progress in resolving NPLs throughout the euro area, the flow of lending weakened, which further exacerbated the growth problems.

Despite the considerable growth sacrifices in the peripheral economies, adjustment of the real exchange rates remained limited. The reason for this is that while the correction in wages in the southern countries moved towards an adjustment in the real exchange rate, the real exchange rate for the most competitive German economy also depreciated due to the nominal depreciation of the euro exchange rate and this resulted in a further increase in Germany's significant trade surplus.

The countries less strongly impacted by the crisis which still had adequate economic policy leeway would have been able to facilitate the adjustment of the euro area more effectively with measures focused on fiscal and income policy.[8] Accepting temporarily larger fiscal deficits and wage increases would have softened the downturn in the peripheral economies, improving the region's long-term growth prospects.

The West is a loser in the currency war

At first glance, it appears that only the European Union is on the losing side in the duel between the US dollar and the euro. But there are also shifts occurring between the developed countries and the emerging countries stemming from the differing rates of economic growth, and the euro area is a loser in this process.

Even before the crisis, the share of the euro area was declining slightly, but the 2008–2009 financial crisis and ensuing economic crisis exacerbated this decline. The Anglo-Saxon economies, in particular the USA and Great Britain, also lost ground vis-à-vis China, but this took place at a much slower rate than the losses of the euro area. While the 'Asian Tiger' countries – South Korea, Taiwan, Hong Kong and Singapore – maintained their position vis-à-vis their competitors, China was gaining ground against both the economies in the Anglo-Saxon countries and the economies of the euro area (Figure 16).

---

[8] The various theories and concepts of differentiated integration, and including the so-called "two-speed" Europe for example, are summarised in Holzinger et al. (2012): Differentiated Integration in the European Union: Many Concepts, Sparse Theory, Few Data. Journal of European Public Policy, 2012.

The rise of the West seen in the last 500 years and especially since 1820 and its triumph compared to China and India was was also supported by the institutions in Western Europe.[9]

Figure 16. PPP-based GDP of different country groups, share of total

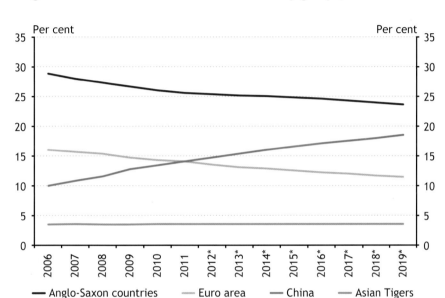

Asian Tigers: Hong Kong, Singapore, Thailand, South Korea; Anglo-Saxon countries: Australia, Canada, New Zealand, UK, USA

Source: IMF WEO, April 2014   * *estimate*

[9] Researchers identify various kinds of reasons behind economic development. Some (e.g. Acemoglu et al. 2005) emphasise the role of the system of political and economic institutions. Others (e.g. Weber, 1930) underline the role of culture and religion. Others yet (e.g. Spolaore et al. 2013) focus on the role of geographic conditions in the transmission of cultural and social traditions which explain different paths of economic development. See: Acemoglu et al. (2005): Institutions as the Fundamental Cause of Long-Run Growth. In: Aghion et al. (eds): Handbook of Economic Growth. Vol. 1A, North Holland, Chapter 6, pp. 385–472 and Spolaore et al. (2013): How Deep Are the Roots of Economic Development? Journal of Economic Literature, Vol. 51 No. 2, pp. 325–369, as well as Weber (1982): A protestáns etika és a kapitalizmus szelleme: Vallásszociológiai írások. Budapest, Gondolat.

The essence of these institutions is rooted in Christianity and the individualist spirit of Europeans, which spurred Europe's people, cities and nations to expand geographically and compete physically and intellectually. Six European achievements played a key role in Europe's success: competition, science, ownership rights, medicine, the consumer society and the work ethic.

The Western work ethic, one of the main sources of which is reformed Christianity, made it possible for work, savings and investment, and for lending, interest and profit to become central aspects of life for Western people. Up until the birth of Protestantism, Western people worked so they could live. After that, however, they lived so that they could work and the same still holds true in the USA today. The ideas of the Renaissance, Reformation, Industrial Revolution and Enlightenment were all nourished by the concept of competition; intellectual competition preceded mass market competition, leading to national markets and ultimately to nation states. The fragmented nature of power in Europe resulted in wars, which spurred technical innovation. During the first decades of the 19th century, the internal power struggle propelled Western Europe upwards and made it the ruler of the world.

It is an exciting fact that this success occurred in a very concentrated geographical and temporal range. In the Industrial Revolution, 38% of the inventions occurred between the start of the Reformation and the French Revolution, and 80% of the great figures of Europe's scientific revolution were born in a geographical hexagon demarcated by the cities Glasgow–Copenhagen–Cracow–Plymouth–Marseille–Naples, and within one hundred miles of these cities. The real impact of the Reformation was the spread of reading and writing: the accumulation of knowledge preceded the accumulation of capital.

In the West, the financial war between the US dollar and the euro is threatening these Western achievements. The emerging Eastern countries, especially China and the Asian Tigers, have already adopted these Western success factors. All of the global competitors are already drawing on the earlier sources of the West's success, whereas some of these factors are steadily weakening in the European Union in particular. The welfare state is undermining the work ethic, because the flawed European crisis management is generating high unemployment, which weakens the work ethic as a result. Competition in Europe is being hampered by the major enterprises in the large EU countries, which practically enjoy a monopoly position. Internal European competition is hampering the euro in a concealed manner, because the economic agents in weaker euro area members are in an unequal competitive position vis-à-vis the economic agents in the stronger euro area countries. The artificially strong euro does not allow for an overhaul of the structure of the economy, which would be a viable option in the case of a weaker exchange rate for national currency.

The southern zone of the euro area is squeezed between two competitors: the technological competition of the stronger north-western members and the competition of the emerging global competitors exporting cheap mass-produced goods. In the struggle between the US dollar and the euro, it now appears that the euro area is losing more than the US dollar zone, but this struggle is also weakening the position of the latter in global competition.

Euro area investment rate loses out in the US dollar – euro struggle

Due to the nature of the EU's crisis management, investments in the euro area are falling, especially in the euro area's southern zone. Instead of maintaining the level of employment and lowering the rate of unemployment, the EU's crisis management approach focuses exclusively on reducing the fiscal deficit. On the one hand, this lowers the amount of investment financed by the public sector in the euro area members, and on the other hand it has a negative impact on the investments of companies and households as well. Due to falling employment and the rising unemployment rate, the purchasing power of euro area citizens in the euro area declines, in particular for the population of the southern zone affected by the crisis. The decline in purchasing power has a negative impact on borrowing and investments. The fall in investments hinders the transformation of economic structures, since significant new investments in the fields of innovation and R&D would be necessary to achieve this.

Prior to the crisis, the investment rate in the euro area was higher than in the Anglo-Saxon countries, and higher than the investment rate in the USA. During the years of the crisis, the level of investments was roughly comparable, but starting from 2013 the rate of investment in the Anglo-Saxon economies significantly exceeds the level in the euro area. One can expect to see a similar negative deviation in the remaining years of this decade in the euro area, which has a detrimental effect on the euro area's competitiveness, not only vis-à-vis the emerging Asian economies, but also compared to the Anglo-Saxon economies, including the USA and UK in particular (Figure 17).

Figure 17. Investment rate in key global economic regions

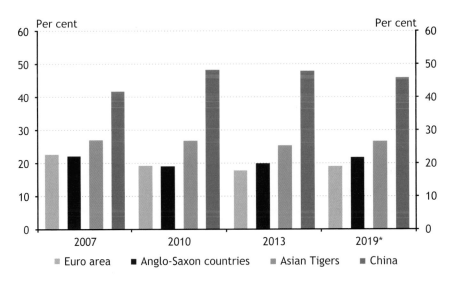

Asian Tigers: Hong Kong, Singapore, Thailand, South Korea; Anglo-Saxon countries: Australia, Canada, New Zealand, UK, USA

Source: IMF WEO, April 2014   ** estimate*

The divergent trend in investment between the Anglo-Saxon countries and the economies of the euro area clearly indicates that the USD area, and even the GBP area, were more successful in managing the crisis than the euro area, since the prevailing level of investment presages the future structural transformation of an economy. The higher the rate of investment in a market economy, the higher the likelihood of implementing competitive changes to an economy's structure in an environment of global competition. In the case of the euro area, the problem is not that the previously artificially high level of real estate investment has fallen, but rather that – due to the euro's artificially strong level for the southern countries – no capacities are being created in manufacturing and modern services, which would be able to take the place of the earlier investments in the field of real estate.

The differing economic policy and crisis management strategies of the two currency areas are also reflected in monetary policies of the central banks. Whereas the US central bank massively increased its money supply and expanded its balance sheet from the very moment the 2008 crisis started to spread, the European Central Bank only took such action to an inadequate degree, with poor timing and only temporarily: accordingly, it made much less use of the stimulating opportunities offered by the loose monetary policy of the US central bank (Figure 18).

The monetary policy of US central bank also assisted in the financing of the private sector: borrowing by the corporate sector in the USA plunged, but from 2010 lending to the private sector, and the underlying investments, started to rise again, as a result of the US response to the crisis. By contrast, lending to the private sector in the euro area declined steeply after the start of the crisis, and following a brief period of expansion, this downward trend has continued.

In the euro area, the central bank was not able to break the steep downtrend in lending caused by the crisis, and this is the reason behind the persistently low rate of investment (Figure 19).

Figure 18. Ratio of the Fed and ECB balance sheets to GDP

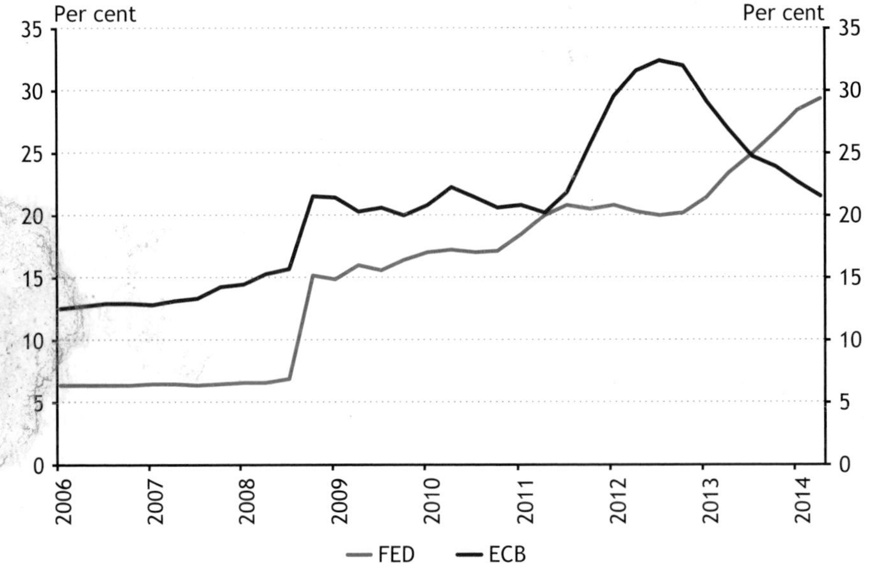

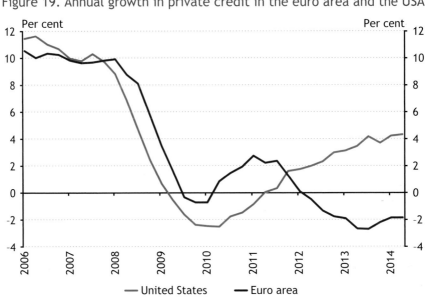

Source: Eurostat, OECD, ECB, Fed

Figure 19. Annual growth in private credit in the euro area and the USA

Source: Fed, ECB   Credit from the whole financial intermediary system

This brings us to the fundamental problem of the euro area: its internal structure is not homogeneous, and there is a distinctive European dividing line in terms of development between the north and the south which runs through the currency area. Consequently, the level of EUR/USD exchange rate and real interest rate which is still suitable for the northern and western group of countries is too strong for the southern part of the area. A major part of the euro area is not carrying out the investments necessary to transform economic structures, because these investments do not offer a return at the given EUR exchange rate and interest rate level. Another factor hindering structural renewal is that the European Central Bank is not providing adequate funding for corporate sector investments. The ECB's post-crisis monetary policy was less and less suitable for meeting the needs of the peripheral countries which suffered the strongest setbacks (Figure 20).

Figure 20. Deviation in the level of interest rates desirable for the euro area core and peripheral countries

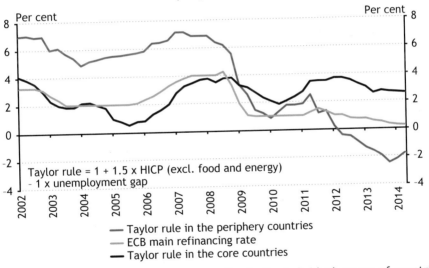

Taylor rule = 1 + 1.5 x HICP (excl. food and energy)
- 1 x unemployment gap

— Taylor rule in the periphery countries
— ECB main refinancing rate
— Taylor rule in the core countries

The Taylor rule illustrates how monetary policy in the individual groups of countries would have reacted to changes in inflation and unemployment, based on past behaviour. The unemployment gap is the difference between actual unemployment and the NAIRU, based on the OECD spring 2014 projection. Calculations based on the study by Nechio (2011).

Source: ECB, Eurostat, OECD

The euro was a joint political programme launched by the French and the Germans, and not a joint economic policy. It would also have been possible to operate a common trade area without the euro, and there are plenty of good examples of this at the global level. European integration could function without a common political framework and a common currency, as evidenced by the example of the trade agreement between the United States, Mexico and Canada. That European integration has been a political undertaking from the very beginning is demonstrated by the fact that the structural and financial foundations for economic integration have only been established gradually. Germany finally gave up its Deutsch Mark which had brought stability and prosperity, with the European Central Bank headquartered in Frankfurt becoming the vigilant guard against inflation.

If the euro had been an economic policy programme, the single currency would have been accompanied right from the start with a common finance minister, a common budget and a common development policy. Upon introduction of the euro, every one inside and outside of Europe believed that German financial discipline would prevail throughout the entire currency union, and consequently interest rates and government bond yields in Greece, Portugal, Italy and Spain fell to historic lows. In the early days, these economies also behaved as if they were parts of the German economy (Figure 21).

Nonetheless, despite introducing the euro, the southern part of the euro area did not become part of the German economy, neither in terms of economic structure, nor productivity, nor export capacity. The political decision backfired: loans became cheap for everyone, and everyone started borrowing, including those who used the cheap funds to improve their quality of life, instead of investing in the renewal of economic structures. Prior to the onset of the crisis, Germany ran an annual trade surplus on the order of EUR 200 billion, a major success in terms of global competition. On the other hand, the other members of the euro area accumulated a trade deficit totalling EUR 200 billion every year.

Figure 21. 10-year government bond yields for core and peripheral countries

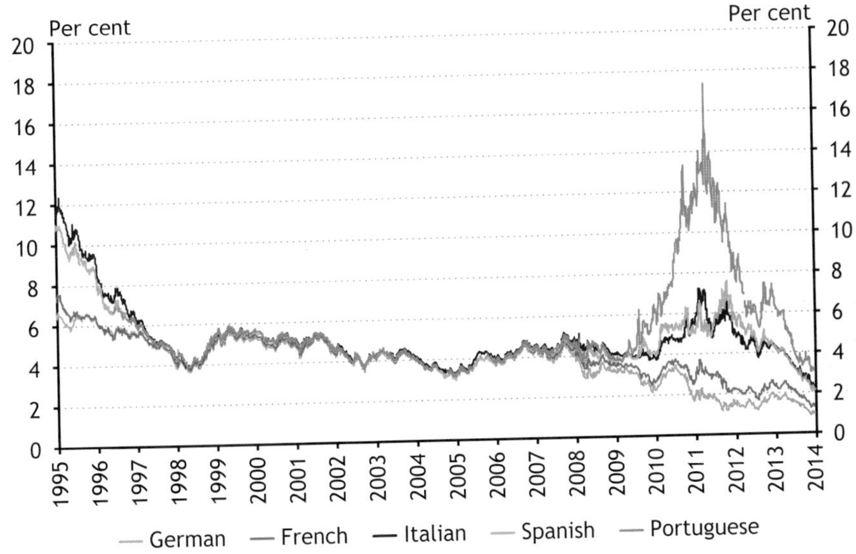

Source: Bloomberg

Economies of different strengths and competitiveness are behind the crisis in the euro area; these economies would not have been included in a common currency area if the decision had been made on the basis of well-founded economic policy and not a political programme. The political decision was motivated by a fear rooted in European history. Europe's leading politicians thought and still continue to think that without an ever closer union and the unifying euro currency the hostility between the large nation states in Europe would resurface. These fears are unfounded, because above a certain level of economic development and standard of living this can be avoided, whereas integration in the Union of a political nature results in a hidden struggle between the nation states and the common institutions, as well as between the centralised bureaucracy of the Union and the citizens.

European Union would benefit from transformation of the euro area

The European Union is competing in terms of growth with the other developed and emerging economies in the global economy. From the perspective of economic growth, the Union's weak point is the euro area, and the weakness of the euro area is caused by the southern group of countries. Up until the financial crisis, economic growth in the euro area's southern members tracked the GDP growth trend in the USA. During the first decade following introduction of the euro, growth in the currency union and within the EU as a whole was fuelled by the investments of the southern members which were based on cheap loans, but did not serve to improve economic competitiveness. The crisis, however, suddenly exposed the real Achilles' heels of the euro area: the differing economic structures of the northern and southern members.

Growth in the southern members suddenly plunged lower, along with investments backing this growth, whereas in the northern members growth returned after the downturn caused by the crisis, albeit this growth remained well below the rates registered in the US economy.

Compared to the US economy, the group of northern countries in the euro area had already exhibited less robust growth performance even before the crisis, but at that time this was balanced by the higher growth rate in the southern group of countries. After the crisis, however, this situation was reversed: the economic performance of the southern group nosedived and the performance of the northern group also did not return to the levels seen before the crisis. Both groups of countries in the euro area, the developed northern group and the weaker southern group, suffer from using a common currency (Figure 22).

Figure 22. Cumulative GDP growth in euro area regions
and other developed economies since 1996

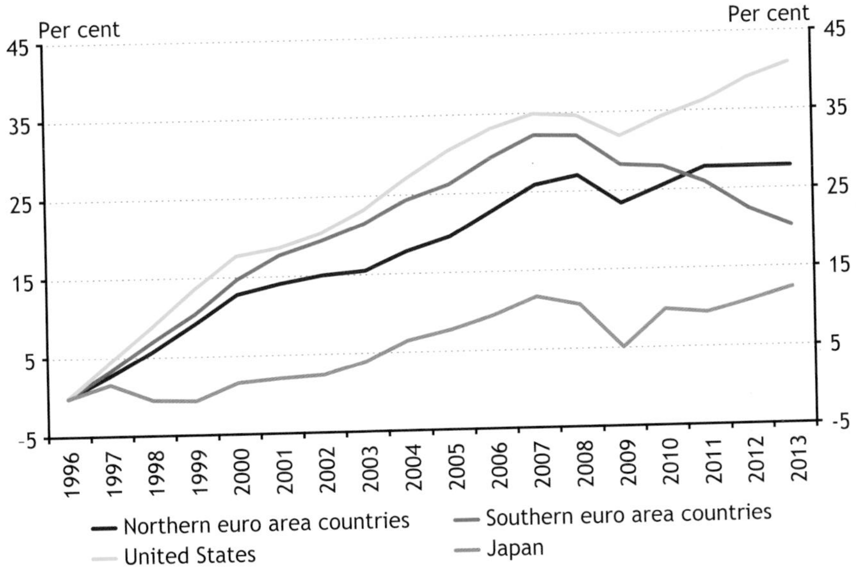

They are not only suffering over the short term, but over the long term as well, as the level of government debt in the group of southern countries jumped considerably higher after the crisis. While the level of government debt prior to the crisis was already lower in the developed northern members of the euro area than in the weaker southern group, the difference in the level of government debt was bearable. By contrast, following the crisis government debt in the euro area rose on a steep trajectory, surpassing 90% of total euro area GDP in 2013. This development, however, was driven by an underlying trend of very rapidly rising government debt in the southern countries and a small increase in government debt in the northern ones (Figure 23).

Figure 23. Debt-to-GDP ratio in the euro area

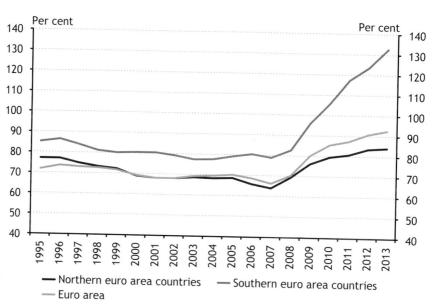

Per cent

Northern euro area countries —— Southern euro area countries
—— Euro area

Source: Eurostat

From the perspective of the euro area's long-term future, one decisive point will be that the southern group of countries is only able to maintain its earlier operation in conjunction with massive growth in government debt, while unemployment rises sharply in these economies and the southern group is characterised by contraction and stagnation, with no progress. The high level of government debt makes the entire euro area vulnerable, because in the event of a normalisation of interest rates up from their historically unprecedented lows or the possible return of global inflationary pressure, the triple-digit levels of government debt in the southern group will become unfinanceable.

Another crisis for the European welfare state is foreseeable, because it will be increasingly difficult to finance the overall stock of government debt in the euro area, and financing the government debt of the countries in the southern bloc of the euro area will immediately trigger a crisis throughout the entire euro area and the entire EU economy if global financing conditions deteriorate. In its current composition, the euro area is not sustainable, because the differences in key economic and financial conditions between the developed northern countries and the weaker southern group of countries are so significant that they will lead to the disintegration of the currency union in the event of a change in the fundamental conditions in the global financial system.

Ultimately, the fate of the euro area will be decided by the difference in labour productivity. Prior to the crisis, the euro did not result in any improvement in labour productivity in the group of southern countries with weaker competitiveness, and there has also been no significant improvement in the wake of the crisis, whereas the euro did lead to productivity growth in the northern euro area countries up until the global financial crisis and thereafter as well (Figure 24).

Figure 24. Real labour productivity by hours worked
in the euro area periphery countries

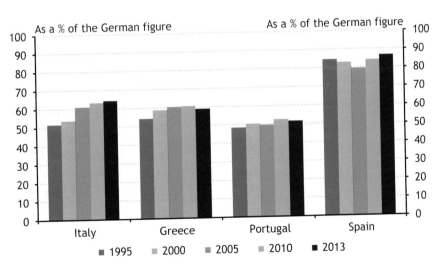

Source: OECD   Calculated using data on 2005 purchasing power parity

Over the long run, Hungarian economic policy must expect that in the years to come there will be no dynamic positive influences from the

European Union, and in particular from the euro area. The euro area will remain mired in crisis as long as it retains its current composition: the crisis will be obvious in the weaker southern countries and remain concealed in the stronger group of northern countries, where it will manifest itself in low growth rates, economic performance falling short of the competition and continuously rising levels of government debt.

The crisis of the euro area peripheral countries and the subsequent prolonged period of weakness has important lessons for EU countries which have not yet joined the currency union, and thus for Hungarian economic policymakers as well. Joining the euro area must occur at a time when the economy is mature enough to resist and manage the asymmetric shocks originating from within the currency area. One important lesson is that it is not enough to satisfy the earlier nominal convergence criteria (the so-called Maastricht criteria). Over the long run, in addition to meeting these criteria, the real economic and regulatory conditions must be reviewed and satisfied appropriately in order for membership to be successful. In respect of the nominal conditions, the criteria relating to consumer price inflation and fiscal balance are of key importance. A rate of inflation which is in harmony with the rate in the euro area core countries for a longer period of time (not just during the year immediately preceding accession) can help to reduce the risk of lending bubbles developing as a result of convergence in yields, while at the same time a stable, low fiscal deficit path (along with a peg of the nominal exchange rate) can provide a suitable buffer for unexpected shocks.

In terms of the real economic criteria, labour market flexibility and export competitiveness are the most important factors. The experiences of the peripheral countries show that in a currency union it is extremely difficult to remedy problems with competitiveness and that this is only possible at the cost of significant growth sacrifices. Accordingly, the long-term benefits of accession can best be exploited with a strong, competitive export sector and networks of domestic suppliers. This can be supported by increasing labour market flexibility, which facilitates adjustment of the real exchange rate taking into account competitiveness aspects. Finally, robust regulatory conditions must also be met in order for membership to be a success. The convergence of yields prior and subsequent to accession generally results in a higher chance of overshooting on the lending market. These risks can be managed by an effective regulatory authority, equipped with a suitable monitoring system and micro and macro-prudential toolsets.

In recent years, Hungary has embarked on the path towards meeting the conditions necessary for convergence in all of the above mentioned areas. As demonstrated by the experiences of the peripheral countries, the indubitable benefits of adopting the euro are accompanied by significant risks as well. Consequently, it is sensible to time Hungary's accession of the currency union at a point when – based on all of the listed criteria – the country is suitably prepared, so that Hungary can be a successful member of the euro area over the long run.

Chapter 2

Economic policy leading to the crisis in Hungary

One of the unique features of the Hungarian crisis was that Hungary was embroiled in a financial crisis well before the global financial crisis even started in 2008. The path leading to this domestic financial and economic crisis was described in detail in my book "From Vanguard to Bringing Up the Rear":[10] at least thirty capital errors in economic policy put Hungary in this situation by 2006. By 2007, the Hungarian economy had the second highest budget deficit and the highest inflation of the twenty-seven EU member states at that time. The rate of growth in the Hungarian economy was far lower than the average rate in the EU, and convergence had come to a standstill.

This early internal crisis was clearly reflected in the fact that Hungarian growth was at one third the level of the average for the Central European region, and consequently Hungary's gap to the region increased rapidly. The crisis on the labour market was reflected by the second lowest employment rate in the EU, while at the same time there were significant inequalities in wealth and income in Hungary.

The problems with the economy were most clearly indicated by the twin deficit, as significant shortfalls were recorded for both the public budget and on the current account. This early, internal financial and economic crisis was clearly the result of Hungary losing its financial balance after 2002. In 2001, the Hungarian budget deficit was still at 4%, while it was already 9% by 2002. Following EU accession, the fiscal balance continued to deteriorate, as the more than 6% budget deficit rose to nearly 10% by 2006: Hungary was already in an economic imbalance

[10] Matolcsy (2008).

well before the outbreak of the global balance crisis in 2008. This crisis in balance is well illustrated by the second element of the twin deficit, the development of the current account balance. Between 2002 and 2008, the deficit on Hungary's current account ranged between 6–8%, and this was accompanied by steady deterioration in external balance (Figure 25).

Figure 25. Current account balance
and general government balance in Hungary, % of GDP

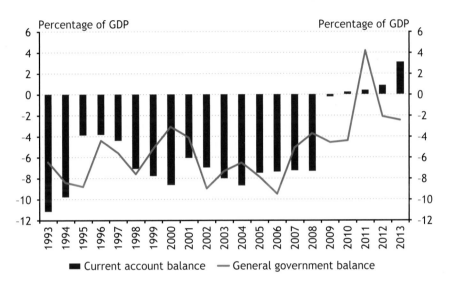

Source: Eurostat, MNB

After 2000, Hungary's financial balance was linked extremely closely to the system of values of the governing political elite: in the case of left-wing, liberal governments, balance deteriorated, while in the case of conservative governments, Hungary's balance improved. Following the election victory of the left-wing, liberal government in 2002, economic policy immediately deteriorated. Instead of making a minor attempt to restore balance, the new government immediately set out to artificially stimulate the economy: instead of hitting the brakes, they stepped on the gas pedal. Naturally, the deterioration in the fiscal balance and the current account resulted in new indebtedness: well before the global financial crisis, Hungary's financial balance was in crisis, leading to a debt crisis. The high twin deficit is the best reflection of the flawed nature of the economic policy pursued after 2002 and before the crisis in 2008, as Hungary showed weaker growth performance than its regional peers, despite the high budget deficit and extremely large deficit on the current account.

The internal crisis from 2002 to 2008 was essentially a crisis in macroeconomic balance. The balance between supply and demand was upset, as shown by the high inflation; the balance in the public budget was upset, as shown by the high fiscal deficit; foreign trade relations were upset, as shown by the high current account deficit; and the imbalances on the labour market remained in place, as shown by the low employment rate and steadily rising rate of unemployment. And all of this occurred at the same time.

On 1 September 2006, the first austerity package came into effect, which – although it did improve the budget situation – still did not fulfil the obligation of a budget deficit of below 3% undertaken as part of Hungary's accession to the EU, even when the crisis erupted. The deficit remained near 4% all the way until 2011.

Between 2006 and 2008, economic policy attempted to address one element of the twin deficit, namely the fiscal deficit, but for lack of measures to address the structural growth problems, no attempt at all was made to remedy the other element, i.e. the deficit of nearly 8% of GDP on the current account balance, all the way until the financial crisis hit. A change in this regard only came after the crisis in 2008 with the IMF-EU agreement, because one of the conditions of the financial bailout was measures to improve the current account balance. Nevertheless, the improvement in the current account balance seen in 2008 and 2009 was not primarily a consequence of economic policy, but rather reflects the automatic effect of the crisis. In the corporate sector, adjustment took place which improved the current account balance, mainly as a result of lower imports in conjunction with an improvement in the trade balance and a decline in the profits of foreign-owned companies. The rising utilisation of transfers from the EU also improved the current account balance (Halpern – Oblath, 2014), (Figure 26).

Figure 26. Net lending in Hungary

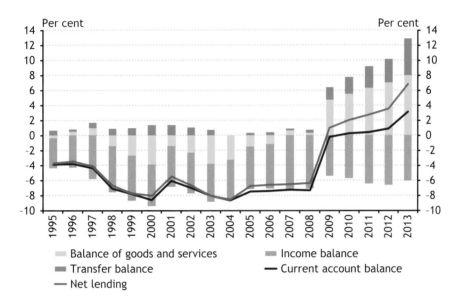

Source: MNB   *As a percentage of GDP*

Another strange and negative feature of Hungarian economic policy was that during the almost five years between EU accession and the onset of the crisis the Hungarian economy was still strongly dependent on foreign funding. This indicates that Hungary did a poor job using the years following EU accession. Instead of using the access to EU funds to reduce the budget deficit, economic policy actually increased the deficit financing of the public budget, while at the same time tolerating significant net borrowing between 2004 and 2008.

Overheated economy financed with external funds

Starting almost immediately following EU accession, Hungary's net external debt rises, and here again a change is only seen when the 2008 financial crisis forces the Hungarian financial system to adjust. The development of the output gap between 2004 and 2008 clearly shows that the flawed economic policy resulted in an artificially overheated economy[11] (Figure 27).

Figure 27. Output gap and net lending according to the financial account

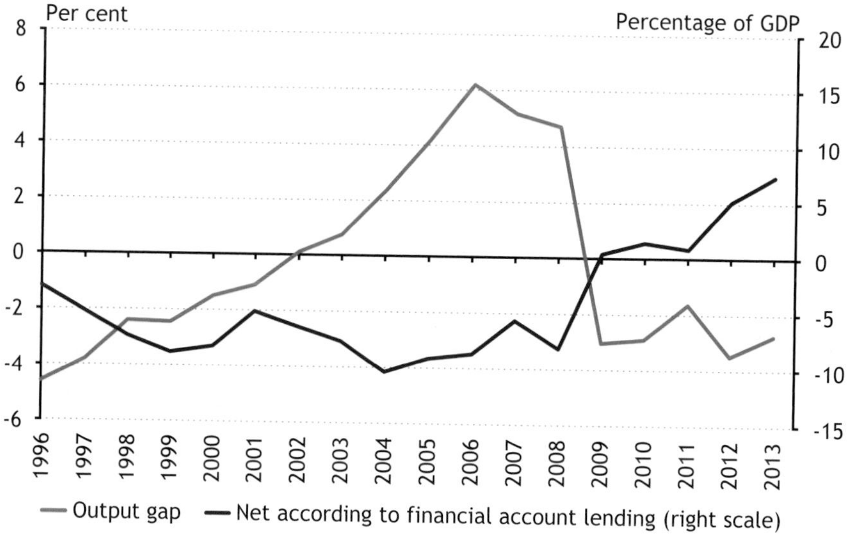

Output gap calculated using the Hodrick-Prescott filter (lambda = 100), based on annual data from 1990. The GDP forecast for 2014-2015 in the September 2014 Inflation Report was used in handling the uncertainty of the end point for filtering.

Source: MNB

[11] In their work, Borio et al. (2013, 2014) noted that financial developments contain important information on potential output and thus on the development of the output gap. Using financial developments, they derive the concept of financial-neutral output, which extends the pre-crisis approach to potential output based on the sustainable utilisation of production factors with financial sustainability.

Strangely enough, the austerity measures enforced from 1 September 2006 also did not lead to any change in this regard: until 2008, the output gap in the Hungarian economy steadily points to overheating. This situation only turns around with the IMF-EU agreement, as the output gap of the Hungarian economy plunged due to the agreement and in parallel with the outbreak of the European economic crisis: the economy moved from being overheated to freezing up. It took quite some time for the Hungarian economy to digest the change of some 7 percentage points in the output gap relative to GDP between 2008 and 2010, as evidenced by the output gap still being around minus 3% at the end of 2013.

There were also external and internal factors behind the overheated economy: the loose fiscal policy, high inflation and rapid accumulation of external debt were also responsible for the overheating. The flawed policies of the central bank and supervisory authority also played a role, as the central bank and regulatory measures made no efforts to restrain the excessive, irresponsible lending. As part of the banking sector's looser lending policies, it was willing to finance a larger portion of the market value of real estate from credit, and in the case of loans to households the banking sector disregarded a safe level of monthly payment-to-income ratios.

Thus, the 2008 global financial crisis struck Hungary when the country was already in the middle of an internal crisis, in which poor economic policy had led to an overheated economy, and structural problems were accompanied by ever greater imbalances. The structural problems in the Hungarian economy are clearly reflected in the development of the current account balance. During the almost one half decade from EU accession to the onset of the crisis, the current account deficit consistently ranged between 6% and 8% of GDP (exceeding 8% in 2004), indicating that Hungary did not use the years after EU accession for structural adjustments, but rather for growth spurred by borrowing, which led to deterioration in both internal and external balance (Halpern – Oblath, 2014).

The lack of structural adjustment is shown by the fact that starting from 2004 the growth of the export share in the Hungarian economy started to slow down compared its regional peers, and from 2007 it contracted. All of this indicates that during the period of EU accession Hungary did a worse job and its peers did a better job in using the financial resources available for transforming the structure of the economy (Figure 28).

Figure 28. Export share in Central Eastern Europe

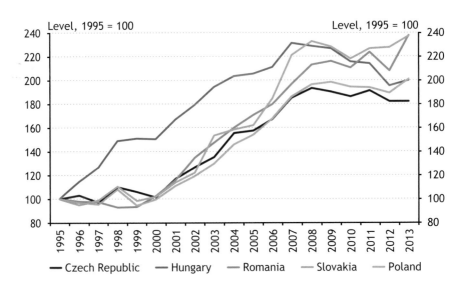

Share of goods and service exports in global imports, at current prices

Source: MNB

Consumption gap signals misguided economic policy

The consumption gap of households, i.e. the deviation of consumption from its long-term equilibrium level, very accurately reflects the quality of economic policy.[12]

---

[12] Estimation of the equilibrium level of consumption is carried out using a vector error correction model. In the model, the long-term level of consumption is determined by households' disposable income, financial wealth and outstanding loans.

Starting from the middle of the 1990s until 2002, right until the moment when the government changed, the consumption gap in the Hungarian economy was consistently negative, as households' consumption fell short of the long-term equilibrium level. The change of government in 2002 triggered a shift in this regard. Liberal budget spending started and as a result, all the way until the consolidation in the autumn of 2006 when the first austerity package was adopted, Hungarian households consumed substantially more than the long-term equilibrium level of consumption. This consumption was financed by borrowing, with foreign currency borrowing playing an increasing role. Until the outbreak of the global financial crisis, the consumption gap was steadily rising, as the household sector again consumed more than the long-term equilibrium consumption and financed this surplus consumption with foreign currency loans (Figure 29)

Figure 29. Household consumption gap in Hungary

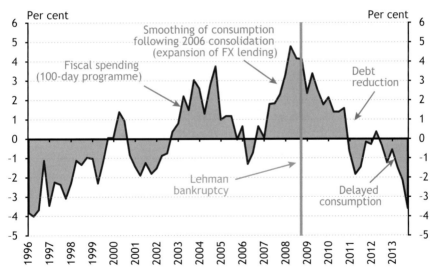

The household consumption gap is the deviation between the level of actual consumption and long-term equilibrium consumption. The equilibrium level of consumption was calculated using a vector error correction model.

Source: MNB, calculations of Endrész et al. (2014)

The 2008 crisis also resulted in a forced adjustment in this regard as well, as deleveraging began. By 2011, the consumption gap had returned to negative territory, as households consumed less than the long-term equilibrium level. The negative consumption gap seen from 2011 on resulted in the accumulation of postponed consumption needs, and we can postulate that during the final years of the decade until 2020 Hungarian households will gradually approach and restore the previous level of consumption. We can also presume that the post-2002 artificial consumption spiral which was fuelled by borrowing will not occur again. Accordingly, it may be possible for Hungarian households to achieve a level and structure of consumption at which the consumption gap will decline to around zero, and thus there will be no significant deviation between actual household consumption and the long-term equilibrium level of consumption.

This is one of the most promising aspects of establishing a sustainable path of macroeconomic balance of the Hungarian economy, because in Hungarian households' system of values the desire for accumulation was always accompanied by excessive risk-taking in the field of borrowing and private investments. Households, however, learned a lesson from the artificial boom in lending in the years after EU accession and before the global financial crisis, and a consumption gap of around zero is now taking shape in Hungary, so it may be possible for households' actual and long-term consumption to reach a state of equilibrium.

Lending to households developed in line with the equilibrium level until 2003. Between 2004 and 2009, however, the actual level of household consumption exceeded the equilibrium level to an increasingly large degree, as foreign currency lending boomed. In 2010–2013, households underwent a period of continuous deleveraging, reducing their new borrowing and repaying their debts. By the end of 2012, actual household consumption approached the equilibrium level, with the ratio of household credit to GDP doing the same by 2013. Consumption-type borrowing was significantly larger than the borrowing of the corporate sector (Figure 30).

Figure 30. Equilibrium levels of the household credit-to-GDP ratio
and the uncertainty of the estimation

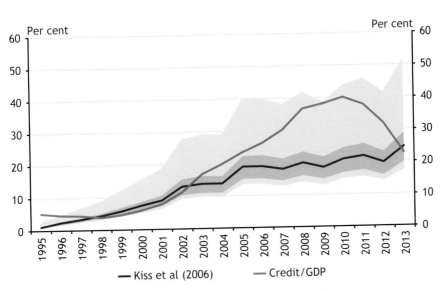

The bands indicated in blue depict the uncertainty of the estimate of Kiss et al. (2006).

Source: MNB, based on Kiss et al. (2006)

Hungary's investment rate lags behind the regional average

From 2005, the investment rate in the Hungarian economy lagged more and more behind the regional average. Although both the regional average and the rate in Hungary show a mild downward trend between 2000 and 2005, from 2005 Q2 the investment rate in Hungary decelerates at an increasingly rapid pace. By contrast, from the end of 2004, investment rates in the regional peers move on an upward trend, all the way until the start of 2008. The mild decline in the regional and Hungarian investment rate from the early 2000s can be ascribed to the slump in the share prices of US tech sector equities in spring 2000. As a result of this, many investment plans were cancelled in the ICT and electronics industries and consequently the output of this industry, which had previously shown the fastest growth rates, dropped off. The bursting of the dot.com bubble had a detrimental effect on the entire region, including the Hungarian economy (Figure 31).

Figure 31. Investment rate in the region and Hungary

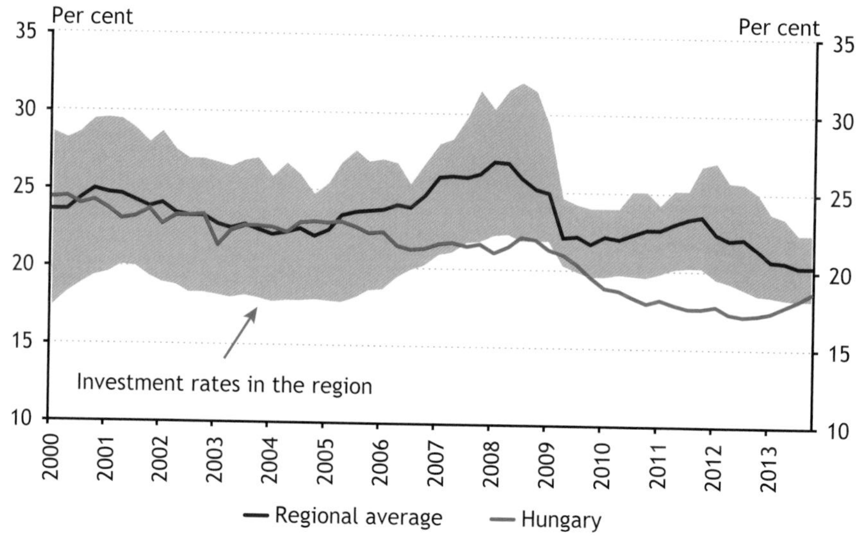

Source: Eurostat

In early 2005, the investment rate in Hungary was still higher than the regional average, ranging well over 20% and moving on a modest uptrend. From spring 2005, however, the investment trend in Hungary turns downward, while the trend in the region starts upwards, leading to the development of a significant gap between the regional and Hungarian investment rates in the period from 2005 to the start of 2009. The regional investment rate approached the level of 28% of GDP, while the Hungarian rate was already heading towards a level of 20%.

As a result of the 2008 global financial crisis, both investment rates shift to a downward path, but the Hungarian rate continues to fall all the way until the end of 2012, dropping to below 20%, while at the same time the average rate for the region stabilises after falling some 5% due to the financial crisis, and then begins rising mildly again from end-2011, before once again embarking on a downtrend due mainly to the economic uncertainties at the global level and in Europe in particular. In Hungary, it was necessary for a recovery in investment to occur in order for the Hungarian investment rate to start rising again, and the trend in investment indicates that the regional rate and the Hungarian rate may be in the same range again around the middle of the 2010s.

The path of investment rates also precisely reflects the sad development that, out of the countries in the region, only Hungary was unable to exploit the advantages of EU accession in 2004, in particular in respect of access to new sources of investment funding. While the range for investment rates typical for the region clearly moves higher after the start of 2005, the investment rate in Hungary starts to drop at exactly that time. That marked the moment when Hungary's investment momentum began to fade, while all of the other competitors in the region gained momentum thanks to the EU and corporate investments. The price of Hungary's flawed economic policy is also indicated by the fact that from the end of 2006 the Hungarian investment rate falls below the lowest rate among the regional peers and stays there until early 2013. Thus, Hungary's performance was worse than the regional investment average in the period 2005–2013: up until 2011 this reflects the consequences of the earlier economic policy, while from 2011 the price of crisis management is seen in the low investment rate.

Hungary's negative development compared to the region is mirrored precisely by the development of investment rates. The Hungarian investment rate of less than 20% in previous years also means that in the years to come the Hungarian economy will suffer from worse competitive conditions in the field of investments compared to its peers in the region. The capacities which were not created due to the investment rate falling short of the regional average cannot be harnessed for production and do not attract further investments. The lower investment rate for around 8 years foreshadows lower GDP growth and export potential in the next 5–10 years.

We obtain an even more accurate picture of the negative consequences of the flawed economic policy by analysing the composition of the Hungarian investment rate which fell short of the regional investment rate (Figure 32).

Figure 32. Deviation of the Hungarian investment rate from the average of the Visegrád countries, by sector

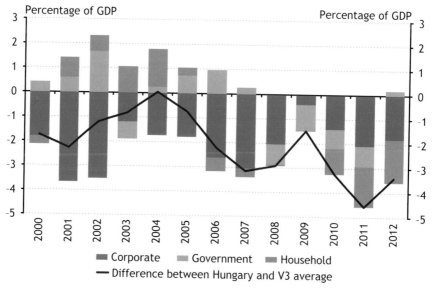

Source: Eurostat

First and foremost, the Hungarian economy performed worse than its regional peers in the field of corporate investments: the quality gap in the structure of investments was even greater than the volume gap.

Thanks to the first Széchenyi Plan, up until 2004 the Hungarian economy's shortfall compared to the corporate investment activity of its regional competitors declined in the field of corporate investments.

After EU accession, however, the investments of Hungarian companies lag behind corporate investments in the regional peers to an ever greater degree. The shortfall was the smallest in 2009, when the entire region was impacted by the global and then the European financial crisis and the ensuing economic crisis. During the period of crisis management, however, Hungary's corporate investment once again falls significantly short of the level seen in the region. As a result of the first austerity programme launched in 2006, the household investment rate already starts to fall and the gap between the investments of Hungarian households and households in the region's other countries widens.

Later, from 2008, Hungarian government investments also fall behind those of governments in the region until 2012, when there is a turnaround in the public sector investment trend and Hungarian public investments gain a small advantage. Prior to the crisis, the deviations in the corporate, public and household investment rates compared to the regional countries precisely reflect the flawed economic policy: compared to the regional peers, investment activity was weaker in the corporate sector, whereas it was stronger in the public and household sectors.

The surplus in public investment, however, resulted in a higher fiscal deficit and higher government debt, however, and the surplus in household investment was mirrored by rising household indebtedness and the rapid increase in foreign currency borrowing in particular.

All of Hungary's production factors lag behind the region

Hungary's potential growth rate increasingly lagged behind the rates for the other Visegrád countries, but the misguided economic policy caused shortfalls on the labour market and in productivity which were even larger than the deficit in investments described in the previous section (Figure 33).

Figure 33. Contribution of production factors to differences
in Hungarian and V3 potential growth

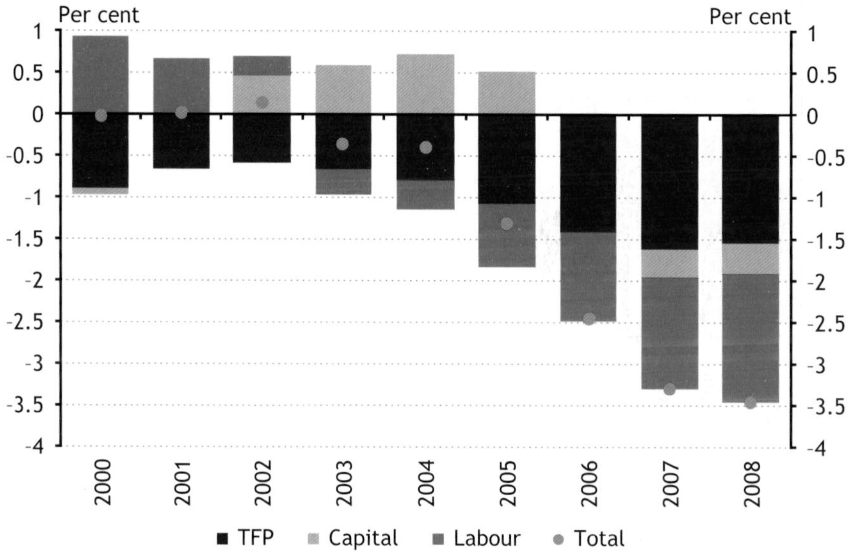

Source: MNB, European Commission (May 2014 forecast)

Together with high unemployment, the low level of employment
and Europe's lowest participation rate meant that the labour market
developed a lag of almost 1 percentage point compared to Hungary's
regional peers. The deficits in investments and on the labour market
were also factors which contributed an additional 1.2 percentage point
gap in terms of total factor productivity in Hungary (Figure 34).

Due to the economic policy errors, the low investment rate, the
extremely low employment and activity rates and the low productivity,
Hungary's potential growth rate was 2% lower than that of its regional
peers (Figure 35).

Figure 34. Activity rate in Europe in 2007

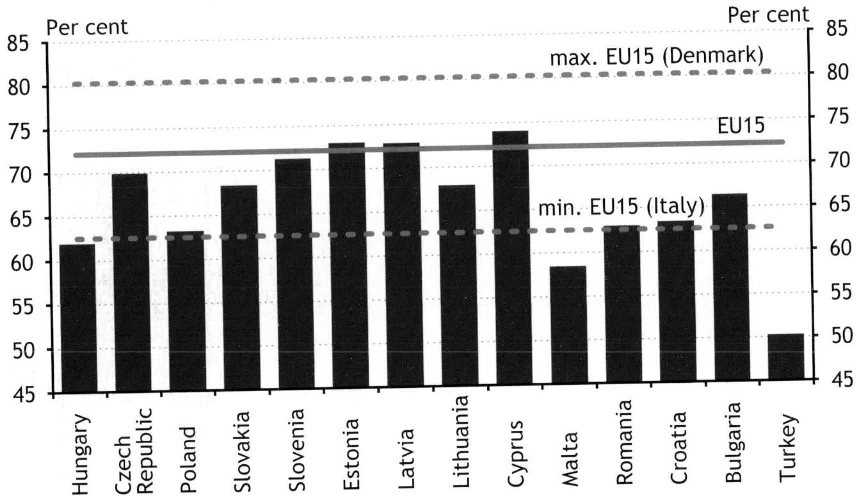

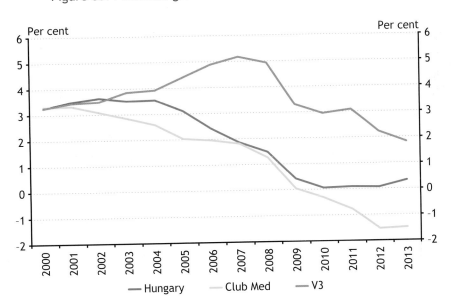

Source: *Kátay (2009), based on Eurostat data*

Figure 35. Potential growth rate in certain country groups

Source: *MNB, European Commission (2014 May forecast)*

After 2002, Hungary fell completely behind the countries of the Visegrád region, with this trend accelerating after EU accession in 2004, and Hungary increasingly resembled the crisis-stricken group of southern peripheral EU countries in terms of its economic fundamentals. While a 2% difference developed between the potential growth rates in Hungary and its Visegrád peers, for the entire period up to 2010 the potential growth rates of the Hungarian economy and the crisis-stricken southern EU countries approximated each other and moved to the same level.

The new direction in economic policy in 2010 also triggered a reversal in this regard. The deceleration in Hungary's potential growth stopped, and from 2012 the rate began climbing again, moving towards the potential growth rates in the Visegrád countries, which had started decelerating in the meantime.

This also reflects the dramatic developments in the Hungarian economy: right around the time of EU accession, it fell behind its group of regional competitors and joined the southern group of euro area countries which later slipped into crisis. Whereas the regional peers reached potential growth rates above 5% around the time of the 2008 crisis and these rates only declined as a result of the crisis, after 2002 Hungary's potential growth rate stalled at a level of 3–4%, before turning sharply downward after 2004 and falling all the way to zero in a long period of stagnation. This is the context for understanding the goal set by Hungary's economic policy after 2010, namely to turn around these trends and bring Hungary back to the group of regional peers.

The price of the flawed economic policy: Hungary's convergence stalled for one decade

After the change of government in 2002, a new economic policy was launched, as embodied by the "100-Day Programme".[13] Fulfilling the election promises begins to impair the budget balance more and more, and then the current account balance, leading to the development of an increasingly large twin deficit. As a result of the twin deficit, the Hungarian economy once again starts borrowing and is characterised by artificially overheated economic growth and a sharp, simultaneous increase in the indebtedness of the government and households. These developments are accompanied by an investment rate falling short of that seen in the regional peers, which is reflected in Hungary's growth potential lagging far behind the potential growth rates in these regional peers. All of this impacted the convergence ability of the Hungarian economy.

After 2002, all of the regional peers were able to boost the pace of convergence, and only Hungary stalled in a range of 65% of the average level of EU development for an entire decade. Starting from a development level lower than Hungary, Poland and Slovakia initially caught up with and then surpassed the performance of the Hungarian economy compared to the EU average, while the Czech Republic was able to build on its historical advantage over Hungary. Hungary's failure in the field of convergence was obvious, as its convergence stalled for one decade after 2003, as the level of development of the Hungarian economy stagnated compared to the EU average, while all of its competitors in the region steadily approached the EU average (Figure 36).

---

[13] After the elections, the new government which came to power in 2002 announced the "100-Day Programme", which mainly consisted of welfare measures that increased the budget deficit. Amongst other things, as part of the Programme, there was a substantial increase in the wages of public employees and university scholarships, along with a one-off payment to pensioners.

Figure 36. PPP-based GDP per capita in the Visegrád countries

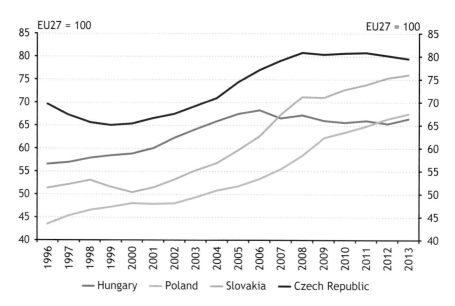

Source: Eurostat.

The situation is even worse if we measure economic performance with gross national income (GNI), instead of gross domestic product (GDP), (Figure 37).

The obvious failure of Hungarian convergence after 2003 can also be ascribed to the fact that, compared to the regional peers and indeed even compared to the Mediterranean members of the euro area, a significantly larger difference developed between gross domestic product and gross national income, i.e. between the incomes available to domestic income earners. Naturally, it is the case that in the Scandinavian countries and indeed with regard to the EU average in the European Union as a whole the national income available to residents is larger than the gross domestic product, because the income from foreign investments is larger than the transfer of income stemming from foreign investments in the given national economy. The large gap between gross domestic product and gross national income highlights one of the weakest points in Hungary's economic convergence, since Hungary was far more indebted than its regional peers: the GDP/GNI difference is reflected in the difference in the investment rate, the difference in the growth rate and ultimately in the difference in the pace of convergence.

Figure 37. GNI-GDP gap by region

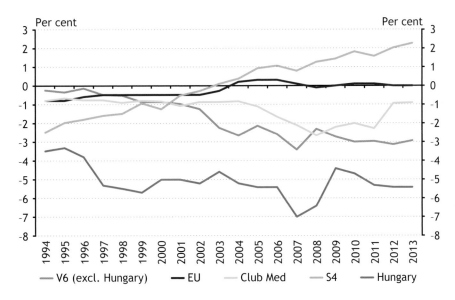

Difference between gross national income and gross domestic product, in proportion to gross domestic product

Source: Eurostat.

Chapter 3

Hungary faces another debt crisis

In the global economy, financial and economic crises have occurred again and again in the last three decades, becoming a natural feature of the capitalist market economy.

At the beginning of the 1980s, the USA was hit by a banking crisis accompanied by high inflation, and the new Fed leadership was only able to bring inflation under control and stabilise the financial system after 1982. In autumn 1987, the US stock markets crashed, which was followed by the stock market crisis in Japan and the banking crisis in Scandinavia. Anglo-Saxon countries and European economies faced an economic crisis in the early 1990s, which resulted in a financial crisis: the British government intervened to protect the British pound, and the Italian lira was also subjected to a speculative attack. This was followed two years later by the Mexican peso crisis, and then another two years down the line by the Southeast Asian crisis, which occurred between 1997 and 1999. In parallel to the Southeast Asian financial crisis, the Russian financial sector collapsed in August 1998, and then the dot. com bubble burst on 7 April 2000 with the NASDAQ crash. Two years later, a financial crisis also hit Argentina (Figure 38).

Analysing the global financial and economic crises over the past three decades, it becomes clear that during the lengthy dot.com boom in the mid-1990s financial analysts and politicians erred in thinking that the capitalist market economy crises were over. The Southeast Asian financial crisis that erupted in 1997 made it clear that the global financial system was indeed increasingly global in nature: if a financial crisis emerges somewhere, it ripples through into the financial systems of all the countries integrated into the global economy – nobody is immune to financial crises. Hungary should have taken this experience into account during the negative shift in economic policy in mid-2002.

It should have been anticipated that financial instability would crop up again, sooner or later, since a financial crisis originating anywhere in the global financial system might eventually impact Hungary.

Figure 38. Countries under financial stress

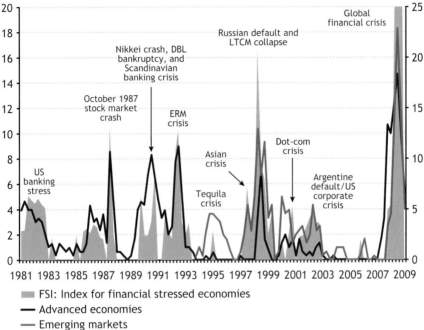

Source: *Global Safety Nets: Crisis Prevention in an Age of Uncertainty (Moghadam, 2010)*

By 2003, the previous notion that global economic growth was feeding off a new resource in the era of information and making development crisis-free had become became obsolete. Information is indeed a very special resource since it increases with consumption, as opposed to all other economic resources, which decrease with consumption. The shift to an information economy, however, did not eliminate the crisis tendencies of the capitalist market economy.

Global economic upturn used for new debt accumulation

Between 2003 and 2008, however, there were some rare moments in the global financial system, when conditions were calm for a short period without any crises. During the exceptionally long period of four to five years without a financial crisis, essentially the only such time during the last three decades, Hungary used the upturn in the external economy to ramp up its debt again: instead of pursuing convergence by means of structural reforms, it borrowed more, leading to a financial crisis. Starting from EU accession (in fact even before then), all of the agents in the Hungarian economy took on debt, which shaped the entire decade between 2004 and 2014.

The government budget generated a high deficit which was primarily financed from abroad, increasing both government debt and external debt, and the banking sector took on even more external debt to finance the new borrowings of households and the corporate sector (Figure 39).

Figure 39. Net debt-type financing by sector

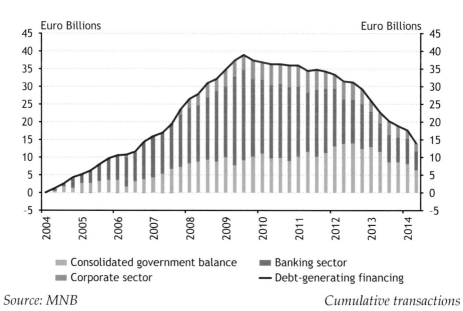

Source: MNB   Cumulative transactions

It is important to note that the corporate sector took on less debt than the other two economic agents. Nevertheless, demand for debt-generating financing in Hungary increased sharply as a result of the new borrowing by the three sectors. In analysing the net debt-type financing of the economic sectors, it becomes clear that the banking system contributed the most to Hungary's new indebtedness.

By virtue of its nature, debt accumulates: in most cases, debts from previous years are financed with new debt, while the interest expenses on accumulated debts increase the financing requirement as well. It is clear that reversing the sharp upward trend in external debt between 2004 and 2009 was a difficult and slow process in subsequent years.

In the period of renewed borrowing between 2004 and 2009, the expansion of Hungary's net external debt reached one third of gross domestic product, an unprecedented level within such a short period of time in the history of the Hungarian economy. In 2009, following the agreement between the IMF and the EU, and as a result of the global financial crisis, an adjustment process inevitably began in the Hungarian economy, but a conscious effort to reduce the debt only started from 2010. Funds amounting to almost HUF 3,000 billion were transferred to the public pension system, and thus to the government budget, during the restructuring of the mandatory private pension fund system. While this lowered government debt, it did not reduce the government's net external debt. Of this amount, some HUF 1,400 billion in government debt was redeemed, which functioned as the catalyst behind the turnaround in government debt in 2011.[14] Directly or indirectly, almost the entire amount of these funds was used to reduce government debt (a smaller portion was transferred to the National Asset Management Agency for asset management purposes).

---

[14] For detailed data, see: State Audit Office (2012): Jelentés az államháztartás központi alrendszerének adóssága és éven túli kötelezettségvállalásának ellenőrzéséről.

New debt accumulated in foreign currency

For lack of any accessible domestic savings, the Hungarian banking system steadily switched to lending more and more in foreign currency from 2004, mainly in Swiss francs. While the quantity of household loans disbursed in forints contracted between 2004 and 2008, household lending in foreign currency, especially in Swiss francs, raced higher. In part due to the weakening of the HUF exchange rate, this trend continued right up until 2010, when the one of the first steps taken by the new government after the elections was to ban foreign currency lending to households. Outstanding foreign currency loans to the corporate sector rose in a similar fashion, but with smaller quantities and mostly with larger collateral: while the vast majority of households did not have any foreign currency income, and therefore had no foreign currency funds to cover the repayment instalments for the foreign currency loans, some of the foreign currency loans disbursed to the corporate sector were backed by export sales revenue, i.e. coverage for the loans in foreign currency.

Volumes of household and corporate foreign currency loans rose sharply between 2004 and 2010, while the volumes of household and corporate loans denominated in HUF both fell relative to GDP. Owing to the low household savings and high budget deficit, forint funds were in short supply, and thus the new debt of the Hungarian economy in 2004–2010 was essentially taken out in foreign currency: this was significantly riskier than using the domestic currency, which increased Hungary's financial vulnerability. Consequently, not only was the increase in outstanding loans relative to GDP from 45% to more than 70% between 2004 and 2010 an unprecedented mistake in Hungarian economic history, the structure of the financing was also extremely risky. It was ultimately the composition of the loans that caused the problems later on (Figure 40).

While forint loans made up the majority of household and corporate debt in 2004, by 2010 most of the lending portfolio was denominated in foreign currency, principally in Swiss francs. It was later seen just how serious an economic policy error it was for households to borrow in Swiss francs.

Firstly, as interest rates on foreign currency loans were low, households borrowed much more than they could actually afford, to finance their current consumption needs. This undermined the balance of trade and boosted the country's external debt, as the indebtedness was not supported by an increase in loan repayment capabilities. At the same time, the imbalance in the current account was exacerbated by the deterioration in the income balance caused by rising interest payments from the external debt, in addition to the mounting trade deficit.

Figure 40. Credit-to-GDP ratio in Hungary

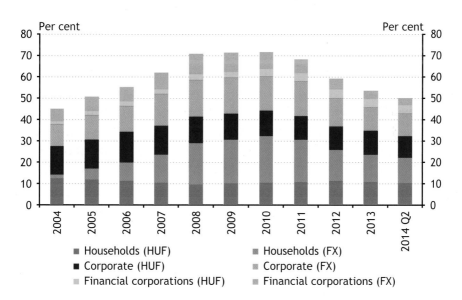

Source: MNB   *Credit institutions and financial corporations*

Secondly, Hungary's vulnerability also rose because the debts in foreign currency steadily increased the exchange rate risk of the private sector; the weakening of the exchange rate during the crisis hit households particularly hard and to a much larger degree than in neighbouring countries.

Thirdly, the indebtedness in foreign currency limited the central bank's room for manoeuvre as the MNB increasingly had to consider financial stability aspects in its decisions. This was one of the main reasons why the MNB was only able to cut its interest rates much later and to a smaller extent. Moreover, the surge in external debt fuelled by foreign currency lending hampered Hungarian economic growth after the crisis erupted: a European comparison shows that larger external debt correlated negatively with economic growth after the crisis.

The risks associated with foreign currency lending immediately had an impact after the outbreak of the global financial crisis, as the Swiss franc turned into a safe-haven currency, since global financial investors looked on CHF as a currency in which they could safely park their financial investments. The CHF exchange rate strengthened, causing the exchange rate risk to materialise for Hungarian borrowers of foreign currency loans.

The Swiss National Bank initially cut its policy rate by more than two hundred basis points, before trying to stop the appreciation of the Swiss franc by gradually lowering the rate to almost zero. This was only achieved by mid-2011, when the Swiss National Bank managed to stop the Swiss franc from appreciating any further by intervening on the FX market[15] and publishing a unique forward guidance (Figure 41).

After 2004, the majority of new borrowing by Hungarian households was comprised of CHF-denominated loans, which meant the global financial crisis in autumn 2008 immediately pushed repayment

---

[15] Aside from intervening daily on the market, the action by the central bank was driven by its commitment to unlimited intervention. See the press release on the exchange rate ceiling: http://www.snb.ch/en/mmr/reference/pre_20110906/source/pre_20110906.en.pdf

instalments up and also increased interest levels. It was a mistake for economic policymakers to assume between 2004 and 2008 that the risk of a financial and economic crisis had disappeared in the global economy. An even greater error was not to anticipate that the euro, the US dollar and the Swiss franc would become safe-haven currencies in the event of a financial crisis. As this had happened before in previous financial crises, CHF appreciation certainly should have been expected again in the event of a new global or European financial crisis. All participants should have known that if a new financial crisis were to occur the Swiss franc would again become a safe-haven currency, which would undermine the financial position of borrowers and thus destabilise the Hungarian financial system.

Figure 41. Interest rates of CHF-denominated housing loans and the Swiss central bank's policy rate[16]

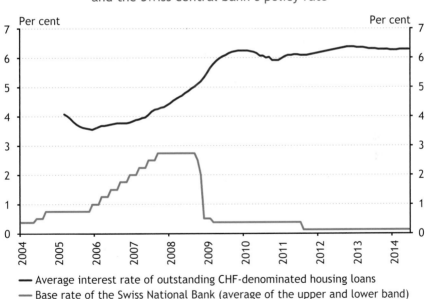

— Average interest rate of outstanding CHF-denominated housing loans
— Base rate of the Swiss National Bank (average of the upper and lower band)

Source: MNB

[16] The cost of funds for Hungarian banks is higher than the Swiss policy rate, as it also contains the country risk. The risk premium rose as the policy rate declined, meaning that raising interest rates on the existing portfolio was not justified, based on MNB calculations.

All of those involved in shaping economic policy made mistakes: the government, the central bank and the financial supervisory authority. From the government's perspective, the Ministry of Finance would have been able to ban households from borrowing in foreign currency by citing households' lack of foreign currency income to cover loans in Swiss franc, euro and yen, as households would thus assume significant exchange rate risk. The central bank should have taken firmer action against households taking out foreign currency loans, as it should have anticipated the related financial risk, the higher country risk on account of the inherited, constantly growing government debt, and the risk associated with declining mortgage collateral in the event of a crisis.

The supervisory authority should have taken the stability risk of the financial system into account as another factor, since a European or global financial crisis would impact the entire Hungarian banking system. At that time, the majority of the banking system was in foreign ownership, and most of its funding came from external capital markets. As an agent in the economy, the banking system would have had an interest in setting limits on foreign currency debt for households and the corporate sector, but instead it did the opposite. Sources of income were not assessed strictly enough during the lending process, down-payments requested from households for foreign currency housing loans were lower than prudent business practices would otherwise have dictated, and the banks were particularly negligent with foreign currency equity loans. Rapid, substantial loss of value in the event of a financial crisis was simply ignored in relation to mortgage collateral.

Households, of course, also erred by believing in the possibility of cheap, risk-free foreign currency borrowing. The reduction of earlier housing subsidies, followed by their cancellation, deprived households of subsidised forint loan alternatives, while the increase in the central bank's policy rate pushed up interest rates sharply on forint loans.

It would in fact have been quite easy to avoid the financial pitfalls of this new borrowing. Corporate sector agents could have set up exchange rate risk guarantees to back foreign trade transactions, mitigating the exchange risk when financing export and import activities. The banking sector should have introduced a similar framework in its own interests. The government, the central bank and the supervisory authority should have prescribed the mandatory establishment and operation of an exchange rate guarantee system in relation to household foreign currency loans.

Key role of large foreign banks in foreign currency lending

The ownership structure of the Hungarian banking system may have played an important role in the increase of household foreign currency loans. Large foreign-owned banks dominated the banking sector at the time of EU accession, while the savings cooperative system which played a significant role in Western Europe was underdeveloped, and the Hungarian-owned banking system accounted for a minority share of the sector.

The rapid increase in foreign currency loans, in particular the rise in household foreign currency loans, was chiefly driven by large foreign-owned banks. With access to cheap funding, foreign parent banks passed on these funds to their subsidiary banks, which identified extremely good business potential in foreign currency lending, as they could disburse cheap funds with a high mark-up. Large and medium-sized Hungarian banks joined the new foreign currency lending business roughly 6–12 months late, but eventually had to jump on the "foreign currency bandwagon" to preserve their market share, because the large foreign-owned banks adopted aggressive lending policies, disregarding prudent and responsible banking operation rules (Figure 42).

Prior to the 2008 crisis, it was chiefly foreign currency lending which generated significant lending growth in the private sector, and thus foreign currency lending was the main source of the banking system's operating costs and profit. The boom in foreign currency lending went hand in hand with looser lending conditions, which meant far riskier customers were also able to borrow. The onset of the crisis caused a change in this respect, as the banks markedly tightened the conditions for extending loans, making it more difficult for even less risky customers to borrow. Forint loans, however, did not fill the gap left by foreign currency loans, nor was there any significant restructuring in the market shares of individual banking segments; instead, what emerged after 2008 was a slow, but steady, adjustment process.

Figure 42. Development of foreign currency loans to households within the sub-groups of Hungarian credit institutions

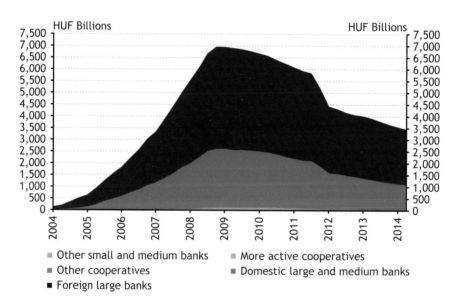

Source: MNB, based on the publication "Átalakulóban a magyar bankrendszer"

The banking groups playing an active role in foreign currency lending – i.e. large foreign banks as well as large and medium-sized Hungarian banks – generally provided their loans using (parent company or capital market) funds from abroad, while boosting their shares of the market.

The growth in lending of these two groups was accompanied by an increase in the loan-to-deposit ratios and thus the financing risks: the dependency of both financial groups on foreign funding increased overall.

The two main groups which played the leading role in foreign currency lending, i.e. the large foreign banks as well as large and medium-sized Hungarian banks, started out from very different positions. While the loan-to-deposit ratio of foreign subsidiaries was higher than 100% for the entire period under review, the loan-to-deposit ratio of large and medium-sized Hungarian banks was initially below 100% and only rose to a risky level during the expansion period. The loan-to-deposit ratio of small and medium-sized banks as well as cooperatives was generally low, both before and after the crisis.

Accordingly, after EU accession in 2004, household foreign currency lending grew the fastest and to the greatest extent. Starting at essentially zero in 2003, the volume of such loans in credit institutions' balance sheets expanded to approximately HUF 7,000 billion. Most of this expansion was seen at large foreign-owned banks.

The volume of household loans denominated in forints loans grew substantially after 2004, with the majority of this occurring between 2003 and 2005 thanks to the state interest subsidies, after which the overall portfolio stagnated until the crisis. Large and medium-sized banks were the largest lenders, but the large foreign banks played a considerable role too (Figure 43).

Figure 43. Development of HUF loans to households within the sub-groups of Hungarian credit institutions

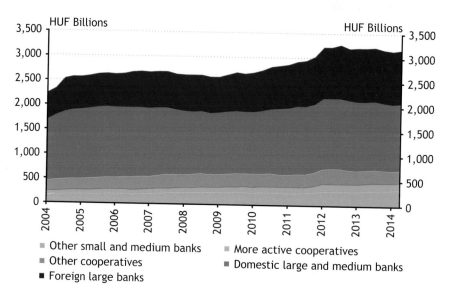

Source: MNB, based on the publication "Átalakulóban a magyar bankrendszer"

In a regional comparison, Hungarian households took on new debt quickly. Between 2004 and 2010, the debt levels of Hungarian households rose steeply until foreign currency lending to households was banned. The vast majority of new household debt was foreign currency debt, so the real question is why did household debt portfolios grow more slowly in the Czech Republic, Poland, Slovenia, Slovakia and even in Romania after EU accession than in Hungary (Figure 44).

Foreign currency loans clearly played the main role in this regard. Hungary saw the highest level of household borrowing in a currency other than the national currency. It is difficult to comprehend the serious economic policy error that neither the government, nor the central bank, nor the financial supervisory authority took any measures to restrict or prohibit foreign currency loans to households, while government institutions in the regional peers regularly limited this practice.

Figure 44. Household indebtedness in the region's countries

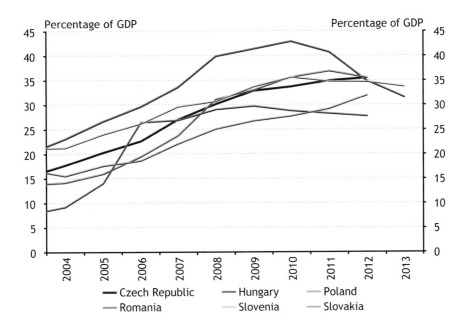

Source: MNB

One of the reasons was that the government used the expansion in household foreign currency loans to replace and substitute subsidised forint loans. A comparison of banking sectors in the region also shows, however, that large foreign banks aggressively built up their portfolio of household foreign currency loans in Hungary, paying little attention to the principles of sound banking operations. Compared to all of the other regional economies, the household sector's loan-to-GDP ratio rose faster and to a higher level in Hungary and this consisted mainly of foreign currency debt, while the Hungarian banking system was exposed to no less risk with the foreign currency lending of Hungarian households than the other regional peers. Thus, the difference stems from the operation of the Hungarian banking system and the dominant ownership share of large foreign banks: the banking system's appetite for short-term gains triumphed over prudent bank lending rules in Hungary.

Figure 45. Net external debt-type financing of the corporate sector

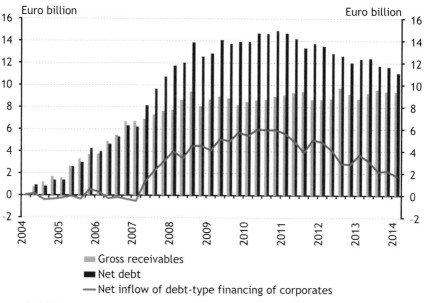

Source: MNB   Cumulative data

Corporate sector also pays high price for indebtedness

The corporate sector lagged behind households in accumulating significant debt. The net external debt of the corporate sector began to rise rapidly from mid-2007, but the trend stalled before the crisis erupted in 2008; the steady growth in net corporate external debt from 2007 until 2010 began to fall again from 2011 (Figure 45).

The net external debt of the corporate sector dropped not only because of the repayment of external loans, but also due to the contracting portfolio of external assets. The decline in net external debt also indicates a narrowing of external funds in the corporate sector. After 2009, the corporate sector became a net financial lender. The Hungarian corporate sector being a net lender brought about a change in the sector's behaviour: the importance of prudence and savings rose in comparison to borrowing.

Figure 46. Net lending from the financial account side

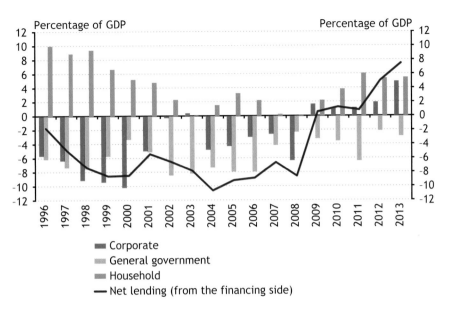

Source: MNB   *SNA-based net lending*

The decade between 2004 and 2014 was characterised by a deterioration and then a subsequent improvement in economic balance. Deteriorating financial balances were observed for all economic agents in the years following EU accession, most strikingly for the state and households, but the corporate sector was unable to escape the trend (Figure 46).

Corporate sector outstanding debt began to rise after 2004, following in the footsteps of households to a smaller extent, but by 2009 it totalled almost 180% of the added value created by the sector. This was followed by a gradual fall in the debt of non-financial corporations. The rates of this growth and decline differ: the debt was accumulated more quickly and to a greater extent than it decreased. The growth in corporate debt was accompanied by increasing interest expenses. This was caused by the financial crisis, which triggered an increase in the country risk, in interest rates, and, for foreign currency loans, in the related repayment instalments (Figure 47).

Interest expenses reflect corporate indebtedness the best, and more specifically the price of taking on foreign currency debt. The mounting financial imbalance at non-financial corporations was also largely due to the growth in foreign currency loans, but the negative impacts of this were less pronounced, because the loan portfolio did not increase as much as for households, and the corporate sector generally had foreign currency income to back up the foreign currency loans. Despite this, interest expenses rose almost threefold from 2007 to 2009, particularly because of foreign currency loans, which meant the Hungarian corporate sector also suffered the negative implications of the deterioration in financial balance.

Figure 47. Debt and net interest income of non-financial corporations (% of value added)

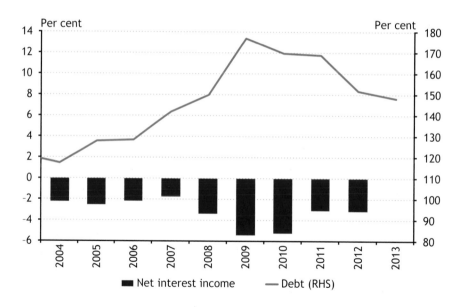

Debt includes securities other than shares, loans and commercial loans.

Source: MNB Inflation Report, June 2014 (based on HCSO and MNB data)

Indebtedness on the high-risk commercial property market

The deterioration in the financial balance of the corporate sector emerged not only because companies rapidly took on significant amounts of debt after 2004, but because many of them opted for cheap foreign currency loans, disregarding the risks, and also because the majority of the excessive lending occurred in relation to high-risk commercial properties.

Between 2004 and 2010 most of the excessive lending and indebtedness in the corporate sector was tied in some way to commercial property developments carrying the highest risk. As seen in the previous section with corporate loan growth, the pace of borrowing picked up here from 2007 as well, mainly in euros and other foreign currencies.

The use of foreign currency loans to finance commercial real estate projects experienced rapid growth from early 2006. This stopped almost immediately at the onset of the crisis and was followed by a steep decline in foreign currency lending for new commercial property developments, but the previous loans remained. To a large degree, the costs of this borrowing and the risk associated with these projects, which were financed primarily with foreign currency loans in the three years between 2006 and 2008, emerged later on (Figure 48).

From an economic history perspective, it is strange that commercial property projects boomed after 2006, since the government introduced the first austerity package from 1 September 2006, the effect of which was already being felt in households' incomes as well as in retail sales figures, i.e. in consumption. The overheating seen in property development was delayed: while households began to take on significant foreign currency debt right after EU accession, it took enterprises a few years to start the excessive borrowing that shook their financial balance. The development of commercial properties started to gain steam right when the cost of the government's flawed economic policy emerged.

Figure 48. Outstanding project loans in the commercial real estate segment in Hungary

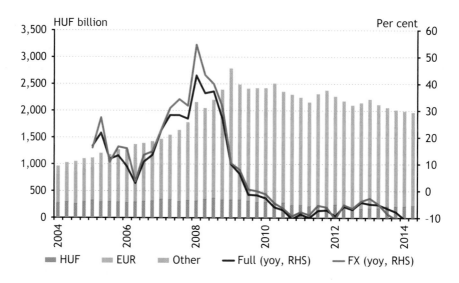

Source: MNB   *Data from the banking system*

Whereas households had acted logically in choosing the very cheap foreign currency loans after 2004 instead of the increasingly expensive forint loans, the corporate sector's decision to take on debt for commercial projects was not rational. Neither the pace of economic growth, nor household consumption trends, nor investment trends in other areas of the government and corporate sector justified ramping up commercial property development. This represents a mistake within a mistake in the tale of new indebtedness, because a macro and microeconomic analysis of the years prior to the 2006–2008 crisis would clearly have shown that the risks associated with commercial property development were rising, while at the same time this segment itself is already one of the riskiest of areas of investment overall.

Price of new indebtedness

Hungary lured itself into another debt trap between 2004 and 2010. All economic agents played a role in this. The surge in government debt due to the fiscal deficit and the rise in household debt because of the growth in foreign currency loans played a key role in this development, but so did the corporate sector, and the most vulnerable point was the excessive lending for commercial property projects. The new accumulation of debt is clearly the result of incorrect economic policy, because the disruption of the fiscal balance caused a surge in government debt, while allowing foreign currency loans resulted in households and enterprises taking on external debt. The financial balance was upset for all three economic agents, but there was one main culprit: the state, and the government's economic policy. The new debt accumulated in Hungary between 2004 and 2010 produced an unsustainable debt path.

In the European Union, Hungary joined the group of countries that were most vulnerable in terms of gross government debt and net external debt (Lane – Milesi-Ferretti, 2001). This meant Hungary broke away from its own group of CEE countries within the EU, the Visegrád Four, because gross government debt as well as net external debt relative to GDP in the Czech Republic, Poland and Slovakia were smaller by orders of magnitude than the corresponding figures in Hungary, though admittedly, they had inherited less debt upon the change of political regime (Figure 49).

For the state, the new debt was reflected in higher government bond yields caused by the higher debt servicing and higher country risk. While this was partially cushioned by the liquidity surplus in the global economy until the crisis erupted, it became that much more pronounced thereafter. For households, the new debt was accompanied by greater financial burdens, as repayment instalments and interest expenses rose by orders of magnitude, especially because of foreign currency loans.

In the corporate sector, the financial situation of groups participating in commercial property developments was shaken, and the interest expenses of enterprises taking on new debt increased sharply. The corporate sector initially benefited from the new debt, and in particular from the foreign currency lending in Hungary financed from cheap external funds, but then it suffered considerably.

Figure 49. Government debt and net external debt in Europe in 2007

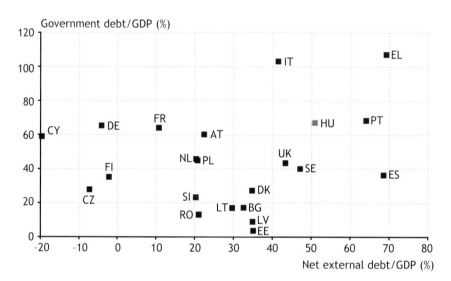

Source: Eurostat

This advantageous situation lasted from 2004 to 2008, but after 2008 the performance of the Hungarian banking sector deteriorated markedly compared to its regional competitors. The previous lack of prudent lending practices resulted in excessive borrowing among all agents in the economy, the price of which was a substantial decline in lending activity compared to the peers after 2008. Lending, and more specifically foreign currency lending after EU accession in 2004, did not reach the same level in any regional neighbour as in Hungary, and then following the 2008 crisis, no regional peer experienced such a rapid contraction of bank lending as was the case in Hungary (Figure 50).

Figure 50. Outstanding corporate loans in Europe

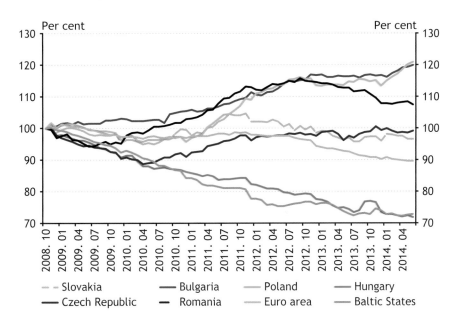

Source: MNB   *October 2008 = 100, banking sector data*

These two aspects are closely related: the excessive lending in an artificially overheated economy subsequently resulted in a significant decline in banks' loan portfolios. The deterioration of financial balance between 2004 and 2008, as reflected by the excessive borrowing by the government, households and businesses, and embodied by the fiscal deficit and the deficit on the current account, later continued in the form of a 'lending diet' for companies and households.

The banking sector strengthened the economic cycles (procyclical approach). During the boom years after EU accession, it increased lending in an irresponsible manner, before scaling back lending quickly and substantially during the downturn that followed the crisis. If the banking system had adopted a "neutral" approach, or even one balancing out the cycles (anti-cyclical approach), then the level of indebtedness would have been lower, and the growth losses caused by the crisis would have been less significant.

The GDP growth rate between 2004 and 2008 was thus higher than if the banking system had acted in a careful and neutral manner, but in the post-crisis period GDP growth was lower as economic agents endeavoured to compensate for their previously excessive borrowing by reducing their loan portfolios (Figure 51).

Figure 51. Annual growth rate of real GDP and annual growth rate of real GDP corrected by the Financial Conditions Index

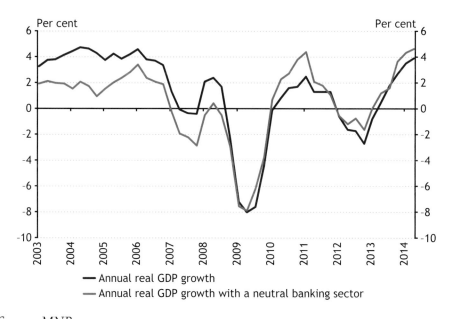

Source: MNB

The real cost of the artificial growth, excessive borrowing and new debt between 2004 and 2008 materialised after the crisis, in the form of higher repayment instalments and interest, a significant drop in loan portfolios within the banking system and slower economic growth throughout the entire economy.

For the banking system, one of the costs of this procyclical approach was the rise in the non-performing loan portfolio and its persistently high level. Credit institutions which had actively participated in foreign currency lending experienced weaker profitability on average and also had a larger non-performing loan portfolio, which stemmed from the lack of prudence before the crisis and excessive risk-taking.

The non-performing loans in the banking system were primarily concentrated at large foreign banks, but the level of non-performing loans rose for the more proactive cooperatives taking part in the lending as well, and generally speaking for cooperatives as well.[17] Non-performing loan portfolios did not rise for small and medium-sized banks, and in fact declined after 2010, which clearly reflects the difference between the small and medium-sized banks (which had operated prudently in a non-procyclical manner) and the large banks (Figure 52).

Households also suffered another distinctive loss: real house prices declined almost constantly in the ten years after EU accession (Figure 53).

---

[17] In the case of cooperative credit institutions, this is linked to underdeveloped risk management practices, and integration between cooperatives is designed to remedy this.

Figure 52. Ratio of non-performing loans (NPL) within the sub-groups of Hungarian credit institutions

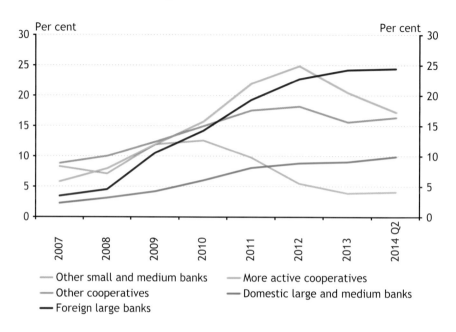

Source: MNB

Households made excessive use of the very risky home construction opportunities financed with foreign currency loans, and thus almost from the first day of EU accession and throughout the entire decade between 2004 and 2014, they suffered losses from the almost 50% decline in real house prices overall. People who built new houses or purchased properties for investment purposes, and financed these projects with loans (especially foreign currency loans) were impacted particularly severely, because real house prices plummeted while foreign currency loan repayments and interest expenses rose significantly. As a result of the indebtedness process, Hungarian households suffered significant losses through several channels during and after the crisis: the value of purchased properties fell sharply, the forint weakening against the Swiss franc pushed repayment instalments up significantly, and the deterioration in general labour market conditions meant less disposable income.

Figure 53. House prices

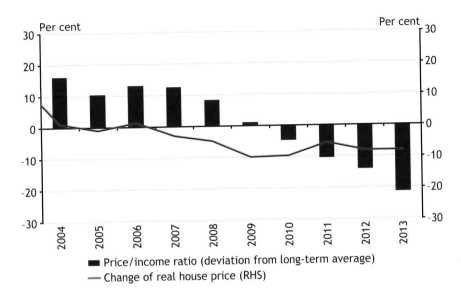

Real house prices are deflated with the consumer price index.

Source: MNB Inflation Report, June 2014 (based on FHB and HCSO data).

Chapter 4

Failed attempts at consolidation

The effects of the negative economic policy approach taken in mid-2002 appeared immediately, as the general government deficit shot higher in 2002. In the years thereafter, a string of negative consequences from this flawed policy became evident, but until autumn 2006 the government did nothing to address the increasingly dire financial imbalances. Then, from autumn 2006 until autumn 2008 it launched its first attempt to restore balance, followed by the second attempt between 2008 and 2010: both of these efforts failed.

In mid-2002, the new government pursued its "100-Day Programme" which led to a lasting deterioration in economic balance, instead of opting for a policy of consolidation after the election year. In the second half of 2002, it still would have been easy to consolidate the budget deficit, which had ballooned earlier during the election year, and to return to the 4% deficit from the previous year. Hungary was not yet an EU member, and thus it was not required to meet the 3% of GDP deficit requirement: the 4% deficit from the previous year would not have represented a deviation from the equilibrium path.

Between 2002 and 2006, however, the government pursued an economic policy which undermined economic balance, by increasing debt for all participants in the Hungarian economy again, increasing the country's gross debt, increasing net external debt, raising the external dependency of the economy with foreign currency lending, and maintaining an imbalanced financial system. As a result of this flawed economic policy, economic balance deteriorated and economic growth also lagged behind the rates in regional countries.[18]

[18] The lag is even more visible, if we filter out the effects of fiscal expansion from the Hungarian growth rates, revealing the economy's underlying growth path. Such calculations were performed by Hornok et al. (2008), showing that without the spending of the central government the rate of Hungarian GDP growth between 2001 and 2003 would have been 1% lower on average than the actual figures.

Hungary dropped out of competition in the region and the opportunity for a decade of economic convergence with the EU average was lost.

Failed consolidation between 2006 and 2008

From mid-2006, attempts were made at consolidation. The goal was to trim back the budget deficit, halt the rising trend in government debt, lower the country's gross debt and arrest the growth in net external debt. The government attempted to improve the conditions of financial balance by applying austerity measures: consolidation of the budget occurred, but balance was not restored. The budget consolidation also proved to be merely temporary, because the combination of the decline in investments, the erosion of consumption growth, the employment sacrifices and the increase in unemployment fuelled the budget deficit.

The attempt to return to an equilibrium path failed, as GDP-proportionate gross external debt steadily kept growing until 2010, just as net external debt also generally increased until the change of government in 2010 (Figure 54).

As we have seen, debt accumulation by economic agents also did not come to an end after the consolidation attempt in 2006, and thus, in addition to lowering the fiscal deficit, economic policy also sustained the borrowing trend by the participants in the economy, i.e. debt accumulation by corporations and households. From 2008–2010, net external debt essentially stagnated, and only started moving on a downward path from mid-2010.

The partial consolidation of the budget (which ultimately failed) was not accompanied by full consolidation of the financial system. In order to achieve this, it would have been necessary to immediately suspend foreign currency lending in the household sector.

This did not occur. Indeed, on the contrary, during the first consolidation attempt from 2006–2008, households' borrowing was continuously overheated and still consisted mainly of foreign currency borrowing. Corporate borrowing also continued to be overheated and was also concentrated in foreign currency loans, and more strong growth was seen in the riskiest segment, i.e. commercial property development loans. As no financial consolidation was undertaken among households and enterprises, the budget consolidation was ultimately doomed.

Figure 54. Ratio of gross external debt to GDP in Hungary

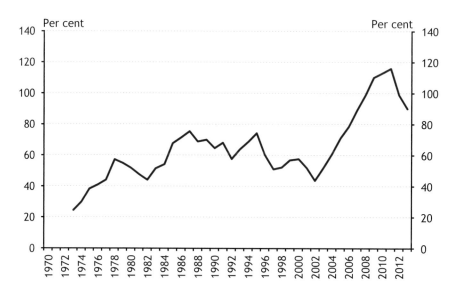

Intercompany loans not included

Source: MNB, World Bank, calculations by Lóránt, K.

From 2004 until 2010, the potential rate of growth of the Hungarian economy continuously declines. This slowdown was driven by all three production factors. While the combination of FDI, overheated household and corporate sector lending and the EU investment funds equivalent to HUF 600 billion received between 2006 and 2008 maintained the growth contribution of capital to the potential growth rate, the rate of potential growth continuously declined until 2010, due deterioration in most of the key factors behind potential growth (Figure 55).

Figure 55. Potential output growth and growth contributions

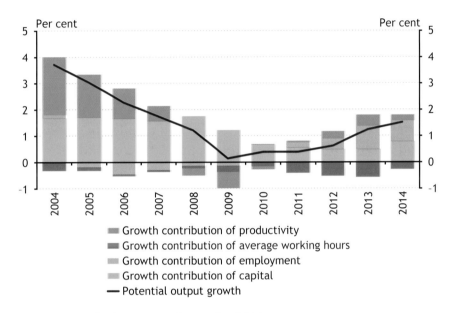

Source: MNB Inflation Report, September 2014

The decline in investments also played a significant role in the failure of the first consolidation attempt between 2006 and 2008. As a result of cutting the budget deficit, a large portion of public investments was cancelled, while at the same time corporate and household sector investments also declined. The fall in the volume of investments was accompanied by a loss of budget revenues, rendering consolidation even more difficult. In a similar manner, the drop in employment and rise in unemployment lowered the chances of consolidation: the budget lost revenues and higher spending was necessary due to the higher rate of unemployment.

Between 1 September 2006 and the end of 2008, in the period immediately before the global financial crisis impacted Hungary, economic policy was unable to halt the increase in gross debt and net external debt. It was unable to return to the 4% deficit level typical for the years around 2000, and was unable to meet the 3% deficit target undertaken as part of EU accession. The policy failed to restore financial balance, but was accompanied by significant sacrifices in the real economy.

Financial consolidation was unsuccessful, and at the same time employment fell and unemployment rose, while investments and productivity contracted. The attempt to restore financial balance entailed growth and investment sacrifices and resulted in employment and productivity losses, because the focus of the consolidation policy was on austerity measures (Figure 56).

Figure 56. Growth rate of investment volume in certain groups of countries

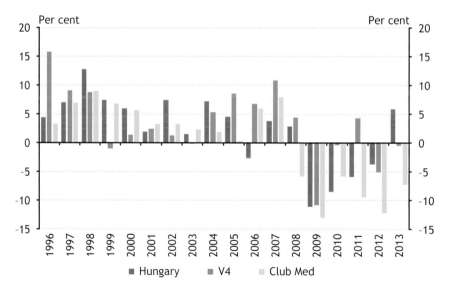

Source: HCSO, Eurostat

In 2006, the government attempted to restore fiscal balance (as embodied by the 3% of GDP budget deficit required as an EU member) primarily by increasing taxes, and within this partly by raising taxes on labour. In fact, it would have been more expedient to launch a full-scale reform of the tax system, shifting the focus of taxation from incomes to turnover and consumption. With the austerity measures, the government tried to reach the targeted deficit of less than 3%, but it did not take into account the unavoidable collateral costs of this policy. The revenue-boosting measures in relation to several kinds of taxes which were used to cut the deficit resulted in a loss of disposable income, and thus reduced consumption and investment, slowed down economic growth, and ultimately narrowed the tax base, leading to a far smaller effect in terms of improving fiscal balance as compared to what was planned.

The austerity-like nature of the consolidation attempt was felt in both investments and consumption, and impacted employment and unemployment, and in both cases the effects were negative. Consequently, tax revenues declined, and thus the measures fell well short of achieving the originally planned improvement in the budget balance.

After introduction of the austerity measures in autumn 2006, the level of consumption began to drop almost immediately, and after a transitional phase, the unemployment rate started to rise from the first half of 2007. From early 2007, the activity rate declines, perfectly reflecting the labour market cost of the austerity measures (Figure 57).

While the country's net external debt rose, this did not result in a higher growth rate compared to Hungary's regional peers. Fiscal consolidation was not supported by revenues from economic growth, because the first consolidation attempt in 2006–2008 sacrificed growth, investments, consumption, employment and productivity, without achieving an improvement in external balance indicators (Figure 58).

Figure 57. Activity, employment and unemployment in Hungary

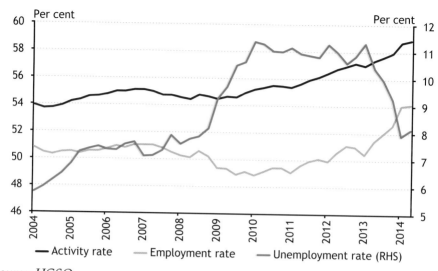

Source: HCSO

Figure 58. Cumulative change in growth and net external debt

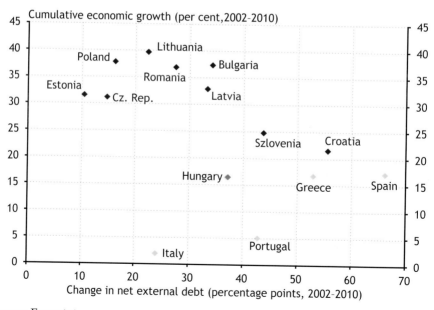

Source: Eurostat

Compared to Hungary, the EU member states, and in particular the countries in the region, recorded better growth performance at similar levels of indebtedness. This was caused by the unfavourable underlying debt accumulation trends, driven by the overheated financing opportunities and the poor structure of utilisation (real estate investments and commercial property development), in currencies other than the national currency (Catão et al. 2013).

Second consolidation attempt between 2008 and 2010

The first unsuccessful consolidation attempt hit a wall in autumn 2008, as the global financial crisis erupted. Due to the flawed economic policy in 2004–2006 and the failed attempt at consolidation in 2006–2008, Hungary became the region's (and indeed the EU's) most vulnerable country at the very moment the global financial crisis started.

The onset of the financial crisis in autumn 2008 and the changes to economic policy as a result of the IMF-EU agreement put an end to households' borrowing and the artificially stimulated economic activity in the private sector as a whole, along with the overheating causing the debt boom. Under external pressure, the government launched its second budget consolidation programme in autumn 2008, because this was the price of the IMF-EU agreement and the international financial rescue package.

Between 2008 and 2010, net external debt as a percentage of GDP did not grow further, but one of the results of this was that the Hungarian economy's output gap dropped steeply. This indicates that the partial consolidation was accompanied by sacrifices in growth, investments, consumption and employment. The sharp drop in the output gap was triggered simultaneously by the second consolidation attempt and the real economic impact of the global financial crisis[19] (Figure 59).

[19] There are debates among economists about the impact of budgetary measures on economic performance, i.e. the degree of fiscal multipliers, but a consensus has broadly emerged that during financial crises and amidst tight credit conditions measures to reduce spending result in a substantial decline in economic performance (Baum et al. (2012): Fiscal Multipliers and the State of the Economy. IMF Working Paper 12/286).

Figure 59. Output gap and external debt

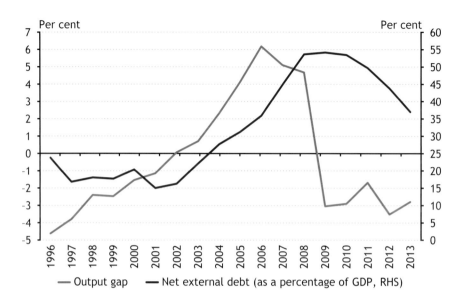

Output gap calculated using the Hodrick-Prescott filter (lambda = 100), based on annual data from 1990. The GDP forecast for 2014-2015 in the September 2014 Inflation
Report was used in handling the uncertainty of the end point for filtering.

Source: MNB

The investment activity of the foreign-owned sector plunged, because
the stock of orders and actual export sales also nosedived. The
ramifications of the second financial consolidation attempt and the
financial crisis transforming into an economic crisis combined together,
resulting in the output gap collapsing from +4.7% to below -3%, in a fall
of around 8%.

The debt accumulation in 2002–2008, the artificially overheated
economic growth and the mounting financial imbalances had
a combined impact when the crisis hit, requiring immediate, significant

balance sheet adjustment throughout the private sector. Viewed from an economic history perspective, this process occurred radically and rapidly between 2009 and 2013.

The first five years of Hungary's first decade in the EU between 2004 and 2014 was characterised by the development of a financing structure resulting in growth in a poor structure and vulnerability due to the flawed economic policy. As a result of this, unsustainable imbalances formed in the Hungarian economy and immediately upon the outbreak of the 2008 crisis the overheating was followed by deleveraging which was even faster than the previous growth in debt.

The accumulation of gross debt by the banking sector in 2006–2008 occurred over a short period of three years, while the reduction of gross debt happened in 2009–2013, over a period of around five years. By the end of 2013, the pre-2006 balance had returned in terms of the banking sector's net external debt. Accordingly, the banking sector experienced two opposite, mirror image half-decades between 2004 and 2014, with the mistakes of the first period leading to the costs of the second period (Figure 60).

The second consolidation attempt in 2008–2010 also failed, because – without the consolidation measures taken by the new government – the budget deficit would have swelled to 7% of GDP in 2010 according to the government's calculations, versus the 3.8% deficit undertaken in the IMF-EU agreement. While the second consolidation attempt did achieve partial results in certain areas of the financial balance (for example, growth in net external debt stopped, balance sheet deleveraging started in the banking and corporate sectors), it did not reach its main goal of restoring fiscal balance. The second effort to restore balance failed even though the government was able to achieve significant savings of almost 4% of GDP on the expenditure side of the budget.

Figure 60. External debt and receivables transactions of the banking sector

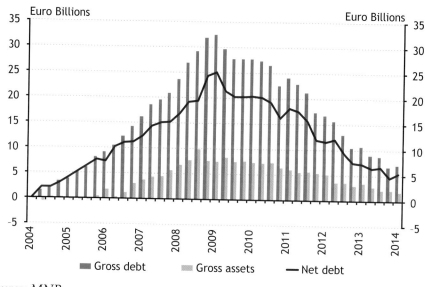

Source: MNB   *Cumulated transactions*

In contrast to the first attempt in 2006–2008, for the most part the government tried to restore overall economic balance by focusing on the expenditure side of the budget, targeting a general government deficit of between 3% and 4%. Similar to the first consolidation attempt, this was unsuccessful in 2008–2010, because the revenue losses stemming from the sacrifices in growth and investment, and in employment and productivity mostly offset the savings achieved on the expenditure side. Both in 2006–2008 and in 2008–2010, the consolidation of the government budget should have occurred on the expenditure and the revenue side.

No tax reform was undertaken in either period, whereas on the revenue side this would have been able to offset the revenue losses stemming from the cuts in expenditures. There was also no real consolidation of the budget, because the attempt to restore fiscal balance was focused only on expenditure side: this is the weak point of economic policy using austerity.

The policy of austerity cannot generate sustained, long-term fiscal balance, because there is always a real economic price to cutting back budget spending. Both the potential and actual growth rates slip lower, the level of investments and consumption falls, and due to the decline in employment and rise in unemployment it is not possible to reduce the state's spending on unemployment benefits.

The failure of the attempts by economic policy between 2006 and 2010 to restore fiscal balance and financial balance in general bears important lessons, because the second attempt was driven by external pressure and the government was serious about lowering budget spending.

Whereas external pressure and government commitment were not tangible aspects in the attempt undertaken in 2006–2008, these were visible in the second phase, but similarly to the first phase only austerity measures were used in the consolidation attempt. Regardless of the strong external pressure and internal commitment, the austerity policies with their flawed approach to consolidation were unable to bear fruit. Revenue losses for the budget generally result from financial consolidation and from budget consolidation in particular. This is unavoidable because the tools used for financial consolidation – termination and reduction of budget spending, structural reforms, reduction of accumulated debts – result in a partial loss of earlier revenues. This loss can be offset by additional revenues from additional growth, which is hardly realistic in the case of budget consolidation, or by new revenues from a new tax system: without these, consolidation is doomed to fail.

Structural reforms initially cost more than they save, and the reduction of budget spending also has a negative impact on revenues. When a government decides to cut one hundred forints in budget spending, this has an impact on consumption and/or on investments: consumption and/or investments, or perhaps savings will decline by one hundred forints.

In the first two cases, the declining consumption and/or investment has tax content: of the one hundred forints not spent on consumption and/or investment, 30–40 forints of direct and indirect taxes are lost for the budget. Thus, in its own right, austerity cannot lead to sustainable financial balance, in particular not in the case of the state budget, and thus, in its own right, it is inadequate to restore balance over the long term.

Prior to EU accession in 2004, the equilibrium level of the budget deficit around 2000 was approximately 4%, and in accordance with the obligations in the Stability and Growth Pact, following accession the targeted deficit declined to 3% of GDP. In the case of an imbalanced budget, it is not possible to achieve a budget deficit of 3% of GDP in a sustainable manner using only a policy of austerity measures. Austerity measures mean a reduction of budget expenditures or an increase in tax revenues. These, however, are accompanied by real economic losses. The larger these real economic losses are, the larger the budget revenue losses they generate as a second-round effect, and thus for at least the first two-three years of the consolidation attempt the loss in budget revenues partially offsets the amount saved by lowering spending, undermining the long-term success of consolidation. In order to combat these effects, in a weak demand environment it is particularly important to optimise the structure of fiscal consolidation.[20]

In theory, it is possible for an austerity programme lasting longer than two to three years to remedy the earlier deterioration in fiscal balance, but this is only the case if there is positive internal and external economic activity during the period in question. The real economic losses related to reducing budget spending, i.e. the declines in growth,

---

[20] It should be noted that intense budget austerity can even increase government debt, as IMF experts have shown in a study. This is because the austerity measures (e.g. spending cuts) result in on the one hand in a loss of revenues, and thus the balance improves by less than expected, and on the other hand GDP declines. If the decline in GDP is significant (i.e. the fiscal multiplier is medium or high), the GDP-proportionate debt ratio may actually increase. See: Eyraud et at. (2013): The Challenge of Debt Reduction during Fiscal Consolidation. IMF Working Paper, 13/67.

investments, employment and productivity, are reversed if strong positive internal and external activity occurs at the same time.

In the EU, however, after the 2008 global crisis, a simultaneous upswing in internal and external economic activity cannot even be expected by the mid-2010s in most of the EU members, and particularly not in those countries where budget consolidation is needed. While there is no need for budget consolidation in Germany, Austria and the Scandinavian EU countries, the need for budget consolidation remains in the euro area's southern countries. At the same time, there is no internal or external economic upswing to assist in mitigating the real economic losses stemming from consolidation in the EU as a whole, and in particular in the euro area's southern countries.

This was also the case for Hungary in the period 2008–2010. The consolidation attempt based solely on austerity measures was supported neither by positive internal nor external economic activity and thus failed. If internal and external economic conditions are not positive during a consolidation attempt, then austerity measures alone should not be used to try to restore fiscal balance: a different set of tools must be used as well. This new toolbox includes a set of unconventional economic policy tools, which was used neither in the 2006–2008 nor in the 2008–2010 consolidation programmes.

As internal and external economic conditions were not robust during either period, it was not possible for the trends in growth, investment, employment and productivity to turn around, and thus fiscal balance could not be restored.

Hungary on the Mediterranean path

From the moment of EU accession, Hungary's economic path was unsustainable: economic growth was founded mainly on non-organic, artificial sources of economic activity, financed from excessive borrowing. After 2004 (actually right after the change of government in 2002), the imbalances that developed in the state budget, the corporate sector and the household sector can all be traced back to the same source: artificially stimulated economic activity. From 2002 all the way until 2010, the fiscal deficit far exceeded the pre-accession level of around 4%, as well as the binding deficit level of 3% after EU accession.

The development of the budget deficit at a higher-than-equilibrium level indicates that the state was spending more than allowed for by fiscal balance: it was artificially stimulating the economy. The current account deficit indicates that a significant amount of external funding was being used for economic growth, investments and consumption: the state was using external funds for stimulus. The significant amount of new household debt and the lesser degree of corporate sector debt indicates that economic agents were not financing their surplus investments and consumption via accumulation, but rather via loans as an artificial source of stimulus.

The key to understanding the operation of the Hungarian economy between 2004 and 2010 is the concept of the credit gap. This shows the change in outstanding loans compared to the equilibrium level of outstanding loans, relative to GDP. The Hungarian credit gap most closely resembles the credit gaps in the euro area's Mediterranean members, but the debt overhang in Hungary was even larger than in the highly indebted Southern euro area members, and the positive credit gap was larger. The positive credit gap indicates that, compared to the GDP-proportionate equilibrium level of outstanding loans, the actual stock of credit was 16–18% higher in 2008–2009: this suggests artificial domestic economic activity fuelled by debt (Figure 61).

Figure 61. Private sector credit gap in an international comparison

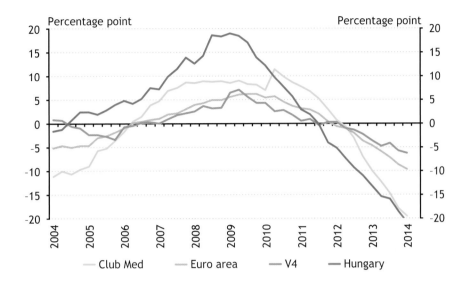

Source: MNB

Hungarian economic agents, especially the state and households, but parts of the corporate sector as well (commercial property development), accumulated debt. This was done in a poor structure (foreign currency borrowing) and these agents used a large portion of the new loans for investments which did not promote competitiveness (real estate investments).

Growth was founded on artificial economic activity, backed by a tacit, but flawed assumption. During the period around EU accession, Hungarian families which took out foreign currency loans believed that Hungary would adopt the euro very soon, and consequently they believed there was no risk involved in borrowing in a currency other than the Hungarian forint. Companies also thought that EU accession would bring a sustained period of dynamic economic growth, with the Hungarian economy firmly on course for economic convergence. Viewed in this light, investment and hiring made sense. The state was the only agent that should have understood that it would not be possible to prosper in the period following accession by allowing an unchecked rise in the deficit.

Because upon accession, Hungary made a commitment to comply with the Stability and Growth Pact, and thus to maintain the budget deficit below 3% of GDP. It was the state which launched the artificial economic upswing by weakening and ignoring the fiscal target, and this signal move by the state was then followed by all economic agents. Many may have thought, if the state is spending, then I will spend too, and if the state sees no risk in borrowing in foreign currency, then the euro must be coming soon, and it makes sense to borrow in euros, or even in Swiss francs.

The artificial economic upturn triggered by the government can be traced back to the change in government in 2002: the initial "100-Day Programme" announced to agents in the economy that the time for consumption and spending had arrived. In 2004 at the latest, however, the state should have improved the fiscal balance, and indeed it should have met the 3% of GDP deficit target. This would have changed economic agents' expectations, and the bubble of artificial activity would have burst. While the bubble on the real estate market in the US economy was the main source reason for the financial crisis, in Hungary the state budget and the government's policies played this role. Several agents participated in the evolution of this artificial economic bubble, as the banking sector, and in particular the large, foreign-owned banks immediately commenced with large-scale foreign currency lending, households and families also threw caution to the wind, and the central bank also put up no resistance. Nevertheless, the main culprit was the state budget and the government's fiscal policy.

Hungary's economic performance during the first decade of its EU membership from 2004 to 2014 was decided right from the start: instead of consolidation, the budget became even more imbalanced. Neither the European Union nor the financial markets punished this, and thus the artificial internal upswing lasted all the way until 2008, when the global financial crisis hit. It was only natural that the government's overspending and choice to disregard fiscal balance was accompanied by debt accumulation by all economic agents, since the upswing created a deceptive atmosphere in the economy.

It is revealing that, of the Visegrád countries, i.e. the regional peers, only Hungary experienced a credit bubble and moved on a debt path based on artificial state-stimulated activity. Other governments in the region did not relax budgetary discipline and did not allow unrestrained foreign currency borrowing (Figure 62).

Figure 62. Household sector credit gap in an international comparison

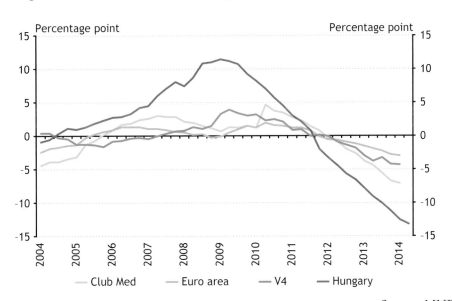

Source: MNB

The first half of the decade from 2004 to 2014 was squandered with a flawed economic policy, resulting in artificially-induced domestic activity, debt accumulation by economic agents, and the development of exceptionally high external and government debt. During the second half of the first decade in the EU, in the period 2010–2014, Hungary executed successful budget consolidation, achieved a government deficit of below 3% of GDP, put an end to household borrowing in foreign currency which was financing the artificial domestic activity, and began reducing the accumulated debts using a complex set of economic policy instruments.

The new economic policy from mid-2010 also built upon the lessons learned from the two unsuccessful fiscal consolidation attempts in 2006–2008 and 2008–2010. It took into account that it was necessary to use both conventional and unconventional economic policy tools to restore economic balance. By using only traditional economic policy to reduce the fiscal deficit it would not have been possible to achieve a sustainable budget balance at a level below 3% of GDP in 2010–2014, because there was no concurrent, positive domestic or external economic activity, and the sources of the earlier artificial upturn had been exhausted.

In respect of the tools used to return to fiscal balance, tax reform played a key role in the period after 2010: it was possible to restore balance using a set of tools which balanced the results on the expenditure and revenue side of the budget. The entire set of economic policy instruments was needed to re-establish fiscal balance, and within this it was necessary to find a balance between tools which reduced spending and tools which increased revenues. Financial balance was achieved thanks to an economic policy which found a balance between the revenue and spending measures and between conventional and unconventional means. Achieving the ultimate result of financial balance was possible because the underlying economic policy approach itself was balanced.

Chapter 5

Financial crisis erupts in 2010

Hungary was in the midst of a complex combination of crises in 2010. It was classified as one of the world's riskiest economies, its government debt swelled to unsustainable levels, companies were confronted with a credit crunch on the domestic lending market, economic indicators signalled hidden structural problems in the economy, the low level of employment and high rate of unemployment pointed to an employment crisis, and Hungarian society was still faced with a demographic crisis. Crisis emerged both in terms of financial balance and growth, leading to a paradigm of "neither balance nor growth".

A combination of crises

These crises were not the outcome of a single year or even a single decade. The pre-1990 planned economy system, the flawed transition to a market economy, and the economic developments in the two decades thereafter all played a key role. The misguided economic policy after 2002 also played a significant role in the evolution of this set of crises, because politics and economic policy set the Hungarian economy onto the wrong track in the years immediately before and after EU accession in 2004. The example shown by Hungary's competitors demonstrates that only Hungary was on the wrong path during the years around EU accession in 2004, as the Hungarian economy fell behind its regional peers in every measure of competitiveness.

Hungary became one of the world's riskiest countries in 2010, as a direct result of the flawed economic policy pursued from mid-2002 and the unsuccessful attempts at budget consolidation, first between 2006 and 2008 and then between 2008 and 2010 (Figure 63).

Figure 63. World's riskiest countries in 2010 and in September 2014

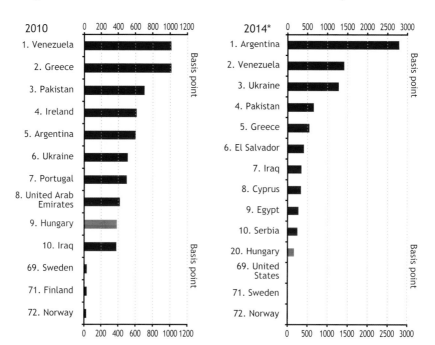

* based on September 2014 data

Source: Bloomberg   *Based on 5-year USD CDS premiums, period-end value*

Hungary was still classified as one of the world's riskiest countries in 2011, but was finally able to exit this vulnerable group as a result of the successful improvement in economic balance in 2013, and then moved further away from the danger zone after the recovery in economic growth.

Hungary was the first country in the EU which was pushed into an obvious debt crisis by the 2008 global financial crisis, and thus the Hungarian economy was the first to request emergency assistance from the International Monetary Fund and the European Union. Without the EUR 19 billion credit line, Hungary would not have been capable of financing its maturing government debt at the end of 2008 and in early 2009, and this credit line was also needed for boosting its foreign exchange reserves and financing the temporary state aid provided to Hungarian-owned banks. In 2010, Hungary was hit by another wave of crisis, which was triggered in part by the revelation around the middle of the year that the planned 2010 budget deficit of 3.8% of GDP which had been agreed in the IMF-EU agreement could not be achieved.

While the political opposition and economists had already pointed out that the budget deficit of 3.8% of GDP was not realistic for 2010, this only became clear to the experts of the EU and IMF,[21] as well as to international financial market experts, after the change of government in 2010. At the level of economic growth planned in the budget, the deficit was expected to reach nearly 7% of GDP, which would have exceeded the target of 3.8% by more than 3 percentage points. Ultimately, however, economic growth turned out to be stronger than estimated in the budget, which would have mitigated this "slippage" somewhat, but would have still resulted in a deficit of 6% in the absence of governmental measures.[22]

The new government recognised the need to lower the 2010 deficit, but the budget slippage was so large that, to a certain extent, reducing the deficit was only possible using unconventional economic policy tools. These tools impinged significantly on the interests of the IMF, the European Union and the international financial markets, as well as those of major domestic corporation agents. The poorly planned budget and management of this situation using unconventional tools triggered another deterioration in the country's risk perception in mid-2010. In addition to the above, this was also caused the crises from previous decades and even by the hidden structural deficiencies in the economy from the decades before 1990.

---

[21] "In mid-2010 it became clear that the budget's deficit target of 3.8 percent of GDP was unattainable due to spending overruns around the elections and revenue shortfalls" – IMF (2011): Hungary. Staff Report for the 2010 Article IV Consultation and Proposal for Post-Program Monitoring, p. 8.
[22] Gazdasági tényfeltáró bizottság (2010): Jelentés az ország állapotáról, and Magyarország konvergenciaprogramja, 2011–2015 (2011)

In 2010, it became clear to the international financial markets and global investor groups that Hungary was truly on the wrong track between 2002 and 2010, since even the second attempt at budget consolidation between 2008 and 2010 was unsuccessful.

In autumn 2009, a 0.9% contraction of GDP was projected in the budget for the next year, but in reality the Hungarian economy had achieved modest growth of 1.2% by the end of 2010. Nevertheless, the 3.8% deficit target was still unachievable even with GDP growth which was 2 percentage points higher than planned, clearly highlighting the failure of the previous government's consolidation efforts between 2008 and 2010. The difference between the planned and actual GDP change was 2 percentage points, representing a difference of about HUF 500 billion. Based on a tax centralisation figure of 40%, this meant about HUF 200 billion in additional revenue for the budget, but without the unconventional measures of the new government the budget still would have closed 2010 with a deficit of around 6%, which would have been unacceptable for the IMF-EU and the financial markets.

The government applied a combination of conventional and unconventional economic policy tools to manage this financial crisis. One of the conventional measures was the budget spending freeze, which reduced the budget deficit on the expenditure side, but was insufficient to reduce the deficit to an acceptable level. Consequently, further measures were necessary. These consisted of unconventional consolidation measures: the bank levy improved the revenue side of the budget by HUF 180 billion, and the crisis taxes improved the budget position by HUF 150 billion, also on the revenue side, while the suspension of transfers to the mandatory private pension fund system for two months also improved the revenue side of the budget by approximately another HUF 60 billion. In addition to this, the government lowered the corporate income tax rate to 10% up to a tax base of HUF 500 million, in the interests of improving competitiveness and stimulating economic growth (Table 2).

The economic policy strategy of immediately addressing the crisis also entailed new expenditure items in the budget, but the magnitude of these did not jeopardise fiscal consolidation. Overall, the quick consolidation of the budget resulted in a correction of around 3% of GDP, taking into account the additional revenue from the higher-than-planned growth.

While the budget deficit did not reach the 3.8% of GDP targeted in the IMF-EU agreement, the 4.3% deficit was still acceptable and was adequate to address the immediate fiscal crisis and the financing problems arising in its wake.

Table 2. Results of the 2010 budget consolidation programme

With traditional economic policy tools	
Budget freeze	HUF 220 billion
Introduction of a 10% corporate tax up to HUF 500 million	HUF -70 billion
With non-traditional economic policy tools	
Bank levy	HUF 180 billion
Crisis taxes	HUF 150 billion
Two-month suspension of transfers to the mandatory private pension fund system	HUF 60 billion
Due to macro-economic developments	
Additional revenue from economic growth	HUF 200 billion
Balance	**HUF 740 billion**

Source: MNB

Growth crisis

The negative economic policy after 2002 had already undermined the potential growth rate of the Hungarian economy in 2004–2005. Furthermore, by 2010 potential output had actually declined to a small degree, before its trend returned to an upward path around 2013. Accordingly, by 2010 the Hungarian economy was in the midst of a hidden growth crisis, caused by the flawed economic policy, which reinforced the distorted economic structure. In 2004–2005, the new growth trend departed from the earlier higher potential growth trend, and according to the forecast it was possible that this shortfall would persist over the long term, indicating that the flawed economic policy errors might cast a shadow over a longer economic history horizon of 10-15 years and would undoubtedly impact the period 2005–2010.

Fellowing years it will become clear whether the Hungarian economy will be able to return to its earlier growth trend as a result of the positive change in economic policy after 2010 (Figure 64).

Figure 64. Estimation of Hungary's potential output gap

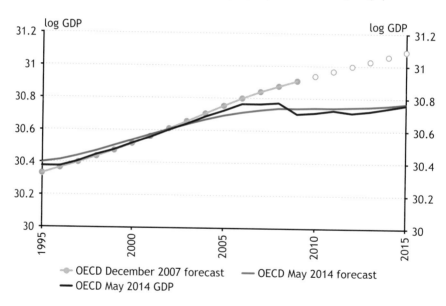

Source: OECD   *In 2005 prices, logarithmic scale*

The growth crisis is also clearly indicated by the divergence in the Hungarian and German growth rates in these years (Figure 65).

Whereas during the period 1998–2005 Hungarian economic growth consistently exceeded the rate of growth in the German economy, after 2006 the output of these two economies diverged more and more from one another. The sharp downturn in 2008–2009 also fits in with this trend, and Hungarian and German economic growth rates only converge again in mid-2013. In terms of Hungary's economic convergence, one of the key aspects was always the degree to which Hungarian GDP growth exceeded economic growth in its largest economic partner, which is also the strongest economy in the EU.

If the Hungarian economy expands at a tangibly faster rate than the German economy, Hungary moves on a trend of economic convergence. If, however, there is a small positive or negative gap in the rate of growth between the two economies, then convergence slows down or stops entirely.

Figure 65. GDP growth in Hungary and in Germany

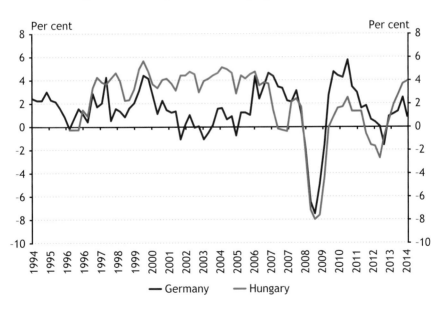

Source: Eurostat

The misguided economic policy approach taken after 2002 already impacted Hungary's convergence path by 2005–2006, as it eliminated the Hungarian economy's growth advantage vis-à-vis the German economy. Indeed, between 2006 and 2013, the Hungarian economy did not converge with the German economy, but actually lagged even further behind. The difference between Hungarian and German GDP growth rates during the period 1998–2014, which is sufficiently long from an economic history perspective, clearly illustrates that Hungary's economic convergence mainly depends on economic policy.

Between 1998 and 2014, Germany's weight in Hungary's foreign trade and economic ties remained almost unchanged, but between 1998 and 2005 this system of economic ties supported economic convergence, whereas after 2006 it was unable to maintain the Hungarian advantage in terms of the difference in the growth rates between these two economies and was not able to support economic convergence.

Starting from 2005–2006, the German economy is already growing faster than the Hungarian economy, and this is actually the result of the negative economic policy after 2002. It was clearly not the quality of the market agents that deteriorated, but rather the nature of the economic policy. It was also proven in the Hungarian economy that – on its own – market self-regulation does not achieve economic convergence. This is fundamentally influenced by the quality of economic policy: proper economic policy results in convergence, while flawed policy leads to a widening gap.

From 2013, the growth rate of the Hungarian economy once again surpasses the rate in Germany. This is clearly the result of the positive new direction in economic policy which was implemented after mid-2010, as the successful consolidation of the budget was the catalyst behind the recovery in economic growth. It was not the quality of the market agents that improved, but rather that they made better decisions, because economic policy steered them in the right direction. Moreover, this new growth did not result in mounting government debt, did not increase the country's external debt and was not based on excessive lending in the corporate and household sectors.

Still, it took 3 years from 2010 to 2013 to complete this successful financial consolidation which provides a solid basis for economic growth in a healthy structure. Just as Hungary's convergence path crumbled over roughly three years between 2002 and 2005, three years were needed between 2010 and 2013 to return to an balanced path, to successfully consolidate public finances and to restart growth again, but this time with a healthy structure (Figure 66).

Figure 66. GDP growth in Europe

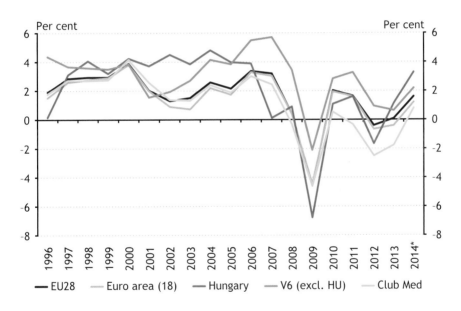

Source: Eurostat, AMECO, MNB   ** estimate*

Domestic lending crisis

The Hungarian economy was confronted with a domestic credit crunch in 2010. As a result of the second attempt at consolidation, the banking sector started to restrain lending in HUF from 2009, and net new lending dropped into negative territory. From spring 2009, Hungarian credit institutions also began to reduce their stock of outstanding foreign currency loans. This means that both corporations and households were paying back more foreign currency loans than they were accumulating. By 2010, the decline in outstanding HUF loans decelerated, while at the same time a significant amount of new foreign currency borrowing occurred, mainly denominated in euro. The stock of outstanding foreign currency loans adjusted for exchange rate effects, however, did not continue to grow, and – after the new government prohibited lending to households in foreign currency – the stock began to shrink at a rapid pace from 2011 (Figure 67).

Figure 67. Cumulated HUF and FX transactions
of the entire credit institution sector from the start of 2008

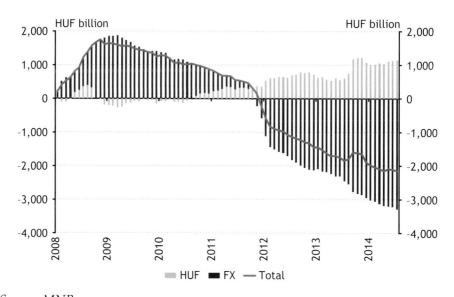

Source: MNB

Thus, agents in the Hungarian economy faced an internal lending crisis in 2010, as net lending slipped into the negative territory, both for forint and foreign currency lending. This situation only changed from the middle of 2013 when the MNB launched the Funding for Growth Scheme; up to then the Hungarian economy was essentially experiencing a domestic credit crunch.

This credit crunch had a particularly severe impact on the sector of small and medium-sized enterprises (SMEs). Whereas double-digit growth in lending before the crisis supported the development of Hungarian SMEs, from autumn 2008 there was a steep decline in lending to the sector, right from the very moment the global financial crisis started. The main reason for this was not that domestic micro, small and medium-sized enterprises immediately felt the crisis and stopped taking out new loans, but rather because the banking sector terminated its lending activities to these economic agents. Compared to large enterprises, banks identified the SME sector as representing a larger credit risk (Figure 68).

Figure 68. Annual credit growth in the SME sector in Hungary

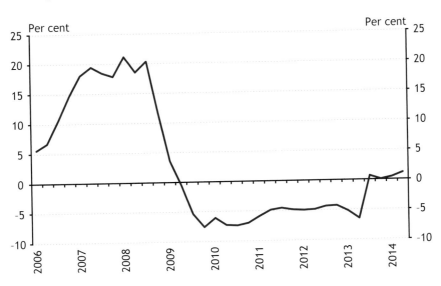

Source: MNB

From mid-2009, the change in outstanding loans to Hungarian SMEs shifted from positive to negative, as the earlier growth in this segment was replaced by the reduction and repayment of loans. By 2010, the credit crunch for the SME sector is clear to see, as these enterprises are forced to reduce their outstanding loans at rates exceeding 5% quarter after quarter. This situation improves somewhat between 2011 and 2013, but the real reversal in the trend comes with the MNB's Funding for Growth Scheme from the second half of 2013.

The credit crunch in Hungary was an unparalleled phenomenon, both in the region and in the euro area as well. While private sector borrowing rates in the Polish, Slovak and Czech economies were even higher than in Hungary, Hungary struggled with the largest decline in outstanding loans in 2009 and the years thereafter (Figure 69).

Figure 69. Lending to the private sector (corporate and household) in the euro area and Visegrád countries, annual change

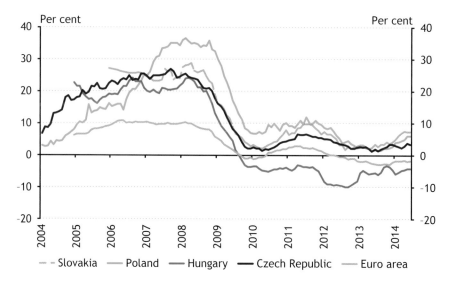

Source: MNB

While pre-crisis growth in euro area corporate lending was slower than in the economies in the region (the annual growth of around 10% was far lower than the annual rates of 20% to 40% recorded in the Visegrád region), the decline in the corporate loan portfolio in Hungary was much steeper compared to the euro area in the period after the crisis. In the case of the euro area, growth in corporate lending "merely" stopped, but in the case of the Hungarian economy annual rates of decline of 0% to 10% were typical.

The contraction in the corporate loan portfolio in Hungary was very significant, compared to its peers and even compared to the members of the euro area. This reflects the severe domestic lending crisis in the years around 2010, because the banking sector's lending activity was not only determined by the indicators (such as loans to individual sectors, and the risk assessment) for the domestic loan portfolio, but also by the country's risk premium, the higher level of government debt and the consolidation of economic policy.

The flawed economic policy ahead of the financial crisis, and the failure of the first and second consolidation programmes resulted in a critical situation in the Hungarian financial system, especially in the banking sector. During the years following the 2008 crisis, the portfolio of non-performing loans (NPLs) in the sector rose continuously, with a particularly strong surge in NPLs registered in household foreign currency loans. NPLs also jumped to critically high levels in parts of the corporate foreign currency loan portfolio and in commercial property development loans.

In the case of the banking sector, an increasingly large portfolio of NPLs became stuck in banks' balance sheets for a long period of time, slowing down the extension of new loans and exacerbating the domestic credit crunch. As a proportion of total lending, the share of non-performing loans overdue by 1–3 years reached 25% and the share of NPLs overdue by 3–5 years advanced into the double-digit range.

This clearly reflects the previous overheated lending, the failures in earlier lending practices, the real risks of the sharp rise in the portfolio of foreign currency loans and the structural weakness in terms of how the loans were utilised (Figure 70).

Figure 70. Distribution of corporate NPLs by time elapsed since becoming non-performing

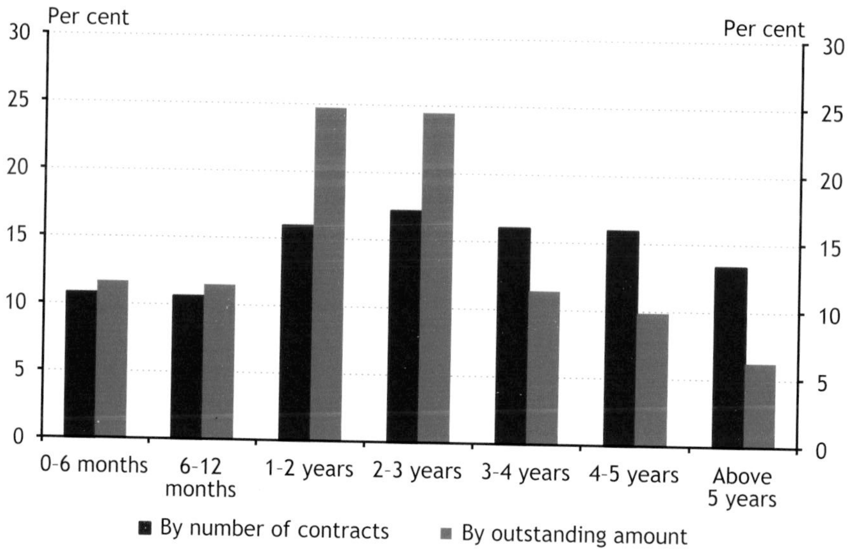

Source: CCIS

As of end-2013

Consumption crisis

The Hungarian economy was confronted with yet another crisis in 2010: the crisis in household final consumption expenditure and public sector consumption.

The first crisis was visible, while the second one was hidden. In 2010, household final consumption expenditure dropped by more than 2%, and although public consumption still expanded mildly, it stagnated at 0% in 2011 and 2012. While there was some modest growth in the Hungarian economy in 2010, household final consumption expenditure contracted substantially (Figure 71).

Figure 71. GDP growth factors

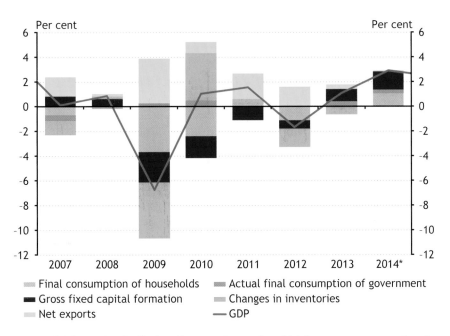

Source: HCSO, MNB (Inflation Report, September 2014)   ** estimate*

This was the result of the second unsuccessful attempt at consolidation in 2008–2010, which focused exclusively on the expenditure side of the budget in attempting to consolidate the budget as a whole. The spending cuts on the expenditure side ultimately reappeared in the decline in household consumption, and then in falling budget revenues.

The other reason for the decline in household consumption in 2010 was the domestic credit crunch. Over the long term, there is a strong set of systemic connections between household income, consumption and credit. The long-term level of consumption fundamentally depends on income and the size of households' wealth. Over the long run, the stock of outstanding household loans (which can be viewed as negative wealth) depends on the level of income and the interest rate on the loans.[23]

If an imbalance arises on the credit market, it also influences consumption demand. In the pre-crisis period, the credit market facilitated the surge in consumption, and higher consumption was accompanied by stronger borrowing. During the first attempt at consolidation in 2006–2008, to a degree, households viewed the fiscal austerity measures as temporary and responded by smoothing out their consumption and by taking on more debt. As a result of this, consumption drifted even further away from its sustainable, long-term path.

When the crisis erupted, which was accompanied by an increase in the risk premium for Hungary and then by a decline in external demand, the repayment burdens of households suddenly shot higher, and households' income and wealth fell. Consequently, consumption and lending remained at levels above the equilibrium. As a result, economic agents had to make balance sheet adjustments (deleverage). Households restrained their consumption and investment expenditures, and focused mainly on repaying their existing debts. The adjustment in consumption

[23] For more, see the analysis of Endrész et al. (2014). The long-term term relationships they estimate are the following (the parameters show how many percentage points a change of one percentage point in the explanatory variable alters consumption or borrowing):

	Consumption	Lending
Income	0.64	1.5
Financial wealth	0.1	0
Housing wealth	0.11	0
Cost of credit	0	-1.34

The adjustment parameters for deviations from consumption and lending equilibrium are the following:

	diff(consumption)	diff(lending)
ecv (consumption)	-0.27	0.72
ecv (lending)	-0.02	-0.05

occurred relatively quickly: in just one single quarter the distance from the equilibrium consumption level declined by one fourth. At the same time, the adjustment of debt is a protracted process, as it only changes slowly due to the long maturity and nature of the loan portfolio.[24] Adjustment had already started in the Hungarian economy by 2010, but the bulk of it occurred during the period of successful consolidation. Again, this indicates the long shadow cast by the previous flawed economic policy.

Hidden structural crisis

As a result of balance sheet adjustment, Hungary's trade balance turned positive in the years after the crisis, but both the import content of exports and the import content of household and public consumption remained high. Consequently, the import exposure of the Hungarian economy is still high.

At the beginning of the 2000s, mostly thanks to the Széchenyi Plan, the import exposure of the Hungarian economy fell, but almost immediately after the adoption of the misguided economic policy approach in 2002 import exposure began to grow again.

The overheated growth based on borrowing also had a poor structure, as reflected by the steady increase in the import exposure of the Hungarian economy after 2003. The import content of public and household consumption also increased, along with the import content of exports. This constituted a hidden structural crisis, which is concealed

---

[24] Hungarian households were more successful in reducing their debts than households in other European countries. The stock of household debt typically hardly changed at all in the euro area countries, and according to the analysis of the European Commission (2014) the stock still significantly exceeded the sustainable level in 2013. The reform of the personal income tax system, which promoted the expansion of disposable income, may have played a role in the good performance in Hungary. In addition to this, the early repayment scheme also facilitated the reduction in debt, mostly for households with financial assets.

by the trade balance and later by the surplus on the current account: the foreign trade vulnerability of the Hungarian economy was high and continued to rise due to the poor economic policy (Figure 72).

Figure 72. Import exposure in the field of goods including import demand generated by exports

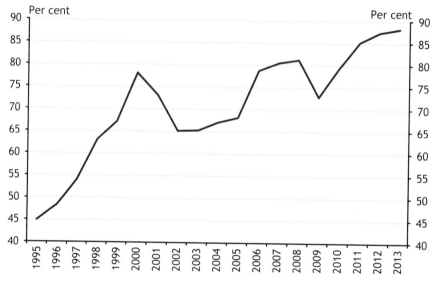

Source: HCSO

In part, this high level of vulnerability is due to the strong dependence on energy imports, which stems to some degree from the low energy efficiency, but also reflects the misguided policy approach after 2002. The post-2002 economic policy did not pay attention to any economic balance indicators at all: it did not focus on external debt, government debt, inflation, or balance on the credit market, and did not monitor domestic structural balance.

In the pre-crisis year, the structure of the economy shifted in an unfavourable direction, as indicated by the increasing import exposure of goods. Instead of public and household consumption and exports showing an increasingly high proportion of domestic products (i.e. agents in the Hungarian economy producing an increasing share of the goods for consumption, investments and exports), the opposite occurred. They produced a smaller and smaller proportion, boosting Hungary's structural vulnerability in economic terms, while at the same time exacerbating the inherited structural weaknesses and dualistic structure of the economy.

The deterioration in Hungary's economic balance started with the loss of financial balance in 2002. First, the fiscal balance was upset. This was followed by a reversal of the previous downward trend in government debt and the country's external debt began to rise. Market balance deteriorated as indicated by the high inflation rates. The balance in lending deteriorated as reflected in the credit gap rising above a sustainable level. And the structure of the Hungarian economy shifted in an unfavourable direction.

Although the deterioration in the economy's internal structure remained concealed, it was reflected in the low rate of potential growth, the low level of employment and high unemployment rate, the low productivity and the high import exposure of goods.

This is also visible if we compare the import exposure of the Hungarian economy with similar data on other economies in the EU. In 2013, Hungary was ranked as one of the top three vulnerable countries in terms of foreign trade, and consequently from an economic structure point of view it was one of the weakest countries. The ranking of Luxembourg is misleading in this regard, and actually the Slovak, Hungarian and Dutch economies exhibit the highest degree of import exposure in the field of goods when compared to the other EU member states. It should also be noted, however, that the members of the EU are also vulnerable, for instance vis-à-vis the US economy, although this vulnerability to foreign trade also includes trade within the EU as well (Figure 73).

Figure 73. Import exposure in the field of goods

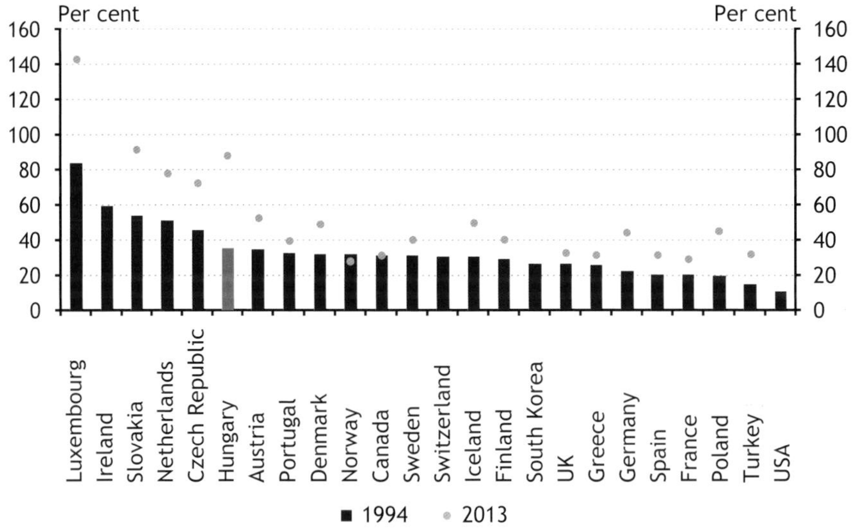

Source: OECD   *Including import demand generated by exports*

In part, the high import exposure calculated for goods in the Hungarian economy stems from the low weighting of the food industry and agricultural production in Hungary. Due mainly to the low weighting of the food industry, the import share of domestic consumption is higher than in France, Italy, Spain and Greece, economies where the low import share results from the strong domestic food industries. The high import exposure for goods in the Hungarian economy, i.e. one of the imbalances and weak points in the economic structure, can best be remedied by significantly increasing the weight of the domestic food industry and agricultural production.

During the years around EU accession in 2004, however, the flawed economic policy had the opposite result, because the overheated economic growth with a distorted structure which was financed incorrectly (foreign currency loans) did not primarily create additional capacities in those sectors which would have lowered import exposure via domestic consumption, investment activity and exports, but rather in sectors which increased this exposure.

During the period 2002–2010, the flawed economic policy initially upset Hungary's financial balance and then made unsuccessful attempts to restore balance in the public budget, government debt and external debt. At the same time, it had no choice but to pursue an exchange rate policy which eased the burdens of debt accumulation in foreign currency by the public, corporate and household sectors by way of the artificially strong exchange rate of the Hungarian forint. This increased the vulnerability of the Hungarian economy in the field of foreign trade, because it allowed for and triggered the rise in the import exposure of goods. The rise in import exposure pushed the structure of the Hungarian economy in the wrong direction, thus further increasing the imbalances in the economy.

Ultimately, the financial imbalances triggered further detrimental developments in economic balance in the period 2002–2010. Eight years of failed economic policy clearly show that attention to financial balance is of paramount importance in economic policy, because in the event of problems in this regard economic policy is left with few choices: it only has bad and worse tools left at its disposal to attempt to remedy the financial imbalances.

In the period 2006–2008, the attempt at consolidation obviously failed. Nor did the efforts made in 2008-2010 achieve the desired results, as the actual fiscal deficit for 2010 would have amounted to 6% to 7% of GDP in the absence of any change in economic policy. Internal economic balance also continued to deteriorate during these two unsuccessful attempts at consolidation, since for example the imbalances in the economic structure deepened due to the import exposure of goods.

In mid-2010, the tasks facing economic policy were clear: first, it was necessary to restore financial balance in numerous areas, and then, based on this, it would be possible to move towards restoring balance in the economy.

Employment crisis

The Hungarian economy experienced a visible and a hidden crisis in the fields of employment and the labour market as well. This was manifested in the significantly lower employment rate compared to the EU average and to the North American economies and the rapidly developing Eastern Asian economies, as well as in the low activity rate and the high level of unemployment.

The employment crisis peaked in 2010, because in 2009–2010 the rate of employment in the Hungarian economy sank to the lowest level recorded in almost a decade and a half between 2000 and 2014. It may appear that this resulted from the impact of the 2008 global financial crisis on the Hungarian economy. In reality, however, the exceptionally low level of Hungarian employment was partly due to the failed transition to a market economy after 1990 and partly due to the missed opportunities around the years of EU accession, as well as to the flawed and unsuccessful economic policy (Figure 74).

The economic policy measures affecting the labour market during the period following the change of political regime had a fundamental, defining effect on the structural problems of the Hungarian economy during the last two decades. In 1990, the collapse of export markets and sectors which were uncompetitive under market conditions resulted in falling employment in all of the economies affected in the region. In Hungary, however, the decline in employment went hand in hand with a decline in labour market activity, i.e. groups in society which lost their jobs left the labour market permanently, assisted by economic policy. While this process, which continued all the way until 1997, reduced the social tensions stemming from the economic transition, the structural tensions caused over the long term created a systemic foundation for repeated episodes of imbalance.

It should be noted that the economic policy pursued between 1998 and 2002, which was still able to preserve balance, was able to boost the rate of employment in the Hungarian economy by a small degree by 2003, and the rate remained practically at the same level until 2007.

Between 2007 and 2010, however, as a result of the first and second unsuccessful attempts at consolidation, and due to the impact of the global financial crisis, the employment rate then fell to its minimum point in 2010.

Figure 74. Labour market activity, employment and unemployment in post-transition Hungary

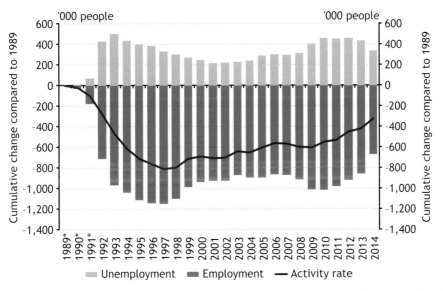

expert estimate

Source: HCSO Labour Force Surveys (from 1992), Statistical Yearbook 1989–1993

An opposite trend in employment is seen in the countries in the region. In the early 2000s, the rate of employment in the countries in the region initially declined as a result of the effect of the economic crises in the wake of the collapse of the stock exchange for the US technology sector, and then after EU accession, the rates began to rise steeply again. This stemmed directly from the fact that these countries were able to take good advantage of the unique opportunity offered by EU accession. Rates of employment in the region and in Hungary moved on divergent trends in the years after accession. Around 2007, the trend in Hungarian employment started to move downwards, as a consequence of the flawed economic policy between 2002 and 2006, and the first attempt at consolidation launched from 2006, whereas the employment trend in the region moved steeply upwards.

Although this development was interrupted by the financial crisis in 2008, the effect was less severe than in Hungary. This also shows that there are two factors behind the decline in the Hungarian rate of employment after 2007: an internal factor, mainly in the form of the economic policy crisis, and an external factor, seen in the impact of the global financial crisis (Figure 75).

Figure 75. Employment rate in the 15-64 age group

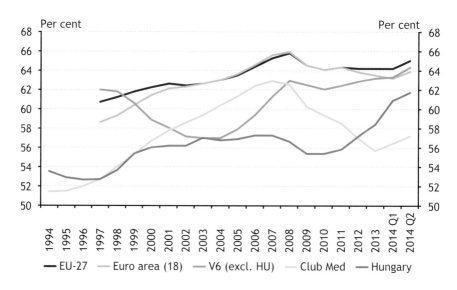

Source: OECD, Eurostat

Since the first factor did not materialise in the countries in the region and only the second factor was at play, the level of employment in these countries rose strongly prior to the crisis, and during the financial crisis employment did not fall as much as it did in the Hungarian economy, which was suffering from a dual crisis. The new direction taken in economic policy in 2010 immediately addressed the financial crisis and pressed forward with a successful programme of fiscal consolidation. At the same time, it immediately began taking measures to resolve the employment crisis: by the second half of 2010, the rate of employment started to climb again, even if only slowly.

Chapter 6

The transition crisis

In the two decades between 1990 and 2010, the performance of the Hungarian economy lagged far behind its regional competitors, in particular compared to the convergence of the Polish and Slovak economies. Two decades is a period which is already significant from an economic history perspective, and thus it is worth analysing the structural and economic policy reasons behind this shortfall.

Hungary departs from the equilibrium convergence path

The two decades between 1990 and 2010 saw a successful transition from a centralised, single-party political system to the political system of a parliamentary democracy, but was marred by failures in the transition from a planned, command economy to a market economy system. This is reflected by the recurrent episodes of financial imbalances and later by the deceleration in economic growth: setting the Hungarian economy on a sustainable equilibrium convergence path was unsuccessful. Economic convergence is measured with the yardstick of the average level of per capita GDP for the later European Union, even though per capita GNI would provide a more accurate picture.

In the period 1990–2013, Hungary was only able to approach the economic output characterised by the average level of per capita GDP for the group of European Union countries to a very small degree, and convergence in terms of per capita GNI was almost negligible (Figure 76).

Figure 76. Per capita GDP and GNI in Europe compared
to the European Union average

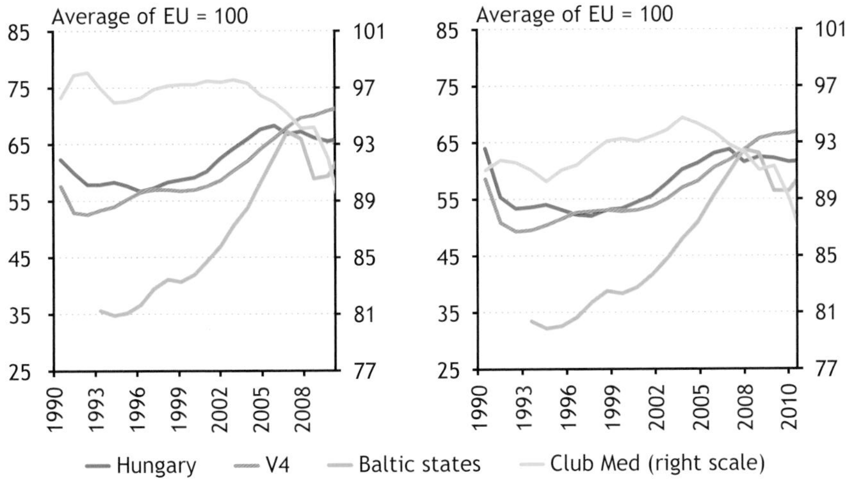

PPP (constant 2011 prices, based on USD data)

Source: World Bank WDI database, Penn World Table, MNB calculations

The failure in convergence is striking when we compare the performance of the regional peers – Poland, the Czech Republic and Slovakia – to Hungary's performance. While the regional peers have quickly moved towards the average level of development in the EU in recent years, the performance of the Hungarian economy has lagged behind in the region. There is also a particularly wide gap between the Hungarian economy's performance during the two decades and the rapid convergence to the EU average by the three Baltic States.

Hungary's deficit in terms of convergence to the later EU average and the regional average is clearly the result of weak growth performance. Aside from some brief periods, the rate of growth in the Hungarian economy fell short of both the EU average, and the average growth performance of the Baltic States and the countries in the immediate region.

The Hungarian growth model proved to be uncompetitive versus the growth models of the EU, the Baltic States and the regional countries.

The most important characteristic of the Hungarian growth model during the two decades between 1990 and 2010 was that economic growth regularly ran into the obstacle of financial balance. When Hungarian growth performance was better than its peers, it had a negative impact on financial balance: the fiscal deficit increased, leading to rising government debt and external debt, while market balance deteriorated and inflation rose (Figure 77).

Figure 77. Economic growth and financial imbalances in Hungary

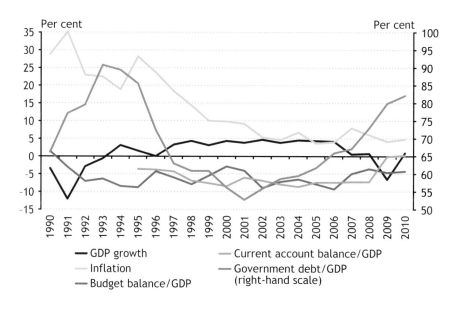

Source: Eurostat, HCSO, MNB, GDMA

Aside from the transition to the market economy in Hungary and the region in the first half of the 1990s, the external shocks which impacted the Mediterranean countries in the EU were essentially identical to the shocks that affected Hungary and its neighbours.

The dominance of internal shocks over external shocks is indicated by the fact that in 1993–1994 the imbalances were not caused by external shocks, but rather by the flawed economic policy of the previous two years and the shock therapy transition to the market. In 1995–1996, the weak growth did not stem from external shocks, but was rooted instead in the necessity to restore economic balance.

The economic imbalances in the period 2002–2006 were not associated in the least with external shocks. In fact, a unique, simultaneous constellation of expansive external activity and a global environment practically free from financial strains were conducive to economic growth. Even viewed from a global economic history perspective spanning back 160 years, it is clear that the economic expansion in the 2000s was quite unique all the way up until the financial crisis in 2008–2009 (Figure 78).

Figure 78. Cycles of financial crises, 1810-2010

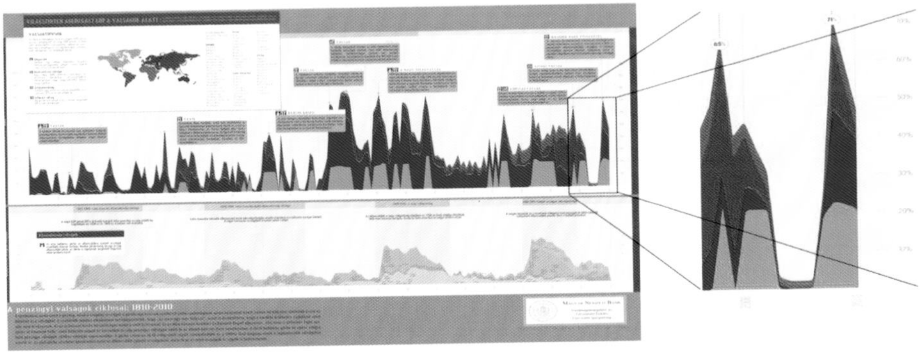

Source: Princeton University Press

Hungary's competitors used this period well, while Hungary's economic policy failed miserably: by mid-2002 economic policy had already departed from the growth path ensuring sustainable macroeconomic balance and by 2008 the Hungarian economy was mired in a dual crisis.

The deterioration in growth in the period from 2007 to autumn 2008 cannot be traced back to any external shock and was actually related to the first attempt to restore economic balance.

Even before the onset of the global financial crisis in autumn 2008, Hungary's growth performance founders and the potential growth rate nosedives (Figure 79).

Figure 79. Annual GDP growth in the Visegrád countries

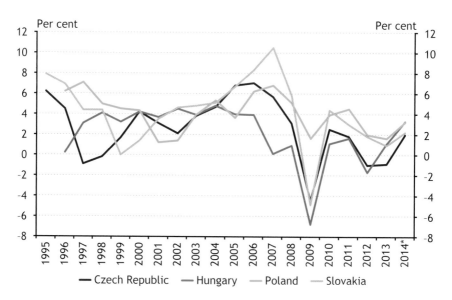

* estimate

Source: Eurostat, European Commission (2014 May forecast), MNB

In the period from autumn 2008 to mid-2010, the Hungarian economy is hit by a major shock. The dual crisis and a policy of restoring economic balance once again leads to a pattern of "neither growth nor balance": a sustainable equilibrium path is not achieved in terms of external debt or the fiscal balance, and at the same time growth slips to a low level. From autumn 2008 to mid-2010, the Hungarian economy almost perfectly replicates the structure seen 20 years earlier: back then, however, the main challenge was to launch the historically important process of transition to a market economy, whereas now the price was being paid for the flawed market transition and the misguided economic policy pursued after 2002 (Figure 80).

Figure 80. General government balance in the Visegrád countries, % of GDP

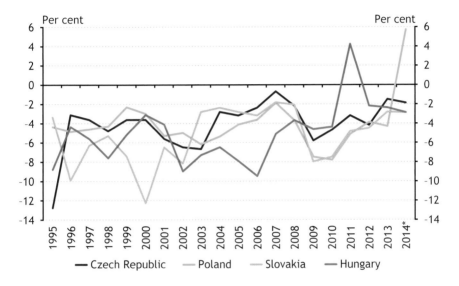

Source: Eurostat, European Commission (2014 May forecast)   * estimate

Can the shock from the transition to a market economy in the early 1990s be compared with the external shock from the 2008–2009 global financial crisis?

While the strength of these shocks was similar, their effects were different. In the 1990s, the rate of employment plunged sharply by international and European standards, due to the misguided economic policy approach to the market economy transition, leading to the fundamental Hungarian paradigm of "growth or economic balance". By contrast, the external shock felt in 2008–2010 occurred in a market economy environment. Strangely enough, the losses seemed natural in both periods. In the 1990s, they appeared to be the necessary sacrifice for transitioning from a non-market economy to a market economy, while in the more recent past they seemed to be the similarly unavoidable sacrifices originating from the global financial crisis. Nevertheless, the countries in the region suffered smaller losses during the market transition in the 1990s as compared to the Hungarian economy, and later the losses inflicted by the global financial crisis were also smaller by orders of magnitude compared to the losses in Hungary.

Moreover, the Polish economy was actually able to weather the 2008–2009 crisis without suffering any contraction at all. For the most part, the reason for these differences can be traced back to the trap laid by the dualistic formula of "economic balance or growth" in Hungarian economic policy: economic policy itself was responsible for steering Hungary's economy into a dead-end in the two decades between 1990 and 2010.

During the period of economic history when transition occurred (1990–2010), the fundamental economic policy error was that it failed to take into consideration employment as the key third factor, in addition to economic balance and growth. If growth was strong, employment appeared to automatically rise, but by international standards it actually consistently remained at low levels. If efforts were made to restore balance in response to external shocks, the rate of growth began to fall and at the same time employment also weakened. This was seen clearly in the period 2006–2008, when the level of employment dropped as a result of the first consolidation attempt. This was followed by the financial shock, and then employment fell yet again, due to the impact of the second attempt at consolidation. At that time, the decline in the level of employment was not as severe as it was during the first half of the 1990s, and there were several reasons behind this. The new, market economy was already more resilient than the earlier command economy, and furthermore several hundred thousand Hungarian employees had found work elsewhere in the EU after 2004: these two factors prevented the Hungarian economy from suffering another dramatic decline in employment during the dual crisis between 2006 and 2010.

Analysis of the transition period from 1990 to 2010 clearly shows the pattern that an economic policy which is focused exclusively on the two factors of balance and growth regularly runs astray. It is no coincidence that the improving growth performance seen during these two decades ultimately upsets economic balance, and restoring or even attempting to restore balance results in growth sacrifices. The reason for this is that the economic policies pursued by the governments in 1990–2010 (with the exception of the policies between 1998 and 2002) did not take into consideration the third main component of economic policy: the labour market (Table 3).

Economic policies in Hungary were only able to achieve temporary successes during the two decades of transition, because out of the three key components of economic policy – economic balance, growth and employment – the third one was disregarded.

The entire period 1990–2010 was marked by rates of activity and employment which were significantly lower than the international and European Union averages.

Table 3. Growth and economic balance

	Growth	Economic balance
1990	zero point = TRANSITION	
1. 1991-1992	⇩	⇩
2. 1993-1994	⇧	⇩
3. 1995-1996	⇩	⇧
4. 1997-2001	⇧	⇧
5. 2002-2006	⇧	⇩
6. 2007-2008	⇩	⇧
7. 2008-2010	⇩	⇩

Source: Compiled by author

The actions of the governments using various economic policy tools in the individual political cycles generated substantial differences in respect of government debt, external debt, inflation, fiscal deficits, the credit market, the trade balance and the current account balance, but – aside from a few years around 2000 – the economic policies of the various governments during the entire period between 1990 and 2010 made no efforts to achieve a rapid, tangible increase in activity and employment rates.

When the economic policies were exceptionally flawed, the rates of employment and activity sank even lower, and the rate of unemployment rose higher: this was seen during the first half of the 1990s and in the period 2006–2010 at the time of the first and second failed attempts at consolidation (Figure 81).

Figure 81. Employment rate and government debt in Hungary, 1990-2014, % of GDP

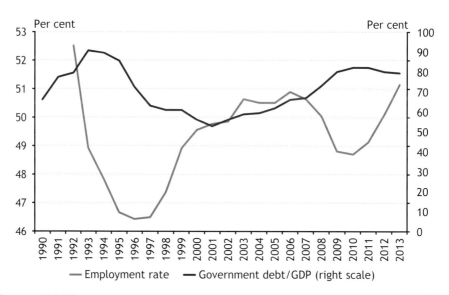

Source: HCSO   * estimate

Starting from mid-2010, an economic policy is implemented in Hungary which focuses equally on all three of these key components. At the heart of this economic policy is the formula "growth + employment = sustainable balance" (G+Em=SB): the macroeconomic achievements in the period 2010–2014 demonstrate that this formula works.

The new economic policy formula: G+Em=SB

From 1990 to 2010, Hungarian economic policy did not use this formula for successful economic convergence, but from mid-2010 it started to. It can be stated that the unsuccessful attempts at consolidation between 2006 and 2008 and even more so between 2008 and 2010 did not result in further large-scale declines in employment and a sharp drop in the activity rate, with a related surge in unemployment, because the structure of the labour market had changed fundamentally in the meantime, since several hundred thousand Hungarian employees had found jobs elsewhere in the European Union.

Without this, the ultimately unsuccessful consolidation attempts executed in the old economic policy framework would have led to substantial new imbalances on the labour market, quickly raising unemployment and lowering the level of employment.

The new economic policy applied immediately from mid-2010 was able to reverse the deterioration in financial balance almost from the very moment it was applied, because the underlying trend in employment had already turned positive. Starting from mid-2010 for three years economic policy focused on financial balance, which it was able to restore thanks to special, unconventional measures. The bank levy, the crisis taxes, the sector-specific taxes and the transition to a system of indirect taxation actually played a decisive role in restoring balance in the government budget and breaking the upward trend in government debt.

The successful financial consolidation in Hungary was truly remarkable, because – simultaneously with reaching a fiscal turning point in 2011 and later maintaining the budget deficit below 3% – the level of employment and the activity rate constantly rose, while the rate of unemployment declined. While it may appear that the new system of public work programmes was responsible for this, corporate sector employment also began to expand from the end of 2012, demonstrating that the new economic policy formula worked (Figure 82).

Figure 82. Old and new economic policy approach

Old economic policy formula → Economic balance

New economic policy → Growth + Employment = Sustainable balance

Source: Compiled by author

The new economic policy applied from mid-2010 simultaneously achieved a sustainable, acceptable budget deficit (defined as a fiscal deficit below 3% of GDP since EU accession), restarted growth, lowered external debt and broke the upward trend in government debt, while at the same time labour market balance steadily improved. Precisely this has created a sustainable economic model for the decades after 2010 in Hungary, because the improvement in the fiscal balance achieved using a combination of conventional and unconventional tools and the return of economic growth has resulted in steady gains in the rate of employment, which means that this new economic policy formula may prove effective over the long term.

Within this framework, the rise in employment is the ultimate guarantee for sustainable fiscal balance, because the combination of expanding employment and accelerating economic growth generate additional revenues for the budget. In part, these new budget revenues can be used to lower government debt, and in part they can be applied to further stimulate economic growth. During the two decades of transition between 1990 and 2010, however, this economic policy formula was not applied, and consequently the situation was always characterised by either "balance or growth" or "neither balance nor growth".

It was not possible to achieve convergence with any other growth formula

In the two decades between 1990 and 2010, Hungary's economic convergence was not only a failure because a flawed formula was applied for financing the economy, but also because the growth formula was mistaken. Economic convergence, even if it starts, cannot be sustained in any economy if no solution is found to the dilemma of simultaneous financial balance and economic growth. As seen in the example of Hungary, resolving this dilemma is not possible without a high rate of employment, because without this economic growth does not generate adequate revenues for the state budget to move towards a state of balance: this leads to the paradigm "either balance or growth".

The question, however, is how does one achieve a steadily high rate of employment, which renders the "balance and growth" formula sustainable. Reaching financial balance does not automatically create a high level of employment. One of the reasons for this is that achieving financial balance, i.e. restoring a sustainable budget deficit level, must occur by siphoning off demand from the economy either on the expenditure or on the revenue side, but most often on both sides of the budget (negative fiscal impulse[25]). Measures intended to improve

---

[25] The fiscal impulse measures how much financial resources fiscal policy withdraws or adds to the economy over the short term. For more, see Kiss (2011).

economic balance reduce both consumption and investment demand in the economy, and consequently have a negative impact on employment. Consolidation measures on the revenue side of the budget generally take the form of tax increases, which result in a withdrawal of income – either directly if they affect consumers or individual taxpayers, or indirectly, if they affect the corporate sector – and thus a contraction in demand.

Generally speaking, policies aimed at remedying financial imbalance not only have an impact on the state budget, they also impact the banking sector. It is often the case that balance in the state budget and the credit market deteriorates at the same time, and consolidation measures are necessary to address both. This means that, in the case of a programme to remedy the imbalances, it is also not possible to compensate the for decline in demand in the economy resulting from fiscal consolidation by way of additional borrowing.

A growth structure which takes into consideration labour market equilibrium leads to the achievement of a high rate of employment. This is accompanied by sacrifices in productivity, either due to a slowdown in the previous rate of productivity growth or due to stagnation in productivity in the economy in question. Economic growth is accompanied by an increase in the level of employment when the growth affects all segments of the labour market, including groups in the most disadvantaged situation.

In the case of Hungary, the imbalance on the labour market is not only indicated by the high level of unemployment, and the persistently low activity and employment rates, but also by the high rate of long-term unemployment, the extremely low employment rate among women, and the also particularly low level of employment among low-skilled persons and workers over 50. These groups of workers are also similarly represented in the level of unemployment. Taken together, these aspects characterised the market economy transition between 1990 and 2010.

The failure of the market transition in the field of economic policy occurred, because no solution was found to the contradiction and mutually exclusive nature of financial balance and economic growth. Economic policy was unable to find a solution to the flawed formula of financial balance or economic growth and apply the correct formula of financial balance and economic growth, because it only focused on two factors and disregarded the third factor, the labour market. The dilemma of economic policy could not be resolved with a low rate of employment.

However, looking at the period of economic history between 1990 and 2010, it can be seen that the growth formula was also flawed, because the economic growth did not reach those groups which played a significant role in the imbalances in the labour market, even during periods of relatively strong GDP growth. There was one exception to this, with the economic policy and growth structure applied around 2000, as 240,000 new jobs were created in the Hungarian economy between 1998 and 2002: in that phase economic policy and the structure of growth mitigated the imbalances on the labour market.

During these two decades, economic growth did not result in convergence because it regularly undermined financial balance, but at a deeper level convergence was also unable to succeed because it did not result in social advancement, i.e. it did not create work opportunities for significant parts of society. Hungary also experienced social crises even at times when there was no crisis in balance or in growth: the imbalances in the labour market continued and sustained a hidden social crisis, even though this crisis was not reflected in the macroeconomic indicators.

The main reason for this was that the policies between 1990 and 2010 did not allow for the development of a structure for economic growth which would have raised employment in Hungary in a sustainable and dynamic manner.

The unsuccessful market transition in 1990–2010 and the failure of economic convergence are related to failures in politics. The mistakes of political decision-makers played a role in this. During the first half of the 1990s, two governments from opposite sides of the political spectrum allowed a market economy transition, which resulted in convoluted developments and lukewarm reforms. This transition made possible the dismantling of state property in such a manner that most of the areas removed from state control came under foreign ownership. It allowed the dismantling of state monopolies in such a manner that these were mostly replaced with foreign monopolies, for example in the energy sector and in the telecommunications sector. It allowed the corporate structure from the pre-1990 planned economy, which was built on the dominance of large state-owned enterprises, to be replaced by the dominance of global multinational corporations in the Hungarian economy, instead of developing a strong structure of small and medium-sized enterprises. Right from the start of the 1990s, it also allowed the indebtedness of the old system to be replaced with new indebtedness, and consequently the losses from the market economy transition would eventually manifest themselves in new borrowing (Figure 83).

Even though economic policy targeted the reduction of government debt from the mid-1990s all the way until mid-2002 (backed by consensus among the political forces in the country) and significant progress was made in this regard between 1996 and 2002, this tacit agreement was later abandoned. In the period 2002–2010, accounting for roughly one half of the two decades of the market economy transition, this consensus was disregarded and Hungary once again embarked on a path of borrowing in the fields of government debt, external debt, foreign currency loans, by households and to a lesser extent in the corporate sector.

Between 1990 and 2010, the new democratic political system also allowed the hidden unemployment from before 1990 to turn into open unemployment.

Figure 83. Market transition: Convoluted developments
and lukewarm reforms - 1

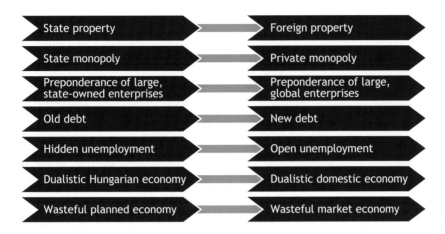

Source: Compiled by author

In this case, the phenomenon itself, i.e. that the previously hidden unemployment within enterprises turned into market unemployment, was not the problem. The problem was that the system did not mitigate the extent and depth of this unemployment. The pre-1990 system functioned with a significant level of unemployment within enterprises; even if a person had a job, there was no actual work, and thus the real unemployment was concealed. In the post-1990 system almost one and a half million jobs disappeared in the first half of the 1990s, which essentially made sustainable economic convergence impossible for two decades. In the system after 1990, not everyone previously unemployed within companies became unemployed in the statistical sense, since economic policy tacitly allowed several hundred thousand people to exit the labour market and become inactive through early and disability retirement. One of the consequences of this was that the Hungarian economy was stripped of a large labour reserve; another was that social spending related to the large number of beneficiaries placed an excessive burden on the budget.

While it was possible to build on this labour market for a few years, it was impossible to do this for two decades, as it was marked by widespread, deep imbalances.

Not only were the employment and unemployment figures negative, the depth and structural divisions also exhibited unfavourable tendencies.

Furthermore, politics allowed the operation of an economic formula which allowed economic growth to continue in a dualistic structure. In the pre-1990 system, this was embodied on the one hand by coexistence of the large state-owned enterprises and the emerging new private companies. On the other hand, the operation of the economy was modern in terms of the economic sectors, but had a dualistic structure in terms of the level of productivity and innovation within the sectors. Starting from the early 1990s, a new dualistic structure quickly developed in Hungary, with the economy characterised on the one hand by a foreign-owned sector working with high productivity and innovation capacity, and on the other hand a domestically-owned sector of micro, small and medium-sized enterprises, with far weaker performance than the foreign-owned sector.

In the period 1990–2010, Hungary's unsuccessful attempt at convergence was constantly perched on one leg: the convergence experiment was based on the developed export sector operating with a high level of capital, a highly trained labour force and strong innovation capacity. The deeply dualistic structure of the Hungarian economy fundamentally limited its growth capacity and convergence chances.

With the exception of the period 1998–2002, from 1990 until 2010 Hungary's democratic politics allowed the earlier, pre-1990 wasteful planned economy to be replaced with a wasteful market economy.

The political failures were manifested in flawed economic policy, which resulted in a poor growth structure, because growth did not reach the groups responsible for the imbalances in the labour market, and ultimately missed out on the economic convergence which started from time to time, because the social advancement behind it was not strong enough. Without work there can be no wide-scale social advancement, and without this there is no strong, broad middle class, upon which successful economic convergence can be built. Ultimately, economic convergence brings social advancement, but this stalls if it fails to initiate upward mobility for individuals, families and communities in wider and wider parts of society right from the very beginning.

The less developed an economy is, the larger the likelihood of rapid growth. In 1990, the Hungarian economy was one of Europe's moderately developed economies and economic convergence occurred within Europe. Thus, convergence with the developed European countries took off from a less developed position, which was a favourable starting point in terms of the rapid economic growth necessary for convergence. Compared to the shocks from the 20th century, the downturn in the Hungarian economy in the first half of the 1990s was not severe and was far smaller than the economic losses caused by the First World War, the Great Depression of 1929–1933 and the Second World War (Figure 84).

Figure 84. Link between economic development expressed
in per capita GDP and economic growth

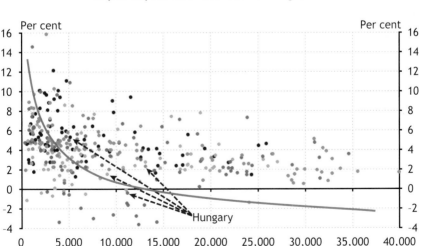

Source: Penn World Table, World Bank, WDI database

The internal economic shock which occurred in the first half of the 1990s was significant, and its strength is reflected by the mass closures of the old state-owned enterprises and the appearance of new, mass unemployment on the market, along with a historically unparalleled drop in the level of employment.

From the perspective of the failed convergence attempt in the period 1990–2010, it was not a problem that the acceleration of economic growth was regularly accompanied by a current account deficit, because this was also the case for most successful convergence attempts. The occurrence of the twin deficit, i.e. the simultaneously high deficits on the current account and state budget, caused convergence to stall by requiring consolidation measures to re-establish balance, and due to the poor economic policy this was also accompanied by growth and employment sacrifices. The imbalances on the labour market which developed in the early 1990s were exacerbated by the employment sacrifices in 1995–1996, and then in 2006–2010 as well (Figure 85).

Figure 85. Connection between GDP growth and current account balance

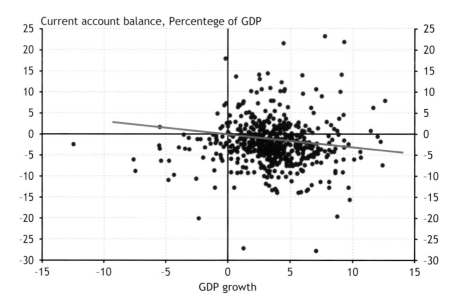

Source: IMF-IFS, WDI

The growth formula which had proven flawed over two decades was not flawed because it caused the current account deficit (this was a common phenomenon in converging countries), but rather because in addition to this it did not take into account fiscal balance, and thus caused a twin deficit, while at the same time failing to address the low level of employment.

Looking at the average for longer periods of time, we see a positive correlation between economic growth and fiscal balance (Figure 86).

Figure 86. Connection between GDP growth and budget balance

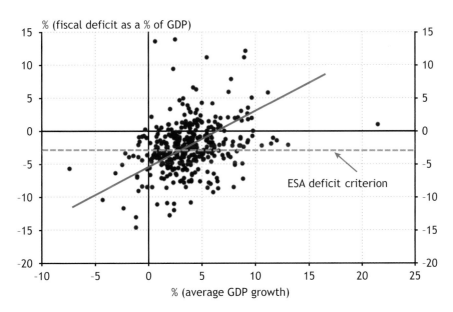

Source: IMF-WEO, WDI

In part, this may be because economic policy integrates automatic stabilisers into the budget, and in part the procyclicality of budget revenues may also be a reason. The positive correlation means that it is easier to maintain fiscal balance in conjunction with a higher growth rate, thanks to the higher revenues. Accordingly, Hungarian economic policy constantly ran into the obstacle of the "balance or growth" formula over the two decades, because the growth performance was weak. This resulted in lower budget revenues than possible and necessary and generated an almost always large budget deficit; consequently, it was not possible to take budgetary measures to stimulate growth.

When a government did attempt to stimulate the economy, as in the period 2002–2006 (Hornok et al., 2008), it had even worse consequences. The high budget deficit initially generated a growth surplus. As we saw, from a historical perspective, it was at that time that the rate of Hungarian economic growth exceeded the rate of growth in the German economy by the greatest degree. However, the accumulation of debt by all economic agents in Hungary was behind this, and after some time this generated a need to rectify economic balance. The ensuing consolidation measures entailed larger growth and employment sacrifices than the original positive stimulus. To a lesser degree, this stop-and-go cycle occurred several times over the last twenty years (Figure 87).

Figure 87. GDP-proportionate budget balance in Hungary

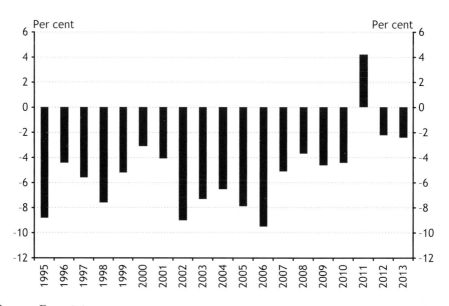

Source: Eurostat.

The high fiscal deficit accepted by economic policy resulted in a surge in government debt, while indebtedness vis-à-vis the banking sector was the factor driving the investments and consumption of both the household and corporate sector.

It is clear that the Hungarian economy was unable to utilise its resources for economic convergence during the decades between 1990 and 2010, because it was unable to deploy budgetary tools to support growth, just as it was also unable to use the current account deficit to assist convergence.[26] There are two reasons for this: it attempted to converge with a flawed growth structure and it made excessive use of both resources at times.

The weak, dualistic growth structure was created by the convoluted developments and lukewarm reforms executed during the market transition, which replaced the earlier, poorly functioning economic system with a different economic system, but one which also operated with similarly low efficiency. If an ownership structure which maintained a balance between domestic and foreign ownership had been instituted in the place of the earlier, mainly state ownership, it is certain that the level of employment in the Hungarian economy would not have fallen so low and then would have started rising quickly again.

If the state monopolies had not been replaced by private monopolies, regardless of whether these were owned by non-residents or residents, then market balance would not have been upset: the Hungarian economy would not have experienced steadily high inflationary pressure. If the path from an economic structure based on the dominance of state-owned enterprises had not led directly to the dominance of global multinational corporations, and instead the high numerical share of domestic micro, small and medium-sized enterprises had been matched by a similar weighting of their economic performance, then growth would have spread throughout the Hungarian economy.

---

[26] See, for example, Obstfeld et al. (1996), Chapter 7.

The other reason was the occasionally excessive "utilisation" of the two financial growth resources, fiscal expenditures and the current account deficit, to spur economic growth and to maintain the earlier rate of growth. If during the period 2002–2010 the left-wing, liberal governments had not used economic policy tools leading to debt accumulation in the interests of economic growth (of these, the rise in government debt and the accumulation of foreign currency debts were perhaps the most detrimental), then the debt levels would be much lower in terms of external debt and government debt, and for private debtors, and consequently the potential growth rate would be higher.

Social transition was also unsuccessful in Hungary

In the two decades between 1990 and 2010, Hungary executed a market economy transition which did not result in tangible convergence with the developed European economies. The economic policies pursued during this transitional phase were the main reason for this. These policies were founded on the false idea that politics and the government should have more "leeway", depending on whether or not the political forces were able to have the governments in power apply economic policies leading to economic convergence and social advancement.

With the exception of the short period between 1998 and 2002, the governments actually did not function in accordance with their fundamental mandate: in democratic systems, the mandate given by society is to create employment opportunities and ensure social advancement. The governments believed that their mandate was to achieve economic growth facilitating economic convergence, which would then automatically generate mass social advancement (Figure 88).

Figure 88. Social transition: Convoluted developments and lukewarm reforms - 2

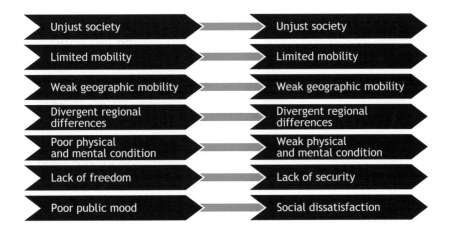

Source: Compiled by author

In Europe, successful periods of economic history are associated with a different period, the period between 1945 and 1990. During that time, there were actually several instances of successful economic convergence and social advancement in Europe: this was experienced by the Bavarians and the Swabians, the Austrians and the Scandinavians, by the Northern Italians and by the Catalans. Before 1990, however, significant changes had also occurred in the field of economic convergence, not only in the formerly socialist countries, but at the global level and within Europe as well.

In Europe, a new, neo-classical, liberal economic school of thought took over the leading role from the earlier social market economy school of thought. This change rearranged the roles of the state and the market, resulting in fundamental changes in the "balance of power". In the successful cases of economic convergence in Europe in previous decades, it was always the state that played the leading role, as it shouldered significant economic development, ownership and employment responsibilities. Economic convergence moved hand in hand with wide-scale social advancement, because the social market economy model consciously paid attention to this aspect. One of the reasons why economic convergence was successful was that it was accompanied by broad social advancement. In addition to high employment and rising consumer incomes, growth was founded on European economic integration, but the key aspect was the steady expansion of the domestic market. In the 1980s, the social market economy model was shaken, as the role of the state shrank and the role of the market grew: no longer was there a strong link between economic convergence and wide-scale social advancement.

During the Hungarian market transition in the 1990s this resulted in a major change: it was natural to view the market as having priority over the state, since the historical task at hand was to develop a market economy, but – due to the mandatory use of this new school of economic thought – the state was to play a much smaller role, as compared to the previous successful examples in Europe. After 1990, the scope of the flawed economic policy provided to the governments did not require a steady increase in employment, the reduction of the rate of unemployment, and the mass acquisition of marketable knowledge and skills.

In the decades between 1990 and 2010, with the exception of a brief period, Hungary actually accumulated democratic deficits, because the governing political elite did not use the state institutions, governance and economic policy in the interests of the electorate. In actual fact, every government was given a mandate for successful economic convergence and widespread social advancement. Whether explicitly or implicitly, these mandates would have meant balanced finances, dynamic economic growth and a labour market moving towards a balanced state, along with the low inflation characterising market balance. For the most part, however, these two decades were marked by imbalances. The imbalance on the labour market runs through the entire course of these two decades, and the market imbalance between supply and demand was also typical for almost the entire time frame, due to the high inflation. Similarly, these two decades are also consistently marked by the imbalance in public finances, and by alternating periods of brief, dynamic growth and periods of weak or falling economic performance.

Figure 89. Due to the exponential nature of growth, every percentage point counts => it is never too late to launch reforms

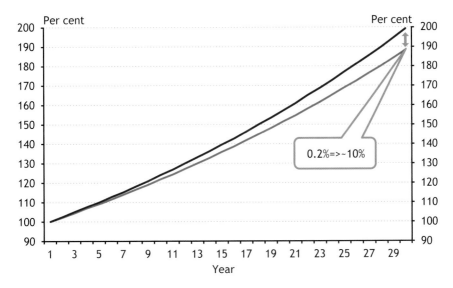

Source: MNB

As a result of the flawed politics, democratic deficits and the resulting unsuccessful economic policies during the period 1990–2010, Hungary missed out on significant economic growth. Due to the exponential nature of economic growth, every tenth of a percentage point counts for the economic growth performance, standards of living and convergence success of later periods. While it is possible that annual growth which is lower by a couple of percentage points in a given year appears to be acceptable or only seems to be a rounding error, if this becomes a persistent phenomenon it can result in significant differences in development levels in just a few decades (Figure 89).

Figure 90. PPP-based per capita GDP in Poland and Hungary

Estimated data from 2013 for Hungary and from 2011 for Poland.

Source: IMF WEO, April 2014

Comparing the actual and anticipated performance of the Polish and Hungarian economies between 1980 and 2015, looking at GDP growth rates for a span of 35 years, shows how quickly the economic policy mistakes during a relatively short period can result in changes in a country's growth or competitiveness position (Figure 90).

The performance of the Polish economy fell far short of the Hungarian economy in the 1980s, and a similar trend was seen all the way until the middle of the 1990s, as Hungary's economic performance was better than that of Poland. The turnaround occurred sometime around the mid-1990s, and starting from that point, to varying degrees, the performance of the Polish economy was better than Hungarian performance.

A massive change then happens around 2005, and from then on the Polish economy pulls ahead, while the Hungarian economy still grows modestly for a bit, but then slumps and falls short of the Poland's growth performance all the way until another change occurs in 2014.

The turning point after which Polish growth performance is better than Hungarian growth can already be seen around the middle of the 1990s. This is related to the two different kinds of economic policy pursued in these countries. Hungarian economic policy accomplished the transition to a market economy by shock therapy and the rapid transition of ownership structures, the market and the economic structure, which was accompanied by significant sacrifices. During the first half of the 1990s, Poland applied an economic policy which avoided or softened shocks, and paid attention to economic balance and growth. The transition to the market was accomplished with shock therapy in Hungary and with an economic policy of gradual adjustment in Poland in the first half of the 1990s.

This resulted in the change in the growth trend in 1995, and these two kinds of economic policies are reflected in the better Polish economic growth. A similar, but even more radical and more unfavourable change in the growth trend occurred for these two economies in 2005, when Poland's previous growth path turns sharply higher, while the Hungarian economy was unable to even maintain its modest, earlier growth and turns downward in terms of per capita GDP. Similar to the case of the first change in the Polish-Hungarian growth trend in 1995, this was not the result of a single year.

While the first change in the growth trend in 1995 reflects the previous several years and the consequences of the market economy transition from 1990, the 2005 change in the trend also reflects the economic policy differences around the time of EU accession in 2004. It precisely reflects the consequences of the worsening Hungarian economic policy after 2002, as the negative effects of the immediate deterioration in economic policy after mid-2002 became apparent over three years: fiscal balance was disturbed, government debt and external debt surged higher, the accumulation of foreign currency loans began, employment stagnated at low levels, investment momentum faltered, and the actual and potential growth rates fell.

In terms of per capita GDP, Polish and Hungarian economic growth turned in opposite directions on two occasions during the three decades: in 1995 and 2005. In both cases, it was not a single year that triggered this change in the trend, but rather the differences in the preceding three to four years. To a significant degree, these two economies and two countries shared almost identical operating conditions, and thus we must ascribe the differences in growth performance and the two breaking points in the growth trend to the differences in politics and economic policy.

Part Two

Successful crisis management in Hungary after 2010

Chapter 7

Crisis management strategy

Hungary found itself in a crisis of multiple dimensions in 2010. These included the Hungarian variant of the post-2008 global financial crisis, the first failed attempt at crisis management between 2006 and 2008, the impacts of the flawed economic policy between 2002 and 2006, and twenty years of misguided market transition from 1990 to 2010, which exacerbated the crisis. There was an obvious fiscal and financial crisis, a hidden structural crisis, a social crisis due to the lack of progress in convergence and advancement, an evident political crisis due to the failures during the two political cycles from 2002 to 2010, and an underlying political crisis due to the democratic deficits of the period 1990–2010, while at the same time, there was also a deep, underlying moral crisis. A strategy had to be developed to address this complex crisis situation.

Foundations, values and objectives of the strategy

First, it was necessary to manage the fiscal and financial crisis, and consequently the government's first actions stopped the financial and economic developments which were leading to a budget deficit of 6–7%. The complex crisis was also the result of two decades of flawed economic policy, and thus the government also announced a fundamentally new economic policy. At the heart of this was that economic policy is based not only on two pillars, namely economic balance and growth: it also incorporated an increase in the level of employment and a decline in the rate of unemployment as its third pillar.

As part of its crisis management strategy, the new government made it clear that it would use its two-thirds political mandate to launch structural reforms. This was perhaps the most important point in the crisis management strategy, because it was aimed at more than just restoring financial balance over the short term.

This policy envisions long-term financial balance through rising employment, a recovery in growth and the execution of structural reforms necessary for economic balance.

With immediate structural reforms, the government wished to achieve radical changes in key areas of the economy, as a result of which the sustainable financial position serving as the basis for higher employment and a recovery in growth would already in place by end of the 4-year political term.

The crisis management strategy used the economic finding that the flawed formula of "balance or growth" was behind the failed economic convergence between 1990 and 2010. Another new insight in the strategy was that budget revenues had to be supported by a new tax system. Behind this insight was the understanding that, in the interests of creating jobs and employment, and stimulating investment and the accumulation of human capital, it was necessary to reduce taxes on income, while at the same time replacing these taxes on income with indirect taxes, in order to ensure fiscal balance. Full-scale tax reform was an essential part of the crisis management strategy. It later turned out that this played a decisive role in the success, just as the lack of this component was a decisive factor in the failure of the earlier consolidation programmes.

Another part of the crisis management strategy announced in mid-2010 was that the earlier debt accumulation trends must be addressed, initially to put an end to further growth and then to reduce the level of accumulated debts. It was clear that borrowing by the household sector in foreign currency had to be ended immediately. Reduction of the debts accumulated between 2002 and 2010 was necessary in order to be able to safely finance the government debt. Reduction of the portfolio of households' foreign currency loans was also necessary, as the high debt servicing burdens limited households' consumption, and in the event of further declines in household consumption (which accounts for around 60% of GDP), it would have been impossible to raise employment and lower unemployment.

Another consequence of the other components of the strategy was that the level of household and public consumption must be maintained in the interests of successful tax reform, because an increase in budget revenues from indirect taxes on consumption was at the heart of this new tax system. It would not have been possible to move to a new tax system, which was absolutely necessary in order to restore fiscal balance, if at the same time household and public consumption had plunged, along with the tax revenues from these two areas.

As another element of the crisis management strategy, the government also announced the return to an earlier, successful economic period: the new economic policy returned to the principles and solutions of the Hungarian model which began to take shape between 1998 and 2002. Finally, one key element of the crisis management strategy was that it was only allowed to use economic policy tools which avoided austerity measures and thus maintained political stability.

In addition to the economic policy programme to address the crisis, there was another programme for managing the social crisis. The government made it clear that it was exercising political control on the basis of a new theory of social philosophy. The foundation was that the liberal socio-political system is replaced with a national socio-political system, the rule of law is founded on a new constitution, full employment was the goal in the economy, social fairness and competitiveness was linked together in the economic policy, the foundation for the organisation of society was respect for human dignity and the politics of bearing responsibility together.

The new social philosophy and the new economic policy are intertwined: central to both of them is the understanding that performance always stems from competition and work, and accordingly this economic policy makes work a central factor alongside competition. From this, it follows that the operation of the economy, society and the state must be centred on work. As part of the crisis management strategy, it was stated that the highest priority of economic policy is to create 1 million new, tax-paying jobs in Hungary within one decade.

Avoiding austerity measures and maintaining political stability

The crisis management strategy was based on the idea of simultaneously managing the financial-budgetary crisis and an economic and social crisis which had been simmering for decades. It follows from this that the only economic policy tools which can be used are ones which maintain political stability. Political stability was necessary in order for the government to be able to launch the crucially important structural reforms and more importantly to be able to complete these reforms.

Structural reforms involve higher costs at the beginning as compared the results they generate, but over a horizon of two to three years and in particular over a four to five-year horizon, this reverses and the results exceed the expenditures. Social and political stability is needed for structural reforms and without this stability, it is not possible in a parliamentary democracy to execute and complete the necessary changes.

An entire political cycle is needed for structural reforms. If, however, social and political stability is lost, it is not possible to apply even just one single element of the new economic policy formula: stalled structural reforms automatically hinder the expansion of employment, leading to stagnation, which prevents the creation of the economic and financial resources for sustainable economic balance. The crisis management strategy was the reason for the decision that it was not worthwhile to continue the 2008 IMF-EU agreement with a new agreement, because the logic of the IMF did not allow for successful crisis management (as later demonstrated by experiences in Europe).

The reason for that is that the IMF and the European Commission both applied a flawed crisis management strategy in the countries which received an IMF-EU safety net. Those countries followed consolidation policies founded on fiscal austerity measures, which were unable to restore economic balance, sacrificed growth and resulted in political instability.

This is clear from the structure of the austerity policies applied in the euro area. The national economic policies controlled by the European Commission and/or the IMF included pension cuts, tax increases and more privatisation. In some places, real estate taxes were levied, in others there were cuts to family allowances, spending on benefits was reduced, public sector wages were cut, housing subsidies were scaled back, and many other measures were taken, the combination of which upset the social and political stability of the euro area members in need of crisis management (Figure 91).

Figure 91. Austerity measures in the euro area

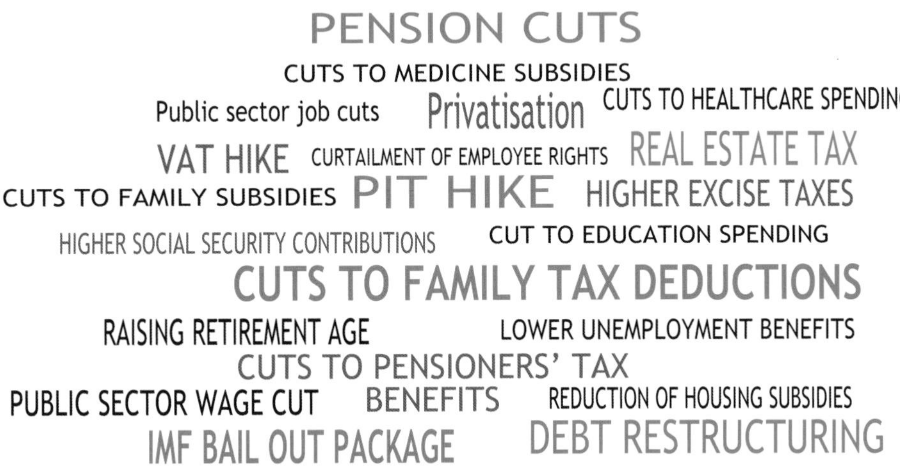

PENSION CUTS

CUTS TO MEDICINE SUBSIDIES

Public sector job cuts   Privatisation   CUTS TO HEALTHCARE SPENDING

VAT HIKE   CURTAILMENT OF EMPLOYEE RIGHTS   REAL ESTATE TAX

CUTS TO FAMILY SUBSIDIES   PIT HIKE   HIGHER EXCISE TAXES

HIGHER SOCIAL SECURITY CONTRIBUTIONS   CUT TO EDUCATION SPENDING

CUTS TO FAMILY TAX DEDUCTIONS

RAISING RETIREMENT AGE   LOWER UNEMPLOYMENT BENEFITS

CUTS TO PENSIONERS' TAX

PUBLIC SECTOR WAGE CUT   BENEFITS   REDUCTION OF HOUSING SUBSIDIES

IMF BAIL OUT PACKAGE   DEBT RESTRUCTURING

Source: NGM

All of the crisis management strategies applied in the euro area between 2011 and 2013 were based on significant austerity measures. The austerity measures enforced in Italy and Ireland amounted to 4% and 5% of GDP, respectively, and to 6% of GDP in Portugal and Spain, while the budget changes and consolidation (essentially constituting austerity measures) in Greece reached almost one sixth of the country's GDP. The policy of fiscal austerity, however, did not bear fruit in these five euro area members: budget deficits remained high, government debt continued to grow, and a high social and political price was paid for the unilateral, traditional austerity policies (Figures 92–93).

Figure 92. Austerity measures in the euro area
Between 2011 and 2013; as a percentage of GDP

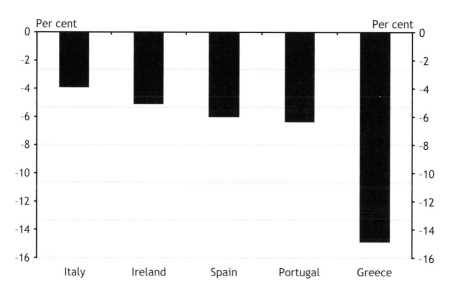

Source: European Commission, Report on Public Finances in EMU 2013, European Economy, 4/2013, (p. 115)

All crisis management strategies are based on the assumption that sustainable economic balance and growth are only possible with deep-reaching, successful structural reforms. The euro area's crisis management, however, did not recognise that time – at least one political cycle – is needed for this, and thus it is necessary to maintain social and political stability. In order to maintain stability one must avoid austerity measures, because these come at the cost of sacrifices in employment, consumption and investment. In a context of falling employment and rising unemployment, and falling consumption and investment, it is not possible to undertake structural reforms, as they will stall and reverse direction in the absence of political and social stability. This has occurred and will likely continue to occur in the coming years in several EU member states.

Figure 93. Public debt in crisis-stricken euro area member states, % of GDP

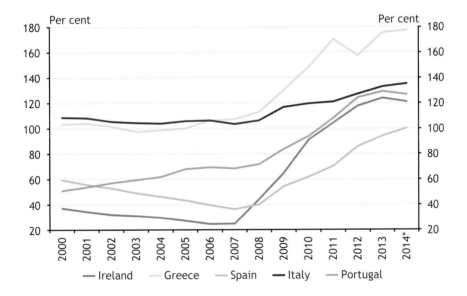

Source: Eurostat, European Commission   ** estimate*

From mid-2010, it became clear that the International Monetary Fund and the European Commission would only support Hungary's crisis management if such was based on strong austerity measures, and thus Hungary's economic policy was left on its own. Hungary's partners in Europe did not accept the logic, according to which political stability was necessary for structural reforms, along with calm social conditions, which would be upset and undermined by austerity.

Managing the crisis without internal and external drivers

Hungarian crisis management was also confronted with the fact that no upswing was expected in the global and European economy during the crisis management period; the generally positive economic performance was not likely to return and Hungary's crisis management efforts could not expect to rely on external drivers.

The assumption proved correct that the major economic downturn in 2009 would be followed by recovery in the global and developed European economies in 2010, but starting from mid-2011 another deceleration of economic activity took shape (Figure 94).

Figure 94. Economic indicators in Hungary's export markets

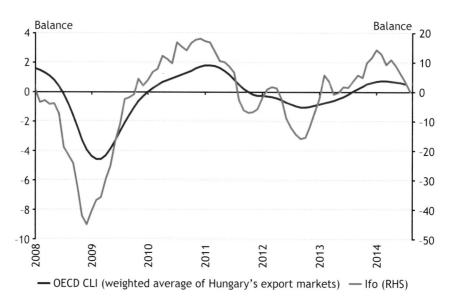

Source: OECD, Ifo

In addition to the lack of positive external factors, Hungary's crisis management could also not rely on internal drivers. Due to households' high debts, it was not possible to stimulate domestic consumption, a factor which has a substantial impact on economic and labour market trends and balance. The structure of household indebtedness was a larger burden for household consumption than the corporate debt burden was for corporate investment, because, due to the high ratio of foreign currency loans, there was not as much natural cover and foreign currency income to back the higher debt servicing requirements for households (Figure 95).

Figure 95. Indebtedness of households and non-financial corporations, % of GDP

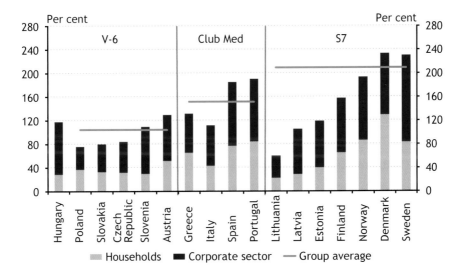

Source: Eurostat   2014 Q2; for Austria and Norway: end-2013

Neither households nor companies, neither consumption nor investment functioned as a factor to stimulate the economy. Consequently, economic policy focused on one single factor: preventing another collapse in consumption, and thus fostering a domestic environment for a future upswing in investments. The indebtedness of Hungarian households was not substantially higher than in the other economies in the region. It was the structure of household debt in Hungary which was far less favourable, due to the high ratio of foreign currency loans, the maturity structure and the nature of the indebtedness. The last aspect is related to real estate investments, mainly in the form of household debt from foreign currency borrowing: during economic downturns, real estate investments do not generate the funds for repaying loans, and even during upturns they do not automatically do so.

If households had taken on debt, even in foreign currency, to expand their entrepreneurial and knowledge capital, their significant burdens would sooner or later have been backed by entrepreneurial income and higher incomes stemming from a higher level of knowledge.

The higher level of corporate debt compared to the regional levels meant that they had revenue to service these debts, but the revenues and profits calculated when the investments were planned would not materialise during times of external and internal economic deceleration.

The crisis management strategy devised in mid-2010 also expected that consumption growth would be hampered for quite some time by the reduction of the debts accumulated between 2002 and 2010, due to the size of the household debt, its structure and the nature of its use.

Of the EU members, the Hungarian economy exhibited one of the largest degrees of household indebtedness during the period of economic upturn between 2001 and 2008, and thus it was foreseeable that it would only be possible to offset this over a similarly long, 7–8 year period of debt reduction. Indeed, due to the mistakes in Hungarian economic policy, the household loans-to-GDP ratio increased by 30% in the period 2001–2008, marking the highest and largest degree of indebtedness in the countries in the region, with the worst structure. As a result, households had already started adjusting before the 2008 global financial crisis, by lowering their consumption (Figure 96).

Hungarian households already suffered a large drop in consumption before 2008, as – in addition to the budget consolidation measures – the reduction of the large amount of accumulated debts with a poor structure already eroded consumption before the crisis. The crisis management strategy formulated in mid-2010 already took into account that the massive burden of household indebtedness from before 2008 would result in a strong reduction in consumption by households, not only during the period before the crisis, but in the years thereafter as well.

Thus, a new economic policy had to be pursued from mid-2010, one which did not burden the process of financial adjustment on households with additional adjustment needs, since a new policy of austerity would certainly have triggered a plunge in household consumption.

This was the goal of restructuring the mandatory private pension insurance fund system. This move brought forward an annual amount of around HUF 300–400 billion in household income which would have been available decades later, while at the same time the flat-rate tax reform increased disposable income by some HUF 300–400 billion.

Figure 96. Change in household loans-to-GDP ratio before the crisis and recovery in consumption following the crisis

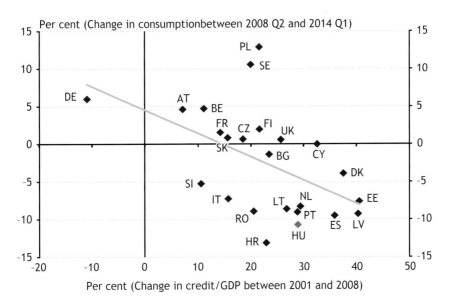

Source: Eurostat

The secret to Hungary's successful post-2010 crisis management was that it was capable of improving the fiscal situation and the financial situation of households at the same time. It disbursed income to households via the 16% flat-rate family taxation, but also found new resources on the revenue side, in the form of income from restructuring the private pension fund system. Additionally, the new indirect taxes on consumption and other components of the tax reform also generated new revenues for consolidating the budget.

Economic policy had to walk a fine line in maintaining financial balance, because the budget revenues allowed to flow to households had to be offset by budget revenues which did not have a negative impact on consumption or investment.

Transformation of the pension fund system can clearly be viewed as such a source of revenue, but the bank levy, the crisis taxes and other sector-specific taxes imposed as part of the new system of tax burden sharing also did not render investment activities by corporations and/or households impossible, even though certain sectors needed some time to adjust. The reason for this was exactly the high level of indebtedness from the past and its structure. Probably even without the bank levy, credit institutions would not have continued lending to enterprises and households, since neither of these sectors would have been able to strongly increase its investments compared to the actual data, simply because neither sector was in the midst of a new debt accumulation phase, and instead found itself in a period of deleveraging.

Opportunities to lower external debt

In mid-2010, Hungary's economic policy was in search of debt reduction tools which could simultaneously lower the country's external vulnerability without having a negative impact on domestic consumption and investment. Rapid reduction of external debt was not a viable path, as its real economic cost would have been too high:

forcing debt reduction would certainly have involved an additional decline in investment and consumption (Catão et al., 2013). Net external debt can fall in conjunction with balance sheet adjustment by all sectors, which involves real economic losses. At a given level of net external debt, certain sectors, such as the government, the corporate sector and households, are only able to reduce their external debt at the expense of each other: in a zero-sum game, this would have had a negative impact on the economic activity of one of the agents, in one of the sectors.

Economic policy did, however, have some scope to reduce gross external debt. This policy anticipated that external dependence would decline in the case of gradually rising demand for government securities by domestic sectors and a smaller stock of government securities holdings by non-residents.

Another advantage was that reduction in gross external debt would help to improve an indicator of great significance in terms of the country's risk perception, a favourable development from the perspective of the international financial markets. Lower gross debt comes hand in hand with a reduction in the country's gross financing requirement, and this lowers the country's vulnerability, while from the financial markets' point of view it helps to maintain the social and political stability necessary to follow through with structural reforms (Lane et al., 2007).

A reduction of gross external debt can also be achieved with a reduction of foreign assets, and coordinated economic and monetary policy is necessary for this. In terms of domestic agents, the central bank has the largest amount of external assets, thanks to its FX reserves. Between 2004 and 2011, external assets – mainly consisting of FX reserves – steadily increased. As a result of the EUR 19 billion available within the framework of the IMF-EU agreement, FX reserves rose, but gross external debt also increased at the same time as foreign assets. It was possible to reduce Hungary's gross external debt by repaying the state's FX liabilities and increasing domestic HUF financing as part of the 2014 self-financing programme. These measures, however, lowered the level

of the central bank's reserves, and thus net external debt did not change
(Figure 97).

In addition to FX reserves, banks' foreign assets also continuously rose
between 2004 and 2009. Immediately after the 2008 crisis, domestic
sectors started their balance sheet adjustment, and as a result between
2009 and 2014 the Hungarian banking sector's stock of foreign assets
steadily declined, which may have contributed to the reduction in gross
external debt.

Figure 97. Debt-type foreign assets of various economic sectors

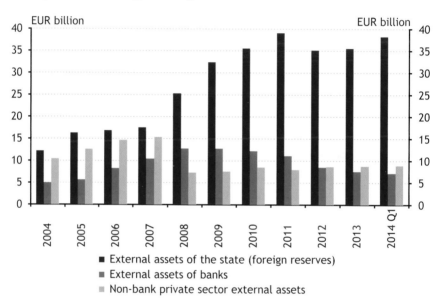

Due to a change in data collection, there is a break in the time series for non-bank
private sector foreign assets in 2008.

Source: MNB

Another method of lowering gross external debt is to channel
households' foreign assets into the domestic economy. The 2008 crisis
marks a sharp dividing line in terms of the development of the foreign
assets of the third sector, the non-bank private sector, in the years before

the crisis and years after it. Whereas the stock of foreign assets of the
non-bank private sector rose steadily and strongly in the period 2004–
2007, from 2008 the accumulation of foreign assets is much slower. The
role of households is crucial in non-bank private sector foreign assets,
as they hold foreign assets equivalent to 7% of GDP, if one also take
into account assets held indirectly. This is a significant stock of foreign
assets, consisting of assets held directly and indirectly (via investments),
(Figure 98).

Figure 98. Direct and indirect financial assets of households at end-Q2 2014

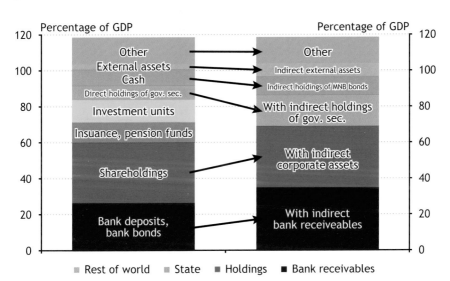

In accordance with the financial accounts, the receivables stemming from transformation of the private pension insurance fund system are contained in households' other
financial assets.

Source: MNB

The crisis management strategy launched in mid-2010 also anticipated
a reduction in net external debt, but at a pace slower than the decline
in gross external debt and over a longer horizon. The easiest way to
achieve an increase in Hungary's external financing capacity and

a reduction in net external debt is by boosting the trade surplus. In order to achieve this, inflows of foreign direct investment, the reinforcement of domestic sectors' export capacity and, naturally, favourable external demand is needed, in addition to high financing capacity. Another tool which is more difficult, but should be applied in any case is the reduction of the deficit on the income account on the current account balance.

Around the crisis, Hungary's income balance was unfavourable, with a deficit of 6–7% of GDP, meaning that significant amounts of funds were withdrawn from the Hungarian economy annually. The high deficit on the income balance indicates the initial weaknesses of the real economy and financial system. This deficit also includes the profit repatriation of the earlier foreign direct investments from two decades. It is worthwhile to divide this into two groups: foreign ownership in the field of domestic monopolies and foreign investments which created export capacities, mostly in the corporate sector. While the former is clearly a negative component of the income balance deficit, the latter is the source of economic convergence.

The government's new economic policy anticipated that it would be possible to reduce the deficit on the income balance if the high profits generated by domestic monopolies were lowered and if the share of foreign ownership in these domestic monopolies declined, as profit repatriation would fall due to both.

A reduction in Hungary's net external debt, however, is not only facilitated by a decline in gross external debt, a cut in the high profits on monopoly businesses and reduction of profit transfers. It also helps if financial market investors purchase government securities at lower yields. This option would also have been available in mid-2010, if good cooperation had developed between the government and the leadership of the MNB. In this case, the leadership of the MNB at that time would probably not have raised the central bank base rate to 7%, which further increased the deficit on the income account. The higher base rate was passed through (as the effect of monetary transmission) to yields on short-term government securities and to deposit and lending rates in the banking sector. All of this also had the impact of increasing yields on medium and long-term government bonds.

Finally, Hungary's net external debt can be reduced by increasing FDI. With this in mind, from the start the crisis management strategy counted on investments in Hungary by foreign investors.

Transformation of labour market structure

The employment component of the crisis management strategy was based on the three-way structure of the Hungarian labour market: producers of goods and services for the domestic market, internationally integrated producers, and agents in activities paying no taxes on the local market and the unemployed. At the centre of this was the understanding that it would only be possible to create one million new jobs in Hungary by 2020, if an employment strategy was pursued which offered all of the major groups on the labour market employment opportunities.

For employees at multinational companies, an increase in FDI represents an improved employment opportunity. For micro, small and medium-sized enterprises producing for the domestic market, preventing a sharp drop in consumption and a steady improvement in domestic economic activity helps to secure existing jobs and opens up new employment opportunities.

For non-tax-paying workers on the domestic market and those registered as unemployed, the allowances in the tax system and the measures to reduce tax evasion open up new possibilities. Public work programmes are a way to create new jobs for unemployed people who are outside the labour market.

This possibility is opened up by tax reform which addresses structural unemployment on the labour market. The Hungarian labour market is fragmented, both with regard to the markets (global, European and regional markets, and domestic and local markets) and to the situation of employees (Figure 99, cf. Figure 75).

For employees without secondary education, for women and for workers over the age of 50, the rates of activity and employment are significantly lower than the international, European and regional levels of unemployment.

It was necessary to implement an employment policy and tax reform which primarily addressed the distortions on the labour market, with an emphasis on providing job opportunities to workers most severely affected by unemployment.

Figure 99. Unemployment in the 15-64 age group

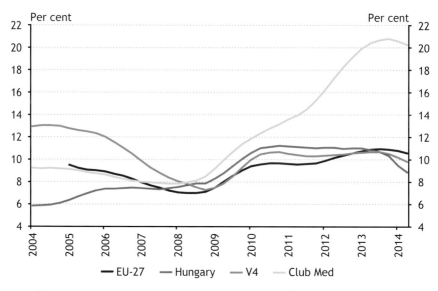

Source: Eurostat   *Four-quarter moving average*

In mid-2010, the new economic policy and need for crisis management was confronted with the situation that the employment rate in the Hungarian economy was the second lowest in the EU. Structural factors were the main reason for this low employment and high unemployment level. The new economic policy formula at the heart of the crisis management strategy was "expanding employment + recovery in growth = sustainable economic balance". Accordingly, as the first and most important part of this formula, it was necessary to increase employment, and structural reforms were needed to do so.

This was the common ground of the crisis management strategy and the new social philosophy. Both are focused on work, and thus on increasing the level of employment and reducing the rate of unemployment.

As part of the new crisis management strategy, it was necessary to resolve a theoretical contradiction between maintaining political stability, the new social philosophy and the economic policy aiming to restore macroeconomic balance. Financial balance had to be restored in such a manner that political stability was maintained, because only in this way was it possible to carry through with structural reforms. All three goals had to be met at the same time, because the general experience from the EU crisis management and Hungary's two unsuccessful attempts at consolidation in 2006–2010 was that if one of the goals was missed, the other two were jeopardised. Without achieving results on the labour market it would not be possible to uphold political stability, and without this stability it would not be possible to follow through with structural changes, and without such changes restoring economic balance would be short-lived.

In order to simultaneously achieve the three goals, it was necessary to prevent a slump in consumption, and consequently it was not possible to follow a programme of austerity. At the same time, to achieve the three goals new perspectives had to be opened up for foreign investors, for domestic micro, small and medium-sized enterprises, and workers who could not be employed in these two sectors, by way of public work programmes.

Figure 100. Employment rate by education

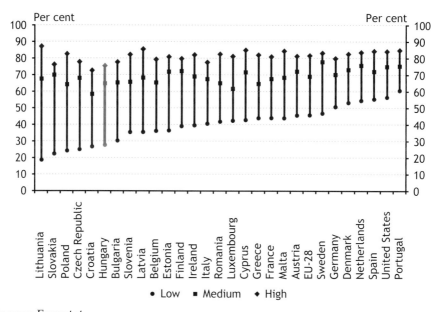

Source: Eurostat

In Hungary, a substantial portion of labour market reserves can be found in groups of workers with low education and in groups outside the labour market. Similar to the labour markets in Lithuania, Slovakia, Poland, the Czech Republic and Croatia, unemployment is highest among those with low education on the Hungarian labour market, and the rate of employment is the lowest in this group. This also represents labour reserve, and thus the crisis management strategy only had to find tools which boost employment among low-skilled workers and groups of potential employable workers, by way of public work programmes (Figure 100).

The strategy anticipated that rising employment among those with low education would result in a productivity loss: there is a link between the additional employment of lower educated workers producing low added value and the change in the level of productivity. The less lower educated labour an economy uses to produce goods of lower added value, the higher the level of labour productivity and vice-versa (Figure 101).

However, in line with the new formula at the heart of Hungary's crisis management strategy, and specifically with goal of expanding employment, it was worthwhile to bear these productivity losses in the interests of higher employment. This was even the case if the route to achieving this higher level of employment was public work programmes. In harmony with the new economic policy, this also follows from the new social philosophy, which centres on work instead of unemployment benefits.

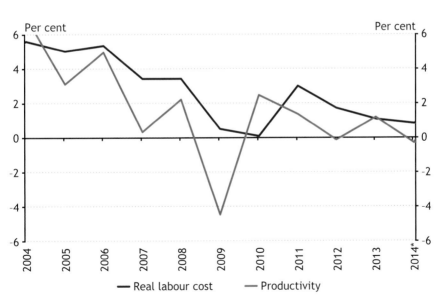

Figure 101. Development of productivity and real wage costs in the private sector

Source: MNB calculations based on CSO data   * estimate

Crisis management without a reform of monetary policy

In mid-2010, Hungary was faced with a peculiar economic policy dilemma. After 2008, all of the global economies forced to respond to the crisis, ranging from the Anglo-Saxon countries, to the euro area and Japan, radically altered their monetary policy in each and every case.

In most of the economies affected by the crisis, the central banks operate independently of governments, but the economic policies pursued by the governments and the monetary policies applied by the central banks are coordinated in the interests of crisis management (Figure 102).

In mid-2010, it was clear that Hungary was in a quite unique situation in terms of its crisis management: the central bank did not support the economic policy announced by the government, would not participate in crisis management and would not depart from its earlier orthodox, conventional monetary policy. Accordingly, the country had to succeed in consolidating the budget without a change in monetary policy.

Figure 102. Central bank rates in developed economies

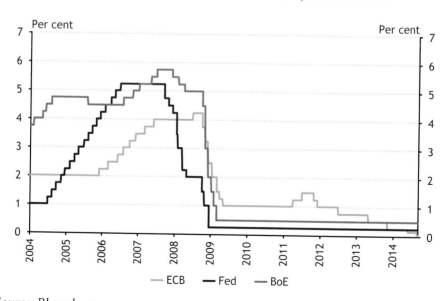

Source: Bloomberg

After 2008, many of the developed market economies engaged in crisis management benefited from the change in monetary policy by their respective central banks: the central banks in the Anglo-Saxon countries, the European Central Bank and Japanese central bank all used new, unconventional tools to support crisis management. Although it was not yet apparent in mid-2010 that, instead of providing support, the Hungarian central bank would make decisions running counter to the government's efforts (e.g. increasing the base rate), one thing was clear in terms of crisis management: in Hungary's response it would not be possible to coordinate economic and monetary policy, and thus fiscal consolidation could not count on support from a change in the monetary stance.

In mid-2010, when the new strategy was formulated, it was also obvious that this lack of coordination would later be reflected in a deterioration in the financial conditions for the real economy in Hungary. If the Hungarian central bank did not change its monetary policy during the period of fiscal consolidation, then it would certainly not lower the base rate to historically low levels, contrary to many smaller and larger central banks in the global economy, and consequently it would not be possible for the lower level of interest rates needed for a recovery in consumption and investments to evolve.

Indeed, the companies in the real economy in Hungary, and in particular the micro, small and medium-sized enterprises, had to carry out their adjustment with higher borrowing costs compared to their competitors in the region and the EU.

By mid-2010, a significant difference had developed between the levels of interests rates for economic agents in the euro area and in Hungary in relation to loans over one million euros, primarily as a result of the high base rates, the high debt levels, the high government debt, the high risk premiums and the central bank's exchange rate policy (Figure 103).

Figure 103. Interest rates on new corporate loans
in Hungary and the euro area

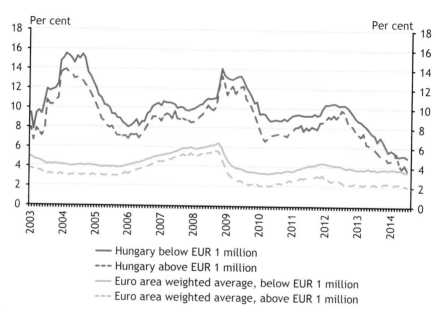

Hungary below EUR 1 million
--- Hungary above EUR 1 million
Euro area weighted average, below EUR 1 million
--- Euro area weighted average, above EUR 1 million

Source: MNB, ECB

While companies in the real economy in the euro area could access credit at interest rates below 4% on average, the Hungarian corporate sector paid average rates of 6–8% for loans over one million euros during the period of financial consolidation. Furthermore, all the way until the decisive change in the central bank's monetary policy, i.e. until the start of the rate-cutting cycle in August 2012, the level of interest rates steadily increased, and by mid-2012 Hungarian economic agents were facing rates on loans of almost 10%.

The gap between euro area and Hungarian conditions on loans less than one million euros was even larger: in mid-2010, Hungarian companies faced rates of almost 10%, whereas rates for borrowers on the euro area market were around 4%. This mainly had a negative impact on SMEs, which is precisely the group of companies with which economic policy wished to achieve the expansion in market-based employment:

during the period of crisis management, new jobs were created much slower than possible due to the extremely unfavourable convergence conditions, and specifically owing to the credit conditions.

An even more unfavourable situation developed for enterprises in relation to the EUR/HUF exchange rate. By mid-2010, when crisis management started, the average EUR/HUF exchange rate had risen to a level of nearly EUR/HUF 280, from EUR/HUF 260 in 2000 and EUR/HUF 250 at the time of EU accession. At first glance, this indicates that Hungarian companies suddenly received support via the exchange rate for an export-oriented investment and business policy. However, if we look at the development of the real effective exchange rate (REER) behind the nominal EUR exchange rate (the REER also takes into account the differences in inflation, unit labour costs and productivity between the euro area and Hungary), it is clear that the actual REER in 2008 for economic agents in Hungary was at a level of about 80% of the REER in 2000.

This was a substantial constraint for the vast majority of companies in terms of pursuing an export-oriented business policy which would improve the trade balance and facilitate GDP growth and rising employment, and thus another possible route for the crisis management strategy was blocked (Figure 104).

Thus, the REER developments did not adequately support the micro, small and medium-sized enterprises which, when entering the external markets focused on export-oriented business and the supporting investments. Furthermore, the relatively stable HUF exchange rate maintained by the high central bank policy rate created a false sense of security and thus contributed to the wide spread of foreign currency lending and the rising vulnerability of the economy. Taking into account the weakening in Hungary's export markets and the amount of accumulated foreign currency debt, the depreciation of the exchange after 2008 was only able to play the stimulating role it would be expected to have in a small, open economy to a limited degree.

Figure 104. Real effective exchange rate
and the average EUR/HUF exchange rate

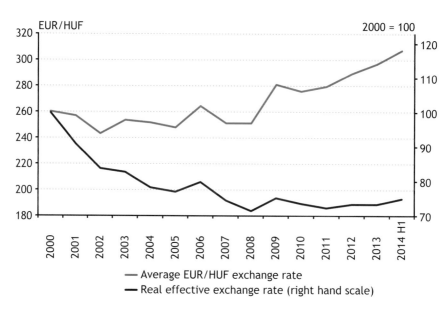

Source: MNB   REER (PPI basis)

In mid-2010, successful budget consolidation and crisis management were almost faced with a Gordian knot in terms of the external and internal conditions. There was no additional demand from the external markets, and it was not possible to conclude an IMF-EU agreement, due to the related risk of austerity measures. Moreover, there was not one single factor left which could trigger positive dynamics, help increase employment and support economic growth, due to the accumulated internal debts, the indebtedness of corporations and households, the particularly unfavourable REER and borrowing conditions which were significantly worse than for competitors in the euro area.

Chapter 8

New economic policy

In 2010, Hungarian economic policy returned to a pragmatic approach. At the centre of this is the understanding that work, capital and knowledge (technology) create new value. In contrast to this, redistribution, i.e. when income is redistributed via the state budget from one social group (where value was created) to another social group (where value was not created), does not create new value, although the distribution of such may approach the social optimum, which may contribute to the better utilisation of economic potential, and thus the creation of new value. This is true for the group of unemployed on the labour market, but is not true for those raising children, because child-raising creates new value: children are a family investment in the future. Similarly, in the case of pensioners, who belong to the social group of the inactive, pensions paid through the public budget do not represent redistribution, because this was already created as new value earlier by the pensioners.

A return to pragmatic economics

Returning to a pragmatic approach in economics meant that it was once again necessary to focus economic tools on job creation, instead of on social redistribution, and within this in particular on benefits related to unemployment. If we look at the sources of growth, the pragmatism of the new economic policy becomes apparent.

GDP growth derives from the expansion of employment, the strengthening of competitiveness and the proportionality of income redistribution within the society. The creation of new value is behind the expansion of employment. The strengthening of competitiveness is backed by the new value created by work, with this value involving greater capital and more advanced technology and knowledge than previously.

Proportional redistribution of income within the society contributes to economic growth: the broader the distribution in society of the incomes derived from the goods produced, the stronger the society's capacity to consume and invest (Figure 105).

Figure 105. Sources of growth

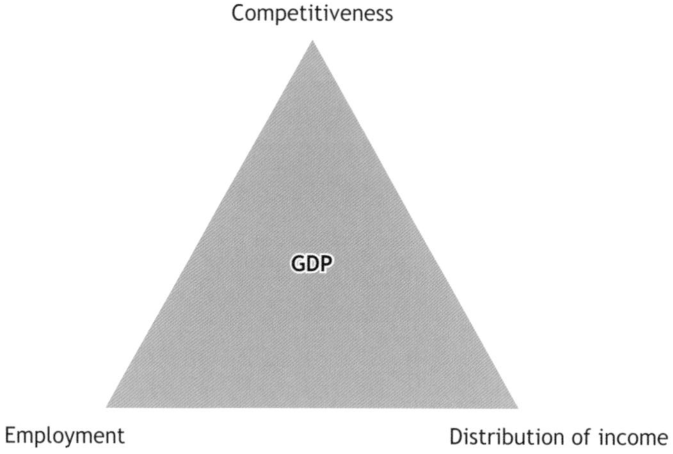

Competitiveness

GDP

Employment   Distribution of income

Source: Institute for Economic Growth

One common feature of the Anglo-Saxon, the European and the Asian convergence models is that three main resources play a role in economic growth: the expansion of knowledge, the application of new technologies and the reinforcement of social capital. The expansion of knowledge requires the re-evaluation and transformation of the role of education and training, and within this ensuring life-long learning, (re-) training and quality higher education are the most important aspects. The application of new technologies is the most visible source of growth in an economy, and consequently the spread of new technologies and innovation must be accelerated and broadened within the framework of families and communities, and in the operation of the state.

Social capital – cooperation between individuals and communities, self-confidence, public confidence, optimism, morals and a good public atmosphere – are the most important invisible source of economic convergence and social advancement.

As a result of the long-term, destructive consequences of socialism from earlier decades, the supply of social capital is nowadays much worse than the supply of money, credit, and ownership, i.e. the supply of material forms of capital goods.

If only a narrow group of society enjoys the new income stemming from new value, consumption and investment will expand precisely in this group, but the degree of such expansion will lag far behind the consumption and investments backed by the income of broad groups in society. If only a narrow group in society accumulates new incomes – as is occurring in the current US economic and social model – then consumption shifts towards luxury consumption, and investments move in the direction of wealth-generating investments. Both of these increase a given economy's potential growth rate to a far lesser degree, and indeed they result in a slower expansion of employment due to more subdued consumption and investment growth.

The return to a pragmatic economic approach was also reflected by the fact that the new government's new economic policy immediately took measures to boost employment and reduce unemployment: it started expanding the sources of GDP growth right away. Similarly, an immediate decision was made to lower the disproportionalities in the distribution of income: this meant cutting back social redistribution via government transfers. These two decisions reinforced the sources of potential growth, but the expansion of employment first took place, using the tool of public work schemes, in the group of low-skilled workers, which initially resulted in productivity sacrifices. According to this pragmatic economic thinking, however, it was worthwhile to bear this short-term sacrifice in the interests of a long-term gain, because the combination of rising employment and more proportional distribution of income results in higher levels of consumption and then investment: after the short-term sacrifices, the conditions for a rise in productivity are established within 3 to 4 years.

If we delve deeper into the sources of economic growth, we find that the growth and income-generating capacity of an economy is fundamentally influenced by the available real assets (natural resources, infrastructure, machinery), the amount and quality of accessible human capital, the technologies applied and the quality of the management principles, as well as the social capital and characteristics of its institutional system. Naturally, national assets include both physical components (natural conditions, capital goods, infrastructure components, real estate and other physically tangible assets) and human resources (the active population employable on the labour market). The production capacity and productivity of real and human capital is fundamentally influenced by the level of the applied technologies and education (information in the field of knowledge capital), (Figure 106).

Figure 106. Sources of economic growth

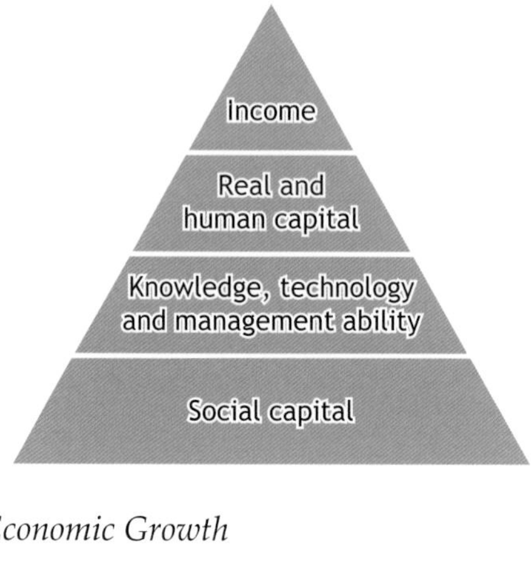

Source: Institute for Economic Growth

Based on all of the above, it is possible to define the fundamental logic of the nature of the current Hungarian economy: the trap of social capital.

Economic success in the 21st century is no longer mainly founded on economic factors; it rests on the social factors of morals, public confidence, self-confidence, cooperation, optimism, families' transmission of values and reliability. Without economic success, these social factors decline, and spiritual-physical illness take a terrible toll in economic losses. It is not possible to achieve rapid growth with declining social capital: the circle is closed. The root of the current problems in the Hungarian economy is that the economy is missing roughly one million tax-paying jobs. This only allows for a rate of GDP growth which is lower than the feasible level, and consequently the budget is missing out on a large part of the possible and needed revenues: either growth or economic balance suffers[27] (Figure 107).

Figure 107. Social capital trap

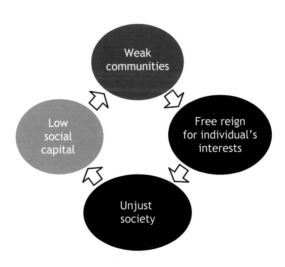

Source: Cséfalvay et al. (ed.), 2009

While the flawed economic policy in 2002–2010 expanded the real estate portion of national assets, by way of new home construction,

[27] This topic is discussed in detail in Cséfalvay et al. (ed.) (2009), Kopátsy (2011) and Kopp et al. (2011).

renovation and real estate investment for business purposes, it did so in an unsustainable financing structure and furthermore in such a way that did not result in long-term growth in productivity. Over the long run, the simultaneous expansion of the quantity and quality of human capital would have resulted in a more favourable increase in national assets, rather than debt-financed investments in real estate and infrastructure. This did not occur, however.

There is also another hidden economic relationship behind the gradual and continuous deterioration in Hungarian macroeconomic data between 2002 and 2010.

In addition to the available real and human capital, social capital also has a profound impact on economic growth. Such capital can include factors such as the trust between social groups, the strength of family bonds, the strength of communities, positive, forward-looking thought, willingness to take risks, the prioritisation of community interests over the interests of the individual, etc.[28] It was in this field that the greatest degree of deterioration (instead of improvement) took place in the period 2002–2010. This already surfaced in the political instability in autumn 2006, and was reflected in society's lack of confidence in the governing political powers. It could be seen in the behaviour of groups of workers which left the country and took advantages of EU accession in 2004, as well as in the weaker-than-potential growth in consumption and investment.

The real reason that Hungary slipped off its convergence path that started at the end of the 1990s and suffered a significant deterioration in its macroeconomic indicators compared to the region and the developed EU economies was that the growth trend in social capital initially stalled and then turned sharply downwards between 2002 and 2010.

---

[28] On the role of confidence, see e.g. Akerlof et al. (2009): Animal Spirits: How Human Psychology Drives the Economy, and Why It Matters for Global Capitalism. Princeton University Press.

The investment trend broke in the first half of 2005, followed by a break in the consumption trend due to the first austerity package in September 2006, the political instability in autumn 2006 resulted in a clear breaking point in the accumulation of social capital, and in autumn 2008 Hungary was the first EU member to request an IMF-EU safety net. On the one hand, these are sources of the negative developments in social capital, and on the other hand they are the indicators of such developments, but the reasons were also the decline in social capital in the period 2002–2010.

Similarly, during the two decades of transition between 1990 and 2010, the weaker-than-possible accumulation of social capital was a constant factor, because this entire period – except for the short time between 1998 and 2002 – was consistently marked by mistaken economic policy and flawed social policy. Over the two decades, every indicator of public and business confidence exhibited a significant negative deviation compared to similar regional and EU indicators, reflecting the lack of social capital.

The accumulation of economic and social values goes even deeper, if, in addition to looking at human capital as sources of economic growth, we also analyse the accumulation of talent capital at a society's disposal and the moral standards governing economic and social relations.

Value created by work is necessary for the expansion of national income and national assets, and in addition to the accumulation of physical capital, knowledge capital must also be built up. Furthermore, there are two other sources of economic growth which are also intangible: talent and morality. One of the hidden economic relationships in every economy is that one unit of talent is now able to create several times more value in comparison to any previous social form or economic structure. When the economy and society was based on the land and physical strength, then the simple difference in physical strength was the decisive factor between two economic agents: along with the land itself and the slow, but steady progress in technology, physical strength was the key point in the accumulation of economic value.

From the second half of the 20th century, however, an economic structure developed, in which the difference between two workers was not their physical strength, but rather the level of knowledge and skills, in particular their motivation, individual skills and talents which are utilised throughout their entire lives (Kopátsy, 2011).

Looking at talent, it is no longer the case in today's global market economy that there might be differences of three or four times between two modern workers, because differences of a thousand times or even a million times can develop between an innovator who makes a technological breakthrough and a worker performing semi-skilled labour (Kopátsy, 2011).

Yet another relationship is even more important: the evolution of moral values which function like a compass. If the members of society and economic agents do not deem the operation of politics and the economic elite to be ethical, it leads to an invisible decay of the fabric of social capital, generating mistrust and the tacit withdrawal of cooperation in both the economy and society (Figure 108).

Figure 108. Moral-Knowledge-Talent

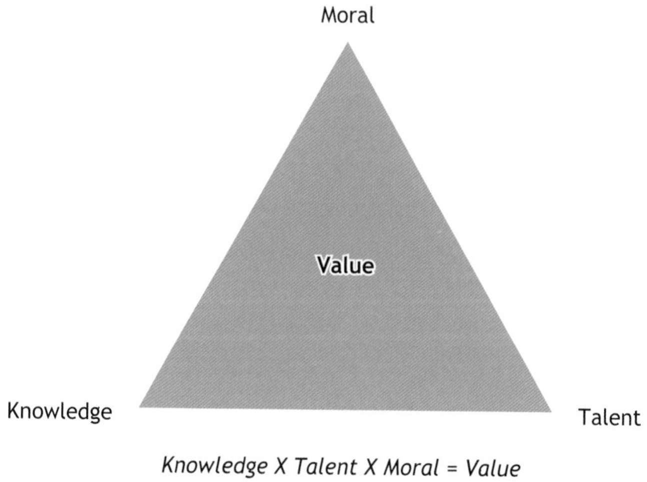

Knowledge X Talent X Moral = Value

Source: Kopátsy (2011), Institute for Economic Growth

In the period 1990–2010, members of society and economic agents consistently took a suspicious view of the moral compass: figures in politics and the business elite did not enjoy the recognition and support of society which is unquestioned in the Anglo-Saxon and Scandinavian system of values. Surveys on values conducted regularly in the period 1990–2010 and the indicators of economic activity also show that a system of moral values detrimental to social capital was manifest in two decades of worse economic performance compared to the country's peers and in the fact that several hundred thousand were employed abroad after 2004. The post-2010 consolidation and stabilisation was able to succeed, because an underlying change in morals also occurred in Hungary: it was no longer natural to expect benefits instead of work, it was no longer natural for the banking sector and domestic monopolies to reap extra profits, it was no longer sustainable to carry on with unfair foreign currency lending, and it was no longer natural for the central bank not to support the government's economic policy.

New economic policy and a new system of values

In many cases, deep behind the economic success of nations, countries, communities and companies we see that erstwhile disadvantages were later transformed into advantages. Between 1950 and 1973, due to its lack of raw materials and energy supplies, Japan relied on its earlier level of industrial development in its successful bid for economic convergence. In respect of the drivers of convergence, Japan's only available resource was labour, and its convergence was built on this. It took this difficult starting position and transformed it into an advantage by the beginning of the 1970s.

Similar developments were later seen in the Four Asian Tigers (Singapore, Hong Kong, Taiwan and South Korea): despite the complete lack of raw materials and energy reserves, natural resources and inherited capital, these economies were actually able to succeed in convergence precisely because of these shortfalls. Their success was due exclusively to the labour force, the increase in knowledge capital, good utilisation of the talents available to society, the dominance of a clear, accepted system of moral values and proportionate distribution of income.

The accumulation of social capital paved the way for the expansion of national wealth and national income.

Similar relationships are seen in the examples of successful European convergence, such as the achievements of the Bavarians, Swabians, Tyroleans, Scandinavians and Catalans, as well as the successes in the last two decades by the Baltic States, the Poles and the Slovaks. In each case, the countries in question started from a disadvantaged position, because they did not have natural resources and inherited capital amongst their sources of economic growth. They harnessed the accumulation of knowledge capital, the application of technology, the expansion of social capital, good utilisation of talent and a clear system of moral values for their success.

In the case of Hungary, for the period 2010–2030 it will be possible to build upon this new approach, which seeks out weaknesses in order to forge them into strengths. The moderately developed Hungarian infrastructure can be raised to a developed level using EU and foreign investment, and this involves strong investment dynamics, which is a good source of growth. Hungarian SMEs suffer from a lack of capital, and thus it makes sense to focus a substantial portion of EU funds on this group, as a result of which strong corporate dynamics will back up economic growth. The income level of Hungarian society is low and the domestic market is small, but following the re-establishment of balance and renewed economic growth consumption dynamics can be expected to be continuously stronger than in the past with a better structure: this can function as a sustained source of economic growth (Figure 109).

In 2010, economic policy returned to the philosophy in place between 1998 and 2002, when as part of the first Széchenyi Plan the compass-like effect of using sources of investment was effective: the country's potential advantages must be turned into real advantages.

Figure 109. Disadvantages and advantages

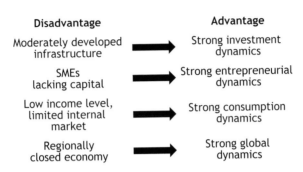

Source: Institute for Economic Growth

This philosophy and economic approach was hardly applied in the period 1990–2010, and was especially disregarded by the flawed economic policy between 2002 and 2010. That misguided policy used new borrowing almost exclusively as a source for growth, and failed to exploit the potential advantages of the geographical location, the country's thermal water reserves, the Hungarian minorities in the Carpathian Basin and Hungarians' innovative way of thinking. Had it used these, then the governments during that period would have applied the majority of the EU funds in the period 2004–2010 to economic development, because it is within the economy that the country's geographical location, thermal waters, the enterprises and R&D binding the Carpathian Basin into a single economic area, and the sources of innovation can be put to good use. Another one of the underlying, hidden reasons why Hungary's economic performance lagged far behind that of its peers in 2002–2010 and 1990–2010 is that Hungary did not built on its strengths, it did not attempt to transform its potential advantages into real ones, and also did not harness its weaknesses and turn them into strengths (Figure 110).

Figure 110. Potential and real advantages

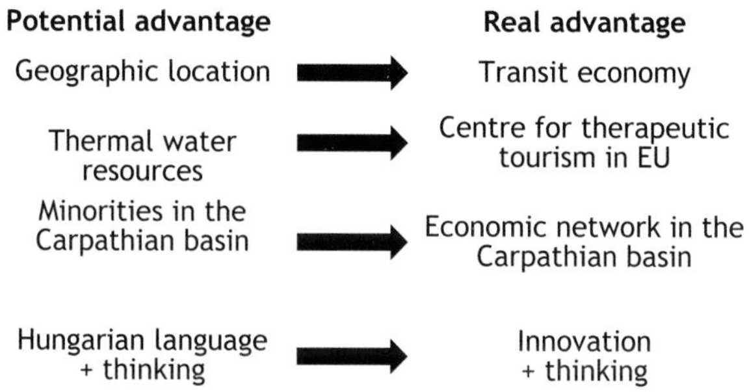

Potential advantage		Real advantage
Geographic location	➡	Transit economy
Thermal water resources	➡	Centre for therapeutic tourism in EU
Minorities in the Carpathian basin	➡	Economic network in the Carpathian basin
Hungarian language + thinking	➡	Innovation + thinking

Source: Institute for Economic Growth

In 2010, Hungary's economic policy returned to a pragmatic economic approach and re-applied the successful recipe for convergence used between 1998 and 2002, but the most meaningful change was that it established a new economic policy formula. Aside from the brief period between 1998 and 2002 when 240,000 new jobs were created, economic policy steadily followed a simplified and ultimately doomed formula between 1990 and 2010. The crux of this formula was economic balance, and within this fiscal balance, and the result would be growth and economic convergence.

Based on the neo-liberal economic philosophy, even before 1990 a Hungarian economic formula was established, according to which it was first necessary to achieve economic balance, and then after this the Hungarian economy, moving on a balanced path, would automatically embark on a growth path, and balance and growth would open up the opportunity for economic convergence and social advancement.

This logic, however, would only be able to function, if at least the Western European, but preferably the Anglo-Saxon and East Asian levels of employment had been typical in the Hungarian economy during those two decades. The formula "economic balance = growth" works with a high level of employment, but does not work in the case of low employment, because the upturn in growth undermines fiscal balance due to the low employment. Consequently, programmes to cut back budget spending are launched, which hamper growth, leading to the situation of "neither balance nor growth" (Figure 111).

Figure 111. Old (1990-2010) and new (2010-) formulas for Hungarian economic policy

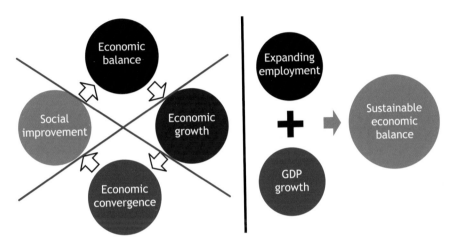

Source: Institute for Economic Growth

Why does low employment lead to this situation? In part, the reason for this is the distribution of income: if in a society significant groups within the groups of potential labour do not participate in the creation of new value, i.e. if their incomes stem from redistribution via the budget, it will lead to a distribution of income which is disproportional. Due to the unequal distribution of income, the consumption of social groups which obtain significant new income from economic growth increases and this consumption is primarily centred in imported goods: this upsets the trade balance.

If substantial numbers of people from the group of potential labour do not participate in this newly created income, the consumption base narrows and large social groups do not feature as consumers of domestic goods and services on the domestic market. In the two decades from 1990 to 2010, the rate of employment in the Hungarian economy was below or around 60%, while the average rate was 65% in the EU countries, 75% in the Anglo-Saxon economies, and 85% in the rapidly converging East Asian economies, including China (Figure 112).

Figure 112. Employee income as a percentage of gross value added

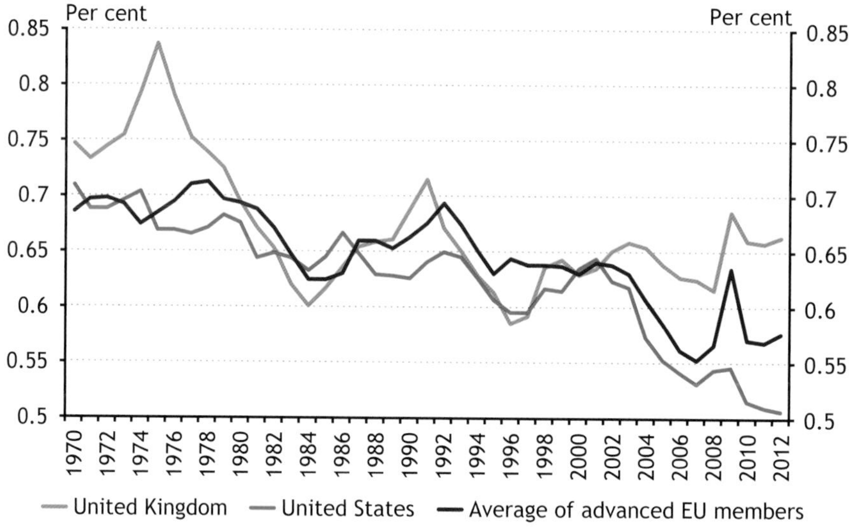

Source: OECD

Due to the low level of Hungarian employment, the supply of domestically produced goods and services did not meet with broad-based demand based on labour income. In certain small groups of society, economic growth generated surplus demand for import goods, and within this for luxury goods, but this had an unfavourable effect on the trade balance. The new economic policy immediately moved to integrate groups which had been pushed out of the labour market, initially by way of public work programmes and later with training programmes to support market-based employment.

The flawed economic policy formula applied between 1990 and 2010 failed to understand that sustainable economic balance was possible if the level of employment in the economy reached at least the 65% average level of the EU members. Naturally, starting with an undeveloped economic structure, sustainable balance also requires that an economic policy focused on work and the accumulation of knowledge capital be applied, rather than one centred on the welfare state style of budget redistribution. Due to the flawed economic philosophy, the cyclicality of "growth or balance" prevailed throughout the period 1990–2010, as the structure of growth repeatedly undermined fiscal balance, and the programmes to restore balance hampered economic growth.

Figure 113. General government net borrowing, % of GDP

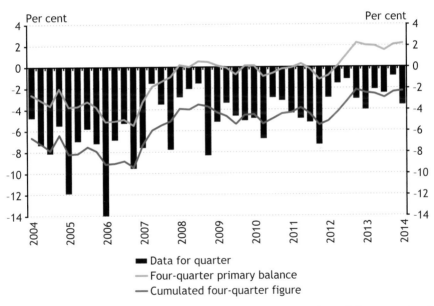

Source: MNB   *Quarterly and four-quarter data*

The fundamental economic relationship of the two decades of transition was that below a certain low level of employment, i.e. at levels at least lower than the 65% rate of employment in the EU, growth does not automatically result in economic balance, and that economic balance also does not automatically generate growth.

Economic policy may not be built on these two factors alone: employment must be included as the third factor. In 2010, Hungary's new economic policy was founded on three factors: establishing balance, expanding employment and exploiting sources of growth.

This policy recognised that one-off attempts to improve economic balance were not what was needed. Sustainable economic balance was needed: a budget deficit lower than the targeted 3% of GDP was needed over the long run, in order for government debt to decline (Figure 113).

In addition to immediate measures to improve balance, at the same time the new economic policy launched programmes to boost employment. During the period of budget consolidation and economic stabilisation from 2010 to 2014, employment increased continuously, helping to establish balance and supporting a return to growth. Naturally, over the long term a rate of employment no less than the 65% rate in the EU will contribute to sustained economic growth and sustainable balance.

Chapter 9

Reforms and innovations

From mid-2010, Hungary changed its direction in terms of structural reforms and economic policy innovation. During the two decades of transition from 1990 to 2010, it appeared that Hungarian governments always introduced structural reforms and economic policy innovations. The fact of the matter is, however, that they applied neo-liberal economic principles and conventional economic policy measures during the transition from the centrally planned economy to a market economy. These reforms actually created a mirror image of the earlier, non-market economy structures. Market-based private monopolies replaced state monopolies, the place of hidden unemployment in companies was taken by market unemployment, and the system of dominant large domestic enterprises was replaced with a corporate sector based on global and European multinational corporate groups. This, however, was unsuitable for economic convergence and wide-scale social advancement, just as the planned economic policy applied under the previous centralised, one-party political system had been.

These were distorted structural reforms, undertaken in the spirit of a conventional, traditional, neo-liberal economic policy approach. A proper structural reform policy would have been pursued if the new market economy had built up a high level of employment in the private sector and ensured a low rate of unemployment, and if a strong system of micro, small and medium-sized enterprises had been fostered in addition to strong domestic competition and strong large enterprises, instead of monopolies.

The new economic structure which developed during the distorted market economy transition in 1990–2010 was actually the result of an unsuccessful structural reform policy, which was in fact not founded on economic and monetary policy innovation, but rather merely applied the predominantly neo-liberal tools of the 1980s and 1990s.

Within this economic philosophy, it was natural that government regulation needed to be reduced and that the operation of the government had to be based on the flawed concept of market self-regulation. In this framework, it was also natural that the government be controlled by strong market and business groups, including first and foremost the banks and the foreign-owned energy supply companies which took the role of domestic monopolies. It was natural that economic policy did not notice that sustainable balance and sustainable economic growth could not be achieved without a high level of employment and a low rate of unemployment.

In mid-2010, a profound change occurred in this flawed Hungarian economic philosophy and the misguided economic policies built on it. This turning point hinged on a new economic philosophy and a new economic policy, and this was an indispensable precondition for launching structural reforms and innovations. The new government's economic policy centred on structural reforms and innovative approaches which had been lacking in the previous two decades and which were absolutely necessary to achieve a turning point in economic balance and growth (Figure 114).

The structural reforms which were needed had to result in immediate, sustainable fiscal consolidation. As it was no longer founded on a strategy of just two factors, but rather three factors, the new policy had to apply a supplementary programme supporting employment growth in the corporate sector and tax measures to strengthen employment and entrepreneurial spirit, in parallel with the public work programme. Domestic inflationary pressure had to be reduced, the risks and burden of foreign currency loans had to be mitigated, and it had to be ensured that government debt was financed via the financial markets, rather than by way of a new IMF-EU agreement.

Figure 114. Reforms and innovations

New tax concept · 50% debt brake · **Reduction in government debt** · 10% corporate tax · New Széchenyi Plan · Planning · Széll Kálmán Plan I-II · 16% personal income tax · 27% VAT · Improved engineering training · Growth Plan · Exchange rate cap · Bank levy · New formula for economic policy · Public work · New Labour Code · Strategic agreements · Job Protection Action Plan · Innovation tax scrapped · Reduction of utility costs · Premium government bonds · Crisis taxes · FX debt redemption with HUF · MNB-HFSA merger · Opening to Eastern markets · New Land Act · Funding for Growth Scheme · Ministry for National Economy · Carpathian Basin economic zone - Wekerle Plan · Curtailment of unemployment benefits · Free economic zones · New National Economy Plan · MNB rate-cutting cycle · R&D spending over 1% · Early repayment scheme · Break-even MNB result · Freeze on budget residuals · Family tax benefits · Crisis management without IMF · Reduction of bureaucracy · Stabilisation Act · "Szép" Card · EU 14-20 planning - 60% for economic development · Repayment of IMF loan · Dual-track vocational training · Flat-rate taxation · New support for sports · Public education reform · Abolition of small taxes · Private pension fund reform

Source: MNB

In order to press forward with successful structural reforms, it was first necessary to resolve the fundamentally dual nature of reforms: without structural reforms, it is not possible to achieve sustainable economic balance and lasting growth over the medium to long term, but during the initial phase structural reforms increase budget expenditures (e.g. insofar as they appear in new investments and increases in R&D and education spending) and lower revenues (e.g. insofar as they involve lower taxes on income). Structural reforms are necessary, because the economy is faced with the challenge of balance and/or growth, but reforms initially render the situation more difficult and only help with the solution later.

The key to the solution is the revenue side of the budget: new revenues were needed for the budget, to offset the paradoxical effect. This had to be done in a way that consumption and investment did not continue to nosedive, as this would have jeopardised budget consolidation.

New markets were also needed, because the domestic market opportunities were not adequate for sustainable fiscal balance and restarting economic growth, while at the same time the EU member states were also exhibiting sluggish dynamics: these new markets mostly needed to be found outside the European market. Finally, the programme of structural reforms had to be launched in such a way that social and political stability was by no means threatened, because in this case there is a real possibility that the reforms launched will slow or even stall, even with a two-thirds majority in Parliament (Figure 115).

Figure 115. Conventional crisis management

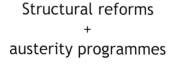

Structural reforms
+
austerity programmes

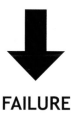

FAILURE

Austerity programmes cause political instability, governments weaken and/or fail, and consequently structural reforms decelerate and/or end.

Source: Compiled by author

Hungary's new economic policy achieved all of this: it was able to launch structural reforms in certain parts of the economy and society in such a manner that these did not run into any social or political limitations. The government placed the burdens from the first phase of structural reforms mainly on monopolistic sectors which had reaped large profits in Hungary in the previous two decades (Figure 116).

Figure 116. Unconventional crisis management

Structural reforms

+

burden sharing

SUCCESS

*Burden sharing maintains political stability
and thus governments win time for structural
reforms and eventually establish sustainable
financial balance over the long run*

Source: Compiled by author

The source of the structural reforms was really defined by the new
system of public burden sharing, which financed Hungary's structural
renewal via the bank levy of almost HUF 200 billion, roughly HUF 160
billion in crisis taxes and a string of other sector-specific taxes (Figure
117).

Only in one area was it impossible to launch structural reforms in
2010: the monetary policy of the central bank. In 2013–2014, it became
clear how much the MNB was able to support fiscal consolidation and
economic growth in Hungary, but only in the case that it completely
renewed its set of monetary policy instruments. This was the course
followed by the central banks in developed countries after 2008, in
particular by the Anglo-Saxon central banks (the Fed in the USA and
the Bank of England), by the Japanese central bank and by the European
Central Bank as well (albeit less effectively). From 2010 to the spring of
2013, Hungary's structural reform programme was unable to rely on
such support (See Figure 102).

Figure 117. Bank levy in certain countries, % of GDP

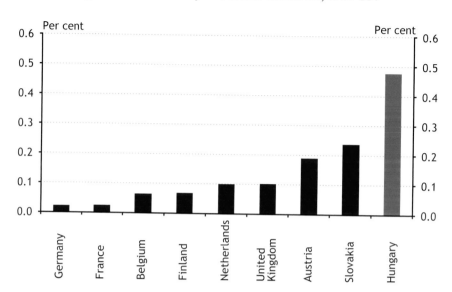

Source: European Commission

Nature of structural reforms

After the launch of structural reforms, they cost more for the budget than they generate during the first phase. Later, this turns around and they bring in more than they cost for the budget in additional spending. Another characteristic of structural reforms is that almost from the moment they are introduced they result in changes in areas which are crucial for fiscal consolidation and economic growth. By definition, structural reforms lead to deep changes in the economy and society by changing the institutional framework, legal environment and rules of operation.

It is worth looking at two examples of how structural reforms work and how they trigger changes in several areas of key importance in term of economic and social renewal.

One of the greatest weak points of the Hungarian economy is the high level of governmental redistribution. Following the introduction of the personal income tax system in 1988, Hungary operated with a much higher ratio of redistribution compared to its regional peers in the market economy transition period of 1990 to 2010. While the Slovak, Romanian and Bulgarian economies exhibited redistribution rates barely higher than 40% of GDP, and even Poland and the Baltic States had rates less than 45%, the rate of redistribution through the central budget in the Hungarian economy was around 50% of GDP and at times even higher than that.[29] The higher level of budget redistribution compared to the regional peers was a competitive disadvantage, because it involves more tax collection and thus a higher tax-to-GDP ratio, both in the corporate sector and in the household sector. This hinders corporate and household investment, while the high taxes on incomes hamper growth in household consumption (Figure 118).

Figure 118. Redistribution rate and per capita GDP, 2009

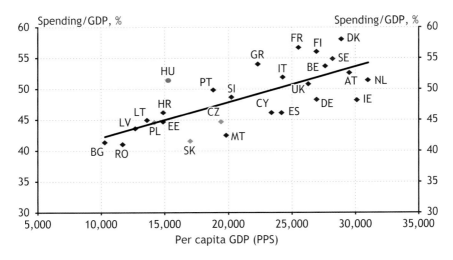

Source: Eurostat

[29] Kiss et al. (2009) performed a detailed comparison of the degrees of government redistribution, in the course of which a "common denominator" was found for the differing budget settlement methods of the Visegrád countries. According to their analysis, disregarding the special features of settlement and interest expenses, Hungary's level of spending now only slightly exceeds that of the regional peers.

Even so, the Hungarian economy's level of redistribution was still slightly lower than in some developed EU countries operating welfare state systems.[30] This could have functioned as a potential competitive advantage for Hungary in the period between 1990 and 2010. One form of this could have been the high level of FDI from the European Union, but this did not actually stem from the relatively competitive level of redistribution, but rather from the government tax concessions granted on investments.

Figure 119. Interest expenditure in the EU
and the Central European region, 2009-2011

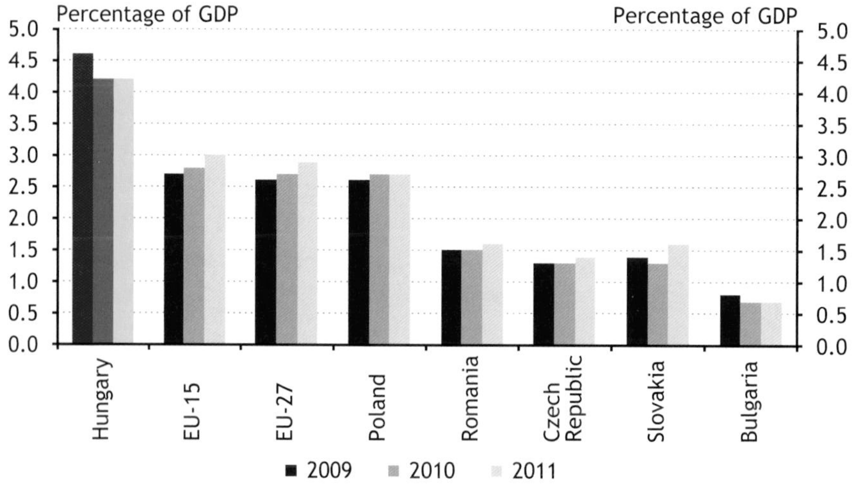

Source: Eurostat

Thus, in the period 1990–2010 Hungary was at a competitive disadvantage compared to its direct competitors in the region due to the higher level of tax centralisation, and at the same time was at a similar competitive disadvantage versus the Anglo-Saxon countries and emerging East Asian economies as its indirect competitors, which

[30] In Hungary, GDP-proportionate fiscal expenditures are lower for example than in France, Denmark and Sweden, but higher than in Germany.

were operating with a clearly lower level of redistribution compared
to Hungary.

The high degree of tax centralisation, i.e. the high level of redistribution
through the budget, can be traced back to two main factors. First, due
to the high level of government debt, more taxes had to be collected
from taxpayers to service the interest, as compared to an economy with
a lower level of government debt and a better financing structure than
that of Hungary (Figure 119).

Compared to Poland, the Czech Republic, Slovakia and Romania, the
level of Hungarian government debt was already far higher in 1990,
and later – aside from a brief period in 1997–2001 when the government
debt ratio fell – the difference between the regional peers' level of
government debt and Hungary's debt-to-GDP ratio even increased
further. This was clearly a competitive disadvantage versus the region,
in several respects (Figure 120).

Figure 120. General government debt in Central Europe

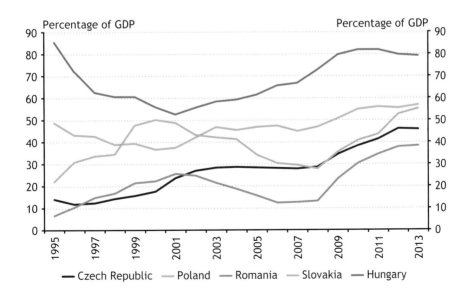

Source: Eurostat

The higher level of government debt results in higher annual interest expenditures, which is already a competitive disadvantage. However, the higher debt-to-GDP ratio compared to the competitors also causes a competitive disadvantage by increasing Hungary's vulnerability and dependence on financial markets. While this does not appear as a disadvantage during periods of generally positive economic activity at the global and EU levels and when liquidity is abundant on the markets, every setback on the financial markets and every crisis situation immediately highlights the vulnerability of the Hungarian economy, due to the high government debt-to-GDP ratio. This is what happened during the 2008 global financial crisis and during the Greek financial crisis starting from spring 2010, and this was seen again during the financial crises in the euro area's southern countries, such as Portugal, Spain and Italy.

Furthermore, it is not only financial and economic crises inside and outside the EU that affect Hungary's vulnerability due to its high debt-to-GDP ratio, but political crises as well. After successful financial consolidation, in 2013–2014 the effects of the Ukrainian political crisis and the Ukraine-Russia tensions were felt, and these developments had a strong impact on the financial markets, and through these markets on the Hungarian economy, which still has a high level of government debt.

It is also worthwhile to analyse the other factor behind the high level of redistribution and tax centralisation on the basis of an example. The Hungarian economy inherited a distorted labour market from the pre-1990 planned economy system, in which very significant levels of unemployment within companies had accumulated. This came to the surface in the first half of the 1990s, because more than 1 million jobs disappeared from the Hungarian economy in the first phase of transition to a market economy, mainly between 1991 and 1994. Further distortion of the labour market was caused by the termination of another 300,000 to 400,000 jobs at the time of the Bokros programme in 1995–1996, and consequently during the first half of the decade of the market economy transition, the number of employees in the legal sector was about 1.5 million lower than before 1990 (Figure 121).

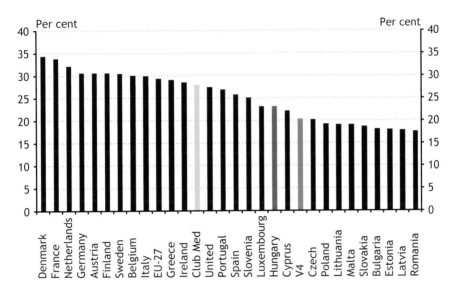

Figure 121. Social protection expenditure in the European Union, % of GDP, 2010

Source: Eurostat

Among the inherited structural weaknesses on the labour market, we find a high level of long-term unemployment, low employment among young people and women, a far lower employment rate among people over 50 compared to the EU and high unemployment among low-skilled persons.

These labour market developments were also reflected in the exceptionally high ratio of disability pensioners by international standards: in Hungary, in the 20–64 age group the ratio of people receiving disability benefits to the working age population was by far the highest in the developed economies, as represented by the OECD countries (Figure 122).

Figure 122. Per cent of population aged 20-64 years
receiving disability benefits

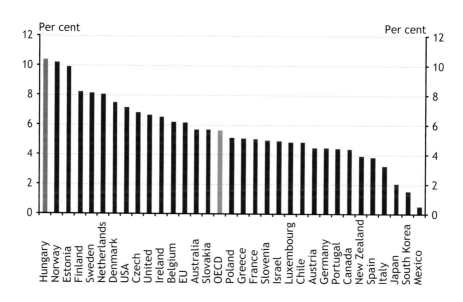

Source: OECD   2010 or last available year

During the two decades between 1990 and 2010, and in particular under
the left-wing government in 1994–1998, the solution to removing some
groups of workers from the labour market (without social tensions)
was to allow them early retirement and status as disability pensioners.
While this ensured a smooth social transition over the short term, it also
naturally increased budget expenditures over the long run, and played
a role in the development of the "neither balance nor growth" formula,
and in consistently hindering the emergence of a positive "balance and
growth" formula.

Compared to gross domestic product, disability benefits were high
in Hungary, and for example even though disability pensioners also
represent a very large group in the Slovak and Lithuanian economies,
the GDP-proportionate level of disability benefits was the highest in
Hungary (Figure 123).

Figure 123. Disability benefits, % of GDP (2008)

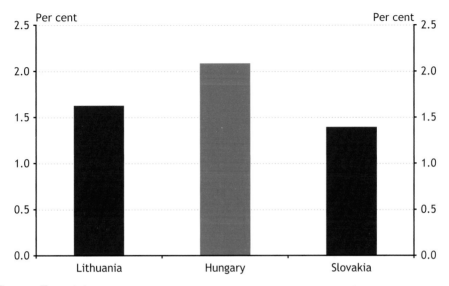

Source: Eurostat

As a result of the distorted labour market, the new economic policy inherited a situation in 2010, in which immediate budget consolidation was necessary while at the same time almost 800,000 workers who were receiving disability benefits and were mostly younger than the pension age were missing from the labour market.[31]

If economic policy succeeds in reducing the high government debt-to-GDP ratio, it is possible to lower the tax-to-GDP ratio through the decline in interest expenditures. Naturally, this has a positive effect on investment and consumption, as well as on job-seeking and employment. Similarly, if employment policy is able to reduce the distortions on the labour market, the activity and employment rate may rise, unemployment may decline, and as a result budget expenditures may fall, while revenues increase.

---

[31] Total beneficiaries of old-age pensions and pre-pension age disability pensions and disability benefits.

One structural reform carried out in a single area can have a positive effect on a range of other areas, and if reforms are launched in several important areas, they multiply each other's positive effects.

Széll Kálmán Plan

In spring 2011, Hungary published its comprehensive plan for structural reforms, known as the Széll Kálmán Plan. In mid-2010, based on the new economic approach and new economic policy strategy, the new government began formulating its programme for structural renewal, resulting in the plan released in spring 2011.

The starting point of the Széll Kálmán Plan was that the government immediately use its strong two-thirds parliamentary majority to launch structural reforms and changes, because these were needed to support fiscal consolidation and a recovery in economic growth. If a government does not initiate structural reforms at the start of the cycle, the opportunities to do so decline as the cycle progresses. Naturally, the new government – backed by a two-thirds parliamentary majority and willing to face conflicts with the corporate sector due to the nature of its new economic policy and the consequences of EU policies and its policy of public burden sharing – had to have the political courage needed to launch structural reforms in areas which might affect social and political stability (Figure 124).

In mid-2010, the new government took the reins of power in Hungary and assessed all of the elements of the new economic policy from strategic and socio-political perspectives, including fiscal policy, the new development policy and the question of structural reforms. It became clear that all of the accumulated structural weaknesses from the two decades between 1990 and 2010 had to be addressed at the same time with structural reforms and that a structural turnaround had to be launched. It was not sufficient to try isolated reforms or a little bit of reform, it was not expedient for the long-term set of goals to postpone the reforms, or to merely concentrate on a few more significant reforms.

Previously, the consensus-based economic idea was that one major change, one reform could be undertaken in each political cycle, but not more, because the dual effects of the reforms would be detrimental to the budget, growth and political stability. This is an error, however, and the opposite is actually true: if a government only undertakes one reform, it misses out on the mutually supportive effect of the reforms, and this is why results are delayed, threatening balance, growth and political stability. We have seen this in the EU's failed crisis management efforts and we saw this with previous Hungarian reforms: the governments only received a mandate for one cycle because they failed to undertake the critical amount of structural reforms. The 2006 elections were an exception in this regard, but in this case the public only became aware of the true economic situation in the autumn of that year.

Figure 124. Hungary's new economic policy

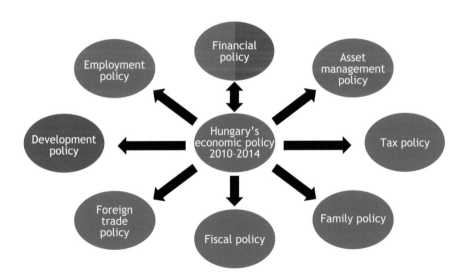

In the figure, the green shaded area refers to the reforms launched and completed during the period 2010-2014; red shading refers to reforms which were launched during the period.

Source: Compiled by author

The advantage of the Széll Kálmán Plan was that it initiated structural changes simultaneously in the most important parts of society and the economy: the critical amount of reforms were launched and consequently it was possible to consolidate the budget and stabilise the economy in the span of a single political cycle.

The character of the Széll Kálmán Plan announced in spring 2011 is reflected by the kind of changes it effected from the perspective of budget consolidation, and these changes were then seen in the 2012 Budget Act. As a result of the Széll Kálmán Plan, the 2012 budget balance improved by 1.56% of GDP according to the approved budget law, and thus the structural reform programme not only helped reinforce Hungary's long-term competitiveness, it also had a positive effect over the short term and facilitated budget consolidation (Table 4).

Table 4. Effect of the Széll Kálmán Plan on the budget balance in the budget bill of 2012

	HUF billion	As % of GDP
Employment and labour market	158	0.54
Pension system	42	0.14
Public transport	26	0.09
Higher education	12	0.04
Health care	83	0.29
General and local government financing	44	0.15
Fund for the Reduction of State Debt	90	0.30
Total	455	1.56

Source: Big Reform Book. The Hungarian Path of Growth and Employment Leading to Sustainable Development, p. 58, February 2012.

The first phase of the Széll Kálmán Plan, together with the later Széll Kálmán Plan II, made a significant contribution to successful budget consolidation and the recovery in economic growth, because it simultaneously supported improvement in fiscal balance and steadily strengthened incentives to work and incentives to create jobs in the corporate sector.

Chapter 10

Fiscal and budgetary policy

The new approach to economic thought in mid-2010 was based on the understanding that the failure of economic convergence and social advancement in the two decades after 1990 was mainly due to the constant see-saw of deteriorating financial balance and stagnation in economic growth. It was rightly recognised that this was caused by the low employment and activity rates as well as the high level of unemployment. This could be partly attributed to the fact that workers' willingness to work was low, as was the motivation of the corporate sector to create new jobs.

One of the reasons for this is the high redistribution ratio of the budget compared to the surrounding countries, i.e. Hungary's most direct competitors, which necessitates a high level of tax centralisation. The heavy tax burden reduces the motivation for employment and job creation through the taxation of income; this is where the weakness of the tax system and the labour market meet. If the tax system penalises employment and job creation, low employment and high unemployment prevail, just like other distortions of the labour market.

Fiscal consolidation

The new economic policy added tax reform to the structural reforms, thereby putting an end to the philosophy of the previous two decades, which primarily viewed taxation as a budgetary, revenue-generating tool and not as a basic economic policy instrument. A safe tax reform was needed, i.e. one that reduced the tax burden on the income of businesses and individuals without rendering fiscal consolidation impossible. A tax reform was needed that would overcome the low motivation instilled into labour market participants in the previous two decades.

Moreover, the motivation and the ability for employment and job creation had to be boosted at the same time. The tax system would have increased the willingness to work in vain, if the motivation and ability to create new employment opportunities did not improve among Hungarian micro, small and medium-sized enterprises.

Tax centralisation had to be reduced and at the same time the taxation of income had to be restructured, while simultaneously ensuring that the tax reform also supported fiscal consolidation (Figure 125).

Figure 125. Tax centralisation, % of GDP

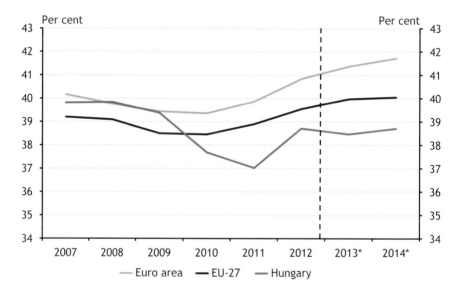

Source: European Commission, AMECO database   * estimate

The second attempt at fiscal consolidation after the 2008 crisis – which finally proved unsuccessful – already incorporated a tax reduction element (PIT) and increased VAT, but it did not undertake a comprehensive tax reform. Due in part to this, the attempt resulted in a 7% budget deficit in 2010. One of the most important structural reforms of the new government was the tax reform, and in particular the introduction of the 16% flat-rate family tax system.

The structural reform programme and the tax reform were fundamentally interdependent: neither of them would have been successful without the other. The main goal of the structural reform programme was to increase Hungary's competitiveness over the long term, which required successful fiscal consolidation and a recovery in economic growth. The third economic policy element was the expansion of employment and the reduction of unemployment, and therefore a trend change was needed in labour market participants' attitude to work. This required a reduction in taxes on income. After the flat-rate tax system was fully phased in, the general government reduced its revenue from personal income taxes by more than HUF 400 billion, which substantially improved the motivation of labour market participants, employees and employers to seek employment and create jobs.

Nonetheless, fiscal consolidation also required other revenues that would offset the HUF 400 billion missing from the budget due to the introduction of the 16% flat-rate family tax system. It was expected that over the medium term, the higher pace of growth resulting from fiscal loosening would boost budgetary revenues as well,[32] but the immediate fiscal consolidation needs required the government to find new, temporary revenue sources until the dynamic economic growth automatically led to higher budgetary revenues. The economic policy stimulating job creation and employment by way of the HUF 400 billion tax cut would have been ineffectual, if fiscal consolidation been not implemented at the same time. In such a scenario, it would have been necessary to hamper the emerging growth with further budgetary measures, and the misguided economic policies of the previous two decades would have emerged again.

---

[32] Based on the microsimulation model previously developed at the MNB, Baksay et al. (2014) concluded that over the long term, approximately 80% of the tax relief would be recovered through additional tax revenues generated by stronger economic growth.

One of the most important features of the tax reform between 2010 and 2014 was that it was able to considerably cut taxes on income for labour market participants, while offsetting the revenue losses with new sources of revenue.[33]

Since 2011, as a result of the decisions on tax reform taken in mid-2010, taxes on labour have been reduced substantially, while taxes on capital also dropped. Meanwhile, indirect taxes have risen considerably, and new sector-specific taxes have been introduced (Figure 126).

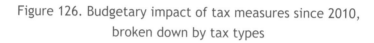

Figure 126. Budgetary impact of tax measures since 2010,
broken down by tax types

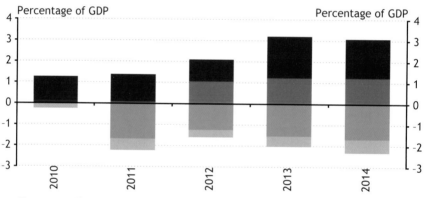

■ Sector specific taxes (surtaxes payable by certain economic sectors, bank levy, financial transaction duty, tax on insurance, tax on collision insurance, public utility tax, income tax on energy suppliers)
▪ Taxes on capital
■ Taxes on consumption and turnover
■ Taxes on labour

The diagram shows the static budgetary effect of the measures in cash flow approach.

Source: Csomós et al. (2014)

---

[33] The shift of the focus of taxation away from taxes on labour can be observed in many countries, and when this is not coupled with a rise in taxes on capital, it is in line with the suggestions of studies on the theory of optimal taxation (IMF Fiscal Monitor, 2013).

The additional revenue generated by the new indirect taxes and by the rise in existing taxes would not have been sufficient for successful fiscal consolidation, because the new economic policy lowered taxes on labour to a larger extent, while also reducing taxes on capital. The revenue loss from the 16% flat-rate tax and the 10% corporate tax could not be offset by the indirect taxes alone. This would have caused short-term inflationary pressure of such an extent in the economy that would have jeopardised the success of fiscal consolidation and may have led to another drop in consumption.

The new sector-specific taxes introduced within the framework of the new system of public burden sharing – i.e. the crisis taxes, the bank levy, the financial transaction tax, the telecommunications tax, the insurance tax, the accident tax, the utilities tax and the so-called Robin Hood tax – not only offset the revenue losses caused by the reduction of income taxes but also significantly contributed to fiscal consolidation by generating more revenue for the budget than was lost due to the reforms (Figure 127).

It is important to note the magnitude of the changes: the reduction of taxes on labour amounted to nearly 1.5% of gross domestic product in 2011–2014. This represented a significant cut in income taxes for both employees and employers, which led to a genuine expansion of employment and contributed to the fall in the rate of unemployment.

The rise in indirect taxes in 2012–2014 only increased inflation temporarily, in 2012, and did not have any lasting second-round effects. The Hungarian economy would have entered on a downward path of inflation even without the subsequent government decisions to reduce utility prices. The tax reform – one of the central elements of the structural reform programme launched by the new economic policy – was successful because it supported employment and job creation by temporarily allowing inflation to rise, but at the same time steadily contributing to fiscal consolidation through the sector-specific taxes.

Figure 127. Sector-specific taxes

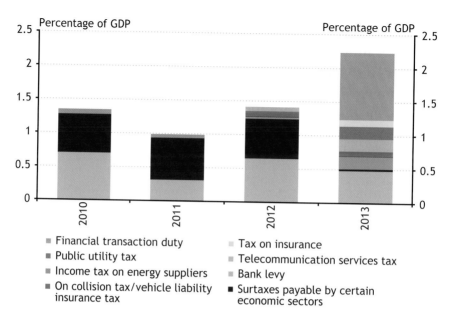

- Financial transaction duty
- Public utility tax
- Income tax on energy suppliers
- On collision tax/vehicle liability insurance tax
- Tax on insurance
- Telecommunication services tax
- Bank levy
- Surtaxes payable by certain economic sectors

The figures show accrual based data. The negative impact on bank levy revenue due to the early repayment scheme was taken into account in determining bank levy revenue for 2011.

Source: Eurostat, National Tax Lists

Fiscal policy

In mid-2010, Hungary was in the midst of a complex crisis and required immediate fiscal consolidation. The urgent need for measures was due to two factors. First, in accordance with the IMF-EU agreement concluded in autumn 2008, Hungary had to achieve a budget deficit of 3.8% of GDP in 2010, while the actual deficit was planned to be around 7% of GDP, since the Parliament passed the Budget Act with this target in autumn 2009. Since revenues were overestimated and expenditure was underestimated in the 2009 Budget Act, the basis for the budgetary crisis that came to light in mid-2010 was already laid in 2009.

In the end, the errors in budgetary planning became obvious, despite the fact that economic growth was considerably stronger than forecast in the Act. In planning the budget, the government projected a 1% contraction in 2010, but in fact the economy expanded by 1%. Despite the extra revenue generated by this unexpected growth, the budget deficit could still have reached 7% of GDP, instead of the officially planned 3.8%. Even though the International Monetary Fund and the European Commission approved the unfounded 3.8% deficit target for the 2010 budget, in mid-2010 they also realised that the deficit might indeed come in at around 7%.

Second, Hungary was the only EU member state that had been continuously subject to the excessive deficit procedure since accession. This was the penalty for constantly breaching the requirement of the Stability and Growth Pact stipulating that the deficit-to-GDP ratio should be kept below 3%. By spring 2010, it had become obvious to almost every international and Hungarian institution analysing economic policy that the 3.8% deficit target would not be achieved in 2010. Before the change of government, the opposition had repeatedly pointed this out to Brussels and the International Monetary Fund, and capital market participants clearly saw that the targets of the 2010 budget were unattainable. Immediate fiscal consolidation was also necessary because the International Monetary Fund and the European Commission could hardly tolerate a difference of this magnitude in the deficit level stipulated in the agreement: in the midst of the Greek crisis that erupted in spring 2010, they might have accepted a minor divergence from the target, but could not tolerate a deficit ratio of 7% of GDP.

There was, however, a third reason why the Hungarian government was compelled to undertake fiscal consolidation in mid-2010. Compared to its peers, Hungary's competitiveness deteriorated between 2002 and 2010, which was reflected by the country's fall in competitiveness rankings. By mid-2010, from the perspective of international competitiveness, Hungary had clearly become the "sick" economy of the region. To a great extent, the deteriorating competitiveness was due to the poor and unpredictable fiscal policy (Figure 128).

Figure 128. Region's ranking in IMD Fiscal Policy Index (2010)

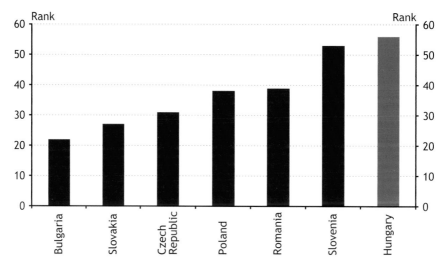

Source: IMD

While the Bulgarian, Slovak, Czech, Polish and Romanian budgets all ranked among the first 40 in competitiveness and the Slovenian budget was ranked 53rd, Hungarian fiscal policy was in 56th place. As a result of the misguided economy policy between 2002 and 2010, the new indebtedness and the failure of crisis management, Hungary took last place in regional fiscal policy rankings.

Of the Visegrád countries, Hungary had recorded the largest budget deficit before the IMF-EU agreement was concluded, i.e. before autumn 2008. Between 2002 and 2008, the Hungarian budget deficit exceeded the deficits in the other Visegrád countries every year. This changed after 2008 (Figure 129).

When the crisis erupted, on account of the previous misguided economic policy, Hungary was forced to cut the deficit to keep government debt on a sustainable path, i.e. it had to implement a procyclical fiscal policy, which curbed overall demand, thus not mitigating but rather exacerbating the contraction in GDP.

By contrast, the prudent fiscal policies followed by the other Visegrád countries enabled them to relax their budgetary discipline in reaction to the crisis, i.e. to pursue anti-cyclical policies, thereby limiting the effects of the recession. After 2008, Hungary ran the smallest budget deficit in the region, but this entailed substantial sacrifices in growth over the short term.

Figure 129. Fiscal balance in the new EU member states

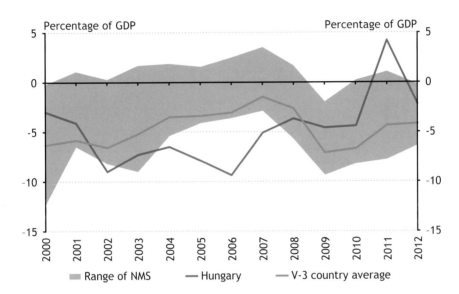

Source: Eurostat

Hungarian fiscal policy was on the wrong path long before the 2008 global financial crisis, contributing to the extremely high deficit levels every year. Indeed, it proved clearly unsustainable when the crisis erupted, and that is why Hungary had the poorest assessment in terms of fiscal policy in 2010. In this context, it is understandable that although the first fiscal consolidation measures were met with considerable resistance from enterprises in the Hungarian corporate sector – the banking system and those business groups on which the bank levy and the crisis taxes were imposed – global capital market participants appreciated the promptly introduced programme that improved the fiscal balance and was ultimately able to reduce the 6–7% inherited deficit to slightly more than 4% (Figure 130).

Figure 130. Fiscal balance in the EU and Hungary, % of GDP

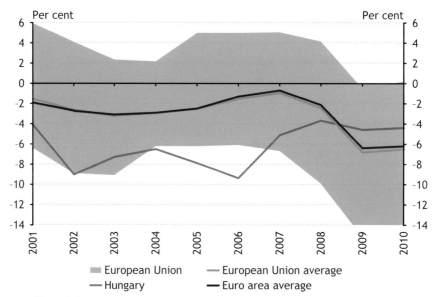

Source: Eurostat

The first steps of fiscal consolidation

When evaluating the first steps of fiscal consolidation, one needs to bear in mind that in Hungary the government redistribution ratio has traditionally been high compared to the regional peers. While it is true that if we adjust this for interest payments, the difference becomes smaller, but nevertheless the ratio of public expenditure to GDP ratio still exceeded that of other Visegrád countries. Of course, the ratio of government redistribution was higher in several member states of the European Union than in Hungary, however, these are not only developed countries but also member states that were later hit the hardest by the crisis. Thus, the standard or example set by these countries can hardly be considered appropriate for Hungary to follow.

The relatively high expenditures as compared to Hungary's level of development were only one side of the coin that, in their own right, would not have caused an unsustainable budget deficit. Aside from these high expenditure levels, what caused the extremely high general government deficit?

The answer lies in the competitiveness review that takes into account the revenue side of the budget as well. This shows that as regards tax avoidance, Hungary fared the worst in the region. The Czech and the Polish economies were the top performers, and even the Slovak economy was among the first 40 in the global ranking, while Hungary came in 55th place[34] (Figure 131)

Figure 131. Key weaknesses of the Hungarian tax system, based on the IMD taxation factors in 2010

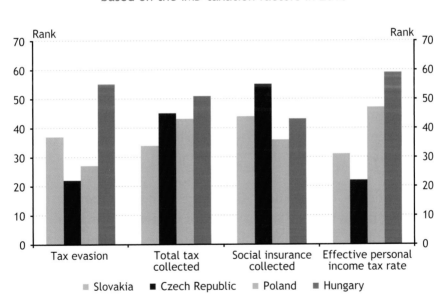

Source: IMD database

[34] Schneider (2013) paints a somewhat brighter, but still very negative picture when stating that the hidden economy generated 22–25% of GDP during the crisis (and even more before that), while this proportion was 15–18% in Slovakia, 16–20% in the Czech Republic and 24–28% in Poland. Studies on the subject estimate that 10–17% of the workforce is employed illegally in Hungary (Elek et al., 2009; Benedek, 2012).

The high level of tax avoidance is the symptom of an earlier vicious circle in Hungarian fiscal policy. Substantial tax revenue was needed to cover the expenditures, which was intended to be collected through high tax rates, especially through high taxes on labour. High tax rates, however, encouraged tax avoidance, and attempts were made to offset the resulting revenue loss with further tax increases. Thus, those actually paying taxes were faced with very high tax rates, while a significant segment stayed in competition on the market by tax avoidance and tax evasion. In addition to the irresponsible expenditure-side budget management, tax avoidance was in large part responsible for the fact that for years before 2008, Hungary ran the largest general government deficit in the region. Due to these factors, Hungary ranked the lowest in competitiveness in the region as regards total tax collection.

Therefore in 2010, the need for immediate fiscal consolidation was underscored by the Hungarian budget structure, in which the extremely high tax burden – as compared to the regional peers – was coupled with a distorted and inefficient tax system. Although taxes on income were very high – as reflected by the highest rates of personal income tax and social security contribution in the region – widespread tax avoidance prevented the revenue side of the tax system from offsetting the expenditure side, and ensuring a deficit close to 3%. The Hungarian economy was overtaxed with respect to income, while at the same time undertaxed with regard to indirect taxes. Tax avoidance was rife both in terms of taxes on income and indirect taxes, while taxes on labour were the highest in the region. The concept for the tax reform was based on the above-mentioned realisations: taxes on labour had to be reduced, indirect taxes had to be increased, and at the same time the control and supervision of taxation had to be strengthened.

In mid-2010, reducing the 20–25% share of the hidden economy in total output (Schneider, 2013) was a key element of consolidation.

The first steps were taken in 2010, and in the following years increasingly effective measures were introduced, generating more and more revenue for the budget. All of these measures could have been adopted in the previous years, when government debt surged and the general government deficit reached extreme levels. Yet, the governments at that time were not willing to adopt them (Figure 132).

Figure 132. Size of the hidden economy in 2010, % of GDP

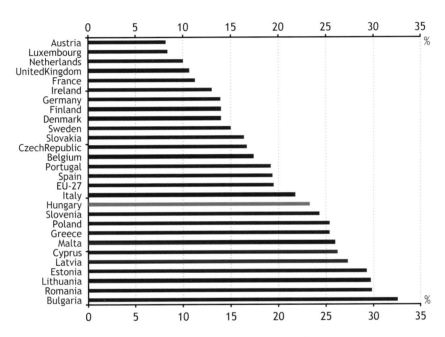

Source: The Shadow Economy in Europe (Kearney, 2013)

In an EU or international context, agents in the Hungarian banking system and external investors holding monopolies in Hungary enjoyed exceptionally high profit rates. While taxes on labour were extremely high, Hungarian economic policy considered it natural that non-resident investors in the banking system and in strategic sectors functioning as domestic monopolies could reap extra profits of 20%. In addition to the dualistic structure of the Hungarian economy, this also indicated weak competition in the banking sector. Supervisory authorities were not able to counter the dominance of domestic monopolies, and therefore, the profit rates of the various economic agents were heterogeneous.

The logical step of the tax reform put an end to the practice of overtaxing a large part of the economy, while undertaxing the smaller portion that enjoyed high profit rates.

The distortion of the Hungarian tax system was perceptible in virtually all its main components: in taxes on human labour, in corporate tax, indirect taxes as well as the taxation of sectors generating extra profits. That is why levying the sector-specific taxes – in accordance with the new system of tax burden sharing introduced within the framework of the new economic policy – was necessary and possible. In 2010, the new bank levy and the crisis taxes already improved the balance of the budget by HUF 360 billion in total, thereby substantially shrinking the high level of the inherited budget deficit.

This, however, would not have been enough to considerably improve the Hungarian budget for 2010, and therefore – as part of the immediate consolidation measures – the government re-channelled the contributions paid to the mandatory private pension fund system into the budget. As a result, the HUF 30 billion of private pension fund contributions that flowed into the public pension scheme in both of the last two months of 2010, provided an additional improvement of HUF 60 billion for the budget. The objective of the new fiscal policy was sustainable consolidation, and re-channelling the private pension fund contributions for two months did not suffice for that: the private pension fund scheme had to be completely overhauled (Figure 133).

The mandatory private pension fund system was introduced on 1 January 1998, which was clearly detrimental to the Hungarian general government, since the budget thus lost revenues of more than 1% in GDP terms annually. This amount was paid to the new mandatory private pension fund system, while the general government had to perform its payment obligations regarding previously acquired pension rights, although the funds for such purposes were depleted.

In fact, the introduction of the mandatory private pension fund system benefited the banking sector, since private pension funds collecting the contributions from members who were required to enter the private pension fund system were mainly established by credit institutions.

For almost 15 years after it was set up, the rate of return for members of the mandatory private pension fund system was a mere 1% in excess of inflation: the gains actually increased the profit of the banking system.

Figure 133. Use of assets transferred from private pension funds to the government

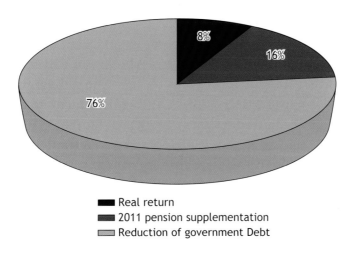

Excluding assets of remaining members; due to fund operations, their 2014 assets differ from their 2010 assets.

Source: Act CLV of 2012 on the Execution of Act CLXIX of 2011 on the 2011 Budget of the Republic of Hungary

In 2010, a budgetary reform was launched, during which the revenue and the expenditure sides were consolidated separately. On the revenue side, the tax system was transformed and a comprehensive tax reform was implemented. The scope of the sector-specific taxes introduced in 2010 was later expanded, taxes on income were substantially reduced, and the significance of indirect taxes increased considerably. The efforts to curb the shadow economy that pays no taxes was stepped up, and except for the wealth tax, the general government used all the tools available for the consolidation of the revenue side of the budget.

The fiscal consolidation of the expenditure side also covered basically every possible area. In mid-2010, the first and most important step towards consolidating the expenditure side was the cancellation of a portion of previously planned government expenditure. In 2010, the government cancelled expenditures of HUF 220 billion in total within the framework of the consolidation programme. One of the characteristics of the Hungarian general government is that it carries over a significant amount – HUF 400–500 billion in 2010 – every year for expenditures foreseen in previous budgets but not yet used. These include current expenditures and investments. Since the Hungarian budget does not contain a separate investment budget, it was difficult to determine in mid-2010 which government investments were truly needed, which of them were secured by various lobby groups, and which of them should be launched to establish competitive government services. The cancellation of HUF 220 billion improved the Hungarian general government deficit by almost 1% of GDP, thereby contributing to successful fiscal consolidation.

Sustainable fiscal policy

The real transformation in Hungarian economic history in 2010 was when the economic policy abandoned the idea of "balance or growth", since fiscal consolidation in 2010–2011 did not entail a setback in growth, and in fact expanded employment and reduced unemployment. Although GDP contracted in 2012, this was due to several unique factors. GDP shrank in almost all EU member states in 2012, and economies outside the European Union also experienced a double-dip recession. Following the recession in 2009, the economic output of developed countries fell again in 2012, but to a lesser degree, while GDP growth in emerging countries decelerated to a similar extent. This unfavourable event curbed Hungary's growth through its foreign trade relations.

A further decrease in GDP of around 0.8% was caused by a deterioration in agricultural production due to adverse weather conditions. In addition, due to their declining market shares in the world economy, certain international corporations in the electronics sector reduced capacities that previously contributed 0.3–0.4% to Hungarian GDP. And of course, the two one-off items that boosted the disposable income of the private sector in 2011 could not be repeated in 2012 (the payment of real interest and the refunding of HUF 250 billion of VAT in accordance with the decision by the European Court of Justice because of the wrongful practices of the previous governments). The bulk of the tax reform occurred in 2012. This resulted in an inflation rate of 5.7%, which led to a drop in real income and consumption.

The new economic policy approach introduced in 2010 exhibited its effect immediately: before and after the exceptional slump in 2012, it did not entail a sacrifice in growth, in fact, it contributed to the expansion of employment and the reduction of unemployment (Figure 134).

This was enabled by a fiscal reform and a budgetary policy that explored new revenue sources which did not have a negative effect on the economic performance of the areas concerned. Although some tried to find a direct link between the highest bank levy in the European Union and the decline in lending in the Hungarian credit institution sector between 2010 and 2014, this was actually caused by natural balance sheet adjustments. Between 2010 and 2014, the banking sector adjusted the unsustainably large stock of outstanding loans accumulated between 2002 and 2010, as well as the poor loan structure caused by the high proportion of foreign currency loans.

Figure 134. Number of government employees and employment rate

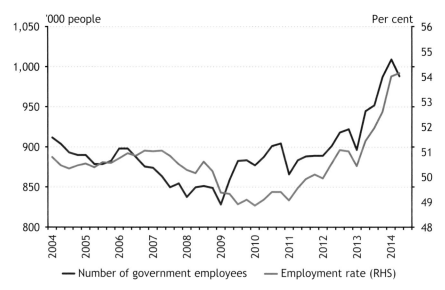

Source: HCSO, Labour Force Survey

Had the Hungarian bank levy been not introduced or had it been smaller, it would not have changed the situation significantly. The banking sector would have still reduced its loan-to-deposit ratio, and the stock of foreign currency loans would have contracted as well.

Why can we state that without the bank levy, the sectoral and crisis taxes or the reform of the private pension fund system, the budgetary situation would have been worse than after the successful fiscal consolidation?

The Hungarian budget needed the annual HUF 180 billion from the bank levy between 2010 and 2014 for successful fiscal consolidation, as it would have been impossible to keep the fiscal deficit below 3% of GDP without this revenue. Had fiscal consolidation been unsuccessful, interest rates, CDS spreads and yields on government securities would have been even higher. It is true for the whole period after 2010 that if fiscal consolidation had failed, the stock of new loans would probably have been even lower and the existing stock of loans would have been reduced at a much faster pace. Thus, the bank levy did not hinder but indirectly fostered lending by not increasing interest rates or risk premiums further through another botched fiscal consolidation. Furthermore, without the annual revenue of HUF 180 billion from the bank levy and the successful fiscal consolidation, financing the general government would have become more difficult and more costly. Without the sector-specific taxes, another sovereign debt crisis – which would have entailed a financial crisis impacting the real economy – could have been hardly avoided.

This may have been prevented by an additional IMF-EU agreement, but this would not have made Hungarian fiscal policy sustainable because it would have required further sacrifices in growth and employment, as demonstrated by earlier experiences in Hungary and by the events unfolding in the other programme countries.

The introduction of the highest bank levy in the EU actually laid the foundation for the positive trend reversal in lending by supporting successful fiscal consolidation: in 2010, this was not visible but in 2014 it was obvious.

There is a similar link between the crisis taxes and economic performance. At first, the investment activities of the domestic monopolies subject to the crisis taxes – energy providers, the telecommunications and retail sectors – were curbed by the new taxes introduced between 2010 and 2014. The effects were, however, again contrary to what was expected: had fiscal consolidation failed, these economic agents – or at least the corporate groups in the retail and telecommunications sectors – would have been less or not at all likely to make new investments. The performance of these two sectors subject to the crisis tax is directly linked to the disposable income of households spent on consumption. If that decreases, the domestic market of these corporate groups shrinks, which results in the postponement or cancellation of investments.

Energy providers are special, since families' and households' electricity consumption and other energy use related to housing and heating is less elastic to changes in income than in the case of other sectors. By contrast, the corporate sector is quick to react to economic cycles: in times of downturn, businesses scale down or postpone their planned investments. From the perspective of energy providers, household consumption responds less to a change in GDP than the corporate sector. Had fiscal consolidation been unsuccessful, another recession would have hit Hungary between 2010 and 2014, since the high rate of inherited government debt and its expensive financing structure as well as the extra financing need due to a deficit of more than 3% would have caused GDP to shrink.

The new budgetary policy introduced in mid-2010 was successful because it found new revenue sources that did not hinder the economic performance of the affected sectors, such as the banking and retail sectors, and the domestic monopolies. The performance of these sectors depends on the income levels of the Hungarian economic agents. In the banking sector, the balance sheet adjustment that started before 2010 continued. Households and businesses would not have taken out more loans even if the bank levy had not been not imposed. In fact, without the bank levy consolidation would have failed, which would have triggered a new crisis, and the prolonged recession would have further eroded real income, consumption and investments.

Restoring fiscal balance was the result of the new budgetary policy, the tax system and the economic policy introduced in mid-2010, which paved the way for a recovery in investment, consumption and growth between 2013 and 2014.

Chapter 11

Tax reform in Hungary

During the two decades of transition between 1990 and 2010, the Hungarian tax system did not meet any criteria that can be expected from an efficient tax system at the macroeconomic level.[35] It did not help Hungarian economic policy onto a path of sustainable balance, nor did it support sustained and dynamic economic growth. In fact, the Hungarian tax system before 2010 was actually dampening employment and job creation by overtaxing income from these areas. The "punitive" nature of the tax system was also demonstrated by the fact that it allowed a considerable hidden economy to operate without paying taxes, thereby causing a competitive disadvantage for the legal, tax-paying portion of the economy, both on domestic and international markets.[36]

Aims of the tax reform

The function of the Hungarian tax system before 2010 played a major role in the recurrence of the economic policy paradigm of "balance or growth". The main reason for this was that, along with a social security system which was unreasonably generous towards the economically inactive, the Hungarian tax system before 2010 prevented a significant, sustained rise in the employment rate and a substantial, steady fall in unemployment. By penalising employment and job creation – apart from the short period between 1998 and 2002 – it did not even make it possible to preserve the already existing jobs.

[35] The characteristics of a well-functioning tax system in an open economy are detailed in Mirrlees et al. (2010) and Mirrlees et al. (2011).
[36] Certain studies found that in 2010, the size of the hidden economy in Hungary was more than 23% in GDP terms (Schneider, 2013). The widespread nature of tax avoidance is illustrated by the findings of Elek et al. (2012), according to which more than 50% of minimum wage earners concealed part of their income.

Interestingly, this did not only apply to the period of quick transition to the market economy using shock therapy in the first half of the 1990s. The Hungarian tax system consistently hindered work, and thus employment as well, until 2010. Apart from the years around 2000 when 240,000 new jobs were created, job creation did not prove to be a lasting success in any political term or economic/investment cycle until 2010. The high unemployment and low employment rates kept recurring.

Indirectly, it was the operation of the Hungarian tax system which prevented economic policy from embarking on a path of sustainable balance and sustained growth, because the tax system restrained the employment rate. The government measures and economic policies implemented between 1990 and 2010 did not focus adequately on employment and unemployment. Governments and economic policymakers thought that it was enough to strive for a balanced budget, and to use investment and especially foreign direct investment to foster economic growth. In the economic policies of 1990–2010 (apart from the policies around 2000 which took into account domestic demand and the domestic market), foreign direct investment was given priority, which resulted neither in a tangible rise in the employment rate nor a reduction in unemployment.

The reason for this was that foreign direct investment stemmed from three sources: from global corporate groups investing in the real economy and mainly bringing in new technologies, from corporate acquisitions in the domestic monopolies, and from the financial sector. In the case of the latter two, due to the nature of the investment, no notable improvement in the employment rate could have been expected. The energy and telecommunications sectors as well as public services (from waste collection to waterworks) have poor job creation potential. In the global economy and according to the examples in economic history, the number of new jobs does not grow dynamically in these sectors. Similarly, foreign corporate groups, credit institutions and insurance companies investing in the financial sector do not create many jobs either: their activities require special knowledge and they generate a substantial profit with few employees.

The foreign direct investment which injected new capital into the real economy did not create jobs at a rate able to offset the loss of around 1.5 million jobs in the first half of the 1990s, because by definition, investments operating with the use of modern technologies and high productivity cannot address the weakness of the Hungarian labour market originating from its composition as regards the qualifications of workers. At the same time, Hungarian SMEs with more labour-intensive production processes were not able to integrate into global production chains. The tax and economic structure – which developed as a result of the prevailing strongly dualistic structure of the economy – increasingly struggled to provide suitable jobs to low-skilled workers.

The Hungarian tax system's concealed but most probably strongest impediment to supporting economic balance and growth and increasing employment was that it did not distinguish between the qualifications and circumstances of labour market participants in terms of taxes on labour.

While it applied one of the highest tax and contribution rates to human labour in the developed OECD countries, the tax system did not take into account the millions of workers whose jobs, due to lower productivity, cannot generate the necessary income for such high taxes. While global corporate groups were able to generate the revenue necessary to pay the high taxes on labour, this was less feasible for businesses producing for the domestic market and impossible for businesses producing for the local market or those only surviving in the grey economy: these businesses either moved towards the hidden economy or postponed their investment and business decisions which could have created new jobs for low-skilled workers (Figure 135).

Figure 135. Ten largest average tax wedges in OECD countries in 2009 for childless, average wage earning taxpayers

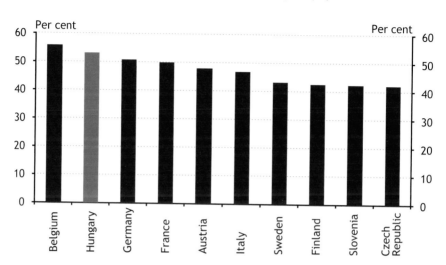

Source: OECD Tax Statistics

In mid-2010, the new government and economic policymakers listed the ten most important goals of tax reform. Directly and/or indirectly all of the goals were linked to an economic policy that would eliminate the factors inhibiting work and employment among labour market participants through the tax reform. Both in the case of employers and employees, a change in business planning related to labour had to be achieved, in order to bring about a trend reversal in the second lowest employment rate among the EU member states and in the double-digit unemployment rate through changes in the tax system. In mid-2010, a political and economic policy concept was embraced that sought to successfully manage the fiscal policy crisis, to prevent a government debt financing crisis and to lay the foundation for a trend change in employment and growth (Figure 136).

Figure 136. Change in average tax wedge in OECD countries (2009-2013)

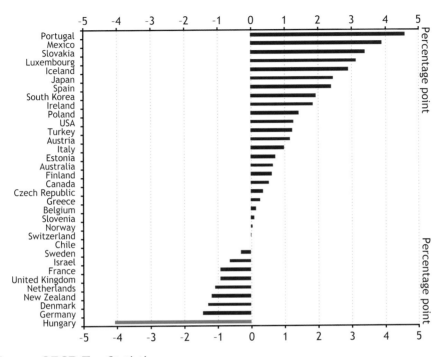

Source: OECD Tax Statistics

Among the aims of the tax reform, budget consolidation was the top priority in mid-2010: this was to be achieved through the bank levy and the sector-specific taxes. Coupled with this, the second most important goal was to immediately boost motivation for job creation: in 2010, this was supported by the 10% rate of corporate income tax that benefited micro, small and medium-sized enterprises, and in the following years it was reinforced by the flat-rate family tax system and the Job Protection Action Plan as well as a number of tax allowances within the framework of special employment programmes. The tax reforms also aimed to increase the motivation of employees for work: this was encouraged by the flat-rate family tax system as well as by the integration of the minimum wage and public work wages into the personal income tax system. The standardised taxation of personal income assists the motivation for employment in and of itself, because it removes the immediate drag of a progressive tax regime triggered by the higher tax brackets that individuals enter as a result of their additional efforts.

Taxing income from public work and the minimum wage from the corporate sector to the same degree motivates employment in the corporate and the public sector equally. The 16% PIT rate – the third lowest in Europe – and the substantial drop in marginal tax rates reduced the advantage of the hidden, tax-avoiding economy over the formal economy as regards employment.

In fact, the flat-rate tax system proved the most effective tool between 2010 and 2014 for raising the employment rate and reducing unemployment, because it was able to eliminate the hindrances for employees and employers alike, while at the same time addressing the differences between the hidden and the formal economy.

One of the stated intentions of the tax reform was to encourage child-rearing: this was promoted through the family-centred flat-rate tax system.

The tax reform, which unfolded from mid-2010 until the end of 2014, sought to create a level playing field for businesses within the private sector. In the field of domestic monopolies, no special, sector-specific taxes were introduced by the tax reform other than the ones engaging them in public burden sharing.

In the target system of the tax reform, another element was present from the outset: the requirement of achieving sustainable balance by restructuring tax revenues. In mid-2010, it was obvious that the general government deficit should not only be improved and later balanced in 2010 and 2011 with a deficit below 3% of GDP, but also that this should be achieved in a manner which is sustainable over the long term. On the one hand, this called for immediate fiscal consolidation, while the expansion of employment had to be constantly supported by boosting the motivation for employment and job creation, and the unemployment rate had to be steadily reduced.

Due to the characteristics of the Hungarian labour market, however, this was not feasible under the previous tax regime. The tax reform was launched at a time when the employment rate was so low and the unemployment rate was so high that long-term sustainable economic balance could not have been achieved by the previous tax system with its proportions of taxation. In the political term between 2010 and 2014, it was unrealistic to expect 1 million new jobs to be created, by virtue of which the fiscal balance would have automatically moved onto a sustainable path. Therefore, the tax reform also endeavoured to incorporate a fast-acting "sustainability" model into the revenue structure: the share of indirect taxes was increased further, while taxes on income were cut. The reason for this was that the income generated in the hidden economy (avoiding taxation) could also be taxed through consumption. Another advantage of indirect taxes is that they do not distort the saving and investment decisions of economic actors, and they usually entail relatively low administrative costs, as a result of which they are less detrimental to economic growth. However, indirect taxes increase inflation in the first year when they are introduced and when they are raised – which has an adverse effect on consumption and investment in such years – but in the following years, they do not affect growth dynamics, yet they continue to generate the extra revenue to improve balance[37] (Figure 137).

Although in international comparison, the revenue from consumption taxes was high in the inherited tax system, this was further increased by the tax reform which aimed to tackle the extensive hidden economy and the low employment rate. Hungary could not be expected to reach the average employment rate of the EU, i.e. 65%, in four years. Accordingly, higher tax revenues generated from the new income from the new jobs

[37] For the distorting and growth-related effects of the various types of taxes, see OECD (2009).

could also not be anticipated, and thus the new budgetary revenues for the general government had to be collected from the expansion of consumption and turnover.

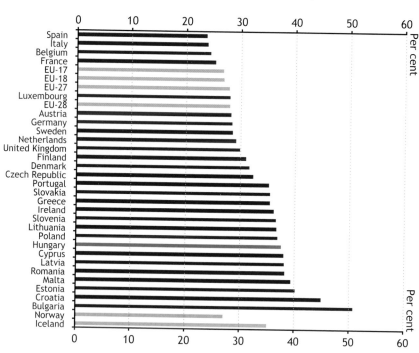

Figure 137. Ratio of consumption tax revenue
to total tax revenue in 2009 (in %)

Source: Eurostat

The tax reform also aimed to promote investments, since new investments create new jobs, which in turn contribute to sustainable fiscal balance: this was to be fostered by the various tax allowances granted to investors, the 10% corporate income tax and the introduction of the small-business tax scheme.

The tax system also endeavoured to expand the tax bases, since in the inherited tax system, due to the extensive hidden economy and various tax exemptions, the tax bases – as the revenue sources for the different tax types – were narrower than possible.

Finally, the tax reform also expressly sought to take a step towards the "most modern" ecotaxes: this was the rationale behind the various sector-specific taxes linked to the environment and the supply of healthier food.

Additionally, the Hungarian tax reform also had an implicit intention which was not linked to economic policy: to transform public thinking. On the one hand, the government expected people to accept that among the economically active population the income for living should be earned through employment. On the other hand, it was expected to be acknowledged that during employment, extra efforts should produce proportionately higher net income. In Hungary in the decades after 1990, higher-than-average income and wealth was deemed suspicious by the state, and aroused aversion and jealousy in society. This public attitude, which entrenched itself during the decades of the socialist era, is an impediment in and of itself to sustainable fiscal balance, and to the economic policy path based on sustained economic growth and high employment rates. It is an impediment because it hinders, in a concealed manner, investment and consumption, the acquisition of knowledge for earning higher income, and wealth accumulation.

The highly progressive taxation of income in Hungary, together with the system of generous budgetary transfers, undermined these values. Although it feigns fairness and claims that it serves the purpose of making the internal income distribution in society more proportionate, in fact progressive taxation does not appreciate the accumulation of capital by individuals and households through earning additional income – be it entrepreneurial or labour income – and it perpetuates the disconnection from the labour market. Since the second half of the 20th century, the lack of appreciation for the accumulation of capital by society has clearly been the greatest obstacle in the field of human capital, i.e. knowledge accumulation: the progressive taxation of income primarily hampers the acquisition of new knowledge, thereby curbing investments by businesses and also restricting household investments.

According to labour market surveys, better expertise – which is measured by qualifications and degrees, and by how these can be utilised on the labour market – ensures higher income for the individual, the families and for the employee's workplace as well. Therefore, if a progressive tax regime levies higher taxes on higher income, it does not encourage knowledge accumulation for achieving higher income, but penalises it through the lack of appreciation for the time, money and effort invested into the process. The greatest advantage of a flat-rate tax system is that it eliminates this concealed hindrance from Hungarian society: the jealousy does not disappear, but it is mitigated by the positive motivation and feedback. In the 16% flat-rate family tax system, if someone earns twice as much as another employee because the former's knowledge capital is twice as large, that person does not pay four times as much personal income tax anymore, only twice as much, which strengthens the motivation for knowledge accumulation. If this becomes a widespread phenomenon, the entire society will re-assess their values: higher income and better knowledge will not provoke doubt, but command respect and appreciation in the majority of society.

Economic theory and past success stories from economic history clearly demonstrate that every economic success is ultimately underpinned by a society's value system and internal culture. If the culture of jealousy persists in a society, that in itself hinders the accumulation of capital, especially the build-up of knowledge capital, even though this is the only social factor that can interrupt, halt or even reverse an economy's convergence processes.

In the economic policy cycle of 2010–2014, the system of indirect taxes was overhauled as well: the reform centred around raising the standard rate of VAT. Economic policy also attempted to levy an even higher,

35% VAT rate on the consumption of luxury goods. However, this effort failed in the face of resistance from the European Union.

Impacts of the tax reform

The primary thrust of fiscal consolidation was therefore the tax reform, since over the short term, only considerably higher tax revenues could help to achieve successful consolidation. The expansion of employment started right at the onset of the cycle, and the economic-psychological effect of the structural reforms also appeared early on: labour market participants felt the change in government policies immediately. Although the adjustment to the new policies started, the budget was actually consolidated in 2010–2011 by the new tax revenues and the higher rates of previously existing taxes. Three main revenue sources played a major role in this: the sector-specific taxes, the higher revenues from indirect taxes and the transformation of the previously mandatory private pension fund system, i.e. the rise in contributions to the public pension system (for more on sector-specific taxes, cf. Figure 126).

The sector-specific taxes introduced within the framework of the Hungarian tax reform also underwent a peculiar evolution between 2010 and 2014. In 2010, the bank levy as well as the crisis taxes imposed on the three sectors operating with a high profit rate were introduced instantly, and they generated new revenues of almost 1.5% of GDP for the Hungarian general government, even in the first year already. In 2011, the Hungarian budget's revenues from sector-specific taxes diminished because banks could write off the share borne by credit institutions in the first phase of the foreign currency loan settlement – i.e. the introduction of early repayment at a fixed exchange rate – from the bank levy.[38] In a transitional year, the tax reform acknowledged

---

[38] Financial institutions were able to reduce their bank levy obligation for 2011 by 30% of the losses they incurred due to the fixed-rate early repayment scheme. They were entitled to request a refund from the Hungarian tax authority from 31 January 2012. Therefore, the tax allowance reduced the bank levy obligation for 2011, but the cash-based refund claims were settled in 2012.

that another economic segment, i.e. households were also in distress, and that the price of managing household indebtedness should be channelled through the sector-specific taxes. The revenues from these taxes – amounting to almost 1.5% of GDP in 2010 – contributed substantially to fiscal consolidation, and in 2011, the lost revenue from these taxes was offset by the private pension fund system reform launched in the meantime, which generated new budgetary revenues of HUF 360 billion annually.

In 2012, the full amount of the earlier bank levy facilitated consolidation, and telecommunications and accident taxes were added to the system of sector-specific taxes. The evolution of sector-specific taxes reached its peak in 2013, when the financial transaction tax was introduced, and thus the revenue from these taxes (totalling 2.25% of GDP) helped complete Hungarian fiscal consolidation. The utilities tax and the insurance tax were also sector-specific taxes first levied in 2013 that taxed revenues in domestic monopolies.

In addition to these taxes, the higher revenues from indirect taxes and the pension system reform – that generated HUF 300–400 billion in extra revenues for the Hungarian general government in 2010–2014 – constituted the revenue sources for fiscal consolidation. All three were necessary for a successful and sustainable general government revenue structure, because the budget would not have been able to raise this amount of new revenue from exports – due to the external economic upswing – or from domestic income that increased through the expansion of the domestic market.

The internal transformation of the tax system considerably lowered the inherited tax system's obstacles to employment and job creation. In the case of certain groups, the Hungarian tax wedge – which was extremely large compared to the international average and even the EU average, and which significantly hampered job creation and employment – shrank considerably between 2010 and 2011 (Figure 138).

The targeted tax allowances introduced for the old, the young and the unskilled ensured a lower-than-average tax wedge for these groups, and they exerted an especially marked effect. Similarly, the tax wedge for career-starters, pregnant women and those returning from unemployment was well below the average for 2014, and the same was true for the tax wedge of those rearing children. All of this together clearly shows that the most important goal of the Hungarian tax reform was met: the incentives for employment became stronger. During the consolidation and stabilisation period of 2010–2014, the Hungarian labour market was characterised by expanding employment and shrinking unemployment.

Thus, the tax reform fulfilled its purpose as it improved the motivation for employment and job creation.

Figure 138. Tax wedge in Hungary in 2014

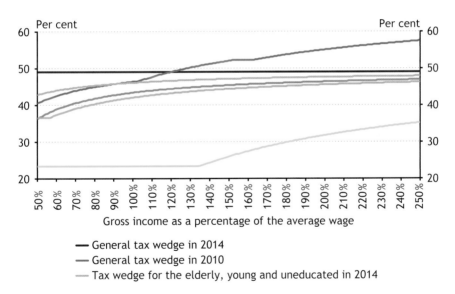

Gross income as a percentage of the average wage

— General tax wedge in 2014
— General tax wedge in 2010
— Tax wedge for the elderly, young and uneducated in 2014

Source: Csomós et al. (2014)

In the decade between 2004 and 2014, the tax reform fundamentally changed the structure of tax revenues in Hungary. Despite the ultimate failure of the second attempt at consolidation in 2008–2010 (without immediate fiscal consolidation the general government deficit would have exceeded 7% of GDP, instead of the planned 3.8%), the most important tool of the tax reform, i.e. the boosting of revenues from indirect taxes already started to take effect in that period. Similarly, taxes on labour as well as the weight or proportion of income tax and social security contributions to all tax revenues started to be reduced in 2008 (Figure 139).

Figure 139. Changes in the structure of tax revenues (2006-2012)

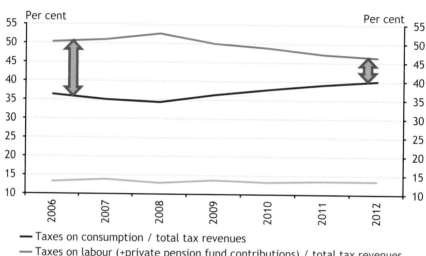

— Taxes on consumption / total tax revenues
— Taxes on labour (+private pension fund contributions) / total tax revenues
— Taxes on capital / total tax revenues

Mandatory private pension fund contributions were also taken into account in taxes on labour.

Source: Csomós et al. (2014)

Two periods were crucial for the Hungarian tax reform: the years between 2008 and 2010, and between 2010 and 2014. While the first phase did not bring about sustainable fiscal consolidation, the second did. The principal reason for this was that the adjustment of the proportions in the tax system in 2008–2010 were not coupled with a complete overhaul of economic policy. Had that been the case, the first steps in the transformation of the tax system and especially the tax structure would have coincided with a new policy of public tax sharing and measures for increasing employment and curbing unemployment. Although a hidden tax reform started in 2008–2010, it did not generate results over a 2 or 3-year time horizon because it was not launched in a new political and economic policy context. It remained stuck in the old system, trying to consolidate the budget through new tax revenues.

Between 2008 and 2010, the employment rate dropped and unemployment rose, i.e. despite the introduction of the tax reform, economic policy made sacrifices in growth and employment once again and did not manage to restore fiscal balance either. As a result of the tax reform that started in 2010, the proportion of the taxes on labour decreased significantly, and by 2012 it was similar to the share of indirect taxes. Consequently, the Hungarian general government collected almost the same amount of revenues from indirect taxes, which the hidden economy cannot avoid, as from taxes on labour. This was not only a quantitative but a qualitative change as well. By 2012, the motivation for employment and job creation among corporate sector actors reached such a high level, that in the second half of 2012 business decisions leading to a recovery in growth were taken, although at first this was not apparent.

While the attempt at tax reform in 2008–2010, lacking the political and economic policy measures to support it, entailed losses in growth and employment and did not manage to consolidate the budget by 2010, the next phase of the tax reform in 2010–2012, which lasted exactly as long, achieved this goal. The chief reasons for this were that the complete transformation of the tax system continued in a new political and economic policy context, the general government collected extra revenues through the new system of public burden sharing, and the pension reform established a sustainable public pension system. The former three-tiered pension system – which was composed of a public pension system, the mandatory private pension funds and the system of voluntary private pension funds – was in itself a major obstacle to long-term, successful, sustainable fiscal consolidation. The annual revenue losses of HUF 300–400 billion – which continued to rise – left a gaping hole in the Hungarian budget, which could have only been plugged over the long term by tax measures that would have entailed further sacrifices in employment and growth.

The decisive component of Hungarian crisis management in 2010–2014 was a comprehensive tax reform, which contributed to fiscal consolidation through new revenues, and at the same time strengthened the motivation for employment and job creation in the corporate sector. Thus, the new economic policy achieved fiscal consolidation without sacrifices in growth and employment. In fact, the tax reform clearly assisted the expansion of employment and the reduction of unemployment even in the short term, and therefore it was the most efficient Hungarian structural reform in terms of forging a new link in economic policy between the increase in employment and the recovery in growth on the one hand, and a genuinely sustainable fiscal balance on the other hand.

While Hungarian tax reform successfully contributed to fiscal consolidation and economic stabilisation, it also had a concealed effect: it started to quietly transform the value system of society. During the years of transition to the 16% flat-rate family taxation, there were constant public debates about the new system. It displayed the courage of the new government that it was open to the debate, despite the fact that this did not seem politically advantageous, although the tax system's economic policy benefits were obvious. It is characteristic of the new economic policy that it exclusively regards the new tax system from an efficiency perspective, not from a social solidarity one, because it does not aim to mitigate social inequalities through the tax system, but rather through education and work as well as other tools expressing community cohesion.

Reducing social inequality is the task of the welfare system, the internal solidarity of the members of society and social institutions, especially churches and local governments. If a moderately developed country with a low employment rate and a distorted labour market uses the system of income tax to address differences in income and wealth, it sacrifices economic efficiency for the sake of social solidarity, and this can only end in failure.

The Hungarian economy was able to succeed with its sustainable fiscal consolidation and the potentially sustained recovery in growth between 2010 and 2014 because it built its structural reforms around a comprehensive tax reform. This tax reform, in turn, focused on economic efficiency instead of social redistribution and solidarity.

Social impact of the tax reform

The most important social impact of the successful Hungarian tax reform was that political stability was maintained during fiscal consolidation and economic stabilisation. That is why structural reforms could be adopted that ensured sustainable balance and steady growth.

In the years after 2010, the social value system and public thinking have changed as well, although in a concealed manner, which is only discernible in indirect factors. Between 2010 and 2014, the thinking of the general public in Hungary was centred around work, which was designated as a central social objective by politics and the government. The creation of one million new jobs by 2020 is a true vision: it sets both a target and a deadline. The new government recognised that a large number of new jobs is required to restart economic convergence and get social advancement under way. Earlier, general public thinking did not concentrate on work, and some people believed that leading a lifestyle relying on social redistribution was tantamount to working.

Initially, it was only acknowledged that there was an economic rationale behind the reasoning that one million new jobs were necessary for a long-term, sustainable fiscal balance and steady economic growth.

This utility-based, rational approach later became widespread, and the social value system changed to a certain degree. However, this change only marked a return to the healthy, work-centred value system which had characterised Hungarian society for centuries.

It was precisely in 1990–2010 (again with the exception of the short period between 1998 and 2002) when the basic Hungarian value system was wrongly abandoned. The basic Hungarian values include the appreciation and respect for work, which is, strangely enough, not best reflected in the performance of the economy, but that of culture.

In international comparison, Hungarian society has created the greatest and most varied collection of folk art objects and culture in the past centuries. In some small villages in Transylvania, so much national wealth was generated over decades in the form of clothes, furniture and other works of folk art that it is on par with the village's economic output over many years. The treasure of Hungarian folk art attests that Hungarian society used to be heavily work-centred, even at times when there were not enough jobs on the local or national labour market. People used their free time for creating culture, and they replaced or supplemented local jobs and the low supply of available jobs on the labour market by generating cultural wealth (Kopátsy, 2000).

As a result of the tax reform, a breakthrough was achieved in managing the distortion of the labour market. The measures of the Job Protection Action Plan hinged on the economic realisation that the weaknesses of the Hungarian labour market were perpetuated by the low employability of certain groups of workers (Figure 140).

The low employment rate of the low-skilled, women and those over the age of 50 demonstrates that the large groups on the labour market cannot be incentivised for employment with the same tools. In the case of an employee with multiple degrees working at the Hungarian subsidiary of a global corporate group, and in the case of the workers who have not completed basic education and are only capable of physical work, the same tax system cannot be effective, especially if human labour is taxed equally. That is why the targeted tax allowances introduced as part of the Job Protection Action Plan represented a breakthrough in this field.

These allowances acknowledged the differences in the skills and circumstances of the actors on the labour market, thereby actively helping the preservation of existing jobs for those already in employment, and supporting the creation of new jobs for disadvantaged groups on the labour market. Another important feature of tax allowances is that they are not removed at higher income levels, and thus they do not increase the marginal tax wedge.

Figure 140. Number of employees receiving targeted social contribution allowance under the Job Protection Action Plan (2013-2014)

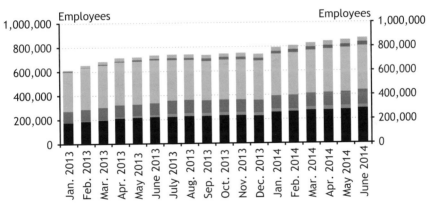

- Employees employed during or after the disbursement of maternity benefits
- Employees employed after a long period of job-seeking
- Employees above the age of 55 years
- Employees below the age of 25 years with more than 180 days of previous employment
- Employees below the age of 25 years with at most 180 days of previous employment

Source: NGM

The Hungarian tax reform in international context

Developed and developing countries actually started to transform the taxation of personal income in 1980, and moved towards a tax system centred more around indirect taxes. While in the 1970s, developed and developing countries reacted to the economic and social shocks of the two oil crises by strengthening the progressive nature of taxation, economic efficiency was later given priority over social redistribution.

Between 1980 and 2010, the progressive character of personal income tax more or less continuously decreased in both country groups (Figure 141).

Figure 141. Ratio of direct to indirect tax revenue

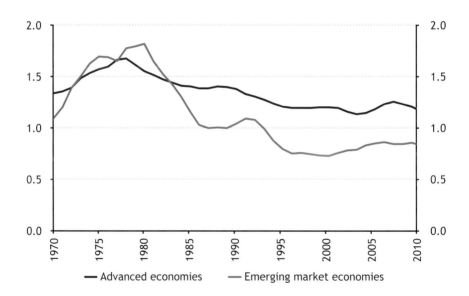

Source: IMF Fiscal Monitor October 2013 database

The Hungarian tax reform fits into this international trend, but it brought about a more significant turning point: with the introduction of the 16% flat-rate tax, the progressive quality of personal income taxation was abolished, and the lost budgetary revenues were offset by consumption taxes.

Similar to Hungary's regional competitors, all of whom pushed through radical tax reforms between 1990 and 2010, a comprehensive tax reform was implemented in Hungary in 2010–2014 that actually compensated for the static nature of taxation policy between 1990 and 2010. Due to the inaction of Hungarian economic policy, in the case of groups that are characterised by stronger ties to the labour market and a higher participation rate, the marginal tax wedge – which is vital in terms of work intensity, income concealment and strengthening the motivation for employment and job creation – lagged far behind its regional competitors until 2013 (Figure 142).

Figure 142. Marginal tax wedge for a single childless person at 100% of average earnings

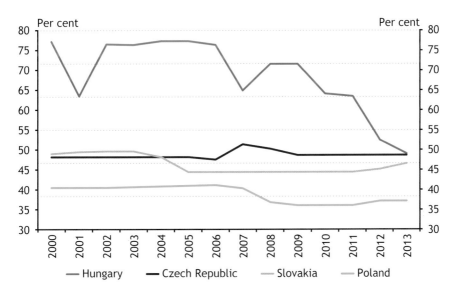

Source: OECD

The Hungarian economy was at an obvious competitive disadvantage against its regional competitors in terms of the tax system due to the high marginal tax wedge, i.e. because income for additional work was burdened with a far higher tax rate than by the competitors.

Among the members of the European Union, the Hungarian tax reform initiated in 2008 and completed in 2010 brought a clear competitive advantage. While in 1995–2008 a clear and steady shrinking trend of the PIT rates in the highest brackets was observable, between 2009 and 2014 – on account of the 2008 crisis – the average rates in the highest personal income tax brackets increased not only across all EU countries, but in the developed EU member states as well (Figure 143).

Figure 143. Development of the maximum statutory personal
income tax rate (2000-2013)

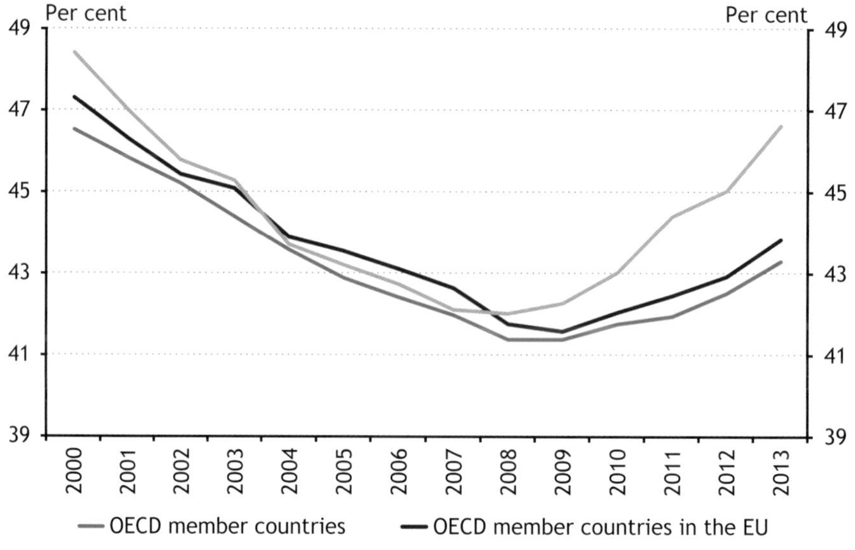

— OECD member countries   — OECD member countries in the EU

Source: OECD Tax Database   *Simple averages*

The highest tax rate rose especially strongly in the developed EU members, i.e. they gave wrong answers to the crisis in terms of their tax systems, and especially the progressive nature of personal income taxation. They repeated the mistake of the 1970s, when developed countries also increased the progressive character of the PIT system. When battered by the waves of crisis in 2008–2014, just like in the 1970s, they introduced social solidarity measures in a situation that should have been improved in terms of economic efficiency: they gave priority to social redistribution over economic efficiency. As a direct consequence, the employment rate dropped and the unemployment rate rose in the European Union. Meanwhile in Hungary, the progressive taxation of personal income tax was abandoned, and in fact, the 16% rate is one of the lowest in the European Union.

Thus, Hungary has gained a competitive advantage against the other EU member states – and also compared to its regional competitors – in one of the most important fields of the tax system, personal income taxation.

It is interesting to compare the Hungarian tax system that was shaped by the tax reform, and the system used in countries on the southern flank of the euro area.

The Hungarian tax system gradually decreased tax centralisation from approximately 40% in 2009 to 37% in 2011. From 2011, tax centralisation climbed slightly, and in the crucial year of fiscal consolidation, 2012, it was close to 39%, but it did not reach its baseline level of 40%, measured in 2009. According to the forecast of the European Commission, the Hungarian tax burden will fall again in 2015 to 38%, i.e. between 2009 and 2015 it will have actually fluctuated around 38%. By contrast, although the level of tax centralisation in Greece, Portugal and Spain was very low when the crisis erupted, with the exception of Spain – where it is projected to be around 34% in 2015 – it has almost reached the Hungarian level. Of the southern euro area countries, the Italian tax burden shows a different picture, however, their level of tax centralisation is characteristic of the developed countries in the European Union. Actually, Italy reacted to the crisis by increasing the tax burden (Figure 144).

Nonetheless, the truly intriguing phenomenon is that the countries hit by the euro area crisis after the 2008 global financial crisis, with the exception of Italy – i.e. the Greek, the Portuguese and the Spanish economies – maintain tax collection levels even lower than in Hungary. In fact, the southern countries of the euro area did not use tax reform in their attempts at fiscal consolidation, and they failed in their endeavours to consolidate public finances. With the exception of Italy, all of these countries ran a fiscal deficit higher than 3% of GDP after 2008. In the years when Hungary successfully consolidated its budget, i.e. between 2010 and 2012, these countries were not able to do so.

The main reason for this was that they sought to consolidate their budget without a tax reform.

Figure 144. Tax centralisation in Hungary and the Club Med countries

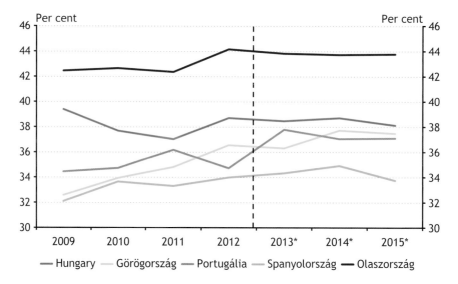

Source: European Commission, AMECO database   ** estimate*

An even more profound reason for their failure was that they did not utilise the revenues from raising indirect taxes. Compared to the Hungarian consumption taxes, tax rates are lower in all euro area member states, especially in the southern countries. In these countries, governments did not want to burden low-skilled and low-income social groups with higher indirect taxes, and did not see the economic link between fiscal consolidation and new revenue sources, especially the higher revenues from indirect taxes.

It is similarly interesting to compare the southern euro area countries with the four Visegrád economies as regards tax burden (Figure 145).

Figure 145. Tax burden as a percentage of GDP

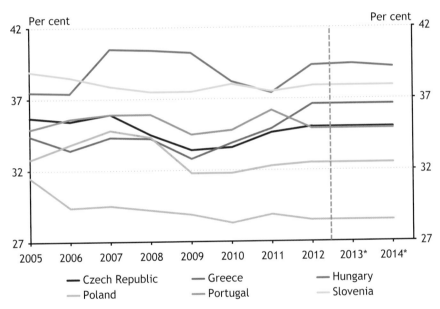

Source: Eurostat   * *estimate*

It can be seen that after the crisis, the tax revenues of the Greek budget in GDP terms sank to the level of Polish tax centralisation, which was not a result of tax cuts but of soaring unemployment and nosediving employment. The misguided and failed Greek crisis management entailed sacrifices in growth and employment, and thus budgetary revenues and the level of tax centralisation plummeted. During the years of the botched crisis management, the Greek economy was characterised by an unsustainably high budget deficit and rising government debt. Meanwhile, not even economists debated the fact that with a full-scale tax reform, especially by increasing the weight of indirect taxes, the budget could be consolidated. The comparison of the Visegrád countries and the countries on the southern flank of the euro area from the perspective of tax burden provides a clear lesson: while the former group of economies operate with a budget deficit of approximately 3% of GDP and a government debt-to-GDP ratio of 60%, the latter group faces a budget deficit well over 3% and constantly rising government debt, even though the level of tax centralisation is similar in the two groups.

From the perspective of the tax burden, Hungary outperformed both groups because it successfully consolidated its budget and stabilised its economy between 2010 and 2014, while managing to decrease tax centralisation (as early as 2010). It came close to reaching the level of the tax burden in the Visegrád countries, i.e. its regional peers – with the exception of the significantly lower Slovak tax burden – while at the same time putting an end to the rise in government debt and even slightly reducing it, and bringing down the budget deficit to a sustainable level of less than 3%. All of this was possible because of the comprehensive Hungarian tax reform, which, in addition to reducing tax centralisation, introduced substantial new budgetary revenue sources in the form of sector-specific taxes as well as the new indirect taxes on consumption. Meanwhile, it resulted in a turning point in the tax structure in 2012, when the revenue collected from indirect taxes almost equalled revenue from income taxation.

Chapter 12

Foreign currency lending crisis in Hungary

The roots of the household foreign currency lending crisis between 2010 and 2014 stretch back to the change of government in 2002. There was a negative economic policy shift in Hungary in mid-2002, as fiscal balance deteriorated, and the need for budget reform emerged in 2003. The government was reluctant to implement fiscal consolidation in the year before EU accession, and the central bank pushed through some monetary intervention instead, endeavouring to counter the government's overspending with a double-digit base rate of interest. In theory, the double-digit interest rate should have restrained budget spending because it made budget financing more expensive, which resulted in a negative spiral for the budget deficit and government debt.

This prompted the budget to break away from its previous trend of gradually reducing the ratio of foreign currency debt within government debt. Instead, at first the government stopped the downtrend, and then from 2005 it began to increase the ratio of foreign currency debt, replacing the more expensive forint financing with cheaper, foreign currency financing that seemed more affordable. Financing the budget in foreign currency was significantly cheaper than in forints because by 2003, the short and relatively mild global recession of the previous years had given way to an economic upswing, while the increasingly expansive monetary policies of the large central banks resulted in an unusually ample supply of liquidity on the global markets, including the European capital markets. The abundance of funds on the global capital markets, which both stemmed from and was the reason for the global economic upturn, facilitated the seemingly cheap spending by the government. The price ultimately paid though, was higher in every respect. Hungary began to take on more debt again (Figure 146).

Figure 146. Share of FX debt in general government debt in Hungary, 1998-2012

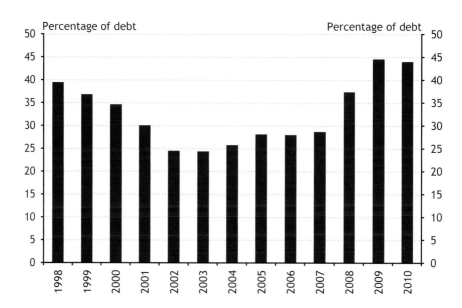

Source: Eurostat

The process snowballed, moving at an increasingly fast pace. Between 1998 and 2002 when the foreign currency ratio was reduced, new debt was essentially financed only in forints, but there were also cases of maturing foreign currency debt being replaced with forint funds. This trend reversed in the second period between 2002 and 2010, when the budget covered part of the deficit and some maturing forint debt with the issuance of new foreign currency debt.

The new debt accumulated in Hungary between 2002 and 2010 not only meant that Hungarian government debt relative to GDP rose from 53% of GDP in mid-2002 to 85.3% of GDP in mid-2010 – in itself a dramatic amount of new debt – but also that the ratio of foreign currency debt within this government debt increased from 25% in 2002 to 44% by 2010. Consequently, not only the much higher level of government debt relative to GDP generated a much higher risk for Hungary than before, but also the vulnerability of this debt owing to the elevated share of foreign currency debt.

The period between 2002 and 2008 was broadly characterised by expansive economic conditions at the global level and ample liquidity. Financing with foreign currency seemed to be a cheap, safe option, but as mentioned above, this was a very unique and exceptional period of economic history over the last 160 years: one could hardly expect it to last forever, and moreover, specific preparations should have been made for when riskier times and crises sooner or later returned to the global economy and the capital markets (Figure 78.)

This is exactly what happened from 2007 to 2008: a new situation emerged over the year from September 2007 in the run-up to the eruption of the global financial crisis in autumn 2008. The new indebtedness trend in Hungary was the result of the irresponsible economic policy which tipped the fiscal balance in 2002 and then constantly tolerated high fiscal deficits, negligently ignoring the risk of foreign currency debt which was chosen as the solution.

By tolerating the high budget deficits, the state and economic policymakers sent a signal to agents in the economy: feel free to take on debt. The signal from the government's economic policy that this debt could be taken out in foreign currency as opposed to the national currency entailed an even greater risk. And that was not all: the state and economic policymakers not only indicated that taking on foreign currency debt was an option, they expressly supported borrowing in foreign currency instead of forints. Taking a look at the global economy and EU member states, in comparison to Hungary, one finds few examples of countries in which, between 2002 and 2010, economic agents – the state, businesses and households alike – switched to such an extent from borrowing in the national currency to taking on debt in foreign currency, with all the added exchange rate risks. It was also rare in the global economy and in European Union economies for economic policymakers to allow indebtedness to reach such a significant and increasing level in a currency other than the national currency.

The Hungarian state had a wide range of instruments at its disposal to restrain and curb borrowing by households and enterprises in foreign currency once it started. Despite this, the central bank did nothing to limit foreign currency borrowing. Between 2002 and 2010, the government and particularly the Ministry of Finance took no action with a view to limiting and stopping households and enterprises taking on debt in foreign currency. It still could have done this, even though it had found a path for itself which seemed to offer a solution, but was in fact a dead-end, namely raising the ratio of foreign currency debt within government debt.

Why did no public institution, i.e. the government, the supervisory authority or the Magyar Nemzeti Bank, intervene against households and the business sector taking on debt in foreign currency? Once again, the answer can be found in the flawed economic policy. The misguided turn in economic policy in 2002 immediately upset economic balance in the same year, and in the period to 2010 the Hungarian budget deficit exceeded the sustainable level in every single year. The government should have immediately deployed a fiscal adjustment policy to restore the balance upset by the flawed economic policy, but this would have entailed growth and job losses according to the economic policy thinking between 1990 and 1998. Even the successful economic policy pursued in 1998–2002 suggested that growth coupled with higher employment is only possible if economic balance improves.

In fact, between 1998 and 2002, government debt relative to GDP declined, economic growth was durable and dynamic, while employment rose, all at the same time. From mid-2002, this led economic policymakers to draw the conclusion that if the imbalance was treated with a fiscal adjustment programme, Hungary's economy would head towards an unwanted financial crisis in the year prior to EU accession and in 2004, instead of being a success story ready for accession. Thus, according to the old economic theory and policy, budget consolidation would have triggered an immediate crisis as early as 2003–2004.

Economic policymakers actually made no attempt to redress the balance in 2003–2004, because the growth and employment cost of this would have jeopardised EU accession: both the referendum and the EU membership process. Moreover, the other acceding countries were clearly enjoying an economic upswing in the years preceding accession on 1 May 2004 and in the years thereafter. As with previous EU accession rounds, inbound foreign direct investment increased in the 2–3 years before accession, new capital market sources became available, and households and enterprises increased their spending as EU accession pushed confidence and sentiment indicators up. Economic policy did not wish to curtail this progress and found a way out for all the agents in the national economy; this is what led to the rise in new debt and the rise in foreign currency lending.

Figure 147. Open FX balance sheet position of the private sector and net external debt

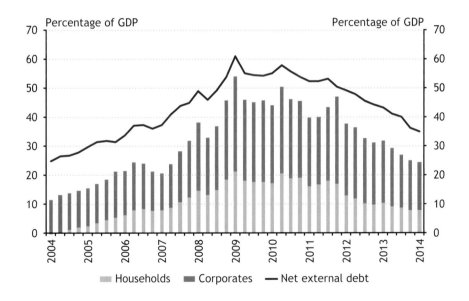

Source: MNB   *Data prepared using BPM6 methodology from 2013 Q1*

Households and families built up an increasing portfolio of foreign currency loans after 2004, in particular via real estate investments.

The corporate sector accumulated an even larger stock of foreign currency loans, while non-residents took on a high level of exchange rate risk between 2004 and 2007, which then decreased until 2010. This stood in contrast to the state, which steadily raised its proportion of foreign currency in government debt. Since all of the economic agents – the state, households and the corporate sector – took part in building up the stock of foreign currency loans, Hungary's net external debt between 2004 and 2009 rose significantly and continuously (Figure 147).

The rise in households' foreign currency lending impaired the country's external vulnerability in various ways. In addition to households' strong demand for loans, the elimination of the liquidity constraints and the low foreign currency interest rates facilitated a much higher level of borrowing. All of this resulted in consumption growth that exceeded income growth, which exerted a negative impact on the trade balance. The unprecedented level of borrowing had an adverse impact on households' net financial savings, furthermore this burdened the economy at a time when the budget was steadily accumulating massive deficits.

Owing to the high net borrowing which was partly attributable to high consumption, Hungary was still heavily dependent on external sources of finance, but the method chosen created new risks for the Hungarian economy. In contrast to the FDI financing that was common in the early 2000s and in parallel to the expanding foreign currency lending, the country relied increasingly on debt financing instruments, which came with significant renewal and interest risks. One of the factors behind this was that banks partly resorted to foreign loans to raise the funds needed to provide households with foreign currency loans. Another key factor in the process that significantly worsened the country's external vulnerability was the particularly high ratio of foreign-owned banks in

Hungary, which found it easy to channel cheap foreign currency funds from their parent banks to Hungarian households (Figure 148).

Figure 148. Structure of external financing

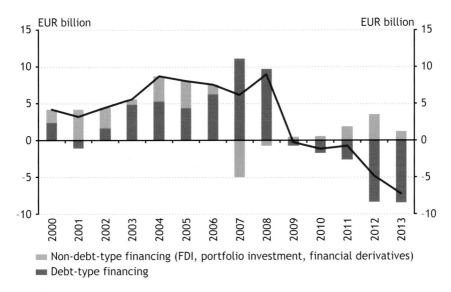

Non-debt-type financing (FDI, portfolio investment, financial derivatives)
Debt-type financing

Source: MNB

Starting from 2009, balance sheet adjustments in the household and corporate sector began, with financial institutions following suit in the background. This was primarily what triggered the fall in Hungary's net foreign debt, but the exchange rate risk on foreign currency loans previously taken out by households and the state materialised: as the exchange rate weakened, these foreign currency loans became an increasing burden for the budget and families. Even with contracting net external debt, Hungary's financial risk rose because the two main agents in the economy, the state budget and households, faced rising repayment instalments expressed in forints.

The damage caused by the flawed economic policy could have been mitigated if the accumulation of foreign currency loans had been stopped from September 2006 with the first attempt to rectify Hungary's economic balance. The government made a political decision in mid-2002 when it triggered a negative shift in economic policy, and likewise when it permitted an artificial economic upswing in the Hungarian economy in the years prior to EU accession on 1 May 2004 that was built on debt, and particularly high-risk foreign currency debt.

A similar political decision was made in the period after accession as no consolidation policy was adopted either in 2004 or in the year after accession to restore the balance.

It later transpired that in order to win the 2006 elections the governing political party decided not to launch a new economic policy before the elections, as this would have come at the cost of growth and employment sacrifices and involved admitting to the previously flawed economic approach. Reducing the budget deficit began only from 1 September 2006, during the first attempt to restore economic balance, which ultimately failed because it was not aligned with a comprehensive change of economic policy for the better. The government returned to its flawed post-1990 economic policy of "balance or growth", and failed to incorporate the third element of raising employment and reducing unemployment.

Even under the old economic policy it would have been possible to stop the accumulation of households' foreign currency loans. This could have been incorporated into the logic of the first programme to restore economic balance between 2006 and 2008, but it did not happen. There was another significant increase in foreign currency lending between 2006 and 2008 in particular, both for households and enterprises: lending in foreign currencies should have been terminated immediately for the former from 1 September 2006. This would have stalled the pace of consumption, which was constrained and reversed anyway by the austerity package, and putting an end to households' foreign currency lending would in all likelihood have triggered an immediate recession in the Hungarian economy. Although this happened slowly, step-by-step during the first consolidation attempt between 2006 and 2008, the recession would certainly have been deeper if households' foreign currency lending had been stopped: despite this, the economic policymakers back then should have made such a decision as a matter of obligation.

Moving along the economic history timeline, however, the decision to ban foreign currency lending to households should finally have been taken during the second attempt to restore economic balance between 2008 and 2010. The reason for this is simple: the US financial crisis in 2007–2008 culminated in a global financial crisis in autumn 2008, and the currencies that became safe havens were the very currencies that the Hungarian economy was indebted in. The Swiss franc naturally became a safe-haven currency compared to other national currencies during a financial crisis. This could have been assumed between 2002 and 2008 as well because financial crises do not disappear forever, and crisis was already a fact in autumn 2008.

The deterioration in economic balance caused by the flawed economic policy led to growth and employment losses between 2008 and 2010 while ensuring that the financial crisis persisted for one of the key agents in the private sector: families. In striving to handle the public finance crisis and trying to reach the targeted budget deficit as per the IMF–EU agreement based on austerity measures, the foundations for a lengthy financial crisis were laid for other two economic agents: enterprises and households, but particularly for the latter.

The crisis dragged on in the European Union and the years after 2008 were characterised by an economic downturn, preserving the Swiss franc's role as a safe-haven currency, the vulnerability of the Hungarian national currency and the exchange rate risk of the Hungarian economy. Under such circumstances it should have been compulsory to reorganise the structure of government debt as well as the borrowing structure for enterprises and especially households: channelling borrowings from foreign currency to forints. This should have been compulsory even if it came hand-in-hand with further consumption and investment sacrifices, because economic policy should not strive towards achieving a simple improvement in balance, but instead target the long-term sustainability of such.

During the second attempt to restore economic balance in 2008–2010, economic policy did not target a balanced state of public finances, and instead aimed for the impossible: improving the state budget without a new recession. Why did economic policy not try to lay the foundations for a sustainable, balanced Hungarian budget between 2008 and 2010?

Once more, the explanation is a political decision: elections were held in Hungary in 2010. Not all economic agents have a vote: the state and enterprises do not, but households and their family members do. While families were under increasing pressure from their Swiss franc debt, which accounted for the majority of the debt in foreign currencies, economic policy suggested that the situation was only temporary. But that was not the case. The severe, prolonged nature of the situation should have been acknowledged by immediately stopping household lending in Swiss francs, euros and the yen.

Previous debts taken on in Swiss francs were increasingly a problem for families, because the Swiss franc exchange rate had markedly appreciated versus the forint, which meant the net salaries of Hungarian workers expressed in Swiss francs declined sharply.

While net salaries expressed in Swiss francs totalled CHF 800 in 2008 based on a relatively weak Swiss franc exchange rate, the same Hungarian net salaries in 2009–2010 amounted to merely CHF 680–690 expressed in Swiss francs, as the forint had depreciated considerably against the stronger Swiss franc in the meantime (Figure 149).

Figure 149. Development of monthly net average wages in Hungary, in CHF

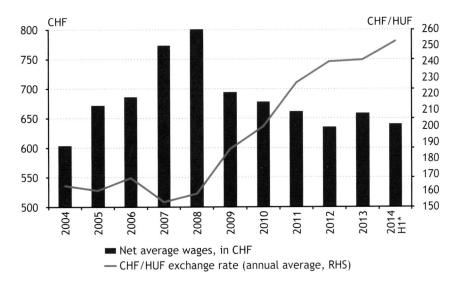

Net average wages, in CHF

CHF/HUF exchange rate (annual average, RHS)

Source: HCSO, MNB   ** excluding family tax benefit*

The Hungarian net salaries calculated in Swiss francs are based on changes in the exchange rate and wage increases: Hungarian net salaries calculated in Swiss francs fell by 20% after 2008, initially sparking a latent and then a fully open foreign currency loan crisis for households. The reason for this was that the roughly one million households with foreign currency loans saw their repayment instalments rise by this amount. The additional income derived from wage increases would have compensated for the additional burden on families up to an exchange rate of roughly CHF/HUF 200, assuming an average rate of CHF/HUF 160 when the loan was disbursed.

In mid-2010, the new government immediately put a stop to household foreign currency lending, prohibiting credit institutions from disbursing loans to private individuals in foreign currencies. Households' outstanding foreign currency loans began to decline from 2010, facilitated by government measures: the early repayment scheme, the exchange rate cap system, the new measures from 2014 to reduce household foreign currency loans, and finally the conversion into forints of the entire household foreign currency loan portfolio. Although this process began from mid-2010, Hungary still had the highest level of household foreign currency debt in the middle of 2014, with the exception of Romania. While almost 63% of the entire outstanding loans of Romanian households was in foreign currency (most of which was euro loans), the corresponding figure for Hungarian households was 56%; by contrast, barely any foreign currency loans can be found at Czech households. In Slovakia there was no such demand even before the introduction of the euro, while the debts accumulated by Polish and Bulgarian households in foreign currency were significantly smaller than in Romania and Hungary.

The extremely high ratio of non-performing loans among Hungarian households is a logical conclusion of this, while the government's decisions targeting the winding-up of foreign currency loans resulted in a low profit margin for the credit institution sector (Table 5).

Table 5. Indicators of banking sectors in regional comparison

	Ratio of FX loans in the household sector** (July 2014)	Ratio of non-performing loans* (2013 Q4)	Credit/ deposit ratio	ROE (2013 Q4)
Hungary	56.0	14.0	106.9	-0.4
Czech Republic	0.1	5.2	77.9	11.4
Poland	30.5	6.0	106.4	10.0
Slovakia	0.0	3.8	95.6	10.0
Romania	62.7	17.9	100.6	0.0
Bulgaria	36.9	18.6	97.9	4.4

Source: MNB, ECB, IMF   * September 2013 data for Czech Republic
                               ** June 2014 data for Czech Republic

The increase in foreign currency loans among Hungarian households was a very complex phenomenon: alongside the state, both credit institutions and families made irresponsible decisions between 2002 and 2010. We have already seen the state's irresponsible role and the underlying motives, as the response of the flawed economic policy was to shift the structure of government debt towards foreign currency debt. This irresponsible approach was only made worse by the government failing to stop household foreign currency lending during the two unsuccessful consolidation attempts between 2006 and 2010, due to the predictable growth and employment sacrifices: attempts were made to rectify the errors of the previous economic policy using adjustment tools that were also flawed. Credit institutions were irresponsible with their lending too, as they did not responsibly review the wages and income behind loan applications, ratios of debt to equity which were acceptable within the framework of prudent lending were skewed towards loans, and borrowers were consistently presented to be in a better position than they were after the 2008 financial crisis, based on their declining net salaries expressed in Swiss francs.

Families were at fault too with the rise in foreign currency loans, because they did not take the exchange rate risk into account and were not prepared with regard to the conditions accepted upon drawing the loan either. As it transpired during the legal resolution in autumn 2014, only rarely did the foreign currency loan contracts comply with the criteria of prudent lending, transparency and fairness.

Yet these pitfalls were not just apparent afterwards, they were clear upon borrowing the money too, and yet households did not consider the conditions of unfair borrowing thoroughly enough.

The behaviour of all three agents – the government, credit institutions and households – which were instrumental in households' foreign currency loans growing to become one of the greatest risks in Hungarian economic history had the same effect: a rising volume of debt in foreign currencies with no regard for the consequences. However, there were different motives behind this concerted behaviour.

The state and government policy were playing for survival, since they wanted to lessen the price of the two consolidation programmes between 2006 and 2010 by maintaining the growth of household borrowings: under the given financial conditions, however, this meant pushing families towards foreign currency debt.

Credit institutions were clearly motivated by trying to maximise their profit, using cheap foreign funds to build up an increasing stock of loans among Hungarian households, exploiting the price difference between the foreign currency and the national currency, i.e. the interest margin.

The motive of families was also clear: they took out foreign currency loans to increase their wealth and improve their standards of living, and chose what seemed to be the cheapest source to do so. The behaviour of Hungarian households was actually derived from Hungarian societal values. Hungarian values are quite special within the European and even global system of values because individual values are very strong in Hungary, similar to Anglo-Saxon societies. Hungary is the world's fifth most individual society, preceded in the ranking by four Anglo-Saxon countries, where the values and interests of individual success are even stronger. Within value frameworks for the individual, the accumulation of wealth by the individual and the family precedes everything: in societies living by these values it is not the risks but the opportunities that families consider, and if there is a chance to accumulate wealth quickly with seemingly acceptable conditions, they take it.

The individual Hungarian values attached to the accumulation of wealth by individuals and families were strengthened by the Hungarian real estate market undergoing a crisis in the 1990s, as the number of new home constructions had fallen to roughly one fifth by the end of the decade. In 2000, the new housing programme of the first Orbán government was launched, which boosted the volume of forint real estate loans in the Hungarian financial system. If this housing system based on forint loans had been maintained from 2002 to 2010 then there would not have been the same increase in household foreign currency loans. It was probably so easy to lead households down the foreign currency loan path because there is a very strong wealth accumulation value at play, and because neither the state actors nor the financial system agents warned the borrowers about the risks. Thus, living in a system of values where people are open to opportunities and take minimal account of the risks, Hungarian households opted *en masse* for drawing foreign currency loans, a decision that ultimately proved to be dramatically flawed.

Hungary essentially experienced the same situation as the US property market, on a smaller scale but with similarly dramatic consequences: households in the USA accumulated debt in the national currency, the US dollar; the emergence and subsequent bursting of an artificial property market bubble caused the US and then global financial crisis in 2008. However, while governmental measures in autumn 2008 contributed to the bursting of the artificial US property market bubble, Hungarian economic policy failed to take any action until the middle of 2010: households' foreign currency lending was simply not stopped. This was the joint responsibility of the institutions acting on behalf of the Hungarian state and failing to make the decisions – the government and particularly the Ministry of Finance, the banking supervisory authority and the central bank – and shows the significant difference between the Hungarian situation and the US financial crisis.

There, the government and the banking system began to treat the causes of the financial crisis when it erupted, i.e. the artificial property bubble and the irresponsible financial lending.

By contrast, in the almost two years after the crisis erupted neither the government nor any other state body nor the banking system took the responsibility for the previously flawed conduct. This two-year delay played a significant role in the household foreign currency loan problem remaining the most significant economic policy risk between 2010 and 2014, during the ultimately successful period of budget consolidation and economic stabilisation.

Foreign currency loans - price of delayed action

We saw that the renewed increase in Hungarian debt began from 2003, particularly the rise in foreign currency loans among all three economic actors. For households this should have been stopped right at the start, as the state bodies did in Poland and Austria. This was not implemented between 2002 and 2006, i.e. during the first political cycle of the flawed economic policy. The second opportunity would have been 1 September 2006, when the first consolidation programme was launched: immediately tightening the conditions for foreign currency lending to households should have been a mandatory element at that point.

The third chance came in autumn 2008: under the IMF-EU agreement the creditor and the beneficiary (Hungarian government) should have included the immediate termination of households' foreign currency loans under the second consolidation programme. Again, this failed to happen. Finally, in the middle of 2010, one of the first measures taken by the new government was the de facto ban in lending to households in foreign currency, which also signalled the start of the reduction in household foreign currency loans over several years.

Hungary paid a significant price for this: the lengthy period raised this price, while all of those involved in the flawed foreign currency lending had to pay their part of the foreign currency loan crisis. The state paid for the initially hidden and then obvious household foreign currency loan crisis with a prolonged deterioration in economic balance between 2002 and 2010.

Budget revenues declined, and therefore the weaker domestic consumption derived from the increase in household foreign currency loans and the changes in exchange rates and interest rates upset the budget balance.

Economic policy also paid in terms of investments. Hungary's investment rate started to decline from the second quarter of 2005, which was partly influenced by economic actors bringing future investments forward in many areas during the artificial economic upturn after 2002: both the corporate sector on the market for commercial real estate and households setting up homes brought medium and long-term investments forward. The investment rate fell in subsequent years on account of the investments completed early. This was characteristic of the entire period between 2002 and 2010: investments were brought forward by the population mostly from 2002 to 2007, while the corporate sector pushed forward with commercial real estate investments in the years after EU accession.

The flawed economic policy and the poor business policy of credit institutions were costly for the banking sector too, as the ratio of non-performing loans deteriorated steadily and significantly among foreign currency loans. From 2007 onwards, the ratio of non-performing loans to total loans in the banking sector skyrocketed, increasing roughly eight-fold. This was partly due to the deteriorating portfolio of foreign currency loans, which in turn can be explained by the worsening household income situation caused by exchange rate and interest changes (Figure 150).

It is clear that the surge in non-performing loans in the Hungarian banking sector between 2007 and 2013 was unparalleled among regional countries, which was a direct consequence of the Hungarian banking system having the highest ratio of foreign currency loans to total loans in the entire region. Slovakia already had the euro, Poland banned the disbursement of foreign currency loans to households, and the low domestic interest rate in the Czech Republic meant that foreign currency debt was not a competitive alternative.

Thus, Hungary was the only one of the Visegrád countries to accumulate such a level and degree of foreign currency lending within the entire portfolio of banking sector loans, which resulted in a marked deterioration in the loan portfolios after the onset of the global financial crisis. The surge in non-performing loans in the Hungarian banking system is almost identical to the deterioration in loans observed in other crisis EU countries.

Figure 150. Ratio of non-performing loans to total outstanding loans and changes therein in certain countries

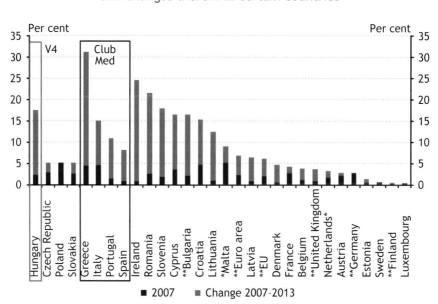

Source: IMF, FSI   *Between 2007–2013; * 2008 data; ** 2012 data*

While Hungary was the only country in the region which experienced a such a large-scale increase in the ratio of non-performing loans to total loans in the banking sector, similar deterioration was observed in the euro area members Greece, Ireland, Italy, Portugal and Cyprus. This

"southern" phenomenon was also characteristic of the Baltic states –
with the exception of Estonia – and of the credit institution systems in
Romania and Bulgaria. However, deterioration in the quality of loan
portfolios, i.e. sharp increases in NPL ratios, were not typical in the
developed economies: Finland, Sweden, Austria, Belgium, Germany,
Holland and the other developed economies did not experience the
same decline in portfolio quality as the Hungarian banking system, nor
did the euro area as a whole.

While the average loan portfolio deterioration – i.e. the rapid increase
in non-performing loans – was significant in the euro area and the
European Union as a whole (the non-performing loan ratio rose around
2 1/2-fold by 2013 compared to 2007 in both cases, i.e. compared to the
last "calm" year before the crisis), this still fell considerably short of the
plunge in quality seen with Hungarian loans.

Figure 151. Bank profitability (ROE) in international comparison

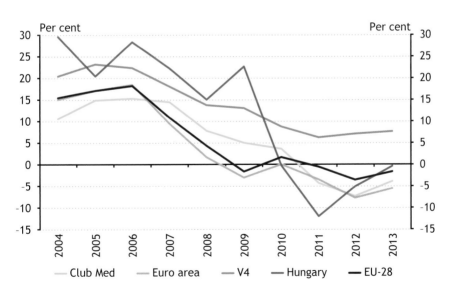

Source: MNB

The changes in Hungarian credit institutions' loan portfolio, i.e. the rocketing growth in the NPL ratio within total loans, caused a hidden financial crisis in the banking system. This hidden crisis emerged into the open in 2009, as the structural deterioration in the loan portfolio coupled with the financial and economic crisis after 2008 heavily impacted profits in the Hungarian banking system.

The earnings position of credit institutions in the Visegrád Four countries also deteriorated between 2007 and 2013, but only in the Hungarian banking system did it reverse the strongly positive figures deep into negative territory (Figure 151).

The southern euro area countries experienced a deterioration in their portfolios similar to the Hungarian banking system, and a resultant plunge in earnings, but after some delay: while the largest drop in profits for the Hungarian banking system was recorded between 2009 and 2011, this only occurred in 2010–2012 for the southern euro area states. The banking system's earnings position which was close to of the euro area and the EU average did not exhibit a similar degree of deterioration, though the profit ratio of the EU and the more developed euro area countries plummeted in 2008 from around 10% in 2007; however, apart from the second plunge in 2012, the average profit rates of the banking systems are still around zero.

The deterioration in the earnings position of the Hungarian banking system was far worse than in all other groups of EU countries and this was not just because the banking system's reaction only took short-term interests into account, but also because it was greedy: the participants in the Hungarian banking system earned high profit rates through high-risk projects financed by foreign currency lending, but particularly under the conditions of the artificial economic upturn.

The two are closely linked to each other: the profit rate of the Hungarian banking sector plummeted to the greatest extent within the whole of the European Union between 2009 and 2011 because it had previously been artificially high. It is no coincidence that the Hungarian budget consolidation programme launched in mid-2010 under the new system of public tax sharing imposed the highest bank levy of all EU member states, and was the first to do so. The reason for this was that the Hungarian banking system had disregarded the rules of prudent lending and disbursed loans without any constraints, returning to the basic inclinations of the financial system, i.e. motivated by greed. Although the bank levy of roughly HUF 180 billion per year reduced the banking system's profit rate between 2010 and 2014, another key factor was that this profit rate was previously maintained at an unacceptably high level artificially.

In fact, in autumn 2008, during the second consolidation attempt as part of the IMF-EU agreement, the Hungarian banking system's profit rate even rose higher compared to before. Instead of Hungarian economic policy involving the banking system in the fiscal consolidation, as was the case later on with the bank levy, it proceeded to create an even more favourable position during the IMF-EU agreement: foreign currency lending to households was not banned, and by far the highest profit rate throughout the European Union was accepted in the Hungarian banking sector during the crisis.

The trend of the Hungarian banking system's profit rate between 2007 and 2014 is very revealing. Two tendencies always characterise the financial system in every economy: greed for profit and an inclination for crisis. These are two sides of the same coin: when a bank or the entire banking system of an economy abandons responsible lending and prudent banking behaviour, the given bank or banking system of the economy immediately lurches towards a new financial crisis. This is why the state, and more specifically the state institutions supervising the banking system, the ministries of finance and the central banks, must constantly keep watch over prudent banking operations: if this does not happen, the basic inclinations of the financial system take over. There was no such vigilance in Hungary between 2002 and 2010, which enabled the two tendencies of the Hungarian financial system, and within this the Hungarian credit institution system, to take over: removing the constraints and abandoning the golden rules of prudent lending. This paved the way for the initially hidden and then open credit crisis in Hungary.

The abandonment of cautious lending practices in the Hungarian banking system between 2002 and 2010 also resulted in an open credit crisis in Hungary, albeit with some delay. When lending is growing, the quality deterioration of a given portfolio is not as noticeable, but as the portfolio matures and is exposed to external shocks, the costs of bank lending that disregarded the previously prudent lending rules suddenly surfaced, resulting in a rapid and substantial worsening of the loan portfolio quality.

In the case of the Hungarian banking sector, the delayed deterioration in the loan portfolio and the resultant decline in profitability are related to the postponed and delayed response from economic policy.

If the balance sheet adjustment process in the banking system had begun from 1 September 2006, i.e. with the first budget consolidation programme, then during the open crisis after 2008, i.e. after the global and euro area financial shocks, the financial loss to the banking system would have been smaller by some orders of magnitude. This delayed impact is seen in the steady deterioration in the ratio of loans rated below average in the Hungarian banking system as a whole between 2009 and 2014 (Figure 152).

Yet besides the state, (and) more specifically the budget and the banking system, the third party also paid a high price for the increase in foreign currency loans: the burdens on households rose significantly and across the board when the risks previously accepted ultimately materialised. The global and euro area financial crisis after 2008 simply brought the hidden crisis in the Hungarian financial system to light, because lending in Hungary between 2002 and 2008, i.e. before the crisis, consistently ignored the golden rules of prudent lending.

Figure 152. Volume of loans with below-average portfolio quality
in the banking system

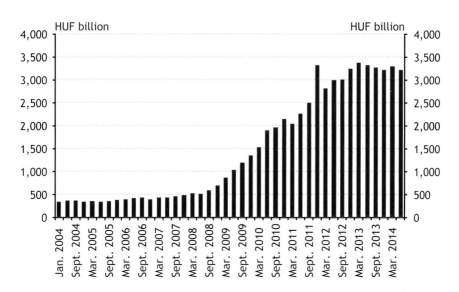

Source: MNB Supervisory Authority

The crisis exposed the previously hidden loan crisis: it resulted in a rapid restructuring of loan portfolios and earnings positions in the Hungarian banking system, which was caused by the worsening position of debtors.

Among the population, those living from average incomes encountered a considerable increase in their payment burdens in the years after the 2008 crisis. According to a survey ordered by the MNB in 2013, the payment-to-income ratio of families earning around the net average wage was approximately 25–30% of the given household's income, but even for the households earning more than the average net income, families had to pay 20–25% of their net income on repayments (Figure 153).

Figure 153. Households' payment-to-income ratio, by income category

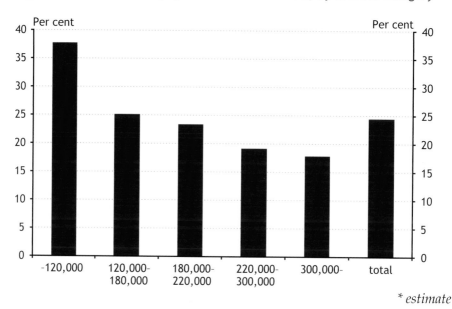

estimate

Source: GfK, MNB (2013 survey)   Quintiles

The surge in interest rates played an instrumental role in the rise in payment instalments, which realised previously assumed risks and brought them to the surface. After the crisis, interest rates rose suddenly on account of the higher country risk, the financing risk for government debt and the high budget deficit, creating a hidden and visible financial crisis for several million households. Interest expenses leapt not only for foreign currency loans but also for forint loans.

The early repayment scheme and the exchange rate cap scheme were exceedingly useful in reducing the foreign currency debt of the population. While households' foreign currency exposure rose steadily and continuously between 2006 and 2010 – with the growth in associated collateral, i.e. household foreign currency deposits, clearly not keeping up pace – households' foreign currency debt contracted sharply between 2010 and 2013, thanks largely to the action of the government (Figure 154).

Figure 154. Households' FX debt, % of GDP

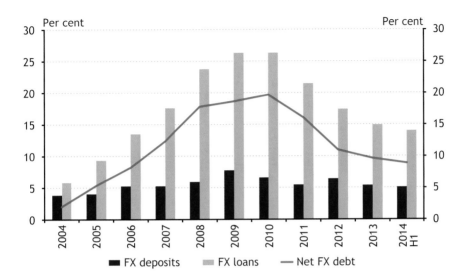

Source: MNB

The early repayment scheme significantly increased net household savings as part of the burden from earlier foreign currency loans dropped out of the family budget, with a knock-on effect on disposable income. Families saved the majority of this income, and later invested some in government securities, thereby reducing the country's dependency on external funding (Figure 155).

As a result, households' net financial savings rose most sharply from 2008 to 2011 in Hungary. Households' net financial savings increased from what was typically around zero relative to GDP in the years before the crisis to more than 3% after the crisis erupted (Figure 156).

A crucial factor in this increase was that households became more cautious in the wake of the second budget consolidation programme launched after 2008, responding to external and internal shocks with savings.

Figure 155. Net savings of households

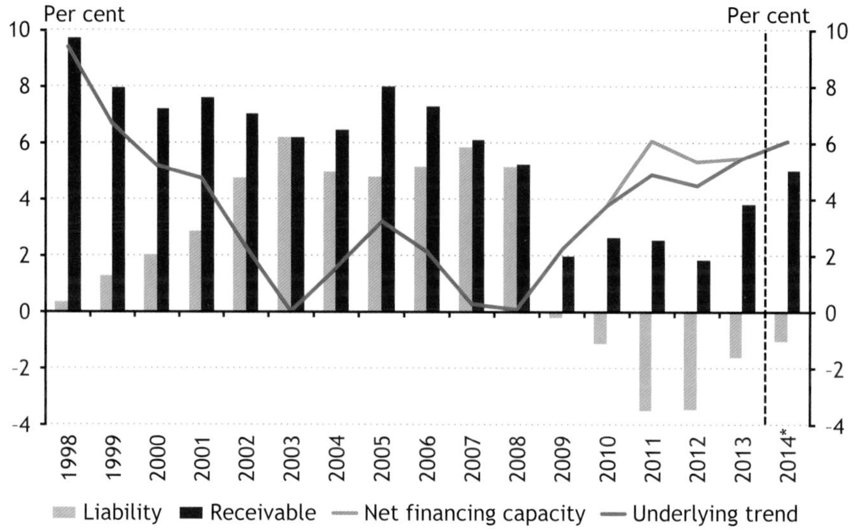

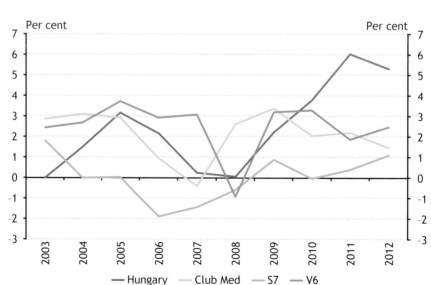

Source: MNB   *SNA indicator, * estimate*

Figure 156. Households' net financial savings as a % of GDP in Hungary and various country groups

Source: Eurostat

Economic policy would not have achieved this alone, the global financial crisis after 2008 played a significant role in the growth of savings. From 2011, however, the trend continued following a brief decline, with increases in both net and gross savings. This improvement was facilitated by tax relief, a stronger precautionary motive and the payment of real yields. The swings in the CHF/HUF exchange rate presumably also played a role in the increased savings, with families putting more aside in reserve to cope with the frequent changes in repayments, as the precautionary motive gained prevalence.

The early repayment scheme also had a major influence on household saving processes. This is because the net financial savings and wealth of households rose under the early repayment scheme, with the value of the forgiven debt i.e. the difference between the free market and the set exchange rate. The funding of the early repayment scheme also impacted on saving processes: roughly one third of the scheme was financed by the population using forint loans, with the remainder coming from financial savings, mainly bank deposits and investment units.

Although the 2011 early repayments reduced gross household financial savings on a temporary basis, the previous trend soon returned. Thus, ultimately the early repayment scheme may also contributed to the increase in savings: on the one hand, the population postponed consumption spending to build up savings cushions on account of the programme, while after the programme households began to rebuild the financial assets used for the early repayment (Figure 157).

Figure 157. Factors behind changes in the credit gap

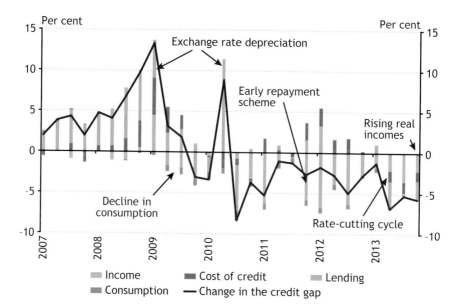

Source: MNB estimate

Corporate deleveraging with foreign currency loans

An increase in corporate lending was observed not just in Hungary from the start of the millennium, but also throughout other countries in the region and even in the euro area. This trend was partly supported by economic growth as the investment activity of enterprises expanded, but the growth of companies brought about a higher financing requirement in general, due to the greater need for current assets, for example.

The lending growth in the emerging countries in Central and Eastern Europe also resulted from convergence with the core countries as well as the deeper financial intermediation so the loan portfolio increased relative to GDP as well. This was all helped by the activity of the financial intermediary system since the period under review was characterised by relatively low financing costs and brisk cross-border lending, either directly or via subsidiary banks. This regularly took on the form of foreign currency lending in countries lacking funds, such as Hungary.

One difference between the increase in corporate and household foreign currency lending is that some of the enterprises taking on foreign currency debt had deposits in the given currency, which provided natural cover for fluctuations in exchange rates. Until the crisis broke out, however, an increasing proportion of Hungarian SMEs – generally those without foreign currency income – took out new loans in euros and Swiss francs, which made the sector increasingly vulnerable to exchange rate depreciation.

Corporate lending around Europe threw on the brakes from 2009. The eruption of the crisis and the economic recession set back both the supply and demand for loans. Growth rates settled at much lower levels, and in many cases turned negative. In the Baltic States for example, where growth was previously particularly strong, the rate declined by 5% annualy, with a similar trend observed in Hungary too. From 2011, lending slumped in countries blighted by the sovereign debt crises, i.e. also in southern euro area states. The increase in outstanding loans stalled in Italy in 2011, stagnating portfolios began to contract in Greece, Spain and Portugal, and in 2014 these countries still experienced downward trends. Growth had returned by this point in the other EU countries, mainly the northern states, but also in several CEE countries.

Hungary suffered one of the sharpest declines in the corporate loan portfolio. Although corporate lending experienced similar growth in many countries of the region prior to the crisis, these states recorded expansion again between 2011 and 2014 (Figure 158).

Figure 158. Corporate lending by the credit institution sector

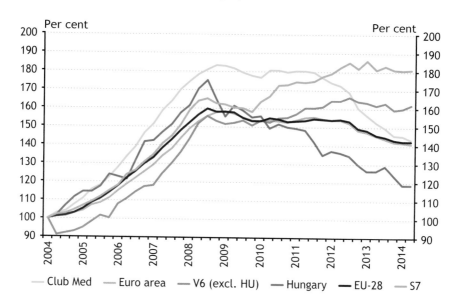

Loans extended by credit institutions, 2004=100%, data not adjusted for exchange rate effects

Source: MNB

The vulnerability of enterprises owing to foreign currency loans presumably influenced the decline in outstanding Hungarian corporate loans outstanding. At the end of 2008, roughly three quarters of the entire corporate loan portfolio was composed of debt from companies that had no export sales revenue providing natural hedging. In their cases, the weakening of the exchange rate increased the regular debt service burden owing to their poorer profitability, while it also raised the debt on their balance sheets due to the higher indebtedness. This vulnerability led to deleveraging at companies, and a decline in their economic activity.

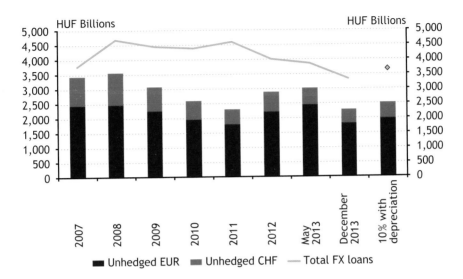

Figure 159. Volume of corporate FX loans

Source: CCIS

After the crisis broke out, there was a gradual decline in these unsecured foreign currency loans from 2009. Foreign currency debts with their high vulnerability risks began to rise in corporate balance sheets again from 2011, as the sovereign debt crisis escalated and the forint weakened. As a result of there, another deleveraging process at companies could have been triggered.

Recognising this risk, the MNB made the refinancing of foreign currency loans into low-interest forint loans part of the Funding for Growth Scheme. Thus between May 2013 and the end of 2013, the stock of unsecured, "toxic" loans declined by around 30% in corporate sector balance sheets.

The growth in foreign currency lending between 2004 and 2008 played a huge role in the indebtedness of the Hungarian private sector. Foreign currency debt exposes borrowers with unhedged positions to substantial exchange rate risk, which may have become a source of systemic risk vulnerability, owing to the large portfolio involved.

The aggregated foreign currency loan portfolio of households and enterprises amounted to just short of EUR 23 billion when the crisis broke out, before both sectors underwent significant deleveraging. By 2014, the stock of "toxic" foreign currency loans was on the decline as private sector agents steadily reduced their debt and the favourable alternatives of the Funding for Growth Scheme took effect (Figures 159 and 160).

Figure 160. Outstanding private sector FX loans from foreign and domestic sources

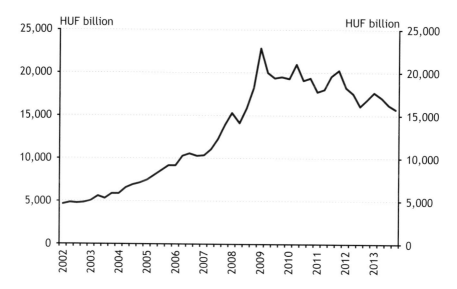

Source: MNB

Part Three

Economic stabilisation and turnaround

Chapter 13

Fiscal turnaround and consolidation

In the period of the Hungarian economic history from 1990 to 2010, sustainable economic balance was not achieved during one single political term. The best performance was attained in 1998–2002, when acceptable level of fiscal deficit evolved, with the exception of the 1998 and 2002 election years.

In 1990, the transition to a market economy started off with a budget surplus of 1.4%.[39] Due to the collapse of the Eastern markets and transition by shock therapy, a brief period of crisis developed, but in 1991 the budget deficit was still at 3% of GDP, a level which in the history of the Hungarian state budget was only reached again following the fiscal turnaround in 2011. Economic balance was broken in the following political cycle, and in the 1994 election year a budget deficit of more than 8% of GDP was registered (Figure 161).

The sharp rise in the budget deficit always resulted from the fact that economic policy was not able to maintain the earlier level of employment, and set the trap of "economic balance or growth" at the beginning of the market economy transition in the 1990s. Looking among Central and Eastern Europe countries, essentially every one of them underwent a period involving unavoidable employment losses due to the switch from the Eastern markets to the Western markets and the change-over from the planned economy to a market economy.

In every country in the region, the previous non-market economy system meant that the economy operated at a level of employment

---

[39] The statistics avaible for the early years of economic transition use a different methodology than the later statistics from 1995 on, and thus the level of budget deficit can be derived from several, slightly differing sets of statistics. Barabás et al. (1998) present detailed information on economic policy during the period of economic transition.

close to full employment, with a very low rate of unemployment: this was however artificial and unsustainable. The Hungarian economy suffered the largest lossesdue to the transition, because the transition to the market economy was not carried out in a slow, organic manner, but rather by shock therapy.

Figure 161. Budget balance in Hungary, % of GDP

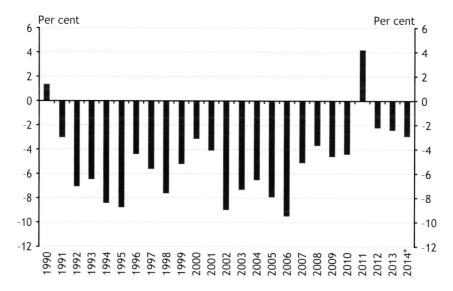

Source: Eurostat, MNB

During the two decades of transition between 1990 and 2010, deficits swelled every time there was an election year. During the three years between the two election years, more modest or more significant budget consolidation took place, depending on the political term, but this was not sustainable and ran into the cyclical spending for the election year again. The budget deficit of more than 8% of GDP in 1994, however, was not the result of election-year spending, but rather reflected the impact of the previous 3–4 years of shock therapy market transition, i.e. the loss of one million jobs. In 1995–1996, the Bokros package tried to restore economic balance with a shock therapy approach, but this was unsuccessful and the Hungarian economy once again ran a budget deficit of 8% in the election year.

In contrast to this, the three middle years of the 1998–2002 political term, i.e. 1999, 2000 and 2001, saw good performance in terms of the budget balance: after inheriting a deficit of over 8% of GDP, the deficit level was successfully lowered to 3–4% during this cycle.

The negative economic policy shift carried out in mid-2002 and the new government's election promises, however, then resulted in a record-setting budget deficit of 9% of GDP. This represented a key turning point in economic policy from the point of view of Hungary's macroeconomic balance. Between 1990 and 2000, the country underwent two shock therapies. During the first cycle, the impact of the shock therapy transition to the market economy was reflected in the imbalances, followed by the renewed shock therapy from the Bokros package. Under the first Orbán government, successful budget consolidation started of and by the middle of the term fiscal deficits were around 3–4% of GDP, and thus the second decade of market economy transition looked promising from the perspective of sustainable economic balance. This process was interrupted in 2002: instead of proceeding with the fiscal consolidation necessary in an election year, the Medgyessy government pursued a policy of redistribution, allowing the fiscal deficit to get out of hand: instead of applying the brakes, they hit the gas, and the deficit ballooned.

After 2002, fiscal deficits of 6–8% of GDP were seen in both election years, as well as during the three "middle years" between the election years in 2002 and 2006. The misguided, incorrect economic policy applied after mid-2002 allowed for deficits for the entire 2002–2006 term. During the first political term of the second decade of transition to the market economy, i.e. under the Medgyessy government and the first Gyurcsány government, Hungary's performance was worse than during the shock therapy transition period between 1990 and 1994, as well as during the period of austerity policies between 1994 and 1998.[40]

---

[40] by Orbán and Szapáry (2006) pointed out well the unsustainable of fiscal policy in 2006.

On the whole, the Hungarian budget was characterised by imbalances in the two decades between 1990 and 2010 and showed negative tendencies. Massive fiscal deficits were regularly run during election years, and subsequently, the deficit of 8–9% of GDP always pushed the next cycle into programmes aimed at restoring fiscal balance. Another characteristic of the two transition decades was that the three "middle" years between two election years also exhibited unsustainably high fiscal deficits. The flawed Hungarian economic policy pursued after mid-2002 was a turning point, because it resulted in significantly higher consolidation needs for the next political term by generating deficits even larger than the fiscal imbalances accumulated during the first decade.

In 2010, an immediate change in economic policy was necessary to address the fiscal imbalance: this change happened, and consequently as early as 2010 it was possible to achieve a deficit of 4.3% of GDP, instead of 7% of GDP.

The real turning point came in 2011: excluding one-off items, Hungary's budget deficit finally came in below 3%. Such quick, successful consolidation was unprecedented for the decades between 1990–2010, and furthermore it was achieved without benign external or internal economic conditions. This consolidation occurred without a safety net from the IMF-EU, was not accompanied by a contraction in GDP, and employment actually increased while unemployment fell. This allowed political stability to be maintained and structural reforms to be launched. The significance of this rapid and successful consolidation is enhanced by the fact that it was not only the assets returned from the private pension system to the public system that helped achieve the below 3% deficit. According to the EU statistical methodology valid at that time, the budget recorded a surplus of 4.3% of GDP as a result of the assets transferred from the private pension funds, because according to the ESA-95 statistics, it could have been accounted for as fiscal revenues. In the interests of comparing the individual years, it is worth examining how the balance would have developed without the one-off items (Figure 162).

Figure 162. Corrected EDP balance for 2011, in accordance with the ESA-95 methodology valid at that time, % of GDP

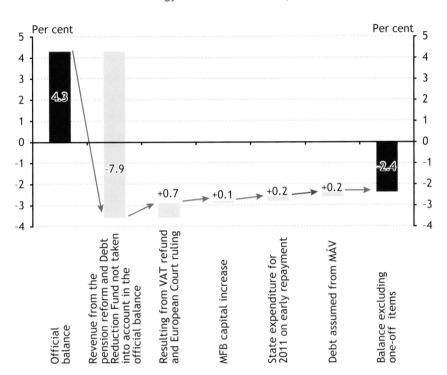

Source: Eurostat, and author's work based on the NGM release of 3 April 2012

We can arrive at the real extent of the deficit by deducting from the budget surplus the private pension fund revenue, which the ESA statistics accounted for above and beyond the part in the cash-flow budget (HUF 460 billion), and, in order to present the corrected deficit, by correcting the expenditure side by items which could be viewed as one-off items, because they did not occur annually. The largest deficit-increasing one-off item was the VAT refund of around HUF 250 billion, due to the ruling of the European Court.[41]

---

[41] The proceeding was launched in 2007 by the European Commission, because in its view Hungarian law did not comply with the principle of tax neutrality in relation to VAT refunding.

It should be noted that the EU's statistical methodology has charged in 2014 and with the application of the ESA-2010 rules the 2011 balance also changed retrospectively. Consequently, instead of the surplus of 4.3% of GDP, the data according to the new methodology show a deficit of 5.5% of GDP.

According to the previous methodology, the persons returning to the public pension system together with the savings transferred to the state improved the fiscal balance at the time of the transaction in 2011, as one-off revenue. According to the new statistical rules, the pension fund assets (amounting to 9.6% of GDP) may not be recorded as revenue in 2011. Instead, they must be accounted for as an "advance contribution on pension benefits" and this resulted in a 5.5% deficit. This does not, however, influence the balance calculated without one-off items, because this did not originally take into account the bulk of the private pension fund assets, which appeared in the cash-flow budget, in the amount of HUF 460 billion, equivalent to 1.7% of GDP. Thus, starting with a different ESA balance the same corrected deficit is derived as shown in Figure 162 (Figure 163).

After the fiscal turnaround in 2011, Hungary consistently maintained its budget deficit below 3% of GDP, and after this turning point this has been the new trend. Furthermore, 2014 was the first election year in the quarter century between 1990 and 2014 when the Hungarian budget deficit remained below 3% of GDP.

This was due to several factors: the successful fiscal turnaround, the government's strict policy of preserving economic balance and the successful operation of the new economic policy formula. As usual when the budget is prepared prior to an election year, the government made a political decision on the fiscal balance for the election year. In 1993, 1997, 2005 and 2009, the governments in power made a political decision to allow an increase in the budget deficit (in 2001 under the first Orbán government, it was not such a decision which caused the large deficit during the election year, but rather the redistribution launched in mid-2002). By contrast, in 2013, the second Orbán government did not make a decision to allow an increase in the budget deficit during the 2014 election year. Quite the contrary: the government's decision was not to prepare an election budget, and instead to target a budget deficit of less than 3% of GDP during the election year.

The new economic policy formula also had an impact, as it was possible to maintain the budget deficit at less than 3% of GDP during the 2014 election year, because the level of employment was increasing and the rate of unemployment was falling from quarter to quarter.

Figure 163. Corrected EDP balance for 2011, in accordance with the ESA-2010 methodology in force since 2014, % of GDP

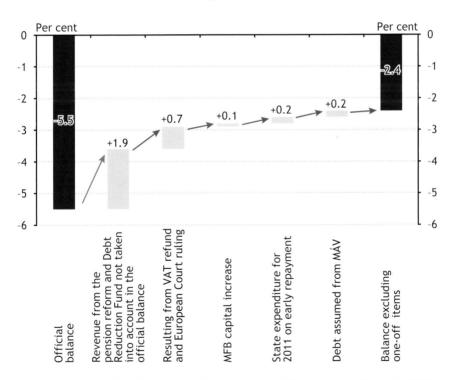

Source: Eurostat, and author's work based on the NGM release of 3 April 2012

Elements of the successful budget consolidation

Between 2010 and 2014, Hungary carried out successful fiscal consolidation. This occurred in four stages. In 2010 the inherited budget deficit of over 7% was lowered to 4.3%, in 2011 a fiscal turning point was reached, even without the one-off effect of reforming the private pension fund system, in 2012 a record low deficit of 2.3% was achieved as a result of the new economic policy, and in 2013 the decision was made not to prepare an election-year budget for 2014.

Each of these four stages was necessary to set Hungary on the path of sustainable fiscal balance between 2010 and 2014.

This successful fiscal consolidation used a large number of tools, eight of which deserve special attention (Figure 164).

Figure 164. Factors of budget consolidation, 2010-2014

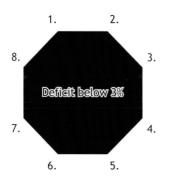

1. Taxation of consumption

2. Széll Kálmán Plan I

3. Széll Kálmán Plan II

4. Budget freezes

5. Transformation of the private pension fund system

6. Flat-rate, family PIT

7. +400,000 jobs

8. Special taxes

Source: MNB

In the period 2010–2014, following the fiscal turning point, the transition to the flat-rate family taxation system had an increasingly noticeable effect, as the stronger motivation to work and create jobs generated additional revenues for the budget. This revenue did not appear primarily in the form of personal income tax. Instead, owing to the fledgling recovery in growth from mid-2013 it appeared in the form of higher payments related to wages stemming from employment, in higher corporate tax revenues and steadily increasing indirect tax revenues.

The recovery in growth that occurred in 2013 also resulted in rising consumption, followed a few quarters later by a rebound in investment, and all of these factors generated additional revenues for the budget, mainly through indirect taxes. The stronger incentives of the flat-rate family tax system were a hidden, but decisive, underlying factor behind all of these developments.

The successful consolidation was backed by an effective policy of structural reform. In terms of its components, the complete reform of the tax system contributed directly and significantly to fiscal consolidation and to the achievment of the sustainable financial balance. The successful labour market reforms had a similar effect, but made an indirect contribution to sustainable economic balance. Thanks to these reforms, employment steadily rose and unemployment declined, resulting in rising revenues from employment and falling expenses related to unemployment.

The consolidation between 2010 and 2014 could have been successful because the state moved ahead with consolidation at both levels, i.e. the central government and the general government, including the decentralised local governments. In relation to the local governments, the new economic policy first moderated borrowing, before consolidating the debts of local governments and making further borrowing subject to authorisation.

On the expenditure side of the budget, changes in government spending also made a substantial contribution to the successful consolidation. In 2010, total budgetary spending of HUF 220 billion was frozen, and in the years thereafter spending items were regularly frozen in the budget.

The earlier complete transformation of the private pension fund system was an indispensable precondition and basis for the successful fiscal consolidation. In 2011, this move contributed to the reduction of the public debt ratio by approximately HUF 1,400 billion, which also lowered the budget's interest expenses. Even more importantly, the pension reform generated additional revenues amounting to up to 1.3% of GDP in every fiscal year.

Due to the HUF 360–400 billion in additional revenue for the public pension system, this structural reform measure played an important role in fiscal consolidation in its own right, but it also had a strong impact through other hidden channels.

Essentially, in the course of transitioning to the flat-rate family tax system the budget revenues declined by the same amount as they increased due to transformation of the private pension fund system: the effect of both of these measures was around HUF 300–400 billion during the consolidation years. The growing size of the mandatory private pension fund system would have resulted in an increasingly large hole in the budget: as the age cohorts enter the labour market, they pay part of their contributions to private pension funds, while at the same time persons who retire receive all of their pension benefits from the public system. Without the pension reform, newer and newer cohorts would have entered the mandatory private pension fund system, while more and more groups of employees would have retired, and thus the public pension system would have suffered more and more from maintaining the mandatory private pension fund system.

The other factor is even stronger: through the flat-rate family income tax system the government motivates child-bearing, and in doing so it redistributes an increasing amount of personal income from the budget to families with children. Within the fiscal consolidation, we see an example of consolidation: economic policy harmonised the structural reform measures of the pension system and the tax system, replacing budget revenues lost on the one side with revenues gained on the other.

In each and every year, the successful fiscal consolidation between 2010 and 2014 relied on expanding employment and the related decline in unemployment. During the years of consolidation, the rise in employment and the decline in the rate of unemployment increasingly shifted away from public labour towards the private sector, and thus supported the return to fiscal balance and the transition to sustainable economic balance to an ever greater degree.

Last, but not least, the expanding system of sector-specific taxes amounting to 1–2% of GDP was an indispensable source of the successful fiscal consolidation. Furthermore, these sector-specific taxes generated new fiscal revenues in such a manner that this policy did not cause any employment or growth losses at the same time. The sectors of the economy upon which sector-specific taxes were imposed would not have created more value or implemented higher investments, if there had been no sector-specific taxes. In the banking sector and the financial sector in general, a strong balance sheet adjustment was under way, and this would have occurred anyway even if there had there been no bank levy. In the energy sector, the sector-specific taxes really did not impact performance, and only resulted in a reduction in the profit level of the companies operating in this sector. In relation to retail sales and the financial transaction tax, in neither case did the economic performance (i.e. the level of employment and traditional payments to the budget) of the groups of enterprises involved decline due to the sector-specific taxes.

These aspects present the most important characteristics of Hungary's successful budget consolidation between 2010 and 2014. The new economic policy used a new formula, in which employment played the key role, and in doing so it clearly broke with the pattern of austerity measures applied in the past to improve economic balance. The consolidation needs which regularly appeared in the period 1990–2010 were always accompanied by employment and growth sacrifices, because an attempt was made to reduce the fiscal deficits with general austerity measures. The broad policy of austerity measures, however, generally had a negative impact on the labour market and growth factors.

By contrast, the consolidation policies applied between 2010 and 2014 did not apply general austerity measures. On the contrary, the new economic policy incorporated general elements of economic stimulus into the government's policy. One of these general elements stimulating economic activity was the introduction of the flat-rate family tax system and the set of labour market reforms to boost employment and lower unemployment.

Thus, while the structural reforms and measures to improve fiscal balance did not contain any elements which worked according to the earlier logic and consequently entailed employment and growth losses, the elements providing general support to economic activity were applied consistently in the course of fiscal consolidation.

These had an offsetting effect, not generally, but specifically in relation to the targeted burdens imposed on specific economic sectors. The system of sector-specific taxes represented a departure from the previous economic policy not only in the sense that a new system of sharing tax burdens was introduced, but also to the extent that financial balance was restored in Hungary using a targeted set of revenue-increasing measures, rather than a general programme of austerity.

Successful consolidation by mitigating cyclical fluctuations

Hungary's successful fiscal consolidation can be traced back to an economic policy which simultaneously achieved a budget deficit below 3% of GDP and stabilised the economy. Steps to stabilise the economy were constantly a part of the fiscal consolidation, as the structural reforms signalled the central role of employment, the new tax system provided incentives for employment and job creation, and the production-centred investment policy helped to stabilise the structure of the economy.

The successful fiscal consolidation was backed by a similarly successful programme of economic stabilisation, which contributed to a steady improvement in the balance by closing the output gap. During the financial and economic crisis, the output of the Hungarian economy fell back, and large numbers of jobs and companies were terminated. As a result, the cyclical component of the deficit turned negative in the 2009 and 2010 budgets (Figure 165).

Figure 165. Hungarian budget balance and its cyclical component, % of GDP

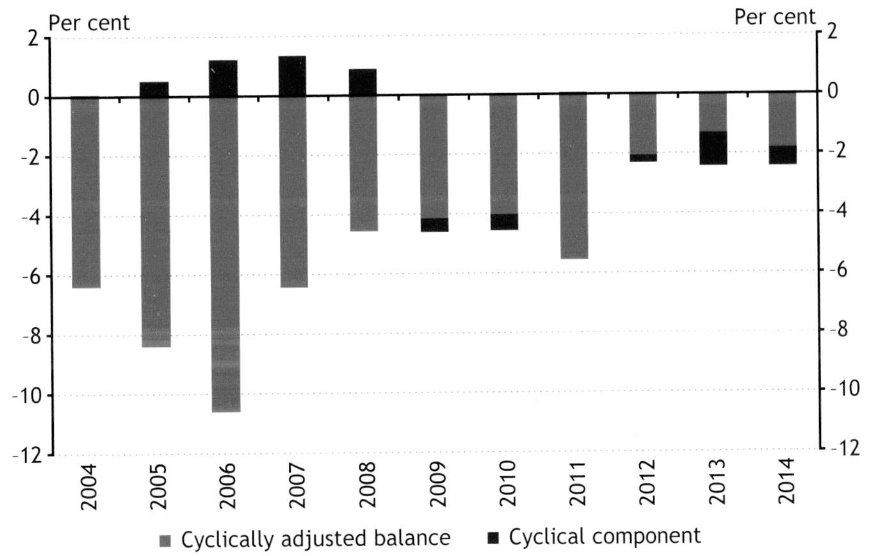

Source: MNB

Following the steep decline in 2009, a brief period of improvement started in the Hungarian economy, which automatically happens after every crisis: after the downturn, economic output, investments and consumption bounce back to the previous levels. Another aspect was that the downturn in 2012 was mild and was also felt by the EU economies. Although the Hungarian GDP contracted by 1.7% in 2012, it was not negative economic policy which caused this, but rather one-off factors partly related to the deterioration in the external economic climate. Agricultural output fell by 20%, which lowered domestic economic performance by 1–1.2% itself compared to the previous year. In the electronics sector, foreign production capacities were terminated or relocated to other countries, and this also had a negative impact on economic output.

At the same time, as part of the tax reform, the transition to the flat-rate family income tax system and the system of indirect taxation started, resulting in an inflation rate of 5.7%, which decreased real incomes and consumption.

The declining performance of the Hungarian economy in 2012 does not show any deviation compared to the trend for the EU member states, and indeed even compared to the overall global economic trend. The decline was not primarily due to the Hungarian economic policy. Hence, the stabilising economic factors continued to have an effect in the Hungarian economy, but these were offset or even exceeded in part by the negative effects from the global economy, and in part from the European economy, and also by the poor year for agriculture.

During the fiscal consolidation, the cyclically adjusted balance also fell significantly, and in 2012 the negative external factors exceeded the one-off negative internal factors. The sustainability of the successful Hungarian fiscal consolidation is facilitated by internal economic stabilisation, which contributes to steady improvement in the balance by closing the output gap.

Hungarian fiscal consolidation was an exceptional event

The significance of Hungary's successful fiscal consolidation between 2010 and 2014 is also underlined by the fact that it not only resulted in a turning point in Hungarian economic history compared to the decades of transition from 1990 to 2010, but also that it was a unique performance among the EU members.

Similar to the Hungarian economy, in the years before the crisis
unsustainable macroeconomic imbalances were mounting in Greece,
Ireland, Portugal, Cyprus, Romania and Latvia. Together with Hungary,
after the outbreak of the crisis in 2008 these countries needed assistance
from the IMF-EU, with Hungary being the first to call for help. Of
this group of seven IMF programme countries, only three economies
succeeded in consolidating their budgets in the period 2010–2014:
Hungary, Romania and Latvia.

In the case of the other IMF programme countries, fiscal consolidation
was included as a requirement of the programme, but these other four
countries were not successful in this regard[42] (Figure 166).

Figure 166. Fiscal balance in IMF programme countries and EU-28, % of GDP

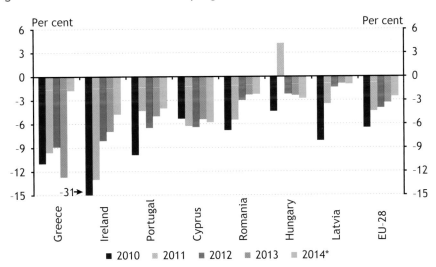

* Hungarian data is the MNB forecast presented in the September 2014 Inflation Report;
source for other countries is the AMECO database.

Source: AMECO, Eurostat, MNB

---

[42] The independent institution assessing the operation of the IMF also acknowledged
that during the crisis the IMF made mistakes in assessing the situation, for example in
2010–2011 it recommended fiscal consolidation too early in the developed countries
(IEO–IMF: IMF response to the financial and economic crises: an IEO assessment, 8
October 2014).

Consolidation of the Hungarian state budget differed significantly from the consolidation undertaken in the other IMF programme countries: it did not follow the economic policy of austerity, of the IMF–EU agreements, but rather relied on a unique Hungarian model. We can also say that Hungary departed from the earlier group of IMF programme countries from autumn 2010, as it properly ended the IMF-EU agreement, while the other countries remained stuck in the IMF-EU aid programmes.

Hungary's successful fiscal consolidation can be seen as an even greater achievement from an economic history perspective, because it was essentially accomplished without an IMF-EU safety net after 2010 (Figure 167).

Figure 167. Fiscal balance in certain country groups, % of GDP

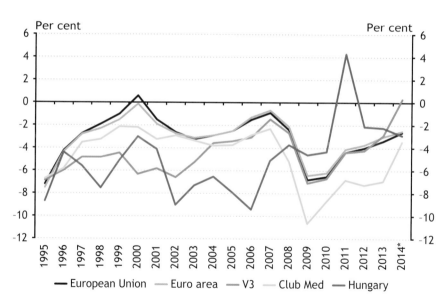

Source: Eurostat, European Commission, Spring 2014 forecast   * estimate*

Among EU member states, most of the non-IMF-EU programme countries were also unable to achieve sustainable economic balance.

In many countries, problems were experienced because the fiscal consolidation did not result in sustainable economic balance, since lowering the budget deficit led to growth and employment sacrifices. Hungary did not accept growth and employment sacrifices in the interests of sustainable balance, whereas many other member states did. These sacrifices, however, could not result in sustainable fiscal balance, because the deterioration in political stability slowed and put an end to the structural reforms.

The role of the exchange rate in economic stabilisation

In small, open economics, changes in the exchange rate play a key role in economic developments. Changes in the nominal exchange rate alter inflation, while real economic processes, such as competitiveness and import demand, are influenced primarily by changes in the real exchange rate. In addition to these traditional channels, in the case of the Hungarian economy it is also necessary to carefully monitor the effects exerted through the significant accumulated amount of debt denominated in foreign currency. Depreciation of the exchange rate can alter the macroeconomic effects through the revaluation of debt burdens (so-called balance sheet effects) and through changes in the situation of the banking sector.

The unsustainable imbalances in the Hungarian economy before the crisis were also clearly reflected in the development of monetary policy conditions. The undisciplined fiscal policy and the total lack of coordination between fiscal policy and monetary policy resulted in massive imbalances in the real economy and the basic structure of the economy. Fiscal policy regularly found opportunities to lower the deficit using measures that fuelled inflation, which essentially rendered it impossible for the central bank to achieve its inflation objectives. At the same time, the central bank attempted to mitigate inflation and maintain the economy's ability attract external funds by using nominal interest rates which were extremely high in a regional comparison. In combination with the high inflation, the high policy rate resulted in a real exchange rate path which increasingly deviated from the real appreciation stemming from real economic convergence (the equilibrium path) and generated a persistent, large deficit on the current account balance. In retrospect, the final result can be right by described as a catastrophe.

The high level of HUF interest rates had an almost neutral impact on the sector of mainly foreign-owned large enterprises which operated with a high import share and typically secured financing through parent bank connections, but at the same time there were serious consequences for domestic SMEs.

Excessive appreciation of the HUF exchange rate further exacerbated the problems of competitiveness in the economy, and maintained or even intensified the existing dualistic economic structure. In the corporate sector, the appreciating real exchange rate had a negative impact on producers competing with imports, which were in a difficult situation due to globalisation anyway, and eroded price competitiveness on the export markets.

In the case of Hungarian SMEs, it was essentially impossible to earn the high HUF interest with new investments while remaining profitable, and accordingly the sector either postponed its investments, thereby reducing its medium-term growth capacity, or assumed the exchange rate risk and incurred debt in foreign currency. The dire consequences of this latter decision became apparent after the outbreak of the global crisis. The investment performance of domestic SMEs indebted in foreign currency which did not have any natural hedge deteriorated significantly after 2008 and was significantly weaker than the investment performance of similar-sized companies which did not have an open foreign currency position.

Based on the experience of the previous current account crises, in any economy struggling with a high current account deficit and large external debt, depreciation of the real exchange rate can substantially facilitate adjustment of the financing situation and put an end to the overvaluation of the domestic currency. In the case of the Hungarian economy, however, it could have quickly become a double-edged sword. Due to the widespread indebtedness in foreign currency, sudden depreciation of the exchange rate would result in deterioration of debt sustainability and the perception of financial system stability, before it had any favourable effect on competitiveness, and thus lead to rising risk premiums. Consequently, the Hungarian economic policy could use the option of real depreciation only very cautiously and prudently.

Following the crisis, the real exchange rate of the forint depreciated, alleviating the previous overvaluation. In addition to the depreciation of the nominal exchange rate, the strong adjustment of other nominal economic variables, such as wages and inflation, also played a role in the process.

Since 2009, Hungary's external economic position has seen a lasting improvement on a scale which is significant even by international standards. Depreciation of the real exchange rate also may have played a key role in this process, in addition to the decline in domestic demand inevitably associated with deleveraging. A depreciated exchange rate and falling HUF interest rates (in particularly thanks to the FGS) improved the competitiveness of domestic SMEs, the positive effects of which are seen over the short run in the decline in the economy's specific import demand. The longer-term effects may result in a decline in SMEs' significant shortfalls in terms of productivity.

Naturally, on the other hand, depreciation renders consolidation of the debt path more difficult. While the impact on the fiscal balance is moderate, the re-pricing of existing debt retards the decline in the debt ratio, but nevertheless this indicator still moved on a downward trajectory.

Figure 168. Development of exchange rates in the region

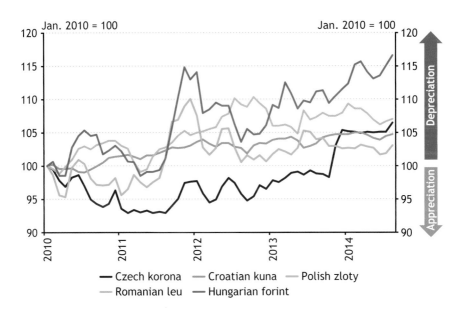

Source: Eurostat   *Monthly average exchange rates versus EUR*

At the same time, in case of private debtors, the series of government measures – the exchange rate cap and early repayment scheme for households, and the FGS funding available to replace foreign currency loans for companies – gradually lowered the sensitivity to changes in the exchange rate, which will disappear almost completely for households with next year's conversion into forints.

On the whole, the economic policy of stabilisation in recent years also gradually put an end to the imbalances arising in the field of monetary policy, without jeopardising debt sustainability and financial stability. The real exchange rate was able to move closer to the level justified by economic fundamentals, and HUF-based financing became the main factor in the financing decisions of domestic private agents. Looking forward, this latter development may also reinforce the traditional mechanism of monetary policy transmission.

Consolidation of the state budget increased economic freedom in Hungary

The trend for Hungary's economic freedom stabilised and then turned around during the period of fiscal consolidation and economic stabilisation.

Between 2008 and 2010, the freedom score of the Hungarian economy declined to a great degree, and then from 2010 onwards a similarly strong trend reversal was seen, as the degree of freedom in the Hungarian economy began to rise. It became easier to found a company, ownership rights were strengthened, and Hungary's ranking in terms of entrepreneurial and financial freedom improved compared to the previous years. Despite the unconventional economic policy measures, from mid-2010 economic regulation as a whole became more favourable for companies, according to international measurements and comparisons. Successful consolidation of the state budget was also one of the deep underlying factors behind this change in the trend. Although government spending remained high at nearly 50% of GDP, leaving the Hungarian economy near the bottom of the ranking, the economic freedom score still improved as a result of the decline in taxes on income and the budget emerging from a level associated with financing risks (Figure 169).

In 2010, the risk of a fiscal deficit of over 7% of GDP was replaced with an actual deficit of nearly 4% of GDP, demonstrating that the unconventional economic policy measures had successfully hindered a renewed surge in the deficit and thus prevented a budget crisis. As a result, the freedom of the economy rose, because the room for manoeuvre in economic policy increased due to fiscal consolidation.

Figure 169. Economic freedom score of the Hungarian economy

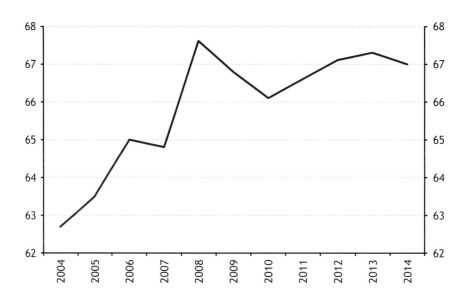

Source: Heritage Foundation

By 2012, just one year after the fiscal turning point in 2011, the degree of freedom in the Hungarian economy returned to the level of the region's countries: the Czech Republic was ranked ahead of Hungary, while Slovakia, Romania and Poland were all ranked behind Hungary in respect of economic freedom. While the level of economic freedom declined at the global level in 2011, Hungary's ranking in the 179 countries included in the survey improved from 51st place in 2010 to 49th place in 2011, when the fiscal trend was turned around. The successful fiscal consolidation bolstered the economic freedom of the Hungarian economy through direct and indirect factors, including in particular the lower tax burden on incomes.

Chapter 14

Turnaround in Hungarian employment

In economic history, it rarely occurs that in the span of just weeks or months an economic policy change causes a turnaround in a macroeconomic indicator, especially an important economic indicator. This is particularly rare in the case of labour market indicators, since – in addition to the cyclical position of the economy – the development of indicators is determined by strong long-term trends: the economic structure, the structure of employment and education, age, the age distribution of the working population and geographic mobility. The inherited weaknesses of the Hungarian labour market were actually preserved after the change of political regime, and manifested themselves in the labour market via an increasing number of distortions.

Following the change of regime, the labour markets in all of the countries in the region suffered a shock due to the collapse of the Eastern export markets, and the dismantling and transformation of the system of domestic enterprises which were uncompetitive under market conditions. Up to 1994, employment declined by almost 1 million in Hungary, and then between 1995 and 1997 it dropped by almost 200,000 persons, partially as a result of the set of austerity measures known as the Bokros package. Aside from the period between 1998 and 2001, Hungarian economic policy was unable to stop this loss of employment, all the way until 2010.

In contrast to the experiences of other economies in the region, Hungarian economic policy attempted to address the social tensions stemming from falling employment using the uncomplicated, short-term solution of easing the rules allowing workers to become inactive. While these measures lowered unemployment over the short run, they had a fundamental impact on fiscal leeway and the labour market opportunities associated with economic growth over the long-term period of decades.

The drastic rise in the number of inactive workers (mainly persons in early and disability pension) resulted in significant, long-term additional expenditures for the budget, while the number of employees subject to income taxation declined substantially. In parallel with this, the skills and work ability of employees becoming inactive who were otherwise of working age declined in proportion to the number of years spent in inactivity, which also reduced the long-term potential growth capacity of the economy.

Figure 170. Change in the number of active, employed and unemployed since 1989

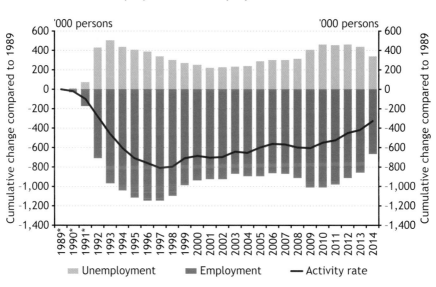

1989–1991 expert estimate

Source: HCSO, Labour Force Surveys (from 1992), Statistical Yearbook (1989–1993),

In the 2000s, after the 1998–2001 period, neither labour market activity nor domestic employment rose during the period of faster economic growth, which in fact was financed by excessive debt accumulation.

Instead of hiring new workers, companies preferred to produce their rising output by utilising their labour and capital inputs more intensively (Figure 170).

During the period, the lack of improvement in labour market conditions (despite the rapid growth) can also mainly be traced back to poor economic policy decisions. Conditions allowing workers to become inactive were left relaxed, and the actual pension age was significantly lower than the pension age specified by law. On the one hand, the generous government benefits available to working-age inactive persons represented an unfinanceable burden for the budget over the long run, while on the other hand, recipients of benefits stayed away from or simply did not appear on the labour market. In parallel with this, the high budget expenditures generated an overriding necessity for the government to obtain budget revenues, despite the high fiscal deficit. One regular source of such revenues was to raise taxes and contributions on labour.

As a result of this process, the tax burden on labour reached one of the highest levels in the OECD. In the progressive tax system, the high tax burden also affected a wide swath of society, since it was often the case that even workers earning near the average wage fell into the highest tax bracket. The high taxes acted as a particularly strong disincentive for families with above-average incomes, and resulted in a high level of income concealment.

As a result of this process, in 2007 prior to the global financial crisis and three years after EU accession, Hungary had one of the lowest labour market activity rates in the EU. In the Czech economy, which is roughly the same size as the Hungarian economy, there were almost 1 million more persons on the labour market than in Hungary.

The problems on the labour market affected well-defined groups of society. These included the young, pre-pension age persons, women of child-bearing age and low-skilled workers. In the case of these groups, the activity rate regularly fell short of the averages in the developed EU countries and was generally lower than the corresponding levels in Hungary's regional peers as well.

It was obvious that – on the supply side – labour market reform had to focus on the employment and employability of these social groups, in addition to scrapping the system of bad incentives (government benefits and the progressive income tax system). In order for employment to be able to rise in conjunction with an increase in labour supply, it was necessary to shape the demand environment accordingly. Achieving this, however, was particularly difficult in the wake of one of the century's most serious economic crises, in an environment marked by prolonged anaemic demand. Consequently, in addition to lowering the costs of labour, it was also necessary to increase the flexibility of the labour market (Figure 171).

Figure 171. Activity rate for certain social groups
in Hungary and regional countries

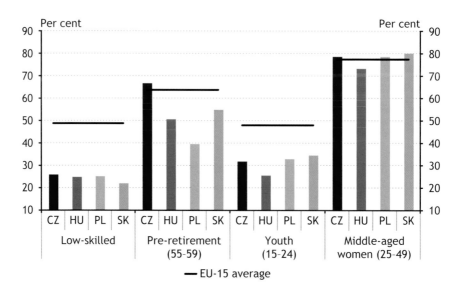

Source: Eurostat

In a rare moment in Hungarian economic history, from mid-2010 employment begins to rise strongly, while at the same time the level of unemployment begins to steadily decline. Considering the significant structural weaknesses in the Hungarian labour market, how was it possible for the change in government to essentially immediately effect a turnaround in employment in the Hungarian economy?

Three main factors played a role in this: the Hungarian system of values, the period of recovery and the new economic policy.

The Hungarian system of values is clearly centred on work, with individual and family wealth accumulation playing a central role in life's goals: this is achieved by work. It is perhaps no coincidence that the saying "Anyone who doesn't work shouldn't eat!" is popular among Hungarians. Market surveys clearly show that Hungarian workers are much more afraid of losing their jobs compared to the EU average. This reflects the fact that Hungarians primarily see their individual and family goals and increases in their income and wealth as being attainable through work. Naturally, the importance of work is even greater for groups outside the labour market, for the unemployed, and for groups of active age: people without a job may even want a job more strongly than those who wish to keep their job.

During the long period of flawed economic policy and failed budget consolidation attempts between 2002 and 2010, the principles of work and employment which are so important in the Hungarian system of values were not the main focus of economic policy. Prior to the 2008 financial crisis, this policy allowed for a steady decline in the labour intensity of production, and then the unsuccessful attempts to manage the financial crisis further weakened the labour market, with the introduction of extra taxes on labour and fiscal austerity measures which triggered a sharp drop in overall demand. The new government, however, had already proven in the period 1998–2002 that economic policy was capable of creating a large amount of new jobs. It continuously pressed for this political and economic policy goal during the period of flawed economic policy between 2002 and 2010, in its role as the opposition political force, and during the general elections it stated this as one of its basic objectives: placing higher value on work and new jobs was clearly a top priority of the new government.

The second reason was the brief recovery period. In 2008, Hungary was hit by two crises: the internal crisis stemming from the flawed economic policy between 2002–2008 and the failed attempts at consolidation, and the global and European financial crisis which erupted in autumn 2008. As a result of these two crises, Hungarian GDP contracted by more than 6.5% in 2009, huge numbers of SMEs went bankrupt or were liquidated and jobs were steadily lost. According to the theory of economic cycles, short and long periods of upturn are followed by setbacks, which are then followed again by periods of recovery. In the Hungarian economy, the significant declines in 2009 were followed by a short rebound in 2010–2011. During recovery periods, economic output improves first and afterwards (with a delay) labour market indicators also almost automatically improve compared to the crisis year: in line with this, in 2010 Hungarian economic indicators essentially automatically improved following the steep falls in 2009.

The third reason was the government's new policies and economic policy, as the value of work, employment and job creation immediately increased based on the new formula. This falls into the category of economic psychology. Economic psychology has a strong effect on all economies and has a particularly strong effect in Hungary. Society and economic agents always pay very close attention to the explicit and implicit messages of the government.

The explicit message for labour market participants for most of the period 1990–2010 was that economic policy considered fiscal balance and economic growth as the central aspects, and did not deem the level of employment and the rate of unemployment as being particularly important. Although this third element did appear for a brief time between 1998 and 2002, the two decades between 1990 and 2010 were dominated by this explicit message. In the economic policy messages, the high level of employment necessary for the healthy operation of the labour market, a low rate of unemployment and a continuous increase in education were not equally important priorities compared to economic balance and growth.

In mid-2010, however, with the government's June programme market agents received a clear message that the new government was serious about its economic policy: the new policy did not respond to the rise in the budget deficit in a manner which allowed growth and employment sacrifices to be expected. Quite on the contrary: in mid-2010, economic policy sent signals to the corporate sector and households which made it clear that starting from 2010 economic policy was no longer focused on two elements, but rather on three key aspects: it targeted sustainable balance with steadily improving employment and durable economic growth.

This explicit message had an immediate effect on market agents. It became clear that, in a rare moment in the history of Hungarian parliamentary democracy after 1990, the government was going to implement the economic policy which it had promised during the election campaign and was actually going to make job creation and employment the core of its economic policy. This was a strong message, as all of the previous deteriorations in fiscal balance had always resulted in a different economic policy than promised by the earlier political elites and governments in their election programmes. The neo-liberal transition to a market economy in 1990–1994 resulted in massive employment and growth losses, even though this is not what the first freely elected government promised in 1990. Similarly, the political programme before the 1994 elections contained no mention of the austerity policies later pursued between 1994 and 1998, which resulted in the loss of several hundred thousand jobs. In the period 1998–2002, the political elite kept its promises, but this was such a brief exception that it did not become a defining factor in society's perception of events.

Steady expansion of employment during consolidation and stabilisation

One aspect of the successful budget consolidation and lasting economic stabilisation that occurred in 2010–2014 was that all of the Hungarian economy's employment indicators improved for the entire period.

Starting from the turning point in the employment trend in mid-2010, the number of employed (adjusted for seasonal effects) continuously rose, and starting from the second half of the cycle unemployment gradually declined. In the beginning, another important factor also undermined developments in unemployment: the ratio and number of active persons on the Hungarian labour market was continuously rising. As a result of changes to labour market incentives, gradual tightening of the pension eligibility rules and transformation of the benefits system, more and more people entered the labour market, while at the same time it became increasingly difficult to become inactive without justification. The extremely low supply of labour, which had previously been the Achilles' heel of the Hungarian economy, began to rise (Figure 172).

As a result of the government's decisions, compared to the pre-crisis level, Hungarian labour supply recorded one of the largest increases among the European economies.

Naturally, in the span of just a few years it was not possible to completely offset the losses accumulated over the last 20 years, and consequently this upward trend must also be maintained in the years ahead, in order for Hungary's convergence to be successful.

As a result of the W-shaped recession in 2012, the rate of unemployment increased slightly. Due to the decline in GDP in 2012, labour market demand did not follow the steady expansion of supply. In parallel with the acceleration of economic growth from 2013, employment began to rise tangibly and consequently the rate of unemployment also began to fall substantially.

Figure 172. Change in number of employed, unemployed and active persons

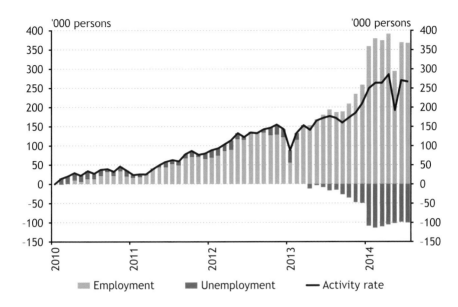

Source: HCSO   *Cumulative change compared to January 2010*

These trend reversals on the labour market, and in particular the increase in the rate of employment, were not a general phenomenon in the EU members: of the group of countries forced to undertake consolidation, employment essentially only increased in the Hungarian economy. This was due to the fact that Hungary successfully managed the fiscal crisis using unorthodox economic policy tools. This is best reflected from 2013, in the fifth year after the 2008 financial and economic crisis. Thanks to the successful consolidation and stabilisation, the recovery in growth and consumption also reinforced the earlier rebound in employment in Hungary starting from 2013.

Examining the international data, the development of the employment and growth data after the crisis correspond to the theoretically expected relationship. We find a positive correlation between these two variables. The number of employed mainly increased in those economies where the effects of the crisis were more moderate, and the pre-crisis level of output was reached or exceeded again during the period of recovery. By contrast, in the countries which suffered severe real economic losses during and after the crisis, the weak growth performance was accompanied by a decline in employment and a related increase in social tensions (Figure 173).

Figure 173. Employment in the national economy and real GDP, 2008-2013

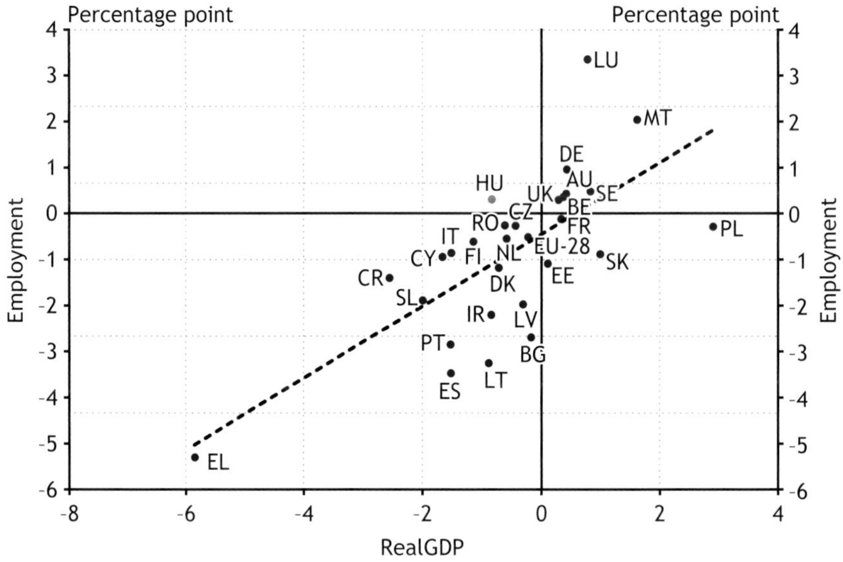

Source: Eurostat   *Average change*

The situation in Hungary was an exception in this regard, however. In respect of the countries where the level of GDP was still lower than the pre-crisis level in 2013, Hungary was the only economy which saw an increase in the number of employed.

Turnaround in the inherited weak points on the labour market

In terms of the inherited weaknesses on the Hungarian labour market, perhaps the greatest problem was the employment rates for low-skilled workers, pre-retirement age persons, the young and women of child-bearing age, as these fell short of the European average. Additionally, the 2008–2009 international crisis, which hit Hungary especially severely due to the flawed economic policy, further exacerbated the employment problems in certain social groups. This was the case, for example, with youth employment.

Figure 174. Changes in the employment rate in the low-skilled group

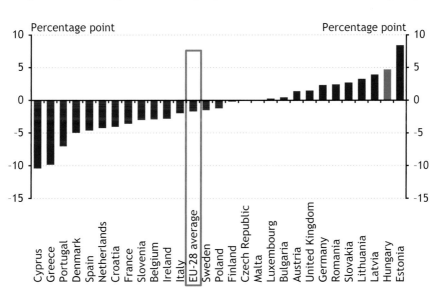

2010 Q2 - 2014 Q2; Croatia has been an EU member since 2013

Source: Eurostat

During the long period of market transition in 1990–2010, aside from a brief 4-year exception, the prevailing economic incentives worked against job creation and employment, and it was these incentives which caused the distortions on the labour market. It is worthwhile to separately examine the rebound in employment which started in 2010 in terms of the situation of the social groups which were struggling with employment problems (Figures 174–175).

Several factors contributed to the successes in boosting the employment of particularly disadvantaged groups during the global crisis. On the one hand, the set of government measures related to labour market participation and employment had a direct effect, and on the other hand, the economic and social philosophy propounded by the government which emphasised work also had an impact, and finally the structure of the measures taken to consolidate the budget also exerted an effect.

Figure 175. Change in employment rate for the pre-retirement age group

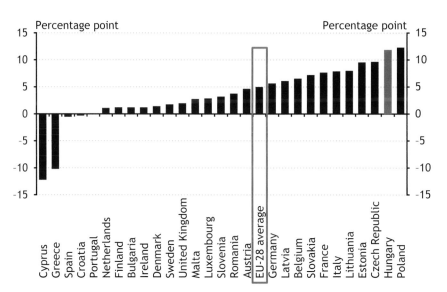

2010 Q2 - 2014 Q2; 55-59 age group, Croatia has been an EU member since 2013

Source: Eurostat

In addition to the steps to promote labour market activity, one must also mention the creation and continuous expansion of the public work programmes, the measures of the Job Protection Action Plan and the changes to the Labour Code. Along with direct intervention, the government is also able to influence the demand side of the labour market with indirect measures. These measures may affect both the costs of employment and the structure of production. In terms of measures affecting the costs of employment, the strongest effect was exerted by the reform of the personal income tax system and the measures of the Job Protection Action Plan. Introduction of the flat-rate family income tax system resulted in a substantial reduction of the Hungarian tax wedge, which was previously extremely high by international standards, and in the amount of employee and employer taxes and contributions on wages.

In its own right, this provided the corporate sector with greater leeway for adjustment in the weak demand environment following the debt crisis, while at the same time increasing net wages for households, even in the case of a more restrained increase in nominal wages.

This was complemented by the measures of the Job Protection Action Plan, the most important of which was to provide companies with an additional, targeted contribution allowance precisely for the groups with the most significant employment problems, thus generally supporting the preservation and expansion of these jobs.

Finally, it is also important to highlight the effects of the budget consolidation on overall demand and economic growth. The experiences with the budget following the crisis show that, during a period when private agents (enterprises, households) are already focused on reducing their debt levels, measures to improve fiscal balance involve larger-than-average real economic sacrifices. This is particularly true when the measures result in direct reductions of budget spending and/ or increase households' burdens to a large degree.

In addition to real economic risks, such measures can also intensify social tensions. Taking all of this into account, after 2010 Hungarian economy policy departed from the conventional set of tools used to manage crises. Instead of immediately cutting expenditures, numerous measures on the revenue side improved the fiscal balance, and at the same time it was possible to distribute the burdens of consolidation across a wider and wider group. Certain corporate groups in Hungary had previously operated with extremely high profitability and thus had greater burden-bearing capacity; it was thus especially important to include these groups in the sharing of public burdens.

The unique nature of the structure of consolidation is clearly reflected by the fact that improvement in Hungarian employment was an exception to the rule for the countries forced into crisis management. Employment losses were registered in the Spanish, Italian and Portuguese economies during crisis management, whereas employment in the Hungarian economy increased from 2010, even after filtering out the effects of public work programmes (Figure 176).

Figure 176. Change in the number of employed in the age group 15-64 compared to 2010 Q1 in the Club Med countries and Hungary

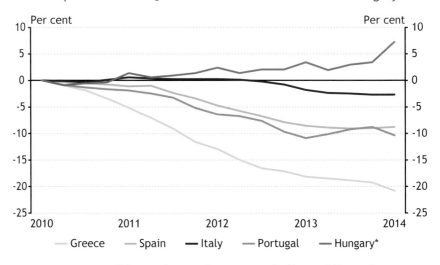

Hungarian employment excluding public work programmes

Source: Eurostat, MNB

This is reflected in the differing results of the two kinds of crisis management. While conventional, austerity measure-based economic policies were applied to restore fiscal balance in the southern group of euro area countries (which failed to lead to sustainable economic balance), Hungary was able to re-establish its financial balance using a new, unconventional economic policy. These two differing economic policy approaches resulted in opposite results in private sector employment. The crisis management approach in the southern euro area countries concentrated exclusively on restoring fiscal balance and on preventing a sovereign debt crisis, while disregarding employment and unemployment. Conventional, orthodox economic policy focuses merely on balance and growth, because it presumes that employment will remain at the earlier high level or does not attempt to boost lower levels of employment, and consequently the adjustment efforts result in employment and growth losses.

This policy fails to achieve its objective of balance, while undermining economic stability and generating socio-political tensions.

Hungary's successful budget consolidation and economic stabilisation in 2010–2014 clearly demonstrates that market self-regulation functions neither on the financial and goods market nor on the labour market. It would not have been possible to achieve a new balance which is better from a social point of view without the state.

The steady increase in employment between 2010 and 2014 was accompanied by successful fiscal consolidation, as economic policy paid close attention to both balance and the employment situation. One of the lessons from Hungarian economic history between 1990 and 2014 is that economic policy always has a significant impact on the operation of the market, but flawed government policy can channel the operation of the market into a negative direction, while correct policy can move it in a positive direction. Equilibrium never develops automatically anywhere on the market as a result of internal self-regulation. Government regulation is needed for this, but incorrect intervention can even worsen the market's otherwise imperfect self-regulation. By contrast, proper intervention can address the shortcomings of market regulation.

The changes in the structure of employment contributed to its expansion. Prior to the crisis, the level of part-time employment was negligible on the Hungarian labour market. This changed during the course of the crisis. Placing some of their workforce in reserve, companies registered full-time employees in part-time positions. As a result, employing these workers cost less and they were also able to adjust to falling demand. This was also helpful later in the recovery period, because these companies did not need to advertise new positions and conduct new hiring when economic activity picked up, since they could simply move their part-time workers back into full-time employment. Generally speaking, more women are employed in part-time positions and this holds true for Hungary as well, albeit during the crisis, male part-time employment also started to rise.

Workers with intermediate-level education comprise the majority of part-time employees, and part-time employment increased the most in this group.[43]

The introduction of the new Labour Code also helped to improve the flexibility of the labour market. It contained new and previously used solutions such as the division of job responsibilities, as a result of which several employees can work on one job, and can have employment relationships with several employers.

---

[43] This topic is discussed in greater detail in Bodnár (2014): Part-time employment during the crisis. MNB Bulletin.

Consolidation and the turnaround in employment helped to reduce the shadow economy

As we saw, the fiscal measures and structure of the consolidation made a fundamental contribution to improving the employment situation. At the same time, the successful turnaround in employment helped to combat the shadow economy, contributing to the long-term sustainability of fiscal balance. The smaller the size of the hidden, non-tax-paying economy, the more revenues are received by the budget. Thus, a reduction of the shadow economy means that the 3% of GDP budget deficit can be achieved in a sustainable manner.

In the period 2010–2015, the effect of public work programmes and the reduction of the shadow economy had a very significant impact on the non-private sector labour market. Although the reduction of the underground economy made a smaller contribution to job creation in the 2010–2011 period, in the four years between 2011 and 2015 this contribution amounted to 50–80%: budget consolidation and economic stabilisation is founded on a continuous decline in the shadow economy (Figure 177).

Figure 177. Ratio of new jobs created in private sector,
and by public work programmes and reduction of the shadow economy

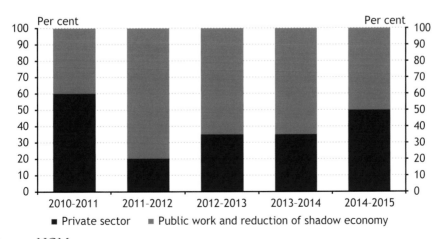

Source: NGM

The reduction of the shadow economy is supported by general measures and special employment tools. When the special employment tools designed to address distortions on the labour market enter into force (e.g. promoting the employment of women, offering public work to persons with low skill levels, providing tax allowances for workers over the age of 50), these measures also expand the group of tax-payers to include groups of employees who had previously been working in informal, unregistered employment.

Chapter 15

A turning point in inflation

In the five years that have passed since the 2008 global financial crisis and European debt crisis, the EU countries have been characterised by a low inflation environment: consumer price increases have fallen steadily short of the 2% inflation targets set by the central banks. The middle of the 2010s has not only been marked by a period of very low inflation rates: the risk of sustained deflation has also emerged as a real danger. Sustained deflation entails the risk that the European Union might replicate the deflationary period seen for the last 15 years in the Japanese economy.

Historically low inflation environment

From the perspective of economic growth, the Japanese economy lost two entire decades, due to flawed economic and monetary policy which was not able to consistently maintain price levels in Japan in a moderate inflationary range. Quarter after quarter, year after year, the level of prices fell in Japan, and consequently consumers postponed their purchases: if money will be worth more tomorrow, then why buy today when you can buy tomorrow.

In the case of the developed economies, the low inflation environment after 2000 can be traced back to several factors. Up until the outbreak of the crisis, commodity and energy prices increased steeply. Similarly, real prices of agricultural goods also increased. At the same time, as globalisation grew stronger, larger and larger amounts of goods from the emerging economies were placed on the markets of the developed economies, and due to the lower labour costs the price level of these goods was significantly lower than the price level of similar categories of goods produced in the developed markets. In line with this, imported inflation was also generally low.

In addition to the disinflationary effect of globalisation, central banks' commitment to fighting inflation was also increasingly credible.

By anchoring inflation expectations, the central banks made a significant contribution to the development of the low inflation environment (Figures 178–180).

Figure 178. Energy and processed food prices
in Hungary compared to January 2000

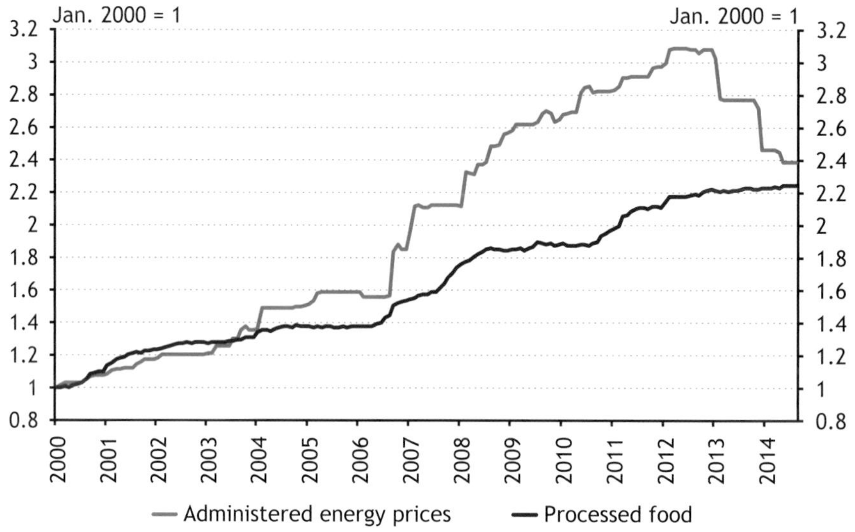

Source: MNB calculations based on HCSO data   Nominal change

Following the global crisis in 2008, the pace of growth and demand in global trade declined, both in the developed and emerging countries. Domestic and imported inflationary pressures both declined, leading to the risk of deflation.

Figure 179. Energy and processed food prices in Hungary

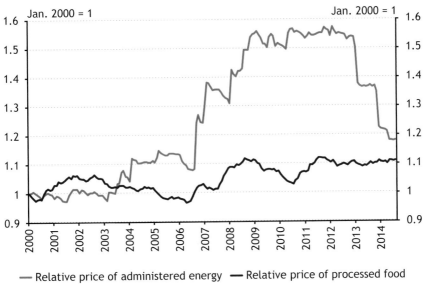

— Relative price of administered energy — Relative price of processed food

Source: MNB calculations based on HCSO data, change corrected with consumer price index

In Hungary, inflation was persistently higher than 3% during the period 2004–2014, but this was mainly due to economic policy and not to the high level of imported inflation. This was partly because food and energy prices consistently played a significant role in the actual rate of price increases, but during the period 2007–2010 (with the exception of the economic recession in 2009) government measures were the key factor driving the actual rate of inflation.

Similarly, inflationary pressure in the economy increased substantially in 2012 as a result of the tax system reform focusing on consumption and sales taxes: this was also related to economic policy and not to an increase in imported inflation (Figure 181).

Figure 180. Changes in major commodity prices, 2000-2014

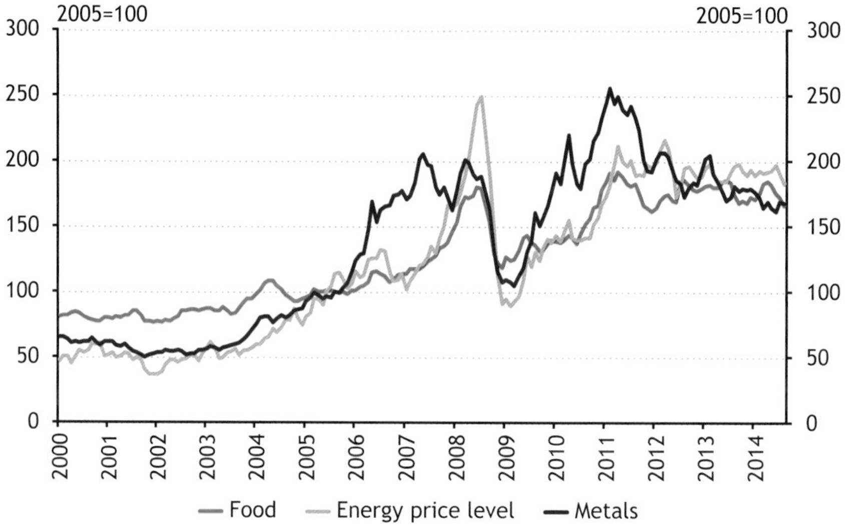

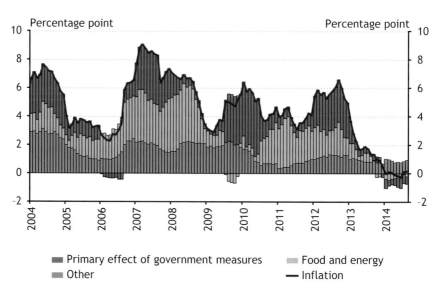

Source: IFS

Figure 181. Decomposition of inflation

Source: MNB calculations based on HCSO data

A turning point in inflation occurred in the Hungarian economy in 2013–2014. Government measures, utility cost cuts, and the reduction in energy prices and costs of public services reduced inflation significantly, and even led to negative inflation rates in 2014.

During the almost quarter century from 1990 to 2014, Hungarian consumer price inflation was mainly driven by five factors: the government's decisions as a regulatory authority, the position of the economic cycle, imported inflation, indirect taxes and inflation expectations.

During the first decade of EU membership from 2004 to 2014, inflation expectations played a very significant role. For the decade as a whole, inflation expectations ranged from 3–8%, and this factor alone maintained the high inflation environment all the way until the turning point in inflation in 2013–2014. Inflation expectations were particularly high during two periods: between 2007 and 2010, and between 2011 and 2013 (Figure 182).

Figure 182. Households' inflation expectations, 2001-2014

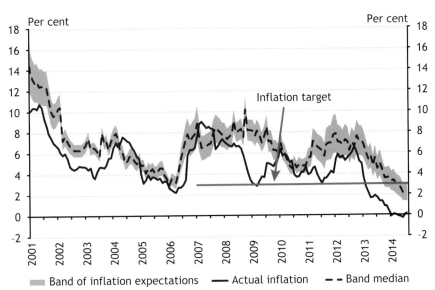

Source: MNB calculations based on data of the EU Commission

The strong rise in inflation expectations was triggered by the relatively high price increases for energy and food, mainly owing to the exchange rate effects which were felt by households. These effects were concentrated in two areas: the role of these two groups of goods is significant in the structure of consumption and perceived inflation, which is why they have such a pronounced effect on inflation expectations.

The trend reversal in inflation seen in 2013–2014 promises to be a lasting development in the Hungarian economy. The factors behind this change suggest that inflation will remain near the central bank's 3% medium-term inflation target over the long run.

No significant inflation is expected in the field of government regulated prices in the coming years, and the transition to the new tax system was completed by 2013–2014. Taking into consideration the steadily low budget deficit, no further increases in indirect taxes are anticipated, and thus this factor will not exert any large degree of inflationary pressure. Imported inflation is low, due to the low levels of inflation in the EU economies, and mainly in the euro area economies, along with actual deflation in some countries. In line with this, inflation expectations are declining: In 2014, consumers expected inflation to be below 3%, while the actual data show that the rate of inflation was below 1%.

In a small, open economy, it is important to also take into consideration the effect of the exchange rate on inflation. After 2009, the impact of changes in the exchange rate on consumer prices declined significantly. This was due to the factors cited above, in particular the development of regulated prices, the cyclical position of the economy and inflation expectations. The subdued demand environment generally limited price-raising decisions, while strict government regulation of prices reduced the immediate inflationary impact in the case of goods with regulated prices. Finally, the ongoing decline in inflation expectations and the generally lower inflation environment will lower the degree and frequency of repricing over the long term, thus also resulting in low pass-through on the whole. In contrast to the experiences prior to the crisis, due to the lower degree of exchange rate pass-through, the gradual weakening of the exchange rate did not jeopardise the central bank's primary goal, i.e. ensuring medium-term price stability.

Development of underlying inflation indicators

During the first decade of EU membership, Hungarian inflation underwent a structural change. The three indicators of inflation – core inflation excluding the effects of indirect taxes, demand-sensitive inflation and sticky price inflation – displayed different developments over the decade, and the differences were mainly caused by the government's economic policy during the year in question.

Between 2004 and 2006, following Hungary's accession of the EU, the three underlying inflation indicators declined, and in particular core inflation excluding indirect tax effects fell from the earlier level of 4% to 1% (Figure 183).

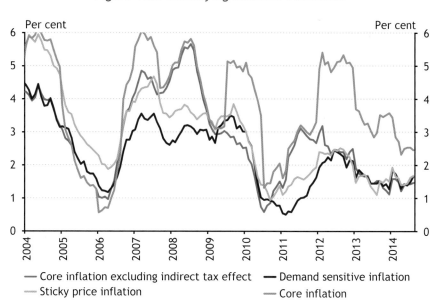

Figure 183. Underlying inflation indicators

Source: HCSO and MNB calculations based on HCSO data

The first half of 2006 mirrored the failure of economic policy. While policymakers tolerated a much higher deficit than the 3% of GDP target during the period 2004–2006, despite the already falling inflation environment they also moved to lower the rate of VAT prior to the elections, creating an even larger hole in the budget. During this period, downward trends were registered for demand-sensitive inflation and sticky price inflation, while at the same time imported inflation was low and consumers' inflation expectations were falling.

This was an auspicious combination of circumstances: in an environment of declining inflation, economic policy benefited from the advantages of EU membership, but at the same time failed to meet the 3% deficit target obligation undertaken upon accession, and the ratio of government debt was also steadily rising.

In the period 2004–2006, several hundred billion forints worth of state investment was financed from EU funds, while the fiscal balance deteriorated in the meantime.

This changed with the austerity programme launched on 1 September 2006, which was simultaneously the first negative turning point in inflation during Hungary's first decade of EU membership. Inflation surged higher, but this was not due to new tax revenues, because the government still did not launch tax reform in the interests of consolidating the budget, even though it increased the middle VAT rate (which had been lowered at the beginning of the year) to the level of the highest VAT rate. The reason for the high inflation was the government's decisions to raise regulated prices. The first attempt to restore economic balance between 2006 and 2008 resulted in higher inflation, but failed to progress with tax reform. It was not the effect of new indirect taxes or the earlier consumption and turnover taxes (aside from abandoning the intermediate VAT bracket) which raised inflation, but rather the result of increases in regulated prices.

These increases in regulated prices mainly benefited foreign-owned energy utilities operating in the monopoly sector and did not benefit the budget, as the GDP-proportionate fiscal deficit remained above 3%. Demand-sensitive inflation surged higher, and sticky price inflation also rose.

The government fuelled this inflation, attempting to thus improve the fiscal balance in a concealed manner. The budget profited from every unexpected increase in the rate of inflation, as inflation generally spreads though the economy and due to price increases budget revenues increase, basically via indirect taxes. During these years, these sources provided the budget with additional annual revenues on the order of tens of billions of forints, but even this was not enough to achieve the deficit target of 3% of GDP. Furthermore, this attempt to improve the balance by way of inflation ran into its own limitations. As a result of the steadily increasing government debt, the debt-servicing expenses of the budget also increased, and thus what the budget gained over the short term from the higher inflation, it gradually lost due to the rising debt-servicing expenses on public debt.

The period of high inflation in 2011–2012 was completely different in nature. At first glance, it may appear similar to the 2006–2008 period, but the rate of core inflation excluding indirect tax effects only reached 3%, compared to the peak of 6% seen during the earlier period. The sustainability of the turnaround in inflation which occurred in 2013–2014 is underlined by the fact that all three of the underlying inflation indicators – core inflation excluding indirect tax effects, demand-sensitive inflation and sticky price inflation – are moving on a concerted downward trend.

As we saw, increases in agricultural product and food prices had a significant effect on domestic inflation in the decade between 2004 and 2014. Above and beyond energy prices (which generated a substantial degree of inflationary pressure due to decisions on regulated prices) and inflation expectations, the increases in agricultural product and food prices actually played the most important role in the rise in consumer price inflation (Figure 184).

Figure 184. Agricultural producer prices

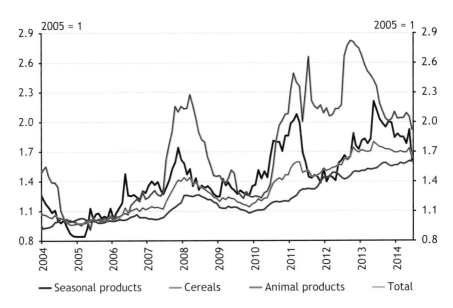

Source: MNB calculations based on HCSO data

Agricultural producer prices were the decisive factor behind the development of these prices.

The price index of seasonal products shows natural fluctuation, while a steadily upward trend is seen for products of animal origin. By contrast, sharp outliers are seen in prices of cereals: in 2007–2008, and then between 2010 and 2011 and then again in 2012–2013, producer prices for cereals jump sharply higher in the Hungarian economy. At the same time, we also find significant imported inflation among the factors determining domestic producer prices.

Industrial producer prices also exhibit similar cyclicality (Figure 185).

Figure 185. Annual change in industrial producer prices

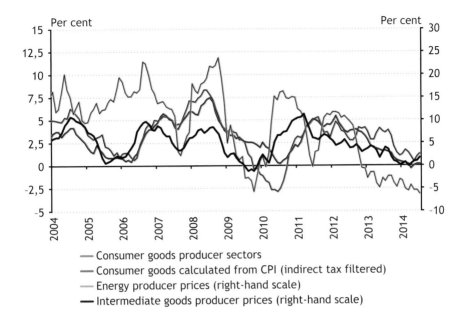

Source: MNB calculations based on HCSO data

The development of prices mainly reflects economic policy and cyclical effects. In the context of rising global commodity prices, the economic policy of allowing energy utilities to reap extra profits was reflected in the high domestic energy prices between 2004 and 2006. In contrast to agricultural producer prices, industrial producer prices moved on a consistently downward path between 2011 and 2014. With the exception of producer prices in the energy production sector, this was also true for consumer goods and for sectors producing intermediate goods. The downward trend in industrial producer prices can mainly be traced back to low imported inflation and weak domestic demand.

Low imported inflation facilitates the turnaround in inflation

Hungary's financial consolidation, and the inflation turnaround in particular, was steadily supported by the low level of inflation in the global economy. During this period, inflation was low in the euro area, in the US economy, in the Central and Eastern European countries and in China as well. The environment of low imported inflation facilitated the turnaround in Hungarian inflation in 2013–2014, and without this factor it would hardly have been possible to implement the reduction of around 25% in energy prices, which contributed to the recovery in consumption, and thus promoted consolidation by way of higher tax revenues from rising consumption.

From 2011–2012, low inflation is seen in the developed economies, the euro area and the USA, whereas inflation in the Central and Eastern European countries was higher than in other groups between 2012 and 2013, due to changes in exchange rates and weakening of the national currencies. During the period 2013–2014, imported inflation also fell in the Central and Eastern European economies (Figure 186).

After 2012–2013, the inflationary pressure stemming from commodities was also weak in the global economy. Projections for oil price futures indicate low inflationary pressure until 2016, and while cereal price futures suggest a rising level of prices, the increases are lower than the previous peaks.

In terms of sustainable low inflation in Hungary, in relation to imported inflation for processed goods the most important inflation forecasts are those in Hungary's most important trading partner, the euro area. In respect of these, the largest outliers are seen in producer prices: in 2006–2007 and in 2008–2009, producer price increases were high, in the wake of the 2008 crisis these prices then declined steeply in 2009, and following a period of recovery producer prices for commodities once again hit a peak in the euro area in 2011. After the period of recovery, from 2011–2012, euro area producer prices steadily decline.

Smaller fluctuations were seen in commodity prices in the euro area, but the trend essentially matches the trend for producer price levels as a whole. The smallest fluctuations were seen in euro area consumer prices in the decade between 2004 and 2014 (Figure 187).

Figure 186. Global inflation trends

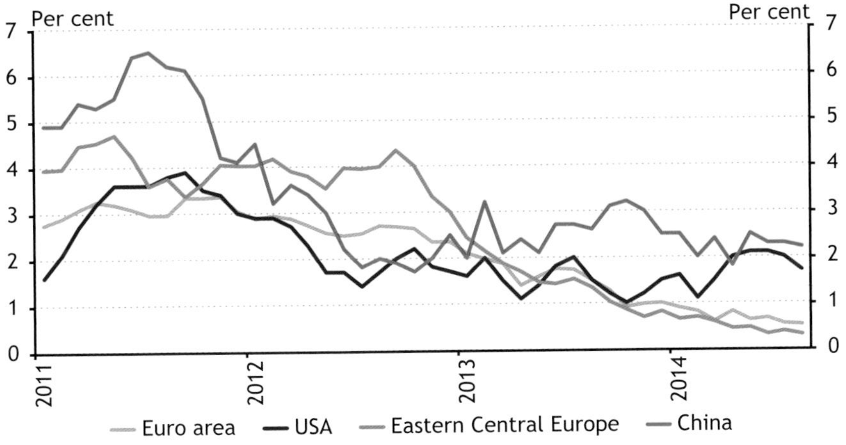

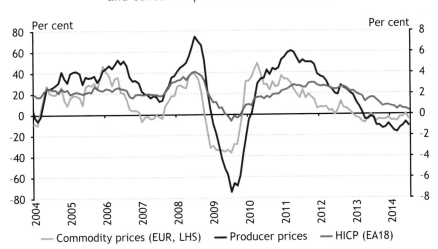

Source: Eurostat, OECD

Figure 187. Commodity, industrial producer
and consumer prices in the euro area

Source: IMF, Eurostat

These reflect cyclical developments in the economy: during stronger upturns the trends rise and during cyclical downturns the trends move on a downward path. During the crisis in 2009, consumer price inflation in the euro area also dipped into negative territory. From 2012, however, the trend in consumer prices moved on a downward path as well. Consequently, the low domestic inflation environment was exposed to the opposite risk, namely the threat of deflation, as indicated by the declines in commodity prices and producer prices in 2013–2014, while consumer price inflation hovered at a rate of around zero.

Decisive impact of government measures in inflation

One of the main features of Hungarian inflation developments is that, in line with the undisciplined fiscal behaviour, government measures were always a decisive factor during the one and a half decades after 2000, until the turning point in 2013–2014. The main role was played by increases in regulated prices, the expansion of indirect taxes and increases in existing tax rates. For one and a half decades, the government's economic policy increased inflation by an average of around 2% annually.

Out of this fifteen years, five individual years stand out: 2004, 2007, the two years period between 2009 and 2010, and 2012. In these years, government measures increased domestic inflation far in excess of the 2% average for the entire period. One feature of the government measures was that the increase in regulated prices and indirect taxes occurred within the framework of fiscal consolidation packages (Figure 188).

In mid-2002, a negative turning point in economic policy was reached in Hungary and consequently the Hungarian state budget immediately moved onto an unsustainable path in 2002. This continued in 2003, and an implicit budget consolidation programme was consequently launched in 2004, as a result of which inflation in 2004 accelerated due to the government measures.

The government's fiscal consolidation which started from autumn 2006 resulted in increases in regulated prices from 1 January 2007, leading to a steep rise in inflation in 2007. This continued in 2009–2010, and during this period there were also government decisions on indirect taxes intended to help restore fiscal balance. These attempts were unsuccessful: it was not possible to achieve a deficit lower than 3%, neither with the implicit budget consolidation using a concealed increase in inflation in 2004, nor with the adjustments implemented in 2007–2008. Similarly, the second attempt at budget consolidation in 2009–2010 was also unsuccessful, despite the fact that economic policy also opted to use inflation as a tool for implicit budget consolidation in this case as well.

Figure 188. Direct inflationary effect of government measures, 2001-2015

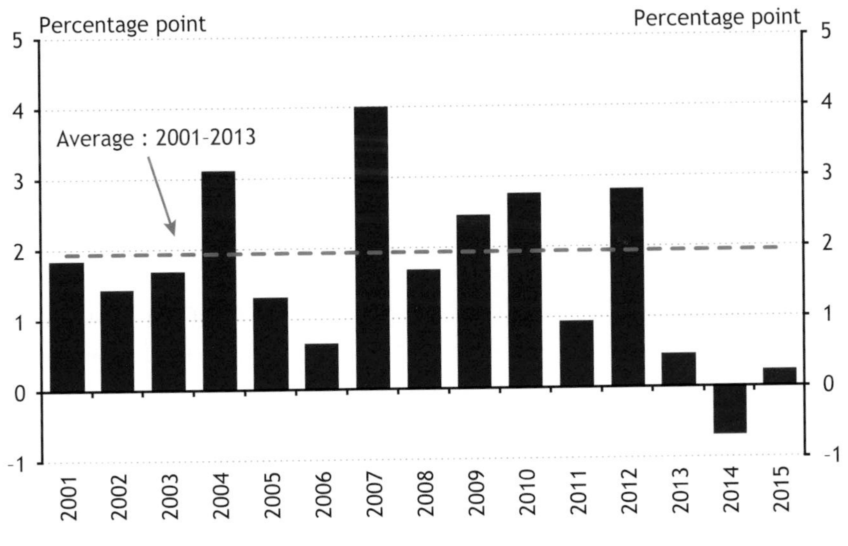

Source: MNB

In 2012, economic policy once again resorted to government measures to improve the budget position and was successful, since the deficit of the Hungarian state budget constantly remained below 3% of GDP in 2012, 2013 and 2014. Indeed, in 2013–2014 there was a major reduction in regulated prices, and the cut in utility prices also made a significant contribution to inflation reaching a turning point in 2013–2014.

Consolidation of the state budget was also achieved, in addition to the substantial reduction in inflation. Economic policy only increased consumption-type taxes significantly in one single year, namely 2012, in conjunction with transformation of the tax system. Following this, the introduction or increase of other kinds of indirect tax did not have a tangible inflationary impact, and consequently reform of the tax system did not jeopardise the turnaround in inflation.

The development of inflation was similar to that of another factor: the path of the central bank's policy rate. As a result of the 24-month rate-cutting cycle between August 2012 and July 2014, the MNB's policy rate fell by 490 basis points. The exchange rate weakening effect of this reduction could have restrained the downward trend in inflation, but this did not occur. In part, the reason for this was that the earlier connection between the exchange rate and inflation changed after 2008: prior to 2008, a forint exchange rate which was 10 forints weaker increased domestic inflation by 1%, but after 2008 the same amount of depreciation only had less than one half of this effect on inflation over a two-year horizon. Via the channel of monetary transmission, the lower policy rate also resulted in lower interest rate levels on the financial and capital markets, reducing the capital costs of investments. In the case of indebted corporate agents, it may have reduced cost-side pressures due to lower interest expenses, and thus lowering the central bank's policy rate increased firms' leeway during a period of debt reduction.

Compared to other groups of EU countries, the Hungarian policy rate declined to a large degree, but nonetheless disinflation was seen in the period from 2012 to summer 2014. While the consumer price index declined by 5.5% in Hungary during this time frame, the decline in the CPI in the southern euro area countries was about half as much and the decline for the euro area as a whole was roughly one third lower during this period, compared to the previous years (Figure 189).

It can be seen that the turning point in inflation occurred at the same time as the central bank's rate-cutting cycle, and the increase in inflation in 2012 was not the result of the reduction of the policy rate during that year, but rather stemmed from the introduction of the higher indirect taxes from 1 January 2012 and the new types of taxes.

Figure 189. Inflation, August 2012 – August 2014

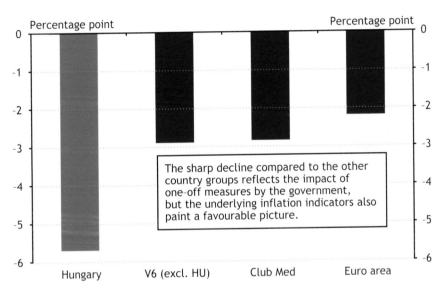

Source: OECD   Harmonised inflation data (based on HICP)

No sign of domestic inflationary pressure in the Hungarian economy

In terms of domestic inflationary pressure, along with the government's economic policy (setting regulated prices, changes to indirect taxes) and the monetary policy (the level of the policy rate, the monetary policy tools used by the central bank), the key factor determining whether or not there is domestic inflationary pressure in the Hungarian economy is the behaviour of consumers.

Instead of taking out new loans, households are making the reduction of old loans the top priority, and the importance of financial savings has also increased in their decisions. This represents a significant change in Hungarian families' financial awareness.

This change in the internal values of society is probably best reflected by the development of households' net financial assets in the two decades between 1994 and 2014. The year 1994 is a good starting point, because by that time the bulk of the shock transition to a market economy had already taken place, but it still precedes the Bokros package which was launched in 1995–1996 in response to the twin deficit. At the very beginning of the 2000s, there had not yet been a surge in irresponsible borrowing and debt accumulation, because although borrowing by the household sector had started, it was still restricted to HUF-denominated loans.

Figure 190. Ratio of households' financial assets to disposable income

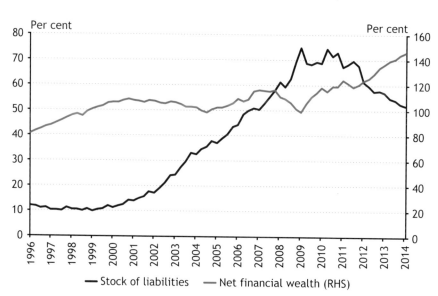

Stock of liabilities   Net financial wealth (RHS)

Source: MNB, HCSO

After 2002, there was a change in the trend both in terms of quantity and quality. The turning point in quantity is reflected in the change of the steepness of the curve, and in the following years Hungarian households increasingly take on debt in Swiss franc and in euro, and to a smaller extent in Japanese yen as well.

The curve rises sharply all the way until 2008, and then, strangely enough, we also see a peak in 2010, but this reflects the higher level of foreign currency debt due to HUF depreciation (Figure 190).

After 2010, the reduction of household debt starts on a trend which is similarly as steep as the accumulation of household debt which was seen earlier. Furthermore, this does not represent merely another (in this case positive) turning point in the quantity of household debt, as a hidden change in quality also occurred. The early repayment scheme which lowered the stock of households' foreign currency loans, followed by the exchange rate cap system and then from autumn 2014 the adoption of new laws paving the way for a final solution to foreign currency loans resulted in a continuous reduction of households' exchange rate exposure, because these measures all lowered the volume of foreign currency loans.

The development of households' net financial assets in the two decades between 1994 and 2014 is mainly related to changes in the loans borrowed by households: before households became indebted, the ratio of net financial assets to disposable income was on the rise, whereas during the period of debt accumulation the level of financial assets fluctuated. After 2010, households' net financial assets move on a steadily upward trend. Nominal incomes and real wages have a smaller effect on the trend and level of households' net financial assets than the quantity and quality of loans borrowed by households. A strong relationship developed between households' net financial assets and borrowing during the two decades between 1994 and 2014. In addition to the tighter lending conditions, this is also why the change in families' system of values is important as well, because in this new system borrowing is considered much more carefully and the importance of financial savings is higher. Accordingly, during a very short period after 2008, Hungarian households switched over to more cautious and prudent financial behaviour, preferring to pay off earlier loans and accumulate new financial savings rather than take out new loans.

From the point of view of inflation, this also means that a large part of households' disposable income was not being used on the market for consumer goods: households focused mainly on buying financial investment products, but also started new investments other than financial investments during the renewed upturn on the real estate market.

In terms of domestic inflation factors, weaker inflationary pressure was generated by increasing real wages on the domestic market compared to the past, because financial investments became a central aspect of families' values, in addition to consumption.

The turning point in inflation in 2013–2014 occurred despite the fact that – due to economic stabilisation – capacity utilisation increased in sectors which are less critical for the development of inflation. The higher level of capacity utilisation in the construction industry was mainly the result of infrastructure investments financed with EU funding. Construction industry output did not increase due to new household borrowing on the real estate market, which would have been a risk factor in terms of inflationary pressure, but rather as a result of infrastructure projects financed with EU funding.

A similar situation was seen in relation to the expansion of output in manufacturing: higher capacity utilisation in manufacturing led to neither direct nor indirect pressure on inflation developments (Figure 191).

Figure 191. Weak demand as the main barrier to output growth

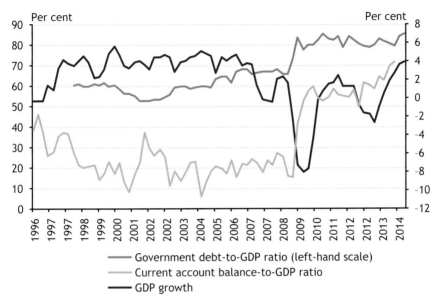

Source: ESI survey   *Deviation from the historical average*

At the time of the recovery in growth and consumption in 2013–2014, capacity utilisation in the services sector also increased, but the level of utilisation in this sector did not reach the levels seen prior to the steep decline in 2009. The combination of weak imported inflation, changes in families' values, successful budget consolidation (obviating the need for additional tax hikes), the steady expansion of households' net financial assets and the adjustment of inflation expectations had the result that a sustainable level of inflation of around 3% was reached in Hungary during the second half of the 2010s, meaning that the turning point in inflation which occurred in 2013–2014 may well prove to be a lasting phenomenon.

Chapter 16

Balance restored in the Hungarian economy

The new politics and economic policy launched in 2010 immediately propelled the Hungarian economy towards sustainable financial balance, but this had to be strengthened from outside to achieve a complete turnaround.

Termination of the excessive deficit procedure

At the time of EU accession, i.e. on 1 May 2004, Hungary – together with the other member states – undertook to abide by the provisions of the Stability and Growth Pact, the most basic of which is keeping the general government deficit below 3% of GDP each year.[44] The Hungarian economy did not meet this target between accession and 2010, as the deficit was higher than 3% every year. As a result, Hungary was continuously subject to the excessive deficit procedure (EDP) in the first decade of EU membership, i.e. until mid-2013.

In the IMF-EU agreement concluded in autumn 2008, economic policymakers also committed to meeting the annual cash flow and ESA budget deficit targets. For 2010, the third year of the programme, the government set a 3.8% target for the general government deficit – i.e. above the 3% it guaranteed at the time of the EU accession – in the regularly reviewed loan agreement.

---

[44] The Treaty on the Functioning of the European Union (TFEU) specifies two requirements: A) The ratio of the planned or actual budget deficit to gross domestic product should not exceed 3%, unless the proportion decreases substantially and continuously, and reaches a level close to the reference value; or unless the excess over the reference value is only exceptional and temporary and the ratio remains close to the reference value. B) The debt-to-GDP ratio should not exceed 60%, unless the ratio sufficiently diminishes and approaches the reference value at a satisfactory pace.

This means that neither the IMF nor the EU considered a deficit of less than 3% to be realistic for 2010, which demonstrates the effects of the misguided economic policy and the failed attempts at consolidation. In autumn 2009, despite the relatively high deficit target, economic policy overestimated the revenues and underestimated the expenses for the 2010 budget: in fact, a general government deficit of 7% was stated in the budget for 2010.

Although Hungary did not meet the deficit target of less than 3% which it undertook at the time of the EU accession or the 3.8% deficit stipulated in the IMF-EU agreement, viewed in the context of the high budget deficits in the EU after the crisis, the deficit of around 4% which was achieved thanks to the political and economic policy renewal in mid-2010 was acceptable both for Hungary's international partners and investors.

In 2011, Hungary reached a fiscal turning point: it was the first time since EU accession that the deficit-to-GDP ratio was below 3% according to the EU budgetary methodology (ESA95) used at that time.[45] It must be noted, however, that this fiscal turning point did not result from the funds from the mandatory private pension fund system. While these accumulated funds assisted in offsetting one-off expenses in 2011, in the following years the deficit was steadily below 3% without them. Nevertheless, transformation of the mandatory private pension system also contributed to the sustained improvement in balance, but not through the transfer of the accumulated funds (i.e. assets), but rather by channelling the annual contributions of HUF 360 billion from 97% of the previous members of private funds into the public pension

[45] The new methodology for national accounting systems, ESA2010, was introduced in the EU in 2014. It included changes to the ESA95 methodology, for example that the funds accumulated by private pension fund members cannot be recorded as revenue in the year when the members opt to return to the state system. This rule had to be applied retroactively as well, and therefore, in 2014, the general government balance for 2011 changed from a surplus of 4.3% to a deficit of 5.5%. According to the ESA-2010 methodology, the transaction does not affect the general government balance in the year of transfer but, peculiarly, in the future when pension payments for members who opted to return to the state system are due.

system. Without this, the deficit would not have been below 3% in each year since 2011. Thus, remedying Hungary's fiscal imbalance was not brought about by the assets, but rather by the income.

In mid-2013, the European Commission removed Hungary from the list of countries subject to the excessive deficit procedure. This was an exceptional success, as Hungary was the only EU country which had been subject to the excessive deficit procedure since accession. In fact, based on its duration, it could even be seen as a double excessive deficit procedure, since Hungary well exceeded the period of a few years the European Council usually sets for correcting the excessive deficit. Hungary failed to meet the EU's 3% deficit requirement not only in the years following accession in 2004, but also in 2007–2008, i.e. before the global financial crisis, during a period of economic upswing (Figure 192).

Figure 192. Countries subject to the Excessive Deficit Procedure (EDP)

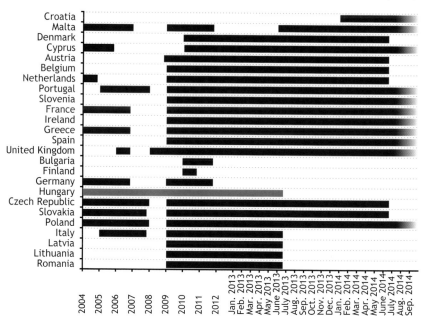

Prior to 2013, truncated years were taken into account by colouring the year in which the EDP was launched, whereas the year in which it ended is left empty.

Source: European Commission

As regards fiscal balance, Hungary saw the worst performance in the years between its 2004 accession and 2010. However, following the fiscal turnaround in 2011, Hungary achieved the greatest trend change in fiscal balance among the EU member states. This was acknowledged by termination of the excessive deficit procedure in mid-2013. The excessive deficit procedures against Italy, Latvia, Lithuania and Romania were also terminated at this time (Figure 193).

Figure 193. Budget balance-to-GDP ratio

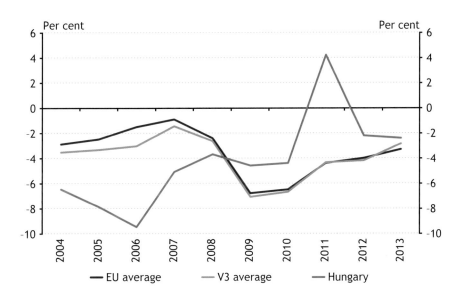

Source: Eurostat

The majority of EU member states remained under the excessive deficit procedure, signalling financial imbalances and an unsustainable budget. From an economic history perspective, Hungary's performance was exceptional in the first decade following its EU accession, which was clearly the positive impact of the new politics and economic policies launched after mid-2010.

According to EU rules, an excessive deficit procedure is launched against a country if actual data or its own prognosis shows that it will breach the deficit threshold of 3%, and the deviation is not small and temporary [TFEU[46] Article 126(2)][47].

At the negotiations with the European Commission in autumn 2012, Hungarian economic policymakers successfully argued in favour of terminating the excessive deficit procedure. The fiscal turnaround in 2011 resulted in a deficit of less than 3%, the deficit target for 2012 was feasible, and the budgetary plan for the 2013 deficit was based on well-founded calculations.

However, the decision-makers of the Magyar Nemzeti Bank published calculations in December 2012 forecasting that the MNB would post substantial losses amounting to HUF 203 billion in 2013. In that case, it would have been necessary for the state budget to cover the loss on the MNB's balance sheet in the following year (2014): this would have generated a new budgetary expense of 0.7% in GDP terms. Since actual data of below 3% and forward-looking budget plan figures for another two years are necessary for the abrogation of the excessive deficit procedure, the positive budgetary outlook for 2014 was undermined by the MNB's loss estimate for 2013 (Figure 194).

The negative prognosis by the MNB was underpinned by several factors. On the one hand, the MNB did not project any further reductions of the base rate, as the decision-makers of the central bank did not support the monthly rate cuts of the rate-cutting cycle launched in August 2012, which was initiated and maintained by the votes of the external members. The projection used a higher rate than the actual base rate turned out to be in the future, and this resulted in additional expenses in the balance sheet of the MNB for two-week bonds (which were later

---

[46] Consolidated version of the Treaty on the Functioning of the European Union.
[47] For details, see: European Commission (2013): Building a Strengthened Fiscal Framework in the European Union: A Guide to the Stability and Growth Pact, Occasional Papers 150.

converted into deposits by the central bank in 2014). The MNB also did not take into account the conversion of certain elements of the currency reserves for debt servicing (e.g. prepayment of the IMF loan) by the state, which had a positive effect on the balance sheet of the central bank, or the resulting profits for the central bank. On the other hand, the forecast was based on a much stronger exchange rate than the actual one, which also pointed to larger losses than were actually realised. At the turn of 2012–2013, the European Commission accepted the profit forecast of the MNB and thus a deficit figure of above 3% for 2014: had that been realised, it would not have been possible to terminate the excessive deficit procedure against Hungary.

Figure 194. Projected and actual MNB losses

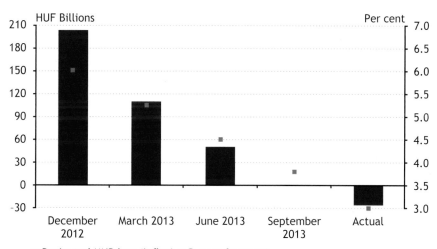

Projected MNB loss (Inflation Report forecast)
Prevailing base rate at the time of forecast preparation (right-hand scale)

Source: MNB   ** base rate for December 2013*

In spring 2013, after notification by the new leadership of the MNB, the European Commission adjusted its assessment of the Hungarian budget for 2014. As a result of the continued rate-cutting cycle, the profits from the state conversion linked to the repayment of maturing FX bonds and the prepayment of the IMF loan as well as other cost-efficiency measures, the MNB's new policymakers projected that there would be no losses by the end of 2013. Consequently, the deficit for 2014 was no longer projected to be above 3%, and it was possible to remove Hungary from the excessive deficit procedure in summer 2013.

Fiscal turnaround paves the way for a revival in consumption

After the negative change in economic policy from 2002, Hungary moved onto a path of unsustainable balance. All three economic agents – the general government, businesses and households – were involved in the new borrowing, and the growing new stock of outstanding loans (which increasingly consisted of foreign currency loans) added a quality risk element into the financial system.

Within the framework of the economic policy launched in mid-2002, this borrowing fuelled an artificial upswing in the Hungarian economy: overspending by the state generated surplus consumption and investment, household borrowing created a real estate market bubble, and the corporate sector reacted to the artificial upturn by bringing forward future investments. All three agents contributed to this artificial upswing, and consequently outstanding loans accumulated rapidly. State institutions – the Ministry of Finance representing the government, the supervisory authority and the central bank – failed to limit the extent of this borrowing or improve its distorted composition which entailed quality risks.

The fiscal situation had to be stabilised between 2010 and 2014, a special period in economic history. The situation was peculiar because the global crisis of 2008 was a debt-based financial crisis. Such crises are caused by the unsustainable debt accumulation of one or more economic agents, which is usually followed by a prolonged phase of debt reduction after the eruption of the crisis. In that phase, economic agents concentrate on stabilising their financial position, i.e. they strive for higher saving rates instead of consumption and investments. Higher propensity to save perpetuates an environment of weak demand.

This was the situation in Hungary as well. Households, and to a lesser extent businesses, were focused on redressing their balance sheets, which dramatically reduced aggregate demand. Fiscal consolidation in itself also lowers the already weak demand. International experiences show that this effect can be especially pronounced if the measures for improving the general government balance affect economic agents which are in the process of adjusting their balance sheets anyway. This realisation also justified the tax measures introduced after 2010. In accordance with the principle of burden sharing, the extra tax revenues for consolidating the budget had to be collected from groups with greater resilience, instead of households in the phase of balance sheet adjustment.

The turnaround in 2010–2014 is especially commendable, because – even though indirect taxes, the new tax types and the higher rates of previously existing tax types played a major role – the consolidation process could not rely on a trend change in consumption or the resulting revenues until mid-2013. Fiscal consolidation was achieved by the transition to an indirect tax regime without expanding the tax base of indirect taxes.

Restoring fiscal balance in Hungary could not rely on inflation revenues either, since (apart from the high inflation rate of 5.7% in 2012, i.e. at the time of transition to the indirect tax regime) the successful fiscal consolidation was carried out in an environment of persistently low and decreasing inflation. In 2013–2014, Hungary's economic balance entered onto a sustainable path in a context of strong disinflation, which was due to the government's utility cost reduction programme and low imported inflation.

Turnaround in economic balance coupled with rising net wealth for households

Hungarian households brought their consumption and investments forward during the artificial domestic upswing between 2002 and mid-2010, financing these expenses by borrowing. While the balance sheet adjustment of the banking system and the corporate sector started at the onset of the 2008 financial crisis, the misguided government decision that failed to limit foreign currency lending postponed this for households.

Between 2010 and 2014, the net financial position of households improved by HUF 9,000 billion: almost one-third of this figure can be attributed to the positive impact of deleveraging, while two-thirds was due to financial investments from current income and the revaluation of existing savings (Figures 195–196).

Figure 195. Households' net financial wealth

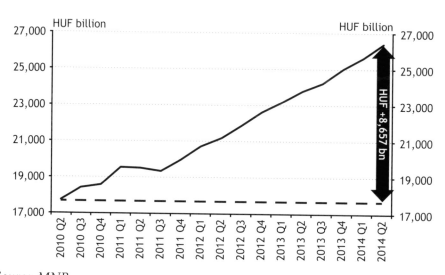

Source: MNB

Figure 196. Components of changes in households' net financial wealth

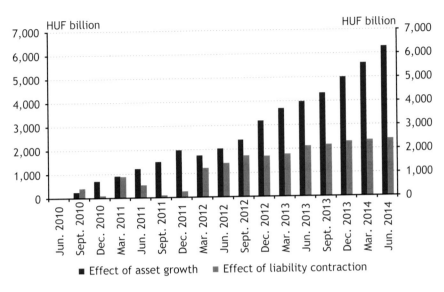

Source: MNB

From the second half of 2010, however, the net financial wealth of households started to expand: a clear trend change could be observed in the financial behaviour of social groups with the ability to save as well as those who had taken out loans.

Although the repayment of loans already increased net financial wealth in mid-2010, the reduction of forint and foreign currency loans gained momentum in spring 2012, partly because of the early repayment scheme. A critical factor in this regard was that the government banned household FX lending, while the high forint interest rates and the inherited outstanding loans limited the scope of new financial obligations, i.e. new borrowing by households.

In late 2012 and early 2013, the transformation of disposable income into new financial investments started: while the reduction of existing forint and foreign currency loans was stepped up, the investment of households' disposable income in financial instruments – primarily in Hungarian government securities – started to pick up.

In Hungarian economic history, there is no precedent of a period in which households' financial circumstances improved at such a pace and to such an extent.

The financial shock resulting from the new household indebtedness between 2002 and 2010 reshaped the driving forces behind the financial behaviour of households: the desire for quick gains was replaced by a focus on stability and security over the medium and long term. This change in behavioural patterns is expected to be a lasting development in Hungarian society, since society brought considerable consumption and investment decisions forward to 2002–2010 from 2010–2020. Looking at the period 2010 to 2020, the artificial upswing experienced in 2002–2010 is not expected to reoccur on the real estate market or in the demand for consumer durables, since families have become more cautious in borrowing, despite the steadily improving forint lending terms.

The repayment of existing loans, especially foreign currency loans, and the financial investment of new income resulted in a positive turnaround in the net financial wealth of households and increased their net lending as well. Due to the accumulation of receivables and the reduction of debts, net lending – the critical determinant of financial security – was enhanced for broad groups in society (Figure 197).

We were also witnesses to another rare moment in economic history. In autumn 2008, the global and European financial crisis hit suddenly, from one moment to the next, and a two-fold financial crisis unfolded in the Hungarian economy: the internal crisis caused by the earlier economic policy intersected with the external crisis triggered by the bursting of the American real estate market bubble. Hungarian households responded immediately to this dual financial crisis: net borrowing, which used to amount to 6% of GDP, ceased instantly after the crisis erupted, and the reduction of debts started. Therefore, the major part of the previously postponed adjustment by households happened in the span of a year.

Figure 197. Net lending of households, % of GDP

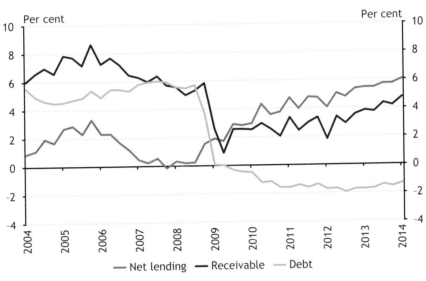

Source: MNB   Seasonally adjusted

This had a significant effect on domestic consumption. The negative economic policy shift in mid-2002 gave a swift boost to consumption and catapulted annual real growth in household consumption to the absolutely unsustainable level of 8%. Even before EU accession, the real growth rate of household consumption started to shrink. It plunged from 8% in 2003 to 2% in the year of accession, and remained at that level until September 2006, when the first attempt at fiscal adjustment was launched to rectify the imbalances.

The volume of consumption dropped again in 2006–2007 during the first attempt at consolidation, which was quickly followed by the second attempt at fiscal consolidation in 2008–2009, again reducing consumption. The two consolidation attempts between 2006 and 2010 pulled down the real growth rate of household consumption into negative territory, with the rate later reaching an exceptional, historic low of -6%. Real household consumption growth climbed from this level until 2011, but it then temporarily returned to negative territory as a result of the third (and finally successful) attempt at consolidation. The successful transition to sustainable fiscal balance in 2013–2014 resulted in another positive development, as the real growth rate returned to a level reflecting the true consumption capacity of households (Figure 198).

The development of households' net financial savings in the first decade of EU membership is similarly intriguing. From the years preceding EU accession until 2005, households' net financial savings steadily increased, but then from that point on, this indicator continuously decreased or stagnated until the end of 2008. The deteriorating income situation after the 2006 consolidation might have played a role in this, together with the fact that households had invested mostly in the real estate market until the eruption of the crisis.

Figure 198. Household consumption and savings, and net external debt

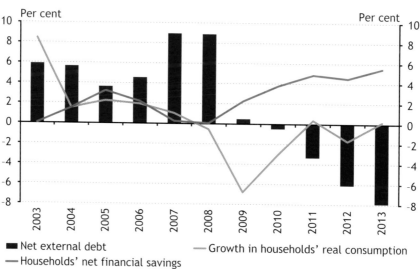

Net external debt
Households' net financial savings
Growth in households' real consumption

Trends in household savings, change in savings and external debt, % of GDP

Source: MNB, CSO

Turnaround in economic balance facilitated by the swift balance sheet adjustment of the corporate sector

The first decade of EU membership was characterised by two distinct phases in the corporate sector's borrowing behaviour. In the first phase, between 2004 and autumn 2008, borrowing increased sharply. The Hungarian corporate sector behaved exactly like the businesses in the region and the euro area: they reacted to the general upswing by expanding their investment and business activities, which called for more borrowing.

While outstanding corporate debt in the EU member states in the region and Hungary followed basically the same trend, in the countries on the southern flank of the euro area corporate debt increased by more than the euro area average, the EU average, the average of the Nordic countries or the average of the CEE countries (Figure 199).

Figure 199. Corporate lending by the credit institution sector

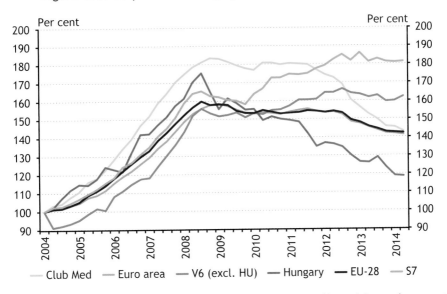

Loans extended by credit institutions, 2004=100%, data not adjusted for exchange rate effects

Source: MNB

The financial crisis that hit in autumn 2008 shattered the roughly homogeneous group of EU member states like a wrecking ball: of course, the average of the euro area and the whole EU followed the same trend, as both areas were characterised by a gradually diminishing level of outstanding corporate debt. By contrast, the Nordic countries – after a quick decrease in corporate debt between 2008 and 2010 – boosted borrowing again: they gave a capital-intensive response to the European and global crisis, i.e. they strengthened their competitiveness by new investments and loans for financing them. Of course, they were better positioned to do so, because they could probably secure better borrowing terms.

In the group of CEE EU member states excluding Hungary, where the EU's top economic performer, Poland, is a major player, the behaviour of businesses did not change significantly between 2008 and 2010: they managed the negative real economy impacts from the EU with a high investment rate and by sustaining the high level of loan financing. Unlike Hungary, the CEE countries did not undertake balance sheet adjustment in the corporate sector entailing sacrifices in employment and growth: they did not need to do so because they utilised the years they spent in the EU between 2004 and 2008 with a better investment and financing structure, and with a lower ratio of foreign currency loans. The southern countries of the euro area maintained the corporate debt stock that was accumulated by 2008 even longer than Hungary's region: they almost "glided through" the crisis in 2008–2011.

Banking sector adjustment through income "optimisation"

The banking sector launched a substantial balance sheet adjustment in autumn 2008. In response to the dual crisis, it adjusted to the decline in consumer and investment loans, coupled with a significant decrease in its external financing. Before the onset of the crisis, a considerable profit rate was achieved on the banking system's external liabilities:

investment in two-week central bank instruments, government securities and FX-denominated government securities purchases as well as FX-denominated lending to households and businesses financed from relatively low-interest foreign currency loans generated sizeable profits for the banking sector. It is indisputable that the profit rate achieved in 2004–2010 by foreign currency lending and external financing was well above the profit rate that could have been realised on forint financing and forint lending, and therefore the banking sector had an interest in maximising external financing and boosting foreign currency lending as much as possible. The widening gap between the interest rate in Hungary and in the euro area after 2008 also presented an opportunity for the banking sector to achieve high profits (Figure 200).

Figure 200. External liabilities of the banking system

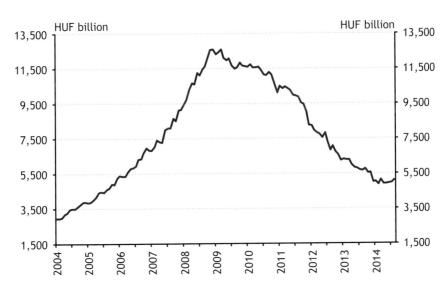

Source: MNB

Due to its external liabilities accumulated since 2002 and the stock of foreign currency loans it extended, the banking system had a distorted interest on the Hungarian money market. The foreign currency loans granted to households only generated steady and substantial profits for the banking system if the loans were repaid, i.e. borrowers did not default. This could be guaranteed to banks by the stability of the exchange rate at a level stronger than the equilibrium level. As we will see later, the nominal exchange rate might have contributed to the fact that the external and internal balance in the Hungarian economy could not be restored, and thus these factors could not support sustained economic growth.

During the balance sheet adjustment of the banking system after the crisis, the situation became even more complex: the considerably higher interest rates on the domestic money market – including the yields on government securities and the central bank's two-week instrument – sustained the banking system's interest in a strong forint exchange rate.

The development of the EUR/HUF exchange rate in the first decade of EU membership, and even over a longer time horizon, highlights a peculiar phenomenon in Hungarian economic history. The nominal EUR/HUF exchange rate shows how many forints one euro buys at the time of conversion. By contrast, the real effective forint exchange rate reflects – in addition to the movement of the nominal rate – the differences of the Hungarian economy compared to its trading partners as regards inflation, productivity and unit labour costs, and accordingly this indicator is better for assessing the effects on competitiveness. Excessive appreciation of the real exchange rate can cause competitiveness issues (Figure 201).

Similar to the experiences of other regional economies, the real exchange rate of the forint displayed an appreciation trend from the mid-1990s until the onset of the crisis. This was basically due to the higher growth rate, i.e. real economic convergence. After 2001, of the countries that joined the European Union in 2004, the Hungarian currency (together with the currencies of the Czech Republic and Slovakia) was among those that appreciated the most in real exchange rate terms. This trend characterised the Hungarian economy at a time when its real economic convergence almost continuously declined and increasingly lagged behind the above-mentioned countries.

Figure 201. Changes in the nominal and real effective exchange rate

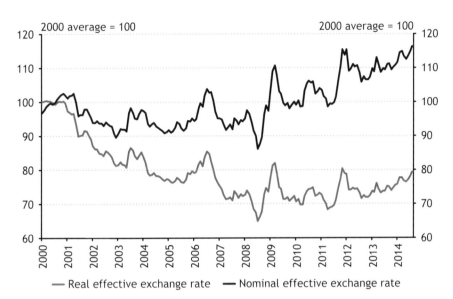

Source: MNB

The phenomenon demonstrates how the sustained imbalances in one segment of a small and open economy, such as the Hungarian one, can have spillover effects in the whole economy, causing serious sustainability and competitiveness issues.

Prior to the onset of the crisis, the real exchange rate increasingly deviated from the equilibrium path that would have been warranted by economic fundamentals. According to some estimates, the Hungarian currency may have been overvalued by as much as 20–30 forints in 2008. This meant that after EU accession, in the ever stiffer competition on the market, a Hungarian business generated less sales revenue in forint terms on each unit of EUR-denominated export than warranted by the differences in inflation, productivity and unit labour costs of the economies.

This difference primarily caused major competitiveness issues for the Hungarian-owned, export-oriented SME sector competing with imported products, contributing to a sustained decline in employment. The experiences of this period offer important lessons. For example, it became evident that an unsustainable budget deficit can indirectly cause distortions and imbalances in many other segments of the economy. This observation was also utilised in the new economic policy launched in 2010. Fiscal consolidation can only be successful and sustainable over the long term if it is coupled with the adjustment of imbalances in other markets (goods, money and labour markets).

In light of the above, it is natural to consider who had an interest in sustaining these imbalances and who profited from them? The distortion was ultimately caused by the state itself. In mid-2002, there was a negative shift in the economic policy of the government, which fuelled an artificial upswing financed from borrowing. Short-term, often politically motivated aspects superseded the arguments for long-term sustainability. This was stimulated by the excess liquidity on global capital markets, where substantial deficits and maturing debts could be financed at lower interest rates, while the artificially stable exchange rate obscured the risks and the actual costs that surfaced after the eruption of the crisis. The duality of high domestic forint interest rates and the stable exchange rate ensured steady and considerable profits for external investors buying Hungarian assets (either government securities or in the form of other synthetic transactions). Later, domestic commercial banks interested in sustaining and improving profitability also saw the lucrative potential of the situation, which was realised through widespread foreign currency lending. A significant mark-up could be achieved on foreign currency loans without a direct exchange rate risk, which, when lending was increasing, constantly boosted banks' profits. Of course, it must mentioned that the initially lower repayment instalments enhanced the possibilities of households and businesses as well, but when the crisis erupted the related exchange rate risk materialised as a major rise in repayment burdens.

Balance restored under unfavourable macroeconomic circumstances

The return to balance in 2013–2014, which finally proved sustainable, and the parallel trend reversals in growth, consumption and investment occurred in a macro environment that was quite unfavourable for financial consolidation and economic stabilisation. The fiscal path became sustainable when it was also assisted by recoveries in growth, consumption and investment.

The steady expansion of employment supported the restoration of macroeconomic balance all along: between 2010 and 2014, 400,000 new jobs were created, more than half of which were in the private sector. Balance was essentially restored via the revenue side of the budget as early as 2011, i.e. the second year of the new economic policy.

At the time this occurred, all of the other economic prerequisites which had played a role in past success stories involving traditional financial consolidation and economic stabilisation were absent. Consolidation and stabilisation was not facilitated by external economic conditions: the 2008–2009 global financial crisis turned into an economic crisis, external economic activity was weak in 2010–2011, and most of the economies in the EU experienced another downturn in 2012.

Restoring economic balance and stability was not supported by a domestic upswing either, because the factors of internal economic activity had no effect. The general government deficit was below 3%, which in itself dampened domestic demand and consumption. Household investment was restrained by the stock of foreign currency loans, which were taken out during the earlier artificial upturn – fuelled by lending – and which became toxic after the risks materialised.

Households, but also businesses, mainly reduced their existing loans instead of taking out new ones. For most of 2010–2014, economic policy could not expect consumption and investment-related factors to assist with consolidation and stabilisation.

The recovery in growth in 2013–2014 was primarily underpinned by strengthening exports, especially the stronger performance of capacities developed through foreign direct investment in the automotive and related industries. Although by 2014 the recovery in growth had spread throughout the Hungarian economy – as several other sectors were growing and consumption started to expand – economic balance had already been restored and the economy had stabilised. In fact, the improvement in economic balance would have been accomplished in Hungary between 2010 and 2014 even without a trend reversal in growth, consumption and investment.

This was a unique phenomenon in economic history, since in addition to these traditional factors, one specific element is usually required for successful fiscal consolidation and economic stabilisation: financial assistance from the International Monetary Fund and/or the European Union. This, however, was not the case in Hungary, because it had properly terminated the previous IMF-EU agreement in autumn 2010 without negotiating a new one. The lack of any other external institutional help was compensated by a factor that ultimately proved decisive: the trust of the international financial markets.

During the consolidation in 2010–2014, financial market sentiment was positive and supportive all along. The international and domestic financial markets expressed confidence in the Hungarian fiscal consolidation by continuously buying Hungarian government securities, although, in fairness, at relatively high yields, which temporarily surged at the turn of 2011–2012. Financial market agents not only showed their trust over the short term, they also expected the improvement in Hungary's economic balance to be sustainable. This was proven by their medium and long-term government securities purchases. In parallel with the rate-cutting cycle of the central bank, it was possible to issue government securities at lower and lower yields in 2012–2014.

On the domestic financial market, the trust of Hungarian households was felt especially strongly. From early 2012 on, Hungarian households' holdings of government securities increased steadily and substantially, which was actively supported by the debt management strategy by developing new assets and by the high yields.

Key elements of the turnaround in economic balance

What then was the ultimate source of the historically swift and successful Hungarian fiscal consolidation and economic stabilisation? What drove this process and ultimately enabled these turnarounds?

The answer is trust. First, trust resulted in the political change during the 2010 elections: the two-thirds mandate of the new government underlined the strong confidence of the electorate. The public's confidence in the government was maintained all along, because the government managed the crisis, restored economic balance and stabilised the economy through structural reforms, a new public burden sharing scheme and a new tax system, instead of resorting to conventional austerity measures. Hungarian citizens put their trust in their own state as voters, as consumers and as investors: this was the primary and most important factor behind this historic success.

A similarly crucial underlying factor was the trust of financial market agents, who purchased Hungarian government securities all along and continued to anticipate that the consolidation and stabilisation would prove successful. They anticipated both, otherwise they would only have purchased short-term government securities with maturities of less than a year. When buying medium and long-term government securities, i.e. with maturities of 3, 5 or 10 years, a financial market investor not only believes that the budget deficit will be below 3% in Hungary for a couple of years, but also that a recovery in growth, consumption and investment will be achieved.

What was the basis for this massive vote of confidence that ultimately played a vital role in Hungary's successful consolidation and stabilisation? Trust was built and maintained through a favourable constellation of multiple factors. The first was that in mid-2010, all economic agents saw that Hungary was in a fiscal crisis, which, due to high government debt, threatened to develop into a sovereign debt crisis over the short term. The new government, backed by a two-thirds political mandate, decided on its style of governance in the first months: it sought to base the crisis management on internal factors, not on external assistance. This inspired the trust of Hungarian society, because people already knew the price and sacrifices entailed by the other scenario, another IMF-EU agreement.

The fact that the Hungarian government endeavoured to achieve consolidation through structural reforms and without an IMF-EU agreement, was actually good news, not only for Hungarian society but also for financial market agents and companies. The earlier crisis management in Greece, and the way of handling the crisis in Portugal, Spain, Italy and other euro area countries did not convince real economy and financial investors – who really vote with their money – that the conventional crisis management of the EU was appropriate and successful.

In fact – although these opinions hardly received any publicity – market agents were truly confident that the conventional crisis management based on austerity measures was unable to be successful. And they were proven right.

Trust was also boosted by the immediate, rapid and determined action of the new Hungarian government. It launched structural reforms in several areas where governments had not undertaken measures or where they had lacked the political will to carry them through. The new tax system in itself signalled to financial and real economy investors that the motivations of labour market participants were changing, while the rising incentives for employment and job creation improved investment conditions. One of the most sensitive fields in the EU's crisis management was the regulation of the labour market. The European Union's excessive use of the "social and solidarity" principle meant that the inflexible and over-regulated nature of the labour market was preserved in virtually all countries in need of reforms. However, the changes to the legislative, tax and various other conditions in Hungary convinced investors that the deepest reforms happened precisely in the most sensitive field of the European economy, the labour market.

Trust was also unwavering because Hungarian crisis management was executed in a stable political environment. The two-thirds majority of the government in Parliament never showed any sign of vulnerability, there was no government crisis nor any hint of political or social crisis in Hungary. This guaranteed implementation of the government's structural reforms: all political forces implement their reforms if their political power is upheld, since in a democratic system they need to account for their decisions, programmes and promises. As the political force that secured a two-thirds majority promised successful crisis management, structural reforms, new jobs and a balanced budget, it could be expected to implement the structural reforms necessary for these if its political power was preserved. Thus, the confidence necessary for consolidation and stabilisation was maintained throughout the reforms.

Another factor facilitated the exceptional fiscal consolidation and economic stabilisation in a concealed but crucial manner: the influx of EU funds into the Hungarian economy.

Of course, the inflow of EU funds constantly improved the macroeconomic indicators essential from the perspective of financial stability, i.e. the current account balance and net lending. Even though the income balance demonstrating the dualistic structure of the Hungarian economy was in deficit all along, the current account balance was constantly in surplus: to external financial investors and real economy investors this was the most positive signal possible in 2010–2014. EU funds played a major role in this: in addition to their actual positive macroeconomic effects, they reinforced trust as well.

EU funds are also one of the greatest reserves for maintaining economic balance and durable economic growth until 2020: in 2007–2013, 15–20% of economic developments was financed from EU funds, and this figure could rise to 60% in the EU's new seven-year budgetary cycle of 2014–2020. The EU funds used during consolidation and stabilisation did not help to expand employment, but they can be expected to do so in the EU's next seven-year budgetary cycle.

Why was this fiscal consolidation different?

The successful fiscal consolidation and the ensuing economic stabilisation was achieved in the Hungarian economy without accumulating new debt. Economic agents – the general government, businesses and households alike – adjusted to the challenges posed by the two-fold crisis not with an expansion of their borrowing, but with precisely the opposite, i.e. its reduction. In this respect, there is a significant difference between the successful fiscal consolidation in 2010–2014 and, for example, the financial consolidation in Hungary of the mid-1920s, which was also successful: back then, consolidation was achieved with the help of League of Nations loans, while it was now possible with domestic and EU funds, flanked by the confidence of the financial markets.

The complete macroeconomic turnaround in 2010–2014 is also fundamentally distinct from the successful recovery in 1945–1947. In 1946, a new national currency, the forint was introduced, which had a momentous impact on crisis management – in terms of restraining inflation – and the recovery. This time, however, no new national currency was introduced in Hungary, and the European currency, the euro, was also not adopted.

The financial consolidation and economic stabilisation by the centralised political regime of the 1970s and 1980s is also in sharp contrast with the return to economic balance and economic stabilisation in 2010–2014. At that time, the precarious balance and the necessary level of economic activity was maintained in each fiscal year and planning cycle at the expense of the future: the country financed the management of the concealed financial and economic crisis from external debts.

By contrast, the economic policy in 2010–2014 used funds from the new public burden sharing scheme, which, however, were retrieved from income generated in the Hungarian economy. The level of new debt did not rise, as consolidation and stabilisation were mainly based on domestic resources. Between 2010 and 2014, Hungary accomplished the most successful financial consolidation and economic stabilisation in the modern economic history of the country. This turnaround was different from all comparable periods, because this time the conditions for a sustainable financial balance and a steadily expanding economy were established. The correction of the distortions in the inherited dualistic economic structure is also under way. This boosts employment, which in turn makes financial balance sustainable and fosters durable economic growth.

Chapter 17

Turnaround in external debt

The deterioration of financial balance and subsequent crisis in the real economy was accompanied by an increase in Hungary's external financial dependency and vulnerability at the time of the misguided economic policy.

Hungary's external debt increases again

In the first decade of EU membership between 2004 and 2014, the accumulation of Hungarian gross debt, particularly gross external debt, can be split into two distinct periods. Hungary's gross external debt and foreign currency debt rose between 2004 and mid-2010, and then fell between mid-2010 and 2014. The negative shift in economic policy after 2002 and the misguided economic policy around the time of EU accession in 2004 left Hungary mired in debt once again (Figure 202).

The southern euro area countries displayed similar growth in gross external debt to Hungary between 2004 and 2010, but used the euro as the national currency. Consequently, the increase in external debt in euros did not imply the same level of vulnerability as the rise in Hungarian external debt in foreign currency (Figure 203).

Analysis of gross external debt by sector clearly indicates that between 2000 and 2002 all three agents – the general government,[48] the banking system, and the corporate sector – reduced their gross external exposure, and then between 2002 and 2009 all three significantly increased their gross external debt. The government's gross external debt continued to rise until

[48] It is important to note that in this chapter the concept of the general government is used in a consolidated sense, i.e. it includes the central bank as well as the public sector.

the end of 2011, as did that of the corporate sector; only the banking sector began to reduce its gross external debt from 2009 onwards (Figure 204).

Figure 202. Hungary's gross external debt and its FX composition

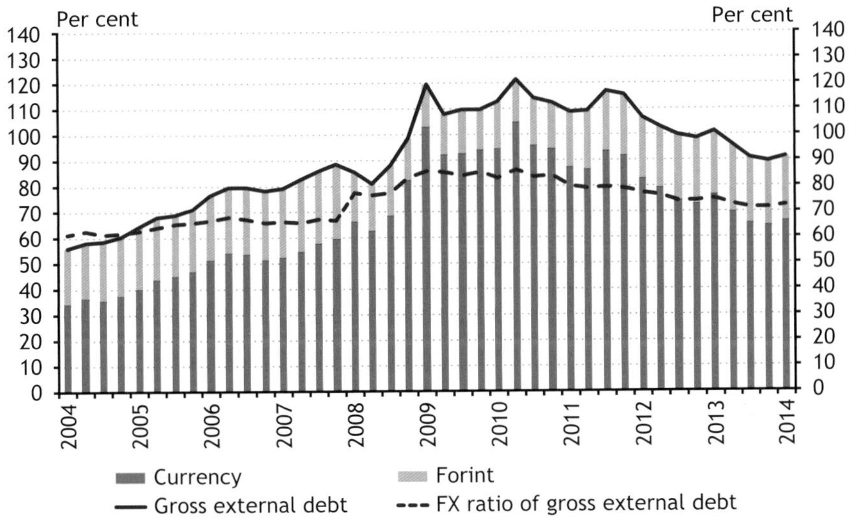

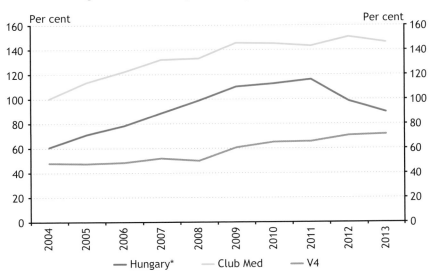

Source: Eurostat, MNB   *Excluding intercompany loans, % of GDP*

Figure 203. Development of gross external debt

Source: Eurostat, MNB   **Excluding intercompany loans loans, % of GDP*

Figure 204. Development of gross external debt by sectors

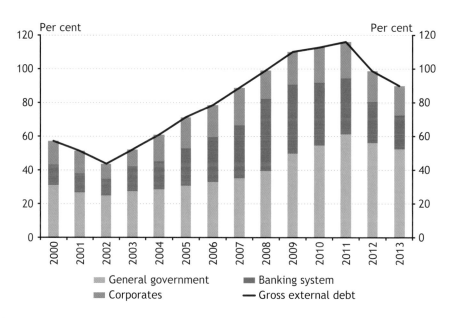

Source: MNB   Excluding intercompany loans loans, % of GDP

For two decades until mid-2010, one of the basic principles of governance was to bring as much external funds as possible into the Hungarian economy, which led to an accumulation of external debt. The country's external liabilities grew continuously between 2002 and 2010, as did the country's interest payment obligations: the Hungarian economy fell into an increasingly uncontrollable debt spiral, and finally, a debt trap.

In the case of Hungary's gross external debt position, the workings of the debt trap are well illustrated in that significant external funds were also needed to refinance existing debt, along with handling the financing demand for the given year. From 2004–2008, some EUR 20–35 billion in external funds were required every year, and Hungarian economic policy only began to adjust when the effects of the crisis emerged. In 2008–2010, gross borrowing fell sharply while the prefix of net lending reversed. The flawed economic policy prior to 2004 and the cost of the consistently unsuccessful adjustment until mid-2010 clearly show that Hungary's debt maturing in the given years rose continuously between 2004 and 2010, hitting record levels of more than EUR 35 billion between 2011 and 2012 (Figure 205).

Figure 205. Net borrowing of the economy

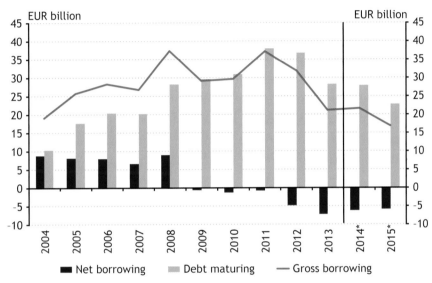

Source: MNB   *estimate*

Subsequently, in the period between 2013 and 2015, maturing debt contracted to an increasing degree, but even in 2015 the country will have to pay off more than EUR 20 billion in external debt.

During the first two years of the successful turnaround in Hungarian economic balance between 2010 and 2014 the country had the highest amount of maturing debt. This two-year period that saw the 2011–2012 budget consolidated, the new tax system, the introduction of structural reforms and other decisive elements influencing the fiscal balance involved the greatest risk in terms of the external debt trap, as the maturing external debt was regularly higher than EUR 35 billion in that period.

Among the structural reforms, Hungarian economic policy made significant use of domestic funds to finance government debt from the beginning of 2012, as a result of which the amount of government bonds bought by households grew constantly and rapidly from early 2012. As a result, some EUR 5 billion worth of foreign currency debt maturing in 2012 was financed strictly in forints, using domestic funds. This factor was behind the quiet financial turning point in 2012, when there was significant growth of EUR 5 billion in net lending. In terms of eliminating the external debt trap, the decisive period proved to be 2011–2012, when the maturing external debt of more than EUR 35 billion per year was successfully refinanced and at the same time the internal restructuring of the government debt framework was launched – shifting from foreign currency into forints, and increasingly towards domestic sectors – and all the reforms playing a role in restoring economic balance were either introduced or continued.

The period between 2011 and 2012 was indeed crucial from the perspective of external debt, since gross borrowing fell sharply from 2011 and net lending continued to improve in 2012; furthermore, the amount of maturing debt also fell markedly after 2012 as the EU-IMF loan repayments began. The period between 2011 and 2013 brought a positive development in gross external debt since both financial indicators that are crucial in terms of the country's vulnerability – net lending and gross borrowing – underwent a positive change in these years.

It is worth considering 2012 from the perspective of the burden which gross interest expenses placed on the Hungarian budget at the time of the external debt turnaround. In 2012, Hungary faced one of the highest gross interest expense-to-GDP ratios in the EU, which was only due in part to the high gross government debt relative to GDP. While the ratio of gross government debt to GDP was high in 2012, the figure of around 80% was close to the EU-27 average. Hungarian gross interest expenses relative to GDP, however, were strikingly high. While the level of gross government debt was "moderately" high, the cost of servicing it was exceedingly so: this stems directly from the make-up of Hungarian gross government debt, and from investors expecting a higher-than-average yield from Hungarian government bonds under the unsustainable economic policy shown above.[49]

The most critical year in the successful management of the crisis between 2010 and 2014 came in 2012, when the second downward branch of the double-dip recession hit the Hungarian economy, tax reforms caused inflation of 5.7%, and real wages, consumption, investments and GDP all fell. At the same time, the Hungarian budget faced the highest gross interest expense obligation relative to GDP in the region, and in fact the third highest among EU member states. Two EU member states had higher interest expenses relative to GDP than Hungary, but these figures in Italy and Greece stemmed from significantly higher gross government debts. The economies of Belgium, Ireland and Portugal had GDP-proportionate gross interest expenses which were close to that of Hungary, largely resulting from their high gross government debt. Hungary thus had the highest implicit interest rate for government debt, calculated as the ratio of annual interest expense and government debt.[50]

Successful fiscal consolidation had already taken place by 2012, and investors expected a deficit of under 3% for this year as well. Thus, the glaringly high gross interest expense cannot be explained with the expected budget deficit: the incredibly poor structure of gross government debt along with the high percentage of external foreign currency debt were key reasons for this. Another important factor was that part of the debt in 2012 (and to a lesser extent thereafter as well) consisted of instruments paying higher interest that were issued during the crisis.

---

[49] Poghosyan (2012) wrote an empirical analysis of the defining factors in government bond yields.
[50] The implicit interest rate can deviate substantially from the yields observed on the government bond market. A substantial part of the debt is always based on fixed-rate government bonds previously issued, the interest rate of which usually differs from current yields.

The strikingly high real interest rate may have made a significant contribution to the high gross interest expenses relative to GDP in the critical year of 2012. In 2011, the Hungarian economy was the 14th riskiest country based on financial system vulnerability, and specifically the high external debt. Whilst Hungary was ranked 14th, the real interest rate – i.e. the difference between the base rate and inflation – in Hungary was the highest in the group of riskiest countries (Figure 206).

Figure 206. Real interest rate in 2011

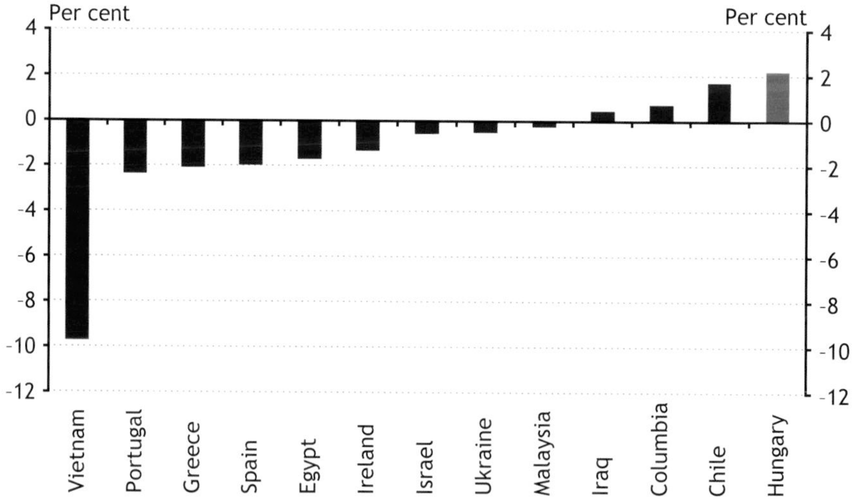

Source: Bloomberg   2011 average (difference between base rate and inflation)

Hungary made significant progress in reversing the upward trend in external debt in 2011–2012, while at the same time offering the highest real interest rate to financial investors of all the countries carrying the largest financial risk. This was the price of the financial market permanently giving Hungarian economic policy a vote of confidence: despite criticism, Hungary received constant funding because it was a reliable debtor and offered a high real rate of interest to investors.

In addition to the moderately high gross debt and gross government debt in Hungary compared to other EU member states, the Hungarian private sector's gross outstanding debt as a percentage of GDP was also moderate in 2010. Thus, it was not because of private sector debt that Hungary became so vulnerable, but rather because of the budget debt and high external debt. The dualistic Hungarian economic structure meant that the debt of Hungarian-owned micro, small and medium-sized enterprises was lower by some orders of magnitude than that of foreign-owned enterprises. Large enterprises generally have export cover to back foreign currency debt, so the negative effect of indebtedness was not as marked in the corporate sector as compared to households.

Figure 207. Outstanding loans of the private sector in 2012, % of GDP

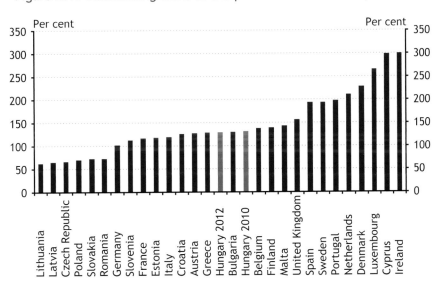

Source: Eurostat

Compared to other countries in the region, however, the gross debt of the Hungarian private sector relative to GDP was higher, as the corresponding figures in Romania, Slovakia, the Czech Republic and Poland stood at around half of the Hungarian private sector's rate of roughly 130% in 2010. In actual fact, Hungary was closer to the southern part of the euro area in terms of private sector gross debt relative to

GDP than it was to its regional peers. Greek and Italian private sector gross debt figures relative to GDP were not far behind the Hungarian level, though the levels in Malta, Spain, Portugal and Cyprus were substantially higher (Figure 207).

Turning point in net external debt

From the perspective of the country's vulnerability, two other factors are even more important than the level of gross external debt: the proportion of foreign currency in the gross external debt, and the net external debt. Hungary's net external debt grew continuously from 2004 until the 2009 crisis, before the crisis prompted a minor decline, but by early 2010 it was already showing an upward trend once again. A sharp turning point in net external debt occurred in mid-2010, when Hungary's outstanding net external debt began to fall steadily after the change of government (Figure 208).

Figure 208. Changes in net external debt and its components, % of GDP

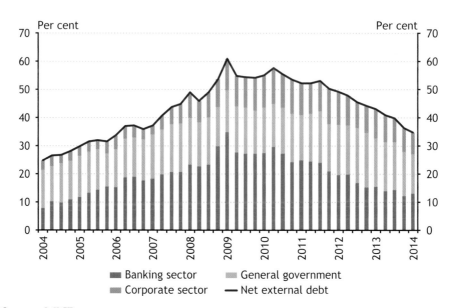

Source: MNB

It is clear that the banking sector played a key role in the accumulation of net external debt between 2004 and 2008. The banking system passed on the external funds received, as the build-up of household foreign currency loans was largely behind the increase in the banking system's net external debt. Households thus only played a definitive role in this process in that the banking system needed to draw significant external funds for the foreign currency loans disbursed to them. The increase in the corporate sector's net external debt was asymmetric: their net external debt relative to GDP stood at around 10%, a position that deteriorated as a result of the crisis; only during the balance consolidation and economic stabilisation period of 2013–2014 did it fall to around 10% once again.

A turning point in Hungary's net external debt occurred in the middle of 2010, after which net external debt relative to GDP fell continuously and substantially, meaning that Hungary's vulnerability underwent a similar improvement. The three previous periods of reduction at end-2006, end-2008 and between 2009 and 2010 were not sustained: the reduction in net external debt relative to GDP came to a halt before the trend reversed, influenced also by the weakening of the exchange rate.

The Hungarian banking system played the lead role in the build-up and reduction of external debt, and more specifically net external debt, which has the biggest impact on vulnerability. While the net external debt of the banking sector relative to GDP hovered at around 5% between 1998 and the beginning of the new millennium, it rose above the 5% mark in the second half of 2002 and increased sharply alongside the rise in household foreign currency lending. The amount of external foreign currency funds used by the Hungarian bank sector grew steeply until the financial crisis of 2008.

By 2008, the net external debt of Hungarian banks stood at 30% of GDP, before dropping from this peak as a result of the crisis when the domestic banking system began to deleverage. The build-up of net external debt, i.e. foreign currency, in the Hungarian banking sector ensued rapidly between 2002 and 2008; during the deleveraging the mainly foreign-owned large banks were equally quick in scaling back their external foreign currency debt, which played the main role in Hungary's vulnerability (Figure 209).

Figure 209. Development of net external debt by sector, % of GDP

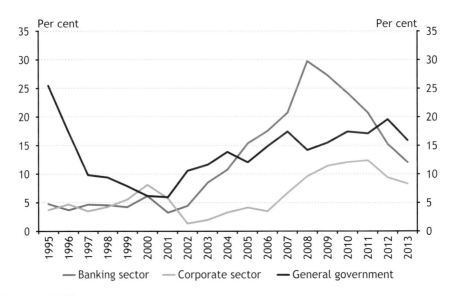

Source: MNB

Of course, households' foreign currency debt taken on primarily for real estate investments was behind the banking system's net external debt. In addition to this, the banking system took out external foreign currency loans to finance government debt and the investments of Hungarian-owned enterprises: growth in household foreign currency loans stalled the most before ceasing altogether in 2010, but the other agents also reduced their borrowing of foreign currency loans in the years following the 2008 crisis.

The increase in net government external debt showed a similar trend as well from the early 2000s, but nothing changed here upon the financial crisis of 2008. Net government external debt initially fell during the first consolidation attempt from 1 September 2006, but then started to grow once again from the beginning of 2008. Growth picked up in earnest with the IMF-EU loan, and depreciation owing to the exchange rate crisis also had a great impact. The upward trend continued until the turning point in 2012, when there was an internal turnaround in the budget, which also played a significant role in external debt, because the previous expansion in net external government debt came to an end in 2012: the Hungarian government's external debt began to contract. This resulted from the change in government debt-financing strategy in 2012: roughly EUR 4.8 billion of foreign currency debt[51] maturing in 2012 was refinanced by the government in forints only.

The first decade of EU membership between 2004 and 2014, indeed the whole period from the beginning of the 2000s, was shaped by the domestic banking sector raising external funds. Households, the government and the corporate sector moved on similar debt paths as the banking sector, yet it is still the banking sector that showed by far the greatest level of external borrowing and then reduction in external net foreign currency liabilities. After all three economic agents – the general government, the corporate sector and households financed by the banking sector – funded their unsustainable operation through external funds, the question arises: would similar debt have arisen with forint-based funding? Would it have been possible to finance a balanced, non-artificial economic upswing in Hungary from domestic funds?

The Hungarian economy was on a growth path maintaining a balance between 1998 and 2002. A balanced budget was created under the economic conditions at the time, since Hungarian government debt relative to GDP fell alongside the budget deficit of around 4%. Economic growth was durable due to decreasing government debt, the balanced fiscal deficit, and rising employment. The 240,000 new jobs created between 1998 and 2002 saw a narrowing of the gap between the rate of

---

[51] In 2012, the Government Debt Management Agency redeemed EUR 1 billion and JPY 45 billion in foreign currency bonds, and SDR 2.9 billion from IMF foreign currency loans, as well as some smaller redemptions to international investment banks (GDMA, 2013).

employment in Hungary – incredibly low in international terms – and that in economies already involved in the European integration process. Every employment and unemployment indicator reflected declining labour market imbalances, paving the way for long-term progress on the growth path ensuring sustainable economic balance.

This trend was disrupted by the negative economic policy turn in mid-2002, as it consistently allowed a deficit that exceeded the sustainable budget deficit, thus reversing the declining trend of government debt relative to GDP. The government thus drove the artificial economic expansion with new debt in every sector of the domestic economy. If the previous path ensuring sustainable growth had continued in mid-2002, domestic funds – household and corporate savings, and domestic funding in the banking system – would have been sufficient to finance domestic economic agents since they had been sufficient to finance the healthy structure of benign economic policy between 1998 and 2002. If there had been no deterioration in the trends from 1998 and 2002, and specifically in the borrowing structure of the three economic agents, and no change in the ratio of forint to foreign currency loans, this would not have been necessary later since EU accession brought non-refundable development funds to the Hungarian economy.

A minor change was indeed already noticeable in the net external debt trends of the government sector and banking sector between 2001 and 2002, but this did not represent a turnaround and could have easily been corrected. The government chose to increase its external debt with its economic policy between 2002 and 2010, but it also drove the corporate sector and, in particular, households and families in the same direction. The Hungarian government did not regulate where and when it should have to limit market agents' external debt using tools of financial regulation. This was not only influenced by the neo-liberal illusion of the self-regulating market, but also by government interests.

The forint and foreign currency loans taken out by households and the corporate sector resulted in additional budget revenues, lessening the burden of the flawed fiscal policy. If households and the corporate sector had not participated in this great external borrowing process between 2002 and 2010, the budget would have displayed a double-digit deficit for the entire period, leading to Hungarian financial bankruptcy even before the 2008 financial crisis. As the misguided economic policy facilitated the country's indebtedness, and particularly the build-up of external debt, it was decided to allow unsustainable deficit levels since the cost of the continually rising government debt was also rising steadily. Following these two decisions, a third one was unavoidable: allowing the build-up of household and corporate sector loans since this source of lending generated budget revenues, which lessened and delayed the recognition and resolution of the unsustainable fiscal situation.

Chapter 18

Breaking the upward
trend in government debt

Over the last one and a half centuries, Hungary has become indebted several times. Within the external debt of the country, external government debt always comprised the greatest burden. It is an economic peculiarity of government debt that the debtor (the state) has very little own income. The source of repayments is actually income withdrawn from the other two sectors in the form of taxes. Government debt is always indirectly assumed by economic agents, in contrast to corporate and household indebtedness, where the companies and families themselves bear the burden. The negative impact of sovereign indebtedness is concealed at first, and only later does it become evident. It gradually increases the burden on economic agents, as debt service payments (the interest and redemption) of government debt rise each year.

Due to the unique characteristics of government debt, economic agents are initially unaware that the state is sliding towards indebtedness. They do not see how the general government deficit in a certain year entails new borrowing, i.e. new indebtedness by the state. In fact, at first, economic agents feel the positive effects. A larger budget deficit means higher government spending, i.e. a fiscal impulse, which, through direct and indirect effects, generates growing demand on the market. Economic agents respond to higher demand by boosting supply: at first, government expenditure contributes to economic growth.

The economy, however, enters on a debt path, and in a few years, unfavourable impacts occur: higher government debt leads to a surge in debt servicing, especially interest payments. The state covers this either with new borrowing, which leads to a debt spiral, or by raising taxes and thus curbing the purchasing power of economic agents.

In the transitional decades between 1990 and 2010, Hungarian indebtedness followed a distinct pattern. The shock therapy transition to the market economy in 1990–1993 caused persistently high budget deficits, as contributions from jobs and state-owned enterprises being terminated were missing. The expenditure side of the budget could not be cut enough to offset the earlier revenues which were now missing: the deficit expanded and government debt rose. Moreover, the economic downturn also increased the government debt ratio.

In the mid-1990s, the government spent the proceeds from the large-scale privatisations of the Bokros package on cutting its accumulated debt, thereby launching the process of government debt reduction. Between 1994 and 1998, the state mainly decreased the accumulated debt from privatisation revenues, but between 1998 and mid-2002, the reduction of government debt was not facilitated by this method, but rather by well-structured budget management. In the macroeconomic context of those times, the general government deficit proved to be at an equilibrium level, because even with a deficit of 4%, the debt-to-GDP ratio – i.e. the government debt ratio – steadily decreased until mid-2002 (Figure 210).

Following the change of government, on account of the misguided economic policy implemented from mid-2002, government debt entered on a growth path again, and it continued to increase until 2010–2011. Even in 1994–1998, the reduction of the Hungarian government debt was primarily achieved through privatisation revenues, but the subsequent left-wing, liberal governments between 2002 and 2010 could not expect proceeds of such magnitude from selling off state assets. The state budget received considerable privatisation revenues between 2002 and 2010, e.g. from selling MÁV-Cargo, the Ferihegy Airport and the state share in MOL, but these were not used for reducing government debt and were spent on current financing instead.

Figure 210. Gross consolidated government debt
(% of GDP) and the exchange rate

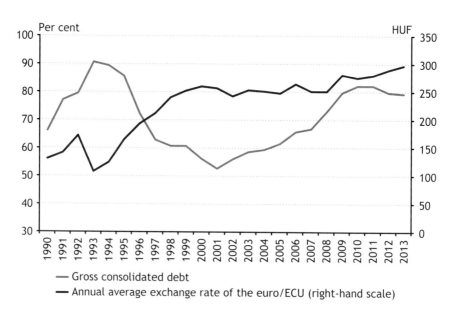

Gross consolidated debt
Annual average exchange rate of the euro/ECU (right-hand scale)

Eurostat was used as the source for annual average exchange rates.

Source: MNB, Eurostat

The rise or fall in the debt-to-GDP ratio is significantly influenced by the exchange rate of the Hungarian forint, but the trend of debt development in a given context of economic growth and yields is defined by the deviations of the budget deficit from the equilibrium level. From an economic history perspective, after adjusting for the exchange rate fluctuations, the trend of government debt is determined by how much the general government deficit diverges from the equilibrium level.

We obtain an even clearer picture of one of the most unique features of the development of Hungarian government debt – i.e. the fact that it is fundamentally governed by political cycles and the economic policies employed – if we analyse the four political terms between 1998 and 2014 with respect to the path of the debt-to-GDP ratio.

Between 1998 and mid-2002, the government debt ratio first stagnated and then started to fall. Privatisation revenues did not play a part in this. In addition to exchange rate effects, it was first and foremost due to the proper economic policy and the economic path focusing on employment and growth. The government debt ratio declined, even alongside the fiscal deficit that had reached the equilibrium level of around 4% (Figure 211).

Figure 211. Government debt ratio under different government cycles

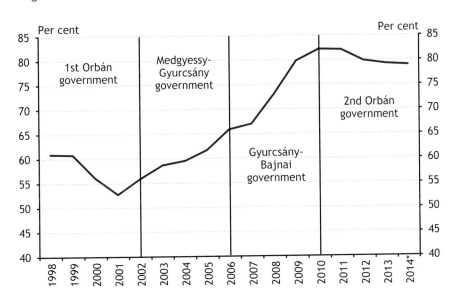

Source: AMECO   * *estimate*

By contrast, in the next political cycle between 2002 and 2006, the Hungarian government debt ratio surged from 53% in mid-2002 to 67% in mid-2006. During that political term, substantial privatisation revenues were collected by the budget, without which the debt ratio would have increased even more steeply. This was undoubtedly the result of a flawed economic policy and a deficit that constantly exceeded the fiscal equilibrium level. After adjusting for exchange rate effects and privatisation revenues, one can clearly see that the new indebtedness was caused by the irresponsible fiscal policy of the political leadership between 2002 and 2006.

Between 2006 and 2010, Hungary experienced a similarly swift slide into indebtedness. This process can be divided into two phases: the first, in 2006–2008, with the rise in the government debt ratio, and the second in 2008–2010, which also included the IMF-EU credit line of almost EUR 20 billion.

Thus, by mid-2010, the Hungarian debt-to-GDP ratio stood at 85.3% and a debt crisis seemed a real threat. One of the most important results of the fiscal consolidation and economic stabilisation in 2010–2014 was that by the second half of the political cycle, the inherited debt-to-GDP ratio of 85.3% was successfully reduced to below 80%.

The concealed burdens of indebtedness

In Hungarian economic history, government debt played an especially distinctive role in the 25 years after 1990. In 1990, Hungary inherited a government debt of around USD 22 billion from the previous era, which was significantly higher than in the case of its regional peers. Therefore, at the onset of market transition, Hungary was at a severe competitive disadvantage compared to the region's economies which were also in the process of transition, because high government debt exerted huge pressure on the general government through high interest payments on the one hand, and Hungary's vulnerability on the financial markets on the other. At the time of the transition to the market economy, the Hungarian government debt ratio was considerably higher than the Czech and Slovak ratios, as well as the ratios in the Romanian, Croatian and Slovenian economies, and – as a result of the shock therapy market transition – the debt-to-GDP ratio reached 90% in the early 1990s (Figure 212).

Figure 212. Inherited government debt in 1990, % of GDP

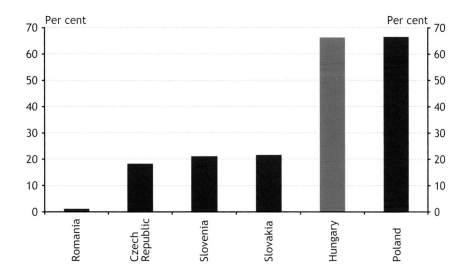

1992 data for Slovakia, 1993 data for Czech Republic and Slovenia

Source: IMF, MNB

There is a strong correlation between the highest government debt ratio in the region at the beginning of the market economy transition and the shock therapy market transition. Due to the inherited government debt of around USD 22 billion, Hungary not only became the most financially vulnerable in the region, but it also had weak bargaining power versus the International Monetary Fund and other international institutions.

The International Monetary Fund advised Hungary in autumn 1990 that it expected a quick and – in today's parlance – neo-liberal market transition for the economy. By contrast, the Polish and Czechoslovakian and later the Czech and Slovak market transitions were not conducted using shock therapy, but rather with economic policies targeting a gradual changeover.

There is a strong link between the market economy transition methods pursued by the regional EU member states and the level of inherited government debt: a high debt-to-GDP ratio demanded shock therapy, while low government debt ratios allowed a gradual transition. Moreover, a significant portion of Poland's government debt was cancelled and other relief programmes were introduced as well, while the government debt ratio of the other regional peers was already well below that of Hungary.

In the case of Hungary, the actual government debt burden was substantially higher than the commonly used GDP-proportionate debt burden: in terms of actual disposable income, Hungarian government debt was 4 percentage points higher in 2010 than the reported figure. This was caused by the significant difference between gross domestic product (GDP) and gross national income (GNI). Gross national income, which measures the balance of income flowing in and out of the Hungarian economy, is a much more reliable indicator than gross domestic product, because it also takes into account that a portion of income generated in Hungary is transferred out of corporate groups and the country by income earners. Government debt is not repaid from generated value but from disposable income, and a part of the income that could be used to redeem government debt and interests is shifted outside the country by income earners in the course of profit repatriation, and therefore in the case of Hungary, the actual government debt burden is well higher than the figures shown by the commonly used statistical methods (Figure 213).

In the mid-1990s, i.e. in the decisive half decade of shock therapy used for market economy transition, the difference between GDP and GNI was significantly smaller, but then, due to the misguided economic policy, high external debt and large-scale profit repatriation by foreign companies, the gap between the two indicators widened. This gap narrowed slightly between 1998 and 2002, but the flawed economic policy implemented after mid-2002 steadily increased the GDP-GNI gap. The new indebtedness after 2002 by all economic agents (but especially by the state) towards external providers of finance led to a significant increase in financing interest payments from the financial system and in profit transfers out of the Hungarian economy.

Figure 213. Government debt as a percentage of GDP and GNI

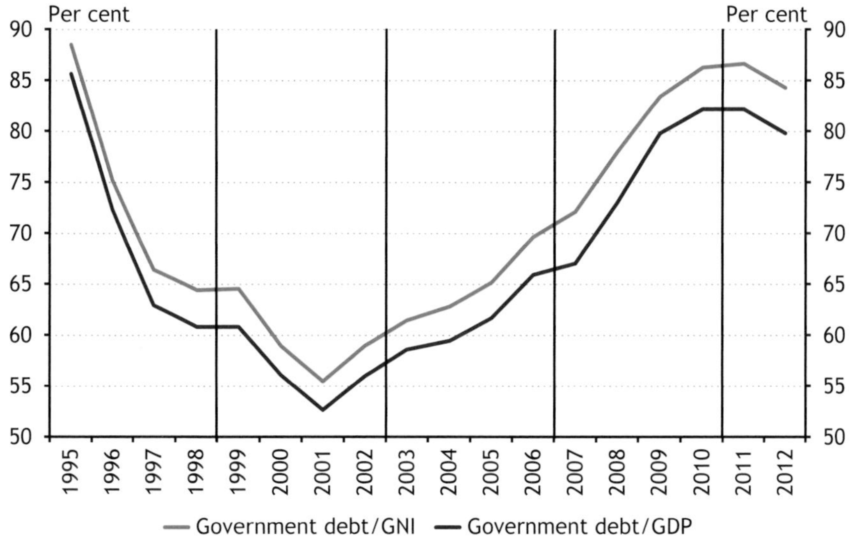

Source: Eurostat

Due to the accumulation of foreign currency loans by the government, the corporate sector and households, interest had to be paid to external lenders, which led to a deterioration of the income balance within the current account balance. The higher the proportion of external (mainly foreign currency) debts in government debt, the stronger the pressure on the income balance and thus on the current account balance (Figure 214).

Another concealed burden of the new indebtedness between 2002 and 2010 was that due to the growing volume and share of foreign currency debts, the GDP-GNI gap widened. This was not only because Hungarian economic agents paid increasingly high interest on the growing debt to foreign lenders, but also because financial institutions transferred a major part of their profits realised on foreign currency loans out of the country before the crisis. Therefore, on the one hand, the new indebtedness by the state after 2002 caused a significantly greater burden than indicated by statistics because of the GDP-GNI gap, and on the other hand, the rise in the share of external investors and lenders in government debt increased the current account deficit through the deteriorating income balance.

Figure 214. Current account balance (% of GDP) and net lending

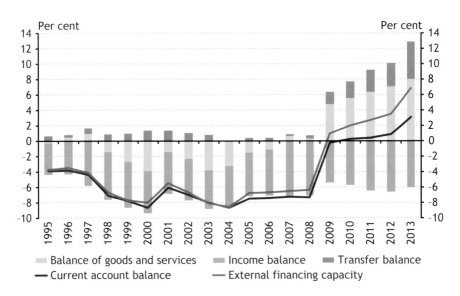

Source: MNB

Turning point in the government debt ratio

Examples in economic history show that when a positive turnaround happens in a macroeconomic indicator that steadily follows a negative trend, the change is sudden and abrupt. Historical examples also show that conversely, negative trend changes happen mainly in a concealed manner, over a longer period. For a country, an economy, a company or a family, trend reversals that result in significant losses over the long term initially do not seem to present a threat or a burden that should be addressed. That is the risk inherent in negative macroeconomic turnarounds: in the beginning, they yield more than they cost, and they are alluring when one seeks short-term gains. Indiscriminate foreign currency lending after 2002 initially improved the terms of borrowing for households and the corporate sector, and while the economy expanded, but the dangers and burdens remained hidden until the risks of Swiss franc indebtedness materialised with the eruption of the global financial crisis in autumn 2008.

Similarly, even one or two years of high general government deficits that entail a slight increase in the government debt ratio and the growing proportion of the latter's external financing do not pose instantly recognisable risks and threats. However, if the irresponsible fiscal policy is not an exception but the rule, it causes a negative macroeconomic turnaround even over the medium term, and leads to new indebtedness by the state.

By contrast, a positive trend reversal cannot be prolonged over several years: there has to be a point in economic history, a period of 6–12 months at most, when the trend change happens. An example for such a moment was when in mid-2010 household foreign currency lending was in effect stopped, and the early repayment as well as the exchange rate cap schemes were introduced. Another decisive moment occurred when foreign currency loans were phased out and the forint conversion programme was launched in 2014–2015.

The turning point in household foreign currency lending was achieved in a single day: with the amendment of a law in mid-2010, the new government practically banned household foreign currency lending. That measure put an end to the build-up of household foreign currency loans. The reversal in the trend was strengthened by the early repayment and exchange rate cap schemes, and finally completed by the phase-out of the foreign currency loans in 2014–2015.

The turnaround in the Hungarian government debt ratio after 2010 showed a similar pattern. The government debt ratio started to decline in the second quarter of 2010, but this reversed in the fourth quarter and the ratio started to climb again. Therefore, the second half of 2010 did not bring a turning point in the Hungarian government debt ratio. Nevertheless, in the first quarter of 2011 the Hungarian debt-to-GDP ratio fell sharply lower because – due to an earlier decision by the government – the mandatory private pension fund system was abolished, and 97% of former pension fund members brought their accumulated assets back into the public pension system.

These funds – together with the real yield that had to paid – amounted to almost HUF 3,000 billion, but this in its own right would not have resulted in an automatic turnaround in the government debt ratio: that required responsible fiscal policy as well. As a one-off factor, the fact that the government spent around HUF 1,400 billion of these funds on redeeming government securities exerted a significant effect on the debt ratio in 2011.

This marked a historic moment for the Hungarian economy: government debt was slashed by HUF 1,400 billion, and by mid-2011, the debt-to-GDP ratio had decreased from 83% to 79%. In the second half of 2011, on account of the weakening exchange rate and the high proportion of foreign currency debt in government debt, the debt ratio temporarily reached its previous level once again, but after that it returned to a declining path, and as of the end of 2014, it has not reversed again during the period of consolidation and stabilisation (Figure 215).

Without the redemption of HUF 1,400 billion of government securities, the trend change in the government debt ratio would hardly have happened in the period of consolidation between 2010 and 2014. This trend reversal supported consolidation and stabilisation, because it lowered the interest expenditure of the budget and increased its revenue. The reform of the private pension fund system enabled the turnaround in the government debt ratio, and – by channelling contributions into the budget that were previously paid to the private pension funds – it generated HUF 300–400 billion in extra revenue for the general government annually. Without the reform of the private pension system, the consolidation between 2010 and 2014 would have been extremely difficult. And without successful fiscal consolidation, economic stabilisation would have been impossible, because with a general government deficit over 3% and a steadily rising government debt ratio, the chances of financing the Hungarian government debt from the financial market would have deteriorated.

There would have been only one possibility: another IMF-EU agreement. However, this would have entailed further sacrifices in growth and employment – just like in the case of the other countries participating in the IMF programmes – which would have also put consolidation and stabilisation out of reach.

Figure 215. Gross ("Maastricht") government debt

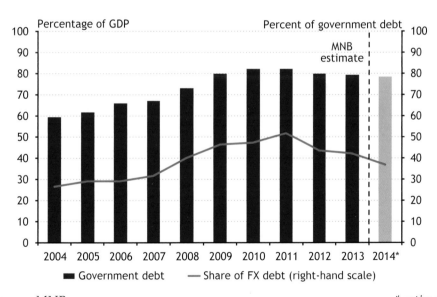

Source: MNB   * estimate

The positive trend reversal in the government debt ratio proved to be a lasting development, which was quite exceptional among the EU member states. Only five member states managed to cut their debt-to-GDP ratio in 2011–2014. Moreover, the reduction of the German, Danish, Latvian and Polish debt-to-GDP ratios was accomplished at far lower government debt levels and in the context of significantly better financing terms. Of the euro area members, only Germany was able to reduce its debt-to-GDP ratio in this four-year period, the other four countries that achieved this are not in the euro area. By contrast, the euro area as a whole saw a significant increase in its government debt ratio, which rose by around 8% of GDP. The southern countries in the euro area were in an almost hopeless situation: their government debt ratio expanded by 15–30 percentage points, with the exception of Italy, where it also increased, but more moderately (Figure 216).

Figure 216. Change in the government debt-to-GDP ratio, 2011-2014*

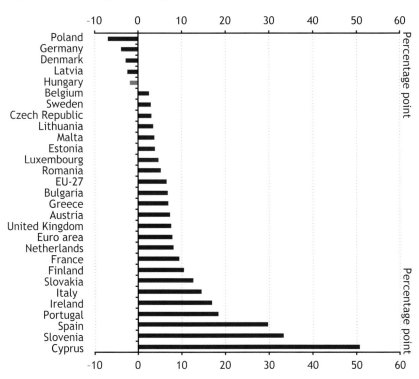

Source: European Commission Spring 2014 forecast, AMECO   ** estimate*

The reduction of the Hungarian government debt ratio in 2011–2014 was an outstanding achievement in the CEE region as well, because despite starting out from a lower level, the debt-to-GDP ratio rose significantly more in the Slovenian and Slovak economies, and even in the Czech Republic. As regards the government debt ratio, Hungary overcame some of its competitive disadvantage in the region, and the turnaround in 2011 – which, in economic history terms, happened in an instant – played a decisive role in this.

Even though Hungary accomplished a significant, positive trend change between 2010 and 2014 in the macroeconomic indicators which had deteriorated as a result of the earlier negative economic policy trends, it was only possible to offset some of the disadvantages accumulated in 2002–2010. The stock of household foreign currency loans put Hungary at a competitive disadvantage throughout the 2010–2014 consolidation period, as did the high level of government debt and its unfavourable financing structure.

The high net external debt was an inherited disadvantage and while a turnaround was observed in response to the 2008 crisis (after this point, Hungary's net external debt decreasd sharply), this burden still posed a financial risk for the country and was thus a competitive disadvantage in the region for several years.

Trend change in the government debt ratio through proper economic policy

Between 2008 and 2014, seven EU states pursued conventional economic policies for consolidation as per their agreement with the International Monetary Fund. Between 2008 and 2010, all of the countries participating in the IMF programme experienced a rise in their debt-to-GDP ratio. While Hungary left the IMF programme in 2010–2014, out of the other countries only Latvia managed to lower its government debt ratio, which increased in all the other participating

EU members. In the case of Cyprus and Portugal, the government debt ratio rose far more between 2010 and 2014 than in 2008–2010. With the exception of Latvia, the other IMF programme countries were not able to reduce their government debt ratio, while all countries pursued an economic policy focusing on austerity measures, as dictated by the IMF (Figure 217).

Figure 217. Change in debt-to-GDP ratio in IMF programme countries

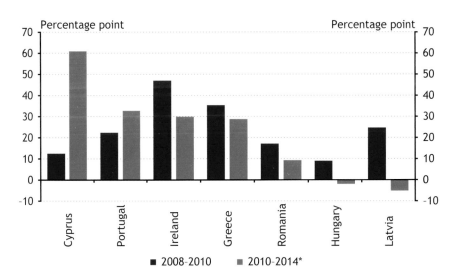

Source: European Commission Spring 2014 forecast, AMECO   ** estimate*

In light of the above, Latvia can be regarded as an exception, and the other countries as the rule. IMF programme countries could not halt the increase in their debt-to-GDP ratio, achieve a turnaround in the government debt ratio or put their government debt on a steadily declining path by introducing austerity measures: conventional economic policy is not suitable for this. All of the IMF programme countries which were forced to carry out fiscal consolidation in a conventional economic policy context suffered growth and employment losses. Consequently, they were not able to bring their deficit-to-GDP ratio below 3%, and without a budget deficit at an equilibrium level, their government debt ratio continued to rise. All of the countries managed to slightly improve their fiscal position, but they paid a considerable price in the real economy for this, and the modest improvement in economic balance was not enough to halt the rise in the government debt ratio.

In the region itself, alongside Poland only Hungary was able to lower its government debt ratio between 2010 and 2014. The debt-to-GDP ratio rose the most in Slovenia, which almost suffered a debt crisis in this period due to the state bailout of the Slovenian-owned (i.e. state-controlled) banking system. The Slovak and the Czech government debt ratio rose substantially as well. The 5–15% rise in the debt-to-GDP ratio did not place these economies at a competitive disadvantage, however, because their level of government debt is still far lower than the euro area average or the Hungarian debt ratio, but these countries did experience on unfavourable trend in terms of their government debt (Figure 218).

Countries in the region pursued economic policies different from those employed in Hungary between 2010 and 2014. No other CEE country – with the later exception of Slovenia – was faced with an immediate need for fiscal consolidation and economic stabilisation, and thus these countries continued to employ their tried and tested economic policies.

It is interesting, however, that Slovakia and Slovenia fared the worst in terms of the government debt ratio in 2010–2014: of the new member states in the region, it was these two economies which joined the euro area. As members of the euro area, their economic policy was in large part subordinated to the European Union and the European Central Bank. Even though Austria is in the euro area, as regards the most important macroeconomic indicators, it resembles Germany, Switzerland and the Nordic economies more than the region. Moreover, Austria was not faced with an immediate need for fiscal consolidation and economic stabilisation during this period.

Figure 218. Change in government debt-to-GDP ratio
in the V6 countries, 2010-2014*

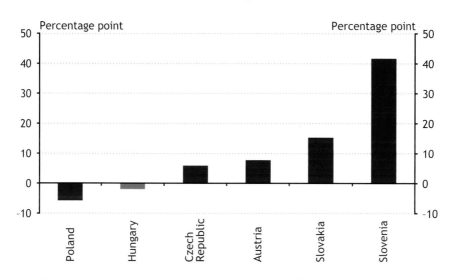

Source: European Commission Spring 2014 forecast, AMECO   ** estimate*

Only Hungary's economic policy diverged from that of the regional economies, especially from the economic policy of those in the euro area. The contrasting results were due to precisely this difference: the independent, unconventional Hungarian economic policy managed to turn around the increasing trend ofthe government debt ratio and reduce it.

By contrast, the three regional economies that are in the euro area, as well as the Czech Republic which had a lower debt level, have increased their debt levels since the crisis. Conventional economic policies did not lead to a turnaround in the debt-to-GDP ratio in the CEE region between 2010 and 2014, while unconventional economic policies did.

Comparing the Hungarian trend reversal in the government debt ratio with the performance of the southern countries of the euro area yields even more convincing results. In 2010–2014, no country in the southern flank of the euro area was able to break the upward trend in the government debt ratio; in fact, the debt-to-GDP ratio soared across all countries. In this period, the government debt-to-GDP ratio increased from 148% to roughly 175% in Greece, from approximately 95% to around 130% in Portugal, from close to 60% to almost 100% in Spain, and even in Italy, where it was already high in 2010, it rose from approximately 120% to over 130%.

By contrast, following the trend change in the government debt ratio, the Hungarian government debt ratio decreased from 82% at the end of 2010, and – after stagnating in 2011 – it continued to contract each year (Figure 219).

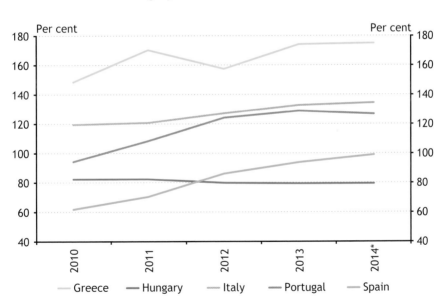

Figure 219. Government debt-to-GDP ratio
in Hungary and the Club Med countries

Source: IMF World Economic Outlook, April 2014   ** estimate*

This comparison also highlights the contrast in the performance of the different economic policies as regards government debt. While the southern countries of the euro area attempted fiscal consolidation by employing clearly conventional methods, Hungary accomplished the successful fiscal consolidation with an unconventional set of tools. The former group necessarily made sacrifices in growth and employment, whereas the unconventional Hungarian economic policy was able to avoid that, which is why fiscal consolidation was successful.

Figure 220. Change in government debt-to-GDP ratio
in Hungary and Europe, 2010-2014*

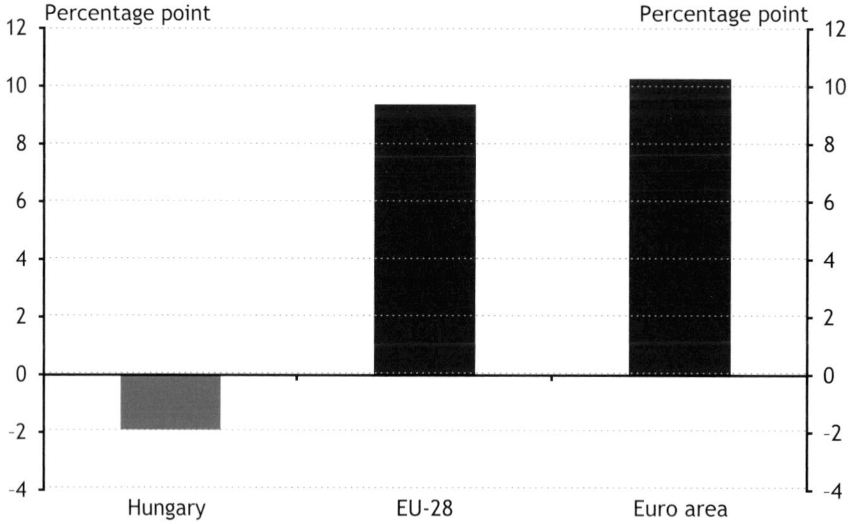

Source: Eurostat, AMECO Spring 2014 forecast   ** estimate*

While in the former group, politicians were not able to launch and implement substantial structural reforms because, as a result of the austerity measures, several governments were toppled, and political and social instability kept surfacing, the unconventional economic policy preserved political stability in Hungary all along: significant structural reforms were completed in the Hungarian economy and society between 2010 and 2014.

Over the long term, only successful structural reforms can lead to a sustainable economic balance, an expansion of employment and sustained economic growth, and these are the only factors that can halt the rise in the debt-to-GDP ratio. If any of these elements are missing, it is not possible to reverse the trend in the government debt ratio, and without that, the debt-to-GDP ratio cannot move onto a downward path. Had fiscal consolidation been not accomplished, the deficit could not have been reduced to below 3%, a level where government debt ratio does not rise anymore. Unless employment is stabilised at a high level and economic growth is steady and positive, no sustainable macroeconomic balance can be achieved, which constantly weakens the budgetary position and necessitates adjustment programmes.

Part Four

Economic stabilisation

Chapter 19

Reorientation of monetary policy

In 2001, the monetary policy framework of the Hungarian central bank was switched to an inflation targeting system and the exchange rate band system, which was maintained until 2008. Aside from the two years after the introduction of the inflation targeting system, the Hungarian central bank and the monetary policy tools used by the central bank were unable to achieve the inflation target in any single year. Credible inflation targeting regimes must be paired with a floating exchange rate system, as otherwise the inflation target cannot be the primary objective of monetary policy. Despite high levels of interest rates and the artificially strong exchange rate, monetary policy was not able on its own to lower Hungarian inflation towards the target. Additionally, until the band system was scrapped, this policy resulted in a more stable exchange rate versus the euro, compared to the other countries in the region, facilitating the strong growth in foreign currency lending (Figure 221).

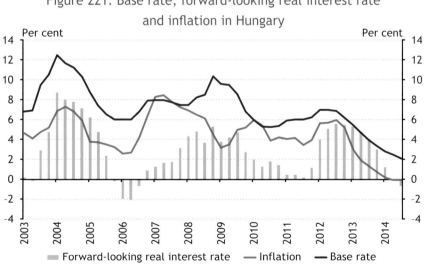

Figure 221. Base rate, forward-looking real interest rate and inflation in Hungary

Source: HCSO, MNB, MNB estimate

In 2003, the central bank responded to the negative turn in economic policy from mid-2002: in reaction to the rise in external debt following the election budget in 2002 and HUF depreciation, the central bank raised the policy rate to 12.5%, an extremely high level from an economic history perspective. With this decision, the central bank gave an economic policy style response to the failure of economic policy and the rapid depreciation of the exchange rate. Intense inflationary pressure was felt in the Hungarian economy as a result of the primary monetary policy anchor introduced in 2001, i.e. the double-digit policy rate used for inflation targeting, the ensuing double-digit lending and deposit rates, and in particular the shift towards foreign currency lending and the impact of tax hikes, which boosted inflation expectations.

Due to the spread of foreign currency lending, the price increases stemming from constant increases in taxes and supply shocks (food prices and the oil price), the correlation between the policy rate in Hungary and inflation was weak, because of the intense distorting effect of inflation expectations until the change in monetary policy. Furthermore, the central bank's policy rate was significantly higher than the neutral rate, and via the monetary transmission channel this substantially increased the expected profit of the domestic goods producers dominating the supply market. Because of the high policy rate and the high lending rates, domestic goods producers were confronted with economic return requirements which were unrealistic and could not be met by most domestic producers; consequently, it constrained the investments of domestic enterprises, thus hampering domestic supply and demand and consequently undermining economic growth.

In addition to this, another negative effect is that the high policy rate results in a strong forint exchange rate, which in turn weakens the export incentives of domestic producers (especially of SMEs), while at the same time increasing the incentives of importers on the domestic market. The role of a high policy rate is to cool down economic activity, but a significant, long-term deviation between the equilibrium level of interest rates and the equilibrium level of the exchange rate distorts the incentives of domestic producers, leading to deterioration of the market balance between supply and demand (Figure 222).

Figure 222. Base rate in Hungary and HUF exchange rate, 2003-2014

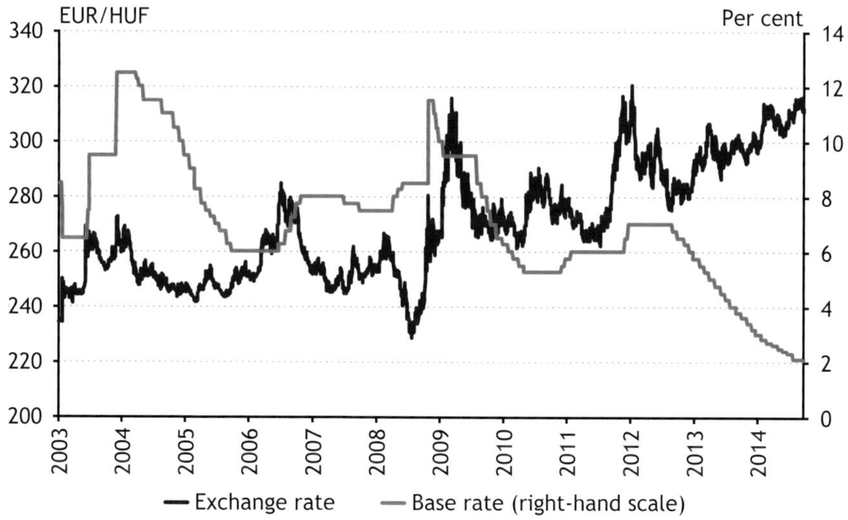

— Exchange rate   — Base rate (right-hand scale)

Source: Bloomberg

The drastic increase in the policy rate by the Hungarian central bank in 2003 should have been based exclusively on the inflation targeting system, but this did not happen, as the central bank attempted to generally restrain economic activity and to stop the depreciation of the forint exchange rate. The central bank stopped the weakening with the high interest rates, but this move was of questionable value for domestic producers and furthermore the overly active exchange rate management may have fostered a false sense of security among Hungarian households, as artificially stabilising the exchange rate for many years facilitated the spread of foreign currency lending. The central bank also did not achieve a general cooling down of the economy, because economic agents turned to foreign currency loans as a result of the dramatic increases in banks' HUF interest rates. The state also began borrowing to a greater and greater degree in foreign currency, and the corporate sector and households also increasingly switched over to foreign currency borrowing.

The central bank's decision in 2003 and the ensuing policy of maintaining the policy rate higher than the neutral level of interest rates would only have worked if the central bank had also been able to prevent the shift by all three economic agents away from HUF loans into foreign currency loans. It would not have been able to prevent the state from doing this, but it could have put a complete end to it for the other two market agents, or at least placed significant restrictions on such borrowing. The tools of the central bank and the supervisory authority would have been sufficient to introduce strong limits on these two market agents shifting their borrowing from forints to foreign currency, but neither authority opted to use these tools.

The leadership of the central bank also maintained this monetary policy during the two attempts to restore fiscal balance between 2006 and 2010. Consequently, in the years after adopting the medium-term inflation targeting system in 2001, central bank policymakers did not stick to the monetary policy anchor: the medium-term inflation outlook was not the sole basis for the MNB's monetary policy decisions, as it also responded to the government's economic policy and developments in the exchange rate. Due to the constant stream of tax hikes which boosted prices, the natural result was that, despite the high interest rate level, the central bank failed to achieve the medium-term inflation target, i.e. price stability.

Between 2003 and 2013, the real interest rate in Hungary was exceptionally high even by international standards. Monetary transmission functioned, because real interest rates and deposit rates were similarly high as real interest rates. This generated an even stronger incentive amongst economic agents to borrow in foreign currency. If the policy rate had been at an equilibrium level, the level of real interest rates substantially lower and forint lending and deposit rates also significantly lower due to monetary transmission, the large difference between forint loans and foreign currency loans – which altered and distorted economic agents' incentives – would not have developed. This was the case, however, and without a doubt there was also one other factor that played a role in this: EU accession in 2004 and the related expectations.

Until 2006–2007, the majority of economic agents expected that Hungary would quickly join the euro. This stretched back to the period 1998–2002: in 2001 the government decided that Hungary would move quickly to join the euro, specifying 1 January 2006 as the first date for accession.

Even though this appeared more and more unlikely after the negative turn in economic policy in mid-2002 (the government first postponed euro accession to 2007 and then to 2008), during the period 2003–2008 many economic agents believed it was a rational decision to borrow in euro, instead of the national currency which was to be replaced in the near future. Indeed, with no expectations of a possible financial crisis (which erupted in autumn 2008), significant changes in the euro and Swiss franc exchange rates did not seem to be a rational anticipation, and consequently borrowing in Swiss franc did not appear completely irrational.

After breaking with the earlier monetary policy in 2001, the monetary policy measures taken in 2003–2013 resulted in significant distortions in the Hungarian economy. Because the policy rate was higher than the equilibrium interest rate, import incentives strengthened, export incentives weakened, reliance on foreign operating capital increased instead of local business development, and the export share of domestically owned micro, small and medium-sized enterprises remained low. With an artificially high policy rate, artificially high lending rates and an artificially strong exchange rate, Hungarian-owned enterprises were unable to take advantages of the new market opportunities opening up in the years following EU accession. While domestic companies which financed their investments with foreign currency loans did not incorporate the conditions related to the distorted HUF lending in their business calculations, they did include a risk factor: the risk of a significant future change in the EUR/HUF or CHF/HUF exchange rate. This hidden risk materialised in late 2008, with a doubly negative impact on businesses which had previously borrowed in foreign currency: they were affected by the crisis at the global, EU and in particular the euro area level after 2008, but they also suffered from the effects of the earlier exchange rate risk materialising.

The real economic distortions resulting from the elevated policy rate, lending rates and exchange rate deviating from the neutral levels were also reflected on the labour market. During the years around EU accession when economic conditions were robust, it would have been necessary to steadily and significantly boost employment in Hungary and to reduce unemployment to a large degree.

The labour market developments seen in this period, however, ran in the opposite direction, even before the first consolidation programme in 2006–2008.

Turning point in monetary policy

From August 2012, the MNB's monetary policy changed: initiating the cycle of interest rate cuts was based solely on expectations that inflation would approach the target over the medium term, and was not motivated by any economic policy, exchange rate or fiscal considerations. The significance of the first steps taken towards this policy change is even greater when one considers that one of the key elements of Hungary's re-establishing economic balance between 2010 and 2014, namely shifting the basis of the tax system to indirect taxes, only occurred in 2012, which was accompanied by a large, but temporary rise in inflation. In all circumstances, monetary policy must be forward looking, and thus decisions made in the present must respond to the anticipated development of inflation in the future. Accordingly, the external members of the Monetary Council, the MNB's supreme monetary policy decision-making body, were correct in assessing that – with the exception of the high 5.7% inflation registered in 2012 – the effect of the shift to an indirect tax system on inflation would only appear in the base year, and that consequently a lower inflation environment could be expected in the period after 2012. Additionally, from June 2012 Hungary's risk assessment improved a great deal.

The change in monetary policy was completed by the new leadership of the central bank in spring 2013. At that time, the MNB returned to the basic principles of monetary policy announced in 2001, i.e. monetary policy decisions were based solely on one single consideration: achieving the medium-term inflation target. As the leadership of the central bank expected low inflationary pressure over the medium term, it announced that monetary conditions would be eased. After the MNB saw that it was possible to fulfil the first two of its three mandates (price stability, financial stability and support of economic policy), it decided to support sustainable economic growth by launching the Funding for Growth Scheme with a volume of almost HUF 3,000 billion to stimulate the economy.

Integration of the MNB and the HFSA paved the way for this turnaround in monetary policy. Stronger coordination of monetary policy and financial regulation also followed from the new law on the central bank, because the new integrated institution had at its disposal a more robust set of tools to ensure financial stability (Table 6).

Table 6. Transformation of monetary policy

CHANGES		
Low inflationary pressure over the medium term	⇨	Expansive monetary conditions over the long term
Support for sustainable growth	⇨	Funding for Growth Scheme (maximum total of HUF 2,750 bn)
Stronger coordination of monetary policy and financial regulation	⇨	Integration of MNB and HFSA
Consideration of the MNB's results	⇨	Positive result in 2013
NO CHANGES		
1 Anchor	⇨	Medium-term inflation targeting
3 Mandate	⇨	Price stability
	⇨	Financial stability
	⇨	Support of economic policy
Conservative management of FX reserves	⇨	High level of FX reserves

Source: MNB

Two major changes occurred in monetary policy starting from spring 2013. First, monetary policy returned to the original strategy from 2001, according to which the inflation target was the primary anchor of monetary policy. The second was that, in the event that price stability was achieved, the central bank could undertake to support the government's economic policy, in accordance with the letter and the spirit of the central bank law, using its reinforced set of financial stability tools. The sequence is also important: price stability comes first, followed closely by financial stability, and only after both of these have been achieved is it possible to support economic policy.

The turnaround in the central bank's monetary policy was motivated by the same basic goals as the government's economic policy: facilitating the expansion of employment and sustained economic growth. The change in monetary policy reinforced the improvement in economic balance, because the central bank no longer generated a loss for the central budget in 2013, and thus helped Hungary to successfully exit the EU's excessive deficit procedure in mid-2013. The central bank's funding programme also backed the recovery in growth. By keeping monetary conditions expansive, the central bank steadily supported the expansion of employment and promoted the turnaround in investment and consumption.

Without the shift in monetary policy in spring 2013, the major successes seen in 2013–2014 would have been delayed, including the return to balance, the recovery in growth and ultimately the rebound in investment.

One aspect of monetary policy that remained, however, was the conservative approach to FX reserves, as the central bank continued to maintain a high level of currency reserves. In 2013–2014, the level of FX reserves was consistently higher than the level according to the Guidotti–Greenspan rule, which is most often taken into account by investors. As part of the turnaround in monetary policy, the central bank followed the basic principle that the central bank's FX reserves must be maintained at a level higher than the minimum required level of reserves, due to the high ratio of government debt, and the high ratio of foreign currency debt within government debt.

This conservative, prudent currency reserve policy promoted the maintenance of expansive monetary conditions over the medium term, because it supported the stability of the domestic financial system.

While the reorientation of the central bank's monetary policy was only completed in spring 2013, this move could actually have occurred much earlier. One particular feature of inflation in Hungary was that the changes in taxes resulted in large fluctuations in the overall consumer price index. In the phases of consolidation following the deterioration in fiscal balance, taxes were increased, especially indirect taxes, and these increases significantly raised the level of inflation during the years they occurred. The unsuccessful consolidation attempt between 2006 and 2008 and then the second attempt in 2008–2010 both used increases in indirect taxes to assist in consolidation, and these always resulted in a substantial rise in inflation during the year of the tax hike (Figure 223).

Figure 223. Development of inflation indicators and the base rate, 2000-2014

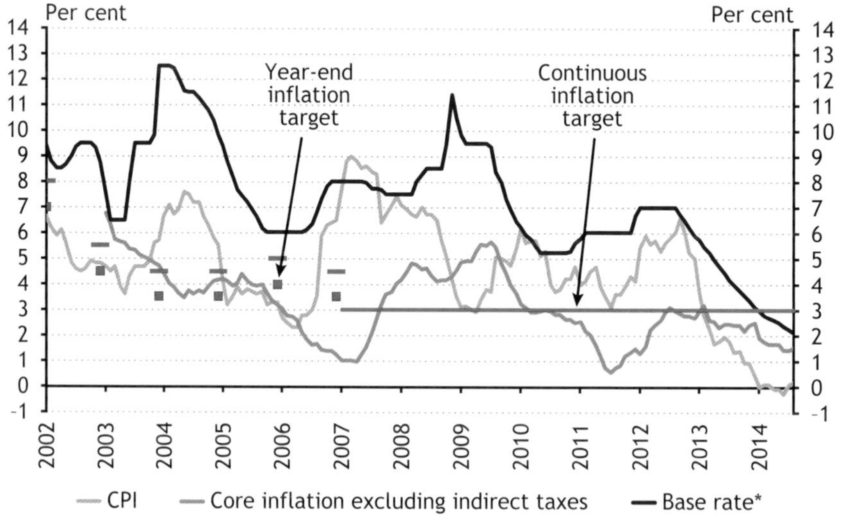

Source: MNB   ** calculated using the arithmetic average for the base rate*

This occurred in 2011–2012, when the successful turning point in economic balance was facilitated by the new kinds of taxes on consumption and by increases in existing indirect taxes.

Even after 2008 it would have been possible to project a trend of lower inflation over the medium term, and thus by the end of 2008 at the latest a shift in monetary policy towards more expansive conditions and efforts to avert the financial and economic crisis could have been started, as was seen at other Anglo-Saxon and EU central banks. This, however, did not occur. The single monetary policy anchor (a high real policy rate for the medium-term inflation targeting system) was also not justified during the period 2003–2006, since the trend in core inflation without indirect tax effects was on a downtrend in this period.

In the years following the 2008 financial crisis, far more expansive monetary conditions could have been applied (and in light of the other factors, should have been applied) in the interests of inflation targeting, because it became obvious that the economic performance of the Hungarian economy was deviating from the long-term output trend. As a result of the crisis, the output gap widened, and corporate bankruptcies, falling employment and rising unemployment all indicated that the Hungarian economy would fall short of the long-term GDP growth trend, and that most of the sectors would underperform their respective growth trends.

The flawed nature of the monetary policy pursued between 2008 and 2013 is reflected by the fact that other EU and global central banks responded to the challenges during the crisis after 2008. Although these responses varied greatly, essentially all of the programmes involved the use of unconventional monetary policy tools. The programmes of quantitative easing (Fed) and qualitative easing (BoJ), the growth-stimulating lending programme launched by the UK's central bank and the steady policy easing by the European Central Bank all show the spread of non-conventional tools.

Hungary's central bank failed to move in this direction, even though the economic conditions were marked by a widening output gap and core inflation adjusted for indirect taxes did not indicate any inflationary pressure, which would have justified implementing a much more expansive monetary policy than was actually pursued.

Precisely for these reasons, the leadership of the central bank should have moved to lower the policy rate even before August 2012, and should not have increased the policy rate to 7% after 2010, and should have considered which other instruments it could have used to support the government's economic policy without jeopardising price stability and financial stability.

Contrary to this, however, monetary policy did not support the government's policy of attempting to restore balance or its efforts to stabilise the economy during the period 2008–2013. Despite introduction of the new economic policy and new system of public burden sharing (in particular the new taxes imposed on the financial sector) following the change of government in 2010, financial stability was not at risk in the Hungarian economy. Neither price stability nor financial stability were in jeopardy from the perspective of the medium-term inflation targeting system: action could have and should have been taken.

If the leadership of the central bank had taken into account the nature of the new economic policy implemented after mid-2010 in its monetary policy decisions, it would have had to introduce new monetary tools directed not against this policy, but rather to support this policy, because the primary goal of the economic policy was to restore economic balance and stabilise the economy. Furthermore, as early as the first half of 2010 and in each and every year thereafter it became clear that the economic policy was achieving the goals it had set. The budget deficit dropped to below 3% of GDP, the ratio of government debt stopped rising and started to fall, and a turnaround was seen in real economic performance in the second half of the cycle. The success in restoring economic balance, supported by the improvement in Hungary's risk assessment, would have been adequate in its own right to provide a basis for a change in the central bank's monetary policy in the period from 2010 to spring 2013.

By contrast, the central bank only launched the cycle of rate cuts in August 2012, and even then this move was only supported by the votes of the external members of the Monetary Council, whereas almost every other global and EU central bank had already taken measures to address the effects of the 2008 global financial crisis far earlier. During the period 2008–2012, it would have been possible to follow the examples set by the Fed, the European Central Bank, the Bank of England, the Swedish central bank, the Russian central bank, the Turkish central bank, and the Czech and Romanian central banks (Table 7).

Table 7. Rate-cutting cycles

Country	Period	Length of cycle (months)	Starting rate level	Final rate level	Reduction (bp)	Interim hold
Romania	June 2004 – September 2005	16	21.25%	7.50%	1375	September-October 2004 (2 months) and May-July 2005 (3 months)
Turkey	November 2008 – November 2009	13	16.75%	6.50%	1025	-
Czech Republic	July 1998 – November 1999	17	15.00%	5.25%	975	February 1999 (1 month), August 1999 (1 month)
Russia	October 2009 – May 2010	8	10.50%	5.00%	550	-
United States	September 2007 – December 2008	16	5.25%	0.25%	500	June-September 2008 (4 months)
United Kingdom	February 2008 – March 2009	14	5.50%	0.50%	500	March 2009 (1 month) and May 2009
Sweden	January-December 1996	12	8.91%	4.10%	481	-
ECB	October 2008 – May 2009	8	4.25%	1.00%	325	-

Source: National central bank websites, MNB

The path of policy rates in the developed economies between 2010 and 2014 clearly reflect the easing of monetary conditions, and only in the euro area was there a limited, brief move in the opposite direction, which was followed by a further reduction of the policy rate (Figure 224).

Figure 224. Central bank rates in developed economies

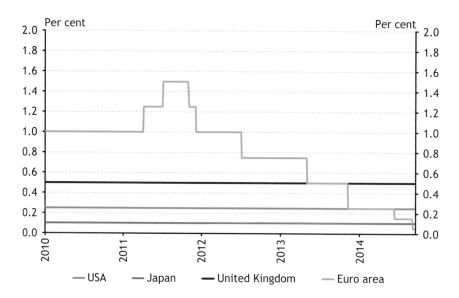

Source: Databases of central banks

Due to the high level of Hungary's government debt and the high ratio of FX-denominated debt within this, it would not have been possible to lower the MNB's policy rate to the levels seen in the developed economies, but it would have been possible to achieve a policy rate of around 2% at any time during the period 2010–2014, as reflected by the results of the 24-month rate-cutting cycle which ended at 2.1%.

The turnaround in monetary policy was made possible by the successful restoration of economic balance and the stabilisation of the economy and the opposite is also true: a shift to looser monetary conditions would have supported the latter two achievements as well. Significant support for the change in the MNB's monetary policy in spring 2013 also came from a hidden factor: the large surplus on Hungary's current account balance. This is considered a "hidden" factor, because it is not usual to take this into consideration as a major factor in monetary policy decisions, whereas its significance in determining the global financial markets' assessment of an economy is equally as strong as other factors such as the fiscal deficit, the rate of GDP growth or the level and composition of a country's debt and government debt. The reason that the current account balance is such an important factor in the financial markets' assessment of financial stability is that as long as a country's current account balance is in the positive domain it may prove to be more resilient to changes in market sentiment.

In 2013, when the MNB's monetary policy shifted, Hungary's position in its group of peer countries was quite exceptional, because there was a significant surplus on the current account. One can see that in Hungary's group of peer countries, the Romanian, Polish and Czech economies run deficits on the current account, whereas the Hungarian economy ended 2013 with a surplus of 3% (Figure 225).

The positive balance on the current account provides an invisible safety net for the changing monetary policy, because it partially compensates for Hungary's competitive disadvantages in the region in terms of its financial-type macroeconomic indicators.

Hungary's government debt level is higher than its regional peers, the composition of the financing is less favourable, the performance of the Hungarian economy was worse during the first decade after EU accession compared the performance of its peers, the household sector's foreign currency loans are a significant financial stability risk and the deficit on the income balance is high. Despite these weaknesses, the surplus on the current account balance, which is backed by the accumulation of a large surplus on the trade balance, "shields" the Hungarian financial system.

Figure 225. Base rate and current account balance in emerging economies

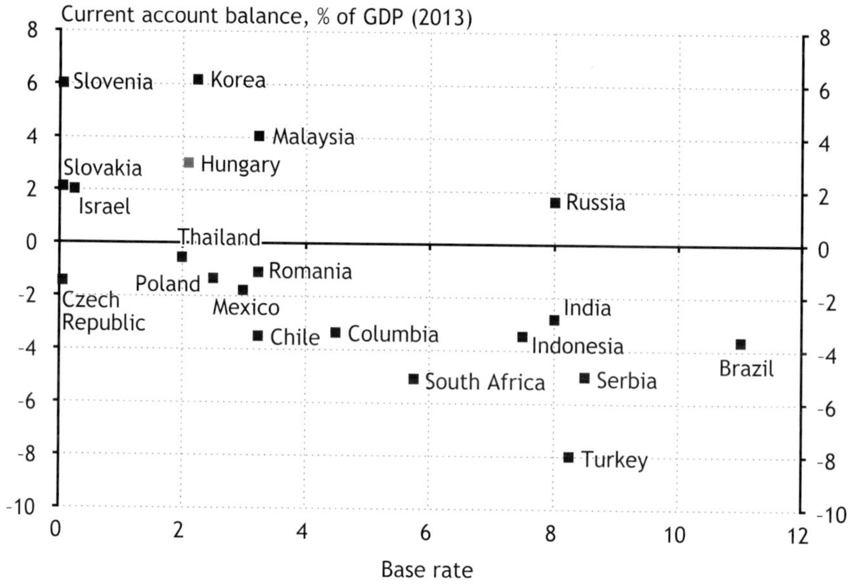

Current account balance, % of GDP (2013)

Base rate

Source: Bloomberg

In using the inflation targeting framework, Hungary belongs to a large international group of developed and emerging economies which apply inflation targeting in their monetary policies. It is clear that Hungary's 3% medium-term inflation target fits in with the monetary policy of a family of larger central banks, but there is still room left to fine tune monetary policy: central banks using the inflation targeting framework tend to define a band for inflation as their target range, in contrast to the Hungarian system which defines a point target.

In the Romanian and Polish systems, the mid-point of the range is defined as a point lower than the 3% medium-term target used in Hungary, and the mid-points in the inflation ranges for the Czech, Swedish and UK systems are even lower than that (Figure 226).

Hungary's inflation targeting system is basically in line with the international examples and reflects a similar monetary policy as its peers in the region.

Figure 226. Inflation targets at central banks using inflation targeting, 2014

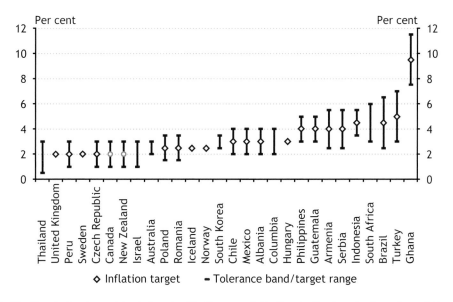

◇ Inflation target   ▬ Tolerance band/target range

In Thailand, the target is defined with the core inflation indicator. In Canada and New Zealand, the emphasis is on the median of the range, which is thus marked with grey circle.

Source: Databases of central banks

Hungarian monetary policy has no exchange rate target

In the inflation targeting system introduced in 2001, it was not possible for the central bank's monetary policy to pursue an exchange rate goal. The exchange rate of the forint only affected monetary policy in one way: via inflation.

Significant changes in the exchange rate only have an effect on domestic inflation developments if these changes are lasting in nature, and consequently monetary policy only needs to monitor the indirect effect of such changes via inflation.

The 2008 financial crisis and the ensuing crisis in the real economy resulted in changes in numerous fundamental macroeconomic relationships in many countries, including Hungary. In the decades prior to the crisis, there was a constant relationship in the Hungarian economy between changes in the exchange rate and inflation: a 10-forint move in the exchange rate resulted in a 0.9% change in inflation. If the exchange rate of the forint weakened by 10 forints compared to the earlier level, inflation was almost 1% higher in the following two years, and this effect was stronger during the first period of forint weakening. The opposite was also true: appreciation of the exchange rate by 10 forints lowered inflation by almost 1%. This relationship, however, did not work in the other direction: if inflation rose owing to increases in indirect taxes or energy prices, there was no pressure on the exchange rate.

After the 2008 financial crisis, there were substantial structural shifts in the real economy at the global and EU level and in Hungary as well. One of these changes was lower output in a number of sectors compared to the earlier economic performance, as a result of which the output gap increased. Surplus capacities mitigate inflationary pressure, because unchanged demand meets with smaller supply on the market. This relationship is more complex, because it has a different meaning in the case of export capacity or domestic production capacity, but the financial crisis, which resulted in a significant contraction in the real economy, and the later restoration of economic balance and stabilisation of the economy all took place in a strongly changing macroeconomic environment in Hungary.

In this changing macroeconomic environment, the earlier relationship between the exchange rate and inflation also changed: after 2008, a 10-forint change in the exchange rate only led to a change of 0.4–0.6% in inflation. Thus, if the exchange rate of the forint weakened by 10 forints, it no longer meant that additional inflation of 1% could be expected, but rather that inflation would increase by 0.5% on average: the effect of the exchange rate on inflation was halved as a result of the crisis.

In addition to affecting inflation, a long-term change in the exchange rate also impacts other factors in a company or a country's economic environment. Thanks to a weaker exchange rate, new export markets may open up, and domestic producers may also be in a more favourable position on the domestic market. Consequently, it may not be possible to meet demand with the existing capacities, and development is necessary. Investment calculations are carried out using the new exchange rate level, and accordingly this has a lasting impact on the strong export incentive and import substituting incentive. If, over the horizon of the calculation, rapid convergence is expected in prices and wages, as well as in economic conditions between an emerging economy and a developed economy, then the stronger export incentive stemming from the weaker exchange rate and the incentive for import substitution may balance each other. However, if no such convergence is expected, then the initial effect may persist over the entire operating lifetime of the new capacity created by the investment: a weaker exchange rate results in a stronger export incentive, higher employment and growth rate, and thus results in stronger investment activity.

Compared to the pre-crisis period, a weaker exchange rate increases inflation to a smaller degree, and as a result of this increases the level of wages, but over the medium term it results in a weaker real exchange rate on the whole. Due to this effect, exports grow and import substitution becomes stronger, as a result of which the utilisation of existing capacities increases, spurring consumption, even without investment. Consequently, however, new investments may also be necessary, and these new investments can target both the domestic market and the foreign markets, leading to further expansion of consumption and a rising pace of GDP growth.

From 2001 all the way until the crisis, exchange rates in the region appreciated sharply, and then in the years following the crisis real exchange rates fluctuated, but essentially remained at the appreciated levels from before the crisis (Figure 227).

Compared to their actual purchasing power and the purchasing power of their EU competitors, the currencies were strongly overvalued and this represented a major competitive disadvantage for all of the economies in the region, with the Hungarian economy suffering from the largest competitive disadvantage.

Figure 227. Changes in the nominal and real effective exchange rate of the forint

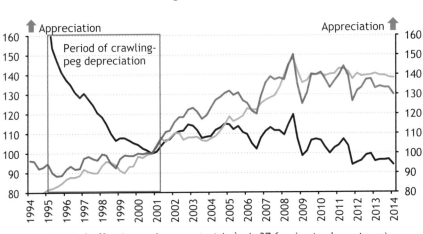

The effective exchange rate indices are determined with 37 foreign trade partner countries.

Source: Eurostat   *2000 Q4 = 100*

Effects of the two-year rate-cutting cycle

At the start of the rate-cutting cycle, inflation still ranged at 6%, but this inflation far in excess of the 3% target was actually caused by one-off factors, and consequently it was possible to launch the rate-cutting cycle. Filtering out the effect of rising food prices caused by increases in indirect taxes and unfavourable weather, inflationary pressure was already moderate in the second half of 2012 from the perspective of underlying developments. Due to the strains in the European banking system in late 2011 and the first half of 2012, the risk perception of Hungary deteriorated as a result of the unfavourable external conditions. From June 2012, the risk perception of Hungary improved greatly and the forint exchange rate appreciated, which reduced the outlook for future inflation, in addition to the disappearance of the indirect tax effects.

From the start of 2013, the underlying inflation trend was already characterised by disinflation, with the main factors in this regard being the disappearance of the indirect tax increases from the base and the reduction of regulated prices in a series of steps. The development of commodity prices on the global market also resulted in similarly moderate inflationary pressure. Due to the high output gap which reflected significant unutilised capacities, inflationary pressure from the real economy was also moderate, and imported inflationary pressure was also subdued.

Accordingly, during 2013 the inflation environment was low, and thus the decision-makers at the central bank made the correct move to continue the rate cuts that had been started in August 2012.

Prior to the start of the cutting cycle, the Hungarian risk premium had declined significantly: in contrast to the development of the emerging market risk premium, Hungary's risk premium was steadily falling and in spring 2013 it declined below the average emerging market risk premium and continued moving away from this average.

This was facilitated by the successful return to economic balance seen after 2010, i.e. the fact that the 3% GDP-proportionate budget deficit target was consistently met (Figure 228).

Figure 228. MNB base rate, and development of domestic
and emerging market risk premiums

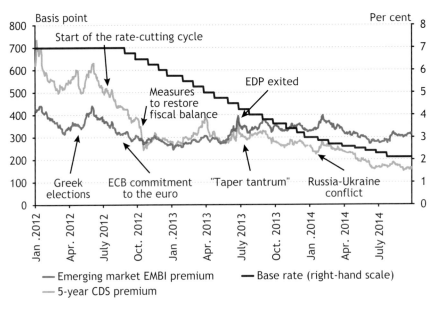

Source: *Bloomberg*

The turnaround in the budget paved the way for a significant, lasting improvement in Hungary's risk perception, which in turn supported the rate-cutting cycle. In 2012, according to the EU methodology, the deficit on the Hungarian state budget declined to 2.3% of GDP, marking a sharp decline from the period 2002–2009, when the budget deficit averaged 6.7%.

Looking at the "environment" in which the rate-cutting cycle occurred as shown in Figure 228, it is clear that the risk premiums of the emerging markets were considerably higher than the Hungarian risk premium at the start of the cycle, and in 2014 the Hungarian 5-year CDS premium was already lower than the risk premium for the emerging markets. The rate-cutting cycle was supported by the decline in Hungary's 5-year CDS premium, and accordingly the shift in the MNB's monetary policy did not have a negative impact on Hungarian risk premiums. Indeed, the relationship was actually the opposite: the stable, predictable monetary policy, including the very gradual, but resolute rate-cutting cycle, reinforced the downward trend in Hungary's risk premiums.

Monetary transmission functioned efficiently through the interest rate channel during the rate-cutting cycle, as banks reduced their household and corporate lending and deposit rates in line with the cuts in the policy rate. This also indicates that the policy rate of 7%, which was substantially higher than the level of equilibrium interest rates, had allowed or prompted banks to pursue an interest rate policy which distorted the economic structure and restrained economic performance. It can be seen that the level of interest rates on household time deposits is the closest to the base rate, and a similar case is seen with regard to corporate time deposits, as these two deposit rates essentially exactly mirrored the rate-cutting cycle (Figure 229).

Figure 229. MNB base rate and the development of interest rates on household and corporate credit/deposit products

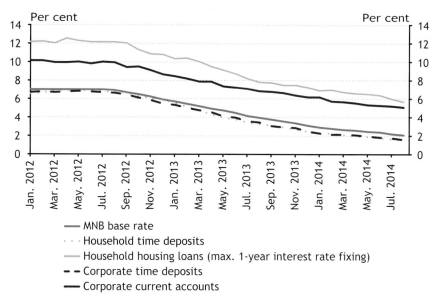

Source: MNB

The rate-cutting cycle reduced this distortion, which was caused by the undershooting of the central bank's medium-term inflation target: in 2013–2014, the Hungarian economy experienced strong disinflation, and consequently monetary policy "undershot" the 3% inflation target, while the lower base rate mitigated this distortion

The 24-month rate-cutting cycle made a large contribution to economic growth in 2013–2014: in just two years, it increased Hungarian GDP by 1.1 percentage points. In 2013, the rate-cutting cycle may have increased average inflation by 0.4% and by 1.1% in 2014. The effect of the interest rate reductions by the central bank was reflected in prices with a lag, which typically amounts to one year; accordingly, the effect of the rate-cutting cycle will also be felt in the development of inflation in 2015. Without the 24-month rate-cutting cycle, 2014 inflation would have been around -1%, leading to deflation in the Hungarian economy, which would have posed a threat to the turnaround in consumption and growth.

The cycle of interest rate cuts also had a positive effect on the price and cost-based competitiveness of the Hungarian economy as compared to the region. The rate cuts made investment loans more affordable, boosted export incentives and thus facilitated the expansion of employment and reduction of unemployment, and contributed to economic growth. The cycle of rate cuts carried out over 24 months had significant macroeconomic impacts, since it resulted in 1.1% higher inflation on the whole, averted the risk of deflation, boosted GDP by 1.1% and thus reinforced the recovery in growth.

The rate-cutting cycle did not undermine households' propensity to save, as households' net financial savings increased during the cycle. Due to deleveraging after the crisis, one of the traditional economic relationships did not hold in the Hungarian economy, because savings did not decline as a result of falling deposit rates in response to the cuts in the policy rate. One of the reasons behind this may be that the substitution effect outweighed the income effect. According to the theory of permanent income, if a lower interest rate environment prevails over the longer term, households will offset the ensuing decline in interest income by increasing their savings. Despite the falling interest rates on loans, households' propensity to borrow remained subdued, and households have shown a long-term adjustment in their behaviour. In respect of consumption, this change was also perceptible during the rate-cutting cycle: households no longer sought to expand their consumption based on borrowing (including borrowing in foreign currency), as the income freed up by the 16% flat-rate family tax system played the key role, along with rising employment and increases in wages. Households' net savings increased during the rate-cutting cycle, while at the same time the economy's net lending grew, and simultaneously household consumption began to expand right from the very start of the interest rate cuts (Figure 230).

Figure 230. Household consumption and financial savings,
and the development of net lending

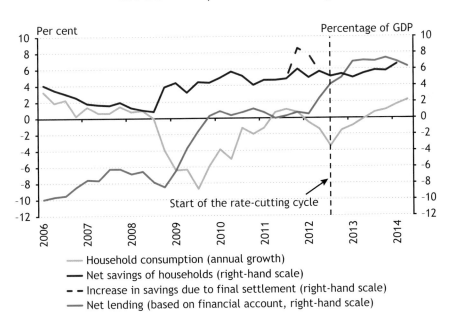

Source: MNB, HCSO   *data from financial accounts*

One important result of the rate-cutting cycle was that – despite the level of the base rate being 490 basis points lower than before – the country's net lending remained high, which helped to lower the risk premiums.

The positive real economic effects of the rate-cutting cycle are also highlighted by the fact that the low base rate was not accompanied by a surge in imports, and thus there was no deterioration in the trade balance.

At the same time, the financing costs for HUF-denominated debt also fell, because the yield curve for government bonds shifted lower in response to the predictable central bank monetary policy and the successful consolidation programme which restored sustainable economic balance. The financing of public debt became cheaper and more secure, as a result of the steady downward shift in the yield curve for HUF government bonds and the shift in favour of forint in financing government debt. The lower forint interest rate expenses cut the deficit on the income balance, which contributed to the improvement in external balance.

Reference yields on government bonds fell by an average of 390 basis points during the rate-cutting cycle.

There was a sharp decline of 400–460 basis points in yields for maturities of less than one year, with the long end of the yield curve falling by 280–370 basis points. Naturally, the interest expense reducing effect of the fall in yields initially affects short-dated bonds, and then later newly issued, longer-dated instruments, and the situation is similar for variable-rate assets, with the decline in yields ultimately propagating through an increasingly large portion of the debt.

The positive effects of the rate-cutting cycle on government bond yields manifest themselves over a period of several years. In the course of one year, roughly one third of Hungarian government debt is repriced, increasing to a ratio of 55% over three years and after nine years some 90% of all Hungarian government debt is repriced.

Due to the cuts in the base rate, interest expenses as a percentage of GDP have declined by 0.2% since 2012 and this trend will continue in the coming years. Assuming complete repricing, a steadily low level of yields, and an unchanged debt structure and HUF exchange rate, the long-term effect of the 24-month rate-cutting cycle will reduce the budget's annual interest expenses as a percentage of GDP by more than 1 percentage point. Due to the rate cuts, in the years after 2014 the budget's annual interest expenses may be HUF 300 billion lower, thus lowering the GDP-proportionate interest expenses by roughly 20-25%.

As a consequence of the low base rate, interest rate conditions on the financial market also declined. Compared to the earlier base rate of 7%, this move improved the profit of the MNB by almost HUF 350 billion, and one of the positive consequences of this is that the MNB's operations did not post a loss in 2013 and thus did not burden the budget. There is a realistic possibility that the MNB will be able to post positive results in the coming years as well, thereby reducing the risks to budget expenses. With a base rate of 7%, due to the stock of sterilisation instruments, mandatory reserves and government deposits, the MNB's interest expenses would have been substantially higher in the period between August 2012 and July 2014: in fact, maintaining the base rate at 7% would have resulted in an unsustainable central bank balance sheet, and covering this expense from the budget would have led to a deficit of over 3%.

The interest rate cuts reduced the central bank's interest expenses, because lower interest had to be paid on the two-week policy instrument, while the rate cuts also had a dampening effect on the stock of the policy instrument as well (Figure 231).

Figure 231. MNB interest savings

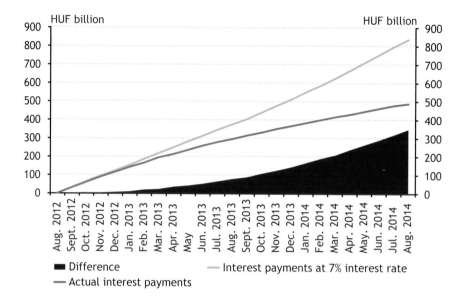

On the stock of sterilisation, mandatory reserves and government deposits (cumulative values)

Source: MNB

During the rate-cutting cycle, the decline in yields on 3-month government paper consistently matched the reduction in the base rate, whereas this was not initially the case for 5-year government bond yields, which subsequently tracked the declines for a long period, and then deviated from the path of the base rate during the final one third of the rate-cutting cycle: this also underlines the success of monetary transmission, since the base rate mainly affects short-term yields of less than one year. At the same time, the decline in long-term yields indicates that investors consider the monetary policy to be credible and believe that the interest rate level lower than the historical average is sustainable over the longer term (Figure 232).

Figure 232. 3-month and 5-year reference rates and development of the base rate since early 2012

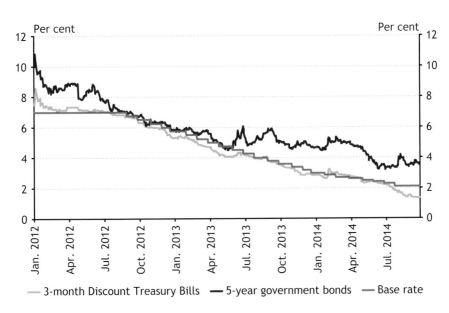

Source: GDMA, MNB

The reduction of the policy rate took place in the context of a consistently high level of FX reserves, and thus did not jeopardise financial stability. While interest rates were being lowered, the level of Hungary's international reserves always exceeded the key indicators monitored by investors. By contrast, prior to the crisis, the level of reserves was lower than the level of short-term external debt. This is proven by the vulnerability of the government's economic policy after 2002 and the economic policy after 2003: neither the government nor the central bank expected that there might be a change in the simultaneous economic upswing being seen at the global level and in the EU, as well as in the abundant liquidity on the financial markets. The relatively low level of central bank reserves was a hidden risk, which immediately materialised during the financial crisis in 2008. During the period of rate cuts, however, the significantly higher level of Hungarian international reserves compared to the past actually reinforced financial stability.

Chapter 20

Turnaround in lending

In the years before the 2008 financial crisis, there was a rapid increase in the credit-to-GDP ratio in the Hungarian economy, as a result of the shift to a flawed economic policy. It is worthwhile to compare the rate of growth in banks' lending to the private sector (non-financial institutions and households) with the rates seen in other countries which had previously experienced a financial crisis. Figure 233 shows the development of the credit-to-GDP ratio before and after the crises for the entire sample and for countries which were characterised by foreign currency borrowing and high levels of government debt.[52] Distinguishing between the latter two items is particularly important, because Hungary was faced by both of these problems.

In Hungary, the credit-to-GDP ratio increased faster than the average of the countries under review. In the third year before the crisis (2005 in the case of Hungary), domestic indebtedness was already higher, and at the onset of the crisis it exceeded the earlier average by 15 percentage points. At the same time, one striking aspect is that the private sector credit-to-GDP ratio rose to an even higher level than that before the crisis in the countries which were characterised by foreign currency borrowing (Figure 233).

During the financial crisis, deleveraging occurred in these countries, as a result of which the volume of outstanding debt declined slowly, but decisively. In Hungary, however, even in the fourth year after the crisis there is still no sign of this occurring, primarily because depreciation of the forint (especially vis-à-vis the Swiss franc) offset the contraction in banks' supply of credit in relation to the ratio of outstanding debt to GDP.

---

[52] Balog et al. (2014): Credit crunch in Hungary between 2009 and 2013: Is the creditless period over? Hitelintézeti Szemle, November 2014.

Figure 233. Private sector loan-to-GDP ratio around financial crises
in different groups of countries

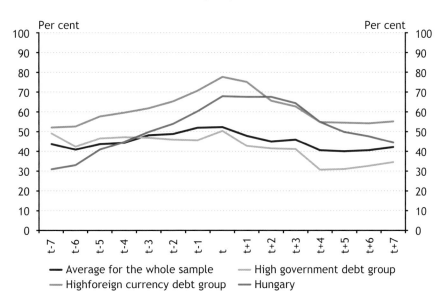

Per cent

— Average for the whole sample   — High government debt group
— Highforeign currency debt group   — Hungary

Based on a sample of 30 countries; total loans extended by the credit institution sector

Source: Balog et al. (2014)

An examination of the corporate loan-to-GDP ratio shows that the
corporate sector did not play the main role in the new accumulation
of debt which resulted in macroeconomic imbalance. During the first
decade after EU accession, the corporate loan-to-GDP ratio for the
Hungarian corporate sector remained between 20–30% and then briefly
edged over 30%, before subsiding back to its historical range. In the
period 2004–2014, corporate loan-to-GDP ratios in Poland, Romania,
the Czech Republic and Slovakia remained consistently below the
Hungarian corporate sector's loan-to-GDP ratio, but the difference
was not significant: compared to its peers in the region, the Hungarian
corporate sector did not cause a lending bubble or borrow irresponsibly.
By contrast, a significant increase in corporate sector borrowing was
seen in the euro area, in particular the southern group of euro area
members, and Slovenia, along with Bulgaria after 2008.

To a large degree, corporate borrowing in the southern euro area countries was responsible for the development of the corporate loan-to-GDP indicator in the euro area (Figure 234).

Figure 234. Corporate loan-to-GDP ratio

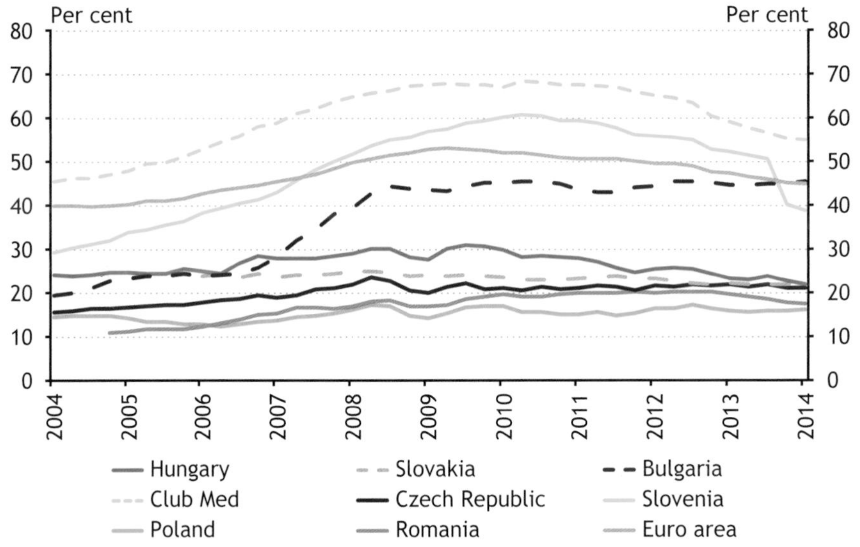

Source: MNB   Intercompany loans not included

Thus, compared to the region, Hungary's corporate sector did not borrow excessively in the first decade of EU membership, and at the same time exhibited a substantially lower level of debt compared to the euro area and in particular the southern euro area members, as well as Slovenia and Bulgaria. Hungary's non-financial corporate sector was not the chief culprit behind the deterioration in financial balance: the parties mainly responsible were the public budget on the one hand, and households on the other, with the banking sector as the driving factor behind the latter, due to its interest in pushing foreign currency lending.

In the years following the 2008 crisis, Hungary exhibited significant adjustment in terms of corporate lending compared to the EU and the region, as the indicator for domestic corporate loans to GDP and the overall stock of outstanding corporate loans declined after the crisis.

A similar degree of deleveraging was seen in the Baltic economies, whereas the degree of adjustment in the euro area and most of the countries in the region was smaller than in the Hungarian corporate sector. The reason for this is that – aside from the Bulgarian economy – the ratios of corporate loan to GDP were lower: outstanding corporate loans actually still increased in the EU members in the region, with the growth stopping for one or two years during the crisis, but looking at rise for the four-year period after the crisis the level of corporate debt has risen. Compared to the countries in the region, the larger degree of deleveraging in Hungary was probably mainly caused by the banking sector's restrained lending due to the high loan-to-deposit indicator and the weak domestic demand resulting from the protracted crisis (Figure 235).

Figure 235. Change in the outstanding corporate credit during the years of the crisis

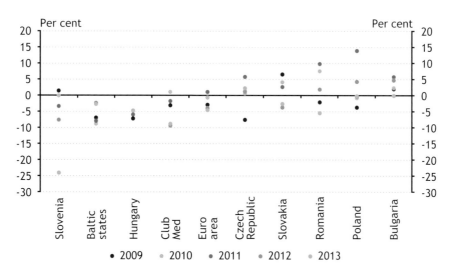

Source: MNB   *Exchange rate adjusted values*

Declining lending turned into a major barrier to the development of the Hungarian corporate sector in the years after the crisis, and this was only justified to a limited extent by the higher stock of foreign currency borrowing compared to the regional peers. In reality, an artificial credit crunch developed in the Hungarian economy in the first years after the 2008 crisis.

Not only was there a different trend in stock indicators, such as the corporate loan-to-GDP ratio, and in outstanding corporate loans compared to the region (i.e. a credit crunch in the Hungarian economy in the years after the 2008 crisis), lending conditions also deteriorated significantly compared to the region in this period. Compared to the countries in the region in the years after the 2008 crisis (and prior to the crisis as well, but the situation deteriorated further after the crisis), Hungarian companies were only able to draw loans over EUR 1 million at substantially higher interest rates compared to their competitors in the region. Whereas companies operating in the region were able to take out loans at rates of 4–8% after the crisis, Hungarian firms could only draw a loan of over EUR 1 million at rates of 6–14% (Figure 236).

A similar difference was seen for loans under 1 million euros, which is the size of loans mainly available to micro, small and medium-sized enterprises. While small enterprises operating in the EU members in the region could access loans at rates of 4–8%, small Hungarian firms had to pay rates of 7–14%.

This clearly shows that the credit crunch affected the entire range of loans accessible to the corporate sector and also essentially made borrowing impossible for SMEs, which play the dominant role in employment. These quantitative and qualitative differences compared to the regional peers already existed before the crisis, and this major competitive disadvantage in domestic and regional corporate lending envirement persisted all the way until mid-2012.

Figure 236. Interest rates on loans over and below EUR 1 million to the corporate sector in V4 countries and in Hungary

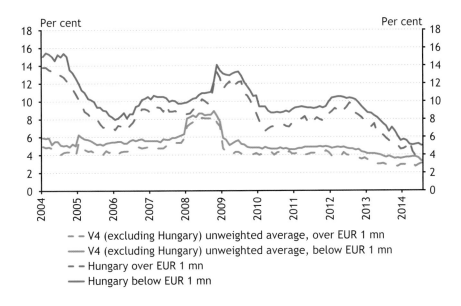

- - V4 (excluding Hungary) unweighted average, over EUR 1 mn
—— V4 (excluding Hungary) unweighted average, below EUR 1 mn
- - Hungary over EUR 1 mn
—— Hungary below EUR 1 mn

Source: ECB

The high budget deficit and rising level of government debt undermined the country's risk rating, which increased the cost of borrowing. The central bank, struggling unsuccessfully with inflation which was steadily higher than the target, kept nominal interest rates high. On the one hand, this made borrowing in the domestic currency almost impossible to access, and on the other hand, it provided greater leeway to the banking sector in the pricing of foreign currency loans as competitive products to forint loans.

In respect of borrowing, Hungarian firms were at a similar competitive disadvantage compared to companies in the southern euro area members, because Hungarian firms also faced far higher lending rates than the companies in the southern euro area economies. The largest difference developed in the period 2008–2010. The reason for this was the forced, rapid balance sheet adjustment of the banking sector, which began to reduce the high loan portfolio irresponsibly accumulated during the crisis years, including the stock of outstanding foreign currency loans (Figure 237).

Figure 237. Average interest rates on corporate loans below and over EUR 1 million in the Club Med countries and in Hungary

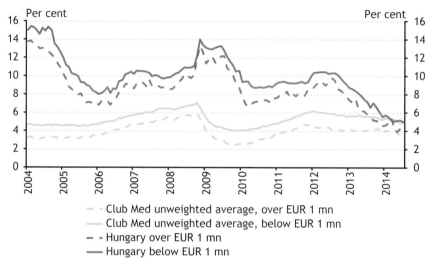

Source: ECB

It is clear that the Hungarian corporate sector was basically not responsible for the new accumulation of debt which led to macro-economic imbalance, as the indicator for domestic corporate loans to GDP was not considerably higher than in the regional economies which are best for the purpose of comparison. Nevertheless, domestic companies suffered from the ramifications of banks' balance sheet adjustment, as they paid the price for the irresponsible borrowing by the government and households when banks turned to deleveraging. This price was the credit crunch, the lack of affordable loans for small companies in particular.

Although Hungary's companies in the real economy did not take part in the new accumulation of debt which upset economic balance, they bore the brunt of the consequences.

There is a clear-cut relationship between the unsuccessful fiscal consolidation efforts in 2006–2008 and 2008–2010 and the situation of Hungary's corporate sector. Since the budget consolidation attempts were based on austerity measures and resulted in growth and employment sacrifices, domestic demand weakened and investment conditions deteriorated. With the forint exchange rate artificially distorted from its equilibrium level and the substantially higher levels of the policy rate and lending rates in comparison to the competitors, the austerity measures created a more difficult situation for precisely that economic agent upon which the attempts to restore balance depended: the corporate sector. Ultimately, no attempts at fiscal consolidation can be successful if employment does not expand and if there is no durable economic growth, but the policy of austerity sacrificed both of these, and the steady deterioration in business conditions rendered the consolidation attempts unrealistic.

The credit crunch in Hungary

A credit crunch occurs in an economy when lending by the banking sector to agents in the economy suddenly drops dramatically. This is a phenomenon occurring on the supply side, as the banking sector fails to provide an adequate quantity and quality of lending, despite demand for credit. The Hungarian financial system is bank based, and the role of the capital market in corporate financing is secondary. This means that larger companies with better credit ratings can still access loans from foreign banks and intercompany loans, while smaller, typically Hungarian-owned businesses can access domestic bank financing, but not loans from foreign banks. As financing via the capital markets is not available to the sector of Hungarian small enterprises, small domestic businesses can actually only obtain loans from the domestic banking sector, and if the banks stop lending, credit for these companies dries up.

A large portion of smaller companies borrowed in foreign currency, but at the same time they did not typically have natural cover in the form of export revenues, and thus hidden risks were built into the financing right from the very beginning. After the crisis, we see a protracted decline in lending to both the household sector and the corporate sector.

Although outstanding lending actually increased still in 2009 owing to revaluation driven by forint depreciation, developments pointing to a credit crunch already started in 2009, if one looks at the flow indicators (gross and net new lending), which are more important from a real economy perspective. With stabilisation of the exchange rate and further tightening of lending conditions, the credit crunch also becomes apparent in the stock indicators starting from 2011.

While the degree of contraction was comparable with what was seen in other countries hit by severe financial crisis and was also comparable with other economies characterised by high level of government debt and/or foreign currency exposure, the credit crunch in Hungary was more prolonged than in other economies in similar situations.

Starting from the fourth year after the crisis, the average stock of outstanding loans in economies in a similar situation already started increasing, whereas in Hungary the GDP-proportionate stock of outstanding private sector loans continued to decline in the fifth year after the crisis, all the way until the end of 2013.

The decline in outstanding household loans was also driven by a natural contraction in demand, based on the shift towards more cautious decision-making by households. By contrast, in the corporate sector it was more the case that supply narrowed, while at the same time demand also fell during the crisis management efforts, in part because the banking sector focused more on short-term lending and in part because economic growth decelerated.

Part of the banking sector's internal adjustment strategy was to reduce the maturity of corporate loans. According to the MNB's financial conditions index, deleveraging by the banking system reduced economic growth by 1% on average during the five years in which lending contracted. This may have resulted in the loss of 20,000–25,000 jobs in the private sector. Such a prolonged freeze in lending was not seen in any of Hungary's regional competitors.

As a result of the continuous decline in outstanding corporate lending, the cyclical position of corporate lending slipped into negative territory from 2010–2011, meaning that outstanding lending to the corporate sector fell short of the "equilibrium" level.

By the end of 2013, the credit gap (which denotes the deviation of GDP-proportionate lending from the trend or equilibrium values) was moving in a range of -5 to -10 percentage points (Figure 238).

Figure 238. Corporate credit gaps

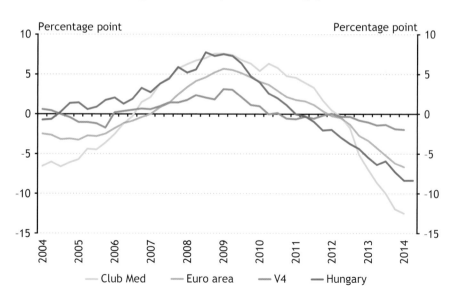

Credit gaps calculated with HP filter

Source: MNB

The severity of the credit crunch in Hungary was reflected by the fact that it lasted significantly longer and was deeper than similar phenomenon seen in other EU economies and it had dual nature: it clearly had a dramatic impact on the sector of small domestic enterprises. Another peculiar feature of the Hungarian credit crunch was that while the banking sector reduced lending substantially over an extended period, its lending ability, capital adequacy and liquidity situation were all satisfactory, and thus it would have been able to lend, but it did not.

To a great degree, the reason for this was that large, foreign-owned banks played the dominant role in the Hungarian banking sector, and the parent banks had to constantly increase capital at their subsidiary banks to cover the ongoing and expected losses. Funding was only withdrawn to the extent that it did not result in serious liquidity problems for their subsidiary banks, which tended to operate with high loan-to-deposit ratios.

Capital and liquidity was apparently available for lending, but the propensity to lend was lacking, and thus the credit crunch dragged on.

During the protracted credit crunch between 2009–2013, the Hungarian banking sector sought out customers with the best credit ratings, avoided riskier debtors and refrained from taking on even the smallest amount of risk. Lending to the domestic corporate sector was almost completely restricted to the largest corporate groups which had secure markets and were considered to be risk-free, and consequently lending shifted even more strongly toward large enterprises, while SMEs were typically only able to take out loans at an extremely high premium. The sector of large enterprises was mainly foreign owned, and – based on its financial reserves and creditworthiness – was already in a better position in terms of access to corporate loans as compared to SMEs, and thus the credit crunch essentially only impacted the domestic SME sector for 5–6 years. The real burdens of the banking sector's deleveraging were shifted to small Hungarian firms in the corporate sector by the predominantly foreign-owned, large banks.

Escaping the credit crunch - the Funding for Growth Scheme

Prior to the launch of the Funding for Growth Scheme, Hungarian companies were in a much worse position in terms of borrowing than companies in other EU economies. While outstanding corporate lending in the Polish, Bulgarian, Czech, Romanian and Baltic economies expanded after the crisis and before 2013 (a decline was only registered in Slovakia), prior to the Funding for Growth Scheme Hungary's situation in terms of the contraction in outstanding lending was on par with the worst-positioned euro area countries, and in particular its group of southern members. Prior to fiscal consolidation and economic stabilisation in 2010–2014, Hungary was actually on an unsustainable balance and growth trajectory together in a group with the Mediterranean countries and had fallen far behind its peer region, while the unfavourable situation in lending for the corporate sector persisted all the way until mid-2013 (Figure 239).

Figure 239. Annual change in corporate loans before and after the FGS

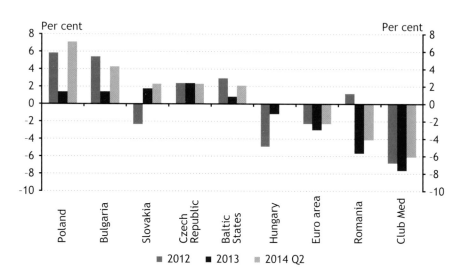

Source: ECB, MNB

In terms of fiscal balance, the path of government debt, employment and unemployment and the launch of structural reforms, Hungary exited the group of Mediterranean countries between 2010 and 2012 and returned to the level of its regional peers, and in particular to the level of the other three Visegrád countries, but with regard to corporate lending the situation of Hungarian companies continued to be identical to that of the southern euro area group until mid-2013.

The Funding for Growth Scheme was then launched in mid-2013, resulting in massive changes by as early as the end of that year. In contrast to the Baltic economies and the regional peers (with the exception of Romania), outstanding corporate lending in Hungary continued to contract, but the contraction was substantially smaller than the decline seen in corporate lending in Romania and the Mediterranean countries. At the end of 2012, the decline in outstanding corporate loans in Hungary was very close to the decline seen in the Mediterranean countries, but by the end of 2013 the situation had already turned around, as access to corporate lending began to recover to the regional level and left behind the conditions in the southern euro area members.

Moreover, this was not just a recovery in quantitative terms, as the conditions of the Funding for Growth Scheme, in particular the 2.5% interest rate and the maximum term of 10 years, also resulted in a significant improvement in qualitative terms.

The Funding for Growth Scheme fostered a complete turnaround in lending to SMEs. After its launch in the middle of 2013, the programme resulted in a positive turnaround in overall lending to SMEs in just three months during the first phase. All the way up until mid-2013, the stock of outstanding loans to domestic SMEs was contracting by rates of 4–6% quarter after quarter, and from the fourth quarter of 2012, before the Funding for Growth Scheme, the pace of contraction in outstanding loans to SMEs actually accelerated. The sharp break in the trend of outstanding lending to domestic SMEs between the fourth quarter of 2012 and the second quarter of 2013 reflects the massive turnaround triggered by the Funding for Growth Scheme. By the first half of 2013, the credit crunch had essentially put an end to lending to Hungarian micro, small and medium-sized enterprises, but the central bank was then able to successfully break out of this situation in the span of just a few months.

It is also clear that without this programme the decline in outstanding loans to the overall group of SMEs would have continued, which again underlines the importance of breaking out of the credit crunch (Figure 240).

Figure 240. Corporate lending forecast

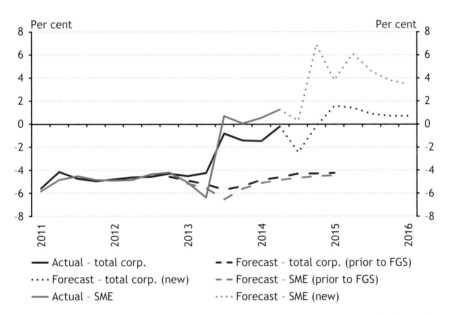

Source: MNB   *Transaction based, yoy*

The central bank's programme also resulted in a reversal of the trend in overall corporate lending. As the credit crunch mainly impacted the segment of SMEs, it was correct for the programme to focus on this segment, and later in 2013–2014 the stock of outstanding corporate loans then started expanding as a result of the successful restoration of economic balance and economic stabilisation.

The success of the Funding for Growth Scheme is indicated by the fact that the largest amount of growth loans financed with central bank funds was borrowed by micro, small and medium-sized enterprises in the domestic sectors which were most severely affected by the credit crunch.

Loan refinancing was significant in the first phase of the Funding for Growth Scheme, but the extension of new loans also began, with enterprises in sectors which had been starved of funding borrowing the largest amounts of these two types of financing (Figure 241).

Figure 241. Average quarterly borrowing prior to FGS and new loans in the first phase of FGS, by industry

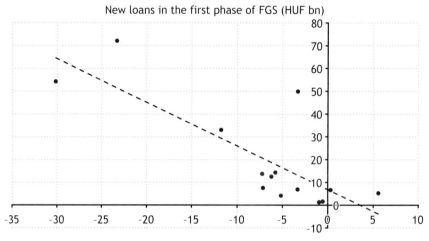

The horizontal axis displays the average net flow of corporate loans before the FGS (2009 Q1 - 2013 Q1).

Source: MNB

The Funding for Growth Scheme was able to finally overcome the credit crunch on the Hungarian lending market. Developments in quarterly lending growth show that the central bank's programme did not merely solve the earlier, artificially induced credit crunch for just a few months, but rather over the medium term. With this, the central bank's lending programme achieved a turnaround in corporate lending.

Figure 242. Factors contributing to the changes in credit conditions in the corporate segment

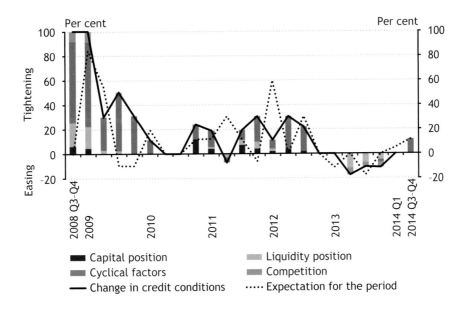

Net percentage balance of respondents tightening/easing credit conditions weighted by market share. Contribution of given factors to the tightening/easing that took place, normalised to the net percentage balance of respondents reporting tightening/easing.

Source: MNB, based on banks' responses

According to agents in the banking sector, the most important factors in the development of lending are the capital position, cyclical factors, liquidity factors, competition and expectations. The combination of these factors determines changes in lending based on responses from domestic banks. As a result of the global and EU crisis which started in autumn 2008, the banking sector's lending activity was naturally dominated most strongly by cyclical factors, but liquidity aspects also played a key role. One can see that expectations also turn around completely between end-2008 and 2009, as it became clear that the Hungarian financial sector would be severely impacted by the crisis. Expectations were also affected by the IMF-EU agreement and the increasingly obvious need for deleveraging by banks (Figure 242).

The cyclical factor continued to be strong all the way until mid-2010, and then between end-2010 and mid-2012 cyclical factors once again played an important role, albeit to a smaller degree. Looking at reports from the banking sector, one can also see that in 2013 lending conditions were fundamentally determined by banks' liquidity position, which is another reason that the central bank's lending programme was so important, because it expanded the funds available for lending. According to the responses from the banking sector, the Funding for Growth Scheme was not yet sufficient to turn around the liquidity situation.

Significance of the Funding for Growth Scheme

Neither the government nor the banking sector was able to solve the credit crunch in Hungary: only the Magyar Nemzeti Bank was able to achieve this in the second half of 2013. The reason for this is that the government was unable to launch an economic stimulus programme, as it had to maintain the balanced fiscal conditions. The banking sector was engaged in its balance sheet adjustment, and thus there were essentially no other agents on the supply side of the credit market aside from the central bank. After 2008, global central banks launched a number of programmes for quantitative and qualitative monetary easing, and the lending scheme of the Hungarian central bank became yet another member of this group of programmes.

Another factor underpinning the MNB's lending programme was that without economic stabilisation, the stock of NPLs in the Hungarian banking sector would have continued to increase, as a result of which risks to financial stability would have arisen, thus jeopardising the fulfilment of the MNB's legally defined mandate. A lending programme by the central bank was clearly justified by the need to sustain fiscal consolidation and prevent risks to financial stability.

In terms of global central banks, the programme launched by the central bank of the United Kingdom provided the pattern for the Funding for Growth Scheme. At the same time, there are considerable difference between the two economies, not only in terms of their respective sizes, but also with regard to the structure of their banking sectors and real economies. The Hungarian economy is characterised by a strong dual structure: due to the dramatic differences between the large export-oriented enterprises under foreign ownership and the typically domestically-owned micro, small and medium-sized enterprises producing for the Hungarian market, it was necessary to concentrate the MNB's programme on the SME sector. Consequently, the Funding for Growth Scheme was designed as a targeted SME credit programme.

At the same time, the programme was also intended to address some of the distortions in lending which had developed in the decades between 1990 and 2010. The dual nature of lending was the strongest of these distortions: the domestic SME sector's share of lending was far smaller than its contribution to GDP. The geographical distribution of lending to SMEs was also far more concentrated than the distribution of SMEs in the Hungarian economy, and in terms of quantitative and qualitative aspects SMEs also suffered from competitive disadvantages compared to large enterprises.

In the first phase of the FGS, of the roughly HUF 750 billion in loans extended, HUF 230 billion was used to refinance foreign currency loans, roughly HUF 180 billion was used to refinance existing HUF-denominated loans, and the volume of new loans amounted to almost HUF 300 billion. As a result of the new loans, by the third quarter of 2013 the net change in corporate lending by the banking sector as a whole approximated HUF 600 billion, marking the highest value since the onset of the crisis.

Figure 243. Annual growth rate of lending in the corporate and SME segments

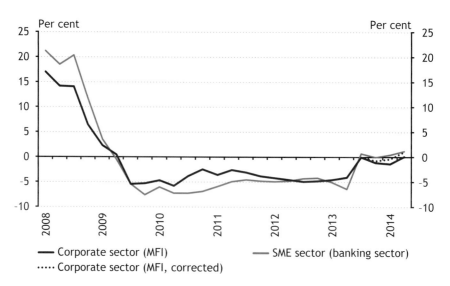

In the case of the overall corporate sector, the time series is based on transactions, while the SME data is based on estimated transactions from 2013 Q4.

Source: MNB

The annual growth rate of outstanding corporate loans also improved significantly by international standards, primarily in the SME sector. Loan refinancing played the most important role in the first phase of the FGS, which helped to bolster the stability of real economy agents participating in the lending programme and thus supported overall economic stabilisation via direct and indirect channels. More than one half of the new loans flowed into manufacturing, commerce and real estate, the three economic sectors in which lending had contracted the most during the crisis (Figure 243).

The Hungarian credit crunch was a highly concentrated phenomenon: large enterprises were not affected, while the SME sector was hit hard, all sectors of the economy were impacted and the high level of interest rates on earlier HUF-denominated loans and the risks inherent in foreign currency loans were threats to economic stabilisation.

Refinancing of the earlier loans with high interest rates and unfavourable structure (high share of foreign currency loans) helps to improve companies' debt repayment ability, and consequently the first phase of the FGS facilitates economic stabilisation, not only over the short run, but over the medium term as well. With refinancing of the forint loans, repayment burdens decline and thus companies are able to repay a larger amount of loans. With refinancing of the foreign currency loans, companies' financial position improves, exchange rate risk is eliminated, and consequently companies' credit rating improves, thus increasing their chances of being able to access new loans from banks.

Breaking out of the credit crunch played a very important role in the stabilisation of the economy in 2013–2014, which was manifested in the recoveries in growth, consumption and investment, along with improvements in labour market indicators and Hungarian competitiveness. This stabilisation was also promoted by the central bank's interest rate cuts and improving economic activity, but these would not have been sufficient in their own right to overcome the credit crunch in Hungary: only the FGS was able to achieve this.

The FGS not only boosted the volume of lending, it also resulted in a substantial improvement in the structure of the loan portfolio. The lending programme offers HUF-denominated, long-term, fixed interest rate loans. During the first phase of the programme, companies used some HUF 230 billion to refinance foreign currency loans, thus reducing the exchange risk of the corporate sector's overall outstanding loan portfolio. In the first phase of the FGS, the average maturity of the loans extended was 6.9 years, whereas during this period the average maturity of the overall SME loan portfolio was hardly more than 2 years. Thanks to the first phase of the FGS, the ratio of forint loans within the overall loan portfolio rose from 43% to 51%, and the average maturity of the loans increased to 3.5 years, approximating the pre-crisis level.

The fixed interest rate charged on the FGS loans (max. 2.5%) resulted in such repayment burdens which can be planned over the long term. All of this together represented a qualitative improvement in the level of risk in SME loans in Hungary, as the risk level of the SME loan portfolio declined and the financial position of SMEs improved.

The first phase of the FGS generated GDP growth of approximately 0.5%, created new jobs and typically helped to protect existing jobs.

Figure 244. Government SME financing programmes
and total FGS loans outstanding

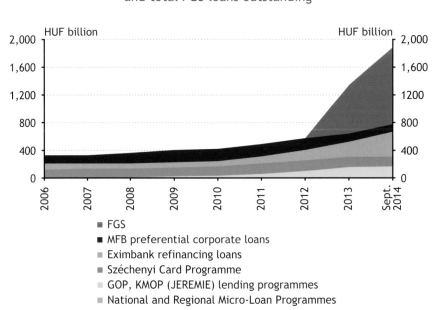

Figures for Eximbank for 2006-2008 are estimates.

Source: Data from operators of subsidised programmes, financial reports of credit institutions, MNB

The two phases of the FGS provided loans to almost 19,000 enterprises, with a value of almost HUF 1,300 billion. The first phase lowered exchange rate risk and companies' interest expenses, while boosting competition in the banking sector at the same time. The second phase was concentrated on reinforcing growth, as 97% was extended in new loans, with 61% of this accounted for new investment loans. One third of the new loans extended in the second phase went to micro enterprises, with one in three of the loans having a value of less than HUF 10 million.

Thanks to the central bank's lending programme, growth spread to all groups of enterprises, sectors and geographical areas.

Together, the two phases of the Funding for Growth Scheme may have boosted Hungarian GDP growth by 1%, and including the similar additional growth of 1% from the rate-cutting cycle, the central bank supported and provided almost one half of the GDP growth in the growth recovery seen in 2013–2014.

In terms of its size and effect, the central bank's lending programme was exceptional, as illustrated in Figures 244–245.

Figure 245. Distribution of outstanding SME loans

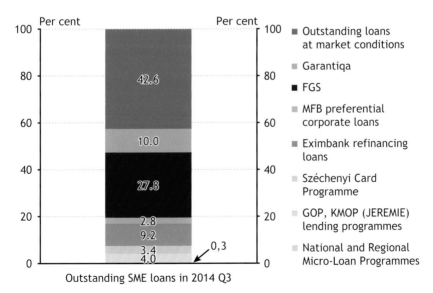

Outstanding SME loans in 2014 Q3

Source: MNB

Without the central bank's lending programme, the stock of outstanding loans would have contracted in 2013–2014, jeopardising the recovery in economic growth (Figure 246).

Figure 246. 12-month cumulative transactions for corporate lending by the credit institution sector

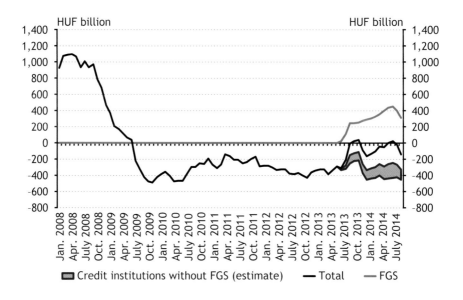

Source: MNB   *12-month transactions, sum*

Chapter 21

Recovery in consumption and investment

The successful consolidation and economic stabilisation in 2010–2014 proceeded in accordance with the strict rules of economics. In mid-2010, the new economic policy immediately started with financial crisis management using conventional and unconventional tools. First, the anticipated GDP-proportionate budget deficit of 7% was reduced to nearly 4%, preventing a fiscal crisis. As a second step, the growth in the ratio of government debt was halted using an unconventional policy tool, i.e. transformation of the private pension fund system, and the GDP-proportionate ratio of government debt was even set on a downward trend using some of the private pension fund assets.

As a third step, from mid-2010, the new policy spearheaded an increase in employment and a decline in the rate of unemployment, thereby laying the most important foundation for sustainable economic balance and later stabilisation of the economy right at the start of the consolidation process. Neither sustainable economic balance nor lasting economic growth is conceivable in Hungary without constant expansion in employment and an employment rate in Hungary which is higher than the 65% average in the EU.

Fourth, the accelerated reduction of household foreign currency loans started in autumn 2011, with the early pay off scheme. With regard to successful consolidation and subsequent economic stabilisation, this was important, because the improvement in consumption would not have been possible without a reduction in households' foreign currency debts. If households had continued to use a high share of their income for principal and interest payments, no recovery in consumption would have occurred before the end of 2014, and without this, economic stabilisation would not have been possible.

Fifth, starting from mid-2010 the new economic policy resulted in a steady increase in economic agents' income, as the 10% corporate tax rate yielded more income for companies and the 16% flat-tax rate for families left more income for households.

From the perspective of consumption, this was decisive, because from 2011 the new personal income tax system alone increased the household sector's net income by some four hundred billion forints annually. This facilitated the accelerated reduction of forint and foreign currency loans, expanded financial savings and was felt by ever larger groups in society over time, with the result that consumption grew. Introduction of the flat rate tax system was not intended to trigger an immediate improvement in consumption as this was not realistic in 2011–2012, but it did arrest the decline in consumption and helped households to deleverage. By 2012, the new system had also fostered a significant increase in households' holdings of government bonds, and thus the surplus income of households supported financial consolidation to an increasing degree, as government debt financing was based more and more on domestic funding.

According to the logic of economics, all of these steps eventually resulted in a reversal of the consumption trend. This occurred in 2013, and one more factor was required: the other economic policy measures were not allowed to extinguish the five policy steps which served as the foundation for the rebound in consumption. In 2012, the key year in the switch-over to the indirect taxation system, an inflation rate of 5.7% developed as a result of the tax increases, and during the same year this impact offset the effect of surplus income, but this impact was restricted to just one year: a reversal of the consumption trend in 2013 was already on the horizon.

The consolidation and stabilisation in 2010–2014 was able to generate sustainable economic balance and durable economic growth by 2014, because there was a recovery in consumption in 2013–2014. Ever larger groups in society successfully reduced their earlier debts and boosted their financial savings. Backed by this, it was only a matter of time before consumption turned around and this occurred in 2013 (Figure 247).

Figure 247. Volume indices of retail sales

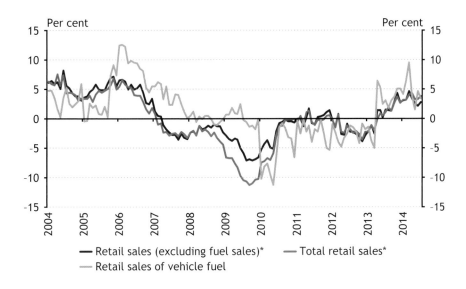

Seasonally adjusted annual change *Adjusted for the distorting effect of transformation of the tobacco shop network.

Source: MNB calculations based on HCSO data

In terms of sustainable balance and long-term economic growth, the only question was whether or not the improvement in consumption would be a lasting phenomenon. A positive outcome was ensured by the combination of the steady expansion of employment, the continuous rise in real incomes, the decline in inflation to a historical low in 2014 and the government programmes aimed at the resolution of the remaining household foreign currency loans. On the expenditure side, household consumption spending accounts for more than one half of Hungary's GDP, with public consumption and benefits-in-kind contributing another approximately 20% of GDP. Thus, the development of consumption always has a major impact on economic growth. Despite the small domestic market and the high export-to-GDP ratio, domestic consumption fundamentally determines the level of production and the propensity to invest of Hungarian-owned micro, small and medium-sized enterprises which are crucial in employment.

The trend reversal which occurred in consumption in 2013 and then the improvement in consumption, which solidified during the successful restoration of balance and economic stabilisation in 2013–2014, will play a dominant role in sustainable balance and GDP growth in Hungary in the years to come.

Furthermore, there is a close connection between the expansion of employment and growth, and the expansion of employment and a rising level of consumption. The more durable the expansion in consumption, the stronger the effect on economic growth, and sustained economic growth underpins steady expansion in employment, because after a improvement in consumption which proves to be sustained it is almost certain that there will be a recovery in investment. These relationships held true during Hungary's period of consolidation and stabilisation: the sustained recovery in consumption was followed with a delay by a turning point in the downward trend in investment and then by a rebound in investment.

The relationship between household consumption and the development of real incomes in the period 2004–2014 clearly reflects the effects and direction of the economic policy decisions, and the consequences of the debt cycle. Due to the fiscal austerity measures adopted from mid-2005, and especially during the second half of 2006, Hungarian households' real income started to fall much earlier than the onset of the global crisis. At the same time, however, there was no corresponding decline in household consumption during this period. The reason was this was the ongoing borrowing by households, which occurred more and more in foreign currencies, along with the relaxed credit conditions. Households corrected the loss of income and the related negative effects on consumption by taking out new loans. The motivation behind this decision, which was regularly supported by the government's communications, may have been that the decline in the real value of incomes was simply a transitory phenomenon, after which a faster outflow of income would occur. The transitory nature of this process is now well known (Figure 248).

Figure 248. Household consumption expenditure and disposable income

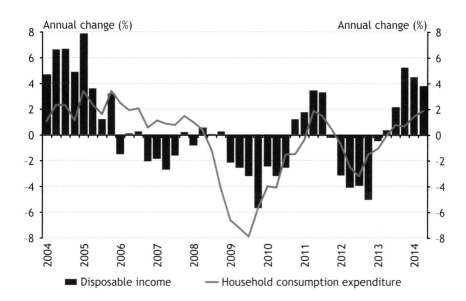

Source: HCSO, MNB estimate

The combination of the global economic crisis and the string of austerity packages which hit the household sector resulted in a significant decline in households' real income, in a trend which continued until 2011 when the personal income tax rate was reduced. In addition to falling real incomes, the previously accumulated foreign currency loans also generated increasingly large burdens on households.

For a very long period of time, the overwhelming need to reduce debt determined consumption demand, which – due to deleveraging – has fallen short of the development of real incomes almost continuously since the crisis. The debt accumulated prior to the crisis thus cast a long shadow over Hungarian economic growth through this channel. According to the latest estimates, household debt may approach a level considered to be sustainable by 2014–2015, and thus positive developments in household real income may once again play an increasingly significant role in the strengthening of consumption.

Upturn in families' incomes supports economic balance

During the first decade in the EU, the development of employees' regular wages in the private sector reflected the nature of economic policy.

The corporate sector has already adjusted the surplus incomes stemming from the flawed economic policy after mid-2002, and the private sector did not follow the path of surplus income paid out in the public sector between 2002 and 2004.

During this period, the volume of outstanding household loans rose sharply along with the ratio of foreign currency loans, and this fuelled an artificial upswing on the real estate market. Additionally, consumer loans also increased and the extension of home equity loans also grew. Both of the these are used to finance consumption, and consequently companies with a staff of less than 50 producing goods for the domestic market experienced an upturn, in response to which they expanded their production and services and raised their wages. This trend was broken in 2007, as the impact of the austerity package from September 2006 was felt. From then on, the index of regular wages in the SME segment drops steeply, reaching its low point in the crisis in 2009 (Figure 249).

Figure 249. Annual index of regular wages in the private sector

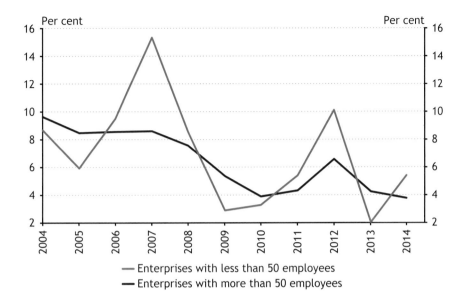

Annual average, 2014 calculated based on the first 7 months.

Source: HCSO

The index of regular wages for companies with a staff of more than 50 shows a more balanced development, with some degree of time lag. While the index for the SME segment was still rising, the index for larger companies was stagnating, and then following the change in trend in 2007 it also begins to move lower, reaching its low point in 2010. From mid-2010, both indices begin moving higher, and then as a result of the economic setback and consolidation, in addition to the decline in agricultural production, both indices decline again from 2012. From 2013, the index of regular wages for companies employing less than 50 persons starts to rise again, while the index for large companies – which mainly reflects the impact of weaker economic conditions at the global and European level – drifts moderately lower.

In terms of economic balance, one factor which had a significant impact during the consolidation between 2010 and 2014 was that the renewed fall in the index of regular wages for companies with less than 50 employees (which play the dominant role in household earnings) was restricted to a brief period concentrated in 2012. For three of the four years of consolidation and stabilisation, gross wages paid by the SME segment reinforced the other economic policy measures designed to increase household income, and only had a negative effect in one single year.

Analysing the use of household income, one sees that the rate of households' net financial savings first declines steadily between 2004 and 2007, then stagnates in 2008, and then continuously rises again, essentially in response to households' reaction to the crisis and then from 2010 as a result of rising incomes and falling debt levels. The development of household investment is particularly interesting. During the austerity programmes and the crisis, the rate of household investment drops substantially, and thus postponing investments was the most important channel of balance sheet adjustment. This only changed in 2014.

As a result of the change in economic policy from mid-2010, households' disposable income rose sharply. This was mainly due to the changes in the tax system, along with economic growth and the income-increasing effect of rising employment (Figure 250).

This leads us to one of the main sources of the successful consolidation and economic stabilisation in 2010–2014. Households' disposable income increased, and regardless of what they used this income for it supported the consolidation of public finances and stabilisation of the economy.

Figure 250. Creation and use of additional income, 2010-2014

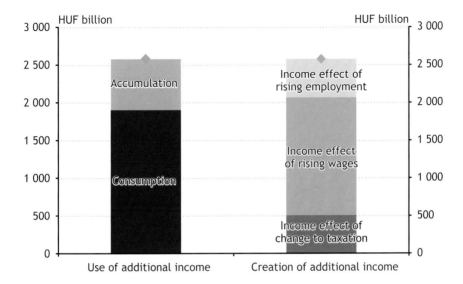

Source: MNB

The structure of how households used their disposable income indicates that most of the additional income was used for consumption, while gross saving increased financial savings, and net debt repayment (as the balance of new borrowing and repayment of existing debt) also accounted for a substantial amount. At the same time, households lowered their new investments, and thus – despite obtaining additional disposable income – they were more cautious and made responsible decisions, reflecting the change in households' financial thinking and behaviour.

Another reason that the consolidation of public finances was successful in 2010–2014 was that large portions of Hungarian society which obtained additional income immediately reacted to the change in economic policy. They did not proceed with their earlier practices of making new investments and use their new income for those purposes and instead did the opposite, increasing their financial savings, becoming net repayers of debt and catching up on consumption which had previously been postponed. This change can be seen throughout the entire period of consolidation and stabilisation and was backed by the changes in households' values.

Figure 251. Use of household income

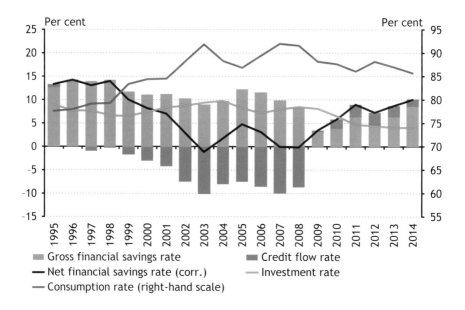

As a proportion of disposable income, savings trends

Source: MNB

Looking at the two decades between 1994 and 2014 (after the period of shock therapy transition to a market economy), for the first time the rate of consumption returns to the trend seen prior to shocks caused by transition. From 1994 to 2003, the role of consumption steadily rose in the use of households' income, which is mirrored by the continuously rising trend in the consumption rate.

Between 2003 and 2005, the rate of consumption declines, as households spent their income on investment. Households not only took on new debt, they also used a larger portion of their disposable income on investment in real estate. In line with this development, the rate of net financial saving fell sharply (Figure 251).

As early as 2002, the share of households' financial savings in the use of income started to decline. After this, 2005 was the only year until the crisis during which the rate of households' financial saving reached the psychologically important level of 4–5%. In the years after 2010, the rate of households' financial saving was steadily over 5%, indicating that a change had occurred in households' financial decision-making (Figure 252).

Figure 252. Households' use of income

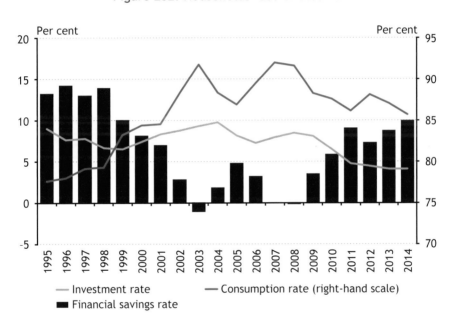

Source: MNB   *As a proportion of disposable income*

In Hungary, the ratio of household debt to GDP is around 30%, putting the country in the middle of the field in terms of debt accumulation by this group in the EU.

Strong relationship between growth and investment

GDP in Hungary began to contract sharply starting from the first quarter of 2006, as the growth rate plunged from 4% into negative territory. From there, growth then struggled back to a modest rate of 2%, but returned to a negative trend again after the crisis. The structure of investment, which deteriorated during the years of flawed economic policy, resulted in decelerating economic growth starting from the first quarter of 2006 and caused economic contraction in the post-crisis years. In 2009, the Hungarian economy contracted by almost 7% as an average for the year (Figure 253).

Figure 253. Growth and investment

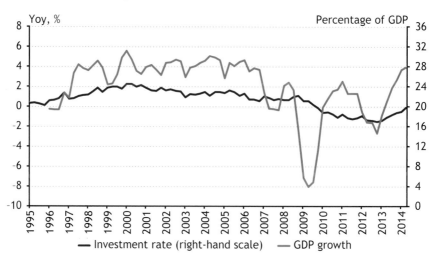

Source: HCSO

There is a strong connection between economic growth and investments: higher GDP-proportionate investment rates support longer-term potential growth, in addition to immediate short-term growth. Along with the investment rate, the composition of investment also has a significant effect on growth, as higher investment in machinery allows for faster growth, while a high share of construction investment leads to slower growth (Figures 254–255).

Figure 254. Machinery-type investment and GDP growth

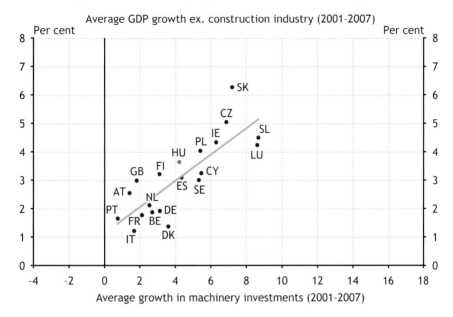

Figure 255. Construction-type investment and GDP growth

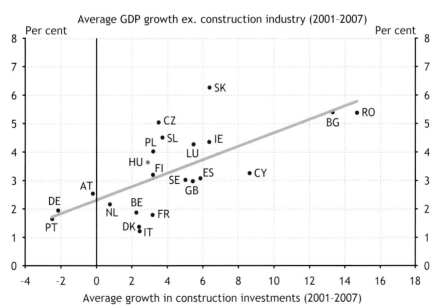

Source: Eurostat

Over the longer-term, investment in buildings may result in lower growth in productivity compared to machinery-type investment. This is especially the case if the construction-type investment is centred on the residential market.

Shock therapy and the structure of investment

Within the region, for the period 1990 to 2010 there is a hidden relationship between economic success and the pace of transition to a market economy. The faster that countries undertook the transition to a market economy, the more they used shock therapy and measures which resulted in growth and employment losses during the transition. These later upset economic balance and over the long run they shaped the paradigm of "neither growth nor balance" and in better years the paradigm of "growth or balance". According to economic logic, in the case of economies of similar size and with similar basic characteristics, which are situated within a narrow geographical region, the use of shock therapy as the method of transition to a market economy fundamentally affects the position of the economies compared to their competitors over the longer run.

During the transition to the market economy, Hungary suffered from competitive disadvantages compared to its peers in respect of at least three points. The first point was the level of inherited government debt. Although the public and even persons working within the government were not aware of the specific figures in the decades before 1990, the Hungarian economy (which was struggling with increasingly serious structural and competitiveness problems) had accumulated massive debts by the end of the 1980s. Amongst the formerly socialist countries, Hungary started the change of political regime with one of the highest levels of debt. While most of the other countries asked for and received debt forgiveness during the transition to a market economy, the Hungarian state did not. The inherited government debt fundamentally limited Hungary's fiscal leeway. Any external or internal shocks almost immediately called attention to the unsustainable debt path, thus requiring repeated fiscal adjustment measures (See Figure 212).

The second point was the labour market consequences of the transition period. The collapse of the Eastern markets and uncompetitive socialist enterprises resulted in a sharp increase in unemployment in all of the affected economies. In Hungary, the number of employees declined by around 1 million over a span of 5 years. In contrast to the developments in the Czech Republic, Slovakia and Poland, most of those who lost their jobs did not remain on the labour market and instead took advantage of the relaxed conditions for early and disability pension to leave the labour market and become inactive. While this solution did help to reduce the social tensions resulting from the transition over the short term, over the long run it resulted in a sustained decline in employment, which made it almost impossible to maintain growth and balance over a longer period of time (cf. Figure 170).

The third point was the flawed execution of privatisation. The privatisation which took place in numerous sectors of great importance to the national economy did not contribute to boosting competitiveness. Essentially, state monopolies were replaced with market monopolies and oligopolies in sectors ranging from energy to banking to telecommunications. Along with the weak regulation of competition, the solution led to an excessive outflow of income and preservation of the strongly dualistic economic structure. These three aspects of the shock therapy strategy used in Hungary determined the Hungarian economy's convergence opportunities for several decades to come.

Compared to the regional peers, the differences in Hungarian infrastructure were not significant enough to be able to explain the poor investment/productivity outcome. It was clearly the period of shock therapy transition in 1990–1994, the new market structure of the new market economy and the strongly dualistic nature of such which caused the negative performance for Hungary.

It may take decades for Hungary to overcome the competitive disadvantages and the deficits which developed in the fields of investment,
productivity, market structure and labour market conditions and in
order for this to occur it will need an investment rate of at least 25%
and high ratios of investment in technology and machinery.

Moreover, the high investment rate and the strong investment in
machinery and technology must be spread throughout the whole of
the economy for this to occur.

Financial crisis and investments

The 2008–2009 financial crisis redefined the relationships between
investments and savings in the global economy. Investment and savings
in the countries impacted by the crisis declined for a long period.

Figure 256. Investment and savings rate following financial crises, % of GDP

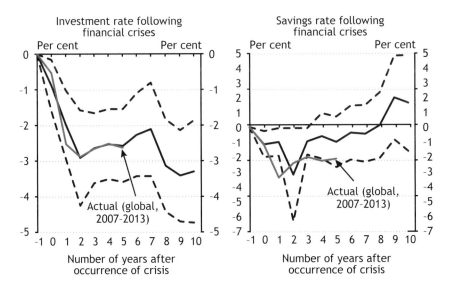

The dashed lines mark the 90% confidence interval of the estimated effects.

Source: IMF World Economic Outlook 2014 April, Chapter 3

Compared to the year prior to the 2008–2009 crisis, the decline in the saving rates in the global economy lasted for 1–2 years, unless it returned to the pre-crisis level within the next few years. This was true for the countries affected by the economic crisis, regardless of whether they were mildly impacted by the crisis or were hit by a strong shock.

In part of the group, the previously robust economic growth was replaced by stagnation, while in the other part of the group growth nosedived by up to 6%. In both cases as well as in the transitional cases between the two extremes, the saving rate dropped sharply in the span of 1–2 years, followed by a trend reversal and an increase, and then stagnation at a level which was lower than the pre-crisis level (Figure 256).

By contrast, the path of GDP-proportionate investment rates looks very different. Following the recovery in consumption and growth in 2013–2014, household investment in Hungary is only expected to return to the earlier level by the end of the decade, whereas households' financial savings are projected to steadily increase. This has contrasting effects for the sustainable consolidation of the public budget: it leads to lower budget revenues from household investment, but increases the amount of household funds that can be used to finance government debt. Starting from early 2012, households' holdings of government bonds have increased continuously and consequently the sustainability of budget consolidation can draw on households' increased demand.

In the countries most strongly impacted by the global economic crisis, public savings fell and budget deficits rose after the crisis, while private savings increased over the long term. The state and families behave differently, with different responses to the shock from the crisis (Figure 257).

Hungary's successful budget consolidation is particularly valuable in light of the relationship between the crisis and the fiscal deficits, because even in the group of countries in the best position which were impacted by the crisis the fiscal deficit rose, whereas Hungary was able to achieve a deficit of under 3% of GDP in 2011. From an economic history perspective and considering the global economy as a whole, the improvement in Hungary's macroeconomic balance is unusual because a positive shift in economic policy was sufficient for the country to achieve the deficit target of 3% of GDP by the end of 2011.

Figure 257. Public and private savings in the years following the financial crisis, % of GDP

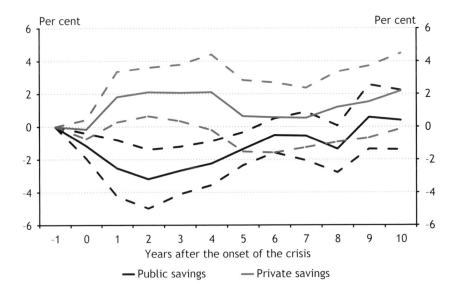

The dashed lines mark the 90% confidence interval of the estimated effects.

Source: IMF World Economic Outlook 2014 April

Analysis of global crises also shows that the recovery period following the 2008 crisis was generally weaker than similar periods seen in the past (Figure 258).

Compared to the 1991 and 2001 recessions, the period after the 2008 financial crisis was marked by very slow recovery in economic performance. One factor in this regard was the long-term changes in demand, i.e. that the corporate sector and households did not return to the earlier practice of irresponsible borrowing even after they had reduced their existing debts. One aspect may be that the rescue measures undertaken were not fiscal in nature, but rather monetary: it is easier to channel money to final users via the budget than it is with central bank money. In the latter case, the money does not flow from the banking sector to companies and households. This, in turn, can change the structure of growth and also highlight the limitations in lending by the banking sector.

Figure 258. Business cycles, based on the US Conference Board composite index (1)

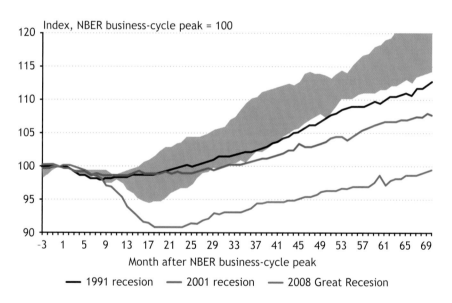

The grey band covers the path of the index during the four business cycles identified between 1960 and 1982. The composite index contains data on employment, industrial production, income, and manufacturing and retail sales. An index value of 100 marks the peak of the business cycles identified by NBER.

Source: Siems (2013), Dallas Fed

Another reason for the slower rebound after the 2008 financial crisis and the longer recovery period was the changing economic paradigm between the West and the East. The emerging countries in the global economy, especially the large East Asian economies, are increasingly taking over the global market positions of the developed Western economies, which hampers the recovery of the developed countries.

Figure 259. Business cycles, based on the US Conference Board composite index (2)

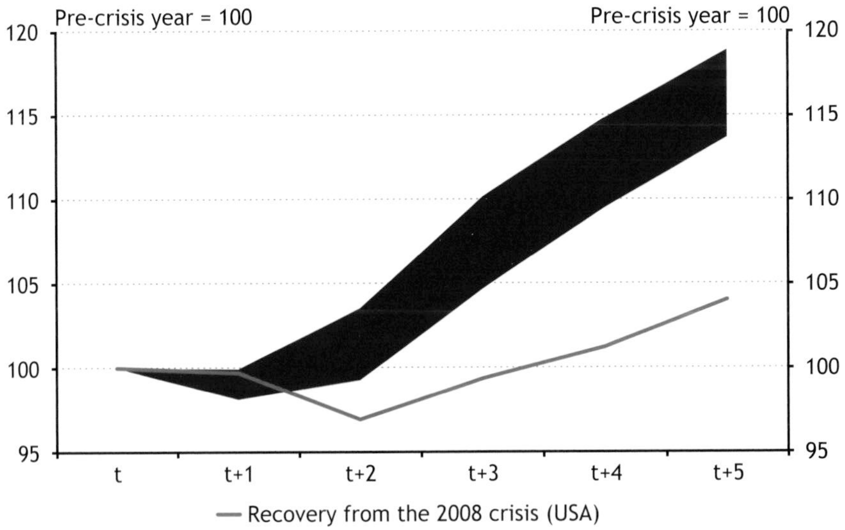

Source: MNB

This global transformation was also behind the large US, Anglo-Saxon and euro area financial bubbles which developed in the 2000s, because in contrast to the production of goods, the construction of houses cannot be globalised: it can only happen locally, in California or Las Vegas. The real estate and stock market bubbles that were concentrated in the USA, the Anglo-Saxon countries and the southern part of the euro area were able to develop because economic policy in those countries did not find any other sectors with which it would be possible to sustain positive economic performance by expanding domestic demand or increasing global market share (Figure 259).

By contrast, in Hungary a peculiar Hungarian credit bubble developed almost simultaneously with EU accession,[53] whereas the expansion of EU markets and EU development funds could have led to additional demand for domestic producers of goods. Once again, the dual structure of the Hungarian economy is a factor here: in this structure, most of the economy was unable to participate in the distribution of work within the European Union, due to geography, the number of companies and employment. Over the short term, EU integration only resulted in additional demand for most of the Hungarian economy if the flawed economic policy also simultaneously stimulated domestic economic performance by artificial means. This is precisely what happened. Despite the wider opening of the EU markets, most of the participants in the real economy did not focus on these opportunities and concentrated instead on developing the domestic market, which was being driven by debt. The flawed economic policy played a role in this regard, along with the significant deviation in the exchange rate from its equilibrium level, the distortions caused by the banking sector, the diversion of demand into foreign currency borrowing by the state and the inherited dual structure of the economy. Most of the first decade of Hungary's membership of the EU was marked by an economic policy which was similar in terms of its effects and even its solutions to the economic policies pursued in the USA, the Anglo-Saxon countries and the southern euro area members, which caused the financial crisis. The Hungarian financial crisis was more severe, because this policy increased the ratio of government debt from an already high level and steadily boosted external debt.

---

[53] Strangely enough, the large-scale lending to households in Hungary did not result in the development of a real estate bubble, and there were several reasons for this. First, as we saw earlier, most of the lending promoted growth in consumption and thus resulted in less pressure on the real estate market. Second, in contrast to the countries listed above, the response of the real estate market did not occur mainly in prices, but rather in volumes.

Looking ahead, for almost the next three decades after the 2008–2009 crisis, the equilibrium growth rate of lending may fall short of the average growth rate from before the crisis. In addition to the initially small portfolio of loans, the rapid growth in lending before the crisis was a factor contributing to the credit bubble, and this was a decisive aspect in Hungary. It can be assumed that Hungary's credit-to-GDP ratio will move towards the current median credit-to-GDP ratio of the euro area members, in parallel with convergence towards the level of income in the euro area (Figure 260).

Figure 260. Long-term projection of the household credit-to-GDP ratio

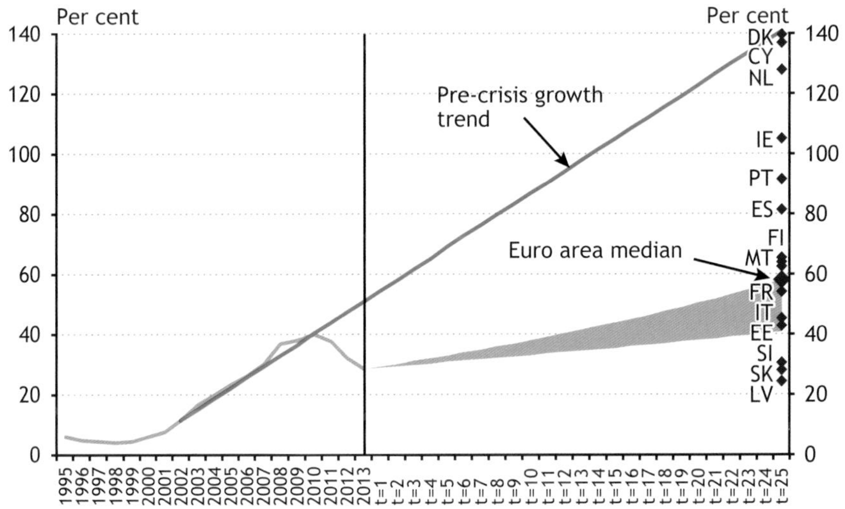

Source: MNB

Based on these trajectories, the portfolio of household loans may expand at a rate of 7%–10% annually in nominal terms, which is slower than the pre-crisis growth rate. From an economic history perspective, this is a positive development because according to the projection there will not be another episode of unsustainable household borrowing in Hungary over the horizon of almost a quarter of a century. With regard to gross fixed capital formation, however, this means that households will make a smaller contribution to investments compared to the pre-crisis years.

Looking at gross fixed capital formation in the various sectors from 2000 to 2014, we can see that gross fixed capital formation as a percentage of GDP falls below 20% in 2009 in Hungary owing to result of the crisis, but after 2010 it is clearly the decline in the gross fixed capital formation of the household sector which keeps gross fixed capital formation below 20%. This is a healthy development, because the previous high share and rate of household investment was an artificial phenomenon.

It is also visible that, filtering out the artificially high level of household investment, i.e. looking at the post-crisis rate of household investment, GDP-proportionate gross fixed capital formation would have been lower than 20% from 2002: during the years after 2002, economic policy was only able to maintain gross fixed capital formation for the overall economy at a level above 20% by artificially boosting households' investment in real estate (Figure 261).

Figure 261. Breakdown of gross fixed capital formation by sector, % of GDP

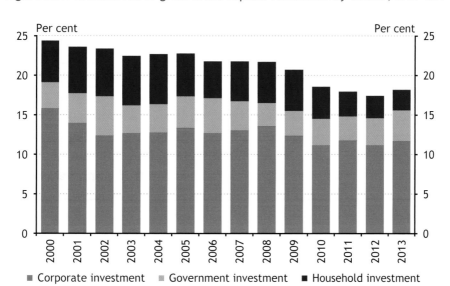

Source: MNB

While corporate sector gross fixed capital formation as a percentage of GDP ranged from 12% to 14% in the period 2002–2010, the 5–6.5% rate of gross fixed capital formation for the household sector includes an artificial component amounting to 2–3% of GDP: the level of household gross fixed capital formation was higher by exactly this amount, compared to what it would have been without the artificial credit bubble. Since large parts of Hungarian society drew forward their real estate investments which were necessary in the following years and even decades, and also financed speculative investments in the real estate market with their borrowing, it is highly unlikely that that the GDP-proportionate level of households' gross fixed capital formation will rise back to the pre-crisis level in the coming period of almost twenty-five years.

Crisis management in the context of low gross fixed capital formation

One of the striking aspects of the consolidation and stabilisation achieved between 2010 and 2014 was that it occurred in parallel with a steady decline in gross fixed capital formation, all the way up until the rebound in investment which was seen from the end of 2013. Indeed, during the period 2010–2014 up until the trend reversal in consumption from the end of 2013, final consumption was only in positive territory in 2011, meaning that consolidation and stabilisation took place in an environment characterised by declining final consumption and gross fixed capital formation. In contrast to this, the positive trade balance consistently supported the success of these two undertakings: consolidation was supported by the taxes on additional revenues, and stabilisation was buttressed by the export capacities created by way of foreign direct investment (Figure 262).

Figure 262. Contribution to domestic GDP growth

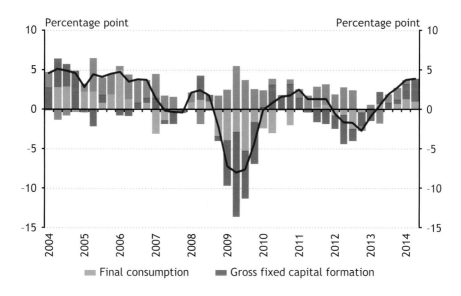

* Difference between export and import data on contribution to GDP growth.

Source: MNB Expenditure approach, compared to the same period of the previous year

Thus, achieving economic balance and stabilisation in 2010–2014 occurred in an unusual environment, as the traditional sources of support – consumption and gross fixed capital formation – were absent for most of the period. Until the recovery in consumption in 2013 and the turnaround in investment in 2014, no domestic catalysts were available, albeit growth was supported by the additional exports and consolidation of the public budget was made possible by the new tax system.

Unusual developments were also seen in investments in the private and public sectors: public sector gross fixed capital formation reached a record-setting level in 2010, and this level was only reached again as a result of the infrastructure developments financed with EU funding which rose after 2012, while private sector gross fixed capital formation practically stagnated during the period 2010–2012. The peak in public investment in 2010 also shows that the government's attempt to consolidate the public budget between 2008 and 2010 was not made at the expense of public investment (Figure 263).

Figure 263. Volume index for investment in the private and public sectors

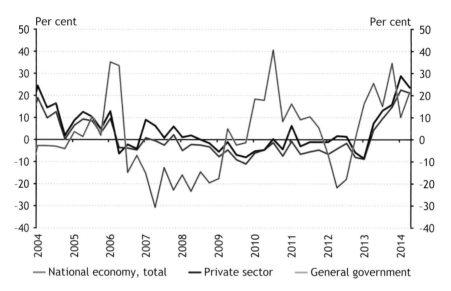

Source: HCSO   *Compared to the same period of the previous year*

The decline in gross fixed capital formation resulted from termination of the artificially high level of household and corporate sector real estate investment. Investments fell sharply in the period 2008–2011, and the main factor behind this was the decline in real estate transactions. The post-crisis adjustment of investment mainly centred on the reduction of real estate investment, indicating that there had been an artificial bubble on the real estate market, and consequently that the rate of gross fixed capital formation of over 20% was exaggerated and artificial (Figure 264).

Figure 264. Components of change in investment, 2008-2011

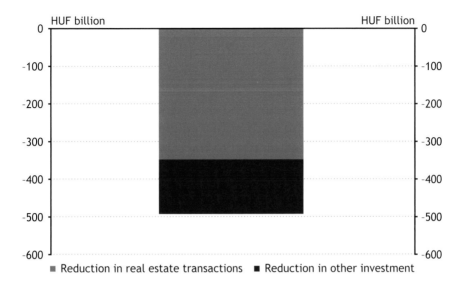

Source: HCSO

Due to high proportion of foreign currency lending, the financing structure was particularly disadvantageous. Owing to the weak connection between growth and construction, it is clear that the artificially high rate of gross fixed capital formation was backed by an upswing in real estate development which was poorly financed and marked by low efficiency in terms of supporting economic growth.

Chapter 22

Recovery in growth in Hungary

A recovery in growth took place in the Hungarian economy in 2013–2014. During the period of consolidation and stabilisation in 2010–2014, Hungarian GDP only contracted in one single year, in 2012. The 1.7% contraction that year was identical to the overall average contraction and the average contraction in economic performance in the euro area. With the steep decline in GDP in 2009 and a renewed drop in 2012, the developed countries experienced a W-shaped recession. Although GDP did not decline in the robust Polish, Czech and Slovak economies, contractions were registered in Croatia and Slovenia, and the contraction in output recorded in Hungary was average for the region.

There were different reasons in each country for the recession in 2012. In Hungary, the 20% drop in agricultural production was responsible for roughly one half of the contraction, relocation of industrial production capacities to other emerging countries accounted for another 0.3–0.4% of the decline, and about 0.5–0.6% was caused by financial consolidation, the rising inflation in response to increases in indirect taxes and the resulting decline in consumption.

By 2013–2014, however, Hungary reached a turning point in the growth trend. This reversal was supported by several indicators all pointing in the same direction. Steady expansion of production capacities in the vehicle manufacturing industry had a major impact on this recovery, and accordingly the export growth were a major factor. More rapid use of EU funds also supported the rebound, and thus developments in the construction industry and related branches financed with EU funds was the second key factor. The expansion of consumption also had an impact through the channel of retail sales and growth in domestic tourism.

Growth was also driven by the upturn in domestic lending, which occurred due to targeted lending to small enterprises via the central bank's lending programme.

After posting declines of around 5% in the previous quarters, corporate lending started to expand again. This lending is spreading through the economy, affecting corporate groups which participate in the expansion of domestic consumption, suppliers of export companies, the construction and transportation industry, as well as agriculture and the food industry. The central bank's lending programme results in a change in the industries which were previously hit the hardest by the credit crunch: this is a hidden reason for the recovery in growth, as the loans for small businesses specifically alleviate the earlier lending bottlenecks.

As a result of this, a rebound in investment already occurred in the Hungarian economy in 2014, with the previous 16–17% investment rate rising to above 20% in Hungary. All of the factors behind the recovery in growth played a role in this. Consequently, the recovery is self-sustaining: the growth in gross fixed capital formation is supported by infrastructure developments financed with EU funds, the growth in consumption and turnaround in lending to SMEs combine to generate an additional increase in investments and the expansion in investments support the aforementioned turnarounds.

Small enterprises expect growth recovery

The development of investments by Hungary's SMEs and the confidence index for this sector also reflected the recovery in growth which occurred in 2013–2014. From 2012, the confidence index for SMEs began to rise sharply and the rate of improvement then increased further in 2013, along with SMEs' planned investment volumes, which increased mildly in 2012 and then began to rise at the same pace as the improvement in the confidence index in 2013–2014. Thus, the turnaround in economic conditions was accompanied improvement in sentiment and expectations. This is natural, as more and more agents in the Hungarian economy started to believe that the new economic policy launched in 2010 would be successful (Figure 265).

No new austerity measures were introduced in 2010, and it was actually possible to bring the impracticable fiscal deficit down to a manageable level, thanks to the new system of sharing public burdens.

The steady upward trend in the deficit was stopped in 2011, and then between autumn 2011 and winter 2012 the Hungarian economy successfully withstood a significant attack by the financial markets. The financial position of households improved thanks to the early repayment scheme, introduction of the exchange rate cap, and more than HUF 100 billion in income from the flat-rate tax system, and the combination of these factors paved the way for an upturn in SMEs' business expectations.

Figure 265. Amount of planned investment stated at beginning of year by Hungarian SMEs and the confidence index in early 2014

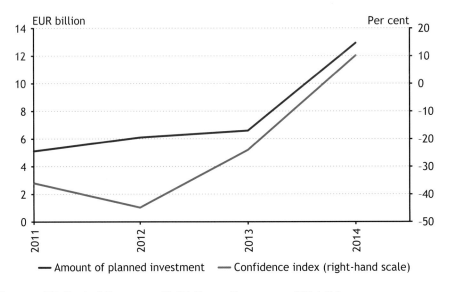

Source: GE Capital European SME Capex Barometer, 2014 Q1

The expansion of the export sector based on foreign direct investment (in particular the expansion of vehicle production capacities) and the rapid utilisation of EU funds would not have been sufficient to drive the recovery in growth in 2013–2014, because these were unable to improve the confidence and expectations index of the SME sector. The growth recovery would have been impossible without the SME sector, because it was also not possible in the past: the automotive industry had been growing in previous years and the utilisation of EU funds had been increasing year after year, but still no turnaround occurred.

In 2013–2014, the positive effects of all of the important economic policy measures came together and led to a turning point. The new tax system played a key role in the improvement in the confidence and expectations index of SMEs, along with the first steps to reduce household debt. A positive effect was also felt from the new government debt financing strategy which was launched in early 2012 and appreciated the value of government bonds for the household sector. Starting from early 2012, households' holdings of government bonds rose significantly and continuously, which assisted the recovery, because it reinforced households' sense of security when investing in government bonds. The rebound in investment by SMEs would not have occurred without the central bank's lending programme, despite the improvement in the indices for confidence and planned investments: without access to affordable loans, there would not have been improving sentiment among SMEs.

During the period 2010–2014, one of the most important lessons from Hungary's financial consolidation and economic stabilisation was that there is no single magic word which leads to success; numerous key economic policy and monetary measures must be coordinated in the interests of achieving a turnaround.

Recovery in growth with rising employment

The recovery in growth was also driven by the steady improvement on the labour market. Starting from mid-2010 and taking into account seasonal factors, employment increased continuously and the rate of unemployment declined in the Hungarian economy.

The public work programmes were not initially a factor, as these were only announced by the government after 2011. The labour market situation first improved due to the brief recovery period following the economic downturn in 2009 and as a result of the new economic policy announced by the new government. It is hard to overstate the importance of the latter aspect, as it became clear to economic agents in mid-2010 that the new government was really going to take a different approach to politics and economic policy.

It did not launch new austerity programmes and actually alleviated the recessive impact of earlier measures, for example by introducing the 10% rate of tax for small businesses. It shifted from the earlier general approach to managing the financial crisis to a more targeted approach, for example by introducing the bank levy and crisis taxes. For the broad majority of market participants and in particular for the domestic SME sector this sent the message that there would not be another recession and that the business environment would improve.

Thus, it was mainly the improvement in business expectations which drove the positive developments on the labour market in 2010. From mid-2010, right from the very beginning of the new political approach and economic policy, employment started rising and unemployment began to decline. This was reinforced by the measures taken on the labour market in the years thereafter, such as the new Labour Code, the system of vocational and adult training, the Job Protection Action Plan, steps to improvement the employment of women and the new tax system. From the start, the new economic policy addressed the legacy of distortions on the labour market using a set of tools which supported employment, beginning with sentiment and expectations from mid-2010 and then turning to parts of the labour market where the rate of employment in Hungary was dramatically lower than the EU average.

The improvement of internal structure of the labour market facilitated consolidation and played a major role in stabilisation as well. The opposite is also true: financial consolidation promoted the expansion of employment, because it generated additional budget revenues. The flat-rate tax system added one million taxpayers to the tax base, and even participants in public work programmes paid the 16% flat tax on their incomes, whereas income tax had previously not been paid on unemployment benefits. The continuous growth in employment supported economic stabilisation even more strongly, because it steadily reinforced the incentive to work and create jobs in the Hungarian economy.

From mid-2010, a recovery begins to emerge in the planned investments of the SME sector. This was partially driven by the improvement on the labour market, while the improvement in sentiment was supported by the shift in motivation.

In the period 2002–2010, the Hungarian labour market was reflected dichotomy for Hungarian companies: unemployment was on the rise and employment was falling, but the motivation to work was declining even more amongst the low-skilled and other underemployed groups. The fewer the job opportunities, the less they wanted to work. Due to the new politics and economic policy, permanent improvement was seen in this regard, because the new policy reinforced employees' motivation to work via the job-oriented tax system.

The recovery in growth that emerged in 2013–2014 was powered by a continuous change in the motivation, sentiment and expectations trends, which started to take shape for all three participants on the labour market – employees, employers and the state – from mid-2010. This was a masterful stroke of success from an economic history perspective, considering that – starting from a crisis situation and then moving forward with a crisis management strategy of consolidation and stabilisation – employment growth and the reduction in unemployment was not interrupted for one single moment in the period 2010–2014 (disregarding seasonal factors, naturally).

Diversified basis for the recovery

The recovery in growth in 2013–2014 was driven to a great degree by the expansion of exports, which was based on rising external demand. The accelerated utilisation of EU funds which resulted in a rising rate of investment rate played a similar role, along with the central bank's lending programme and growth in FDI (Figure 266).

Figure 266. Changes in export market share

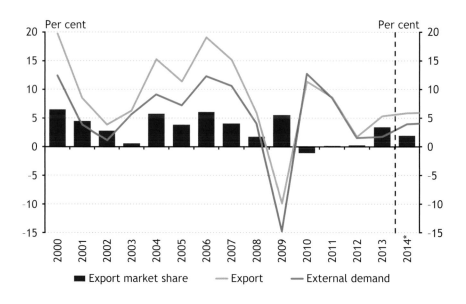

Source: MNB   Annual change, * estimate

After again having steadily declined since 2008, the rate of investment began rising after 2013, and this was a crucial development for the recovery (Figure 267).

Figure 267. Investment rate by sector

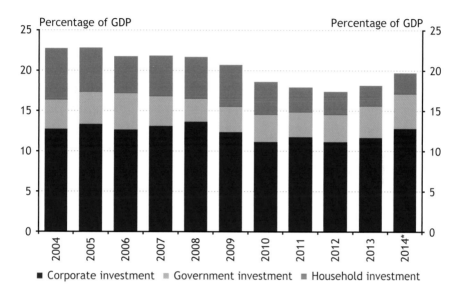

■ Corporate investment   ■ Government investment   ■ Household investment

Source: HCSO, MNB   * *estimate*

The largest change occurred on the labour market: in the period 2010–2012, there was an initial mild decrease in the rate of unemployment, followed by a steep decline, and at the same time, employment steadily rose. The decline in unemployment occurred despite the fact that the number and ratio of unemployed persons returning to the labour market increased. Together, the increase in employment, the steadily rising number of jobs and the improvement in ability to work resulted in a significant number of people who had previously left the labour market returning and seeking jobs. The majority of the employees who had left the labour market do not work abroad, because they have neither the skills nor the other necessary abilities to do so. Most low-skilled workers, unemployed persons over the age of 50 and jobless women are not in a position to exit the domestic labour market and seek employment on the European or global labour market, whereas this is a realistic option for unemployed persons under the age of 25.

The development of the financial saving rate also played a role in the growth recovery. The new economic policy simultaneously boosted employees' willingness to work and employers' motivation to create jobs, while at the same time providing an incentive for financial savings. The rising level of financial savings improved the financial security of families and SMEs. Similar to the situation in the Italian, Spanish, Portuguese and Polish economies, the SME and household sectors are interconnected to the improving confidence and expectations indices, which in turn have an impact on other areas (Figure 268).

Figure 268. Household saving rate and unemployment rate

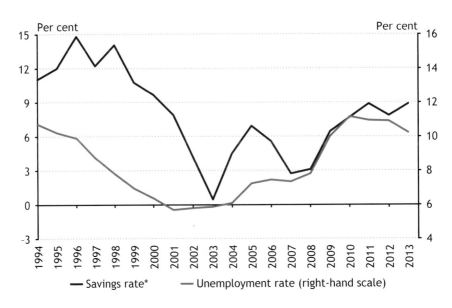

Source: CSO, MNB   * as proportion of disposable income

After the 2008 financial crisis, the household saving rate rises steeply, as families' financial values changed rapidly and significantly. Nevertheless, the saving rate also includes corporate savings, and motivations also changed substantially in this area: for companies, and within this group for SMEs, financial reserves became more important, in contrast to immediate spending or even new investments. As there is a strong relationship between the SME sector and the household sector in the Hungarian economy, the change in motivations and values in both of these sectors generated a strong rise in the saving rate.

Between 1994 and 2002, there was a covariance between the saving rate and the rate of unemployment, as both trend pointed downwards. From 2002 until the onset of the crisis in 2008, both rates continue moving in the same direction, but whereas there is a strong rise in the saving rate, the rate of employment only rises slowly but steadily up until the crisis. After this, in the period 2008–2010, the saving and unemployment rate move on the same trajectory, with the rate of unemployment subsequently beginning to decline mildly and then more strongly.

EU funds backed the recovery in growth

The accelerating utilisation of EU funds was a major source of support for the recovery in growth in 2013–2014.

In 2013, the net balance of financial transfers from the EU reached 5.5% of GDP, which was 1.5% higher than in the previous year. This facilitated the reduction of external debt and the increase in the investment rate.

Net EU transfers initially started rising from the end of 2008 until mid-2010, driven by the accelerated utilisation of EU funds. Later, from the second half of 2012, the balance of transfers begins rising again, fundamentally as a result of increases in net EU grants (Figure 269).

Figure 269. Transfer balance, % of GDP

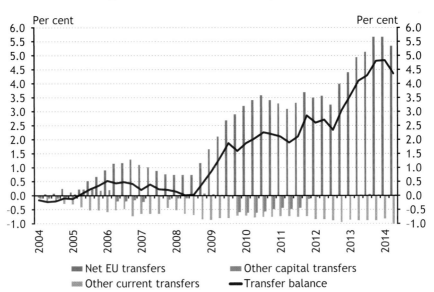

Source: MNB   *Four-quarter moving average*

Following EU accession in 2004, Hungary received a significant amount of EU funding: during the first decade of EU membership between 2004 and 2014, the country obtained financial funding of EUR 30 billion. The flawed economic policy in 2004–2010 and the failed fiscal consolidation efforts constantly relied on the positive net balance of EU transfers and their positive effect on growth, but both consolidation attempts still failed.

Between 2008 and 2010, net EU transfers had a positive effect on investments and the rate of growth, which generated revenues for the general government. Despite this, the government still planned an unsustainable deficit of over 7% for the 2010 budget. The successful consolidation in 2010–2014 also relied on the large and steadily growing net balance of EU transfers, which helped to achieve the sustainable budget deficit of less than 3%.

Comparing these two periods in terms of EU transfers one sees a clear relationship: EU transfers support the budget, but even this is not enough for a deficit of less than 3%, if the economic policy is flawed. The EU funds are a necessary, but not an adequate pre-condition for a deficit of less than 3%, for a decline in the government debt ratio and improvement on the labour market. Without a shift in other areas of economic policy, consolidation and stabilisation will fail even if there are significant transfers from the EU. Even in the case of large increases in the utilisation of EU funds, as was seen in 2008–2010, consolidation and stabilisation was not sustainable.

The situation is similar with inflows of FDI, which are good for the investment rate, economic growth and budget revenues, but are not enough in their own right to solve the problems of consolidation and stabilisation. In the period 2010–2014, FDI made a considerable contribution to successful consolidation and stabilisation, but it occurred in a correct economic policy framework. The positive changes in the economy starting from mid-2010 enhanced the positive effects of FDI and EU transfers. Consolidation and stabilisation strengthened in the context of the improving business climate and improving conditions on the labour market.

One of the important lessons from Hungary's successful consolidation and stabilisation is that external funds are only able to assist in the financial consolidation and lasting stabilisation of an economy and are not adequate in their own right; if they are not supported by sound economic policy, they do not lead to success. Despite the EU transfers and FDI inflows in 2008–2010, financial consolidation was unsuccessful, the ratio of government debt kept rising and employment continued to fall while unemployment rose.

External funding does not solve a country's fundamental financial and economic problems; only internal factors are capable of doing this.

Changes in borrowing supported the recovery in growth

After 2010, a hidden, but steady change took place in borrowing in the Hungarian economy. Following the 2008 financial crisis, the banking sector immediately began deleveraging, resulting in a constant decline in the loan-to-deposit ratio and new loans. The reduction of loans was started initially by the banking sector, followed by households and the corporate sector: the first component of the change in lending was the accelerated reduction of outstanding loans. The second component was the reduction of foreign currency lending, which was initiated by the prohibition on households borrowing in foreign currency from mid-2010. This was followed by the early repayment scheme, the exchange rate cap programme, and from the second half of 2014 the string of measures designed to eliminate households' foreign currency loans.

The third component of the change in lending was the reduction in new borrowing by the household sector, with this due to changes in behaviour, in part by the banking sector and in part by the household sector. Everyone became more cautious, which resulted in a decline in new borrowing by households. A similar trend was seen in the corporate sector, as economic agents in this sector also became more cautious. The deleveraging of borrowing system encountered the diminishing borrowing prosperity.

The fourth component is related to the central bank's lending programme, which made it possible to break out of the credit crunch.

After 2008, one aspect of the change in lending is that – compared to the past – all agents demonstrated more rational, responsible behaviour, but the banking sector participants overshot the goals in deleveraging, while SME sector agents in particular were not able to access credit.

This "overshooting" during crisis management, as reflected in the irrationally excessive reduction of lending activities by the banking sector, was not the result of deleveraging: after 2010, economic policy decisions related to the banking sector played a key role in this regard.

Starting from mid-2010, the lending capacity of the banking sector was continuously high, but its propensity to lend was steadily falling. Although macroeconomic indicators were improving, businesses were faced with steadily worsening credit conditions. The banking sector punished the corporate sector for the bank levy, the early repayment scheme and other economic policy measures. This situation changed with the Funding for Growth Scheme, bringing the final turnaround in lending that was seen in 2013–2014.

The relationship between the development level of an economy and lending is a linear one: a larger loan portfolio is associated with higher per capita economic performance, and higher per capita GDP arises with a higher stocks of loans. The strength of this relationship varies from economy to economy at the global level (Figure 270).

Figure 270. Economic development and lending

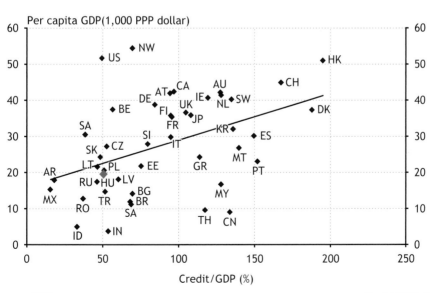

Source: BIS   *End-2012 data*

After the 2008 financial crisis, developments in lending in Hungary restrained the rate of GDP growth. The behaviour of all market agents changed, as fewer agents borrowed compared to the past, leading to a negative change in the credit-to-GDP ratio, and initially this had a hidden effect on the rate of per capita GDP growth. From 2009 this effect became visible, as GDP plunged lower, and from 2010 it once again hampered Hungarian GDP growth in a concealed manner.

A negative impact from the strong relationship between credit-to-GDP growth and per capita GDP growth was seen specifically during the period of fiscal consolidation and economic stabilisation.

In Hungary, corporate lending has a much more pronounced growth impact than household lending. Changes in outstanding household lending also have an effect on growth, but corporate lending is the key factor. In the years around EU accession, corporate lending first expanded up until the first half of 2005, but then declined prior to the first austerity programme launched on 1 September 2006. The sector's behaviour behind the development of corporate lending already reflected the flawed economic policy. EU accession generated a one-off, special economic situation, but despite this the corporate sector's borrowings for investment decline, reflecting the deterioration in domestic business conditions (Figure 271).

Another negative change occurred after the onset of the crisis in 2008 and this decline was of lasting nature. The substantial decline in outstanding corporate loans was also behind the large drop in GDP in 2009, after which there was initially an unsuccessful attempt at financial consolidation, followed by a successful one, accompanied by a steady fall in outstanding corporate loans.

The successful fiscal consolidation and economic stabilisation seen in 2010–2014 was not backed by corporate lending, and indeed the decline in the stock of outstanding corporate loans actually had a hidden negative impact on these efforts. Although corporate lending could expand in certain quarters, the rate of growth for corporate lending was consistently negative over the four years of consolidation.

Figure 271. Decomposition of the Financial Conditions Index

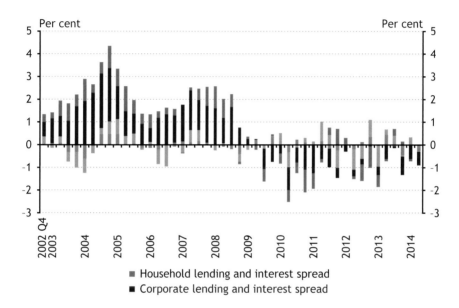

■ Household lending and interest spread
■ Corporate lending and interest spread

The index quantifies the impact of financial conditions through lending on annual GDP growth.

Source: MNB

There is a similar relationship between household lending and consolidation, albeit the connection between household lending and economic growth is not as strong as between corporate lending and GDP growth. The decline in household lending also had a negative impact on the budget revenues needed for consolidation. On the other hand, the policy of consolidation was supported by the rise in households' net financial wealth. Two thirds of the additional income received by families thanks to the tax reform was used for the reduction of debts, and the other one third went into financial savings. Consequently, the share of households in the financing of government debt increased, boosting the security of government debt financing.

Numerous analyses and estimates of the connection between lending and growth have been prepared, and based on these 10% growth in credit supply boosts Hungarian GDP by 1–2% over a one-year horizon. The relationship is similar in the Czech economy, where a 1% contraction in corporate credit supply results in a 0.2% drop in GDP. In every country, there is a positive and a negative relationship between outstanding loans and changes in GDP and while the strength of these relationships varies, the direction is the same (Table 8).

Table 8. Estimations of the relationships between lending and growth

Countries reviewed	Sectors reviewed	Quantitative link
Hungary	Corporates	Credit supply 10 per cent growth over a one-year horizon boosts GDP by 1-2 percentage points
Czech Republic	Corporates	1 per cent reduction in credit supply results in 0.2 per cent contraction in GDP
Bulgaria, Czech Republic, Estonia, Poland, Latvia, Lithuania, Hungary, Romania, Slovakia, Slovenia	Total outstanding lending	1 per cent growth in credit supply results in 0.1 percent economic growth
Sample of 47 countries	Total outstanding lending	10 per cent higher credit-to-GDP ratio results in 0.14 percentage point higher per capita GDP growth
Sample of 71 countries	Total outstanding lending	Increase in credit-to-GDP ratio from 50 per cent to 60 per cent results in higher per capita GDP growth
Sample of 74 countries	Total outstanding lending	10 percentage point increase in the credit-to-GDP rate results in 0.37 percentage point higher per capita GDP growth
Sample of 75 countries	Total outstanding lending	With regard to the credit-to-GDP ratio, if a country moves from the lower quintiles of the sample to the median, the rate of per capita GDP growth can be 1.4 percentage points higher over the long term. In instable countries, however, the link can be negative over the short term.

Source: MNB

During the crisis, the role of lending became much more important in terms of growth. Crisis management was far easier in developed economies which saw an increase in lending, compared to crisis management in an environment characterised by a reduction in lending. During the year of the crisis, in the developed economies, crisis management which was accompanied by lending growth resulted in a difference of around 3% in terms of GDP compared to crisis management without lending growth. This relationship also persisted into the second year of the crisis: GDP growth with an expansion in lending was 1.5–2% higher than the recovery seen without lending growth (Figure 272).

Figure 272. Real GDP growth (median) around crisis periods

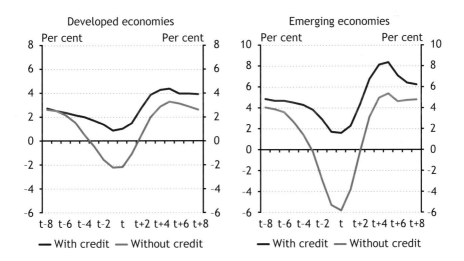

Eight quarters before and after trough

Source: Sugawara et al. (2013): Credit-less recoveries: neither a rare nor an insurmountable challenge. World Bank Policy Research Working Paper, WPS 6459

In analysing financial and economic crises, Sugawara et al. (2013) found an interesting difference between the post-recovery trend without lending growth and with lending growth. Creditless recovery can occur more rapidly than a recovery with lending growth, because the former tends to start from a deeper recession. At the same time, over a longer period a recovery without lending is slower, because postponed investment due to the absence of credit have a negative impact on the economy's long-term growth potential, in addition to short-term growth. Based on international experiences in crisis management, it is clear that Hungary's consolidation and stabilisation in 2010–2014 was far more difficult in an environment without lending growth (and actually occurred in conjunction with a contraction in lending) than it would have been, had lending even just stagnated or increased. Hungary actually underwent a creditless recovery, because there was no growth in outstanding loans for almost one-half decade following the crisis, but fiscal consolidation and economic stabilisation was nonetheless successful.

Deleveraging appears to be stronger in Hungary than in other countries in a similar situation. Prior to the crisis, outstanding loans to non-financial corporations in Hungary grew faster than the global average, and the increase in outstanding loans was faster and larger than seen in the countries with high ratios of government debt as well as compared to countries with high levels of foreign currency exposure. This indicates that the Hungarian economy was not actually impacted by a single financial crisis, but rather by several financial crises in the period before the 2008 financial crisis and indeed after this crisis as well. The Hungarian economy was simultaneously suffering from high public debt and high foreign currency exposure, in conjunction with a fiscal deficit stubbornly above 3% and a portfolio of household foreign currency loans involving particularly acute risks (Figure 273).

Figure 273. Non-financial private sector credit-to-GDP ratio before
and after banking crises (percentiles)

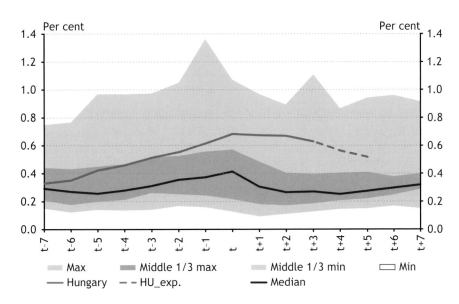

Percentiles, the horizontal axis is divided into years, where "t" marks the year of the crisis.

Source: MNB

In 2008, it was actually a banking crisis which developed in Hungary, because the previous loan-to-deposit ratios had become unsustainable, along with the earlier set of conditions for lending and the prospective growth path of lending. This hidden banking crisis began when foreign currency loans were canceled and became visible in autumn 2008. It was followed by deleveraging during the years after the crisis. It was only natural for this to be stronger than the global average and to be stronger than the deleveraging by the banking sectors in the countries with high levels of government and high levels of foreign currency exposure. This is why consolidation and stabilisation in Hungary was more difficult in the other economies which faced crisis management.

The recovery in growth proved to be difficult because Hungary had "brought forward" a significant amount of growth performance in the years prior to the 2008 financial crisis compared to other countries in the region: the stronger expansion in outstanding loans indicates that growth was brought forward. This growth in outstanding loans was artificially fast and large, and there is a close relationship between lending growth and economic growth: part of the GDP growth registered in the years prior to 2008 was artificial growth which was brought forward.

Central bank lending programme necessary for a recovery in growth

There is a strong correlation between growth and lending, and this relationship is stronger in the Hungarian economy than in other countries. Due to deleveraging by the banking sector after the crisis, the high stock of households' outstanding foreign currency loans and the need to consolidate the budget, there was essentially only one actor left in the Hungarian economy which could launch the turnaround in lending necessary to reverse the growth trend: the Hungarian central bank. From mid-2013, the turnaround in lending started with the central bank's Funding for Growth Scheme, focusing on the domestic SME sector which was hit hardest by the credit crunch.

From autumn 2008 until the end of 2009, the overall rate of corporate lending growth slowed, and remained negative as outstanding loans continued to contract until the launch of the central bank's lending programme in mid-2013 (Figure 274).

Figure 274. Transaction-based growth
in the banking sector's corporate lending

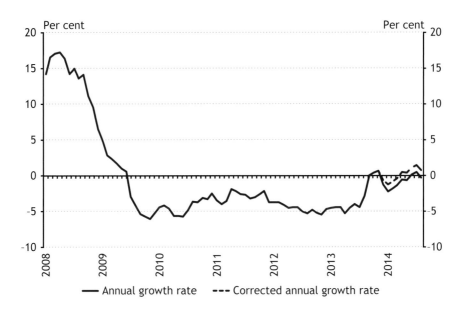

The corrected line is adjusted from one-off factors (shareholder's loan repayment of a bank's affiliated company).

Source: MNB

The central bank's lending programme which was initiated in mid-2013 resulted in an immediate, significant increase in outstanding loans to the SME sector, and a turnaround in lending to SMEs was seen within just a few months. After the reversal in the trend, the change in lending to the SME sector remained consistently positive, and as we saw in the case of the fiscal turnaround and the recovery in consumption, the growth path remained on a sustainable positive trend in the area impacted by the credit crunch even after the turnaround in lending to SMEs (cf. Figure 243).

While the central bank's lending programme did not result in a turnaround in lending to large enterprises, the turnaround in SME lending did reverse the negative trend in lending to the corporate sector as a whole. Since the funds disbursed through the FGS could be used for investment purposes, refinancing of existing HUF-denominated loans with high interest rates or the refinancing of existing foreign currency loans, the central bank's lending programme must also be seen as a breakthrough not only in quantitative terms (in relation to the expansion of outstanding loans to SMEs), but also in qualitative terms. It achieved growth in SME lending, while at the same time improving the structure of loans to SMEs. The combination of lower forint interest rates and the refinancing of foreign currency loans generated a major improvement in the financial situation of more than 10,000 companies.

Figure 275. GDP growth contribution of the output of key economic sectors

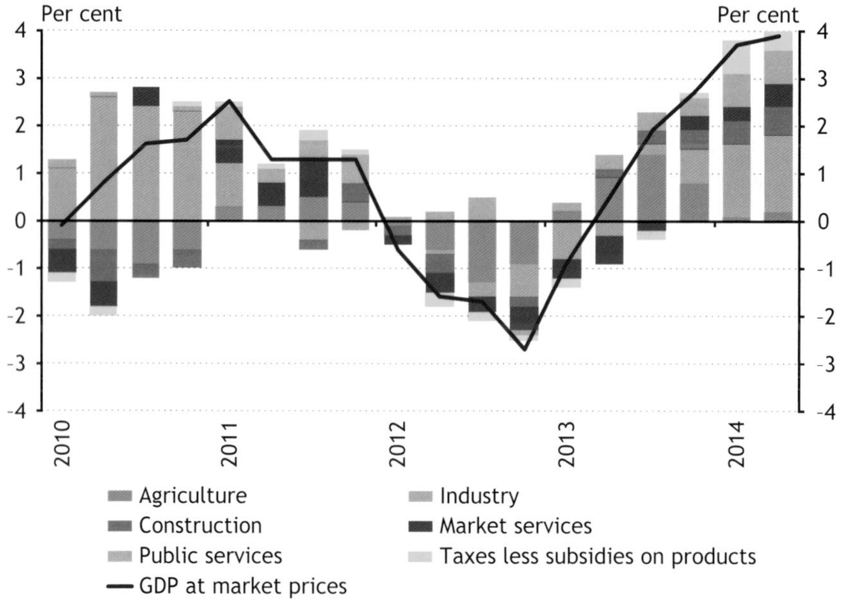

Source: CSO

The greatest success of the central bank's lending programme was that it intervened in a targeted manner precisely where the strongest potential growth capacity was hindered by the worst access to credit.

As there is no growth without credit, in the years following the crisis the growth potential of the Hungarian economy was deteriorated the most by an asymmetric situation: the sectors which still had the best growth potential in the years after the crisis were the ones which had the most restricted access to new loans.

The turnaround in lending to the SME sector triggered by the central bank's lending programme launched in mid-2013 was another factor behind the recovery in growth seen in 2013–2014. This is reflected by the relationship between the sectors contributing to growth and the sectors which played the key role in the FGS. The sectors which contributed the most to the recovery in growth in 2013–2014 were the ones which borrowed the most within the framework of the FGS (Figure 275).

Real economy as the key factor

Manufacturing, market services, agriculture and the construction industry played the main role in the recovery in growth in 2013–2014. Amongst these economic sectors, the recovery in the construction industry was financed by EU funds and the upswing in manufacturing (in particular in the automotive industry) was financed by FDI, but the rising supply of credit via the FGS played a role in all of the sectors. Investments, net exports and the improvement in consumption were a major factor in the growth recovery seen in 2013–2014. The central bank's lending programme played a role in the expansion of net exports, investments and consumption, respectively.

The increases in the exports of the domestic automotive industry played a significant role in the growth recovery, as these were able to offset and actually overcompensate the negative effects from declines in the electronics industry (Figure 276).

Figure 276. Industrial output in the automotive and electronics sectors

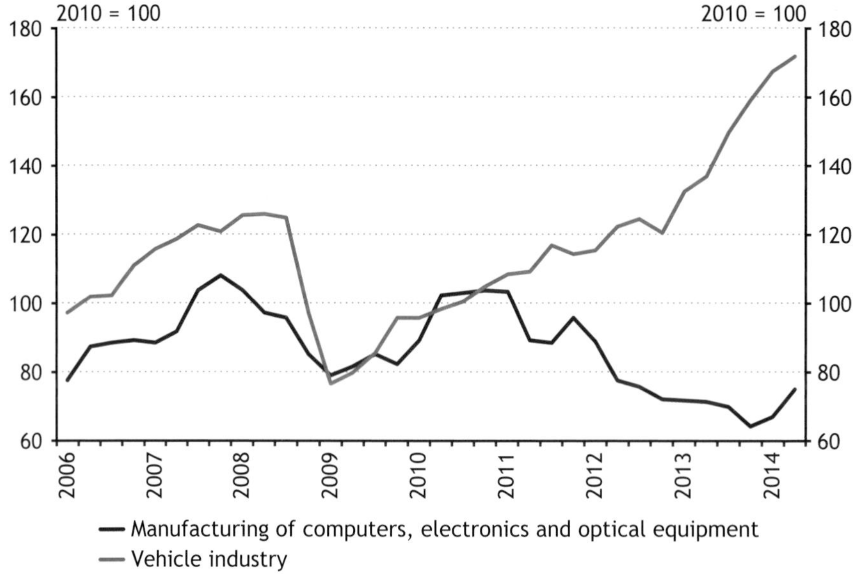

2010 = 100   2010 = 100

Source: HCSO

It can be seen that whereas the domestic automotive manufacturing industry grew without interruption up until the crisis in 2008, the growth trend in the electronics industry already broke at the end of 2007. Both of these two industries reach their low point in early 2009, but from then output only expanded steadily in the automotive industry, whereas the output of the electronics industry contracted after a brief period of stagnation. During the period following the crisis, however, the positive performance of the automotive industry was able to offset the negative performance of the electronics industry. Another factor that played a major role in the 2013–2014 growth recovery was the shift in structure in industry, and within this in manufacturing: without the strong rise in automobile manufacturing it would probably not have been possible to turn around growth in 2013–2014. In the vehicle production industry, the group of domestic suppliers includes more and more Hungarian SMEs which participated to a large degree in the FGS programme, and thus the automotive industry would not have been able to expand so strongly and play such stabilising role without the SME suppliers which took part in the lending programme.

Similar to the situation with the automotive industry, the dynamic expansion of foreign trade in modern services was also a key factor facilitating the recovery in growth (Figure 277).

Figure 277. Development of world trade in goods and traditional and modern services

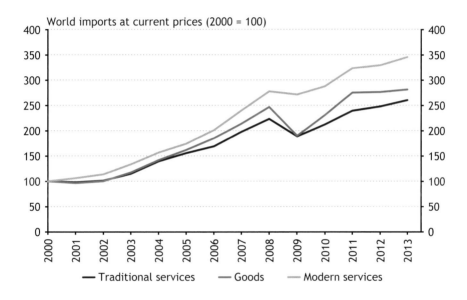

Source: WTO   *Traditional services: tourism and transportation*

As the Figure shows, the gap between traditional services and modern services widens from 2000, and while foreign trade in traditional services grows up until the start of the crisis, the amount of foreign trade in modern services expands at a faster rate. Moreover, during the crisis, the volume of foreign trade in both of these types of services declines, but the drop in traditional services is far more severe, whereas the decline in modern services is modest. Following this, both of these groups of service companies see a strong rise in their foreign trade. In the period 2010–2014, a significant gap opens up between these two service sectors: modern services are more competitive than traditional services.

Looking at the period of almost one and a half decades from 2000 to 2014, a similar difference is seen between the trend lines for goods and modern services. The crisis after 2008 resulted in a sharp downturn for domestic enterprises involved in the production of goods, followed by a period of rapid recovery. After 2010, growth is seen both in goods production and modern services, but a larger gap develops between the output of these two sectors.

Another positive aspect of the central bank's lending programme is that it provided the funding needed for the expansion of foreign trade in modern services, since most of the companies involved in this sector are SMEs and the ownership structure is also characterised by a Hungarian majority ownership.

Figure 278. Link between share of services sector and per capita GDP

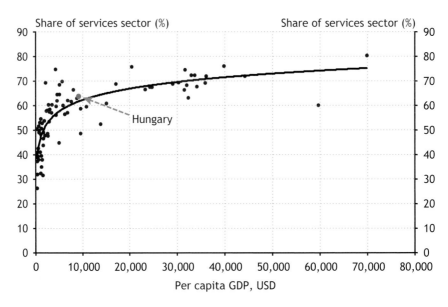

Data for the average between 1993 and 2007.

Source: MNB calculation based on WDI data

Since the share of the service sector in the economy increases in conjunction with the level of economic development, putting traditional and modern services back on a trajectory of strong growth following the crisis will be a key factor in terms of future economic growth in Hungary (Figure 278).

The Hungarian economy is particularly well suited for development of the service sectors, because a flexible, creative workforce is the biggest competitive advantage. New companies play an important role in both traditional and modern services, because new needs and the corresponding new capacities are almost constantly appearing in the field of services. While companies producing goods also continuously take part in the process of development and innovation, the pace is faster in the service sectors and is really a typical characteristic of all participants, with this process being more important in the field of modern services, as compared to traditional services.

The Hungarian workforce, especially the younger generations, are clearly the most open to modern services. Furthermore, in the two decades after EU accession many young working-age Hungarians moved abroad, mainly to EU countries, and their best employment prospects upon returning to Hungary will be in the fields of traditional and modern services.

In terms of the future outlook for Hungary's potential growth, one of the greatest reserves will stem the confluence of modern services and the generation of young workers, in particular the several hundred thousand young workers who left Hungary for other EU countries. Altough young Hungarian employees previously working abroad are returning to agricultural and food industry companies producing intermediat products (for example craft wines) and a similar trend has been observed in enterprises manufacturing goods, especially among Hungarian firms supplying the automotive industry, but upon returning to Hungary, workers who have been employed abroad will the most opportunities in the service sectors, and especially in modern services.

The true significance of the recovery in growth is that it will make this confluence possible.

The steadily improving economic environment in Hungary and the constant growth of the service sector (including the sector of modern services which require foreign language skills) will open up increasing opportunities for the generation of young people who are employed abroad.

Hidden factors behind the recovery in growth

Among Hungarian economists, it is considered bad style to mention the EUR/HUF exchange rate as a significant source of growth. This stems from a false economic presumption based on neo-liberal doctrine: a weaker exchange rate only has an effect on competitiveness over the short run, and not over the medium to long run. By contrast, the correct economic relationship is that anything that has an impact over the short run also has an effect on the subsequent periods, because the decisions made within a given framework influence the results of the next period and have an effect on the decision-making basis of individuals and enterprises.

After the 2008 financial crisis, the fundamental economic relationships characterising the Hungarian economy changed to a great degree. Prior to the 2008 financial crisis, a change of 10 forints in the EUR/HUF exchange rate generated a change of 0.9% in inflation, whereas after the crisis the same change in the exchange rate only resulted in a change of 0.3–0.5% in the annual rate of change in consumer prices. If the domestic currency weakens by 10 forints versus the euro, this results in inflation in the following two years being 0.3–0.6% higher. It can be assumed that the inverse is also true, but there is no empirical evidence in this regard.

Similarly, there is a positive relationship between a weaker exchange rate and GDP growth. A depreciation of the forint by 10% boosts the level of Hungarian GDP by 0.5%–0.8%, and again it can be assumed that the inverse is also true. The effect on growth exerted by a weaker exchange rate occurs over at least two years, but the decisions made by businesses and households over this two-year period also influence growth in the following years.

The relationship between a 10% depreciation of the exchange rate and the development of GDP is the strongest in the Czech, Croatian, Romanian and Polish economies. The effect on growth of a weaker exchange rate is also significant in the UK, Hungarian and euro area economies, but less so than in the former group.

We consider a weaker exchange rate to be a new exchange rate prevailing over a two-year period. In the case of the Hungarian economy, for the entire period of consolidation and stabilisation the prevailing exchange rate was 20–30% weaker than the previous, artificially strong exchange rate of the forint, and this may have had a substantial effect on growth in the Hungarian economy. The most important hidden factor driving the reversal of the growth trend in 2013–2014 and the recovery in growth as a whole was this weaker exchange rate. Owing to financial consolidation, the exchange rate of the forint began moving away from the earlier, artificially strong level towards an equilibrium level, which was also promoted by the central bank's rate-cutting cycle. Accordingly, from a growth perspective, the exchange rate prevailing during the period of stabilisation was much more favourable compared to the earlier rate.

The most important aspect of the recovery in Hungarian growth is that the economy has shifted towards economic growth in a more healthy structure. While the artificially boosted economic upswing and debt-financed growth seen during the period 2002–2008 resulted in significant distortions to the already dualistic structure of the Hungarian economy, the recovery in growth in 2013–2014 put the Hungarian economy on track for growth with a healthy structure. It was no longer risky foreign currency loans which drove growth, Hungarian economic conditions were no longer marked by unsustainable fiscal and government debt paths and instead the focus turned to reducing debt and a creditless recovery.

The healthy forint exchange rate, the targeted lending programme by the central bank and the utilisation of EU funds also provided considerable support for this new healthy growth structure.

Accelerat of the utilisation of EU funds allenate the credit crunch when the central bank's lending scheme was launched, but this alone was not able to resolve it because the bulk of EU funds was not used to finance economic development and was consequently unable to overcome the credit crunch which had arisen in the corporate sector.

One of the other factors behind the recovery in growth which was hidden, but had a significant effect was the increase in households' financial wealth. Households' net financial wealth is the difference between households' financial liabilities and their financial investments. The higher the level of households' net financial wealth, the greater their financial independence, the stronger their sense of security, and the more they participate in economic growth via consumption and investment.

Households' net financial wealth grew until 2007 and then after the onset of the crisis it temporarily declined as a result of revaluation caused by the weaker exchange rate, before starting to steadily rise again in the years following 2008.

In the period after 2007–2008, real estate loans account for a significant part of households' overall financial liabilities, but the negative impact of consumer loans and other loans on households' net financial wealth was even greater (Figure 279).

Figure 279. Household financial wealth

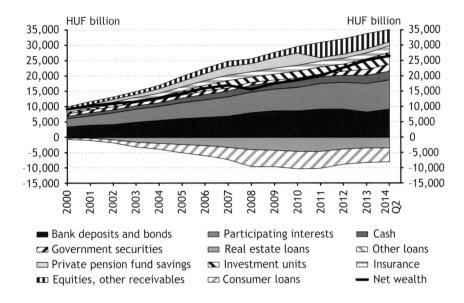

Legend:
- ■ Bank deposits and bonds
- ▨ Government securities
- ▢ Private pension fund savings
- ▥ Equities, other receivables
- ▥ Participating interests
- ▥ Real estate loans
- ▨ Investment units
- ▨ Consumer loans
- ▥ Cash
- ▧ Other loans
- ▢ Insurance
- ▬ Net wealth

Source: MNB

Thus, the 2008 financial crisis caused the internal exchange rate risks inherent in the portfolio of foreign currency loans to materialise. As a result of this, the portfolio of outstanding consumer loans and other loans suddenly jumped higher, along with the debt servicing burdens. After the 2008 crisis, households' adjustment pressures over the short term also facilitated the expansion of consumer and other loans, since they were only able to cover the level of consumption reached earlier and the repayment of earlier loans by taking on new loans.

After the onset of the crisis, households' share in bank deposits and outstanding bonds increases, all the way until the shift in households' investment in government bonds seen at the start of 2012. In the period 2013–2014, households increasingly withdraw their money from bank deposits and other bonds and put it into government bonds, partially due to the higher yields on government securities and partially due to the increase in confidence as a result of the successful fiscal consolidation (Figure 280).

Figure 280. Composition of households' financial savings and the GDP-proportionate level of their gross financial assets

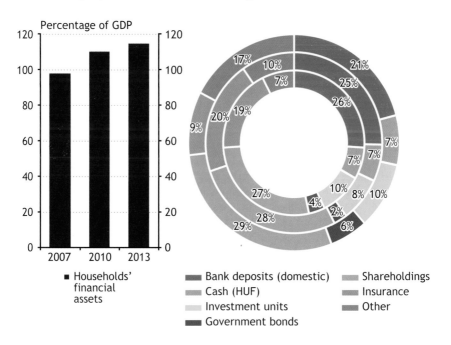

The size of the item other accounts receivable was significantly impacted by the fact that, according to the ESA-2010 methodology, the claim from private pension funds which was terminated in 2011 turned into a receivable from the state.

Source: MNB

Growth in households' net financial wealth initially decelerates during the period 2010–2014, before starting to steadily rise on a trend faster than the trend seen after 2000; this had a significant, hidden effect on consolidation and stabilisation. Households' financial investments were concentrated more and more in government bonds, which raised the share of HUF-denominated, domestically-owned holdings in government debt, facilitating consolidation. While households' reluctance to take out real estate loans did not contribute to stabilisation, it did help with financial consolidation, since households' financial wealth was held in investments which were considerably more liquid than in the past. All of this bolstered households' confidence, supporting the rebound in consumption in 2013 and the turnaround in investment in 2014. After 2010, the reduction of consumer and investment loans was a major determining factor in the development of households' net financial wealth.

The development of households' financial assets reflects the change in households' financial behaviour, as the shares of bank bonds, investment fund shares and cash shifted during the first decade of EU membership between 2004 and 2014. The most significant changes were seen in the period 2008–2014: bank deposits are replaced with government bonds, investment fund shares become popular again and holdings of cash steadily rise. One of the major factors behind the successful financial consolidation in Hungary between 2010 and 2014 was households' growing confidence in the public budget and the state in general (Figure 281).

Figure 281. Changes in households' financial assets

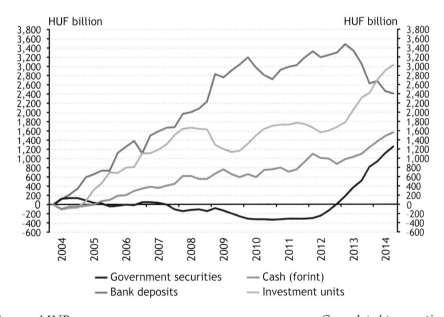

Source: MNB   *Cumulated transactions*

After the recovery in growth in 2013–2014, the real question for the years ahead is whether the turnaround that has been achieved is sustainable, and if so, at what pace in the future. Following the 2013 growth recovery, more and more positive factors are coming together and pointing towards a rate of Hungarian GDP growth which is sustainable and relatively high compared to the country's regional peers. On the expenditure side of GDP, one of these factors is the anticipated continuous growth in household consumption, because the reduction in outstanding household loans continues to be substantial and rapid, along with the steady rise in households' disposable income. The measures to settle and convert outstanding foreign currency loans which were launched in 2014 will make a major contribution in this regard as well. The steady increase in employment and the reduction in unemployment also increases households' disposable income. To an increasing degree, this disposable income is flowing into consumption, resulting in a self-sustaining cycle of consumption.

The uninterrupted growth in households' net financial wealth results in steadily strengthening confidence, which supports both growth in consumption and investment activity (cf. Figure 195).

In the period 2010–2014, the business climate in Hungary actually continuously improved (despite the competitiveness indicators lagging behind the region), because the successful fiscal consolidation was followed by lasting economic stabilisation. While this was not an exception for the Central European region, it does offer a competitive advantage when looking at the European Union as whole and in particular the members of the euro area.

The upturn in investments behind this recovery in growth is due to investments by domestic economic agents and to the inflow of foreign direct investment. Together, these may result in a rate of investment of around 20% during the years following the recovery in Hungarian growth. The rebound in lending may initially have a similar effect in the SME sector, followed later by the sector of large enterprises.

Successfully breaking out of the credit crunch in 2013–2014 triggered a turnaround in lending, which is expected to be finished with the complete restructuring of the ownership structure of the banking sector in the period 2014–2016.

In terms of achieving a sustainable growth trajectory in the years ahead, there are a number of other factors in reserve. With the steady improvement in the business climate, more and more Hungarians currently working in the global and EU economies may decide to return to Hungary. Accordingly, the steady quantitative and qualitative improvement in labour supply may also support employment growth in the years ahead.

Productivity growth is another hidden source of growth for the future (Figure 282).

Figure 282. Productivity and private sector employment

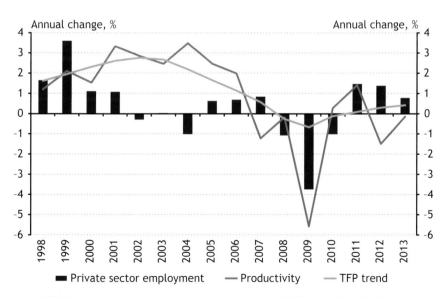

Source: MNB   *TFP calculated in hours worked*

After the period 2008–2009, we see a phase of quick recovery in productivity: in order to achieve this, a mild rebound from the earlier losses suffered in private sector employment was sufficient, which indicates that the Hungarian private sector already had internal productivity reserves during the period before the crisis.

This relationship was temporarily interrupted in 2011–2012, when employment in the private sector increased, but productivity fell nevertheless. The reason for this was the introduction of the public work programme. In fact, the relationship between expansion of employment in the private sector and productivity continued to be valid, but this was obscured by the low level of productivity of employees in the public work programme.

Figure 283. Estimated savings attainable by boosting efficiency in health care in 2017, % of GDP

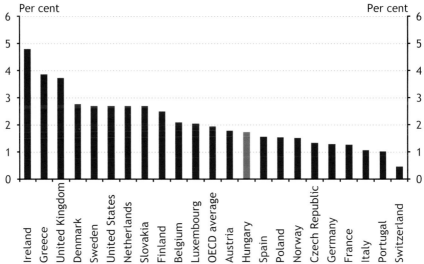

Source: OECD – Health care systems: efficiency and policy settings (2010)

According to an OECD survey, Hungary has very significant reserves in terms of savings which can be achieved via the improvement of efficiency. Utilisation of efficiency reserves in the Hungarian economy could result in GDP growth of around 2% by 2017, primarily by mobilising the reserves available through the reduction of bureaucracy and administration. There are also significant efficiency reserves available via boosting Hungarian life expectancy, which may improve the quantitative and qualitative structure of Hungarian employment (Figure 283).

Chapter 23

Hungary catches up with the region

Geographically, Hungary has always been part of the Central European region, but in terms of economic development it was sometimes a front-runner, while at other times it lagged behind in the two decades between 1990 and 2010. In 1990, it entered the market economy and Western integration as the vanguard of the region at a time when the Czech Republic and Slovakia had not separated, the Yugoslav federation had not broken up, and Poland and Romania were the worst economic performers in the region. By 2010, the roles were reversed. The first two decades in the market economy were utilised best by Poland. Slovakia and the Czech Republic fared impressively, Romania improved its position, and Croatia and Slovenia performed well in the first two decades of independence.

Hungary lags behind the region

By contrast, Hungary fell behind the CEE region during the period of flawed economic policy 2002–2010, and it resembled the southern flank of the euro area on account of its financial indebtedness, the artificial domestic upswing as well as the internal and external imbalances (Figure 284).

This is clearly demonstrated by the performance of the economy in the years after the 2008 financial crisis. Due to the huge accumulated financial burden, Hungarian indicators were close to those of Croatia, Italy and Portugal, they lagged behind the Romanian and Czech figures and were far worse than the Polish and Slovak GDP data. Compared to the region, poor GDP growth and a weaker and more protracted recovery was observed in Hungary after 2008, which was the result of the misguided economic policy before 2008.

From the years around the 2004 EU accession until 2008, just like in the Baltic states, Hungarian economic growth was fuelled by an artificial domestic upswing financed by external indebtedness, which had already become unsustainable in both the Hungarian and the Baltic economies even before the crisis.

Figure 284. Development of GDP in 2014 versus 2008 in certain countries

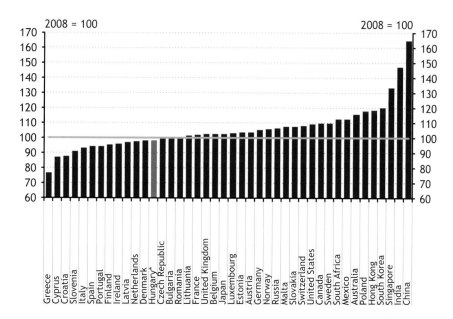

* Calculated using the estimates from the September 2014 Inflation Report.

Source: IMF WEO, April 2014

Between 2010 and 2014, Hungary gradually caught up with the CEE region's economic performance at a slower pace than the Czech and the Romanian recovery, but it fared better than the southern countries of the euro area which were in a constant state of crisis: Hungary returned to its natural region.

The development of gross external debt to GDP displayed a trend similar to economic growth. It can be seen that Hungary's gross external debt to GDP soared because of the poor economic policy between 2004 and 2008. As a result of the 2008 global financial crisis, the internal risk of foreign currency borrowing materialised, and the ratio of Hungarian gross external debt to GDP was around 150% in 2009.

By contrast, the gross external debt-to-GDP ratios of Poland and the Czech Republic hardly changed in 2004–2008, although they increased slightly in 2009 due to the financial crisis in the previous year. However, the gross external debt-to-GDP ratios of around 60% in Poland and 50% in the Czech Republic were far lower than the gross external debt of Hungary (Figure 285).

Figure 285. Ratio of gross external debt to GDP in the Visegrád countries

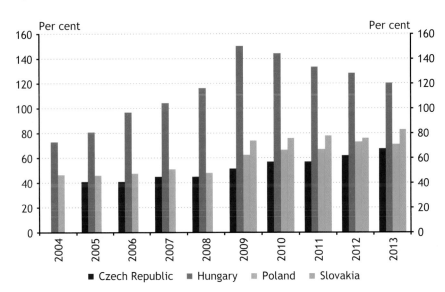

Source: Eurostat   *Including intercompany loans*

After 2009, the reduction of the Hungarian gross external debt-to-GDP ratio started, while the Polish figure passed the threshold of 60%, and stood at around 70–80%. The gross external debt ratio of the Czech Republic also rose marginally, entering the 60–80% band relative to GDP in the years after the crisis.

Hungary becomes the most vulnerable in the region

Hungary also fell behind the region in 2004–2008 as regards gross debt to GDP. While GDP growth in the region was not fuelled by an artificial internal upswing and considerable indebtedness, all of the economic agents in the Hungarian economy were heavily indebted: in addition to the sharp rise in the government debt ratio, the external debt ratio almost doubled. Between 2010 and 2014, Hungary approached the region in terms of external debt, but the earlier misguided accumulation of debt still caused a considerable competitive disadvantage compared to the other economies in the region.

Compared to its peers in the EU, the Hungarian financial system was much riskier, because using currencies other than the national currency posed an exchange rate risk. The financial vulnerability of Hungary was compounded by the loans in Swiss franc and a smaller proportion of loans denominated in yen. Household foreign currency loans were taken out mainly in Swiss franc, and if one takes this into account, the share of foreign currencies used in the Hungarian financial system was higher by orders of magnitude than in other regional countries.

The set of measures targeting the reduction of household foreign currency loans – the early repayment and exchange rate cap schemes, the decisions by the Curia (Hungary's supreme court) and the new laws facilitating this process – will fundamentally improve the situation of the Hungarian financial system in the years ahead, because they eliminate the greatest risk from system, i.e. the risk posed by households indebted in Swiss franc. Even after implementing such measures, the proportion of foreign currencies used in the Hungarian economy will remain high as compared to other regional countries, especially compared to the Polish and Czech economies, but if household Swiss franc loans are phased out, this proportion will not deviate much from the regional average. When the problems with the household foreign currency loans are resolved, i.e. when foreign currencies are phased out, Hungary will catch up with the region with respect to the use of the national currency as well.

Looking at overall outstanding loans in the CEE region, the proportion of USD and EUR-denominated loans is 55–75%. Hungary lags behind the region with respect to the financial system, and this is perhaps best illustrated by the fact that, compared to the ratio of the euro, the ratio of the Swiss franc in household and corporate foreign currency loans is far higher than the regional average (Figure 286).

Figure 286. Development of outstanding foreign currency loans in the household and corporate segments in the CEE region, % of GDP (January 2014)

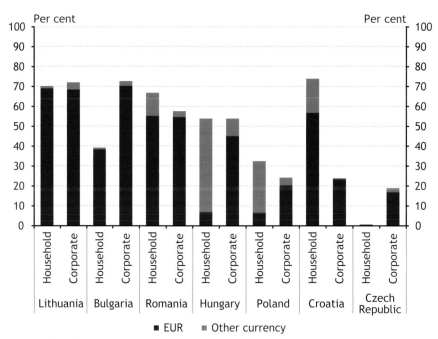

Source: ECB, CNB, HNB

We saw that the proportion of foreign currencies in household and corporate loans is far lower in the Polish and Czech economies, and the vast majority of foreign currency loans are denominated in euro (with the exception of the Polish portfolio of foreign currency loans). In Croatia, household deposits are predominantly in foreign currencies, and thus the aggregate foreign currency exposure of Croatian households is significantly lower.

The detachment from the regional financial system is highlighted even more by the comparison with the Romanian, Bulgarian and Lithuanian economies. In Hungary, households' outstanding foreign currency loans were mainly denominated in CHF and not in EUR, and this mistake was not made in the other CEE economies. Only the Polish portfolio of household foreign currency loans contains a higher proportion of Swiss franc loans than the regional average, but even the Polish figure is half of the Hungarian ratio.

Figure 287. Share of banks' external funds, % of GDP

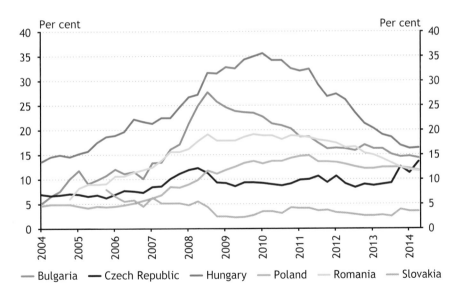

Source: ECB, Eurostat

The Hungarian financial system started to catch up with the region in mid-2010, at the moment when the earlier accumulation of loans was halted by banning household foreign currency borrowing. The external financing risk of the banking system steadily decreased from mid-2010. By 2014, the Hungarian banking system increasingly resembled the financial systems in the region with respect to financing risk.

While the external financing exposure of the Hungarian banking system increased steeply between 2004 and 2008 as banks' external funds as a proportion of GDP rose substantially, the external financing risk stagnated in 2008–2010, and then it declined sharply (Figure 287).

It can be seen that in the Bulgarian economy – similar to the Hungarian trend – banks' external funds relative to GDP expanded dynamically for some time, but in Bulgaria the adjustment after the 2008 financial crisis was more momentous than in the Hungarian financial system. The Czech, Polish and Romanian financial systems did not accumulate external funds in the banking system in a proportion similar to the Hungarian one, and therefore these banking systems' external financing risk did not come close to the Hungarian level at these regional competitors. Consequently, they had to reduce the financing risk from a lower level after the 2008 financial crisis.

Return to the region

The regional comparison conclusively demonstrates that the Hungarian financial system fell behind the region in 2004–2010 in terms of the external financing risk, and then in 2010–2014 it returned to the regional risk level. By 2014, with respect to banks' external funds in proportion to GDP, the Hungarian banking system was very similar to that of its regional peers.

This was a decisive factor in drastically reducing the vulnerability of the Hungarian banking system by the end of 2013, as compared to the level at the onset of the financial crisis. It emerges clearly that the proportion of foreign currency loans in the banking system in 2008 was by far the highest in Hungary. The country's banking system was also a leader in terms of the loan-to-deposit ratio, while it was second only to the Romanian financial system as regards the proportion of external funds, and the ratio of non-performing loans corresponded to the regional average. The latter indicates that although the risks inherent in foreign currency lending materialised with the eruption of the 2008 financial crisis, they did not "pass through" to borrowers at that time, only in the following years (Table 9).

Table 9. Regional comparison of banking sector vulnerability indicators

2008	Share of FX loans (%)	Loans/ deposits ratio (%)	Share of banks' external funds (%)	NPLs (%)	CAR (%)
Hungary	67.4	144.8	26.4	3.7	12.9
Poland	34.2	114.8	6.9	3.4	11.3
Slovakia	18.8	82.6	5.1	1.7	11.2
Czech Republic	9.1	82.8	10.5	4.7	11.6
Romania	54.7	130.8	30.4	1.5	14.1
Bulgaria	56.3	130.6	21.6	4.8	14.9

2013	Share of FX loans (%)	Loans/ deposits ratio (%)	Share of banks' external funds (%)	NPLs (%)	CAR (%)
Hungary	54.2	105.6	15.2	14.7	17
Poland	30	102.6	3.7	6	15.3
Slovakia	0.4	93.2	3.3	3.8	16.5
Czech Republic	9.5	76.6	9.8	6.7	16.6
Romania	61.2	101.3	20.4	21	18.1
Bulgaria	60.9	96.8	12.7	19.5	16.9

Source: National central banks

In 2013, the ratios of foreign currency loans in the Romanian and Bulgarian banking systems were higher than in Hungary. As regards the loan-to-deposit ratio, Hungary was near the Polish and Romanian figures, and with respect to the proportion of external funds, it was close to the Romanian and Bulgarian levels. Although the share of NPLs expanded considerably compared to 2008, it remained below the Romanian and Bulgarian level.

In fact, financial systems in the region split into two groups. With respect to the indicators showing the vulnerability of the banking system, Slovakia and the Czech Republic became the top performers by the end of 2013, Poland and Hungary were catching up to them, while the vulnerability of the Romanian and Bulgarian banking systems remained high. A significant adjustment took place in the Hungarian banking system. The situation in late 2013 will continue to improve in the years ahead because the proportion of external funds continues to decrease substantially, the loan-to-deposit ratio is falling and the share of foreign currency loans is contracting rapidly, which can be expected to entail a reduction in the ratio of NPLs.

Hungary's risk premium also displays a similar trend. The Hungarian risk premium dropped from the earlier high CDS level that signalled a fiscal and government debt financing crisis to a lower level reflecting the successful crisis management (Figure 288).

It can be seen that biggest drop in the Hungarian risk premium occurred in 2012 when GDP contracted, and real income and consumption declined. Thus, the Hungarian risk premium plunged in the decisive year of transition to the new tax system, when inflation temporarily spiked. This merely appears to be contradictory, since 2012 proved to financial market participants that the general government deficit below 3% in 2011 was not a fleeting success, but that it would be repeated in 2012 as well.[54]

[54] According to data from 2011, the Hungarian budget was in surplus or, adjusted by one-off factors, in a deficit below 3%. In 2014, the EU adopted the ESA-2010 methodology, which changed data series retroactively as well. The new methodology does not take into account the transfer of the assets accumulated in pension funds, and therefore the official figures without the one-off factors show a budget deficit of over 5%.

Figure 288. 5-year sovereign CDS premiums in the Visegrád countries

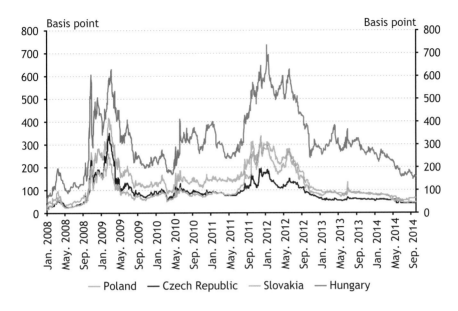

Source: Bloomberg

As regards the current account balance, Hungary fell especially far behind the region. Even in the years before the EU accession, Hungary was one of the worst performers in terms of the current account balance, which was mainly due to the mistakes during the transition to the market economy. However, in the early 2000s, the Hungarian current account deficit was 6%, which was not significantly higher than in other regional countries, with the exception of Austria and Slovenia. Austria's current account balance is characteristic of a developed and successful economy, in which a surplus in the trade in goods and the income balance was able to transform the current account deficit to a substantial surplus. The main driver behind this was precisely Hungary's region, as Austria utilised the region's business opportunities through trade and capital investments (Figure 289).

Figure 289. Current account balance in the Visegrád countries, % of GDP

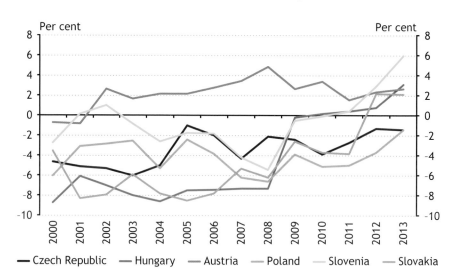

— Czech Republic   — Hungary   — Austria   — Poland   — Slovenia   — Slovakia

Source: Eurostat

With the exception of the Slovenian economy, the region started the 2000s with a current account deficit, and by the time the 2008 financial crisis unfolded, the Slovenian current account also showed a considerable deficit. It can be seen that in the early 2000s, only the Slovak economy's current account deficit was larger than the Hungarian deficit, and by 2007–2008, Hungary's current account deficit became the largest in the region.

Two key factors contributed to this: the mismanaged 1990s, i.e. the flawed market economy transition and the botched years before and after EU accession. After increasing sharply from 2002 and exceeding 8% of GDP, the Hungarian current account deficit stagnated at 7% (the highest in the region) until the onset of the crisis. The particularly swift and successful adjustment in the Hungarian current account balance started at this time, which was due to the expansion of exports and the balance sheet adjustment by the banking system. In autumn 2008, the Hungarian banking system abandoned its earlier expansionary policy based on external financing, and returned to cautious lending practices during its balance sheet adjustment. The substantial improvement in the current account balance between 2008 and 2010 can be mostly attributed to this.

The success of the consolidation between 2010 and 2014 is also demonstrated by the comparison of the Hungarian current account balance with the regional peers. In times of misguided economic policies, the Hungarian current account balance was the worst in the region, but when the right economic policies were pursued, the current account balance was on par with the best economies in Europe.

In the period of consolidation between 2010 and 2014, the improvement in the Hungarian current account balance was comparable to the Slovenian and Slovak progress, while the Czech and the Polish current account remained in deficit. The development of the current account balance over 15 years highlights two similar stories in the region: the Hungarian and the Slovenian current account balance followed a similar pattern in this period. The 2008 financial crisis was a turning point for both economies.

Before the crisis, both countries' economic policy was characterised by irresponsible borrowing. Later, the current account balance was improved by the banking sector's balance sheet adjustment, and the positive turnaround in Hungarian economic policy helped to sustain the upward trend of the current account.

Despite the similarities, however, there is a significant difference between the two countries: Slovenia uses the euro, while Hungary does not. Slovenia actually resembles the southern euro area countries with its poor performance preceding its current account crisis. The Slovenian economy also fell behind the Central European region, but, due to its membership in the euro area, it was protected by a financial safety net all along. Nevertheless, the use of the euro also imposed constraints on the Slovenian economy, because without a national currency devaluation could not help export companies. Hungary also lagged behind the region as regards the current account balance and economic and financial processes, but – since it was not in the euro area – it did not have a financial safety net. Nonetheless, forint depreciation (while exacerbating the situation of foreign currency borrowers) may have contributed to the improvement in the trade balance. Thus, for Hungary, catching up with the region in terms of the current account balance was even more important than for Slovenia, because the high government debt ratio and the consistently high net external debt made the economy persistently vulnerable, while the country was not secured by the euro area's financial safety net.

The current account balance is perhaps the best indicator of economic policy, as it includes basically all important factors that determine economic balance and growth. The balance of trade in goods reflects the situation of the real economy, while the income balance accurately indicates financial balance. One of the worst current account balance data series – that of Hungary – of the years preceding the 2008 crisis illustrates the deterioration in both areas: the duality of the economy, the banking system's external indebtedness and its interest in financing the artificial upswing.

Another substantial change is apparent from the 15-year history of the regional current account balances: those economies in the region that accomplished a successful current account adjustment, are "closing in" on Austria. While the Austrian current account balance steadily improved from the mid-2000s until the crisis, the current accounts of the countries in the region constantly deteriorated: the current account of the Czech Republic, Poland and Slovenia displayed the greatest fluctuations.

Following the 2008 crisis, however, the current account balances of Austria and the other regional economies started to develop in opposite directions: the Austrian current account balance first weakened, and then in 2010–2014 it recovered to some extent, but did not reach the considerable pre-crisis surplus relative to GDP. By contrast, economies in the region improved their position relative to the Austrian economy significantly – although to various degrees – with respect to the current account balance. Slovakia and Hungary made the best progress. The current account surplus of over 4% in Slovenia does not mark as substantial an improvement from the initial current account balance of approximately zero as in the case of the other two economies. Alongside Hungary, Slovakia made the most remarkable improvement in terms of the current account balance compared to the benchmark figures measured in the early 2000s: as regards the current account balance, the Hungarian and the Slovak economies converged the most with Austria.

Hungary becomes the vanguard in the region

This improvement is reflected in net lending as well. By 2013, Hungary had one of the best values for net lending relative to GDP among the EU member states. While average net lending relative to GDP in the euro area was 2.4%, the Hungarian figure was over 6% (Figure 290).

As we saw, the Slovenian and the Slovak economies displayed similarly swift, successful balance sheet adjustments, which was reflected in the current account balance and net lending at the same time. With the region's best figure in this important financial indicator, Hungary became one of the top-performing EU member states. In the years ahead, this is expected to be maintained, as the income balance – which is predicted to improve as a result of the elimination of household foreign currency loans – will support it.

The overhaul of the banking system's ownership structure may also contribute to this, as should the return of prudent lending conditions in the banking system.

Figure 290. Net lending in European Union countries in 2014, % of GDP

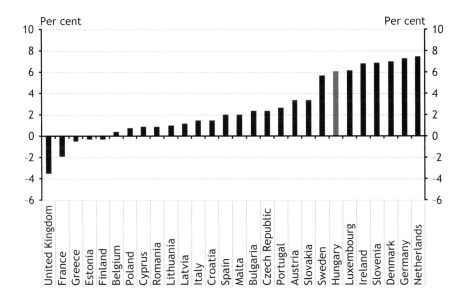

Source: Based on the European Commission 2014 Spring forecast

As has been shown, of the countries in the region, Hungary's net lending – i.e. the financial risk based on the development of the current account and the capital account – improved the most. After the 2008 financial crisis, net lending improved in the Hungarian, Polish and Slovak economies. Meanwhile, the Czech economy did not experience such a rapid improvement, which was mainly due to the income balance that was in even worse shape than in Hungary (Figure 291).

In the case of Hungary, both the balance of goods and services and the transfer balance improved after the crisis, which was not true for the trade balance of Poland, and the foreign trade of Slovakia also showed an uneven picture in 2008–2014. The transfer balance improved substantially in all four economies following the 2008 crisis.

Figure 291. Current account and capital account developments
in Visegrád countries, % of GDP

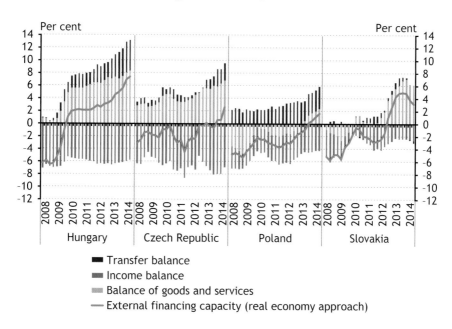

Source: MNB, Eurostat   *Four-quarter figures*

The national currencies of Slovakia and the Czech Republic displayed no or only slight real depreciation in terms of the ULC-based real exchange rate. By contrast, with respect to the ULC-based real exchange rate, the Hungarian currency depreciated the most (Figure 292).

Of course, this was partly due the earlier overvaluation, but the real exchange rate trend in the two groups may exert a significant impact on the relative competitiveness of regional countries. It has been demonstrated that, as a result of the flawed economic policy, the forint became overvalued compared to the equilibrium EUR/HUF exchange rate, which played a role in the emergence of imbalances and real economy distortions. This overvalued EUR/HUF exchange rate started changing after the crisis, especially after 2010, and the new exchange rate suggested a shift towards the equilibrium level.

Figure 292. Development of ULC-based real exchange rates in the region

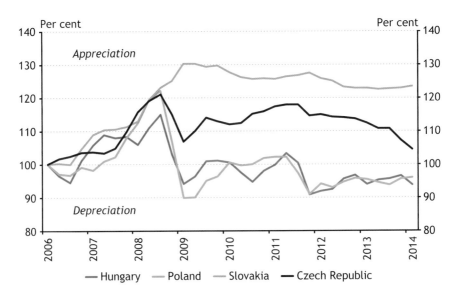

Exchange rate index calculated based on 37 foreign trade partners. 2006 Q1 = 100

Source: Eurostat

The equilibrium or disequilibrium real exchange rate – which in addition to unit labour costs captures inflation and the change in productivity as well – has a marked effect on the competitiveness of the Hungarian economy, especially when conflicting trends can be observed in the country's natural region (Central Europe and the CEE countries). From the perspective of economic growth in the coming years, one of the hidden reserves of the Hungarian economy is that the EUR/HUF real exchange rate has started the adjustment process, which will naturally lead the artificially overvalued national currency towards the equilibrium exchange rate level.

One of the greatest hidden reserves of the Hungarian economy within the region is that economic policy and the central bank's monetary policy have shifted towards more balance in finances and the real economy. The reorientation of monetary policy by the central bank in

2013 made it clear that the Hungarian central bank has only one anchor when taking its monetary policy decisions: the medium-term inflation target. This means that it does not have an exchange rate target, i.e. when making monetary policy decisions, the exchange rate is only taken into account if it affects the medium-term inflation target.

As long as the 3% medium-term inflation target is not jeopardised by the development of the exchange rate, the central bank considers the exchange rate on the financial markets as exogenous to monetary policy.

Economic policy and monetary policy have the same goals: a balanced budget, an equilibrium base rate, equilibrium commercial bank interest rates, an equilibrium real exchange rate and market balance (inflation around 3%). In the region, the harmony between economic policy and the central bank's policy has become a competitive advantage, and in the case of the Hungarian economy, this harmony was already achieved in 2013–2014.

Figure 293. Change in the number of employed
in the age group 15-64 compared to 2010 Q1

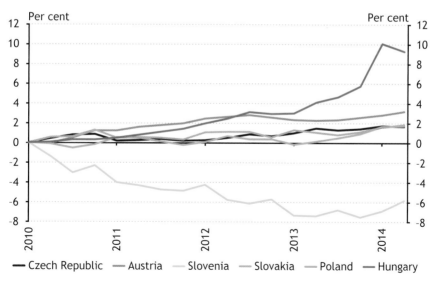

Source: Eurostat   Seasonally adjusted data

In a regional comparison, the development of employment between 2010 and 2014 was similarly positive. Among the economies of the European Union, the employment rate expanded the most in Hungary, which can be attributed to several factors.

Of course, in terms of the countries in the region, Hungary's employment rate was the lowest at the time when crisis management was launched in mid-2010. The very low employment rate and the high unemployment rate in mid-2010 was fundamentally influenced by the economic policies of two periods. They reflect the forced and misguided market economy transition between 1990 and 1996, as well as the flawed and failed economic policy targeting the re-establishment of economic balance in 2002–2010 (Figure 293).

Despite the low base it started out from, the fact that Hungary was the top performer in the region proves that its crisis management was successful in restoring economic balance and growth, in the financial system and in the real economy as well. A counterexample for this is the plummeting employment rate in Slovenia, which started from a high level in 2010, but as a result of the response given to a similarly ill-advised economic policy, then tumbled in 2010–2014. It is clear that at the time of the EU accession and when Slovenia joined the euro area the country's economic policy deteriorated to a similar degree as in Hungary, but Slovenia – as a member of the euro area – was not able to address this with a new economic policy combining conventional and unconventional elements. Although Slovenia's financial balance improved, in the meantime the stability of the real economy was undermined. A fiscal turnaround was accomplished, but economic stabilisation was not, which was reflected by the drop in the employment rate.

The stagnating employment rate in Poland in 2010–2014 is puzzling, since in terms of the other macroeconomic indicators the Polish economy was the top performer in the region. The employment rate in Poland had been low in an EU context, but it increased between 2010 and 2014 because the economic crisis in 2008–2010 did not affect the Polish economy. In the years following the crisis, the Polish economy was unable to raise its persistently low employment rate and to reduce the consistently high unemployment rate, despite strong GDP growth and a healthy financial system. The development of the Hungarian and Polish employment figures in 2010–2014 illustrates the basic difference between the two economic policies: in Poland, employment was not given as much weight as economic balance and growth.

Polish economic policymakers – unlike their Hungarian counterparts – did not launch public work programmes or structural reforms aimed at the transformation of the labour market. The Polish economic policy was primarily based on the traditional "economic balance and growth" formula, but it managed to avoid the peaks and troughs caused by economic policy in Hungary between 1990 and 2010, and actually remained fairly stable. The market economy transition in Poland was not achieved by shock therapy but, conversely, by a gradual, multi-stage process. The positive effects of this are observable in macroeconomic balance, in growth, in the financial sector and in the real economy as well. In fact, the Polish economic policy relied heavily on the export of labour for several decades, especially around EU accession in 2004: there is a strong presence of Polish workers primarily in Western European economies, but also in the global economy.

Hungarian economic policy was forced to follow a new path from mid-2010, because it was faced with the combined impacts of the failed market economy transition of the first half of the 1990s and of the similarly failed and flawed economic policy between 2002 and 2010. Although the Hungarian workforce is also increasingly taking up employment in EU member states (albeit not in such large numbers as the Polish), the Hungarian employment rate is even worse than the Polish. In fact, the success of the Polish economic policy conceals a weakness: no turnaround was accomplished in employment, even though the results in economic balance and growth in the 25 years after 1990 are exemplary.

The fact that Hungary accomplished the best improvement in terms of the employment rate is important, because without that sustainable economic balance and durable economic growth cannot be achieved. The less advantageous initial position presented the opportunity to start a new political era and launch a new economic policy, and in the end, despite its earlier disadvantage, Hungary produced better results than its peers in the region.

Chapter 24

Lessons from Hungary's successful crisis management

Under the previous system prior to 1990, the Hungarian economy was already characterised by a dual structure, consisting of a foreign-owned corporate sector producing mainly for export and a Hungarian-owned SME sector focused primarily on the domestic market. The sector of large enterprises was open to the economies operating under Soviet system, while the hidden sector of small companies concentrated on the domestic market. There were many SMEs operating, which were actually artificially integrated into the large, state-owned enterprises. During the restructuring of ownership which occurred after the change of political regime in 1948, the SMEs which had previously been privately owned were generally integrated into a large enterprise with its headquarters in Budapest.

One feature of the dualistic structure of the economy prior to 1990 was that most of the large enterprises were not real large enterprises, because they operated as an artificial conglomeration of small and medium-sized companies. Another aspect of this dualistic structure was that the Hungarian economy was similar to that of a developed economy in terms of its sectoral structure, but at the same time it lagged far behind the performance of developed economies in terms of technology and productivity. Viewed from the outside, the structure of the Hungarian economy was developed, with a high share of industry and manufacturing. The ratio of sectors involved in the second wave of industrialisation, such as the chemicals industry, vehicle manufacturing, electronics and the production of medical equipment, was similar to the ratios in developed countries, but the quality indicators lagged behind the performance of such countries.

In the pre-1990 system, the small share of private ownership only resembled the fledgling stage of a later market economy. Thanks to economic reforms, at the beginning of the 1980s the steadily perfected planned economy regime opened up internally to allow market economy structures.

As the independence of the internal units of large, state-owned enterprises increased, a unique kind of "management ownership" developed, and the sphere of privately-owned micro and small companies which were not state owned became stronger and stronger.

It was with this peculiar economic structure featuring numerous dualistic dimensions that Hungary began its shock therapy transition to a market economy in the early 1990s. The Soviet system collapsed in 1989–1992, the Eastern markets suddenly disappeared for the large, state-owned enterprises, and the shock therapy approach to transition used privatisation as its main tool for constructing a system centred around private ownership.

Theoretically, several different approaches could have been taken. It would have been possible to legalise the earlier "management ownership" using a unique form of management buy-out, by means of which the managers and employees of the internal, decentralised units of the previously state-owned enterprises would have become the owners of the SMEs which would have been privately owned.

The state's ownership in strategic sectors could have been maintained. The later "privatisation" in the Czech Republic, for example, was based on an earlier Hungarian proposal: the Czechs reorganised the old large state-owned enterprises into state holding companies. Later, over a longer period of time of 5–15 years, the assets of these holding companies were privatised, and by doing so the Czech Republic was able to avoid the sharp decline in assets triggered by the shock therapy transition to a market economy. The shock therapy approach resulted in an immediate, sharp depreciation in state assets, as the external markets disappeared and domestic demand also plunged, and consequently the market value of the state's assets decreased dramatically. In the case of shock therapy, this loss of assets is concentrated in a period of just a few years, whereas with a steady, gradual transition to a market economy the impact appears over a span of 5–15 years, and the prolonged nature of the decline also helps to mitigate its extent.

The third solution would have been for the privatisation by the state to steer state assets towards the private sector which had formed between 1980 and 1990. In this case, the micro and small companies operating in the "second" economy could have been the purchasers.

Hungary's transition to a market economy, however, opted for a fourth solution: the majority of the previously state-owned companies were sold to foreign investors. This already started during the first political cycle in 1990–1994, but the transfer of strategic groups of enterprises into foreign ownership mainly occurred during the second political cycle between 1994 and 1998. There was a dramatic loss of assets in the previously state-owned enterprises, in part due to the collapse of the Eastern markets and in part because large enterprises which were not interesting for foreign investors were closed down. Producers for the domestic market also shrank to a fraction of their earlier value, due to the plunge in domestic consumption.

Hidden and obvious imbalances

In the pre-1990 political system, imbalances developed in line with the economic policy and investment cycles: there was no market control in the planned economy system and thus nothing limited the internal propensity towards imbalance. The shock therapy transition undertaken in the first half of the 1990s established market control, but added a new factor into Hungary's economic structure which tended to be vulnerable to imbalances, as low employment and the new duality in the market economy environment generated a steady cycle of deterioration in economic balance.

This occurred in 1994–1995, when the twin deficit indicated that the paradigm of "balance or growth" had resurfaced in the market economy environment. The consolidation programme executed in the mid-1990s reined in the rampant government debt using the proceeds from privatisation, but this attempt at consolidation also resulted in growth and employment losses and reinforced the dualistic structure of the economy. Between 2002 and 2010, economic policy upset balance in all parts of the economy, with high budget deficits, a massive increase in government debt, high inflation and a large current account deficit, and then attempted twice to redress some of these imbalances. These attempts were unsuccessful, because the employment and growth sacrifices reinforced the hidden tendency towards internal imbalance which was inherent in the economic structure.

In the years prior to the 2008 crisis, a number of underlying factors laid the groundwork for the later crisis, such as the deviation of the EUR/HUF exchange rate from the equilibrium rate, the artificially high policy rate and HUF lending rates, and the spread of foreign currency lending. The key to solving the dualistic structure of the economy would have been to recapitalise the Hungarian-owned SME sector, providing these companies with inexpensive funds and stronger supplier relationships and steering them towards new markets. This would have increased the level of Hungarian employment first to the EU average, and then to 65% and later 70%–75%, resulting in sustainable economic balance and lasting economic growth. The consolidation attempts before and after the crisis moved in two different direction and it was only natural for them to fail as a result.

Any economic policy which attempts to remedy regularly occurring financial imbalances at the expense of sacrifices in the real economy, including losses in the field of employment, is flawed, because it increases the internal imbalances in the economic structure and reinforces its dualistic nature. The excessive fiscal deficit, the rising ratio of government debt, higher-than-equilibrium inflation and a negative income balance (which generates constant pressure on the payments balance) are obvious manifestations of the imbalances in the Hungarian economy.

All of the external imbalances result from the internal imbalances. The Hungarian economy operates with serious internal imbalances in terms of its economic structure, ownership structure and financial system. The strongly dualistic nature of the economic structure leads to obvious imbalances, because most of the agents in the economy are Hungarian-owned small businesses. Due to the low productivity and less advanced technological level, this group does not generate enough revenues to protect against a high fiscal deficit.

The ownership structure of the Hungarian economy is also distorted, because there is a high ratio of foreign ownership in strategic sectors and in particular in the field of domestic monopolies. The profits generated in these areas regularly lead to high income outflows, which regularly cause an imbalance on the income balance, resulting in an unstable balance of payments.

The imbalance in the financial system is reflected in the fact that there is a high ratio of foreign-owned credit institutions in the financial system as a whole, and there is a high ratio of external funds in the banking sector's funding. The imbalanced financial system results in pressure on the state budget, the government debt and the income balance, and via this channel on the balance of payments. Its natural internal principle is the maximisation of profit, and to achieve this it makes economic agents running into debt in currencies of countries which are more developed than Hungary, thus causing regularly occurring imbalances for all three economic agents. The Hungarian financial system, with its imbalanced ownership and funding structure, finances the Hungarian state budget and Hungarian government debt, uses external funding to a greater extent than actually required by the Hungarian economy and, within a flawed economic policy framework, finances an artificial upswing in economic activity.

In the 1990s, economic policy incorrectly supported the evolution of this imbalanced economic structure. In the new market economy system, this led to an imbalanced structure in the real economy and the financial sector. This hidden imbalance manifests itself in the financial imbalance and the vulnerability to inflation. In the Hungarian economy, all of the imbalances reflected in the external, visible and ultimately financial macroeconomic indicators stem from this internal, hidden underlying economic imbalance.

Capital and economic balance

According to the internal logic of economics, there can be no other relationship between external balance/imbalance and internal balance/imbalance. A goods-producing economy creates the income which is either able or unable to establish an equilibrium level in the field of the state budget or government debt, in the field of foreign trade and flows of income, and between supply and demand on the markets. Internal imbalances in the real economy and the financial sector lead to the above-mentioned macroeconomic imbalances for the state and the market.

As a result of the inherited dualistic structure, the shock therapy transition to a market economy and the flawed economic policy during the two decades of transition from 1990 to 2010, economic balance in Hungary regularly deteriorated. Economic policy attempted to resolve these problems using internal resources, but later realised that it was more comfortable to use external resources: it gradually got the Hungarian economy addicted to external capital and external financing.

Without external financing, the Hungarian economy would not have been able to achieve the average 21% investment rate during these two decades; relying exclusively on internal resources, the investment rate in the Hungarian economy would probably have been substantially lower. If we look at three decades, i.e. the period between 1984 and

2014, we can see that Hungary's net lending deteriorated precisely at the start of the transition to a market economy in 1990: it was only with external funds that both the state and other economic agents were able to sustain the investment rate above the 21% average for the three decades or finance consumption which had been delayed in the past.

With the exception of the years after the 2008 crisis, the investment rate in Hungary consistently ranged between 20% and 25%, which is a rate suitable for sustained growth, from an economic history perspective. On the other hand, there was significant fluctuation in savings: the average saving rate of 19% of GDP actually moved between 10% and 25% during the three decades, in relation to the overall savings of economic agents. Following the market economy transition in 1990, the GDP-proportionate saving rate for the Hungarian economy drops steeply, as both companies and households responded to the deterioration in their income situation by saving less (Figure 294).

Figure 294. Saving and investment rate in the Hungarian economy

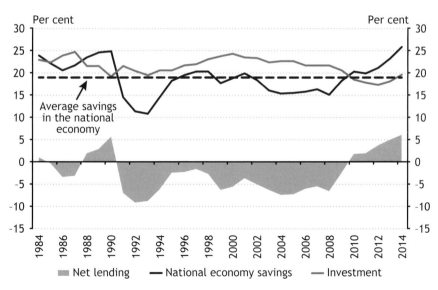

Source: HCSO, MNB   *percentage of GDP*

Despite this, the investment rate remained consistently above 20% of GDP between 1990 and 2008, and thus external funds were used to finance a significant portion of the investment activity, instead of domestic savings. In the period 1990–2008, the need for external funds in the Hungarian economy was consistently high, exceeding 5% for long periods of time, and the reason behind this was the debt accumulation of economic agents.

During the first two decades of transition to a market economy, economic growth was regularly supported by investments financed from external funds. Prior to the transition to a market economy, the investment rate of over 20% was still financed by internal funds, with the rate of saving ranging from 20–25% of GDP, but this changed with the market economy transition almost immediately, in 1990.

During the first two decades as a market economy and during the period from EU accession until the 2008 financial crisis, one characteristic of the Hungarian economy was that, relying on its own resources, it was not able to maintain an investment rate which results in sustainable, dynamic economic growth. During the period 2002–2008, external debt accumulation fuelled an artificial economic upturn, and due to the higher ratio of real estate investments, the structure of this investment contributed less to economic growth during that period, compared to the investment structure seen previously and thereafter.

From the perspective of economic growth, the period of debt accumulation between 2002 and 2008 was useless and inexpedient, and also proved to be unsustainable as it resulted in deteriorating economic balance.

With this Hungarian growth structure, in order for there to be lasting economic growth and sustainable balance, a kind of foreign capital is required which creates the resources for financing it: this occurs with inflows of foreign direct investment. While the financing of a fiscal deficit using external funds does not automatically create the resources for repayment (similar to the case of external debt behind a rising government debt ratio), households' real estate investments financed using external funds also do not provide a foundation for repayment. By contrast, foreign direct investment can create export capacities, which generally tend to create a basis for repayment. Furthermore, this form of capital financing is final: it does not create a repayment and interest servicing liability, as the payment of profits is registered in the balance of income (Figure 295).

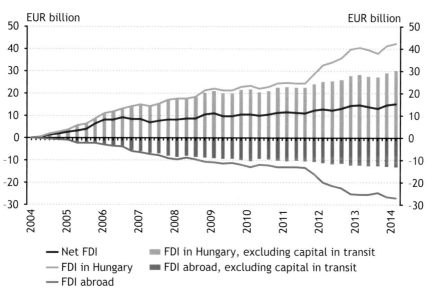

Figure 295. Foreign direct investment (FDI)

Source: MNB   Cumulated transactions

From the perspective of financial imbalances, this is a crucial difference compared to the imbalances which develop with the other forms of external financing, because although the income balance suffers from the transfer of profits, the government budget also obtains some of the income generated in the Hungarian economy via indirect and direct taxes, and the corporate sector and labour market participants also receive some of the incomes generated by the production capacities. In contrast to other forms of financing, the advantages of foreign direct investment far exceed the disadvantage appearing in the income balance (insofar as the investors decide to transfer profit and capital).

In terms of the tendencies towards imbalance which were incorporated into the Hungarian economy right at the very start of transition to a market economy, it is important to consider the extent to which it was possible to mitigate and offset these with "good" inflows of funds. During the years around EU accession, the inflow of foreign direct investment to Hungary increased, as EU membership clearly demonstrated its ability to attract capital.

The stock of foreign direct investment in Hungary is significantly higher than in the EU members in the region, and even higher if compared with the southern group of euro area countries. The group of southern euro area members essentially operate with negative FDI: the amount of outward foreign direct investment from these countries is larger than the amount of inward foreign direct investment. For the economies in the southern euro area group, this means that foreign direct investment results in a surplus on the income account in the balance of payments. The situation is even more favourable for the group of Scandinavian countries: the amount of outward foreign investment is substantially higher than inflows of FDI, and the significant export of capital means that a high level of net profit transfers is likely (Figure 296).

All of the economies in Hungary's region struggled with the inherited weaknesses in economic structure during the transition to the new market economy system which generally occurred around 1990. All of the countries had problems with dualistic structures, all of them had hidden unemployment, and all of them suffered from hidden inflationary pressure, but there are two closely related differences which can be perceived.

The first of these was that the ratios of inherited government debt to GDP (after cancellation and debt relief for Polish government debt) were substantially lower than the government debt ratio in Hungary. The second was that, as a result of the high inherited ratio of government debt, Hungary was forced into market economy transition using shock therapy. Its new strategic partners forced this on the country, whereas it was not possible to force this on the other countries, because they did not have this Achilles' heel, in the form of a high financing requirement stemming from the high level of government debt in the case of Hungary.

Figure 296. FDI in various country groups, % of GDP

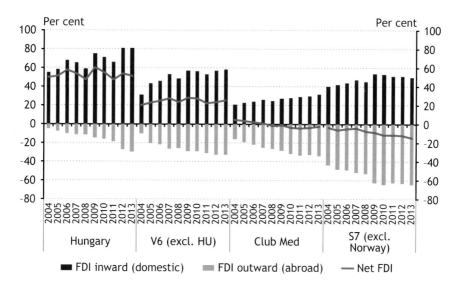

Source: Eurostat

Taking into account all of the economic factors, the logical conclusion is that the countries in the region which were able to adjust the imbalanced economic structure which they had inherited were the ones in which the high level of inherited government debt did not force economic policy onto a path with no alternatives. The government debt ratios in Romania, Croatia, Slovenia, Slovakia, the Czech Republic and ultimately in Poland were considerably lower than the Hungarian level during the early 1990s (the crucial period for market transition), and consequently the financing of government debt did not represent such a strong financial constraint as in the case of Hungary.

In autumn 1990 it was possible to force the Hungarian government into a shock therapy transition to a market economy, because the government had inherited government debt in the amount of USD 22 billion and at that time there were signs of an economic and financial crisis in the European economy as a result of which financing of the government debt was jeopardised: without the support of the IMF it was not possible to finance Hungarian government debt. In return for this support, they requested the implementation of a neo-liberal economic policy conforming with the prevailing global economic train of thought during that period: immediate reduction of state ownership, immediate closure of loss-making enterprises, a reduction of the state's role and the other measures required by the Washington consensus. If the ratio and amount of government debt had not been so high and had not been held exclusively by external agents, Hungary would not have had to embark on shock therapy transition to the market.

During the two decades of transition between 1990 and 2010, the reason that Hungary's economic performance lagged substantially behind the performance of its regional peers (as a result of the recurrent problems with economic balance and growth) is related to the high level of government debt inherited from the pre-1990 system. This is the one side of the coin, the other side is economic policy. Between 1998 and 2002, a well-conceived economic policy was able to achieve financial balance, dynamic economic growth and a substantial increase in employment. Although there were also global financial crises during this period (the Asian financial crisis between 1997 and 1999, and Russia's financial collapse in 1998), economic policy still pursued all three goals simultaneously and established the sustainable economic policy formula of "balance and growth".

Although there was intense pressure on Hungarian economic policy to adopt a strategy of shock therapy in the early 1990s, it was nevertheless basically economic policy errors which caused the evolution of the distorted economic structure. Similar to the case in 1994–1998, the mounting problems with financial balance, such as the twin deficit, i.e. simultaneous fiscal and current account deficits, could have been addressed with the kind of economic policy which was deployed between 2010 and 2014.

The trap of economic orthodoxy

The difference between these two trains of economic thought can be narrowed down to one single aspect: work, and the government's stance on employment and unemployment.

In the Hungarian system of values, work has a very important position, and this was not taken into account by the governments during the decade after the market economy transition. In the period 1990–2010, the rate of employment in the Hungarian economy was the second worst compared to the later peer group of the EU members. The factors which caused this weakness on the labour market should have been individually addressed by government policies. This would have been possible, as the low level of employment among women could have been addressed by increasing part-time work, the low employment rate among low-skilled workers could have been mitigated by training programmes and the low rate of employment among workers over 50 could have been improved with these measures and other special programmes which are used internationally.

At any time during the decades between 1990 and 2010 it would have been possible to treat the weak points of the labour market with various economic policy measures, just as this was done in the period 2010–2014. The value of labour could have been increased within the framework of a new tax system and the value of unemployment could have been reduced; employment among women could have been reinforced using tax measures, and the labour market position of low-skilled workers, young people and workers over 50 could have been improved with special tax measures.

However, trapped in the orthodox school of economic thought in Hungary, policymakers perceived the level of employment as if it were an incurable hereditary disease. The politicians in power between 1990 and 2010, economic policymakers, corporate managers and bank directors, and even theoretical economists (once again, with the exception of economic policymakers between 1998 and 2002) all thought that the pre-1990 company-internal unemployment had merely turned into overt unemployment after 1990, and that this was an immutable circumstance.

The fact that change was possible, however, was demonstrated by the creation of 240,000 new jobs in the period 1998–2002, and the almost 400,000 new jobs created in 2010–2014. For almost all of the quarter century of Hungarian economy history between 1990 and 2014, however, there was a continuous crisis on the labour market, as reflected by the fact the ratios of key groups of workers in employment were far lower than the corresponding ratios at the international, European and regional levels.

The trap of orthodox economic thought stems from an unusual introversion: the politicians, economic policymakers and economists from that period failed to look around in the world and in the region. It was only in 2010 that Hungarian politics and economic policy declared that it was incomprehensible and unsustainable that employment in the Czech Republic was one and a half million higher than in Hungary. The level of employment was only elevated to the same status as economic balance and growth in the government's policies during the period 2010–2014.

Thus, the previous economic policy – which disregarded the central role of work in the Hungarian system of values, ignored clear-cut international experience and took an introverted approach – found itself in a trap: it was completely unable to see the solution, the interests opposing the solution and the desirable direction which economic policy needed to take. Strangely enough, there is another factor behind this trap: forgetting the past. Since there was an almost unanimous opinion among the politicians and economists of that period that every single element of the pre-1990 system was flawed, they failed to analyse one of the characteristics which cannot be seen as unequivocally negative: the artificially high level of employment. In the centralised, planned economy system, the hidden unemployment within companies limited economic efficiency, but strengthened social capital. A secure job without work was better than double unemployment: the social situation of having no job and no work.

The years between 2010 and 2014 represent a new period for the economy, which will probably last several decades, because the governing political elite, the economic policy, and consequently economic thought has abandoned the earlier flawed approach, as the new economic policy and style of government is centred around employment and job creation.

2010 was a milestone in Hungarian economic thought, because this was the first time it was possible to consciously escape the trap which had ensnared economists for the previous two decades. Between 1998 and 2002, economic policy did not consciously work towards resolving the problems on the labour market, it moved in this direction on the basis of conservative, middle-class values, resulting in the creation of 240,000 new jobs. It was only in 2010, however, that Hungary's political and economic elite consciously discarded the previous flawed way of thinking. From that point on, political and economic decisions were no longer determined by the trap of orthodoxy: they were founded on pragmatism.

The close relationship between sustainable economic balance and lasting economic growth became clear and accepted, since deterioration in balance is followed by consolidation, which undermines growth, and employment appears as a third constituent in economic thought. From then on, it was no longer possible to fall back into the old trap.

Raising the value of work and employment represents a milestone in Hungarian economic history, because it was with this realisation that Hungary was actually able to close the two decades between 1990 and 2010. The two decades after 1990 were a period of transition, because the importance of work, employment and job creation, a high level of employment and low unemployment was not recognised in the economy. This new age started at the moment when work assumed its true position in political and economic thought. Thus, the period from 1990 to 2010 was a transitional phase, and a new period of economic history started from mid-2010.

Illusion of the self-regulating market

Hungary's political and economic elite was caught in this trap of orthodoxy which caused the failure, because it accepted the erroneous theory of the self-regulating market. Around the world, a revolution in economic thought occurred in the 1970s with the revival of the fundamental theses of classical-liberal economics, which were integrated into neo-classical liberal theories.

The economic theory of the 1970s abandoned the earlier train of thought which understood the state and the market as being in equilibrium and as each other's partners.

This theoretical and practical break with the past was caused by the over-emphasis of Keynesian theories. Keynes clearly stated that during a crisis the state should spend and during good times the state should save. In cases of deterioration in economic balance, economic recession leading to high unemployment, contraction in consumption and a collapse in investment, the state budget intervenes to support and replace market agents: spending by the state budget appears in lieu of market demand. Keynes warns against this during good times, and viewed deficit spending as a viable strategy during period of economic recession.

In the 1970s, however, high inflation appeared in the developed countries as a result of the two oil price shocks. Consequently, government debt and budget deficits exploded, meaning that a correction was needed. The explanation for this correction in theoretical economics was provided by Friedrich Hayek and Milton Friedman. From the end of the 1970s, the Anglo-Saxon political elite accepted the fundamental precepts of the neo-classical liberal school of thought in economics and as a result this new school of economics was triumphant. In this, the goal was not to achieve equilibrium between the state and the market: market forces took the top priority, based on the economic illusion of the self-regulating market. The transitions to a market economy in the region which started after 1990 were consistently guided by economic policies which accepted this market illusion.

Building on the theory of the self-regulating market, the dismantling of old government regulation plays a central role, along with the idea that there is no need for new market regulation activities by the state. In this understanding, the state is a bad owner, all state ownership is worse than corporate ownership, because the former is not able to exercise self-regulation with self-control, whereas the latter is intrinsically self-regulating. Market enterprises are motivated by profit, whereas state-owned enterprises are not, and therefore a market economy should only contain the former.

Known under the expression "neo-liberal" in European economics terminology, this neo-classical liberal theory – based on the logic of market self-regulation – deemed it necessary to dismantle public services and to replace them with services provided by the private sector. In the field of public services (since these were not offered by market participants and thus could not be self-controlling and self-regulating), it is necessary to replace state institutions with enterprises in education, the healthcare sector and all other fields of public services, because such enterprises provide services to society more efficiently. At the same time, this means that the public good is not better served by public property and public services, but rather by private property and services provided by private enterprises. In this conception, a high level of tax centralisation is always wrong, because it siphons off income from market participants, and – due to self-regulation – these participants are better at using these incomes than the state. This understanding makes no distinction between indirect and direct taxes (i.e. between taxes levied on consumption and turnover, and taxes on income), whereas the above statement does not apply to the former and is only applicable to the latter form of taxes.

In this old/new neo-classical liberal school of economic thought, a public budget deficit is always bad, and accordingly this new economic approach based on market self-regulation rejects the state intervening in a crisis. A later form of this is seen in the EU's approach to crisis management, which tolerates high, rising ratios of government debt, while punishing public budget deficits over 3% of GDP. The neo-liberal school of economic thought assumes that – thanks to self-regulation – the financial system will not induce a crisis and that the financial system's own internal self-regulation is capable of controlling the most intrinsic characteristic of the financial system: the desire for profit. By contrast, excessive spending by the state always leads to a crisis, because it leads to an unsustainable state, an unsustainable public budget deficit and an unsustainable level of government debt.

The neo-classical liberal train of thought tacitly believes that the labour market will automatically generate high employment and low unemployment through the mechanism of self-regulation.

According to the neo-liberal theory, external funding is always good for a country, because both the market agents providing the capital and the market agents using the capital operate within the framework of self-regulation, and thus they will only draw on external funding under the conditions and in the amounts which can be used efficiently.

Market self-regulation is an economic illusion, which is refuted in every respect by reality. In the case of the Hungarian economy, not all forms of external funding are beneficial: the spread of foreign currency lending was only good for the banking sector alone and only efficient in that sector for a short period of time. Market participants (in this case foreign-owned banks) abandoned the conditions for judicious, prudent lending, and self-regulation also failed to function in the sector. Nor is the labour market self-regulating, otherwise the second worst level of employment in the EU could not have developed in Hungary in the period 1990–2010, and there would have been no outstandingly high unemployment among women, young people, people over 50 and low-skilled workers.

The operation of the financial system is what triggered the 2008 financial crisis in the USA, which later spread to become the global financial crisis, followed by debt crises, fiscal crises, and economic and social crises. Indeed, it was precisely the lack of self-regulation by the financial system which triggered the 2008 global financial crisis, just as it was the lack of state regulation which caused the 1997–1999 crisis in Southeast Asia, as self-regulation of the capital market and banking system was also lacking there. The financial system is behind all of the financial crises seen in the last 150 years: no one could have reasonably thought that the financial system, and within this the banking system, would be able to tame its desire for profit via self-regulation.

Nor is a high level of tax centralisation a problem in its own right: the Scandinavian countries and other developed Western European economies have advanced into the group of most developed countries with high levels of tax centralisation. A high level of indirect taxes is actually an advantage in the case of a financial crisis, characterised by imbalances related to a high fiscal deficit or rapidly rising government debt. This is demonstrated by Hungary's successful crisis management, as the transition to the indirect taxation system resulted in significant additional revenues for the budget.

A high fiscal deficit can be accepted temporarily, if the point is to manage a crisis: this was demonstrated by the successful crisis management of the 1929–1933 Great Depression in numerous economies. That said, if the fiscal deficit does remain high for a longer period this actually does lead to long-term imbalances, and thus it may only be used for short periods and in exceptional cases for crisis management purposes.

The last four decades have not confirmed the neo-liberal economic idea that private sector services replacing public services are more efficient: this and the opposite of this also has been evidenced by the success stories in the global economy. Nor has it been proven that privatisation always results in higher efficiency, because there are owners which are worse than the state: those foreign owners who purchase a domestic monopoly in a country and withdraw from the country the income allowing for a high rate of profit, because the domestic monopoly does not require high investments commensurate with the steadily high rate of profit. The reason for this is that only part of the high profit rate of the domestic monopoly stems from amortisation and high asset requirements. The other source of this profit is the lack of competition: viewed from the perspective of the national economy as a whole, the profit stemming from the monopolistic nature of the business would better serve the economy in question, rather than having a private owner withdraw it from the country.

The idea that there is no need for state regulation and that it is worthwhile to dismantle all of the old state regulation is also incorrect: financial crises in particular have clearly shown that a lack of state regulation leads to crisis. Indeed, it is worth creating new state regulation for every new situation, where the risk of deteriorating balance arises. Innovation in the global financial system in the last two decades has brought numerous products to the market which need to be regulated, because they generate imbalances and lead to asset bubbles, but according to the neo-liberal approach, the regulatory authorities in Anglo-Saxon countries do not undertake to regulate these.

The self-regulating market not only proved to be an illusion in view of the facts and reality, it was also found to be incorrect from a theoretical perspective as well.

The market cannot be self-regulating, because for this to occur every market participant would have to have all of the necessary information at all times: this condition does not apply at any time to any private enterprise operating in any sector at all. In order for market self-regulation to function, the individuals and enterprises participating in this invisible, internal and automatic regulation must have all of the information necessary to make good decisions. As this is impossible, self-regulation fails to function: not only in the real world, but in theory as well.

Market self-regulation actually works retrospectively, via self-correction, but this means that the theory upon which self-regulation is based is incorrect. State regulation is necessary if the market only corrects retroactively, because theoretically the cost of a retroactive correction may be higher than that of proactive state regulation: in practice this is always the case.

The failures in Hungary's economic history between 1990 and 2010 also indicate that it is not adequate to leave the matter of a country's economic balance and growth to strong market participants (typically external participants), because short-term desire for profit is natural among private enterprises, but it does not always automatically lead to public good. Indeed, experience in Hungary shows just the opposite: throughout the two decades of transition, the public good would have been better served if the rate of domestic employment had not plunged to the second lowest among the EU members and if unemployment had not risen. Moreover, this public good would have generated results in economic policy and economics, because sustainable balance and lasting economic growth would have facilitated higher employment and lower unemployment.

Since it is only retroactive correction which functions with the logic of the self-regulating market, and this comes at a significantly higher price for the society and economy as compared to proactive regulation and deterrent measures, the theory of the self-regulating market is not a benign one; it is a malignant illusion, which ultimately costs all participants in the economy and the market more than if the governments had prevented the imbalances through proactive state regulation.

During the period 1990–2010, numerous political and economic policy decisions were based on this illusion of the self-regulating market, and this had a significant impact on the economic and social performance achieved during these two decades. If the market creates the common good and not the state, then it is worthwhile to replace state institutions with market enterprises. If private interests serve public interests best, then it is worthwhile to weaken the institutions enforcing public interests and strengthen enterprises representing private interests. If profit expresses the common good better than the value, because private interests are motivated by profit and the common good can be achieved by enforcing private interests, then value must be replaced with profit in all cases. If the financial market is self-regulating and moreover the rate of profit is higher in the financial market than in other sectors, then the focus should be on the financial market in contrast to the real economy. The value of financial investments must be prioritised over real economy investment, since the higher rate of profit in the financial market indicates higher economic efficiency and greater social utility.

If a business enterprise motivated by short-term profit considerations is better than a state operating in line with long-term values, then the time frames must be switched: those will be lost who plans too long time horizon. By contrast, short-term interests which are naturally motivated by profit provide a good compass for business and social decisions.

If external market participants are stronger than domestic economic agents, then they must function more efficiently: domestic agents must be replaced with external ones, because this increases the efficiency of the economy and boosts social utility. According to this train of thought, external capital investment must always be preferred over the capital adequacy of domestic companies, because this is justified by the difference in productivity between the two sectors. If we provide capital to the companies in the best group of the dualistic structure operating with higher productivity and not to the others, this will accelerate economic growth, resulting in more budget revenues, which is good for economic balance.

It was this train of thought that led to the dramatic mistakes in economic policy in the period 1990–2010, because it sustained and even reinforced the dualistic structure of the economy, kept employment low, and raised unemployment to a high level, resulted in an excessively open economic structure and led to a long-lasting deterioration in financial balance by shifting to reliance on external funding.

It would also not have been possible to launch the Funding for Growth Scheme if there had been a deficit on the current account, because this would have undermined confidence in the central bank's change in monetary policy. Furthermore, following the major shift in the current account balance, the reorientation of the central bank's monetary policy became credible and sustainable, thanks to achieving a very positive net lending.

Economic balance and growth

When crisis management was started in mid-2010, economic policy adopted a new formula: first, it addressed the fiscal crisis in the second half of 2010, in 2011 it put a stop to the growth in government debt and then stabilised the debt level, and by mid-2014 it achieved a historically low base rate capable of stabilising the economy, while at the same time it constantly enjoyed the positive current account balance's beneficial effect on economic balance. The turnarounds which led to durable economic growth did not occur at the beginning of the cycle, but rather during the second half of it: the combination of the rebound in consumption, the upturn in employment in the private sector, the trend reversal in investment resulted in a recovery in growth in 2013–2014 (Table 10).

At the end of the crisis management, however, the original formula returned, because the combination of the rise in employment (in addition to the public sector, the increase in employment in the private sector played a more significant role) and lasting growth render the financial balance which has been achieved sustainable.

Table 10 Successful crisis management 2010-2014

BALANCE
1. Government deficit ratio below 3% of GDP
2. No rise in the debt ratio
3. Balance on the goods market and inflation near the central bank target
4. Positive current account balance
5. Equilibrium base rate
GROWTH
6. Positive growth rate
7. Expanding employment and falling unemployment
8. Expanding consumption
9. Rising investment
10. Rising FDI
Σ Growth + Employment = Sustainable Balance

Source: MNB

Based on these aspects, Hungary's crisis management in 2010–2014 can clearly be deemed successful, because Hungary avoided a public finance crisis in 2010, avoided a sovereign debt crisis in 2011–2012, and was able to exit the EU's excessive debt procedure. These three economic facts are reflected in the recognition of the successful fiscal consolidation by the international financial market and international institutions.

Nonetheless, the true value of Hungary's crisis management is not merely that it prevented a financial crisis and stabilised financial balance indicators, but that it achieved this at a sustainable level and in a sustainable structure. The budget deficit of less than 3% results from a revenue and expenditure structure which is sustainable over the long run. Putting a stop to the increase in government debt is also a long-term success, because at the same time the share of government debt denominated in foreign currency is declining and households' share in holdings of outstanding government bonds is increasing.

In addition to the sustainable fiscal footing, it was possible to achieve a lasting decline in the government debt ratio and also to reduce the external exposure of government debt. Market balance and the policy rate are two more aspects which are both similarly lasting and sustainable. Although economic balance indicators can still deteriorate in the case of a dramatic worsening in external economic conditions, this will not occur due to internal factors, and economic balance will not be threatened over the long run by external factors.

The success of Hungarian crisis management is demonstrated by the fact that it was able to simultaneously stabilise financial balance and transform the structure for lasting economic growth. Financial balance naturally supports lasting economic growth, whereas in the two decades between 1990 and 2010 the deterioration in financial balance regularly resulted in economic policy measures intended to restore fiscal balance, which came at the cost of growth and employment sacrifices.

The success of Hungary's crisis management is underlined by the sustainable structure of the durable economic growth. This in turn is based on the sustainable structure of the production and expenditure sides of GDP. Agriculture, industrial production, and within this manufacturing, as well as services all participate in the expansion of GDP, while on the expenditure side consumption and investment both support growth.

Hungary's successful crisis management is a unique phenomenon among EU countries, because it was able to achieve breakthroughs in all of the most important factors at the same time. It simultaneously achieved a sustained increase in employment and a lasting decline in unemployment, along with financial balance and durable growth. In doing so, it actually achieved the formula for a lasting, sustainable economic upturn, because it maintains the fiscal balance below 3% of GDP, preventing a renewed rise in indebtedness, and lowers government debt, while at the same time boosting employment and GDP.

Figure 297. Unorthodox recovery: Unemployment rate (left panel) and annual GDP growth (right panel)

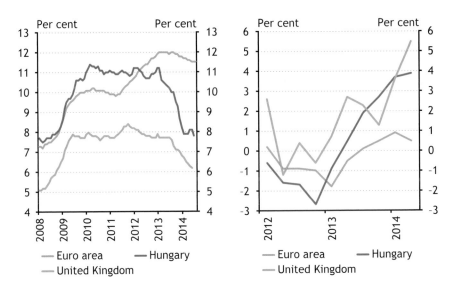

Source: Eurostat   *Harmonised, seasonally adjusted data*

This is an exceptional success compared to the crisis management in the euro area. During the second phase of crisis management in 2013–2014, unemployment fell substantially and steadily and Hungarian GDP was growing, whereas in the euro area countries unemployment rose and GDP essentially stagnated during the same period.

Compared to the UK economy, however, a similar structure can be seen. Unemployment declined in both the UK and the Hungarian economy during the years of crisis management, and GDP rose (Figure 297).

Decline in external vulnerability

The successful crisis management between 2010 and 2014 resulted in a significant decline in the external vulnerability of the Hungarian economy. It resolved the tensions between financial balance and economic growth that plagued the period 1999–2010. This set of measures, which was extremely concentrated from an economic history perspective, was able to establish the conditions for a sustainable upturn in the domestic economy.

In doing so, it led the Hungarian economy out of the dead-end trap of "balance or growth", which had regularly hindered Hungary's economic convergence and social advancement during the two decades since 1990.

The tools used by economic policy to achieve sustainable economic balance and durable economic growth succeeded in preventing financial crisis. The macroeconomic financial indicators of the Hungarian economy – such as the fiscal balance, the ratio of government debt, inflation, the base rate and the current account – are at or very close to equilibrium levels and point to a path of economic convergence, which will be accompanied by social advancement.

Structural reforms: the key to successful crisis management

One of the features of Hungary's successful crisis management in 2010–2014 is that the factors which allowed financial balance to be rectified over the short term also support a breakthrough in growth over the long term. Everything done over the short run to help consolidate the public budget, to stop the rise in government debt and then lower the debt, and to ensure market balance and a positive current account balance also bolsters economic growth and promotes employment over the long run. Structural reform is the economic policy tool which is able to simultaneously affect these mutually related time frames.

Based on economic theory and international examples, there is agreement that structural reforms have an asymmetrical effect over time, in terms of their impact on economic growth: reforms involve sacrifices over the short term, while their advantages typically materialise over longer time horizon. Due to this, one of their characteristics is that that they lead to the paradox of reform: over the short term, structural reforms generate tensions and political instability, and if a government survives this, only then can it enjoy the results of the reforms. This is the traditional view of structural reforms in economics, and, in line with this, structural reforms in the EU member states regularly run into the limitations of the time frame and the resulting political instability.

In numerous cases, governments weakened and collapsed during EU crisis management when they attempted fiscal consolidation by way of structural reforms. Consequently, the majority of these EU member states were not able to follow through with structural reforms which would have generated more benefits over the medium to long range, than they cost over the short run. These governments were unable to follow through with the necessary labour market reforms, could not keep the GDP-proportionate fiscal deficit below 3%, were unable to arrest the increase in the ratio of government debt and were also unable to stimulate lasting economic growth after periods of temporary stabilisation.

By contrast, Hungary's economic policy was able to do all of this at once, achieving a sustainable fiscal consolidation and durable economic growth with the successful crisis management. Indeed, the economic policy deployed in Hungary's crisis management efforts was able to prevent the development of social tensions and consistently maintained political stability. In 2010, structural reforms were initiated by the new government with its new political approach and economic policy on the basis of a two-thirds majority in Parliament, and in 2014 the government was once again voted into power with a two-thirds majority in the general elections. The success of the structural reforms launched in 2010 was one of the reasons for this, because the reforms initiated at the start of the cycle had already led to the breakthroughs and generated the results over the medium term, by the end of the cycle. This is the main reason that the EU's crisis management was unable to attain these results, while Hungary's crisis management was.

The group of EU members which were forced into fiscal consolidation (the southern countries in the euro area, the Irish and Baltic economies and the Slovenian economy) only launched part of the critical amount and composition of the structural reforms, while the other structural reforms necessary to achieve breakthroughs were not initiated or bogged down. In contrast to this, the programme of structural reforms at the heart of Hungary's successful crisis management reached critical mass, both in terms of the amount and the quality, i.e. the composition of the reforms. The structural reforms and economic policy innovations unveiled in mid-2010 covered all of the crucial areas of the economy and the financial sector.

From the financial system to the real economy, from economic policy to monetary policy, from the components necessary for the restoration of financial balance to the components resulting in the recovery in economic growth, each and every reform which was needed was initiated in the Hungarian economy at the very beginning of the 2010–2014 cycle. This crisis management occurred without a safety net from the IMF, and at the same time the country repaid the loans it had previously borrowed from the IMF and EU.

The structural reforms and economic policy innovations contained both conventional and unconventional crisis management tools. The traditional elements included the reforms in the Széll Kálmán

Programmes I and II, the rule on government debt, the labour market reform carried out in the framework of the new Labour Code, the increase in the ratio of household holdings of government bonds and freezes on budget spending items. The unconventional elements included the bank levy, sectoral crisis taxes, taxation of consumption instead of labour, the new tax system, the 16% flat tax rate on families' income, reduction of the corporate tax rate to 10%, the Job Protection Action Plan, the exchange rate cap and the reduction of outstanding foreign currency loans, as well as reform of the private pension fund system. The other structural reforms also interlink with the range of conventional/unconventional reforms. One of the characteristics of the Hungarian structural reforms was that they simultaneously support the conditions for economic balance and growth and are sustainable, i.e. each structural reform upholds social and political stability in each phase.

The success of the reforms can actually be traced back to one single aspect: the critical amount and the quality of their composition. In respect of the reforms which were needed, the crisis management strategy of the EU member states essentially only used traditional tools and used unconventional tools on rare occasion, while at the same time reforms were not even attempted in a number of indispensable areas. The EU's crisis management was actually short on reforms, and was timid and weak: viewed from an external standpoint and from the top down, the tools used for fiscal consolidation appeared brave, but in reality they lacked depth and breadth. They did not affect the welfare state and the outdated internal agreements typical of social market economies, and they did not result in deep-reaching structural reforms in the labour market, in the tax system and in competition.

By contrast, the essence of the Hungarian structural reforms was that they buttressed financial balance and growth with breakthroughs in employment and competition. The difference between the failure of the EU's crisis management and the success of Hungarian crisis management stems from the critical amount and proper composition of the structural reforms, but there is another hidden reason which played a major role in the differing outcomes. According to a simplified approach to economics, financial balance is mainly related to the fiscal deficit and the level of the current account balance, and other balance indicators are typically not taken into consideration. In mainstream economic thought, the equilibrium level of the base rate is a critical element. Consequently, the equilibrium levels for lending and deposit rates, the level of profit achieved in foreign monopoly areas, the rate of profit of the banking sector, and the levels of yields which develop for the financing of government debt are ascribed less importance in assessing financial balance. If, in an economy, the budget deficit is below 3% of GDP and, in the case of an emerging economy, there is a tolerable deficit on the current account balance, then analysts who follow this simplified train of thought in relation to financial balance will not deem a country to be risky.

The role of economic balance

Market balance is measured by inflation, which reflects the quantitative and qualitative factors of supply and demand. On the labour market, balance or imbalance is reflected by the level of employment and the rate of unemployment, as well as by other indicators unique to the labour market, such as the rate of employment among those under 25 and over 50 years of age, the rate of employment among women, the rate of employment among low-skilled workers and the level of long-term unemployment of over one year. In respect of government debt and external debt, the degree of balance/imbalance is measured by a global comparison or an internationally accepted level. In the case of the euro area, a ratio of government debt of less than 60% of GDP is taken as a guideline; a government debt ratio of over 90% is already a risky level and government debt higher than 100% generally indicates an unsustainable debt situation.[55]

In reality, however, the state budget balance and the development of the current account are mutually and significantly affected by the other balance/imbalance indicators of the financial system. The central bank's natural base rate, which is higher than the equilibrium base rate, is transmitted via the monetary transmission channels into lending and deposit rates, resulting in higher interest rates than the equilibrium interest rate level in the banking sector, which hinders lending in HUF. In the decade between 2003 and 2013, for various reasons, the central bank's natural base rate (which was higher than the equilibrium base rate) maintained the lending and deposit rates and the interest paid on the central bank's two-week instrument at artificially high levels, and pushed yields on the government bond market higher. The high base rate ultimately led to high bank interest rates, high levels of two-week central bank interest rates and high yields on government bonds.

Throughout the entire financial system ther was an upward shift from the natural and equilibrium interest rate levels shifted higher, upsetting the internal balance of the financial system, because the economic calculations of market participants were driven not by the natural and equilibrium rates of interest, but rather by artificially high interest rates above the equilibrium level. Not only was this much more expensive for the state, for the corporate sector and for households than the case of equilibrium interest rate levels, it resulted in a permanent, substantial distortion of all market participants' decisions. The central bank's high base rate promoted interest in foreign currency loans, as it kept interest rates on HUF loans at high levels.

---

[55] Countries which are able to maintain a ratio of government debt in excess of 100% of GDP for a sustained period of time are generally ones in which the bulk of the debt is financed from domestic savings, meaning that the lion's share of government debt is held by residents (e.g. Japan, Italy). In these case also, however, it can be seen that the high level of debt is a burden for the economy, which is mainly reflected in low economic growth.

In addition to this distorting effect, the real economy also suffered from the distorting effect of an EUR/HUF exchange rate which was artificially higher than the equilibrium rate. While all of this took place in a concealed manner, it was a constant factor in the decade between 2003 and 2013.

Imbalanced operation of the financial system for an extended period of time in an finally resulted in a "visible" deterioration of financial balance, e.g. a high public budget deficit, ballooning government debt and a deficit on the current account. As a result of the distorting effects on the real economy, the potential growth rate of the Hungarian economy steadily declined, along with the actual rate of growth, and at the same time all of the factors crucial for balance on the labour market also deteriorated.

These effects were reflected in the balance on the current account: a significant difference (deficit/surplus) developed between the average current account balance in Hungary for the period 2003–2007 and the balance during the period 2014–2015. Between 2003 and 2007, net lending reflected an imbalance amounting to 8% of GDP on average. This was caused by all of the imbalances in the financial system: the central bank's base rate which was higher than the equilibrium base rate, commercial interest rates higher than the equilibrium level, government bond yields higher than the natural level of government bond yields, and the internal risks of the accumulation of outstanding foreign currency loans which later materialised.

The success of Hungarian crisis management in terms of restoring financial balance can be traced back to the same reason as the consolidation of the state budget and economic stabilisation. In both cases, all of the factors resulting in the turnaround simultaneously worked in the same direction.

At the same time, the EU's crisis management was unable to achieve sustainable fiscal balance (i.e. a budget deficit permanently below 3%

of GDP: in 2013, nine countries still had deficits higher than 3% of GDP), and was not able to sustain economic growth, i.e. employment. The Hungarian economy was able to achieve this, because it launched and followed through with all of the significant structural reforms necessary to reach a turning point in the financial system and the real economy. The real hidden reason behind the successful consolidation and economic stabilisation is that economic policy and monetary policy combined to apply structural reforms to a number of areas, in which traditional economics sees no need for action.

*** * ***

Hungary's consolidation and stabilisation between 2010 and 2014 was a unique achievement by international standards and from the perspective of economic history, and deep below the surface, there is also another reason: a change in public's way of thinking.

Hungarian voters gave the new government a two-thirds mandate, because the public realised: we have gone astray and we need to make a fresh start.

The governing political elite realised that there was no way out of the crisis save for putting the budget into order. It accepted that a new economic policy was necessary to achieve this, one which would combine unconventional and traditional elements in a whole new way.

The vast majority of Hungary's citizens and enterprises realised that without a complete transformation it would not be possible to escape the crisis, consolidate the budget and reignite economic growth. Everyone accepted that the path to individual, family and communal success was through work.

We must be careful not to forget these realisations, because this better understanding has led to good decision-making, these good intentions have been transformed into good deeds, and from this a stronger Hungary has emerged. If we do not stray from this course, Hungary can look forward to a new future era of successful economic convergence and social advancement.

Appendix

Acknowledgements

Without the Hungarian voters, this book would certainly not have been written: I wish to thank them for their vote of confidence in a new political era and a new economic policy in 2010.

I must express my deep gratitude to Viktor Orbán for entrusting me with the implementation of Hungary's economic policy, first when he was the head of the opposition political forces and ultimately in his role as Prime Minister. I am very grateful that he constantly supported his minister and his team in the face of constant attacks; without his personal confidence and support this book would never have seen the light of day.

I am also indebted to the Fidesz–KDNP representatives for supporting our economic policy individually and as a group, and for believing that this new economic approach was correct, and for backing me unflinchingly in the midst of economic policy debates.

My thanks go the members of the Government from 2010–2014 for their professional and personal support, as the achievements discussed in this work are the fruit of our joint efforts.

The executive staff for economic policy at the NGM and the MNB worked together as a real team to achieve these crucial turnarounds in economic and monetary policy and I am extremely grateful to all of them. First and foremost, my thanks are due to Róza Nagy for standing by me as a friend, ally and the Government's most effective state secretary, and ultimately as the general director of the MNB. Cabinet Heads Helga Wiedermann and Marcell Horváth allowed me to maintain my freedom of thought while bearing the burdens of day-to-day governance and management. Norbert Csizmadia deserves my thanks for his creative thinking which helped our team to explore new possibilities. I wish to thank Ádám Balog for pressing forward with tax reform as my trusted deputy and later supporting the renewal of the MNB's monetary policies.

My thanks are due to all the directors and staff at the NGM for enthusiastically and professionally backing Hungary's economic policy turnaround between 2010 and the spring of 2013. Special thanks go to György Naszvadi and Benő Banai for finding the best solution in consolidating the government budget and for rising above their specialisation in fiscal policy issues to make decisions like true economic policy leaders. I am indebted to Sándor Czomba and Kolos Kardkovács for helping develop the tools that paved the way for the turnaround in the key field of employment.

I must thank the current directors at the MNB for putting their faith in our new monetary policy. I am particularly grateful to Márton Nagy and his colleagues for directing the Funding for Growth Scheme. I also wish to thank László Windisch and his team for providing focused, effective support in transforming Hungary's financial system.

Without the support of the members of the MNB's Monetary Council, it would not have been possible for the components of the new monetary policy to support Hungary's economic policy.

Many, many others also supported and facilitated the birth and final form of this book and I am grateful to them all, including the working group which finalised the book, especially to Dániel Palotai, head of the working group, and to Barnabás Virág and Péter Monoki, who smoothed the author's sometimes rough expression and honed the book's messages. I also express my gratitude to the other members of the working group – Gergely Baksay, Balázs Csomós, Dóra Danyik, Gergely Fábián, Zsuzsa Kékesi, Péter Koroknai, Kristóf Lehmann, Balázs Márkus, Gábor Pellényi, Zita Vajda, Viktor Várpalotai and Balázs Vonnák – for their comments and observations over the weeks and months: finalisation of this work was truly a collaborative intellectual experience.

My thanks go to János Ádám, Dániel Babos, Dóra Bak, Máté Bálint, Csaba Kornél Balogh, Tamás Bánkuty, Lóránt Baracsi, Bálint Dancsik, Péter Fáykiss, Sára Farkas, Júlia Gutpintér, Zsuzsanna Hosszú, Balázs Kertész, Zsolt Kovalszky, Emese Hudák-Kreisz, Gergely Kicsák, Balázs Kóczián, Ádám Martonosi, Dániel Módos, Zsolt Oláh, István Papp, Géza Salamin, István Schindler, Balázs Sisak, Ákos Szalai, Anikó Szombati, Gábor Sztanó, Ákos Vajas and Sándor Winkler for their help in preparing the figures and tables in the book.

I would like to thank Eszter Hergár for her enthusiastic, knowledgable assistance in bringing this work to publication.

Lilla Zsuzsanna Bak, Mrs József Bognár, Eleonóra Németh and Viktória Németh all deserve my thanks for their careful and tireless work in preparing the book.

Special thanks is also due to the editor: Beáta Sólyom's thorough, expert editing was a crucial factor in launching this work on its journey.

I wish to thank my publisher, György Bedő for his usual, but inestimably valuable support in the publication of this book.

Finally, but by no means in the least, I am deeply grateful to my family for their enduring, inspiring support. I thank my wife for standing by me without fail during all of the struggles behind the events in this book, and assisting with the editing in the crucial stages. I thank my sons for the fresh ideas of the new generation, Máté for his original thoughts and solid footing in the new economy, and Ádám for his insights into how the economy really works.

Literature

Recommended literature

Acemoglu, D. – Robinson, J. (2012): Why Nations Fail: The Origins of Power, Prosperity, and Poverty. Crown Business

Acharya, V.V. – Richardson, M. – Van Nieuwerburgh, S. – White, L.J. (2011): Guaranteed to Fail: Fannie Mae, Freddie Mac and the Debacle of Mortgage Finance. Princeton University Press

Atkinson, D.R. – Ezell, S.J. (2012): Innovation Economics, the Race for Global Advantage. Yale University Press

Beck, U. (2013): German Europe. Polity Press

Broad, E. (with Pandey, S.) (2012): The Art of Being Unreasonable, Lessons in Unconventional Thinking. Wiley

Madrick, J. (2009): The Case of Big Government. Princeton University Press

Ormerod, P. (2012): Positive Linking, How Nudges and Networks Can Revolutionise the World. Faber and Faber

Piketty, T. (2014): Capital in the Twenty-First Century. Belknap Press

Reinhart, C.M. – Rogoff, K.S. (2009): This Time Is Different, Eight Centuries of Financial Folly. Princeton University Press

Rodrik, D. (2011): The Globalization Paradox. Oxford University Press

Stiglitz, J.E. (2001): Monetary and Exchange Rate Policy in Small Open Economies: The Case of Iceland. Central Bank of Iceland, Economic Department, Working Papers No. 15

Wilson, P.H. (2010): Europe's Tragedy, A New History of the Thirty YearsWar. Penguin Books

Literature

References

Acemoglu, D. – Johnson, S. – Robinson, J. (2005): Institutions as the Fundamental Cause of Long-Run Growth. In: Aghion, P. – Durlauf,

S.N. (eds): Handbook of Economic Growth. Vol. 1A, North Holland, Chapter 6, pp. 385–472

Akerlof, G.A. – Shiller, R.J. (2009): Animal Spirits: How Human Psychology Drives the Economy, and Why It Matters for Global Capitalism. Princeton University Press

ÁKK (2013): Government Debt Management Report, 2012.

State Audit Office (2012): Jelentés az államháztartás központi alrendszerének adóssága és éven túli kötelezettségvállalásának ellenőrzéséről

Baksay, G. – Csomós, B. (2014): Az adó- és transzferrendszer 2010 és 2014 közötti változásainak elemzése. Köz-Gazdaság, Adózás különszám, 2014/4

Balog, Á. – Matolcsy Gy.– Nagy M. – Vonnák B. (2014): Credit crunch in Hungary between 2009 and 2013: Is the creditless period over? Hitelintézeti Szemle, November 2014

Barabás, Gy. – Hamecz I. – Neményi J. (1998): A költségvetés finanszírozási rendszerének átalakítása és az eladósodás megfékezése. MNB-füzetek 1998/5

Baum, A. – Poplawski-Ribeiro, M. – Weber, A. (2012): Fiscal Multipliers and the State of the Economy. IMF Working Paper, 12/286

Benedek, D. – Elek, P. – Köllő, J. (2012): Adóelkerülés, adócsalás, fekete- és szürkefoglalkoztatás. In: Fazekas K. – Benczúr P. – Telegdy Á. (szerk.): Munkaerőpiaci tükör, 2012. Budapest, MTA KRTK KTI

Bodnár, K. (2014): Part-time employment during the crisis. MNB Bulletin, March 2014

Borio, C. – Disyatat, P. – Juselius, M. (2013): Rethinking Potential Output: Embedding Information About the Financial Cycle. BIS Working Paper, 404

Borio, C. – Disyatat, P. – Juselius, M. (2014): A Parsimonious Approach to Incorporating Economic Information in Measures of Potential Output. BIS Working Paper, 442

Catão, L.A.V. – Milesi-Ferretti, G.M. (2013): External Liabilities and Crises. IMF Working Paper 13/113

Cséfalvay, Z. – Matolcsy, Gy. (ed.) (2009): Jövőkép - Megújított szabadelvű és szociális piacgazdaság Magyarországon

Csomós, B. – P. Kiss, G. (2014): Az adószerkezet átalakulása Magyarországon 2010-től. Köz-Gazdaság, 9(4)

Elek, P. – Köllő, J. – Reizer, B. – Szabó, P.A. (2012): Detecting Wage Under-Reporting Using a Double Hurdle Model. Research in Labor Economics 34: 135-166. Emer

Elek, P. – Scharle, Á. – Szabó, B. – Szabó, P.A. (2009): A feketefoglalkoztatás mértéke Magyarországon. In: Semjén, A. – Tóth, I.J.: Rejtett gazdaság. Be nem jelentett foglalkoztatás és jövedelemeltitkolás – kormányzati lépések és a gazdasági szereplők válaszai. Budapest, KTI Könyvek, 11

Endrész, M. – Kiss, R. – Virág, B. (2014): A lakossági adósságleépítési folyamat helyzete Magyarországon. MNB manuscript

Erhart, Sz. – Kékesi, Zs. – Koroknai, P. – Kóczián, B. – Matolcsy, Gy. – Palotai, D. – Sisak, B. (2015): A devizahitelezés makrogazdasági hatásai és a gazdaságpolitika válasza. Devizahitelezés Nagy kézikönyve, Nemzeti Közszolgálati és Tankönyvkiadó

European Commission (2013): Building a Strengthened Fiscal Framework in the European Union: A Guide to the Stability and Growth Pact. Occasional Papers, 150

European Commission (2013): Report on Public finances in EMU, 2013. European Economy, 4/2013

European Commission (2014): Private Sector Deleveraging: Where Do We Stand? Quarterly Report on the Euro Area, vol. 13 No. 3, 7–19

Eyraud, L. – Weber, A. (2013): The Challenge of Debt Reduction during Fiscal

Consolidation. IMF Working Paper, 13/67

Gazdasági tényfeltáró bizottság (2010): Jelentés az ország állapotáról

Gossé, J.B. – Serranito, F. (2014): Long-run determinants of current accounts in OECD countries: Lessons for intra-European imbalances. Economic Modelling, 38, pp. 451–462

Gourinchas, P.O. – Rey, H. – Truempler, K. (2012): The financial crisis and the geography of wealth transfers. Journal of International Economics, Vol. 88, No. 2, pp. 266–283

Halpern, L. – Oblath, G. (2014): A gazdagsági stagnálás „színe"és fonákja. Közgazdasági Szemle, Vol. LXI, July-August 2014, pp. 757–800

Hayek, F.A. (1945): The Use of Knowledge in Society. American Economic

Review, Vol. 35, No. 4, pp. 519–530

Hoffmann, M. – Kóczián, B. – Koroknai, P. (2013): Developments in the external balance of the Hungarian economy: indebtedness and adjustment. MNB Bulletin, October 2013 special issue, pp. 71–82

Holzinger, K. – Schimmelfennig, F. (2012): Differentiated Integration in the European Union: Many Concepts, Sprase Theory, Few Data. Journal of European Public Policy

Hornok, C. – Jakab, M.Z. – P. Kiss, G. (2008): Through a glass darkly': Fiscal expansion and macroeconomic developments, 2001–2006. MNB Bulletin, April 2008

IEO–IMF (2014): IMF response to the financial and economic crises: an IEO assessment. International Monetary Fund, October 8, 2014 IMD (2010): IMD The World Competitiveness Yearbook. International Institute for Management Development (IMD), Lausanne, Switzerland

IMF (2011): Hungary. Staff Report for the 2010 Article IV Consultation and Proposal for Post-Program Monitoring. International Monetary Fund

IMF (2013): Fiscal Monitor – Taxing Times, October 2013. International Monetary Fund

IMF (2014): World Economic Outlook. April 2014. International Monetary Fund

Kátay, G. (ed., 2009): The causes and effects of low activity and employment in Hungary. MNB Studies, 79

Kearney, A. T. (2013): The Shadow Economy in Europe, http://www.at-kearney.com/financial-institutions/featured-article/-/asset_publisher/j8IucAqMqEhB/content/the-shadow-economy-in-europe-2013/10192 Downloaded: 19 September 2014

Kiss, G. – Nagy, M. – Vonnák, B. (2006): Credit Growth in Central and Eastern Europe: Convergence or Boom? MNB Working Papers, WP 2006/10

Kiss, G.P. – Szemere, R. (2009): Apples and oranges? A comparison of the public expenditure of the Visegrád countries, MNB Bulletin, May 2009

Kiss, G.P. (2011): Moving target indication: Fiscal indicators employed by the Magyar Nemzeti Bank. MNB Occasional Paper 92

Kopátsy, S. (2000): T.E.T.T. A minőség társadalma. Kairosz/ Növekedéskutató, Budapest

Kopátsy, S. (2011): Új közgazdaságtan – A minőség társadalma. Akadémiai Kiadó, Budapest

Kopp, M. – Martos, T. (2011): A magyarországi gazdasági növekedés és a társadalmi jóllét, életminőség viszonya

Lane, P.R. – Milesi-Ferretti, G. (2001): Long-term Capital Movements. NBER Working Paper, No. 8366

Lane, P.R. – Milesi-Ferretti, G. (2007): The External Wealth of Nations Mark II: Revised and Extended Estimates of Foreign Assets and Liabilities. Journal of International Economics, Vol. 73, pp. 223–250

Lane, P.R. (2012): The European Sovereign Debt Crisis, The Journal of Economic Perspectives, Vol. 26, pp. 49–67. Lapavitsas, C. et al. (2012): Crisis in the Eurozone. Verso. Convergence Programme of Hungary, 2011–2015 (2011)

Matolcsy, Gy. (2008): From Vanguard to Bringing Up the Rear – A Chronicle of Lost Years, Éghajlat Könyvkiadó, Budapest

Mirrlees, J. – Adam, S. – Besley, T. – Blundell, R. – Bond, S. – Chote, R. – Gammie, M. – Johnson, P. – Myles, G. – Poterba, J. (2010): Dimensions of Tax Design. Oxford University Press

Mirrlees, J. – Adam, S. – Besley, T. – Blundell, R. – Bond, S. – Chote, R. – Gammie, M. – Johnson, P. – Myles, G. – Poterba, J. (2011): Tax by design. Oxford University Press

MNB (2014): Inflation Report, September 2014

MNB (2014): Report on Balance of Payments, April 2014

Nechio, F. (2011): Monetary Policy When One Size Does Not Fit All. FRBSF Economic Letter 2011–18

Obstfeld, M. – Rogoff, K. (1996): Foundations of International Macroeconomics. The MIT Press. London

OECD (2009): Taxation of SMEs: Key Issues and Policy Considerations. OECD Tax Policy Study, 18. Paris: OECD Publishing

Orbán, G. – Szapáry, Gy. (2006): Magyar fiskális politika: quo vadis? Közgazdasági Szemle, vol. LIII, April 2006

Poghosyan, T. (2012): Long-Run and Short-Run Determinants of Sovereign Bond Yields in Advanced Economies. IMF Working Paper, 12/271

Schneider, F. (2013): Size and Development of the Shadow Economy of 31 European and 5 other OECD Countries from 2003 to 2013: A Further Decline http://www.econ.jku.at/members/Schneider/files/publications/2013/ShadEcEurope31_Jan2013.pdf Downloaded: 14 June 2014

Schularick, M. – Taylor, A.M. (2012): Credit Booms Gone Bust: Monetary Policy, Leverage Cycles, and Financial Crises, 1870–2008. American Economic Review, Vol. 102, No. 2, pp. 1029–1061

Spolaore, E. – Wacziarg, R. (2013): How Deep Are the Roots of Economic Development? Journal of Economic Literature, Vol. 51 No. 2, pp.325–369

Swiss National Bank: Press release on the currency limit: http://www.snb.ch/en/mmr/reference/pre_20110906/source/pre_20110906.en.pdf (accessed: 19 September 2014)

Szapáry, Gy. (2006): Az inflációs célkövetés tapasztalatai Magyarországon. Pénzügyi Szemle, Vol. LI, No. 4/2006

Weber, M. (1982): A protestáns etika és a kapitalizmus szelleme: Vallásszociológiai írások. Budapest, Gondolat

Other literature

Backé, P. – Égert, B. – Zumer, T. (2006): Credit growth in Central and Eastern Europe - New (over)shooting stars? European Central Bank Working Paper Series, October 2006, No. 687

Backé, P. – Ritzberger-Grünwald, D. – Stix, H. (2007): The Euro on the Road East: Cash, Savings and Loans. Monetary Policy & the Economy, Oesterreichische Nationalbank (Austrian Central Bank), Issue 1, 2007

Balog, Á. – Matolcsy, Gy.– Nagy, M. – Vonnák, B. (2014): Credit crunch in Hungary between 2009 and 2013: Is the creditless period over? Hitelintézeti Szemle, November 2014 (Vol. 13), No. 4

Banai, M. – Reisel, W. D. – Probst, T.M. (2004): A managerial and personal control model: predictions of work alienation and organizational commitment in Hungary. Elsevier - Journal of International Management. Vol. 10 (2004). pp. 375–392

Berglöf, E. – Claessens, S. (2006): Enforcement and Good Corporate Governance in Developing Countries and Transition Economies. World Bank Research Observer, World Bank Group, 2006. Vol. 21(1), pp 123–150

Berglöf, E. (2005): What do Firms Disclose and Why? Enforcing Corporate Governance and Transparency in Central and Eastern Europe. In: Oxford Review of Economic Policy, Oxford University Press. Vol. 21(2), pp. 178–197

Bielik, P. et al. (2010): Economics, social policy and citizenship in the European Union -Evidence of V4 countries and perspectives for Ukraine. Visegrad Fund. Nitra, 2010. p. 263

Bogár, L. – Drábik, J. – Varga, I. (2013): Válság és valóság. Éghajlat Könyvkiadó Kft.

Bogár, L. (2012): Háború a nemzet ellen. Kairosz Kiadó, Budapest

Bogár, L. (2014): Tékozló ország. Kairosz, Budapest

Bonin, J.P. – Leven, B. (2001): Can state-owned banks promote enterprise restructuring? Evidence from one Polish bank's experience. Post- Communist Economies. Carfax Publishing, Taylor & Francis Group. Vol. 13, No. 4, 2001

Bonin, J.P. – Wachtel, P. (2004): Dealing with financial fragility in transition economies. BOFIT Discussion Papers, Bank of Finland. No. 22.,2004

Bonin, J.P. (2010): From reputation amidst uncertainty to commitment under stress: More than a decade of foreign-owned banking in transition economies. Comparative Economic Studies, 2010. 52, pp. 465–494

Boros, I. (2014): Árulkodó háttérképek pénzügyekről. Kairosz, Budapest

Brown, L. (2007): Economic and social cohesion policy implementation in Hungary and Poland and its comparison to the conditions of the Czech Republic in programming period 2007-2013. Regionální Studia (Regional Studies). 2007(1). pp. 39–41

Buckley, N. (2013): Confidence returns to maturing central and eastern European economies. Financial Times (online), 07. 11. 2013. (http://www.ft.com/intl/cms/s/0/d246cd7c-4572-11e3-997c-00144feabdc0.html#axzz3LI9kR5p1)

Büttner, D. – Hayo, B. – Neuenkirch, M. (2009): The Impact of Foreign Macroeconomic News on Financial Markets in the Czech Republic, Hungary, and Poland. MAGKS Joint Discussion Paper Series in Economics by the Universities of Aachen, Gießen, Göttingen, Kassel, Marburg, Siegen. No. 03-2009

Büttner, D. – Hayo, B. (2008): EMU-related News and Financial Markets in the Czech Republic, Hungary and Poland. MAGKS Joint Discussion Paper Series in Economics by the Universities of Aachen, Gießen, Göttingen, Kassel, Marburg, Siegen. No. 15-2008

Cienski, J. (2012): What's the point of the Visegrad 4? Poland's Sikorski speaks. Financial Times (online)/ Comment/ Blogs, 05. 07. 2012. (http://blogs.ft.com/beyond-brics/2012/07/05/whats-the-point-of-the-visegrad-4-polands-sikorski-speaks/)

Csaba, L. (2007): The New Political Economy of Emerging Europe (Second, revised, extended and updated edition). Akadémiai Kiadó, Budapest

Csaba, L. (2009): Crisis in Economics? Studies in European Political Economy. Akadémiai Kiadó, Budapest

Csaba, L. (2014): Európai közgazdaságtan. Akadémiai Kiadó, Budapest

Cséfalvay, Z. et al. (2000): A tudástársadalom kiépítésének forrásai Magyarországon a térszerkezetben és a szellemi vagyon növekedésének tényezőiben. A Matolcsy György által vezetett kutatás eredményeiről beszámoló publikáció. Oktatási és Kulturális Minisztérium

Diczházi, B. – Matolcsy, Gy. – Kopátsy, S. et al. (1997): Helybenjárás és szabadesés. Társadalmi Szemle. 52. 1997. 2., pp. 3–16

Egert, B. – Mihaljek, D. (2007): Determinants of House Prices in Central and Eastern Europe. BIS Working Papers, Monetary and Economic Department. September 2007, No. 236

Goglio, A. (2005): In Search of Efficiency: Improving Health Care in Hungary. OECD Economics Department Working Papers. 29 September 2005, No. 446

Goglio, A. (2007): Encouraging Sub-National government Efficiency in Hungary. OECD Economics Department Working Papers. 04 July2007, No. 565

Guerson, A.D. (2013): The Composition of Fiscal Consolidation Matters: Policy Simulations for Hungary. IMF Working Paper. October 2013, WP/13/207

Hemmings, P. (2007): Family Policy in Hungary: How to Improve the Reconciliation between Work and Family? OECD Economics Department Working Papers. 04 July 2007, No. 565

Hostomský, K. – Ženka, J. (2011): The automotive industry crisis as a determinant of regional unemployment growth in Slovakia and Hungary in 2008–2009. Regionální Studia (Regional Studies). 2011(2), pp. 25–31

Jolliffe, D. – Campos, N.F. (2004): Does Market Liberalisation Reduce Gender Discrimination? Econometric Evidence from Hungary,1986—1998. William Davidson Institute Working Paper. April 2004, No. 678

Goglio, A. (2012): Encouraging Sub-National government Efficiency in Hungary. OECD Economics Department Working Papers. 22 July 2012, No. 958

Kierzenkowski, R. (2012): Towards a More Inclusive Labour Market in Hungary. OECD Economics Department Working Papers. 23 May 2012, No. 960

Kiss, Á. (2013): The optimal top marginal tax rate: Application to Hungary. European Journal of Government and Economics. (December2013), Vol. 2., No. 2

Klinger, K. (2014): Polish Style: In-work Poverty. Visegrad Economy Analysis.21 March 2014, (www.visegradrevue.eu/?p=2360)

Kopátsy, S. (2001): Harmadszor Nyugat felé, C–E–T. Belvárosi Könyvkiadó

Landesmann, M. – Altzinger, W. (2008): Introduction to a Special Issue: Relocation of production and jobs to Central and Eastern Europe– who gains and who loses? Structural Change and Economic Dynamics, Vol. 19, No. 1, 2008, pp.1–3

Landesmann, M. – Gligorov, V. – Holzner, M. (2004): Prospects for further (South) Eastern EU enlargement - From divergence to convergence? Michael Landesmann and Dariusz Rosati (eds), Shaping the New Europe: Economic Policy Challenges of European Union Enlargement, Palgrave Macmillan, pp. 315–345

Landesmann, M. – Gligorov, V. (2010): Special topic: Redirecting the growth model in Central and Eastern Europe. Crisis is over, but problems loom ahead. Wiiw Current Analyses and Forecasts, No. 5, Vienna, February 2010, pp. 1–21

Landesmann, M. – Richter, S. (2004): Consequences of Accession: Economic Effects on CEECs. Michael Landesmann and Dariusz Rosati (ed), Shaping the New Europe: Economic Policy Challenges of European Union Enlargement, Palgrave Macmillan, pp. 149–184

Lauçev, J. (2012): Public Private Earnings Differentials during Economic Transition in Hungary. Budapest Working Papers on the Labour Market. 2012/2

Lentner, Cs. (2007): Pénzügypolitikai stratégiák a XXI. század elején. Akadémiai Kiadó

Lentner, Cs. (2013): Közpénzügyek és államháztartástan. Nemzeti Közszolgálati és Tankönyvkiadó

Lentner Cs. (ed.) (2013): Bankmenedzsment – Bankszabályozás, pénzügyi fogyasztóvédelem. Nemzeti Közszolgálati és Tankönyvkiadó

Leustean, L. (2013): Economy and foreign relations in Europe in the early inter-war period - The case of Hungary's financial reconstruction. Eastern Journal of European Studies. Volume 4., Issue 1., June 2013

Matolcsy, Gy. – Palotai, D. (2014): Növekedés egyensúlytalanságok nélkül – Fenntartható növekedési pályára állt a magyar gazdaság. Polgári Szemle. 2014. (10. évf.) 1-2. szám. I. fejezet: Magyarország jobban teljesít

Matolcsy, Gy. (1987): Fordulat és reform. Medvetánc. 1987. No. 2, App. pp. 6–7

Matolcsy, Gy. (1989): Helybenjárás avagy a lendület illúziója - A Fordulat és Reform harmadik születésnapjára. Mozgó világ. – 15. 1989.11, pp. 3–15

Matolcsy, Gy. (1991): A magyar tőkefelhalmozás. Valóság. 1991. (Vol. 34) No. 1, pp. 1–13

Matolcsy, Gy. (1996): A bűnös mintadiák. Kritika - Társadalomelméleti és kulturális lap. 1996. (Vol. 25) No. 12, pp. 13–15

Matolcsy, Gy. (1996): A társadalmi sokkterápia kísérlete 1995-ben. Magyarország politikai évkönyve 1995-ről. Budapest, 1996. (Vol. 8) pp. 232–239

Matolcsy, Gy. (1997): A fonák visszája. Kritika. 1997. (Vol. 26) No. 9, pp. 22–25

Matolcsy, Gy. (1997): Eredeti tőkeátcsoportosítás Magyarországon - A tőkeszivattyúk működése a 90-es években). Századvég. 1997. (Vol. 2) No. 5, p. 37

Matolcsy, Gy. (1998): Economic program of Hungary's mainstream opposition. Interview with economic adviser György Matolcsy. TRANSITION – The Newsletter About Reforming Economies. 1998. Vol. 9, No. 1, pp. 18–19

Matolcsy, Gy. (1998): SOKK (vagy kevés?) Kairosz Kiadó, Budapest

Matolcsy, Gy. (1999): A növekedés határai - közgazdász szemmel. Magyar Tudomány. 1999. (Vol. 44) No. 9, pp. 1063–1071

Matolcsy, Gy. (1999): Globális csapdák és magyar megoldások. Növekedés és globalizáció [Válogatott tanulmányok]. Kairosz Kiadó/Növekedéskutató. Budapest, 1999. pp. 68–104

Matolcsy, Gy. (2004): Amerikai birodalom - A jövő forgatókönyvei. Válasz Könyvkiadó, Budapest

Matolcsy, Gy. (2005): Adókereszteződés – Átalakítás előtt az állami elvonások rendszere. Figyelő. 2005. (Vol. 49) No. 11, p. 21

Matolcsy, Gy. (2005): Gazdaságpolitikai fordulat előtt. Polgári Szemle. 2005. (Vol. 1) No. 6–7, pp. 7–16

Matolcsy, Gy. (2006): Adóreformot, most! Magyarország politikai évkönyve, 2006. (Vol. 19) No. 1, DVD. old.

Matolcsy, Gy. (2007): A neoliberális gazdaságpolitika téveszméi. PolgáriSzemle. 2007. (Vol. 3) No. 7–8, pp. 6–16

Matolcsy, Gy. (2007): Értékrend és politikai stratégia. Polgári Szemle. 2007. (Vol. 3) No. 12

Matolcsy, Gy. (2008): Harmadik sokkterápia. Magyarország politikai évkönyve 2007-ről. II. kötet: Közpolitika. 2008. pp. 707–723

Matolcsy, Gy. (2008): Megújított szabadelvű és szociális piacgazdaság Magyarországon. Magyarország politikai évkönyve, 2008. (Vol. 21) No. 1, DVD. old.

Matolcsy, Gy. et al. (1992): Lábadozásunk évei II. - A privatizáció tapasztalatai Magyarországon. Válogatás a Privatizációs Kutatóintézet tanulmányaiból. Privatizációs Kutatóintézet

Matolcsy, Gy.(1998): A pénzfelesleg kora. Kritika. 1998. (Vol. 27) No. 11, pp.32–35

Matolcsy, Gy. (2000): Hungary's debt. From totalitarian to democratic Hungary: Evolution and Transformation [ed. by Mária Schmidt and László Gy. Tóth]. 1990-2000. New York: Columbia University Press. pp. 232–266

Matolcsy, Gy. (2000): Hungary's debt. Transition with contradictions: The case of Hungary 1990-98. [ed. by Mária Schmidt and László Gy. Tóth]. Kairosz Kiadó

Mihaljek, D. (2009): The global financial crisis and fiscal policy in Central and Eastern Europe – the 2009 Croatian budget odyssey. Financial Theory and Practice. Vol. 33. (3), 2009. pp. 239–272

Moghadam, R. (2010): Global Safety Nets: Crisis Prevention in an Age of Uncertainty. iMFdirect, 9 September 2010

Moore, T. (2007): The Euro and Stock Markets in Hungary, Poland, and UK. Journal of Economic Integration. 22(1), March 2007, pp. 69–90

Nowotny, E. – Mooslechner, P. – Ritzberger-Grünwald, D. (2013): A new model for balanced growth and convergence: Achieving economic sustainability in CESEE countries. Edward Elgar Publishing Ltd.

Prokop, D. (2014): Czech Debt Collection System Creates Poverty And Damages the Economy. Visegrad Economy Analysis. 27 February 2014 (www.visegradrevue.eu/?p=2301)

Revoltella, D. – Mucci, F. – Mihaljek, D. (2010): Properly pricing country risk - A model for pricing long-term fundamental risk applied to central and eastern European countries. Financial Theory and Practice. Vol. 34. (3), 2010, pp. 219–245

Schadler, S. – Mody, A. – Abiad, A. (2006): Growth in the Central and Eastern European Countries of the European Union. IMF Occasional Paper. 1 January 2006, No. 252

Schadler, S. (2010): The Crisis: The not-so-good, the bad, and the ugly (ppt for conference at Center for Social and Economic Research, Warsaw, November 2009). International journal of social economics. Vol. 37. 2010, 1/2, pp. 84–100

Swieboda, P. – Nic, M. (2014): Financial Times (Guest post): Central Europe's golden decade. Financial Times (online)/ Comment/ Blogs, 17. 02. 2014. (http://blogs.ft.com/beyond-brics/2014/02/17/guest-post-central-europes-golden-decade/)

Westover, J.H. (2010): Global shifts - Changing job quality and job satisfaction determinants in socialist and post-socialist Hungary. Emerald - International Journal of Social Economics. Vol. 37, No. 2, 2010, pp. 84–100

Wiedermann, H. (2014): Sakk és póker – Krónika a magyar gazdasági szabadságharc győztes csatáiról. Kairosz Kiadó, Budapest

Yoshino, H. (2009): Financial Policies and Dynamic Game Simulation in Poland and Hungary. IDE Discussion Paper, No. 187, March 2009

Methodological notes

This book is based on information available until 17 September 2014. After that date, there was a revision in the national accounts system in relation to the replacement of the ESA-95 system with ESA-2010, and this had a more significant impact on certain areas compared to normal statistical revisions. This change had a major impact on the statistical time series for the Hungarian budget, as – in contrast to the previous statistical convention – the transfer of assets from members switching from the private pension fund system to the public system is no longer accounted for at the time of the transaction, but is projected forward over several decades. As a result of this, the Hungarian budget balance for 2011 calculated using the European Union methodology changed from a surplus of 4.3% of GDP, according to ESA-95, to a deficit of 5.5% of GDP, according to ESA-2010 (cf. Chapter 13 for a detailed discussion of the issues related to the 2011 budget balance). This statistical revision also affected other macroeconomic time series, but to a lesser extent.

Due to the deadline for compiling the data, the data using the ESA-95 methodology which were available in September 2014 were published in this book. One significant aspect is that the use of the ESA-95 data ensures greater consistency between the data presented in the book and the data available to decision-makers for the period 2010–2014, as compared to presenting the data calculated using the methodology which was introduced later.

Glossary

Activity rate: The ratio of the economically active population to the working age population (usually people aged 15–64).

Actual inflation: Cf. Consumer price index.

Aggregate demand: The sum of planned consumption, investment and government expenditure on goods and services, plus net exports of goods and services (exports less imports).

Aggregate supply: The total of all the goods and services that are offered by producers.

Anchored expectations: When economic actors expect the inflation to be on target over the medium term, even if the current rate of inflation diverges from it, then expectations can be regarded as anchored.

Anglo-Saxon free market model: Also known as Anglo-Saxon liberal capitalism. This system is characterised by a low level of control, state involvement and tax rates as well as a strong focus on free trade. In Anglo-Saxon countries, individualism permeates the free market economy. Such countries include the USA, the United Kingdom, Canada, Australia and New Zealand.

Anti-cyclicality (countercyclicality): Refers to an indicator (e.g. unemployment) that changes in the opposite direction to that of economic performance. An anti-cyclical economic policy seeks to smoothen the cyclical fluctuations of the economy: at times of economic upturn it is restrictive (and dampens demand), while at times of recession it is expansive (and boosts demand).

Appreciation: The domestic currency (or, in other words, the exchange rate) appreciates when demand for the currency increases or its supply diminishes. In such a scenario, less domestic currency is required to buy one unit of foreign currency (and vice versa: more foreign currency is required to buy one unit of the domestic currency).

Automatic stabiliser: An element of economic policy for smoothening economic fluctuations without external intervention. Unemployment benefits are such automatic stabilisers, because they provide income for the unemployed during a downturn, thereby cushioning the effects of the negative shock.

Balance of payments: The balance of payments records the real economy and financial transactions between residents and non-residents. Its components are the current account, the capital account and the financial account. The balance of payments is accrual-based, so transactions are accounted for the time of the transfer of ownership.

Balance sheet adjustment: A balance sheet adjustment occurs when the financial accounts of individual sectors are reorganised due to some external factor. Since the 2008 crisis, major adjustments have been made in the individual actors' accounts; households and businesses are repaying their loans (they are net repayers), while the banking system is reducing its external debt.

Base rate or policy rate: The interest rate that best reflects the monetary policy stance or its change. In the case of the MNB, this is the same as the interest rate of its main policy instrument (currently the two-week deposit in Hungary).

Budget consolidation: Fiscal policy aimed at reducing the budget deficit and government debt.

Business confidence index: Business confidence indices are economic cycle indicators that basically try to capture businesses' assessment and expectations about the economy through representative surveys. Respondents are typically not asked to answer quantitative (numerical) questions, but rather qualitative ones (related to quality and trends).

Business cycle: The successive periods of economic upturn and downturn (or deceleration of growth) where the pace of growth fluctuates around its long-term trend.

Capital inflow: When external actors increase their assets or decrease their liabilities in Hungary, or when domestic actors increase their external liabilities or decrease their external assets.

Capital outflow: When non-resident actors decrease their assets or increase their liabilities in Hungary, or when domestic actors decrease their external liabilities or increase their external assets.

Central bank: The independent institution in charge of monetary policy. In Hungary, this function is performed by the Magyar Nemzeti Bank (MNB). The rights and obligations of the MNB are stipulated in Act CXXXIX of 2013, which is often referred to as the "Central Bank Act".

Changes in inventories: Inventories are produced assets that include the value of goods and services purchased by businesses, finished or semi-finished products as well as unfinished production. Changes in inventories are changes in the stock of inventories during the accounting period.

Competitiveness: It refers to the ability of an economic actor to sell products or services on a given market. It can be interpreted on a corporate, regional or national economy level. If a national economy is competitive, it is present in the world economy with increasingly profitable goods and services. There are several lists and indicators created by international organisations that measure this (e.g. Global Competitiveness Report, World Competitiveness Report).

Consumer confidence index: Consumer confidence indices are economic cycle indicators that essentially try to explore through surveys the population's opinion and expectations about their income levels, consumption and saving behaviour. Respondents are typically not asked to answer quantitative (numerical) questions, but qualitative ones (related to quality and trends). The goal of the consumer confidence index is to assess the confidence level of consumers in an economy as regards the economy's outlook and current status. Accordingly, these indicators can be used to forecast economic developments.

Consumer price index: The most important indicator of inflation. In Hungary, it is measured and published by the Hungarian Central Statistical Office. The consumer price index expresses the price change of a consumer basket consisting of products usually purchased by a typical household compared to the previous period under review. The index may be long-based, that is, annual (if the price change is compared to the previous year) or short-based, that is, quarterly or monthly (if the price change is compared to the previous quarter or month).

Consumption rate: Consumption rate is the ratio of households' consumption expenses and disposable income.

Consumption spiral: The concept introduced by Pierre Bourdieu (1979) characterises the consumer society of modern capitalism with the consumption spiral. Lower-income groups try to mimic the expensive lifestyle of higher earners when they purchase a mass-produced variety of a certain product. Since a wide range of products is available to a wide range of people, the distinctive factor is not the possession or lack of a specific product, but its quality and even more its certain symbolic features. When the lower classes imitate their social superiors, the wealthy start to look for another product or style which has not become widely popular to distance themselves from the others. Thus, as a result of the competition in quality and quantity, the economic sectors producing consumer goods play an increasingly substantial role in production.

Contribution effectiveness: It shows how the actually collected contribution revenue compares to the theoretical revenue calculated on the basis of the wage bill of the national economy and the contribution brackets set out in the legislation.

Core inflation excluding indirect taxes: Core inflation excluding the estimated effects of changes in the VAT, the excise duty and other indirect taxes.

Core inflation: An inflation indicator composed of products, the price development of which is less volatile and mainly shaped by market forces.

Credit cooperative: A credit cooperative is a cooperative credit institution with restricted authorisation for financial and ancillary services. The founding and operation of a credit cooperative requires at least 200 members. Both legal and natural persons may be members of a credit cooperative, but the number of legal persons may not exceed one third of the total number of members. An owner's direct and indirect share in the registered capital of the credit cooperative – with the exception of the Hungarian government, a voluntary institution protection fund acting within its function and the Hungarian National Deposit Insurance Fund – may not exceed 15%.

Credit gap: The credit gap is the current level of loans less their equilibrium level. The equilibrium level of loans can be defined in several ways. One possible methodology is to use vector error correction models, in which the model identifies long-term (so-called cointegrated) connections among several variables. Based on this, a given variable's long-term equilibrium as well as the pace of returning to it can be estimated.

Current account balance: The current account balance contains the trade balance (goods and services), the income balance, and one type of transfers, current transfers.

Cyclical component: The effect of the economic cycle on the general government balance which, for the most part, results in the fluctuation of tax revenues, and for the lesser part, in change in expenditures indexed for unemployment benefits and real variables.

Debt assumption / debt consolidation: From time to time, the general government assumes the debt of other subsystems or organisations in the government sector, if their debt levels become excessive. Debt assumption from the government sector does not affect general government debt or its balance, because the transaction increases expenditures and revenues in equal measure. However, when the general government assumes the debt of an economic actor outside the government sector (e.g. MÁV Zrt.), the transaction adds to its gross debt and deficit.

Debt-type funds: Within liabilities, we differentiate debt-type funds. These include liabilities where a repayment and/or interest payment obligation arises for the recipient (basically loans, deposits and debt securities). A loan is a transaction where the lender provides funds to the borrower who pays back the agreed amount (the debt) by the date set out in the loan agreement. In analysing financial statements, (bank) loans and deposits, as well as some portfolio investments such as bonds and money market instruments are classified as debt-type transactions.

Deflation: A continued, sustained decline in the general price level; "negative" inflation.

Demand shock: An economic shock resulting from a change in demand (e.g. a change in consumption preferences, a pick-up in public investment).

Demand: It represents the relationship between the price and quantity of a desired product. It shows how much the consumer is able and willing to buy a certain product at various possible prices. If the price of a product rises (drops), the demand for it typically declines (increases). A shift in demand may be caused by, among other things, a change in needs, consumer income and the price of substitutes or complements.

Demand-pull inflationary pressure: The pressure to raise prices due to increased demand.

Demand-sensitive inflation: This indicator excludes processed food prices from core inflation (excluding taxes), which might be warranted by the fact that the price changes of processed food depend greatly on the typically highly volatile price development of unprocessed food. Accordingly, demand-sensitive inflation shows the inflation of industrial goods, market services as well as alcohol and tobacco products.

Depreciation: The domestic currency (or, in other words, the exchange rate) depreciates when demand for it decreases or its supply grows.

Disinflation: A decline in inflation, i.e. the rate of increase in the price level; decelerating inflation.

Disposable income: The disposable income of households is the balance of primary income (employee income, capital income) and the redistribution of income in cash. Redistribution includes social contributions paid, social benefits in cash received, income and wealth tax paid and other current transfers. Disposable income does not include social transfers in kind (e.g. free public education) from the government or non-profit institutions serving households.

Distribution of income (redistribution): The secondary distribution of income through a system of taxes and subsidies.

Early repayment scheme: The early repayment scheme enabled foreign currency debtors to repay their loans at preferential exchange rates (EUR/HUF 250 and CHF/HUF 180) between October and December 2011. Coupled with this, the MNB held foreign exchange auctions for banks. Most of the foreign exchange needed for early repayments was acquired by banks from the central bank at these auctions. The early repayment scheme involved around 170,000 household loans with a total value of HUF 1,355 billion.

Economic and Monetary Union (EMU): The Maastricht Treaty outlined the three stages of creating the Economic and Monetary Union. The first stage (from July 1990 to December 1993) was characterised by the elimination of internal barriers to the free movement of capital within the European Union. In the second stage (from January 1994 to December 1998), the European Monetary Institute was formed, which can be considered the forerunner to the European Central Bank. This was also the stage when the financing of the government sector by the central bank was abolished in the member states. In the third stage (from January 1999), the European Central Bank began operations, at the same time when the common European currency, the euro was introduced.

Economic crisis: A significant slowdown or temporary contraction in economic growth.

Economic cycle index: An economic cycle index indicates the direction of basic economic developments and gauges economic performance as well as the cyclical position. Such indices are usually available monthly. Since they often provide information on future developments as well (e.g. confidence indices, information on the stock of orders and contracts), they can be used for forecasting economic developments.

Economic upturn: This refers to the growth stage of the business cycle characterised by the expansion of economic output.

Economically active population: The part of the working age population that appears on the labour market as active or as seeking work.

EDP balance: The general government balance indicator used in the excessive deficit procedure (EDP). Since the changeover to the ESA-2010 methodology, the EDP balance has equalled the ESA balance (earlier, from a methodological perspective, the EDP balance almost equalled the ESA balance; they only differed in the settlement of interest expenditures, which caused a difference in the two indicators of around 0.1-0.2 percent in GDP terms).

Efficiency of tax collection: The ratio of the actual tax revenue and the tax revenue expected based on the tax legislation. This ratio diverges from 1 due to tax evasion.

Employment policy: A public regulatory framework for regulating supply and demand on the labour market. It may aim to balance the supply and demand for labour force, to boost employment or to maintain it at a high level, to facilitate employment for disadvantaged groups of workers, and to improve the working conditions of disadvantaged groups which are already employed.

Employment rate: The ratio of the employed (those having a job) to the economically active population.

ESA balance: The budget balance calculated on the basis of an economic statistics methodology employed in the European Union (European System of Accounts, ESA). One of its important features is that it is accrual-based, i.e. transactions are not listed on the basis of actual transfers, but on the transactions' economic substance.

Euro area: The community of the member states of the European Union that introduced the euro in the third stage of the Economic and Monetary Union. Since 1 January 2015, the euro area has had 19 members: Austria, Belgium, Cyprus, Estonia, Finland, France, Germany, Greece, Ireland, Italy, Latvia, Lithuania, Luxembourg, Malta, the Netherlands, Portugal, Slovakia, Slovenia and Spain.

Excessive Deficit Procedure (EDP): The procedure initiated against member states that miss their budget deficit or government debt targets as set out in the Stability and Growth Pact. Punitive measures can range from a warning to financial sanctions. The aim is to keep the budget deficit below 3% of GDP, and to reduce government debt at a specified rate until it reaches 60% of GDP.

Exchange rate band: The band within which the exchange rate of the domestic currency can move vis-à-vis a major foreign currency or currency basket. The central bank commits to intervene at the floor or ceiling of the band, in order to keep the exchange rate within the band. From June 2003, the exchange rate band was ±15% from the central rate of EUR/HUF 282.36. In February 2008, the exchange rate band was abandoned and since then a floating exchange regime is in place in Hungary.

Exchange rate cap scheme: Since June 2012, foreign exchange debtors can use the exchange rate cap scheme, which helps them to repay their foreign exchange loans at a stable exchange rate which is lower than the prevailing rate (at the exchange rates of CHF/HUF 180, EUR/HUF 250 and JPY/HUF 2.6 in the case of CHF, EUR and JPY loans, respectively) for five years after joining the scheme. The principal in excess of the reduced exchange rate is transferred to a pool account and is considered as a loan of the debtor, while the interest in excess of the preferential rate is jointly borne by the bank and the general government. The loan accumulated on the pool account should be repaid by the debtor in instalments after the scheme is concluded.

Exchange rate risk: The risk for holders of FX-denominated financial assets stemming from the fact that in the case of an exchange rate movement, the value of the assets changes in domestic currency terms.

Expansive / loose monetary policy: A monetary policy where, due to lower real interest rates and/or a depreciated exchange rate as well as the rapid increase of the money supply, aggregate demand grows and inflation accelerates.

Expectations index: Expectations indices are economic cycle indicators that basically assess market actors' (businesses, households) expectations about economic developments.

External debt: The external debt indicator shows the external debt-type liabilities (loans, bonds) of the whole economy (the private sector as well as the general government).

Family tax benefit: A tax benefit related to personal income tax, introduced on 1 January 2011. Individuals may reduce their consolidated tax base depending on the number of their dependants (usually minors). In 2013, the amount of the monthly benefit was HUF 62,500 per dependant in the case of one or two dependents or HUF 206,250 per dependant in the case of three or more dependants. Since 2014, the unused portion of the benefit may be used to reduce personal contributions (with the exception of the labour market contribution).

Financial crisis: A disturbance attributable to fundamental causes that prevents the financial system from exercising its basic allocation function over the long term. A financial crisis may result in considerable costs for the real economy.

Financial imbalance or disequilibrium: The over-indebtedness of one or more economic sectors (e.g. households), or the excessive price hike on certain markets (e.g. stock exchange, real estate market), which is unsustainable over the long term. The spontaneous adjustment (correction) of such poses the risk of creating panic on the markets as well as a significant downturn or crisis. That is why it is best to avoid these imbalances or prevent their development, since adjustments entail disproportionate losses for society.

Financial stability: Financial stability is a state in which the financial system withstands economic or financial shocks and is able to exercise its basic functions (allocating financial resources, managing risks and payments) smoothly.

Financing capacity/requirement: Net financing capacity (net financial saving) means the portion of disposable income that the economy does not spend on consumption or accumulation. A financing requirement refers to a situation where the sum of income and domestic consumption is negative, i.e. when the national economy's expenditure on accumulation (investments and changes in inventories) and consumption exceeds the total disposable income of the country. It is the sum of the current account balance and the capital balance.

Fiscal impulse: The fiscal impulse measures how much financial resources fiscal policy withdraws or adds to the economy over the short term. There is no universally accepted formula for measuring fiscal impulse, but it can be basically assessed by the change in the general government balance adjusted for certain factors.

Fiscal policy: The approach to budget expenditures and revenues from an economic policy perspective (e.g. tax policy, social transfers, public investments). Its primary objective is macroeconomic stabilisation, income redistribution and maintaining certain public services. The fiscal policy of a country is usually determined by the government or the parliament.

Fiscal stimulus: Increasing government consumption or easing the tax burden to stimulate economic growth.

Fixed (peg) or floating exchange rate system: In a fixed exchange rate regime, the central bank undertakes to keep the exchange rate of the domestic currency against a certain other currency or currency basket on a predetermined path with the help of FX market interventions. In the case of a floating exchange rate regime, the central bank does not have an exchange rate target, so the exchange rate is free to move as determined by the forces of supply and demand on the market. The type of exchange rate regime fundamentally defines the options available to monetary policy. Hungary has used a floating exchange rate regime since February 2008.

Flat rate tax system: Taxpayers pay a flat tax rate irrespective of their income levels.

Foreign exchange (FX) reserves: The sum of all FX assets held by the central bank. The main reasons for holding such reserves are to fulfil international investors' expectations related to reserve levels, to meet the government's FX needs for transactions, to ensure the FX market intervention capacity, and, in certain countries, to maintain the exchange rate regime.

Foreign direct investment: Foreign direct investment (FDI) is an external investment by which an investor who is a resident in one country seeks to acquire lasting interest/ownership in a company that is resident in another country. In effect, FDI includes investments that result in an ownership of 10 percent or more for the non-resident investor. If one or more ownership chains start out at the same investor, then all the companies in all the chains are in a foreign direct investment relationship.

Funding for Growth Scheme: The Magyar Nemzeti Bank launched the Funding for Growth Scheme as an element of the monetary policy toolbox on 1 June 2013. At the outset, the programme rested on three Pillars. Pillar I consisted of loans for investment, working capital financing, pre-financing EU funding or the redemption of an SME loan or financial lease originally granted for such purposes. Pillar II comprised forint loans for the redemption of a HUF-denominated or FX-denominated loan or financial lease granted by Hungarian credit institutions to SMEs. Pillar III included foreign exchange tenders by the MNB to help participating credit institutions reduce their short-term external liabilities. Pillar III was terminated as of 1 July 2014.

FX exposure / open position: FX exposure (or, in other words, an open position) of an economic sector is defined as the FX-denominated financial assets less liabilities.

Globalisation index: It shows in an international context how deeply a given country has integrated into the world economy. The Ernst & Young Globalisation Index analyses 20 different indicators from 60 important economies to gauge this. The indicators are grouped into five categories: openness to trade; capital flows; exchange of technology and ideas; movement of labour; cultural integration. These elements are weighted based on the opinions of 992 prominent global business executives.

Government debt: The gross consolidated debt of the government sector at nominal value. Government debt is basically comprised of the deficit from previous years, which may be increased by assumed debts.

Gross domestic product (GDP): The value of the goods and services produced by an economy in a given period without the value of goods and services used in the production.

Gross national income (GNI): This indicator measures the income generated by domestic income earners. For Hungary, it can be derived from GDP by subtracting the income of foreigners and adding EU transfers as well as remittances from Hungarians working abroad. GNI is the better indicator for measuring the total disposable income held by the residents of a given country.

Guidotti–Greenspan indicator: The ratio of the central bank's currency reserves to the country's external debt maturing within a year. If it is greater than 1, it suggests that even if external financing is suddenly cut off, the country would be able to repay its maturing debt.

Household demand deposits: Funds on a current account that can be accessed by the customer at any time. Banks pay lower interest on demand deposits than on term deposits. Demand deposits include liquid deposits that are not linked to a current account, overnight deposits (with a maturity of one working day), traveller's cheques issued by credit institutions, liquid funds (or electronic money) paid in advance in connection with the use of electronic money, as well as sight deposits.

Imported inflation: A continued and sustained rise in the price of imported products.

In such a scenario, more domestic currency is required to buy one unit of foreign currency (and vice versa: less foreign currency is required to buy one unit of domestic currency).

Income balance: The income balance records the income related to foreign investments (interest on debt and profit on equity) and the income linked to working abroad.

Income index: Cf. Wage index:

Indirect tax: Indirect taxes are levied on goods and services, while direct ones are levied on income, profits and wealth. Indirect taxes include the value-added tax (VAT) and the excise duty. Indirect taxes must be paid by the final consumer, but it is collected by the tax authority from an intermediary (e.g. a trading company).

Inflation expectations: The level of inflation expected or planned by economic actors for some future date.

Inflation target: The particular level of inflation in an inflation targeting regime that the central bank undertakes to achieve. The current inflation target in Hungary is 3 percent.

Inflation targeting: A monetary policy framework in which the central bank's primary objective is to maintain price stability. To this end, the central bank sets an inflation target that it undertakes to achieve. The transparency and accountability of the monetary policy pursued by the central bank is an important element of an inflation targeting regime. The Magyar Nemzeti Bank has followed an inflation targeting regime since the summer of 2001.

Inflation: A continued and sustained rise in the general price level, that is, the general price level of goods and services.

Inflationary pressure: Economic developments that fuel inflation, for example a pick-up in demand, accelerating wage rises, rising oil prices or a depreciating exchange rate.

International Monetary Fund: The International Monetary Fund is an institution set up by the United Nations in 1945 and headquartered in Washington, D.C. Hungary has been a member of the Fund since 1982. Its main goal is the promote financial cooperation and exchange rate stability, and to provide temporary financial assistance to its members facing balance of payments difficulties.

Investment rate: The investment rate is the ratio of gross fixed capital formation to gross domestic product, which is usually calculated from current price data. Investments are vital from the perspective of potential growth: the higher the investment rate, the faster the growth of capital stock and thereby the economy may be. It defines the government sector more broadly than international law, since it does not distinguish the public from the private sector based on legal provisions, but based on economic activities. It does not contain unprocessed food, fuels, or products and services the pricing of which is regulated.

Job Protection Action Plan: A set of measures announced by the government in the summer of 2012. Within the framework of the Action Plan, the government introduced two taxes that cut the tax burden on small and medium-sized enterprises (KIVA, KATA), as well as a social contribution tax allowance improving the labour market situation of certain social groups (those aged over 55 or under 25, those returning from parental leave, the unskilled and the long-term unemployed). The measures set out in legislation came into effect on 1 January 2013.

Labour market equilibrium: The labour market is in equilibrium when the demand for labour equals supply. In a market economy, the supply and demand for labour are usually not in equilibrium, which can lead to the emergence of involuntary unemployment.

Labour market tightness: An indicator measuring the ratio of the labour demand of the private sector to the unused labour capacity that can be used to demonstrate the relationship of labour demand and supply. Higher labour market tightness means that fewer people are competing for a given job, which increases the bargaining power of the workers, leading to more substantial wage growth.

Labour productivity: The amount of goods and services that can be produced by one unit of labour.

Liquid asset: An asset that can be turned into cash quickly and at a low cost (including exchange loss). For example, cash and bank deposits are liquid assets.

Liquidity situation: The ratio of the actual and desirable levels of a bank's reserves. A liquidity shortage occurs when the desirable level is higher than the actual one and banks need to resort to loans from the central bank.

Loan-to-deposit ratio: The loan-to-deposit ratio measures the vulnerability of the banking system. It shows what proportion of a bank's loans are financed from deposit-type sources.

Local government debt: The combined debt of local governments and local minority self-governments. When calculated, debts of the individual local governments and minority self-governments owed to each other should be consolidated.

Local government sub-system: As currently provided for in the Public Finance Act, the local government sub-system of the general government includes the following legal persons: local governments, local minority self-governments, associations, regional development councils and the budgetary authorities controlled by such.

M1: The narrowest category of money that comprises the cash in sectors other than monetary institutions plus demand deposits and current account deposits, irrespective of denomination.

M2: A broader monetary aggregate that comprises M1 plus term deposits with a maturity of up to two years.

M3: The broadest monetary aggregate that comprises M2 plus those marketable financial instruments that can be regarded as close substitutes for bank deposits and that are issued by domestic monetary institutions.

Macroeconomic indicator: A set of indicators describing the developments of the whole national economy or its parts (e.g. sectors). Among others, gross domestic product (GDP) or the number of people employed are such indicators.

Marginal tax wedge: The marginal tax wedge shows how much tax should be paid at a given income level for an additional unit of labour cost (gross income plus employer contributions).

Monetary Council: The supreme decision-making body of the Magyar Nemzeti Bank is the Monetary Council. It holds its meetings as required but at least twice a month, announcing its meetings in advance. Its base rate decisions are made at the second meeting of each month.

Monetary policy toolbox: It encompasses all the tools available to the central bank under the mandate of the Central Bank Act for achieving its monetary policy goals. The elements of the toolbox can be used to directly influence interbank interest rates and the volume of central bank money in circulation on the interbank market.

Monetary policy: The part of economic policy governed by the central bank. The aim of economic policy is to promote social welfare by influencing and guiding economic developments. Monetary policy can best support this by maintaining price stability. The main elements of monetary policy are the interest and exchange rate policies.

Monetary transmission mechanism: A mechanism through which the central bank's monetary policy actions affect output and inflation through influencing market participants' decisions.

Monopoly: A corporation that dominates the market of a certain product or service by being its sole producer.

Net financial wealth/position: A stock indicator. Households' net financial wealth is the difference between their financial assets and liabilities.

Net financing capacity: A flow-type indicator. It is financial asset accumulation less the change in financial liabilities (net borrowing).

Neutral interest rate: This refers to the interest rate where 1) the output gap is closed, 2) there is no medium-term inflationary pressure, forward-looking inflation is on target, and 3) risk premiums are developing in line with their medium-term rates. In such a situation, monetary policy does not need to change the base rate for reasons related to inflation, the real economy or stability.

Nominal anchor: The nominal macroeconomic variable (e.g. price level, exchange rate, wages, money supply) targeted by the stabilising economic policy, the projected development of which serves as a guidance or reference for establishing other nominal prices. Accordingly, it is an economic variable that is able to stabilise or "anchor" economic actors' expectations about future inflation. If the nominal anchor is credible, that is, economic actors trust that the monetary authority is able to meet its objective, they will form their expectations of future inflation consistent with that anchor.

Nominal convergence criteria: The nominal convergence criteria (Maastricht criteria) detail expectations about the development of inflation, fiscal equilibrium, the exchange rate and the long-term nominal interest rate. In the case of the budget, the deficit should not exceed 3% of GDP, and government debt should not exceed 60% of GDP. The inflation rate should converge to the internal average of the euro area (it cannot be more than 1.5

percentage points above the average rate of the three member states with the lowest inflation). In the case of the exchange rate, the goal is to reduce fluctuations (participation in the ERM-II exchange rate mechanism) and to maintain stability as well as to lower the interest rate of long-term debt instruments (long-term yields cannot be more than 2 percentage points above the average rate of the three member states with the lowest inflation). The progress of convergence, which is also reflected in these indicators, fosters the functioning of the European common market and promotes its competitiveness.

Nominal effective exchange rate: The weighted (usually with trade) average exchange rate of a certain currency against a currency basket.

Non-debt-type funds: Non-debt-type funds are external debts where no future repayment and/or interest payment obligation arises for the recipient. Due to economic considerations, they include all foreign direct investments (not only equity-type funds, but also intercompany loans that, from a statistical perspective, are considered debt) and one type of portfolio investment, shares.

Output gap: The difference between actual and potential output.

Potential growth: The fastest rate of economic growth that does not entail inflation. The rate of potential growth is determined by the increase in supply-side factors (technological progress, available capital, expansion of the labour force, etc.).

Potential output: The concept of potential output seeks to capture the long-term or underlying production possibilities in an economy. Accordingly, it is either defined as the output accompanying a steady inflation rate or as an output trend. Since potential output cannot be observed, it is either estimated based on the production function or trend filtering, depending on interpretation.

Price stability: The combination of sustained low inflation and anchored expectations. In an environment of price stability, inflation does not play a significant role in the consumption and investment decisions of economic actors.

Procyclicality: The positive correlation between an economic indicator and the rate of change in economic activity (GDP change). From an economic policy perspective, it points to a measure that supports the cyclical position of the economy. A procyclical economic policy is expansive at times of economic upturns, and restrictive during recessions. Its opposite is anti-cyclical economic policy, the advantage of which is that it smooths out the cyclicality of the economy.

Production factors: Production factors are permanently available means of production which can be utilised for the production goods without using up the factor. Macroeconomists typically consider physical and human capital the most important production factors.

Progressive tax system: A tax system in which the average tax rate increases in conjunction with the tax base.

Prohibition of local government borrowing (cap on local government borrowing): Pursuant to the section on the reduction of government debt of Act CXCIV of 2011, the consent of the government is a prerequisite for local government borrowing (excluding loans for the own contribution to EU tenders, debt restructuring, loans maturing within the calendar year, and development loans with a value not exceeding the statutory cap).

Propensity to consume: Propensity to consume refers to the proportion of a potential extra unit of income spent on consumption.

Public employment: The reform of the public employment system started on 1 January 2011, and included the abolition of the public labour programme as well as the public interest and public benefit employment projects, which were replaced by a unified system of public employment. The reform measures sought to create a special form of employment aimed at helping the participants of the programme to return to or enter the primary labour market.

Public good: A product or service the consumption of which is available for all, and the consumption of which does not deplete its available quantity (e.g. public lighting).

Public sector: The group of institutions as determined by the ESA methodology. The conditions for reclassifying institutions from the corporate sector as public sector institutions are the following: 1) state control, and 2) less than half of the company's production costs should be covered by sales revenues (including state subsidies that are granted to all similar producers). Due to the latter requirement, the parts of the Budapest Transport Corporation (BKV) and the Hungarian State Railways (MÁV) making the greatest losses remain in the corporate sector.

Real effective exchange rate: The real effective exchange rate (REER) is the nominal effective exchange rate adjusted for the inflation differential. A change in the real effective exchange rate indicates a change in the competitiveness of a country.

Real interest rate: The so-called ex ante real interest rate is the nominal interest rate less the expected inflation, while the ex post real interest rate is the nominal interest rate less the actual inflation. The one mainly influencing consumption, saving and investment decisions, and hence aggregate demand and inflation is the ex ante real interest rate. Monetary policy can influence future inflation, amongst other things by indirectly changing the real interest rate.

Risk premium: The element of the borrowing rate in excess of the risk-free rate that the lending institution demands to cover – in whole or in part – the expected loan loss.

Saving rate: The portion of households' income not spent on consumption.

Self-regulating market theory: According to this theory, markets satisfy the needs of economic actors without external intervention (state control) at the point where the supply and demand curves meet. Thus, it provides maximum welfare to economic actors.

Small, open economy: From the perspective of economic theory, a country is considered small when it is a price taker on its import and export markets. The measure of openness is the strength of the country's cross-border economic ties and the extent of its external trade. It is typically calculated as the ratio of exports plus imports to GDP.

Social policy: All the government measures aimed at mitigating inequalities between social groups through the reorganisation of the redistribution process.

Stability and Growth Pact (SGP): The goal of the Pact is to contribute to fiscal discipline in the third stage of Economic and Monetary Union, thereby supporting the strong, sustainable growth that reinforces the conditions fostering price stability and the expansion of employment. In practice, this means that member states need to strive for budgetary positions close to balance or in surplus over the medium term, that is, on average in the economic cycle. In accordance with the Stability and Growth Pact, by the start of Stage III of EMU, all member states participating in the monetary union need to present a Stability Programme for their budget that needs to be close to balance or in surplus over the medium term. The Programme also needs to contain the path ensuring that the target is met. The counterpart of the Stability Programme for countries outside the monetary union is the section of the Convergence Programme related to fiscal criteria. Moreover, the Pact determines strict deadlines for the steps of the Excessive Deficit Procedure, and details the types and the severity of the sanctions that can be imposed in Stage III of EMU.

State monopoly: The exclusive right of the state to produce certain goods or supply certain services. It primarily involves public services that the market cannot provide efficiently. A state monopoly's activity usually serves social interests.

Stop-and-go cycle: It refers to the cyclicality of economic activity where restrictive (stop) and expansive (go) fiscal policies alternate. It is usually mentioned when economic policy pursues contradicting objectives or when, during the expansive period, it accumulates excessive imbalances that it is compelled to correct later (stop). Two contradicting objectives may be pursued by alternating restrictive and expansive fiscal policies.

Supply shock: An economic shock resulting from a change in supply (e.g. rising oil prices or productivity).

Supply: It represents the relationship between the price and quantity of a product on offer. It shows how much the consumer is able and willing to buy a certain product at various possible prices. A shift in supply may be caused by, among other things, a change in the costs of production, statutory requirements or technological progress.

Sustainable growth path: Sustainable growth path refers to the potential growth path that in addition to using resources optimally, preserves financial equilibrium, and thus does not lead to excessive, unsustainable debt ratios.

Target horizon: The span of time in which the central bank endeavours to achieve the inflation target or to keep inflation near the forecast rate in an inflation targeting regime.

Tax avoidance: Evasion of tax obligations as per their economic substance. An example for this is the statement of labour income as capital income. It can take an illegal form with a sham contract, or a legal form when an entrepreneur voluntarily reports low labour income. The illegal form is called tax evasion (or tax fraud), while the form exploiting the possibilities (loopholes) in the tax system is called tax planning.

Tax base: The basis for measurement (e.g. wage bill, investment expenditure, etc.) which is theoretically subject to taxation is referred to as the tax base. The effect of exemptions from the tax base is reflected in the fact that the actual (effective) tax rate is lower than the nominal rate defined by law (furthermore, tax evasion can also reduce the effective tax rate).

Tax burden: The total amount of tax on a given tax base.

Tax centralisation: The ratio of tax and contribution revenues to GDP.

Tax rate: A distinction is made between the statutory, marginal and average tax rates. The statutory tax rate is the tax rate stipulated by law for different income or profit levels. The marginal tax rate shows how much tax should be paid at a given income level for an additional unit of income. The average tax rate is the ratio of the tax payable and the tax base.

Tax wedge: This indicator shows the relationship between the total labour cost of an "average employee" for an employer and the net disposable income of the employee. The tax wedge is the ratio of all the taxes on labour (personal income tax, employee and employer contributions, social contribution tax) to the total labour cost (net wage plus taxes on labour).

Tax-adjusted core inflation: See Core inflation excluding indirect taxes.

Taylor rule: A monetary policy recommendation formulated by the economist John Taylor that can be used to determine the optimal level of the base rate taking into account the changes in economic conditions. According to the rule, the central bank should set the nominal base rate considering the divergence of inflation from the price stability target and the deviation of economic growth from its potential level (output gap).[56] The new scheme provides temporary employment to those who have been unable to find work on their own for a long time.

Trade balance: The trade balance records the volume of goods and services exchanged between residents and non-residents. The volume of foreign trade is measured by the Hungarian Central Statistical Office (HCSO) based on customs statistics on the one hand, and the individual reports submitted by larger corporations as regards foreign trade on the other hand. The trade balance is the export less the import of goods and services.

Transfer balance: The transfer balance records other primary income (taxes on products and production, rental fees), secondary

[56] http://www.frbsf.org/education/publications/doctor-econ/1998/march/taylor-rule-monetary-policy

income (unilateral transfers, basically current transfers received from the EU) and the capital balance (mostly capital transfers received from the EU).

Twin deficit: Twin deficit refers to a situation where a country experiences a current account deficit and a budget deficit at the same time. There is no direct cause-and-effect link between the two. It is common, however, that the budget plays a critical role in increasing the current account deficit.

Underlying inflation indicator: An indicator that shows the more persistent inflation trends and is free of the temporary effects not substantially impacting the medium-term outlook on inflation.

Unemployment rate: The ratio of the unemployed to the economically active population.

Volume index: The volume index expresses how much a certain economic variable changes over a given period without the effect of price changes.

Wage index: The rate of wage growth compared to the same period of the previous year.

Washington consensus: Ten neo-liberal economic policy reform proposals for emerging economies formulated by international financial organisations and compiled by John Williamson. The proposals were based on the Latin American financial crises of the 1980s. As the Latin American countries that adopted the socially often costly economic policy proposals were not spared by the financial crises of the 1990s either, the Washington consensus has been strongly criticised. When the output gap is positive, aggregate demand exceeds aggregate supply, and thus real economy developments contribute to higher inflation.

Abbreviations and country groups used in this book

AMECO: Annual macroeconomic database
AR: Argentina
AT: Austria
AU: Australia
Baltic States: Estonia, Latvia, Lithuania
BE: Belgium
BG: Bulgaria
Bn: Billion
BoJ   Bank of Japan
BoE: Bank of England
BR: Brazil
CA: Canada
Capex: Capital expenditure
CAR: Capital adequacy ratio
CCIS   Central Credit Information System
CDS: Credit default swap
CEE-4 countries: Czech Republic, Poland, Hungary, Romania
CH: Switzerland
CHF: Swiss franc
CLI: Composite leading indicator
Club Med countries: Greece, Italy, Portugal, Spain
CN: China
CNB: Česká národní banka (Czech National Bank)
CPI: Consumer price index
CY: Cyprus
CZ: Czech Republic
DE: Germany
DK: Denmark
ECB: European Central Bank
EDP: Excessive Deficit Procedure

EE: Estonia
EL: Greece
EMBI: Emerging Markets Bond Index
EMU: Economic and Monetary Union
ES: Spain
ESA: European system of national and regional accounts
ESI: Economic Sentiment Indicator (European Commission)
ESP: Spain
EST: Estonia
EU: European Union
EU-15 countries: Austria, Belgium, Denmark, Finland, France, Germany, Greece, Ireland, Italy, Luxembourg, The Netherlands, Portugal, Spain, Sweden, United Kingdom
EU-27 countries: Austria, Belgium, Bulgaria, Cyprus, Czech Republic, Denmark, United Kingdom, Estonia, Finland, France, Greece, The Netherlands, Ireland, Poland, Latvia, Lithuania, Luxembourg, Hungary, Malta, Germany, Italy, Portugal, Romania, Spain, Sweden, Slovakia, Slovenia
EU-28 countries: Austria, Belgium, Bulgaria, Cyprus, Czech Republic, Denmark, United Kingdom, Estonia, Finland, France, Greece, The Netherlands, Croatia, Ireland, Poland, Latvia, Lithuania, Luxembourg, Hungary, Malta, Germany, Italy, Portugal, Romania, Spain, Sweden, Slovakia, Slovenia
EUR: Euro
Euro area (18) countries: Austria, Belgium, Cyprus, Estonia, Finland, France, Greece, The Netherlands, Ireland, Latvia, Luxembourg, Malta, Germany, Italy, Portugal, Spain, Slovakia, Slovenia
FCI: Financial Conditions Index
FDI: Foreign direct investment
Fed: Federal Reserve
FGS: Funding for Growth Scheme
FI: Finland
FIN: Finland
FR: France

FSI:	Financial Soundness Indicator
FX:	Foreign exchange, forex
GB:	Great Britain
GDMA:	Government Debt Management Agency
GDP:	Gross domestic product
GER:	Germany
GNI:	Gross national income
GR:	Greece
Gyed:	Childcare allowance
Gyes:	Maternity benefit
Gyet:	Child-raising benefit
HFSA:	Hungarian Financial Supervisory Authority
HICP:	Harmonised Index of Consumer Prices
HK:	Hong Kong
HNB:	Hrvatska Narodna Banka (Croatian National Bank)
HR:	Croatia
HU:	Hungary
HUF:	Hungarian forint
HUN:	Hungary
HY:	Half year
ID:	Indonesia
IE:	Ireland
IFS:	International Financial Statistics
IMF:	International Monetary Fund
IN:	India
IRL:	Ireland
IT:	Italy
JP:	Japan
KR:	South Korea
LFS	Labour Force Survey
LFS:	Labour Force Survey
LT:	Lithuania
LUX:	Luxembourg
LV:	Latvia
MÁV:	Hungarian State Railways

MFB: Hungarian Development Bank
MN   Million
MNB: Magyar Nemzeti Bank (central bank of Hungary)
MNYP: Private Pension Insurance Fund
MT: Malta
MX: Mexico
MY: Malaysia
NAIRU: Non-accelerating inflation rate of unemployment
NBER: National Bureau of Economic Research
NGM: Ministry for National Economy
NL: Netherlands
NPL: Non-performing loan
OECD: Organisation for Economic Cooperation and Development
PIT: Personal income tax
PL: Poland
POL: Poland
PPP: Purchasing power parity
PT: Portugal
Q: Quarter
R&D: Research & development
RO: Romania
ROE: Return on equity
RU: Russia
S-4 countries: Denmark, Finland, Norway, Sweden
S-7 countries: Denmark, Estonia, Finland, Latvia, Lithuania, Norway,
            Sweden
SA: Saudi Arabia
SE: Sweden
SI: Slovenia
SK: Slovakia
SME: Small and medium-sized enterprise
SNA: System of National Accounts
SW: Sweden
SWE: Sweden
TFP: Total factor productivity

TH: Thailand
TR: Turkey
UK: United Kingdom
ULC   Unit labour cost
US: United States
USA: United States of America
V-3 countries: Czech Republic, Poland, Slovakia
V-4 countries: Czech Republic, Poland, Hungary, Slovakia
V-6 countries: Austria, Czech Republic, Poland, Hungary, Slovakia, Slovenia
VAT: Value added tax
WDI: World Development Indicators
WEO: World Economic Outlook

György Matolcsy
ECONOMIC BALANCE AND GROWTH

2015

Print: Prospektus–SPL consortium
H-8200 Veszprém, Tartu u. 6.